Musical Instruments

Musical Instruments

History, Technology, and Performance of Instruments of Western Music

MURRAY CAMPBELL, CLIVE GREATED,
AND ARNOLD MYERS

OXFORD

UNIVERSITY PRESS

OXFORD
UNIVERSITY PRESS

Great Clarendon Street, Oxford OX2 6DP
Oxford University Press is a department of the University of Oxford.
It furthers the University's objective of excellence in research, scholarship,
and education by publishing worldwide in

Oxford New York

Athens Auckland Bangkok Bogotá Buenos Aires Calcutta
Cape Town Chennai Dar es Salaam Delhi Florence Hong Kong Istanbul
Karachi Kuala Lumpur Madrid Melbourne Mexico City Mumbai
Nairobi Paris São Paulo Singapore Taipei Tokyo Toronto

Oxford is a registered trade mark of Oxford University Press
in the UK and certain other countries

Published in the United States
by Oxford University Press Inc., New York

British Library Cataloguing in Publication Data

Data available

Library of Congress Cataloging in Publication Data

Data available

ISBN 0–19–816504–8 (hbk.)

1 3 5 7 9 10 8 6 4 2

Typeset by A. Typesetter
Printed in Great Britain
on acid-free paper by
Biddles Ltd.,
Guildford & King's Lynn

PREFACE

In this book we attempt to describe and explain musical instruments in their various forms: how they work, what they can do, and how they came to be the way they are.

The whole field of musical instruments is vast, and in a single volume a high degree of selectivity is inevitable. We have chosen to devote most attention to the instruments of literate music and its derivatives—instruments built to play in musical traditions transmitted in large part by notated scores and parts. We concentrate, therefore, on the instruments of Western music (now, of course a worldwide phenomenon): orchestral, chamber, and ecclesiastical music, civilian and military bands, dance music and jazz, opera and shows. The recent explosive growth of interest in 'early' music, and in performances using historic or reproduction instruments, is reflected in an emphasis on the historical development of the main types of instrument.

We also refer frequently, but in less detail, to instruments of musical cultures where aural tradition and improvisation are paramount. This does not imply any value judgement about the relative merits of literate and non-literate musical traditions; complex and subtle use of musical instruments is a worldwide phenomenon. So rich, indeed, is the diversity of instrumental forms and performing techniques in non-Western music that it is impossible to offer a detailed treatment in one volume.

The primary function of all musical instruments is to generate musical sound. Two introductory chapters outline the nature of musical sound and the acoustical principles which underlie the operation of musical instruments. The remaining chapters survey the different instrumental families, following broadly the conventional classification of instrumental types (strings, woodwind, brass, percussion, and electronic) with the equally conventional subdivisions. For the principal instrumental types within each family we describe the distinguishing acoustical features, the historical development, the variety of sizes and shapes, and the musical contexts in which they are commonly used. Manufacturing techniques are outlined, and playing techniques and performance practice are described.

Information on pitch notation, equal temperament frequencies, woodwind instrument keywork patterns, and brass instrument nomenclature is given in three Appendices, which are followed by a substantial list of suggestions for further reading. The Glossary/Index contains definitions of technical terms, and brief notes on instruments not discussed in the main text. Acquaintance with the rudiments of musical staff notation is assumed.

The book is designed to be used in two different ways: approached from the beginning, it can be read as a concise survey of the subject; approached through the Index/Glossary, it can serve as a concise dictionary and work of reference.

CONTENTS

ACKNOWLEDGEMENTS

The authors are grateful to the following for their kind permission to reproduce copyright illustrations: Boosey & Hawkes Music Publishers Limited (Figures 1.1, 1.9, 5.14), Edinburgh University Collection of Historic Musical Instruments (Figures 3.5, 3.6, 3.7, 3.8, 3.9, 3.10, 4.1, 4.2, 4.4, 5.4, 5.6, 5.7, 5.8, 5.9, 5.10, 6.4, 6.5, 7.2, 7.3, 7.4, 7.5, 7.6, 7.7, 8.2, 8.4, 8.5, 8.6, 9.2, 9.3, 10.1, 10.2, 10.3, 10.8, 10.15, 10.16, 11.2, 11.3, 12.2, 12.3 photographs by Antonia Reeve Photography, Edinburgh and Figure 5.1 photography by Mark Findlay), Novello Music Publishers Limited (Figure 8.7), Oxford University Press (Figure 12.18), Peters Edition Limited (Figures 8.9, 11.13), Ronald Stevenson Society (Figure 11.12), Peter Tuffy (Figures 10.15, 12.10, 12.12, 12.15), and United Music Publishers Limited (Figure 11.10).

The authors are grateful to the following for assistance given with the text: John Barnes, Marcus Bennett, John Cranmer, Anne Macaulay, Peter Nelson, Guy Oldham, Raymond Parks, Andrew Shivas, Edwina Smith, William Waterhouse, John Webb, and especially to Patsy Campbell, who wrote the sections of Chapter 8 dealing with members of the viol family.

In addition to the texts listed in the Further Reading section, the authors have drawn on the following works: *The Flute and Flute Playing*, by Theobald Boehm (trans. Dayton C. Miller, Rudall Carte, 1922), *The Flute*, by Albert Cooper (Albert Cooper 1980), *Teaching the Flute*, by Simon Hunt (Pan Educational, 1983), and *Bellfounding*, by Trevor Jennings (Shire, 1988).

The authors are grateful to A. Murray Campbell for assistance with line diagrams and to Kelly J. White (Treble Clef Music) for assistance with music examples.

I

Sounds and Sweet Airs

CALIBAN: Be not afeard. The isle is full of noises,
Sounds, and sweet airs, that give delight and hurt not.
Sometimes a thousand twangling instruments
Will hum about mine ears . . .

(Shakespeare, *The Tempest*)

This is a book about musical instruments. The range and diversity of the devices which fall into this category testify vividly to the inventiveness of the human imagination. Yet the tromba marina and the violin, the flageolet and the cathedral organ, the serpent and the synthesizer all share one common purpose: the creation of musical sound.

In order to understand why musical instruments have their characteristic shapes and sizes, and to gain insight into their possibilities and limitations, it is necessary to know a little about the nature of musical sound. In this introductory chapter we discuss briefly how sound waves are generated in the air around an instrument, travel to the ear of a listener, and there evoke the sensation which we call music.

1.1 MAKING WAVES

Squeezing the air

We live at the bottom of a sea of air, more than 400 km deep. Because of the weight of the upper layers of the atmosphere, the air at ground level is compressed; any surface exposed to the air experiences a strong force as a result. The ratio of this force to the area of the surface is called the atmospheric pressure. The internationally accepted unit of pressure is the pascal (abbreviated Pa); normal atmospheric pressure is about 100,000 Pa.

To get an idea of the magnitude of the force which atmospheric pressure can exert, imagine that the f-holes in the top plate of a violin are blocked up and all the air is pumped out of the internal cavity. The force on the top plate due to the external air pressure would be roughly equal to that caused by placing on top of the violin a weight of 500 kg (about half a ton).

Under such an enormous force the violin would of course immediately collapse. In its normal state, however, the violin has open f-holes, and the cavity within is filled with air at atmospheric pressure. This internal air pushes outwards on the top plate with just the same force as the external air pushing inwards, and the two forces balance.

When a violinist picks up the instrument and bows one of the strings, the vibration of the string is communicated to the top plate through the bridge. Later we shall return to discuss the details of this process; at present we concentrate on the effect of the vibration of the violin body on the surrounding air. As the top plate moves upwards, the layer of air in contact with the plate is squeezed against the mass of air above, and the air pressure rises. In a later part of the vibration cycle, the top plate will be moving downwards, and the air pressure will drop. The up-and-down motion of the top plate thus gives rise to a corresponding up-and-down fluctuation in the pressure of the air near the plate.

A microphone is essentially a device for converting variations of air pressure into electrical signals. By measuring the output of a calibrated microphone placed near the violin we can deduce the size of the pressure variations that occur when the violin is played. Such a measurement shows that, even when the violin is bowed very strongly, the atmospheric pressure around the instrument varies by only about 1 Pa. Remembering that normal atmospheric pressure is about 100,000 Pa, we see that the violin causes fluctuations in the air pressure which are never much greater than 0.001 per cent. Fortunately the human ear is extremely sensitive to the pressure changes which occur in musical performance—under optimum listening conditions sounds can be heard which correspond to pressure changes of less than a thousandth of a pascal.

Once the air pressure variations have been turned into electrical signals by a microphone we can use various modern electronic aids to examine their nature. One of the most useful of such aids is the oscilloscope. In this device a light spot is pulled horizontally across a screen at a constant speed, while the electrical signal being studied is made to deflect the spot in the vertical direction. By making the horizontal speed very fast we can examine the signal variation over a very short interval of time; by slowing down the horizontal motion we can see the variation over a longer timescale.

Our interest here is in studying the varieties of sound which can be produced by musical instruments. Figure 1.1 shows a brief excerpt from a full orchestral score: the last page of Bartók's *Concerto for Orchestra*. In this triumphant conclusion to a famous orchestral showpiece the composer calls for sixteen different types of instrument. To illustrate one or two points about the general nature of musical

1.1 The last page of the score of Bartók's *Concerto for Orchestra* (© Copyright 1946 by Hawkes & Son (London) Ltd)

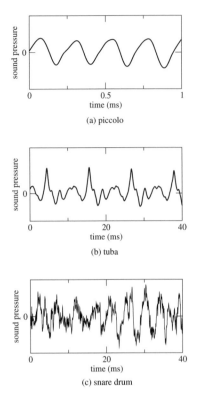

(a) piccolo

(b) tuba

(c) snare drum

1.2 Variations in air pressure created by three of the instruments contributing to the final chord in Figure 1.1

sound, let us isolate and examine three of the component sounds in the final chord—the high C played by the piccolo, the F more than five octaves below played by the tuba, and the unpitched sound of the snare drum.

In Figure 1.2 are shown the oscilloscope traces which resulted when the three instruments were recorded separately, and their sounds were fed in turn to the oscilloscope. For the display of the piccolo's sound the horizontal speed of the spot was chosen so that the complete trace was drawn in only one millisecond (a thousandth of a second, abbreviated ms). In that time the pressure near the piccolo rose and fell just over four times. The most striking feature of the trace, shown in Figure 1.2(a), is its regularity. After 0.24 ms one up-and-down cycle of pressure variation has been completed, and the trace starts to repeat itself. After a further 0.24 ms another cycle is completed, and a further repetition starts. We say that the piccolo's trace is periodic, with a period of 0.24 ms. The shape of the trace is called the waveform; the waveform of the piccolo's sound is a smooth and regular wiggle, close to the simple wave shape known in mathematics as a sine curve.

The number of complete cycles of pressure variation which occur in one second is called the repetition frequency (or, more loosely, simply the frequency) of the sound. Symbolizing the frequency by f and the period by T, it follows that

$$f = 1/T$$

where T is measured in seconds (abbreviated s) and f in hertz (abbreviated Hz). Thus the piccolo's high C, with a period of 0.24 ms or 0.00024 s, has a frequency of $1 : 0.00024 = 4,186$ Hz. The piccolo top C is the highest pitch normally found in orchestral scores; we have seen that this high pitch corresponds to a very fast periodic variation in the air pressure. Turning to examine the recorded sound of the tuba's low F, we find that again the pressure variation is periodic, but the period is much longer. To see the regularity in the trace from the tuba, it was necessary to slow the oscilloscope spot down so that it took 40 ms to cross the screen. The resulting trace, shown in Figure 1.2(b), is a much more complicated and spiky variation of pressure than in the case of the piccolo note, but the pattern repeats itself every 11.5 ms. We can therefore say that the tuba F has a period of 11.5 ms, and a frequency of $1 : 0.0115 = 87.3$ Hz.

The third instrument whose sound we chose to examine was the snare drum. The trace from this sound, shown in Figure 1.2(c), is even more spiky than that of the tuba. This time there is no evidence of a repetitive pattern in the trace; we cannot identify a period, or work out a repetition frequency. Here we have an illustration of a fundamental distinction between two types of sound made by musical instruments: pitched sounds, like the notes of the piccolo and the tuba, correspond to regular, periodic variations of air pressure, while unpitched sounds, like the snare drum roll, are associated with irregular pressure variations without a definite periodicity.

Travelling waves

We saw earlier that the vibration of a violin body causes minute pressure fluctuations in the immediately surrounding air. It is not, of course, necessary to place one's ear very close to the violin to hear the sound—two thousand people filling a large concert hall can simultaneously respond to the vibration of a single instrument. This is possible because the pressure fluctuations do not remain localized around the violin but spread out through the surrounding atmosphere. If a bather standing at the centre of a calm swimming pool starts to move a hand backwards and forwards in the water, a series of ripples radiate from the bather towards the sides of the pool: the bather is making waves. In a similar way, the function of all musical instruments is to make waves. Instead of a variation in the height of the water surface, the wave generated by a musical instrument is an invisible variation in the pressure of the air. Because this type of wave carries the sound of an instrument to the ear of the listener, we call it a sound wave.

In discussing the nature of the sound wave radiating from a violin, it is helpful to imagine that the air above the top plate is divided into a set of layers. The first layer, nearest the plate, will be squeezed first when the plate rises. As a result, the pressure in the first layer will increase. After a short time, the first layer will expand upwards, pressing against the second layer. The pressure in the second layer will therefore increase, a little later than the increase in the pressure of the first layer. In its turn, the second layer will expand against the third layer, causing its pressure to increase. Thus a ripple of increasing pressure will travel outwards from one layer to the next.

In the second half of its vibration cycle, the plate will be falling. This will cause a drop in the pressure of the air in the first layer, since it will have some additional space into which it can expand. After a short time the second layer will find that it is no longer being squeezed so hard from below, and as it expands downwards its pressure too will drop. Slightly later, the third layer will also feel a drop in pressure. In other words, a ripple of decreasing pressure will be travelling outwards behind the ripple of increasing pressure.

After it has completed one cycle of its vibration, the plate will start to rise once more, sending a second ripple of increasing pressure outwards. As these successive ripples wash over a listener some distance away, the listener will experience a periodic rising and falling of pressure which accurately mimics the changes close to the instrument. The set of ripples, which together constitute the sound wave, travel at the speed of sound, which depends on the temperature and humidity of the air; some values for the speed of sound are given in Table 1.1.

Table 1.1 *Some values for the speed of sound*

Conditions	Speed of sound (m/s)
Dry air, 0°C	331.5
Dry air, 10°C	337.5
Dry air, 20°C	343.4
Dry air, 30°C	349.2
Exhaled breath, 25°C	346

Because the speed of sound is not infinitely large, there is a time delay between the vibration of the plate and the arrival of the corresponding pressure ripple at the listener. This delay is obtained by dividing the distance between instrument and listener by the speed of sound. As an example, consider a violinist playing on the stage of a concert hall, and a listener 70 metres from the stage. Taking the speed of sound to be 340 metres per second gives a time delay of 70/340 seconds; the listener hears each note begin about a fifth of a second after the violinist has started to play it.

To help clarify the nature of these rather mysterious invisible sound waves which bring music to our ears, let us imagine an experiment in which we sit eighteen listeners, one behind the other, in the first eighteen rows of a concert hall. Each listener holds a microphone linked to a meter which measures the air pressure.

On the platform, an instrumentalist starts to play a note, and the sound wave radiates from the instrument towards the back of the hall. To simplify the illustration, let us assume that the pressure variation generated by the instrument has a sine curve waveform similar to that of the piccolo shown in Figure 1.2(a). Figure 1.3(a) illustrates the pressures measured by the different listeners at a particular instant. Listener A finds that the pressure is neither raised or lowered by the sound wave. One row behind, B finds that at the same instant the pressure has risen by 3 pascals; in Figure 1.3(a) this is represented by 3 boxes above the line. C sees an excess pressure of 5 pascals on the meter; D registers a 6 pascal increase.

In the rows behind D, the meters held by E and F show smaller pressure rises. Listener G agrees with A: the pressure has the same value as it had before the sound started. The reading on H's meter has dropped by 3 pascals; this is represented by 3 boxes below the line. Two rows further back, J finds a drop of 6 pascals.

Looking at the overall shape of the diagram in Figure 1.3(a), we can clearly see the wave shape in the pressure variation. At the instant represented, a crest is passing D. Another crest, sent out earlier from the instrument, has just reached P. The distance between these two neighbouring crests is called the wavelength, usually symbolized by the Greek letter λ (*lambda*). Here the wavelength is the distance between twelve rows of seats.

It is important to remember that all the pressure measurements shown in Figure 1.3(a) were taken at the same time. The other three diagrams in Figure 1.3 show similar sets of measurements taken at three subsequent times. In Figure 1.3(b) the crest has moved from D to E; in Figures 1.3(c) and 1.3(d) it has passed on to F and then to G. This type of wave, in which a crest moves steadily in one direction, is called a travelling wave.

If we focus attention on P's pressure meter, we see that the excess pressure decreases from 6 pascals to zero in the four stages of Figure 1.3. Continuing the diagram to show later stages in the passage of the sound wave, we would see the pressure at P continuing to fall until it had reached 6 pascals below normal. At that stage the trough of the wave, which started at J in Figure 1.3(a), would just have reached P. The pressure in P's meter would then rise again, eventually reaching once more the peak value of 6 pascals above normal. This would occur when the crest which was at D in Figure 1.3(a) had travelled across the twelve rows to P.

In the time the crest took to travel from D to P, the pressure meter at P showed a change from maximum to minimum and back to maximum. But this time is just the period T of the sound. We also know that the distance between D and P is the wavelength λ. From these two pieces of information we can deduce that the crest travels a distance λ in a time T. The speed at which the crest travels, which is the speed of sound, is thus found by dividing the wavelength by the period. This relationship is expressed in the formula

$$c = \lambda/T$$

where the speed of sound is symbolized by c.

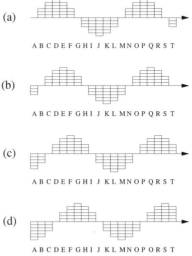

1.3 Four stages in the progress of a travelling sound wave

Remembering that frequency is the inverse of period:

$$f = 1/T$$

we finally arrive at a most useful relationship linking frequency, wavelength, and speed of sound:

$$c = \lambda \times f$$

As an example of the practical application of this relationship to musical instruments, consider an organ which has been tuned when the temperature of the hall was 10°C, but is subsequently played in a concert when the hall temperature has risen to 20°C. The wavelength of the sound from a diapason pipe is controlled by the length of the pipe, which will not change significantly as the temperature rises. We can see, however, from Table 1.1 that the speed of sound changes from 337.5 metres per second at 10°C to 343.4 metres per second at 20°C; this is an increase of nearly 2 per cent. The equation above shows that the frequency will increase by the same percentage: a diapason pipe tuned to the standard A of 440 Hz will sharpen to 448 Hz as the temperature rises. Clearly, if the organ is to play with other fixed pitch instruments, it is important that it should be tuned at the playing temperature.

Standing waves

Returning to our imaginary experiment in the concert hall, let us follow the sound wave as it continues past the listeners, travels over the empty rows behind them, and eventually reaches the rear wall of the auditorium. What happens to the wave then? The details depend on the nature of the hall, but some of the sound energy will bounce off the rear wall, and a reflected wave will retrace its path towards the platform. Assuming that the instrument is still playing, the listeners will then experience the combined effect of the direct wave, travelling from front to back, and the reflected wave, travelling from back to front.

This situation, in which a travelling wave is reflected back along its original path, is of great importance in musical instruments, so it is worth examining closely how the effects of the two waves combine. In Figure 1.4(a) we show the pressures measured by our listeners in the concert hall. The first diagram simply reproduces Figure 1.3(a), showing the distribution of pressures at a particular instant due to the direct wave travelling from the platform towards the rear. The second diagram shows the pressure distribution for the reflected wave travelling in the opposite direction. For simplicity we have assumed that all the sound energy is reflected back, so that the peaks and troughs in the reflected wave are the same size as those in the original wave.

At the instant illustrated in Figure 1.4(a) the crests of the direct and reflected waves happen to coincide at listener D, who therefore measures a 6 pascal pressure increase from each wave, and a total pressure rise of 12 pascals. This effect of the two waves combined is shown in the third diagram. Listener A, in contrast, finds no pressure increase from either wave; neither does G nor M. J finds that each wave separately lowers the pressure by 6 pascals, so that the total drop is 12 pascals. The effect of combining the two waves at this instant is to give another wave with twice as big an amplitude as the direct wave.

How do things look a short time later? Figure 1.4(b) illustrates the situation when the crest of the direct wave has reached F, two rows behind D. The reflected wave has moved two rows towards the front, and its crest has just reached B. When we add the effects of the two waves, shown separately in the first two diagrams, we see something quite remarkable. Listener A now finds the direct wave lowering the pressure by 6 pascals while the reflected wave raises it by the same amount; the net effect is to make no change. D finds each wave raising the pressure by 3 pascals, giving a total increase of 6 pascals. When all the changes are combined we obtain the third diagram in Figure 1.4(b). Comparing this with the third diagram of Figure 1.4(a), we see that the wave has the same shape as before; its amplitude has decreased from 12 pascals to 6 pascals; and, most significantly, its crest does not appear to have moved either to the right or to the left.

As the two travelling waves continue their passage in opposite directions, the crest remains in the same place, and its amplitude continues to decrease. When the crest of the direct wave reaches G, and that of the reflected wave reaches A, we have the situation represented by Figure 1.4(c): the two waves cancel each other completely, and none of the listeners measures a pressure change. Later on, the pressure measured by D would drop until it was 12 pascals below normal; at this time J would measure an increase of 12 pascals. Throughout, listeners A, G, and M would find that the pressure was unchanged at its normal value.

The combined effect of the two travelling waves is described as a standing wave.

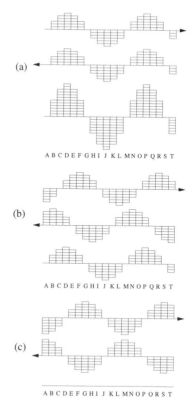

(a)

ABCDEFGHI J KLMNOPQRST

(b)

ABCDEFGHI J KLMNOPQRST

(c)

ABCDEFGHI J KLMNOPQRST

1.4 The addition of two sound waves travelling in opposite directions, giving rise to a standing wave. (a), (b), and (c) show three stages in the cycle of the standing wave; in each case, the first two lines show the contributing travelling waves, whose summation gives the standing wave pattern in the third line

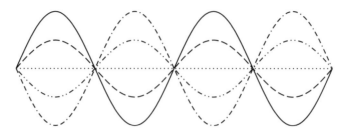

1.5 Five successive stages of a standing wave

The reasons behind this name are fairly obvious. In Figure 1.5 the pressure distributions are shown for five successive stages of a standing wave. There is no suggestion of a crest moving either to the right or to the left; in that sense the wave is standing still. At certain points, called nodes, the presence of the wave makes no difference, since the pressure remains constant throughout. At intermediate points, called antinodes, the pressure rises and falls by its maximum extent.

In our example in the concert hall, listeners A, G, and M happened to be sitting in seats which were at nodes of the standing wave. This means that they would hear no sound from the instrument playing on the platform. D and J were more fortunate in their choice of seats: since they were at antinodes of the standing wave they would hear the sound with maximum volume.

Returning for a moment to Figure 1.4, we can see that while the wavelength is twelve rows, the distance between the node at A and the antinode at D is three rows. This is an example of a general principle of great use in discussing musical instruments: the distance between a node and the nearest antinode is a quarter of the wavelength. It follows, of course, that two nodes are separated by half a wavelength.

Of course the situation in a real concert hall is not as simple as our example: there are sound waves travelling in many different directions, and multiple reflections from different walls. Furthermore, the sound waveforms of real instruments are more complicated than the simple sine curve we have assumed in our discussion. It remains true, however, that a listener walking around in a hall while an instrument plays a steady note can hear significant variations in loudness because of the standing wave patterns in the room.

1.2 THE HEARING PROCESS

A musical ear

In our discussion of sound waves we deliberately sidestepped the issue of subjectivity by giving each member of our audience a pressure meter. We now move on

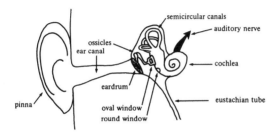

1.6 Anatomical sketch of the human ear

to consider what happens when the sound waves from an instrument fall, not on the diaphragm of a microphone, but on the ear of a musically responsive listener.

We already saw that the human ear is a remarkably sensitive organ, able to respond to a change in air pressure of one part in a hundred million. It is not surprising, therefore, to find that the delicate parts of the hearing mechanism are buried for protection several centimetres inside the bone of the skull.

Figure 1.6 is an anatomical sketch indicating the layout of the different parts of a human ear. The ear flap (pinna) is relatively unimportant, although it does play a minor role in establishing the direction from which a sound comes. When a sound wave arrives at the ear it is channelled down a tube roughly 25 mm long and about 7 mm in diameter. This tube is the ear canal (auditory meatus), and is sealed at the inner end by the eardrum (tympanic membrane). The outer flap and the ear canal together form the outer ear (see Figure 1.7).

The eardrum is a relatively stiff, cone-shaped membrane. When the incoming sound wave reaches it, the eardrum is set vibrating. Not all of the sound energy is passed on to the eardrum, however; some of it returns up the ear canal as a reflected wave. Thus a standing wave is set up in the ear canal. In Chapter 2 we will see that when the length of a tube closed at one end and open at the other is equal to a quarter wavelength a very strong standing wave can be set up. This condition is known as resonance. For the ear canal, resonance occurs at a wavelength of about 10 cm, corresponding to a frequency around 3,000 Hz. This resonance helps to

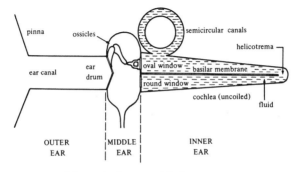

1.7 Schematic diagram of the human ear

make the ear particularly sensitive to frequencies around this value, corresponding to pitches about three or four octaves above middle C.

On the inner side of the eardrum is the air-filled cavity of the middle ear. Three tiny bones (ossicles) bridge this cavity, transferring the vibrations of the eardrum to another membrane which covers the entrance to the inner ear. The three bones act like a lever system, multiplying the minute forces generated by the sound pressure on the eardrum.

The middle ear also acts as a protective shield before the highly sensitive inner ear. When a very loud noise is heard, the brain sends a warning signal to the stapedius muscle, which pulls the ossicles out of their normal alignment. Instead of multiplying the forces sent to the inner ear the lever system then reduces them. This effect is known as the acoustic reflex. Unfortunately there is a delay of about a tenth of a second before the acoustic reflex is fully activated, and it is ineffective for frequencies much above 1,000 Hz. There is little protection from a sound like a cymbal clash, which rises almost instantly to a high amplitude and which contains powerful high-frequency components.

The inner ear contains the most fragile and delicate part of the hearing mechanism. Because it is housed in a spiral tube very like the shell of a snail, it is called the cochlea (the Greek word for a snail). The tube is divided lengthways by a partition called the basilar membrane, along which lies an array of hair cells known collectively as the organ of Corti. Above the basilar membrane is the upper gallery, and below it the lower gallery. An opening in the basilar membrane at the apex of the cochlea connects the two galleries, allowing the watery fluid which fills the inner ear to flow from one gallery to the other.

At the entrance to the cochlea are two windows in the bony wall. The oval window connects the middle ear to the upper gallery, as shown in Figure 1.7. The third of the middle ear bones, called the stirrup (stapes) because of its shape, fits into the oval widow, the surrounding gap being sealed by a membrane. The round window, also sealed by a membrane, communicates between the lower gallery and the middle ear.

When a sound wave arrives at the ear, the vibration of the eardrum is passed to the stirrup, which pumps in and out of the oval window with a piston-like motion. Unlike the air, which can be squeezed into a smaller volume by increased pressure, the fluid in the cochlea is almost incompressible. Thus when the stirrup pushes into the oval window the fluid displaced has to find somewhere else to go. The flexible basilar membrane is pushed downwards in the vicinity of the oval window; the fluid thus displaced in the lower gallery causes the round window membrane to bulge outwards. Although the downward bulge in the basilar membrane starts near the oval window, it rapidly travels along the membrane towards the apex of the cochlea.

When the stirrup pulls outwards on the oval window the pattern is reversed, with the basilar membrane rising and the round window membrane moving inwards. The upward bulge in the basilar membrane races along in the wake of the downward bulge. Thus as the stirrup pumps in and out in response to the sound pressure variations at the eardrum, a rippling motion is set up on the basilar membrane. The hair cells along the surface of the membrane 'fire' as a ripple passes, and the firing of each hair cell generates a tiny electrical pulse. Nerve fibres pick up the pulses and convey the signals to the brain of the listener. With the evocation of the sensation of musical sound the chain of communication between performer and listener is complete.

Rainbows of sound

If you are reading this book in daylight, the page will appear white. This is the colour of the light which streams from the sun and is reflected from the page. But when the sunlight encounters a cloud of raindrops on its path through the atmosphere, the rays are bent and reflected to form a rainbow in the sky. We see then that the light is not, after all, a single colour: it is made up of a spectrum of different colours, from red through orange, yellow, green, and blue to violet. When they arrive at the eye mixed up together, the components of the colour spectrum are not perceived separately, but are fused together by the brain of the viewer to give the sensation 'white'. The raindrops act as a spectrum analyser, separating out the colour components so that the viewer perceives them individually.

There are many analogies between light and sound. Both are types of wave, although the frequencies of light waves are extremely high (around a thousand million million hertz). Of the visible spectrum seen in the rainbow, the red components have the lowest frequencies. The frequencies of the yellow components are somewhat higher, while the violet components have the highest frequencies that can be seen by the eye. The rainbow is in fact a display of the frequency spectrum of the sunlight, with the low-frequency components at the red end and the high-frequency components at the violet end.

A sound, like a beam of sunlight, can be split up into its frequency components. Indeed, the inner ear acts as a sound spectrum analyser, spreading the sound into a musical rainbow along the basilar membrane. The ripples which correspond to low-frequency components are strongest near the apex of the cochlea, while the ripples of high-frequency components have their highest amplitude near the oval window. Since the different regions of the basilar membrane send their signals to the brain through different nerve fibres, the frequency components undergo at least a preliminary sorting out before reaching the brain.

In discussing the musical sensation evoked by a particular type of sound, it is very useful to be able to mimic the behaviour of the ear by analysing the sound into its frequency components. An electronic spectrum analyser performs this task. Earlier we saw how the electrical signal from a microphone could be fed into an oscilloscope to show the waveform of a sound. If, instead, we feed the signal into a spectrum analyser, the screen will display the frequency spectrum of the sound.

Applying this technique to the sounds whose waveforms were examined in Figure 1.2 yielded the frequency spectra shown in Figure 1.8. In these diagrams a particular frequency component is represented by a vertical line. The distance along the horizontal axis represents the frequency of the component, measured in hertz. The height of the line represents the strength of the component. We have not yet discussed how to quantify the strength or loudness of a sound; the decibel (db) scale, which is used in Figure 1.8, will be explained later in the chapter.

Looking first at the sound of the high C on the piccolo, we see that, apart from some low-amplitude 'grass', the spectrum is strikingly simple. There is one strong

1.8 Frequency spectra of the three sounds whose waveforms are shown in Figure 1.2

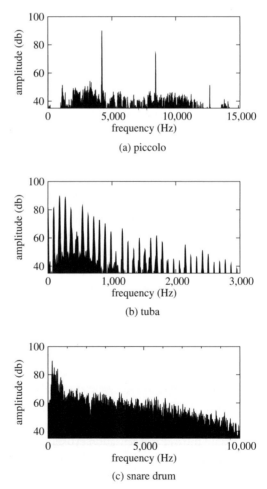

(a) piccolo

(b) tuba

(c) snare drum

component, with a frequency of 4,186 Hz—this, we recall, was the repetition frequency of the waveform. There is another component, considerably weaker, with exactly twice this frequency, and a third, weaker still, with three times the repetition frequency.

The tuba low F boasts a much larger number of frequency components in its spectrum than the piccolo high C. The first major peak again occurs at the repetition frequency, in this case 87.3 Hz. It is obvious from a casual glance at the piccolo and tuba spectra in Figure 1.8 that in each case there is a set of components equally spaced along the horizontal axis; this means that the frequencies of the higher components are simple whole number multiples of the lowest frequency. Such a set of equally spaced frequency components is called a harmonic spectrum, and the individual components are called harmonics.

As its name implies, the harmonic spectrum is fundamental to an understanding of musical sound. It would be a mistake, however, to conclude on the basis of our two examples that all musical sounds had harmonic spectra. When we look at the third example, the snare drum, we see a quite different type of spectrum. The components are very numerous, and are spread almost uniformly along the frequency axis. We could not find a periodicity in the waveform of this sound; nor can we find a set of harmonics in its spectrum. In fact, there is a mathematical result known as Fourier's theorem stating that a periodic waveform must have a harmonic spectrum and vice versa.

A pattern now begins to emerge from our investigation of sounds and their spectra. Musical sounds can be divided into two broad classes: pitched and unpitched. In the score of Figure 1.1, the woodwind, brass, timpani, and strings are all asked to play at specified pitches; in contrast, the snare drum and cymbals, notated on single lines, are expected to produce sounds of indefinite pitch. If we investigate the spectrum of any of the pitched sounds, we will find a set of harmonics (or, in the case of the timpani, a close approximation to one). On the other hand, if we look at the spectrum of an unpitched sound we will not find such a set of equally spaced frequency components.

1.3 THE PITCHES OF MUSICAL SOUNDS

The purpose of a musical instrument is to produce musical sounds. The musical context may be that of Caliban's 'sweet airs, that give delight and hurt not', or it may be the volcanic eruption of a heavy metal rock group; the physical processes giving rise to the sounds are similar, and the same basic vocabulary can be used to describe them. In the concluding part of this chapter we consider the musical terms which are used to characterize a particular note played on a particular instrument, and to reflect briefly on the relationship between these terms and the information that can be gained from measuring equipment like the oscilloscope and spectrum analyser.

A musical score, such as that shown in Figure 1.1, is a recipe for the production of musical sounds. In the last bar of the *Concerto for Orchestra* Bartók has written twenty-eight different notes. The pitches of twenty-six of these are determined by their positions on the stave, while the remaining two are unpitched. The loudness of each of the notes is specified by a dynamic marking (either *ff* or *fff*). The timbre of each sound is controlled by the requirement that the note be played on the instrument listed at the left of the score; for the snare drum and cymbal the method of playing is also specified. We shall look in turn at these three basic qualities of a musical sound: pitch, loudness, and timbre.

Methods of pitch description

The most common method of defining the pitch of a sound is by the position of a note on the musical stave, as in Figure 1.1. This method is based on the division of the audible pitch range into semitone steps. Later in this chapter we will discuss the reasons behind the choice of the semitone as the basic step. At present we merely accept that the resulting set of pitches provides the framework for most Western European music.

Frequently it is convenient to be able to define one of these pitches without drawing a musical stave. Within an octave this can be done by the usual letter names, augmented by sharps or flats. To specify the octave within which the note lies, we will in this book use the 'USA standard system', in which a number is added either as a subscript to the letter or immediately after it. The lowest C on the piano keyboard is labelled C_1; the chromatic scale upwards from this note is described as $C^\sharp_1, D_1, E^\flat_1, E_1, \ldots B^\flat_1, B_1$. The next octave starts with $C_2, C^\sharp_2$, etc. Middle C thus becomes C_4, and the highest note on the normal full- size piano keyboard is C_8. The three notes usually found below C_1 on a piano keyboard are labelled B_0, $B^\flat_0$ and A_0; this octave can in principle be extended down to C_0, but pitches below A_0 are very rare in music.

The USA standard system of pitch description is simple to write, and easy to remember because of its direct relationship with the piano keyboard. There is, however, another system which has been used in many books and articles on musical instruments. This is the 'Helmholtz system'. The original version of the system, introduced by the German acoustician Helmholtz in the nineteenth century, used upper- and lower-case letters with subscript numbers and superscript primes. A modified version, which retains the distinction between upper and lower cases but uses only superscript primes, is now more common. The relationship between the USA standard system and the modified Helmholtz system is shown in Appendix 1.

Pitch and frequency

Earlier in this chapter we compared the sounds of a high note on the piccolo and a low note on the tuba. We found that the high note had a high repetition frequency, the low note a low repetition frequency. It is in general true that the higher the frequency of a note, the higher its pitch. This apparently simple relationship does, however, require some further study.

Let us start with the simplest possible sound: one whose frequency spectrum contains only a single component. This sound, whose waveform is a sine curve, can be readily generated by many synthesizers. If we set the repetition frequency to 440 Hz we have a sound which is internationally recognized as a pitch standard: the A above middle C, which is described in the USA standard system as A_4.

It is important to recognize at this point that pitch is a subjective sensation. By this we mean that, although the frequency of 440 Hz can be electronically generated and scientifically measured with high precision, the response in terms of pitch may vary from individual to individual. Indeed, a single listener hearing the sound through an earphone applied first to the right ear and then to the left may well detect a pitch difference between the two ears. Fortunately, when both ears are used simultaneously the brain is normally able to integrate the signals from the two ears to give a single averaged pitch.

Dependence of pitch on loudness

Another complication in the relationship between frequency and pitch arises because the pitch of a single-component sound also depends to some extent on its loudness. Not everyone experiences this effect in the same way, but most listeners hear a 440 Hz sound drop slightly in pitch as its loudness is increased. The effect is greater for low-frequency sounds; some people find that the pitch of a single-component sound with frequency 100 Hz drops by several semitones when its loudness is increased from just audible to almost painful.

At first sight this finding appears to have drastic implications for the behaviour of instruments which are required to play low-pitch notes over a wide dynamic range. Consider, for example, the opening bars of Rachmaninov's Second Piano Concerto (Figure 1.9). The pianist plays the note F_1 seven times with the left hand, starting pianissimo and making a crescendo to fortissimo. The dramatic contrast between the relentless repetition of this fixed pitch and the shifting harmonies of the right-hand chords would be totally disrupted if the pitch of the bass notes drifted downwards as the loudness increased. Indeed, the very idea of a 'pianoforte'—a keyboard instrument that can play both quietly and loudly—would be impracticable.

Fortunately for the sanity of pianists, it is found that the variation of pitch with

1.9 The opening bars of Rachmaninov's Second Piano Concerto (© Copyright 1901 by Hawkes & Son (London) Ltd)

loudness is strong only for single-component sounds, and is negligible for sounds with many components. Figure 1.10 illustrates measurements of the spectra of three notes played mezzoforte on a grand piano. Clearly none of them are single-component sounds—indeed, it is possible to distinguish more than fifty components in the spectrum of F_1. Thus a pianist can safely indulge in a crescendo without risking an inadvertent modulation.

The harmonic spectrum

Looking again at Figure 1.10, we are faced with a question fundamental to an understanding of musical sound: why should a collection of many different frequency components sound like a single pitch? We already found an important clue in the observation that pitched sounds are associated with a special type of frequency spectrum, called the harmonic spectrum, consisting of a set of frequency components equally spaced along the frequency axis.

The concept of the harmonic spectrum is crucial to the discussion of pitch. As its name suggests, it is also an important idea in the theory of harmony, and it recurs constantly in the description of the acoustics of musical instruments. It is therefore worth pausing briefly to explain how a harmonic spectrum can be recognized and described.

Figure 1.11 illustrates the frequency spectrum of the note A_2 played mezzoforte on a tenor trombone. As with the other pitched sounds we have examined, the frequency spectrum contains a set of sharp peaks. Reading from left to right along the frequency axis, we find the first component at a frequency of 110 Hz. The second component has a frequency of 220 Hz, exactly twice the first. The third component has a frequency of 330 Hz, just three times the first. In fact, the components are spaced at equal frequency intervals, 110 Hz apart: they are therefore a set of harmonics, and the spectrum is a harmonic spectrum.

The first component in a harmonic spectrum is called the first harmonic; it is also often known as the fundamental. The second component, whose frequency is twice that of the fundamental, is called the second harmonic; and so on.

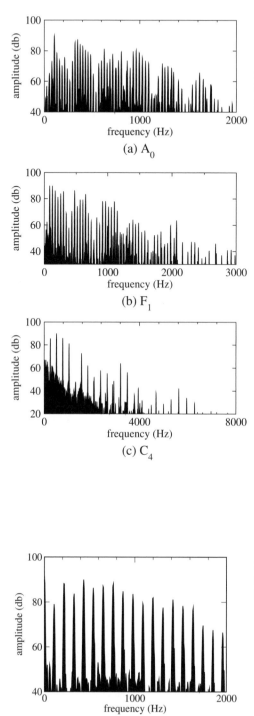

(a) A_0

(b) F_1

(c) C_4

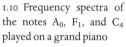

1.10 Frequency spectra of the notes A_0, F_1, and C_4 played on a grand piano

1.11 Frequency spectrum of the note A_2 played on a tenor trombone

Analytic and synthetic listening

It is possible to filter the sound of the trombone electronically in such a way that all the components save one are removed. If, for example, we set the filter to allow only the first component through, we will hear a note a little like a flute organ pipe with pitch A_2. Setting the filter to pass only the second component, we will hear a flute-like note with pitch A_3. The third component will sound at the pitch E_4; the fourth at A_4. Without the filter we are listening to all of these pitches simultaneously; somehow the brain fuses them all together to give a single note, with the pitch A_2.

Actually, it is possible by concentrated listening to hear some of the lower components of a musical note separately, even without the aid of an electronic filter. This mode of listening is sometimes called the 'analytic' mode, to distinguish it from the normal 'synthetic' mode in which the components are fused together. Earlier in this chapter we saw that the inner ear performs a frequency analysis of an incoming sound by spreading its spectrum along the basilar membrane. The six or seven lowest-frequency components of a harmonic series can in principle be distinguished separately because each component sends a signal to the brain from a different region of the basilar membrane. The higher-frequency components, on the other hand, excite overlapping regions on the basilar membrane, and the signals going to the brain are mixed up together. The first seven components are said to be 'resolved' by the ear's frequency analyser, while the higher components are 'unresolved'.

The perceived pitch of a harmonic spectrum

The low-frequency resolved components seem to be most important in determining the sensation of pitch which is aroused by a particular sound. The theory of pitch perception which is generally accepted at present involves a two-stage process. In the first stage the brain considers the individual pitches of the resolved components; this is equivalent to the analytic hearing mode previously described. In the second stage, the pattern of pitches of the resolved components is examined to see whether it resembles the pitch pattern of a harmonic spectrum. If it does, the listening mode switches from analytic to synthetic, and only a single note is heard. If the brain cannot find a reasonable match to a harmonic pattern, it remains in the analytic mode, and each component is heard separately.

Why does the brain search for a harmonic spectrum? It has been suggested that this is the mechanism by which a baby first learns to distinguish the sound of its mother's voice amid the cacophony of noise which bombards its ears. A less charming version of this theory is based on the need for primitive man to listen acutely for the howls and growls of marauding animals. Whatever the reason, it appears that the human brain constantly scans the incoming sound for evidence of a harmonic spectrum, and responds with the special sensation of a synthesized pitch when it finds one.

When we listen to a harmonic spectrum, the pitch we hear is close to that of the fundamental; in fact, for most practical purposes we can assume that the pitch of a set of harmonics is the same as the pitch that would be heard if all components except the fundamental were filtered out. In certain musical contexts, however, the harmonic content can have a noticeable effect on the pitch. For example, a musician playing behind the scenes in an opera house is in danger of sounding flat in the auditorium because the sound which penetrates has the higher harmonics filtered out by the selective absorption of the curtaining and scenery.

One remarkable feature of the brain's pitch processor is its ability to recognize an incomplete harmonic series. If the trombone A_2 in Figure 1.11 is recorded and played back through a portable tape player with a very small loudspeaker, the poor bass response will result in a spectrum with the fundamental at 110 Hz almost totally absent. The brain will still recognize the remaining components as belonging to a harmonic series with fundamental 110 Hz, and the pitch heard will still be A_2. Many synthesizers are capable of generating a 'square-wave' output, whose spectrum contains only the odd harmonics; if the fundamental frequency is chosen to be 110 Hz, the pitch heard will still be A_2 despite the fact that the frequency spacing between adjacent harmonics is now 220 Hz rather than 110 Hz.

The perceived pitch of an almost harmonic spectrum

Musical instruments which are played by plucking or striking do not usually generate sounds with exactly harmonic spectra. Careful measurements of the spectrum of the piano C_4 in Figure 1.10, for example, showed that the second component had a frequency slightly more than twice the first; in fact, the ratio was 2.001 : 1. Similar discrepancies were found in the frequencies of the higher components, each being slightly sharper than the corresponding ideal harmonic. Later we will discuss the reasons for these discrepancies; at this stage we merely note with gratitude that the brain's pitch processor is prepared to ignore them, and to identify the sound of a piano note as having a clear and definite pitch.

Some fascinating experiments using computer-generated sounds have been carried out to explore the limits of tolerance of the brain's pitch processor. It seems that the brain is very eager to find a harmonic spectrum, and is willing to accept quite flimsy evidence. The components can be shifted by nearly a semitone from their exact harmonic values before the brain gives up the attempt to hear a single pitch and reverts to the analytic mode, hearing each component individually. We will see later that this has an important bearing on the behaviour of tuned percussion instruments.

When the brain is trying to make pitch sense of an inharmonic spectrum, it does not treat each frequency component as having equal importance. The perceived pitch is affected most strongly by components in the frequency range from 500 Hz to 2,000 Hz; this range is sometimes called the 'dominance region' for pitch perception. Thus if we modify the exact harmonic spectrum of A_2 shown in Figure 1.11 by sharpening the fifth component slightly, leaving the others unchanged, the perceived pitch of the synthesized spectrum will also sharpen since the fifth component is in the dominance region. Making the same change in the fundamental would not significantly affect the pitch, since the fundamental of A_2 lies well below the dominance region.

Pitch intervals

Whether describing the shape of a melody or analysing the structure of a chord, the concept of pitch interval is vital to most types of music, and predetermined pitch intervals feature in almost all musical instruments. A particular pitch interval corresponds to a fixed ratio of the fundamental frequencies of the notes concerned. If two notes are an octave apart, for example, the frequency of the higher note is always twice that of the lower note. The fundamental frequency of A_2 is

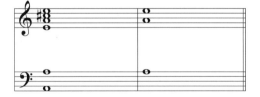

1.12 Individual pitches of (left) the first six harmonics of a sound with pitch A_2; (right) the first three harmonics of a sound with pitch A_3

110 Hz; to jump an octave to A_3 the frequency must be doubled to 220 Hz; to jump a further octave to A_4 the frequency must be doubled again to 440 Hz. The octave is of special importance in music, since two notes separated by this interval have a particularly close relationship. They sound almost like different versions of the same note—this is reflected in the fact that they are given the same letter name. We can view the relationship in a different way by considering the frequency spectra of the two notes. Take the lower note to be A2: its fundamental frequency is 110 Hz, and the first six harmonics are shown in Figure 1.12 (left). The note an octave above is A_3, with fundamental frequency 220 Hz. Its second harmonic is at twice 220 = 440 Hz; its third harmonic is at three times 220 = 660 Hz, as shown in Figure 1.12 (right). The remarkable fact evident from Figure 1.12 is that all the harmonic components of the upper note are already present in the spectrum of the lower note. To jump up an octave from A_2 it is not necessary to add any new sound—we need only remove the odd-numbered harmonics from the spectrum.

If one instrument plays A_2 and another joins in exactly an octave above, the second instrument merely reinforces the even harmonics in the spectrum of the first. It is natural to take the octave as a basic unit for measuring and comparing pitch intervals. In music we are frequently concerned with very small pitch changes, and to measure these we use subdivisions of the octave. On a modern piano keyboard the octave is divided into twelve equal steps called equally tempered semitones. Each semitone can be further subdivided into a hundred cents. The cent is as small a unit as we require, since even under optimum conditions the normal human ear is insensitive to pitch changes of less than three or four cents.

Intervals in the harmonic spectrum

The harmonic spectrum is of importance not only in the perception of sound but also in the practical functioning of many instruments. For example, the natural notes which can be played on a tenor trombone without extending the slide are found at pitches corresponding to the harmonics of $B^\flat_1$. It is therefore worth looking in some detail at the pitch intervals which occur in a set of harmonics.

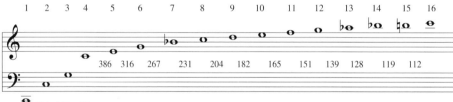

1.13 Pitches of the first sixteen members of the harmonic series with fundamental C_2. The number of each harmonic is shown above the stave; the pitch intervals (in cents) between successive harmonics are shown below the stave. The nearest member of the equally tempered chromatic scale is shown by a semibreve

The pitches of the first sixteen harmonics of C_2 are shown in Figure 1.13. The number of each harmonic is shown above the stave, and below the stave is shown the size of each successive pitch interval in cents.

The interval between first and second harmonics is of course an octave, since the frequency ratio is 2 : 1. The octave, consisting of twelve semitones each of 100 cents, is 1,200 cents wide. The interval between second and third harmonics is the perfect fifth C_3–G_3. Since the frequency of the 3rd harmonic is three times the fundamental and the frequency of the second harmonic is two times the fundamental, the frequency ratio corresponding to the perfect fifth is 3 : 2. When the frequency ratio $f_2 : f_1$ is known the pitch interval can be calculated using the formula

$$\text{pitch interval (cents)} = 3986 \log(f_2/f_1);$$

for a ratio of 3 : 2 the interval is 702 cents.

We can see immediately that the perfect fifth found in the harmonic spectrum is not exactly the same interval as the fifth available on an equally tempered keyboard. The latter interval is made up of seven equally tempered semitones, each of which by definition contains 100 cents; the equally tempered fifth thus contains 700 cents, and is 2 cents narrower than the perfect fifth in the harmonic spectrum.

Several other important musical intervals are found in the harmonic spectrum. The interval between the 3rd and 4th harmonics is a perfect fourth (498 cents), that between the 4th and 5th harmonics is a major third (386 cents), and that between the 5th and 6th harmonics is a minor third (316 cents). Intervals derived from the harmonic spectrum are often called just intonation intervals.

The necessity for keyboard temperament

The intervals between the first six notes in the harmonic spectrum have a particular significance—they can be heard by analytic listening to a single musical note, and can therefore be seen as emerging naturally from the basic fabric of music. On the other hand, it is not possible to tune a keyboard instrument of the conventional pattern to give only just-intonation intervals. The problem is revealed immediately by consideration of the four-note chord C_4–E_4–$G^{\#}_4$–C_5. If the intervals C_4–E_4 and E_4–$G^{\#}_4$ are both just-intonation major thirds, each containing 386 cents, the interval C_4–$G^{\#}_4$ must contain $2 \times 386 = 772$ cents. The octave C_4–C_5 contains 1,200 cents, and on a twelve-note keyboard $G^{\#}$ must be the same note as $A^{\flat}$. Thus the interval $A^{\flat}_4$–C_5 must contain $1200 - 772 = 428$ cents, which is 42 cents (nearly half a semitone) too large for a just-intonation major third.

Another illustration of the impossibility of tuning a keyboard to give only just-intonation intervals is provided by the 'circle of fifths', shown in Figure 1.14. If we start with C_1, the lowest C on a piano keyboard, and take twelve upwards steps of a fifth, we will arrive at the note $B^{\#}_7$. On the keyboard, this note is the same as C_8, which is seven octaves above C_1. The trouble is that twelve perfect fifths add up to $12 \times 702 = 8{,}424$ cents, while seven octaves contain $7 \times 1{,}200 = 8{,}400$ cents. The discrepancy of 24 cents is known as the Pythagorean comma. If eleven of the fifths are made perfect, the remaining one will be nearly a quarter of a semitone too narrow.

Rather than having some intervals ideal and others unusable, keyboard instruments are normally tuned in such a way that the discrepancies are shared out among the different intervals in the scale; this is the process known as temperament. Various methods of temperament will be discussed in Chapter 10. When the sharing is completely even-handed we arrive at equal temperament tuning, in which all semitones are exactly 100 cents. Each fifth has been narrowed by 2 cents

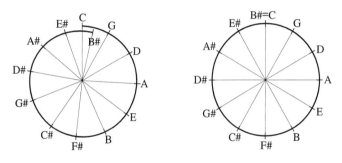

(a) just intonation fifths (702 cents)   (b) equal temperament fifths (700 cents)

1.14 The circle of fifths. The discrepancy between C and B♯ in just intonation is exaggerated for clarity of illustration

to 700 cents; the circle of fifths then closes, in the sense that B♯ and C have the same pitch (Figure 1.14b). The three major thirds in the chord C_4–E_4–$G^{\sharp}_4$– C_5 discussed above will each contain 400 cents; the 42-cent discrepancy has been equally shared out so that each interval is 14 cents larger than its just intonation value.

Pitch intervals in musical performance

Before leaving the subject of pitch intervals it is necessary to issue a warning against the assumption which is sometimes made that there is one ideal size for each pitch interval, valid in all musical circumstances. On a keyboard instrument such as the piano or the organ, as we have seen, the intervals are chosen by the tuner in advance of the performance. On most other types of musical instrument the pitch of each note can be subtly adjusted by the performer at the time of playing, and musicians are well aware that a particular note which sounds in tune in one context may have to be adjusted up or down by several cents to fit a different context.

A pitch interval can appear in music between two successive notes (melody) or between two notes played simultaneously (harmony). The tuning is more critical in the second case because of the phenomenon of beating. This phenomenon is illustrated in Figure 1.15, which shows the effect of adding together two sine wave sounds A and B of the same amplitude but slightly different frequency. The first line shows the signal picked up by a microphone when only sound A is played, while the second shows the signal from sound B alone. The third line shows the signal when the two sounds are played simultaneously.

At the earliest time shown (on the left of the diagram) the two waves are in phase—that is, a peak in A coincides with a peak in B, giving an amplitude for the combined wave which is twice that of either component separately. The frequency of A is higher than that of B, so that as time goes by the two waves get increasingly out of phase. Eventually a peak in A coincides with a dip in B; The effect of A then exactly cancels the effect of B, and the amplitude of the combined wave drops to zero. Still later, A has gained a complete cycle of vibration over B, and the two are once again in phase.

As can be seen from the third line of Figure 1.15, the addition of the two steady notes of slightly different pitch results in a sound whose amplitude regularly rises to a maximum and dies away again. The characteristic effect resembles a series of sound pulses, and each pulse is called a beat. If, for example, sounds A and B have frequencies of 103 Hz and 100 Hz respectively, in one second A will complete three more vibration cycles than B and three beats will be heard. Thus the number of beats per second is equal to the frequency difference between the two notes.

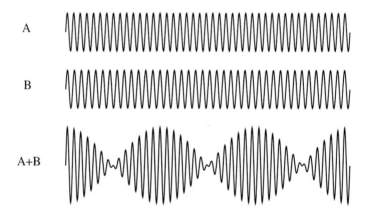

1.15 The addition of two sine waves with slightly different frequencies: the resulting amplitude fluctuations are known as beats

Listening for beats can be a useful method of tuning a unison, for example between two unison strings on a lute—the slower the beat rate, the smaller the pitch difference between the strings. The method is extremely sensitive, since it is possible to hear beat rates slower than one per second. For pitches around A_4, a beat rate of one every two seconds corresponds to a pitch difference of only two cents. In practice, it is usually the sound of beats which betrays an imperfectly tuned unison.

Beats also play an important role in the perception of harmonic intervals other than the unison. A simultaneous octave played by two instruments with rich harmonic spectra contains numerous unisons between pairs of harmonics. Figure 1.16 (left) shows that in the octave C_3–C_4, considering only the first six harmonics of each note, there are three unisons. If the octave is slightly mistuned, each of these now imperfect unisons will beat. In contrast, Figure 1.16 (right) shows that in the major third C_3–E_3 there is only one unison. For this reason a small tuning discrepancy is detected more easily in an octave than in a major third.

The unison between the fifth harmonic of C_3 and the fourth harmonic of E_3 will be perfect when the interval between the fundamentals is a just intonation major third. If this interval is an equal temperament major third there will be a frequency difference of just over 5 Hz between the two harmonics. The significance of this difference will depend on the nature of the spectra of the two notes—obviously if one of these harmonics is very weak the effect on the sound of the interval will be negligible. But if both harmonics are strong the beating will probably be audible, at a rate of five beats per second.

Even if the interval is a just intonation major third, the sound is coloured by interactions between adjacent harmonics. The fourth harmonic of C_3 is a semitone above the third harmonic of E_3, while the sixth harmonic of C_3 is a semitone below the fifth harmonic of E_3. In each case the frequency difference between the pair of harmonics is 33 Hz. While the ear cannot distinguish individual beats at a

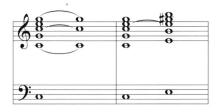

1.16 Interactions between the harmonics of two simultaneously sounded notes. (left) Octave interval: three unisons (shown by slurs). (right) Just intonation major third: one unison (shown by slur)

rate much above ten per second, the 33 Hz fluctuation in loudness contributes a sensation of roughness to the perception of the interval. Other musical intervals can be analysed in a similar way. When a soloist is asked to play an unaccompanied melodic line, the choice of intervals is not constrained by the necessity of avoiding beats. The factors governing the exact choice of intervals between successive notes are not yet fully understood, but tests of what musicians actually play under these circumstances have shown some fascinating and surprising features. There are small but systematic differences between intervals chosen for melodic and harmonic purposes. In particular, the octave used in unaccompanied melody is usually slightly larger than the 'standard' octave so far discussed, whose frequency ratio is exactly 2 : 1.

In Appendix 1 we give a table of the frequencies of all notes from C_0 to B_8 in semitone steps, calculated according to the equal temperament scheme. This set of frequencies provides a useful framework for reference purposes, but it is worth reiterating that many subtle effects determine the exact pitch chosen by a musician in a given context. The ultimate guide must be the musical sensitivity of the performer.

1.4 THE LOUDNESS OF MUSICAL SOUNDS

Pressure amplitude and musical dynamics

Most of the ink on a page of conventional musical score is spent in defining the pitch of each note required. In contrast, the loudness of the note is specified by a dynamic marking which allows the performer considerable leeway in interpretation. There are two fundamental reasons for this relative lack of precision. In the first place, the human ear is much more sensitive to small gradations of pitch than to correspondingly small changes in loudness: a musically trained listener could probably distinguish more than 800 significant steps in the pitch range from C_1 to C_8, but would be hard pressed to distinguish more than fifty steps in loudness from a just audible sound to one which was almost painful. In the second place, the loudness of a note in a given musical context is subject to so many different factors that the composer must rely on the judgement of the player to balance all these factors at the time of performance. In what follows we seek to clarify the nature of some of these factors.

The first dynamic markings to appear in musical scores, at the end of the sixteenth century, defined only two categories of loudness: piano (quiet) and forte (loud). The most obvious factor which distinguishes a note played quietly from the same note played loudly is the amplitude of the pressure fluctuations in the sound wave. The pressure fluctuates much more at the forte dynamic level than it does at the piano level.

By the end of the nineteenth century eight dynamic categories were in common use: *ppp, pp, p, mp, mf, f, ff* and *fff*. Experiments designed to measure the pressure amplitude of a simple sine wave sound as its dynamic level is increased have shown that an increase in loudness from *mp* to *mf* corresponds to an increase in the pressure amplitude by a factor of about 3. To raise the loudness by another dynamic step to *f*, it is necessary to again multiply the amplitude by roughly 3. Extending the experiment from *ppp* to *fff* confirms the general rule: multiplying the amplitude by a factor of about 3 raises the loudness by one dynamic step.

Sound intensity and decibel measurements

In describing a musical performance the word 'intensity' can be used with a variety of subtly different meanings. The word also has a precisely defined scientific meaning which is useful in discussing the loudness of sounds: the intensity of a sound wave is the amount of sound energy passing through an area of one square metre in one second.

For sine wave sounds, the intensity of the sound wave is proportional to the square of the pressure amplitude. This relationship implies that when the dynamic level increases by one step, and the pressure amplitude increases by a factor of just over 3, the intensity increases by a factor of about 10. For a more realistic musical sound with a more complex waveform, the relationship between pressure amplitude and intensity is not so straightforward. Nevertheless, we can still use the approximate guideline that increasing the loudness by one dynamic step is equivalent to increasing the intensity by a factor of about 10.

The remarkable nature of this relationship becomes clear when we remember that the normal dynamic range has seven steps between *ppp* and *fff*. If each step involves multiplying the intensity by 10, then the *fff* sound must be 10,000,000 times as intense as the *ppp* sound. The fact that the human ear operates over such a large dynamic range poses quite a problem to designers of sound-reproduction equipment—it is not easy to build a microphone which can respond adequately to the quietest audible sound without overloading when the intensity is increased by a factor of ten million.

Equal steps on the musical dynamic scale correspond roughly to equal ratios of intensity. When specifying intensity changes in a musical context, for example in an electronic music score, it is therefore convenient to use the decibel (db) scale, since equal decibel steps also correspond to equal intensity ratios. The decibel difference between two sounds with intensities I_1 and I_2 is defined by the formula

$$\text{decibel difference} = 10 \log(I_2/I_1)$$

For our present purposes we need to use only two simple rules: multiplying the intensity by 2 gives a 3 db increase, and multiplying the intensity by 10 gives a 10 db increase. The second of these rules shows that a single dynamic step (for example from *ppp* to *pp*) corresponds roughly to an increase in intensity of 10 db. The dynamic range from *ppp* to *fff* consists of seven steps each of 10 db, giving a total span of 70 db.

The fact that the subjective response to the loudness of sound (as expressed by musical dynamics) is related to the decibel scale helps to explain the law of diminishing returns which operates when we try to increase the loudness of an orchestra or band by bringing in more players. If we double the size of the band we can expect it to generate twice as much sound energy, so the intensity should double: but this will raise the loudness by only 3 db, about a third of one dynamic step. A group of twenty musicians might find it impossible to generate a dynamic level higher than *f* at the back of a large hall; to raise the perceived loudness to *ff* would require an increase in intensity by a factor of 10, and a band of 200 players.

Loudness and frequency: why the piccolo is always heard

The human ear does not respond with equal sensitivity to all frequencies. Variations of air pressure at frequencies below about 20 Hz or above about 20,000 Hz

1.17 Variation of loudness with pitch for a sine wave of constant intensity

do not evoke any sensation of sound, although such infrasonic and ultrasonic waves can produce other effects on the human body. The ear is most sensitive to frequency components around 4,000 Hz, partly because the ear canal has a resonance in this frequency region. Below about 300 Hz the sensitivity deteriorates rapidly; a sine wave with a frequency of 25 Hz requires a million times more intensity than a wave at 1,000 Hz if both are to sound at the *pp* dynamic level. The practical effect is that very low-frequency components in the sound of musical instruments are usually not sufficiently intense to be audible.

As another illustration of the variation of the ear's sensitivity with frequency, let us assume that a synthesizer set up to give a pure sine wave sound plays the descending arpeggio shown in Figure 1.17. The volume control is adjusted so that the first note sounds *mf*; the control is then left at that setting, so that the pressure amplitude and intensity of each note is the same. The loudness, however, will vary in the way indicated by the dynamic markings, reflecting the changing sensitivity of the ear. The dynamic level will drop steadily as the arpeggio descends through the bass clef region, and the last note will be completely inaudible.

The ear's preference for notes above the top of the treble clef has many important consequences in musical performance. A performer on the tuba, which generates most of its sound energy at low frequencies, has to work much harder than the player of the piccolo, whose frequency components lie in the ear's most sensitive region. For the same reason, the Queen of the Night in Mozart's opera *The Magic Flute* could always overcome her adversary Sarastro if the contest were merely to see who could sing the loudest note, since the Queen is a high soprano and Sarastro a bass.

Sound power output of musical instruments

Power is a measure of the rate at which energy is supplied or used. The unit of power is the watt (abbreviated W), familiar in everyday life in rating light bulbs, electric heaters, and amplifiers. In all these cases it is electrical power which is being measured, but the same unit is used in the measurement of sound power. Unless a musical instrument is being played with extraordinary force its sound power output is only a fraction of one watt, so it is more convenient to quote musical instrument powers in milliwatts (abbreviated mW: 1 W = 1,000 mW).

The rate at which an instrument radiates sound energy will clearly depend on how loudly it is playing. Table 1.2 shows the results of some tests in which musicians were asked to play at the dynamic level corresponding to a forte in orchestral music. The remarkable sensitivity of the ear is very evident from these figures: a forte chord from a symphony orchestra is an impressive sound, yet the total sound power involved is only one hundredth of the electrical power needed to run a small light bulb. Another striking feature of Table 1.2 is the large range of sound outputs from players responding to the same dynamic marking. In a forte passage a brass instrument will typically generate about twenty times as much sound energy as a stringed instrument, and about ten times as much as a woodwind. From these figures we can readily see why an orchestra requires a large number of string players in each section, and why Richard Strauss warned that a conductor should never look encouragingly at the brass.

The wide disparity in power output among orchestral instruments is a positive advantage in one sense. A solo performer on violin, clarinet, or trombone strives to achieve the largest possible dynamic range on the instrument by varying its sound power output in a controlled manner. In practice it is impossible to maintain the necessary degree of control over the span of 70 db which we earlier identified with the full dynamic range from *ppp* to *fff*. To achieve this, a player would have to be capable of sounding a note so quiet that it carried only one ten-millionth of the power of the loudest note. The maximum practicable ranges for the instruments quoted in Table 1.2 are shown in the right-hand column; they range from 20 db for the flute to 40 db for the clarinet and horn. These figures are, of

Table 1.2 *Sound power and dynamic range of instruments* (after J. Meyer)

Instrument	Average sound power playing forte (mW)	Practical dynamic range (db)
Violin	0.8	35
Viola	0.5	30
Cello	1	30
Double bass	1.6	30
Flute	1.3	20
Oboe	2	30
Clarinet	2	40
Bassoon	2	30
Horn	16	40
Trumpet	13	30
Trombone	13	35
Tuba	20	30
Full orchestra (without percussion)	250	65

1.18 Excerpt from the first movement of Tchaikovsky's Sixth Symphony, from bar 157

course, only rough guides, and relate to normal orchestral playing conditions. Part of the art of the virtuoso soloist lies in the ability to transcend such limits.

The instrumental palette available to the composer of music for the full orchestra offers much greater dynamic contrasts. In the excerpt from Tchaikovsky's Sixth Symphony shown in Figure 1.18, the orchestration is pared down until, at the end of bar 159, only a single clarinet is playing. The extreme dynamic marking of *ppppp* clearly requires the player to find the quietest sounds possible; the clarinet is well chosen for this task, since it has the largest dynamic range in the woodwind and can be sounded at a power level below that of any other orchestral instrument. The minimum power level at which the bassoon can be sounded is at least 10 db higher, which makes it impossible for the bassoon player to fulfil the composer's demand for an even quieter sound in the second half of bar 160. In practice these four notes are frequently played on a bass clarinet which, like its higher-pitched relative, has exceptional control at very low power levels.

With shattering effect, this exploration of the lower limit of the dynamic spectrum is succeeded by a fortissimo chord from the full orchestra. Dominated by the power of four horns, two trumpets, three trombones, and tuba, and reinforced by a timpani roll, the dynamic level can rise abruptly by more than 60 db. This is a far greater increase than could be achieved on a single instrument, and is close to the maximum useful range of 70 db which we discussed previously. Late Romantic music offers innumerable similar examples of the exploitation of the full dynamic range available from a large orchestra.

Our discussion of pitch ended with a warning against taking calculations of 'ideal' intervals and scales too seriously. An even larger pinch of salt is required to season any suggestion that musical dynamic markings might be replaced by decibel ratings. The problem in both cases is that the human brain operates in a very sophisticated way when interpreting the sounds of music. Thus the listener adapts to the restricted dynamic range of the flute, and is happy to accept that a crescendo from *pp* to *ff* on a solo flute requires a change in intensity of only 20 db; from a full orchestra, this would sound like a much more modest increase in loudness, and a full *pp – ff* crescendo would require an intensity change of around 60 db. The performing situation and the musical context are such important factors that the selection of the sound power required for a given dynamic marking must ultimately be left to the judgement of the player or conductor.

1.5 THE TIMBRE OF MUSICAL SOUNDS

In Figure 1.19 a short excerpt from the score of Beethoven's Fifth Symphony is reproduced. The excerpt starts at bar 59 in the first movement. At bar 63 the first

1.19 Excerpt from the first movement of Beethoven's Fifth Symphony, from bar 59. Note that the clarinet is a transposing instrument, so that the sounding pitch is a tone lower than the written pitch

violins enter with a four-bar melody; in bars 67–70 the melody is repeated by the first clarinet. In terms of pitch and dynamic level these two statements of the melody are identical. The remaining difference is in the character of the sounds, played in the first case by a string section and in the second by a solo woodwind. Timbre and tone quality are two terms often used to encompass the various factors which allow us to distinguish between two notes of the same pitch and loudness. In the following section we review briefly the more important of these factors.

We start by considering the simplest case, a long steady note. Later we will look at the fluctuations, or transients, which are important characterizing features of most real musical sounds.

The frequency spectrum of a steady note

Earlier in this chapter we saw that a steady note with a definite pitch had a frequency spectrum containing a set of harmonics. In Figure 1.20 (a) and (b) we show two spectra recorded by a bass singing the two vowel sounds 'ee' and 'ah' at the pitch G_2. The fundamental frequency of G_2 is 98 Hz; as expected, the components of both spectra are equally spaced at 98 Hz intervals along the frequency axis.

The two notes were sung at the same dynamic level (forte), so the distinction between the vowels must lie in the different timbres of the sounds. Comparing the two spectra, it is clear that this difference of timbre is related to the relative strengths of the different frequency components. In the spectrum of the 'ee' sound the components around 300 Hz and 2,000 Hz are higher (that is, stronger) than the remaining components in the spectrum; in contrast, the strongest components in the 'ah' spectrum are found around 700 Hz and 1,000 Hz.

A line joining the tops of all the component lines in the frequency spectrum is known as the spectrum envelope. If the measurement were repeated, with the same vowels sung at the same pitch, the heights of the individual components would probably be somewhat different, since no two humanly generated sounds are ever identical. The spectrum envelopes would still show the same patterns of peaks and dips, which are the broad features used by the brain to identify the timbre of the sounds, and hence to recognize the vowel as either 'ee' or 'ah'.

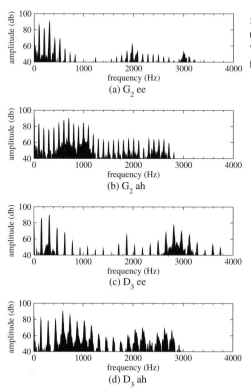

1.20 Frequency spectra of the vowel sounds 'ee' and 'ah' sung by a bass at two different pitches

Formants

Spectra (c) and (d) in Figure 1.20 show the frequency components found when the two vowels are sung at the higher pitch D3. The frequency spacing of the harmonics has increased to 147 Hz, which is the new fundamental frequency. Interestingly, however, peaks in the 'ee' spectrum are still found at around 300 Hz and 2,000 Hz, while those of the 'ah' spectrum are found at around 600 Hz and 1,000 Hz. In the 'ee' spectrum, the second peak is centred on the 19th harmonic at the pitch G_2 and on the 12th harmonic at the pitch D_3. What is important for the characteristic vowel sound 'ee' is obviously not the number of the strongest harmonic but rather its frequency.

A frequency region where the components are always strong, regardless of the pitch of the note being sung or played, is called a formant. From the observations just quoted we can deduce that the sung vowel 'ee' is characterized by formants at around 300 Hz and 2,000 Hz, while the vowel 'ah' is characterized by formants at around 600 Hz and 1,000 Hz. Different formants also characterize the other vowel sounds.

Whether formants are important in the recognition of musical instrument tim-

1.21 Frequency spectra of the notes (a) $B^\flat_2$ (b) F_3, (c) $B^\flat_3$ and F_4, played on a tenor trombone. A formant is evident at around 750 Hz

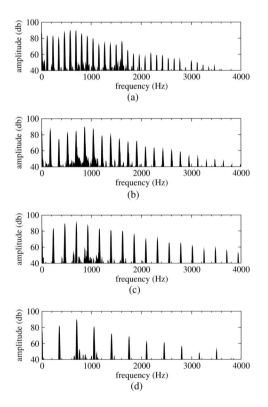

bre is a matter of debate. A resonance in the amplifying system of an instrument will tend to boost whichever frequency components come within its range, giving rise to a formant in the spectra of the instrument. An example of such a formant is evident in the spectra of a trombone shown in Figure 1.21. In each spectrum the component nearest in frequency to 700 Hz is the strongest, with the exception of (b) in which the peak is just over 800 Hz. This formant in the region of 700–800 Hz is related to a resonance in the mouthpiece of the trombone.

Bright and clean, dark and dirty

Pitch and loudness are one-dimensional quantities. By this we mean that if the pitch of a note changes, it must go either up or down—it cannot in any sense go 'sideways'. Likewise, there is a single scale of variation in loudness; a change in loudness is either a crescendo or a diminuendo. Timbre, on the other hand, is a multi-dimensional quantity, in that two notes can differ in timbre in a wide variety of ways. To cope with this diversity musicians have appropriated a large number of adjectives in the attempt to describe subtle shades of timbre. A sound may be bright or dark; hard or soft; broad or narrow; clean or dirty; open or closed.

It has proved difficult to relate these subjective descriptions to obvious features of the sound spectra. However, one verbal scale, in which sounds are described as 'sharp' or 'dull', has been shown to correlate well with the presence or absence of high-frequency components in the spectrum. A sound with strong high-frequency components is described as having a 'sharp' timbre, while one with most of the sound energy concentrated in the low-frequency components is described as 'dull'. Because of the confusion with sharpness in the sense of high pitch, the term 'brightness' is often preferred by musicians. Obviously an instrument with a strong high-frequency formant will tend to have a bright sound. For most instruments the high-frequency components get stronger as the instrument is played louder, so that loud notes have a brighter timbre than quiet notes.

Amplitude envelopes

Early attempts to synthesize the sounds of real instruments proved that, even when the spectrum of the steady part of a note was fairly accurately reproduced, the artificial nature of the note was still very evident. Subsequent research showed that the realism of the synthesized sound was greatly improved when proper attention was paid to the way in which the note started and stopped. In particular, the pattern of change at the beginning of a note—the 'attack transient'—has turned out to be one of the most important clues which the brain uses in identifying the instrument which is playing the note.

As an example of a realistic attack transient, Figure 1.22 shows the signal from a microphone recording the start of the note G_4 played on an oboe. The pressure variation which constitutes the sound wave does not begin immediately at its full amplitude, but grows steadily, reaching a steady state only after about 15 milliseconds. This 15-millisecond period contains the attack transient of the note.

A line drawn to link the upper extremities of the pressure waveform is known as the amplitude envelope. The amplitude envelope is the simplest way of characterizing the attack transient. Early electronic organs did not attempt to repro-

1.22 Oscilloscope trace illustrating the sound pressure changes during the initial transient of an oboe

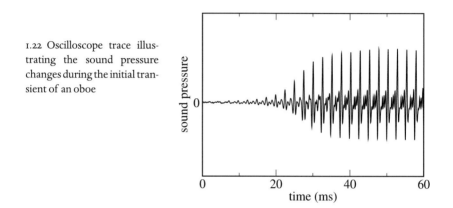

duce the attack transient; the steady state of the note was switched on abruptly by pressing a key. As a result, an organ oboe stop had an unmistakably 'electronic' sound. Modern techniques of synthesis allow the amplitude envelope to be properly reproduced, giving a timbre much more like the real instrument.

Closer inspection of Figure 1.22 reveals that it is not only the overall amplitude that is changing during the attack transient. The shape of the waveform evolves from a relatively smooth wiggle to one with a rapid alternation of jagged peaks and dips. Since the shape of the waveform is related to the spectrum of the sound, it is clear that the spectrum must also be changing during the attack transient. The implication is that the different components in the spectrum are growing at different rates; each component must have its own individual amplitude envelope. The human ear is sensitive to such spectral changes in the attack transient, and to provide a convincing reproduction of a particular instrument a synthesizer must generate realistic amplitude envelopes for at least the first few frequency components.

2

Family Resemblances

The instruments in a symphony orchestra are conventionally divided into four classes: woodwind, brass, percussion, and strings. In an orchestral score, such as that shown in Figure 1.1, the parts are usually grouped in these classes. At the top of the score come the woodwind: flutes, oboes, clarinets, and bassoons are the regular occupants of this section, which in larger orchestras can also include piccolo, cor anglais, E♭ and bass clarinets, saxophones, and contrabassoon. Below this section in the score come the brass: horns, trumpets, trombones, and tuba are occasionally augmented by such specialities as flugelhorns and Wagner tubas. Next come the percussion: a very varied group this, sometimes limited to two or three timpani, but frequently extended to include bass and side drums, gongs, cymbals, triangle, bells, glockenspiel, xylophone, and a wide range of unlikely looking noise-makers. Finally comes the string section: harp and piano if required, then violins, violas, cellos, and double basses.

The discussion of musical instruments in the following chapters of this book is based on this accepted classification scheme. Chapters 3 and 4 deal with the woodwind family; in Chapters 5 and 6 we discuss the brass; Chapter 7 reviews the percussion family; Chapters 8 to 11 cover the strings, including the keyboard stringed instruments; finally, Chapters 12 and 13 consider organs and electronic instruments, which are not normally associated with the symphony orchestra.

In this second introductory chapter we look a little more closely at the varied ways in which musical instruments create their characteristic sounds, focusing especially on those factors which are common to instruments from a particular family. The conventional family names are obviously an unreliable guide in this quest: a saxophone, frequently made of brass, is not considered a brass instrument, while a silver flute without a particle of wood in its construction is accepted as a woodwind instrument. The family resemblances between members of a section are clearly due to something more fundamental than the material of manufacture.

Various alternative schemes for classifying musical instruments have been proposed. A systematic classification scheme originally developed by Erich von Hornbostel and Curt Sachs, and later extended by Francis Galpin, is very helpful in clarifying the crucial similarities and differences between instruments. To use this scheme, we first identify the nature of the basic sound generating mechanism in the instrument. Five different types of sound-generator can be distinguished, and the five corresponding classes form the major divisions of the scheme. Within each class, subdivisions are used to group instruments with similar methods of construction, similar playing techniques, or other features in common.

A simplified version of the classification scheme is outlined in Table 2.1. The first major class contains those instruments whose basic sound generator is a vibrating object, usually a bar, tube, or plate. Members of this class are described as idiophones, a technical term defining the ability of the object to emit its own characteristic sound when excited. The idiophone class includes all the instruments of the percussion section apart from the drums. In the second column of Table 2.1 four methods of exciting idiophones are described. Method (a), striking, is much the most important for the orchestral percussion instruments—indeed, the term percussion implies the act of striking.

The second major class of instruments contains the membranophones, whose essential sound generator is a stretched flexible sheet or membrane. The remaining members of the percussion section of the orchestra, the drums, fall into subdivision (a) of this class, being struck membranophones.

The third major class comprises the chordophones, which have as their essential sound generator a stretched string and therefore come under the general

Table 2.1 *Musical instrument classification scheme*

Major class	Method of excitation	Examples
1. Idiophones: vibrating rigid object	(a) striking (b) plucking (c) rubbing (d) shaking	xylophone, gong, triangle Jew's harp, lamellaphone glass harmonica maracas, jingles
2. Membranophones: vibrating stretched membrane	(a) striking (b) rubbing (c) singing	timpani, bass drum, tabla rommelpot kazoo
3. Chordophones: vibrating stretched string	(a) striking (b) plucking (c) bowing	dulcimer, clavichord, piano harp, guitar, harpsichord violin, viol, hurdy-gurdy
4. Aerophones: vibrating air	(a) air jet (b) mechanical reed (c) lip reed	flute, recorder, organ flue pipe clarinet, organ reed pipe, accordion trumpet, bugle, cornetto
5. Electrophones: vibrating loudspeaker	(a) electronic (b) electromechanical (c) electroacoustic	Ondes Martenot, synthesizer Hammond organ electric guitar

description of stringed instruments. Subdivision (c), the bowed chordophones, includes the standard orchestral string section, while subdivisions (a) and (b), the struck and plucked chordophones, contain important solo and keyboard instruments.

The fourth major class covers instruments in which the basic sound generator is not any part of the mechanical structure of the instrument, but rather a fluctuating air flow. The woodwind and the brass are included in this aerophone class, since the crucial feature of both families is a tube within which a column of air is set into vibration. The musically vital distinction between woodwind and brass appears here in the subdivision based on the method of excitation of the tube. Subdivision (a) includes instruments in which an air jet flows across an edge, and subdivision (b) contains those in which a mechanical reed periodically interrupts the flow; both are described as woodwind. When the player's lips are stretched across a cup mouthpiece to form a lip reed the instrument falls into subdivision (c), and is usually described as brass. If the fluctuating air is not confined by a tube, the instrument is described as a free aerophone. Reed organs (including the accordion) are free aerophones in which a mechanical reed periodically interrupts the air flow, so they fall into subdivision (b).

The fifth major class has increased greatly in importance in recent years. The electrophones are instruments in which the radiated sound is generated by a loudspeaker. The nature of the sound is determined by the electrical signal sent to the loudspeaker, and the source of this signal can be used to subdivide the class. In the purely electronic instruments grouped in subdivision (a) the signal is generated by electrical circuitry with no mechanically moving parts. The electromechanical instruments in subdivision (b) employ rotating wheels as part of the oscillator circuits, but the moving parts are not themselves sound generators. The electroacoustic instruments of subdivision (c) contain elements such as bars or strings which are set into vibration, and the electrical signal is derived from this vibration through a microphone or other transducer.

According to the classification system just described, the electric guitar is clearly an electrophone, since the sound output is generated by a loudspeaker. However, the signal can be pursued back to a pickup which in turn is responding to the vibration of a string, so that the electric guitar can equally be viewed as a chordophone. Many such debates can arise over the subtleties of any classification system, which is bound to embrace ambiguities and exceptional special cases.

In the following pages of this chapter, we will examine each of the five major classes, considering the ways in which the natural vibratory patterns of the instruments affect their musical performance. Although the idiophone class comes first in Table 2.1, our discussion will be simplified if we start instead with the aerophones and chordophones, considering next the idiophones and membranophones, and ending with the electrophones.

2.2 VIBRATING AIR COLUMNS: THE AEROPHONE FAMILY

The acoustical properties of the woodwind and brass instruments, which belong to the aerophone family, are largely determined by two factors: the shape of the air column and the way in which it is set into vibration. We first consider the various shapes of tube found in wind instruments, then turn to look at the methods of excitation.

The shape of a tube, which determines the shape of the air column within it, is best described in terms of its bore. Imagine the tube to be sawn through perpendicular to its axis at a given distance from one end. Looking directly into the sawn-off end we would see a circle, whose area is called the cross section or bore of the tube at that point. In real wind instruments the bore usually changes in a complicated way along the length of the tube, but most instruments can be considered to be made up of sections of tube which are either cylindrical, conical, or flaring to a reasonable approximation. These three shapes, together with sketches of the bores at various points on each tube, are shown in Figure 2.1.

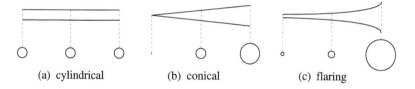

(a) cylindrical   (b) conical   (c) flaring

2.1 Idealized bore profiles of tubes used in musical wind instruments

Whatever the method used to excite the tube, the effect is to send a sound wave travelling down the air column from the playing end. (In the following discussions, we assume that in each case the playing end is uppermost.) When the wave arrives at the far end, what happens depends on the nature of the tube and on the frequency of the sound. If the far end is closed, as it is in a stopped organ pipe or a pan pipe, the situation is quite straightforward. Regardless of the frequency, the sound wave is reflected by the closed end and travels back up the tube.

The simultaneous presence of a direct wave travelling down the tube and a reflected wave travelling back up gives rise to a standing wave. We recall from Chapter 1 that a standing wave has fixed points called pressure nodes where the pressure amplitude is zero, and other fixed points called pressure antinodes where the amplitude of the pressure fluctuation is greatest. The layer of air just inside the closed end of the tube cannot move further down the tube when it is pressed from above, so the pressure rises to its highest value at the closed end. In a later part of the wave cycle, air will flow back up the tube, relieving the pressure on the layer next to the closed end; because no air can flow in from below, the pressure there will drop to its lowest value. It is thus clear that the closed end must be a pressure antinode in the standing wave.

If the far end is open, it is natural to assume that the sound wave will simply travel on out of the tube and into the surrounding atmosphere. When the frequency of the sound is so high that the wavelength is much less than the tube diameter, this is indeed what happens. However, if we gradually reduce the frequency, thereby increasing the wavelength, we find that a larger and larger fraction of the sound energy is getting reflected back up the tube at the open end. For sufficiently low frequencies, practically all the sound is reflected back.

The reflection of the wave at the open end of a tube is closely related to the phenomenon known as diffraction, which is illustrated in Figure 2.2. A very high-frequency wave, with a wavelength short in comparison to the tube diameter, hardly notices when it arrives at the open end of the tube. It continues to propagate forwards in a narrow beam, and a listener would have to stand almost directly on the tube axis in order to hear the sound. In contrast, a low-frequency wave, whose wavelength is much longer than the tube diameter, spreads out almost uniformly in all directions as it escapes the confines of the tube. A listener standing at one side would hear almost as much of the sound as one standing directly in front.

When the frequency of the wave is low enough for diffraction to dominate, a small high-pressure parcel of air pushed out of the open end suddenly finds that, instead of a narrow tube, it has the whole atmosphere to expand into. The expansion causes the pressure to drop rapidly towards the steady value of atmospheric pressure. Correspondingly, when a low-pressure region of the wave arrives at the

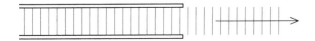

(a) wavelength less than pipe diameter

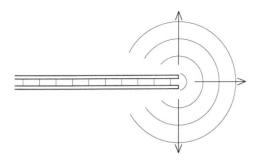

2.2 A sound wave travelling down a tube undergoes little diffraction at the open end if the wavelength is much less than the tube diameter, as shown in (a); it is strongly diffracted at the open end if the wavelength is much greater than the tube diameter, as shown in (b)

(b) wavelength greater than pipe diameter

end of the tube, air from the open atmosphere rapidly flows in to compensate for the pressure drop. At a point just outside the open end, the amplitude of the pressure fluctuations are reduced almost to zero; thus the open end behaves like a pressure node.

The nature of the playing mechanism at the upper end of the tube determines whether it will behave as an open or closed end. The flute embouchure hole behaves like an open end, making a pressure node in the standing wave, whereas reeds behave like closed ends and give pressure antinodes. Knowing whether each end of the tube is a node or an antinode allows us to determine the possible standing wave patterns which can be set up in the tube. These patterns determine which notes can be played on a given instrument, and have a profound effect on their loudness and timbre. The following section describes the standing waves in the different types of tube used in musical wind instruments.

Standing waves in a cylindrical tube

The simplest type of tube has the cylindrical bore shown in Figure 2.1(a), for which the diameter and cross section are the same all along the tube. The flute and the clarinet can be treated as approximately cylindrical, although in both cases there are important deviations which we will deal with later.

We consider first the case of a clarinet-like cylindrical tube with the upper end closed and the lower end open. A standing wave in this tube must have a pressure antinode at the top and a pressure node at the bottom. Some of the patterns consistent with this requirement are shown in Figure 2.3. Each possible standing wave pattern is known as a mode of the cylindrical air column.

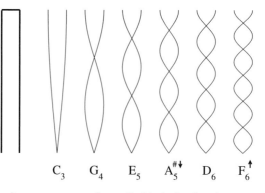

C_3 $\quad$ G_4 $\quad$ E_5 $\quad$ $A_5^{\#\downarrow}$ $\quad$ D_6 $\quad$ $F_6^{\uparrow}$

2.3 The first six standing wave patterns for a cylindrical tube closed at one end. The profile of the tube is shown at the left. The pitch of each standing wave pattern for a tube length of 66 cm is shown below it. *Note*: these and subsequent patterns show the pressure changes in the standing wave, not the displacement of the air. The horizontal separation of the two lines is proportional to the pressure amplitude

The speed at which a travelling wave moves in a tube is not necessarily the same as the speed of sound in open air, values for which were given in Table 1.1. Indeed, the wave may travel faster in one part of the tube than in another. However, the cylindrical tube is one of a special class of tubes for which the speed of sound is almost exactly the same as the open-air speed. For this type of tube the standing wave has the same characteristics as the one we examined in Figure 1.5: nodes and antinodes are spaced regularly along the tube, and the distance between a node and the neighbouring antinode is a quarter of a wavelength.

We can use these characteristics to work out the frequencies of the different modes shown in Figure 2.3. For the first mode, the whole length of the tube L is equal to the distance between node and antinode, which is a quarter wavelength. Thus the wavelength λ_1 must be four times the length:

$$\lambda_1 = 4L$$

The frequency f_1 is given by dividing the speed of sound c by the wavelength:

$$f_1 = c/\lambda_1 = c/4L$$

For example, a cylindrical tube of length 66 cm, closed at one end, has a first mode wavelength

$$\lambda_1 = 4 \times 0.66 = 2.64 \text{ m}$$

Taking the value $c = 345$ m/s for the speed of sound gives the first mode frequency as

$$f_1 = 345/2.64 = 131 \text{ Hz}$$

The corresponding pitch, C_3, is shown on the stave below the first mode diagram in Figure 2.3.

For the second mode of the air column, an additional node and antinode are found within the tube. From the diagram in Figure 2.3 it is clear that the quarter-wavelength distance from one node to the nearest antinode is now only a third of the total length of the tube, so that the second mode wavelength is given by

$$\lambda_2 = 4(L/3)$$

The second mode frequency is then

$$f_2 = c/\lambda_2 = 3c/4L$$

This is just three times the first mode frequency. For our 66 cm example, the second mode frequency is 392 Hz, corresponding to the pitch G_4.

The higher mode frequencies can be similarly evaluated. It turns out that they form the odd members only of a harmonic series whose fundamental is the first mode frequency. The pitches corresponding to the first six modes of the 66 cm example are shown in Figure 2.3.

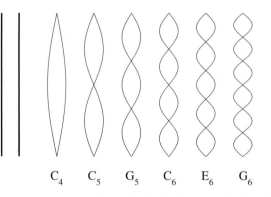

C_4 C_5 G_5 C_6 E_6 G_6

2.4 The first six standing wave patterns for a cylindrical tube open at both ends. The profile of the tube is shown at the left. The pitch of each standing wave pattern for a tube length of 66 cm is shown below it

Let us now consider the case of a flute-like cylindrical tube open at both ends. The requirement that each end should be a pressure node determines the possible standing wave patterns shown in Figure 2.4. For the first mode, the quarter-wavelength distance from node to nearest antinode is equal to half the length, so that the wavelength is

$$\lambda_1 = 2L$$

This is just half the first mode wavelength for a tube closed at one end. In consequence, the first mode frequency is twice as high as it would be if one of the ends were closed:

$$f_1 = c/2L$$

The first mode pitch for a 66 cm tube with both ends open is C_4, an octave higher than the first mode pitch with one end closed.

The second mode of the tube open at both ends has a node–antinode distance equal to a quarter of the tube length. This is just half the value for the first mode, so the frequency of the second mode is twice that of the first. Likewise, the third mode frequency is three times that of the first mode. In fact, the mode frequencies form a complete harmonic series, as shown by the pitches in Figure 2.4.

This discussion provides the basis for understanding many musically significant features of musical instruments. For example, when a clarinet player overblows, the pitch of the note rises by a twelfth because that is the interval between the first and second modes of the air column in that instrument. When a flute player overblows, the pitch rises by an octave for the same reason.

In the later chapters on wind instruments we will explore some of the limitations in this highly simplified picture. At this point we will note only that the 'effective' or 'sounding' length of the air column, which must be used to calculate the correct mode frequencies, is usually considerably longer than the physical length of the instrument. The reason for this discrepancy has already been hinted at in our discussion of the reflection of the travelling wave at the open end of a tube. The pressure node is actually located slightly beyond the end of the tube. For a cylindrical tube the distance from the open end to the node is about a third of the tube diameter; this distance is known as the end correction. The end correction for a partially open end, such as the embouchure hole on a flute, can be much greater.

Standing waves in a conical tube

The oboe, bassoon, and saxophone are examples of instruments for which the tube bore is approximately conical—that is, the diameter increases steadily from the playing end to the far end. The conical tube is another of the special cases for which the speed of sound in the tube is almost exactly the same as the speed in open air. However the travelling waves in a conical tube have a different shape from those in a cylindrical tube. This difference is illustrated in Figure 2.5. In the cylindrical tube the crests and troughs of the wave move forward as a set of parallel planes; in the conical tube they are curved surfaces. To visualize the wave surfaces in a conical tube, imagine that a spherical balloon is gradually being inflated. A circle marked on the side of the balloon encloses a curved surface, whose area gradually increases as the balloon radius grows. In a similar way, the area of the wave surface increases as it moves down a conical tube.

(a) plane   (b) spherical

2.5 (a) Plane wavefronts in a cylindrical tube; (b) spherical wavefronts in a conical tube

When the wave reaches the far end, which we assume to be open, reflection occurs as it does with a cylindrical tube. The reflected wave also has curved crest surfaces, which can be visualized by allowing our imaginary balloon to deflate slowly. The crossing of the direct and reflected waves again gives rise to a standing wave, but because of the curvature of the wave surfaces it is not immediately obvious how the standing wave patterns will relate to those we have seen in a cylindrical tube.

From a careful study of the physics involved it emerges that the standing wave patterns for a conical tube are as shown in Figure 2.6. A comparison with Figure 2.4, which shows the patterns for a cylindrical tube open at both ends, reveals one important similarity between these two cases. The positions of the internal nodes

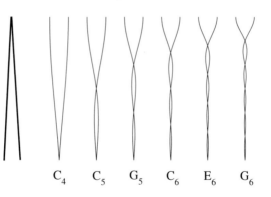

2.6 The first six standing wave patterns for a conical tube complete to the vertex. The profile of the tube is shown at the left. The pitch of each standing wave pattern for a tube length of 66 cm is shown below it

in the standing wave patterns of the conical tube match exactly those in the corresponding patterns of a cylindrical tube open at both ends. For example, in both cases the pattern for mode 3 has a node one third of the way down the tube and another node two thirds of the way down.

There are, however, some highly significant differences between the pressure distributions in Figures 2.4 and 2.6. These differences can be understood by recalling that the conical tube narrows towards the upper end, so that a parcel of air moving up the tube is squeezed through a smaller and smaller cross-sectional area. Thus the pressure changes arising from the oscillating air flows are magnified towards the top of the tube. The extreme case occurs right at the top, where in an ideal cone the diameter is reduced to zero; instead of the pressure node which we found at the top of the open-ended cylindrical tube, we now find a pressure antinode. This is an important difference, since reed instruments like the oboe and the bassoon require a pressure antinode at the playing end.

A more subtle difference concerns the positions of nodes and antinodes. The nodes in the conical tube are at the same places as the nodes in the equivalent open-ended cylinder, but the antinodes are shifted slightly towards the upper end. The distance from a node to the nearest antinode cannot therefore be simply equal to a quarter wavelength. However the distance between two adjacent nodes remains half a wavelength; the distance from the upper end to the nearest node is also half a wavelength, as shown in Figure 2.6.

Using these facts we can calculate the mode frequencies in the same way that we did for the cylindrical tubes. The result is that the frequencies for the conical tube are identical with those for a cylindrical tube of the same length open at both ends. The pitches for the first six modes of a conical tube of length 66 cm are shown in Figure 2.6; it will be seen that they are the same pitches as those of Figure 2.4. Although the conical tube is effectively closed at the very narrow playing end, its mode pitches form a complete harmonic series, in contrast to the odd-member-only harmonic series of the cylindrical tube closed at one end. As a consequence, the oboe and bassoon overblow to the octave like the flute rather than to the twelfth like the clarinet.

Standing waves in a flaring tube

Finally we consider tubes which grow in diameter from the playing end to the far end, but at a rate which increases with increasing distance from the playing end. This flaring behaviour is characteristic of the bell sections of many brass instruments, including the trumpet, trombone, and french horn.

The flaring tube provides a more complicated problem acoustically than either the cylindrical or conical tubes, because the speed of sound in the flaring tube is not the same at all points along the tube. The wave travels faster in a region where the wall is curving strongly outward than it does in a region where the outward curvature is small. Recalling that the speed of a sound wave is equal to the frequency times the wavelength, we can see immediately that for a wave of a certain frequency travelling down a flaring tube, an increase in wave speed must mean a corresponding increase in wavelength. Since the wavelength varies as the wave travels along the tube, the method that we used to work out mode frequencies for cylindrical and conical tubes cannot be employed. In fact, the mode frequencies depend on the detailed profile of the tube bore and are not necessarily harmonically related, as shown by the example in Figure 2.7.

We saw earlier that a travelling wave was reflected at the open end of a cylindrical tube if its frequency was low enough. In a flaring tube the wave may not even get as far as the open end before being reflected; the flare has the effect of

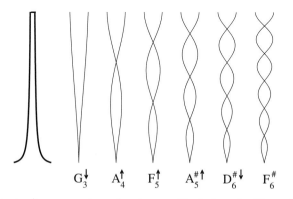

2.7 The first six standing wave patterns for a trumpet-like flaring tube. The profile of the tube is shown at the left. The pitch of each standing wave pattern for a tube length of 66 cm is shown below it

making the tube seem shorter as the frequency of the wave gets lower. By careful design of the flare it is possible to adjust the effective length of the tube for each mode so that the mode frequencies are close to a complete harmonic series.

The trumpet is intimately associated in most people's minds with the notes of the harmonic series, from which fanfares and military trumpet signals are built up. It is ironic that from the point of view of basic acoustics it is the cylindrical and conical tubes which by their very nature generate harmonics—the trumpet-like flaring tube can only do so imperfectly, and even that requires a careful choice of flare. The long 'posthorn' which is sometimes found jostling the horse brasses above the bar of a country inn can look an impressive instrument; but if it is a modern reproduction, the chances are that the flare has been chosen for appearance rather than function, and an unwary trumpeter essaying a fanfare will find some very unexpected notes emerging.

Flute-type excitation: the air jet

Turning now to consider the ways in which a wind player feeds energy into the air column of the instrument, we begin with the type of excitation characteristic of flutes. A ribbon-shaped jet of air is formed by blowing either through a slit, as in the penny whistle, recorder, and flue organ pipe, or through a slit-like gap between the lips of the player, as on the orchestral flute and panpipe (Figure 2.8). In each case the jet flows across an opening which is big enough to prevent a significant build-up of pressure between the inside and the outside of the tube, thus ensuring that the blowing end of the tube must behave acoustically as an open end.

At the far side of the opening the jet strikes the wall of the tube, which in most

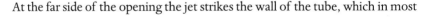

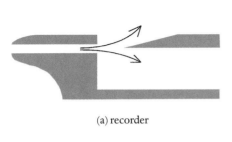

(a) recorder

(b) panpipe

2.8 Creation of a ribbon-shaped air jet by (a) the slotted mouthpiece of a recorder; (b) the lips of a panpipe player

members of the flute family is tapered down so that it presents a relatively sharp edge to the jet. We might expect that the air would divide smoothly, with half of the stream passing above the edge and half below. For a very slow stream of air this is what would happen. In a flute, however, the speed of the air flow is quite high (typically around 30 m/s), and the jet develops a wave-like wiggle.

Let us consider first an air jet formed by a slit and edge system without an attached resonating air column. Two phases of the wiggling motion are illustrated in Figure 2.9. In the first, the jet is deflected downwards at the edge; the resulting build-up of pressure below the edge is partially relieved by an upward air current in front of the slit. The jet emerging from the slit is blown upwards by this air current. As the wave travels along the jet, the upward deflection is carried

(a)   (b)

2.9 Wiggling motion of an air jet impinging on an edge

downstream from the slit. At the time illustrated by the second diagram in Figure 2.9 it has reached the edge. The jet is now flowing above the edge, and the compensatory downward air current in front of the slit is deflecting the emerging jet downwards. This downward deflection will in turn travel along the jet, steering it below the edge and initiating a new cycle of the wiggling motion.

The wiggle frequency of the jet depends on the speed of the air flow, and hence on the blowing pressure. The harder the player blows, the faster the air flows and the higher the natural frequency at which the jet tends to swing up and down. But on a flute the jet is also strongly influenced by what is going on below it, in the air column of the tube. By a suitable choice of blowing pressure the player can use the jet wiggle to excite one of the natural modes of the air column. As the standing wave develops it creates an oscillating air flow in front of the slit which is much more powerful than the jet's own compensating current; jet and air column lock together in a synchronized vibration whose frequency is determined primarily by the mode frequency of the tube.

Let us assume that the first mode of the tube shown in Figure 2.4 has been strongly excited in this way. The air jet is then being switched regularly in and out of the tube at the first mode frequency, in this case 262 Hz. Every second, 262 puffs of air are being sent down the tube. But although this is a periodic variation of the air flow into the tube, it is not a simple sinusoidal variation. If the amplitude of swing of the air jet is strong enough, it may flow entirely into the tube for a significant part of the cycle, during which the flow rate remains approximately constant.

Recalling from Chapter 1 that a periodic waveform is equivalent to a set of harmonic frequency components, we can regard the flat-topped waveform as being made up of a set of simple sinusoidal air flows: one at the fundamental frequency of 262 Hz, another at the second harmonic frequency of 524 Hz, another at the third harmonic frequency of 786 Hz, and so on. Thus the air jet is exciting the tube not just at the first mode frequency but at a whole set of frequencies which are harmonics of the first mode frequency.

We can now see how important it is that the mode frequencies of the tube are at least approximately members of a harmonic series. Looking again at Figure 2.4, we see that the second mode of the air column has a frequency of 524 Hz. Because this is in tune with the second harmonic of the air jet excitation, the second mode of the air column will also be pumped up by the air jet. A similar argument applies to the higher modes. Any mode which is in tune with a harmonic of the first will be strongly excited. Conversely, a mode which is not in tune with a harmonic will be unable to gain much energy from the air jet. When a large number of harmonically tuned modes interact simultaneously with the air jet a strong, stable vibration regime is set up, resulting in a note with a rich harmonic spectrum.

Clarinet-type excitation: the single reed

The crucial feature of all the excitation mechanisms of wind instruments is some means of converting a steady stream of air into a series of puffs with a repetition frequency close to one of the mode frequencies of the air column. In the clarinet this is achieved by the single-reed mechanism. The air stream is allowed to enter the tube through a slit-shaped hole in the side of the tube, just below the upper end. This hole is covered by the reed—a strip of flexible material, usually cane, sealed against the tube wall at one end and free to vibrate at the other (see Figure 2.10).

When the instrument is not being played there is a small gap between the free

(a) open   (b) closed

2.10 Two stages in the vibration cycle of a strongly blown clarinet reed. The arrow represents the flow of air into the instrument from the player's mouth. *Note:* in normal playing technique, the mouthpiece is inserted between the player's lips with the reed facing downwards

end of the reed and the tube wall. To sound the instrument the player puts the end section into the mouth and blows air through this small gap. The increased air pressure inside the player's mouth presses down on the flat surface of the reed; the airstream flowing past the reed also exerts a force on it, in the same way that the air flowing over an aeroplane wing exerts an upward force which keeps the plane in the sky. These forces and the natural springiness of the reed combine to set the reed vibrating; the periodic opening and closing of the gap between the reed end and the wall has the desired effect of chopping the air stream into a series of puffs.

The natural vibration frequency of the reed does not necessarily correspond to the note which the player wants to sound. In fact, the natural frequency of the clarinet reed is usually much higher than the normal playing range of the instrument. But, as with the air jet mechanism of the flute, the single reed is very susceptible to the forces exerted by the standing waves in the air column. Figure 2.3 shows that the reed is at a pressure antinode for all the modes of a clarinet. Once a standing wave starts to build up at one of the mode frequencies, the strong pressure fluctuations at the antinode dominate the behaviour of the reed, forcing it to open and close at a frequency very close to the mode frequency. The resulting variation of air flow into the tube is not sinusoidal, but, as in the case of the air jet, consists of a set of harmonic frequency components.

In Figure 2.3 we illustrated the modes of a clarinet-like tube 66 cm long. This tube has a first mode frequency of 131 Hz. In the first register, the reed will vibrate at a frequency very close to this value. The 2nd harmonic of the excitation, at 262 Hz, does not correspond to one of the air column modes, so that the radiated sound contains very little of this component. The 3rd harmonic, on the other hand, is in tune with the second mode of the air column at 393 Hz, and this mode will also build up strongly. The argument can be extended to show that only the odd harmonics of the excitation find matching air column modes; for the idealized clarinet-like instrument discussed here we would expect the radiated sound spectrum to be almost totally lacking in even harmonics. We will see in Chapter 3 how true this is of real clarinets.

Oboe-type excitation: the double reed

The double reed operates on the same general principle as the single reed. As its name suggests, the double reed consists of two strips of flexible material, bound together at one end around a narrow tube called the staple which is inserted into the playing end of the instrument (Figure 2.11). The reed is placed partly inside the mouth of the player. When air is blown through the narrow gap between the free ends of the two strips, the reed settles into a vibration pattern in which the gap opens and closes with a frequency close to that of one of the modes of the air column to which it is coupled. As with the single reed, the modulation of the air flow into the instrument contains many harmonic components, each of which will contribute to the strength and timbre of the note to the extent that it finds a matching mode of the air column.

Both double and single reeds are classed as inward-striking reeds, which means that an increase in blowing pressure tends to narrow the gap through which the air

(a) open   (b) closed

2.11 Two stages in the vibration cycle of an oboe reed. The arrow represents the flow of air into the instrument from the player's mouth

must flow. If the blowing pressure is increased too far, the reed will close completely and the sound will be cut off. This feature sets an upper limit to the amount of sound energy which can be generated using a given reed, although the chanter of the Scottish Highland bagpipe offers pungent proof that despite this limitation a double reed can still generate a most impressive volume of sound.

Trumpet-type excitation: the lip reed

The type of excitation used on brass instruments is sometimes described as cup-mouthpiece excitation, because the common feature of all such instruments is a mouthpiece across which the lips are stretched (Figure 2.12). We have preferred the term lip-reed excitation to emphasize the essential role of the lips, and to point the analogy between the lip vibrations in a brass instrument and the vibrations of the flexible strips in a double reed instrument.

The similarities between the cane double reed and the lip reed are obvious enough. The brass instrument mouthpiece is placed against the player's lips so that the entrance to the instrument tube is sealed, apart from a small opening

(a) open   (b) closed

2.12 Two stages in the vibration cycle of the lips of a trumpet player. The arrow represents the flow of air into the instrument from the player's mouth between the lips. When a stream of air is blown through this gap, the lips are set into vibration in such a way that the gap opens and closes periodically, modulating the air flow into the tube of the instrument. This is just the process that we saw in action in the double reed.

There are, however, two important differences between the cane double reed and the lip reed. One of these concerns the behaviour as the blowing pressure is increased. We saw earlier that the double reed is an inward-striking reed, closing up completely for a sufficiently large blowing pressure. As can be seen from Figure 2.12, the lips on a mouthpiece appear to behave as an outward-striking reed, being forced more widely apart as the blowing pressure increases. However when the force exerted on the lips by the air flowing between them is also taken into account it appears that the lip motion is more complicated, displaying features of both inward- and outward-striking reed behaviour.

The other difference concerns the nature of the vibrating elements themselves. In the case of an oboe reed, these are small thin strips of cane. The mass and springiness of the strips can be adjusted by scraping, and the player can exert some control during performance by squeezing the reed between the lips, but the motion of the reed is dominated by the forces exerted by the standing waves in the air column. The vibrating sections of the lips on a trumpet mouthpiece are considerably more massive, and a skilled player can use the complex set of muscles around the mouth to adjust the mass, shape, and tension of the vibrating segments during performance. This ability of the brass player to effectively change reeds several times in the course of a single note permits a wide range of loudness and timbre to be employed, and the strength of the lips allows a note to be 'lipped' or 'pulled' some way from the pitch preferred by the air column.

2.3 VIBRATING STRINGS: THE CHORDOPHONE FAMILY

Our discussion of the aerophone family was extended by the necessity for describing the standing wave patterns in several different shapes of air column. Turning now to the chordophone family, we find a more straightforward task. In discussing the stringed instruments covered in this book, the only type of vibrating string which we need to consider is the uniform string, by which we mean a string whose density and diameter are constant along its length. We start by looking at the standing wave patterns which can be set up on a uniform stretched string. We then examine the three important ways in which these waves are generated in musical instruments: plucking, which is characteristic of the harp, guitar, and harpsichord; hammering, which is the method used on the dulcimer, clavichord, and piano; and bowing, which is the staple technique of the violin and viol groups.

Travelling waves on a stretched string

The basic vibrator which characterizes the chordophone family is a string held in
tension between two fixed points on the body of the instrument. Various materials have been used in the manufacture of strings, including silk, gut, metal, and
nylon. In principle, it is possible to use any material which can be formed into a
uniform strand with adequate flexibility and strength. An important distinction
must be drawn right away between the type of wave which is set up in the air column of a wind instrument and that which is important in generating the sound of
a stringed instrument. The wave in the air column of a flute is described as a longitudinal wave, since the particles of air in the column vibrate backwards and forwards along the line of the tube axis. When a string is bowed or plucked, each
individual particle of the string vibrates along a line at right angles to the string

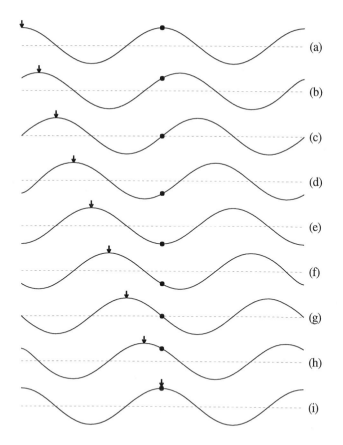

2.13 Nine stages in the progress of a travelling wave on a stretched string. The centre point of
the string is marked by a dot; the position of one crest of the wave is indicated by an arrow

axis. However, the overall motion of the string can be described in terms of waves travelling in both directions along the string. Such waves are called transverse waves, since the motion of the individual particles is transverse to the direction in which the wave travels.

The nature of a transverse wave is illustrated in Figure 2.13, which shows nine successive views of a horizontal string as a transverse wave travels along it from left to right. In each view the dashed line marks the position of the string before the wave arrived. The arrow points to one of the crests of the wave, which clearly appears to move from left to right in the successive pictures. A particular point on the string is marked by a black dot, painted on while the string was at rest. As the wave goes by, the dot moves from its highest point vertically downwards; on reaching its lowest point it reverses direction and moves back upwards. Over the nine views in Figure 2.13 the dot completes one cycle of this transverse vibration.

The speed at which a transverse wave travels along a stretched string depends on how heavy the string is and how much it is tightened. More precisely, the speed c (measured in metres per second) is given by the formula

$$c = \sqrt{T/m}$$

where T is the tension applied to the string (measured in newtons) and m is the mass per unit length of the string (measured in kilograms per metre). The square root in this formula means that the speed of the wave on a string will be doubled if either the tension is increased fourfold or the mass per unit length is reduced by a factor of four.

Standing waves on a stretched string

A wave travelling along the string of a musical instrument is reflected when it reaches a point of support such as a bridge. We then have two waves travelling in opposite directions, the recipe for the creation of standing wave patterns on the string.

In our discussion of wind instruments, the important quantity which varied during the passage of a wave was the pressure in the air column. For the stringed instruments the corresponding variable is the displacement of the string from its rest position. Standing waves on the string are again characterized by nodes and antinodes, but this time they are positions of zero and maximum displacement respectively.

As with the wind instruments, the end conditions limit the possible standing waves which can be established on a string of a given length. If the string is stretched across completely unyielding supports, each end of the vibrating section must be a displacement node. Some of the standing wave patterns consistent with this requirement are shown in Figure 2.14. In these diagrams the undisturbed string is assumed to lie vertically, as on the harp; the horizontal width of the pattern represents the extent of the transverse vibration of the string.

The standing wave patterns in Figure 2.14 appear identical to those for a cylindrical tube open at both ends shown in Figure 2.4, although it must be borne in mind that in one case the diagram represents pressure changes while in the other it represents string displacements. The distance from a node to the nearest antinode in Figure 2.14 is again equal to a quarter wavelength. The same argument used

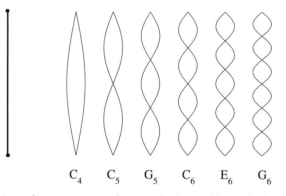

$$C_4 \qquad C_5 \qquad G_5 \qquad C_6 \qquad E_6 \qquad G_6$$

2.14 The first six standing wave patterns for a stretched string. The pitch of each standing wave pattern is shown below it, assuming that the first mode has a pitch of C_4

in the case of the cylindrical tube now shows that the modes of a string of length L have frequencies which form a complete harmonic series, with fundamental frequency

$$f_1 = c/2L$$

The formula previously given for the speed of a wave on the string can be incorporated into the above equation to give an expression for the fundamental frequency in terms of length, tension, and mass per unit length:

$$f_1 = (1/2L)\sqrt{T/m}$$

The pitches of the first six modes of a string tuned to a fundamental pitch of C_4 are given below the relevant standing wave patterns in Figure 2.14. These pitches are exact harmonics of C_4 only if the string is completely flexible and its supports completely rigid. A real string on a real musical instrument does not satisfy either of these conditions exactly. Because the string has some inherent stiffness, and the supports move as the string vibrates, the mode frequencies deviate slightly from their ideal harmonic values. This inharmonicity has some important musical consequences, which will be explored in Chapter 11.

Plucking a string

On the guitar, mandolin, and harp, and in pizzicato playing on the violin, the string is set into motion by plucking. The essence of this action is that the string is pulled into a kinked shape, either by a plectrum or by the finger, and then released.

When the initial motion of a plucked string is filmed by a high-speed cine-camera, an examination of successive frames of the film reveals that two kinks travel in opposite directions away from the plucking point. When each kink reaches the fixed end of the string it is turned upside down and reflected back along the string. The result is a series of zigzag string shapes, as shown in Figure 2.15.

The musical character of the sound of a plucked string depends to a large extent on its frequency spectrum. It is not at all obvious which frequency components are likely to be generated by the complicated motion shown in Figure 2.15, but studies of the physics of vibrating strings have revealed some useful guidelines. The most important is a general rule which states that the motion of the string after its release is made up of the simultaneous vibrations of the natural modes of the string. Whatever the shape in which the string is released, the subsequent motion can be reproduced by adding together in appropriate proportions the different vibration patterns shown in Figure 2.14.

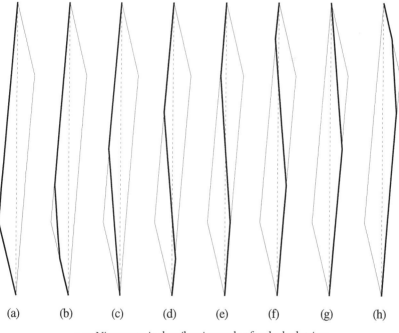

(a)   (b)   (c)   (d)   (e)   (f)   (g)   (h)

2.15 Nine stages in the vibration cycle of a plucked string

The significance of this rule becomes clear when it is recalled that in a particular mode, each point on the string is performing a simple sinusoidal vibration at the mode frequency. If every possible motion of the string can be made up just by adding modes together, the frequency spectrum must contain only components at the mode frequencies. We saw above that for a real musical instrument string the mode frequencies are very close to being members of a harmonic series, and it is this set of slightly inharmonic components that we find in the sound of a plucked string. The deviations from true harmonics are usually much too small to disturb the sensation of a single clear pitch which we expect from a harmonic series.

When a string is plucked, not all of the modes are excited with equal strength. In general the low-frequency modes are set vibrating more strongly than those of

2.16 Frequency spectra for the note G_3 played in three different ways on a Spanish guitar: (a) string plucked by fingertip, distance of plucking point from bridge one fifth of string length; (b) string plucked by fingernail, distance of plucking point from bridge one fifth of string length; (c) string plucked by fingernail, distance of plucking point from bridge one twentieth of string length

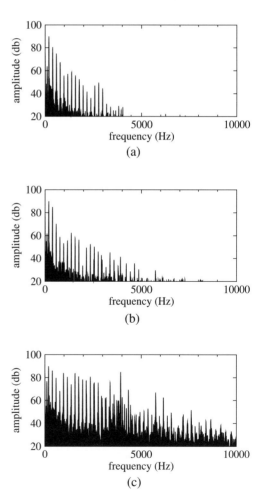

higher frequency. The relative strengths of the different modes can be adjusted by altering the way in which the string is plucked. Moving the point of plucking nearer to one end of the string boosts the high-frequency modes, giving a brighter sound, while plucking near the middle of the string is most favourable to the modes of lowest frequency. Plucking with something soft and rounded, like the fleshy part of a fingertip, favours the lower modes, whereas a hard and sharp object such as a fingernail or a harpsichord quill throws more energy into the upper modes.

These differences are illustrated in the spectra of plucked guitar notes in Figure 2.16. It is important to realize that, on its own, a vibrating string radiates very little sound. This is basically because the thin string is very inefficient at communicating its energy to the surrounding air. A vital further stage in every stringed instrument is an extended body to which the string is coupled through a bridge or some comparable device. The string sets the body vibrating; the large surface area of the body makes it an efficient radiator of sound waves.

The body of a guitar has its own resonances, and as a consequence it radiates some of the string component frequencies more efficiently than others. Despite this additional complication, Figure 2.16 shows clearly that plucking nearer the bridge, or with a sharper plectrum, increases the relative strength of the higher-frequency components in the spectrum.

Another influence of the point of plucking can be seen in Figure 2.16(b). In this case, the distance from the plucking point to the bridge is one fifth of the total string length; the plucking point is therefore a node for the fifth mode (see Figure 2.14). We would hardly expect that the fifth mode would be excited by plucking at a point which is supposed to remain at rest in that mode, and indeed the spectrum in Figure 2.16(b) shows that the fifth mode radiates much less sound than neighbouring modes. The same argument explains the relative weakness of the sound radiated by the tenth mode.

Hammering a string

The hammering action used to excite the string of a dulcimer or a piano is acoustically very similar to the plucking mechanism which we have just discussed. In both cases the string is forced into a particular shape, then released and left to vibrate without further interference from the exciting mechanism. As with the plucked string, the motion of the hammered string is made up of a set of the natural modes of the string vibrating simultaneously. The principal differences between plucking and hammering appear as differences in the proportions of the various modes excited by the two methods.

We saw that in general plucking favoured low-frequency modes rather than high-frequency modes. As a consequence, the high-frequency components in the spectrum of sound from a plucked string were relatively weak. A similar prefer-ence is found in hammering, but for a narrow, hard hammer the falling off in amplitude of high-frequency components is less pronounced than in the plucked case. The situation is quite different for the relatively broad felt-covered hammer typical of the modern piano. We do not expect a particular mode to be excited if a displacement node lies under the hammer. Recalling, however, that the distance between nodes is half a wavelength, we can see that if a mode has a frequency high enough so that the half wavelength is less than the length of the section of the hammer head which contacts the string, at least one node must lie under the hammer. Thus the broad hammer effectively filters out all modes with frequen-cies above this limit.

Another effect which limits the strength of the high-frequency components is related to the finite time of contact between string and hammer. If the hammer head has a soft covering, the string will embed itself in this damping material for a short time before the hammer rebounds from the string. A low-frequency mode will be relatively unaffected, since the contact time will be only a small fraction of its period of vibration. On the other hand, a mode whose vibration period is shorter than the contact time will be damped out.

The influence of the position of striking is comparable to that found in the plucked case. Striking near a fixed end strengthens the upper-frequency modes, while striking near the middle puts more of the energy into the modes of low fre-quency. A given mode will be relatively weakly excited if the striking point is near to one of its nodes. For example, in the spectrum of the piano note F_1 shown in Figure 1.10(b) modes 9, 18, and 27 make only small contributions to the sound; this is because for this string the distance from the hammer striking point to the bridge is one ninth of the string length.

Bowing a string

There is no mystery about the fact that a plucked or hammered string gives a musically useful pitched note. The frequency components in the sound are just those of the natural modes of the string, which are close enough to a harmonic series to persuade the brain to hear them as a synthesized single note.

It is not at all obvious that scraping a hank of resined horsehair across the string should give a musical note. Indeed, as most beginners on the violin are all too aware, there are many ways of bowing a string which produce only squeaks and groans. It is worth exploring in a little detail the interactions between the bow and the string when a steady sound with a clear pitch is being generated.

The first important clue is the rosin (a type of resin) which must be applied to the hair of the bow. It is disastrous to handle the hair with greasy fingers—the bow then merely slides across the string, giving almost no sound. In contrast, well rosined hair sticks to the string, and as the bow is pulled across the string it carries the string with it.

Let us imagine that the bow is applied to a stationary string and pulled very slowly to one side. As the segment of the string under the bow is displaced further and further, the tension force in the string acts more and more strongly in resisting the displacement. This string force is called a restoring force, since it always tries to restore the string to its undeflected position. For a time the frictional force holding the string to the hair of the bow can increase to keep the string attached to the hair, but eventually the restoring force becomes equal to the maximum frictional force that can be supplied by the hair.

What happens then? The bow continues to move sideways, but it starts to slip over the string instead of gripping it. We might imagine that the string could remain in this deflected position, with the frictional and restoring forces just balancing. However, the properties of frictional forces make this impossible. When the hair starts sliding over the string the frictional force drops considerably; the restoring force is now much stronger, and the string is accelerated back towards its undeflected position. As it accelerates, the frictional force gets still smaller. When the string overshoots the undeflected position, the restoring force starts to act in the same direction as the bow, slowing the string down. Eventually the string is recaptured by the hair, and the cycle repeats itself.

We can thus understand why the bowed string should perform a periodic vibration. But what determines the period? We know from experience that whether a violin string is bowed or plucked the note which sounds has the same pitch. This implies that the basic vibration frequency of the bowed string must correspond closely to the frequency of the first mode of the string. So far our discussion of bowing has not involved the string modes at all.

To explain why the stick–slip cycle locks onto the frequency of the first string mode we return for a moment to the illustration of the vibration of a plucked string in Figure 2.15. We saw that after the string was released two kinks travelled in opposite directions along the string. A similar behaviour has been found in studies of the bowed string, with the difference that in the bowed case only a single kink is observed.

The motion of a bowed string through one cycle of vibration is illustrated by Figure 2.17. It is assumed that the bow is being moved steadily to the left. The string passes over a bridge at the bottom of the diagram and over the fixed bar known as the nut at the top of the diagram. In the successive snapshots from (a) to (c) the string is deflected to the right, and the kink is travelling towards the nut. In (d) the kink has reached the nut, and the string is passing through its undeflected position. In (e), (f), and (g) the kink returns towards the bridge, and the string is now deflected to the left. In (h) the kink reaches the bridge, and in (i) it is back at the same position as (a) to start another cycle of vibration.

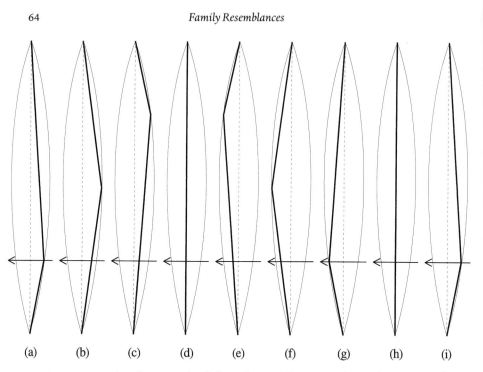

(a)   (b)   (c)   (d)   (e)   (f)   (g)   (h)   (i)

2.17 Nine stages in the vibration cycle of a bowed string. The arrow indicates the position and direction of the bow. When the bow moves in the opposite direction, each string shape is a mirror image of the shape illustrated

The kink is directly underneath the bow at (a). As it passes under the hair it gives an extra tweak to the string in the direction of the bow motion. Just before this, the hair has been slipping, and if the string is being bowed properly the extra tweak is just enough to allow the hair to recapture the string. This initiates the sticking part of the cycle. While the kink travels up to the nut and is reflected back down, the segment of string under the bow remains attached to the hair and moves steadily to the left at the bowing speed. At (g) the reflected kink passes under the string, this time imparting a tweak to the right. By this stage the frictional force from the hair is approaching its limit; the extra tweak is enough to detach the string and start the slipping part of the cycle.

The time taken for the kink to shuttle up and down the string is equal to the vibration period of the first mode. The moving kink thus acts as a timekeeper, triggering the transitions between sticking and slipping at a rate determined by the string's natural vibration frequency.

The frequency spectrum corresponding to the vibration pattern shown in Figure 2.17 is broadly similar to that already seen for the plucked string, with most of the energy in the low-frequency components. There is one crucial difference, however, between the spectrum of a bowed string and that of a plucked or hammered string. We saw that in the plucked and struck cases the components are at the natural mode frequencies, which for a real string are not exact harmonics. In contrast, for a steady note on a bowed string, the motion is an exactly repeating sequence of the stages shown in Figure 2.17. The vibration of the string is therefore exactly periodic, and the frequency components are exact harmonics.

2.4 VIBRATING DRUMSKINS: THE MEMBRANOPHONE FAMILY

We now turn to consider the class of instruments in which the basic vibrating element is a flexible sheet or membrane stretched across a supporting frame. This class is essentially identical to the musical drum family, including timpani, bass drum, snare drum, tom-tom, and tambourine.

One striking feature of the membranophones which we have just listed is that in each case the supporting frame is circular. There is an obvious advantage in avoiding sharp corners which might puncture the membrane, and it is relatively easy to stretch the membrane uniformly over a circular frame. There is, however, a more fundamental property of a vibrating circular membrane which makes it of particular musical significance: under the right circumstances, it can give a sound with a definite pitch. To see how this can come about, we need to explore the standing wave patterns which can be set up on a circular drumhead.

Standing waves on a circular membrane

A flexible membrane under tension can be usefully thought of as a two-dimensional version of a stretched string. When the string is hit by a hammer, transverse waves travel up and down the string, resulting in standing wave patterns at the particular mode frequencies of the string. Similarly, when a membrane is hit by a hammer, waves of transverse displacement travel outwards as circular ripples from the point of striking. On arrival at the fixed circumference of the drum these ripples are reflected back across the membrane. The crossing and recrossing of the ripples creates standing wave patterns at the natural mode frequencies of the membrane.

It is possible to excite a single mode of the drumhead by playing a sine wave signal of the appropriate frequency through a nearby loudspeaker. When this is done, it is found that the mode has a characteristic pattern of nodal lines. Every point on a nodal line is a node—that is, it remains at rest throughout the vibration cycle. The diagrams in Figure 2.18 show the nodal lines for the first ten modes of a circular membrane under uniform tension.

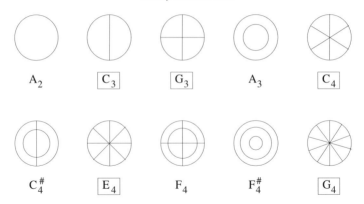

2.18 The first ten standing wave patterns on a circular drumskin. The approximate pitch of each standing wave pattern (taking into account air damping) is shown below it, assuming that the second mode has a pitch of C_3; boxes indicate the modes which contribute to the perceived pitch of the drum

The nodal lines in Figure 2.18 are either circles with the same centre as the drumhead or diameters passing through the drumhead centre. In each case the outer rim is a nodal circle, since the membrane is forced to remain at rest where it passes over the frame. For the first mode the outer circle is the only nodal line. When the membrane is vibrating purely in this first mode, all parts of the membrane are rising during one half of the vibration cycle and falling during the other half.

The second mode has a nodal diameter as well as the outer nodal circle. In this mode the two halves of the membrane on opposite sides of the nodal diameter vibrate with opposite phases, one half rising while the other falls and vice versa. The third mode has two nodal diameters at right angles, dividing the membrane into four quadrants. The fourth mode has no nodal diameters, but in addition to the outer nodal circle has a second nodal circle. The higher modes show the membrane divided into smaller and smaller segments by increasingly complex patterns of circles and diameters.

The vibration pattern created by a blow from a drumstick does not correspond exactly to any of the single modes shown in Figure 2.18. The effect of the blow is to excite many of the modes into simultaneous vibration, each mode receiving an amount of energy determined by the nature of the blow. The frequency spectrum of the sound from the struck drum will contain a component at the characteristic frequency of each excited mode.

We saw earlier that a string struck by a hammer also radiated its characteristic mode frequencies, which in that case formed an almost exact harmonic series. The mode frequencies of the circular membrane are more difficult to calculate because of the two-dimensional nature of the vibrating system. An additional effect known as air damping must also be taken into account. If the membrane were vibrating in a vacuum, the only force on it would be the tension applied by stretching it over its frame. Vibrating in air, the membrane experiences an additional force arising from the resistance of the air, which has the effect of lowering the mode frequencies. This effect is accentuated when the membrane is stretched over a bowl, as it is on a kettledrum.

On a kettledrum tuned to sound the note C_3, the first ten modes have approximately the pitches given in Figure 2.18. It is at once obvious that the modes are closer in pitch than those of a string: the tenth mode has a pitch less than two octaves above the first, whereas the interval between first and tenth modes for a string is more than three octaves. The fact that the mode pitches are not members of a harmonic series is at first sight difficult to reconcile with the knowledge that a drum can give a sound with a single, definite pitch. To understand how the brain of a listener can be persuaded to hear a pitch in the sound of a drum, we must examine the way in which the membrane is struck, and the way in which the sound dies away after the blow.

Striking a drum

The amount of energy given to each mode of the membrane depends on the point at which the membrane is struck. The general rules which we earlier applied to a plucked or struck string can also be used in the present case. Striking near the middle of the membrane favours low-frequency modes, while moving the striking point towards the rim gives an increasing fraction of the energy to high-frequency modes. If a nodal line for a particular mode passes through the point of striking, that mode will not be significantly excited by the blow. The second of these rules shows that striking at the centre of the drumhead will not excite any of the modes with one or more nodal diameters. Of the ten modes shown in Figure 2.18, only the first, fourth, and ninth will be excited by a blow at the centre of the drum.

The normal striking point on a kettledrum head is fairly close to the rim. This is a good point for exciting the modes with only a single nodal circle, and relatively inefficient for exciting the sixth and eighth modes (see Figure 2.18).

Decay rate of drumhead modes

An important feature of the vibration of a drumhead is that not all of the modes decay at the same rate. In general, modes with only nodal circles are more efficient at radiating sound energy than modes with nodal diameters. Thus if the first and second modes are given equal amounts of energy by the blow from the drumstick, the first mode will radiate its energy away in a fraction of a second while the second mode will continue to vibrate for several seconds. The sound of the drum can be considered as having two parts: an initial thump dominated by the rapidly decaying circle-only modes, and a ringing aftersound contributed by the more long-lived diameter modes.

When the drumhead is struck in the centre, none of the diameter modes are excited. All of the vibrational energy imparted by the stroke goes into the circle-only modes, which die away quickly giving a short burst of sound. We earlier described this sound as a 'thump', because it does not seem to have any recognizable pitch.

The pitch of a drum

When the drumhead is struck at the normal playing spot, it is the aftersound which gives the sensation of pitch. The modes which contribute most strongly are the second, third, and fifth, although the seventh and tenth may also play a role. The corresponding pitches are shown boxed in Figure 2.18. These pitches are close to being the second, third, fourth, fifth, and sixth members of a harmonic series with fundamental C_2. From our discussion of the brain's pitch processor in Chapter 1, we should expect this sound to be heard as a note of pitch C_2. In fact, the perceived pitch is an octave higher, for reasons which are not fully understood.

2.5 VIBRATING BARS AND PLATES:
THE IDIOPHONE FAMILY

The idiophone family of musical instruments includes glockenspiel, tubular bells, xylophone, marimba, vibraphone, triangle, cymbals, gongs, wood blocks, and castanets. The unifying feature in this highly diverse group is the inherent springiness or elasticity of the solid object which generates the sound. A string will only vibrate if it is under tension, but in a solid bar or plate there are internal forces which try to oppose any bending of the object. As a result of these forces, transverse standing waves can be set up which result in the radiation of sound.

Before examining the nature of these transverse waves in some simple cases, we should note that longitudinal waves can also be created in solid objects. A longitudinal wave stretches and squeezes the object, rather than bending it. The longitudinal wave patterns in solid rods are very similar to those we found earlier in air columns. The longitudinal modes of a freely supported cylindrical metal bar, for example, have exactly the same patterns as those of the cylindrical air column in Figure 2.4. There is one big difference, however: in a solid object the speed of a longitudinal travelling wave is typically more than ten times greater than the speed in air. For this reason the longitudinal waves in solid objects are usually of too high frequency to be musically useful.

Transverse standing waves on a long thin bar

A tubular bell and a glockenspiel bar seem at first sight to have little in common apart from the fact that they are both made of metal. Acoustically, however, each can be approximately treated as an example of a long thin bar free to vibrate at both ends.   The first five modes of transverse vibration for such a bar are shown

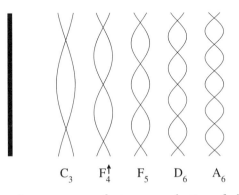

$$C_3 \quad F_4^{\uparrow} \quad F_5 \quad D_6 \quad A_6$$

2.19 The first five standing wave patterns for transverse vibrations of a long, thin bar or rod. The pitch of each standing wave pattern is shown below it, assuming that the first mode has a pitch of C_3

in Figure 2.19. In each case it will be seen that the ends of the bar are not displacement nodes. For the first mode there is a node about a quarter of the length of the bar from each end. For the second mode these two nodes are closer to the ends of the bar, and a third node has appeared at the centre of the bar. For each successive mode an additional node appears.

The frequency of the first mode is proportional to the thickness T of the bar, and inversely proportional to the square of the length L:

$$f_1 = KT/L^2$$

The quantity K depends on the material of which the bar is made. The formula tells us that doubling the thickness will also double f_1, raising the first mode pitch by an octave; doubling the length will reduce f_1 by a factor 4, lowering the pitch by two octaves.

The mode patterns in Figure 2.19 are similar in many respects to the mode patterns for a string shown in Figure 2.14. When we look at the relative pitches of the modes, however, we find a dramatic difference between the bar and the string. Let us assume that we choose a combination of length and thickness to give a first mode pitch of C$_3$ for the bar. The pitches of the next four modes are shown in Figure 2.19. The mode pitches are much more widely spaced than those of a string, and are clearly not members of a harmonic series.

Pitched sounds from struck bars and tubes

A bar struck by a hammer behaves in a similar way to a piano string or a drumskin, in that the motion after the hammer blow is equivalent to a set of the natural modes of the bar vibrating simultaneously. Which modes are strongly excited depends on how the bar is supported and where it is struck. A place where the bar is firmly held will be unable to vibrate, so any mode which contributes to the vibration pattern must have a node at the point of support. On the other hand, the place at which the bar is hit by the hammer cannot be a node.

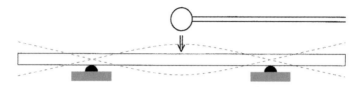

2.20 Method of supporting and striking a glockenspiel bar

We would not expect a struck bar to give a pitched note, since its mode frequencies are far from a harmonic series. Members of the tuned percussion family get round this fundamental problem in a variety of ways. A glockenspiel bar is supported at the two nodes of the first mode, and hit at the centre (Figure 2.20). These conditions are ideal for generating a strong first mode. The higher modes are only weakly excited because they do not have nodes at the supports. In addition, the second and fourth modes are not excited because for these modes the point of striking is a node. The result is that almost all of the sound of a glockenspiel note comes from the first mode only.

On the xylophone, marimba, and vibraphone the bar is not of uniform thickness along its length. Figure 2.21 shows a side view of a typical vibraphone bar, which is cut away underneath in the shape of an arch. This thinning of the bar at the centre has two important musical effects: the frequency of the first vibration mode is lowered, and the pitch interval between the first and second modes is

2.21 Arched undercutting of a vibraphone bar

increased. For a uniform bar the second mode is about an octave and a fourth above the first (see Figure 2.19); by cutting away the underside of the bar this interval can be increased to exactly two octaves. Even if the second mode is not completely eliminated by the method of support, it no longer interferes with the sense of pitch of the bar, since its frequency is the fourth harmonic of the first mode frequency.

The tubular bell is hung from its frame in a way which allows a large number of modes to vibrate freely. It is struck at the end, which is not a node for any of the modes. Thus the spectrum of the radiated sound contains components at many inharmonically related frequencies, giving the tubular bell a fascinatingly ambiguous sound which will be discussed further in Chapter 7.

2.6 ELECTRICAL OSCILLATIONS: THE ELECTROPHONE FAMILY

In the families which we have discussed previously, the pitch of each note on a particular instrument has been determined principally by the resonant vibrations of some part of the instrument. On a guitar, for example, the mass, length, and tension of the top string are chosen so that the natural modes of the string are almost exact harmonics of 330 Hz. This fixes the pitch of the string at E_4.

On an acoustic guitar, the vibrations of the string are communicated through the bridge to the body, which in turn vibrates and radiates a sound wave. On the electric guitar, which belongs to the electroacoustic sub-group of the electrophone family, the string vibrations are transformed into an electrical signal by a pickup; after amplification, the electrical signal is transformed back to a mechanical vibration by the loudspeaker, which radiates a sound wave. In both cases the pitch of the radiated sound is determined by the properties of the string.

In the Hammond organ, which is a member of the electromechanical subgroup, a set of steel wheels are in constant rotation. Near each wheel is a pickup consisting of a small bar magnet and a coil. The circumference of each wheel is cut into a wave-like pattern of peaks and dips. The movement of the wheel generates an electrical signal in the coil; the pitch of the resulting sound depends on the speed of rotation of the wheel, and on how many peaks and dips there are around the circumference.

In instruments of the electronic group, in contrast, the pitch of a note is determined by the properties of the electrical circuits which lie at the heart of the instrument. The methods by which musically useful electrical signals are electronically generated can be divided into two broad classes: analogue and digital. Although all early electronic instruments used analogue techniques, most modern synthesizers and electronic organs use digitally generated signals. We give here a brief outline of both techniques, which are discussed further in Chapter 13.

Analogue techniques

It is possible to construct an electrical circuit which behaves as an oscillator. When such a circuit is energized by the application of a voltage, the current surges round the circuit first in one direction, then in the opposite direction. This alternation of forward and backward current flow continues at a frequency known as the resonant frequency of the circuit.

The resonant frequency can be altered by changing the resistance, capacitance, or inductance of the circuit. The resistance is determined by components called resistors, which turn electrical energy into heat. The capacitance is controlled by capacitors, which store electrical energy during one part of the oscillation cycle and release it during another. The inductance is supplied by wire coils. Thus by switching in different values of resistors, capacitors, or inductors, a single oscillator may be made to generate notes at many different pitches.

The complexity and versatility of the analogue synthesizer was made possible by the development of the voltage controlled oscillator (VCO). In this circuit, the oscillation frequency can be varied merely by altering an externally applied voltage, without physically changing the components in the circuit. Effects such as vibrato, portamento, and pitch bend can easily be obtained by suitably varying the voltage applied to the VCO.

The simplest resonant circuit generates an electrical sine wave. More complex circuits can generate the square waves, triangular waves, and sawtooth waves which form the repertoire of basic signals in a typical analogue synthesizer.

Digital techniques

The explosive development of computer technology in recent years has had a profound impact on many branches of music. A computer is essentially a device for manipulating and storing numbers. The fact that a musical signal can be represented as a sequence of numbers has made it possible to harness advanced and sophisticated computer techniques in order to create, modify, record, and reproduce music. The use of the adjective 'digital' implies that the musical signal is being treated as a sequence of numbers, rather than as a continually varying (or 'analogue') quantity. A device which converts an analogue signal into a number sequence is called an analogue-to-digital converter (ADC).

The process of analogue-to-digital conversion is illustrated by Figure 2.22. The continuous line represents an analogue signal in the form of a triangular wave, rising steadily from 0 to 10 volts and falling steadily back to 0 with a repetition period

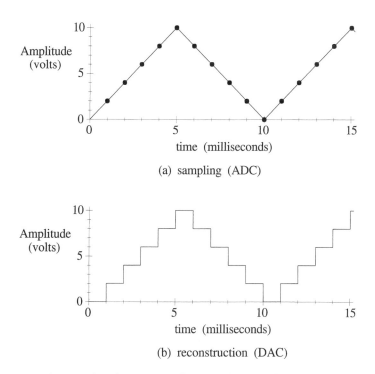

(a) sampling (ADC)

(b) reconstruction (DAC)

2.22 Analogue-to-digital conversion of a triangular wave. (b) Reconstruction of the original waveform by digital-to-analogue conversion

of 10 milliseconds. The converter 'samples' the signal every millisecond. At the first sampling time it registers 0 volts; one millisecond later it registers 2 volts; after a further millisecond it registers 4 volts; and so on. One complete cycle of the triangular wave is recorded as the number sequence 0, 2, 4, 6, 8, 10, 8, 6, 4, 2, 0.

In the above example, the signal is sampled one thousand times in one second: we say that the 'sampling frequency' is 1,000 Hz. To record accurately the nuances of a complex musical signal a much higher sampling frequency would be required. A compact disc is a digital record of a musical performance, and the ADC used to convert the sound into a set of numbers normally operates at a sampling frequency of 44,100 Hz.

The accuracy of an ADC depends also on its resolution—that is, into how many steps it divides the voltage range of the signal. An 8-bit ADC offers 256 steps; a 12-bit ADC has a much finer gradation, with 4,096 steps; while the ultra-fine resolution used in CD recording employs a 16-bit ADC with 65,536 steps.

By using an ADC it is possible to generate a set of numbers corresponding to a pre-existing musical sound. A more intriguing possibility is to start directly in the numerical domain, inventing sets of numbers unrelated to any previously known sound. The use of a sophisticated computer to generate the numbers offers the electronic musician almost limitless creative scope.

However the numbers are generated, they must be turned into a continuous analogue signal before a loudspeaker can realize their musical potential as sound. This process is carried out by a digital-to-analogue converter (DAC). In principle the output of the DAC is a series of steps rather than a smoothly varying signal (Figure 2.22), but the musical significance of this 'staircase effect' is negligible provided that suitably high values of resolution and sampling frequency are chosen.

3
Woodwind Instruments with Reeds

3.1 ACOUSTICAL PRINCIPLES

A reed woodwind instrument consists essentially of a tube, considerably longer than its widest diameter, with a single or double reed at one end. We saw in Chapter 2 that such an instrument is a member of the aerophone family, since the pitches at which it sounds are determined by the properties of the air column confined within the tube.

The tubes used in practical woodwind instruments fall into two categories: approximately cylindrical, and approximately conical. We start by discussing the acoustical consequences of using a reed to excite an exactly cylindrical or conical tube, before considering the musical consequences of the deviations of real instruments from these idealized shapes.

Basic acoustics

When a note is sounded on a clarinet or oboe, a complex interaction takes place between the reed and the standing waves in the air column. Standing waves which have pressure antinodes at the reed cooperate to pump up the amplitude of the reed vibration, which in turn modulates the air flow so as to increase the amplitudes of these standing waves. As the standing waves grow, more energy is lost as heat to the walls of the tube, or radiated as sound. When the instrument is radiating a stable note of constant loudness, a balance has been achieved in which the energy input is equal to the rate of loss.

The requirement that standing waves should have pressure antinodes at the reed makes the blown end of the tube behave as though it were closed. Our discussion in Chapter 2 then leads us to expect that a clarinet-like cylindrical tube, with one end effectively closed by the reed, will have natural mode frequencies which are the odd members only of a harmonic series (see Figure 2.3). For example, a B♭ clarinet with all the side holes closed has a set of natural modes with frequencies close to 147 Hz, 440 Hz, 735 Hz, etc. These are 1, 3, 5 . . . times the first mode frequency of 147 Hz.

When the lowest note on the clarinet (sounding D₃) is played, the reed locks into vibration at a frequency of 147 Hz. The resulting variation of the air flow into the instrument contains all harmonics of 147 Hz, not just the odd ones. The reception afforded to odd and even harmonics by the air column is however very different. Each odd harmonic of the exciting air flow is in tune with a natural mode of the air column, and happily enters into the mutual back-scratching arrangement already described. The even harmonics, in contrast, find no helpful air column resonances at their frequencies, and therefore make only a weak contribution to the radiated sound.

For oboe-like instruments with a conical bore, the natural mode frequencies form a complete harmonic series (see Figure 2.6). Odd and even harmonics of the exciting airflow thus receive an equally favourable response from the air column, and we should not expect to find any bias in favour of odd harmonics in the spectrum of the radiated sound.

The shapes of real woodwind instruments

A real clarinet differs in many ways from the ideal cylinder which was assumed in the foregoing discussion. Figure 3.1 shows the measured bore profile for a typical B♭ clarinet. Although the main part of the tube is cylindrical, there is a noticeable narrowing towards the reed end and a pronounced flaring out at the open end. Nor is a real oboe a perfect cone: Figure 3.2 illustrates a typical bore profile, con-

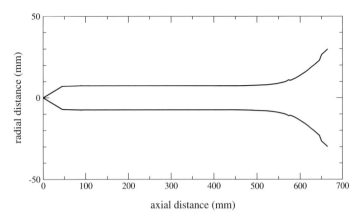

3.1 Internal bore profile of a B♭ clarinet. The complicated inner geometry of the mouthpiece is here replaced by a cone with the same cross-sectional area. Note the difference in axial and radial scales

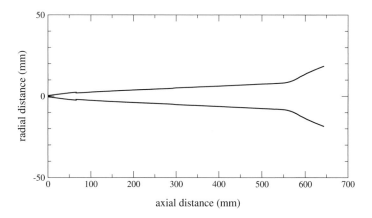

3.2 Internal bore profile of an oboe. Note the difference in axial and radial scales

sisting of several conical sections with different tapers and a final flaring bell. There are also the side holes; even when these are all closed they constitute a series of additional volumes spaced along the tube.

As a result of these divergences, the natural mode frequencies of real wood-wind instruments show small but significant departures from the exact harmonics predicted by the idealized theory. This does not mean that the frequency spectrum of a steady woodwind note will contain inharmonic components: the regular periodic vibration of the reed ensures that a set of exact harmonics is injected into the tube. But the strength of each harmonic in the radiated sound will depend on how close it is in frequency to one of the natural modes of the tube.

The vibration frequency of the reed tends to adjust so that several of the low harmonics are as close as possible to natural modes of the air column. The resulting build-up of a set of strong standing waves is sometimes called a 'cooperative regime'. By altering the blowing pressure and the way that the reed is squeezed by the lips the player can vary the reed frequency to a considerable extent. Since this will move some harmonics closer to air column resonances and others further away, such 'lipping' of the note will alter the timbre as well as the pitch.

An ideal cylindrical clarinet should give a note with only odd harmonics. To what extent is this true of a real clarinet? This question is answered by the measured spectrum shown in Figure 3.3. We can see that the 2nd and 4th harmonics are certainly much weaker than the 1st, 3rd, and 5th, but by the time we get to the 10th harmonic we find that it is much stronger than the surrounding odd components. The reason for this reversal of the expected pattern is that the natural modes have by then got so out of tune that the fifth mode, which should have boosted the 9th harmonic, is in fact in tune with the 10th harmonic.

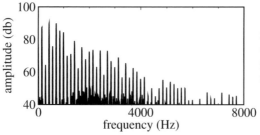

3.3 Frequency spectrum of a note D₃ (sounding pitch) played on a B♭ clarinet

Overblowing

On most woodwind instruments it is possible by a suitable adjustment of blowing pressure and lip control to make the reed vibration lock onto the second natural mode of the air column, instead of the first. This adjustment is described as 'overblowing'. On a conical bored instrument like the oboe the second mode is an octave above the first, so the pitch of the note will rise an octave on overblowing. Further overblowing will make the reed frequency jump to that of the third natural mode, a twelfth above the first. On a cylindrical instrument like the clarinet overblowing will raise the pitch immediately by a twelfth, since this is the interval between the first and second natural modes.

Overblowing is greatly assisted by the opening of a small vent-hole near a pressure node of the desired higher mode. Figure 2.6 shows that in a conical tube complete to the apex, the second mode has a pressure node half-way along the tube. In a realistic oboe, which is more like a cone with the sharp end cut off, this pressure node is nearer to the reed end. What would be the effect of opening a vent-hole at the node? If the second mode alone were activated there would be no variation in pressure at the position of the vent-hole; opening the hole would then have no effect, since both inside and outside there would be constant atmospheric pressure. The same argument applies to the fourth mode, and in fact to all the even modes; opening the vent-hole should have no effect on these modes.

On the other hand, the first mode is trying to maintain a significant pressure variation at the vent-hole. Opening the hole will have two effects on this mode: the amplitude of the standing wave will decrease, and the frequency will shift upwards. There will be similar changes in the amplitudes and frequencies of the other odd modes.

With the vent-hole open, the second mode is stronger than the first, which encourages the reed to lock onto the second mode frequency. This tendency for the sounding note to jump an octave is strengthened by the fact that the odd-numbered mode frequencies are shifted by varying amounts and are no longer capable of supporting the original cooperative regime. In contrast, the fourth mode frequency is unaffected by the opening of the vent key, allowing a cooperative regime based on the second and fourth modes to stabilize the vibration of the reed at the higher frequency.

Side holes and scales

It is possible to make music using only the notes obtainable by overblowing a tube of fixed length. To play an approximation to a diatonic scale, however, it is necessary to overblow to the eighth mode and beyond (see Figure 1.13). Although this technique is commonplace in brass instruments, it is rarely used on wood-wind instruments. Instead, a set of holes is provided along the side wall of the tube. To play the lowest note on the instrument all of the side holes are closed, either directly by the fingers or via a system of keys, levers, and pads. Opening the lowest side hole reduces the effective length of the vibrating air column and rais-es the pitch of the note. Successively opening higher side holes raises the pitch fur-ther, in a series of steps which can be made to correspond to any desired scale by suitable positioning of the holes.

The pitch obtained by opening a particular hole depends not only on the posi-

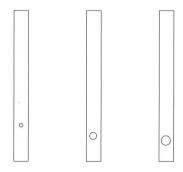

3.4 Three cylindrical tubes, open at both ends, each with a single side hole. The tubes have the same effec-tive (or sounding) length

tion of the hole but also on its diameter. All three tubes shown in Figure 3.4 will sound the same note, since the shortening effect of each hole is the same. The tube on the right has a hole with a diameter almost as big as that of the tube. Opening such a large side-hole is roughly equivalent to sawing off the section of tube beyond the hole; a pressure node is created just below the hole position. The tube in the middle has a somewhat smaller side-hole, and the effective pressure node is some distance below the hole. The tube on the left has an even smaller hole, and the distance from hole to effective pressure node is even greater. The ability to compensate for the shifting of a hole by altering its diameter is very use-ful to the designer of woodwind instruments.

On most modern woodwind instruments the use of side-holes is coupled with the overblowing technique previously described to provide a musical compass of several octaves. The oboe, for example, sounds the note $B^\flat_3$ when all its holes are closed. By successively opening side holes a chromatic scale up to C_5 can be played. This part of the instrument's compass is described as the low register; for all of the low register notes, the reed vibrates at a frequency close to that of the first mode of the air column.

There is no further hole which can be opened to give the next chromatic note, $C^\#_5$. To sound this note, most of the side-holes are closed again to give the fingering for $C^\#_4$; the opening of a vent hole causes the instrument to overblow to the octave above, thus achieving the desired pitch. The chromatic scale from $C^\#_5$ to C_6 is obtained in this way by overblowing from the low register. Since the vent-hole should be at the pressure node of the second mode, there should ideally be a separate vent-hole for each note. In practice, a small perforation opened in the pad covering the highest side-hole is used to vent the notes from $C^\#_5$ to $E^\flat_5$; a vent-hole further up the tube is opened by the 'bottom octave key' for the notes E_5 to $G^\#_5$; and an even higher vent is opened by the 'top octave key' for the notes A_5 to C_6. The notes from $C^\#_5$ to C_6 constitute the upper register of the instrument, in which the reed frequency is close to that of the second mode of the air column.

A further extension of the compass of the oboe (up to A_6 is required by some orchestral parts) is provided by overblowing so that the reed locks on to the third or fourth mode of the air column. This region is described as the high register.

Similar techniques are used on the other reed woodwinds, although the detailed methods of venting vary considerably. In instruments of the clarinet family the second mode is a twelfth above the first, and the low register of the instrument must span this pitch interval. The side-holes therefore continue further up the tube than is necessary on a conical instrument. The relationship between fingering patterns in first and second registers is also less straightforward: a fingering which gives, say, C_4 in the low register of a clarinet will give not C_5 but G_5 in the upper register.

Tables showing patterns of finger-holes and keywork for several currently used and historically important models of woodwind instruments are given in Appendix 2.

Cut-off frequency

Up to this point we have assumed that opening a particular pattern of side-holes on a woodwind instrument reduces the effective length of the air column by the same amount for all its modes of vibration. This is an oversimplification. The effect of an open hole on a wave travelling down the tube depends very much on whether its frequency is above or below a critical value known as the cut-off frequency. If the wave frequency is much below the cut-off, the wave is reflected just below the highest open hole, as described above. As the frequency approaches cut-off, the point of reflection moves further down the tube. If the frequency is above the cut-off value, the wave is not significantly reflected by the open side-hole, but continues on to the lower end of the tube.

The cut-off frequency depends on the diameter and depth of the open side-holes, and on their spacing. The pattern of open holes changes with the note being played, and in general there will be a different cut-off frequency for each fingering pattern. An instrument with large side-holes will have higher cut-off frequencies than an otherwise similar instrument with smaller holes.

Altering the cut-off frequency has a profound effect on the timbre of the instrument. Below the cut-off frequency, the strong reflection gives powerful natural modes corresponding to the shortened tube length. Above the cut-off, we find much weaker modes corresponding to the complete length of the tube. Usually an instrument is proportioned so that the first few modes are below cut-off, and these strong low-frequency modes provide the cooperative regime which stabilizes the reed vibration. The higher harmonics of the exciting airflow lie above the cut-off; the absence of strong modes in this frequency region means that in the internal spectrum of the instrument these high harmonics are much lower in amplitude than the harmonics below cut-off. Raising the cut-off frequency will boost the strength of some of these high harmonics, giving the instrument a brighter timbre. Carrying this process too far will make the sound unacceptably harsh.

The cut-off frequency also affects the fingering of notes in the high register. A note in the low register normally has a fundamental frequency well below the cut-off frequency; since a wave at this frequency is totally reflected at the highest open hole, it is unaffected by the opening or closing of holes much further down the tube. In contrast, the waves which determine the pitch of a high register note may have frequencies above the cut-off, in which case they will run on to the end of the tube. The pitch can then be altered by closing one or more of the lower holes, a technique known as cross-fingering. Because the standing wave patterns above the cut-off frequency are complicated, the effect of cross-fingering can be surprising—sometimes closing an additional hole will make the pitch rise instead of fall.

Radiation of sound

We have seen that in the internal air column of a woodwind instrument harmonics below the cut-off frequency are liable to be much stronger than those above cut-off. In the sound radiated by the instrument, this bias towards low-frequency components is partly offset by the fact that in general high frequencies are radiated more efficiently than low frequencies. This 'treble boost' in the radiation process means that the sound heard by a listener is much brighter than the sound which is picked up by a microphone inside the instrument.

The directional pattern of the radiated sound depends on frequency; once again, the cut-off frequency is a crucial parameter. A component with frequency much below the cut-off is radiated with equal strength in all directions; such a uniform directional pattern is described as isotropic. Practically all the sound energy is radiated from the highest open hole. A component whose frequency is close to the cut-off is radiated in a complex pattern, with the strongest radiation occurring along a fairly wide cone whose central axis is that of the tube. For components with frequencies much above the cut-off, the sound is radiated most strongly down the tube axis. The varied nature of these directional patterns poses a tricky problem for the recording engineer, trying to position a microphone so that one frequency region will not be favoured at the expense of another.

3.2 HISTORICAL DEVELOPMENT

Many of the most primitive instruments known are of the reed type because of the simplicity with which they can be made. Every child knows, for example, that by stretching a blade of grass between cupped hands and blowing across the edge, a loud and quite varied buzzing sound can be produced. A crude form of reed instrument, which produces a squawk when placed in the mouth and blown strongly, can be made simply by splitting the end of a dry length of reed. Little is known about the earliest origins of reed instruments, but it is not unreasonable to assume that techniques such as these were used for the imitation of natural sounds and the accompaniment of religious ceremonies.

Pictorial representations of reed instruments date back as far as 3000 BCE, and the remains of Sumerian silver reed instruments found in the course of excavation in the Royal Cemetery of Ur have been dated at about 2500 BCE. These are cylindrical bore instruments with three side-holes, probably designed to play whole tone scales. Single reed instruments are frequently depicted in Egyptian tomb paintings of the Old Kingdom (around 2200 BCE); double-reed instruments do not seem to have appeared in Egypt until the time of the New Kingdom (around 1500 BCE).

Further developments were made by the ancient Greeks, whose wind instruments were characterized broadly as either aulos (reed) or syrinx (flute). An aulos usually took the form of two pipes, each fitted with a reed and typically about 50 cm long, held one in each hand, usually at a divergent angle, and played together. Players are often depicted wearing a form of halter which covers the cheeks and the outer lips, being held on with a strap around the back of the head. One possible function of such an arrangement is in helping to maintain the pressure in the mouth and to stop the cheeks from bulging. There appears to be convincing evidence that both single- and double-reed versions of the aulos were constructed. Writings of the ancient Greek philosophers tell us that a good deal was known at that time about the art of producing suitable reeds and the mechanics of blowing them.

Rather similar to the aulos was the Roman tibia, dating from around 500 BCE. This was usually made of metal, although sometimes hardwood or even ivory was used, and it incorporated a number of technical refinements which increased its flexibility. For example the side-holes could be opened or closed by means of metal bands, thus allowing the instrument to be preset to play in one of a number of modes. Tibias were used, often by groups of players, to accompany social and ceremonial events ranging from the preparation of food to the engagements of gladiators in the arena.

After the fall of the Roman empire the European tradition of reed instrument-playing seems to have almost completely died out. There is no evidence that knowledge of the classical reed aerophones contributed to the reappearance of double-reed instruments in Europe around the end of the first millennium CE. The catalyst for this development was almost certainly the growing military, political, and social interaction between Islamic and Christian civilizations, which led to the spread into Europe of conical reed instruments already in common use in North Africa and the Near East.

Shawms

The term shawm is used generically to describe a conical bored double-reed instrument. Although no shawm made in Europe before the sixteenth century is known to have survived to the present, images of this type of instrument are found in late twelfth-century manuscripts, and documentary evidence for the use of shawms in Europe is found from the thirteenth century onwards. The shawm is blown in a similar manner to a modern oboe except that the reed itself is held almost entirely inside the player's mouth. Frequently the reed is mounted in a cylindrical wooden holder known as a pirouette. The lips of the player can rest against the front face of the pirouette while maintaining some control of the reed at its base. The use of the pirouette makes it easier to play loudly for long periods of time without lip fatigue setting in, and also protects the player's mouth from damage in the event of the instrument being knocked.

The earliest European shawms were small instruments playing in the soprano range. By the end of the sixteenth century shawms were being made in a range of sizes from the sopranino down to the great bass. The body is generally wooden. Figure 3.5(b) shows a twentieth-century reconstruction of a tenor shawm similar to that illustrated by Michael Praetorius in the *Syntagma Musicum*, published in the early seventeenth century. Pirouettes are not normally used on the bass and great bass, whose reeds are mounted on crooks similar to that of the modern bassoon. The lowest notes on the larger instruments are operated by metal keys, which are usually shielded by a perforated wooden barrel called a fontanelle; this feature is evident in Figure 3.5(b).

The sound of the shawm carries well outdoors and it can compete on an equal footing with brass instruments. A typical fifteenth-century outdoor band might

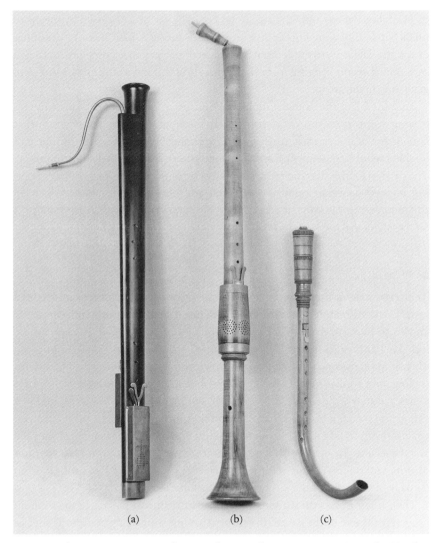

(a) (b) (c)

3.5 (a) curtal (reconstruction: Wood *c.*1980); (b) tenor shawm (reconstruction: John Hanchet *c.*1975) with the crook turned towards the camera to show pirouette and reed; (c) tenor crumhorn (reconstruction: Gunter Korber, *c.*1975). The upper keys on the crumhorn are found only on modern instruments

have consisted of two or three shawms and a slide trumpet or sackbut. In the following century much larger ensembles were employed on ceremonial occasions; in these groups shawms frequently played along with other wind instruments such as cornetts, sackbuts, and curtals.

By the beginning of the seventeenth century the use of the shawm had started to decline in Europe, although shawms continued to be played in German town bands at least until the end of the eighteenth century. Reconstructions of historical shawms are now once again used regularly in performances of medieval, Renaissance, and early Baroque music. Traditional shawms like the Breton bombarde and the Spanish tiple and tenora have continued in vigorous use in many areas of Europe, and conical double reed instruments are important classical and folk instruments in many other parts of the world.

Crumhorns

The most characteristic feature of the crumhorn is the hooked shape which gives it its name (from the German Krummhorn meaning 'crooked horn'). The narrow bore is predominantly cylindrical but widens out towards the lower end. The fingerholes are arranged essentially the same as on the recorder but the instrument is not overblown, so that on an instrument without additional keys the range is just an octave and one note. Its double reed is housed in a wind-cap with a slot in it for blowing through, so the lips are not actually in contact with the reed. However, notes can be articulated by tonguing against the slot, in a similar manner to the recorder. The lower curved section has vent-holes which cannot be reached by the fingers and are therefore permanently open; these have the effect of darkening the tone quality.

The crumhorn was probably developed in northern Germany, although the earliest evidence of its existence is its representation in a picture in Bologna dated 1488. During the sixteenth century it spread throughout Italy, Germany, and the low countries and was played by professional musicians at courts and in town bands. Complete consorts from soprano to great bass were constructed. The narrow bore and small finger-holes give the crumhorn a characteristic buzzing tone. The loudness is fixed by the design of the instrument and the nature of the reed, and cannot be modified significantly by blowing technique. Modern reproductions of the crumhorn vary a lot in the volume of sound which they generate; inconographic evidence suggest that some at least of the original instruments were powerful enough to join in bands containing shawms and trombones.

The crumhorn maintained an important role until the middle of the seventeenth century, especially in Germany; it then suffered a decline as tastes changed and the demand for greater compass and dynamic range increased. There is evidence to suggest that some players did away with the wind-cap and played with the reed directly in the mouth in an attempt to make the crumhorn more expressive.

In the latter part of the twentieth century there was a remarkable resurgence of interest in the crumhorn, due in large measure to the enthusiasm of amateur musicians wishing to play Renaissance music on period instruments. The similarity between recorder and crumhorn fingering, and the fact that the lips are not required to exert any control over the reed, makes the crumhorn relatively accessible to recorder players, although a much higher blowing pressure is required than on the recorder.

The limited compass means that it is not straightforward to find music playable on a consort of crumhorns; there is evidence that sixteenth-century players were used to transposing music into suitable keys, and to editing parts as necessary to bring them within the ranges of the instruments. Many modern crumhorn makers have extended the range upwards by adding one or two extra holes covered by keys; this feature is evident on the twentieth-century tenor crumhorn illustrated in Figure 3.5(c). Although these keys are very useful, there is no evidence of their use on historic instruments. Extra holes covered by keys were sometimes added at the lower end of late Renaissance crumhorns to extend the range downwards.

Other Renaissance reed instruments

In the fifteenth and sixteenth centuries there was an upsurge of interest in the development of new types of wind instruments, especially in Germany and Italy. We have space to mention only a few of the reed instruments which flourished around this time, and which are described in detail in Praetorius's *Syntagma Musicum*.

The cornamusa is a windcapped instrument, similar in many ways to a crumhorn but with a straight tube. The bore is cylindrical, and the lower end is plugged, so that all the sound is radiated through the side-holes. Praetorius describes five sizes of cornamusa; the fingering and compass of each instrument is similar to that of the corresponding crumhorn, although the sound is more subdued.

The racket also has a narrow cylindrical bore, but its unique feature is its method of construction. A central bore is drilled through a short, wide wooden cylinder, with eight similar bores running parallel to the central one and concentrically placed around it. The bores are connected by channels in the caps which seal the top and bottom of the instrument, in such a way that a continuous pipe is created whose length is nine times that of the body. A wide reed on a metal staple is inserted into the central bore, surrounded by an elaborate and decorative form of pirouette.

Praetorius suggested that the bass members of the racket family could play a useful role in doubling viols and other bass instruments in a consort, playing the parts an octave lower than written. The efficacy of this advice has been confirmed by performers using modern reproductions. The racket is a remarkably compact source of very low notes: the great bass racket, with an overall length of only 39 cm from base to pirouette, descends to C_1, which is only a tone above the bottom note of the modern contrabassoon. In the Baroque era the racket was redesigned with a set of cylindrical bores of steadily increasing diameter, connected to give an overall bore equivalent to a stepped cone.

The curtal, or dulcian, also uses the space-saving idea of connected parallel bores, but in this case there are only two tubes involved. The bore is conical, so that the curtal is in principle similar to a shawm bent into a U shape. It is clear, however, from the illustration in Figure 3.5(a), that the instrument is constructed by reaming two conical bores into a single piece of wood, the connection being provided by a cap at the base.

The folded construction of the curtal reduces the need for long key levers by bringing most of the holes within reach of the player's fingers. This is obviously of greatest advantage in the bass range, and within a few decades of the appearance of the curtal in the 1540s the bass member of the family had established a firm foothold both in outdoor bands and in church ensembles. Other sizes, from soprano to great bass, are also described by Praetorius. As the alternative name 'dulcian' implies, the sound is softer and more controllable than that of the shawm. By the time that further technical developments had led to the introduction of the Baroque bassoon in the second half of the seventeenth century, the curtal had already accumulated an impressive repertoire of virtuoso chamber music.

Early oboes

The oboe is a direct development from the soprano shawm. Its origins can be traced to Paris around the middle of the seventeenth century. The primary innovators appear to have been members of the Hotteterre and Philidor families, who were woodwind players at the French court. The oboe, or hautbois, was distinguished from the shawm by its construction in three jointed sections and the absence of a pirouette. Direct control of the reed by the lips meant that a greater degree of flexibility of articulation and volume control could be achieved. The diameters of the finger-holes were smaller than those typical of the shawm, which made it easier to obtain accidental notes by cross-fingering. The new instrument could provide a fully chromatic scale through two octaves, and had a far greater dynamic range than the shawm.

Lower-pitched members of the oboe family were introduced at the French court around the same time as the treble instrument, pitched in C. These included the haut-contre de hautbois, pitched in A, the taille de hautbois, pitched in F,

3.6 (a) three-key oboe (Stanesby senior, London, *c.*1700); (b) Conservatoire system oboe (SML, Paris, *c.*1950), showing keywork added to the oboe in the nineteenth century

and the quinte de hautbois, pitched in D. In the first quarter of the eighteenth century, a version of the taille developed with a curved body and a widely flaring bell; this was known as the oboe da caccia. With the addition of a globular bell, the haut-contre developed into the oboe d'amore, and the taille into the cor anglais, also known as the English horn.

The oboe existed for some years alongside the shawm, each instrument performing its separate musical functions. The shawm was principally used for outside performances and military purposes, while the oboe found its primary use in the court and opera house. During the eighteenth century, two- and three-keyed oboes gained acceptance in the orchestra, and also saw use in the military band; there were, however, few significant design developments in this period. Figure 3.6(a) shows a three-keyed example dating from around 1700.

The turn of the nineteenth century saw the start of a period of mechanization. By 1825, Josef Sellner in Vienna had created his thirteen-key oboe which formed the basis of the highly individual Viennese System, still in use in some parts of Austria. New developments were soon made in France, particularly by the famous Triébert family who produced their Système 5, now known as the thumb-plate model. As well as having a superior mechanism, the new French oboes had a more refined tone than their Viennese counterparts and soon found favour amongst players. By the 1870s Frédéric Triébert had brought out a further modification which he called Système 6; this is now known as the conservatoire model. An example is shown in Figure 3.6(b). The thumb-plate and conservatoire models are the most commonly used today.

After the death of Frédéric Triébert in 1878, his foreman François Lorée set up his own firm and further developed the conservatoire system. He died in 1902, but his work was continued by his son Adolphe Lucien, who brought out the perfected Lorée version of the conservatoire oboe in 1906. This is usually referred to as the conservatoire system Gillet model, after the French oboist Georges Gillet who had much influence on its development. It is used widely in France and the USA, although it does not enjoy the same popularity in Britain.

Early bassoons

The bassoon proper emerged in France around the middle of the seventeenth century, being distinguished from the dulcian by its construction in four sections or joints. These early bassoons usually had just three keys, but during the eighteenth century additional keys were added. Figures 3.7(a) and 3.8(a) show a five-keyed bassoon from the late eighteenth century.

Radical design changes were introduced by the German bassoonist and instrument maker Carl Almenräder, working in collaboration with a close friend Gottfried Weber in Mainz. Weber was a musician, but also a learned theoretician who had published articles on woodwind acoustics. Almenräder was able to conduct experiments in the Schotts Söhne instrument factory, applying the principles passed on to him by Weber; these experiments led to his fifteen-key bassoon. This had an extended range and improved intonation, brought about primarily by enlarging the lower tone holes and moving them closer to the bell, whilst adding

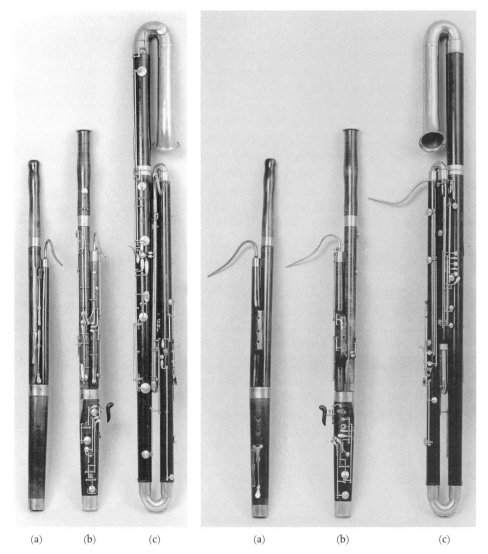

3.7 (left) (a) five-key bassoon (anon., England, *c.*1790); (b) modern bassoon (Heckel, Biebrich); (c) modern contrabassoon (Buffet-Crampon, Paris *c.*1920). Each instrument is viewed from the player's side. The elaborate keywork of the modern bassoon (b) can be compared with the relative simplicity of the Classical-period instrument (a)

3.8 (right) The instruments illustrated in Figure 3.7, as seen facing the player

and relocating certain other keys. Eventually this was followed by his eighteen-key model which had a complete chromatic compass of four octaves.

In 1829 the 17-year-old Johann Adam Heckel entered the Schotts Söhne company, and after two years Almenräder and Heckel founded their own firm. After

Almenräder's death, Johann Heckel continued to manufacture and develop the bassoon; two further generations of the Heckel family followed him. An important innovation that Johann's son Wilhelm introduced was the hard rubber lining of the wing and butt joints. This solved the problem of the wood perishing through condensed moisture.

As with the oboe, there were also corresponding developments of the bassoon in France. With the bassoon the French essentially retained the old instrument and simply added keys; Jancourt in 1847 developed a twenty-two-key model which has been extensively used in Britain and France. In Germany, however, the instrument developed by Almenräder and perfected by the Heckel family represented real design rethinking. The German design is now accepted worldwide as the standard instrument, although there are moves to revive the French model.

Early clarinets

The late seventeenth century saw the evolution of the chalumeau, an instrument which had two of the essential features of the clarinet: a mouthpiece with single reed, and a cylindrical bore. The chalumeau body was very similar to that of the Baroque recorder, with seven finger-holes and a thumb-hole; like the recorder, it was usually constructed with a separate foot joint. Because of the effectively closed end provided by the reed, however, the chalumeau overblew to the twelfth rather than to the octave. This necessitated the addition of two keys to bridge the gap between registers, although in fact the instrument was primarily designed to play in the fundamental register. It was frequently but not invariably blown with the reed against the upper lip.

The clarinet proper came into being about 1700, its invention being attributed to Johann Christoph Denner, a woodwind instrument maker of Nuremberg. His new instrument was very similar to the chalumeau but featured a speaker key, operated by the left thumb, which facilitated overblowing. Access to the upper register was also made easier by a reduction in mouthpiece size, and the foot joint was replaced by a bell. In the early eighteenth century the chalumeau and clarinet coexisted, and the distinction between the two is frequently unclear in the records of that period. However, the essential feature of the new clarinet was that it was designed to play in the overblown register, whilst being rather weak in the fundamental register. The chalumeau, on the other hand, was strong in the fundamental register and could overblow only with difficulty. The terms 'chalumeau register' and 'clarinet register' are still retained to describe the fundamental and overblown registers of the modern clarinet.

The early Denner clarinets, pitched in D, had only two keys, and were thus reliant on cross-fingerings for the semitones. Like the chalumeau, the early clarinets were usually played with the reed uppermost; this technique has surprisingly little effect on performance, despite the fact that it rules out tonguing techniques as we know them today. Players could also choose to play them with either left or right hand uppermost, two separate holes being provided for the lower-hand little finger. It was intended that the unused hole should be plugged with wax or a peg. The mouthpiece and barrel were made in one piece out of the same wood and were regarded as the top section of the instrument, rather than as separate entities. Reeds were tied on with twine, a practice which is still common in Germany.

Around the mid-eighteenth century, deeper-pitched instruments in C, B♭, and A came into use; these had four or five keys and a wider bell, similar in size to the one on a modern clarinet. By this time the mouthpiece and barrel had still not been separated, and it was common practice to have what was effectively a pair of clarinets using a single lower section but alternative upper sections of different length. An interchangeable upper section was known as a *pièce de rechange* or *corps de rechange*. The custom of holding the instrument with the left hand uppermost had now become firmly established. Near the end of the century the practice of separating the mouthpiece from the barrel became standard, and further keys appeared. Figure 3.9(a) shows a typical six-keyed boxwood clarinet from this period.

The beginning of the nineteenth century saw the introduction of a number of new keys, and the thirteen-keyed instrument developed by Ivan Müller became the standard instrument of the period. Müller also invented the metal screw ligature for clamping the reed in place. The Boehm system, which is used almost universally today, was developed by Hyacinthe Eléonore Klosé, a clarinet professor at the Paris Conservatoire working in collaboration with the Paris instrument maker Louis-August Buffet. Their early model was exhibited in 1839 and a perfected version was introduced to the public in 1843. Boehm, in fact, had little to do with its design, although the new instrument incorporated some of the mechanical features that Boehm had used on his early flutes, particularly the ring keys. The new system provided duplicate fingerings in abundance and abolished many of the earlier cross-fingerings and the associated sliding from key to key necessary with the Müller model. The 1843 model remains essentially unchanged today except for improvements in sonority brought about by changes in bore dimensions and in the size and location of finger-holes.

Adolphe Sax also introduced ring keys to the Müller design, while retaining its fingering system, and a number of other instrument makers continued to experiment and make improvements. Eugène Albert of Brussels became famous for manufacturing this design, which is often referred to as the simple or Albert system. Derivatives are still used to some extent in Germany; they are occasionally described as 'Oehler system', after Oskar Oehler (1858–1936) who significantly developed the German clarinet.

3.9 (a) typical six-keyed boxwood clarinet in B♭ (Lawson, London 1794); (b) twentieth-century wooden Boehm system clarinet in B♭ (Selmer, *c.*1950); (c) metal Boehm system clarinet in B♭ (Hawkes, *c.*1925). The metal example gives an indication of the narrow bore of the clarinet, cylindrical for most of its length

Adolphe Sax

Adolphe Sax was born in 1814. He was the son of Charles-Joseph Sax, an instrument maker who had a factory in the town of Dinant, on the river Meuse 75 kilometres south of Brussels. Adolphe was a student of flute and clarinet at the École Royale de Musique in Brussels, and also worked in his father's factory. He was one of the great innovators in musical instrument design. Because of the enormous popularity of the saxophone, the name of Sax is normally associated with this instrument, but it should not be forgotten that he also invented the saxhorns and brought out new designs for a number of other instruments including the clarinet, bassoon, and trombone. In 1836 he completed his improved design for the

(a)   (b)

3.10 (a) alto saxophone (Selmer, *c.*1950); (b) alto saxophone (Couturier, *c.*1880). Note the automatic octave keys with single touchpiece in (a) and the two octave keys with independent touchpieces in (b)

bass clarinet with its saxophone-like shape; previously it had been constructed in a doubled-up shape similar to the bassoon.

In 1841 Adolphe Sax first exhibited a new instrument based on a wide conical bore and a single-reed mouthpiece. This idea probably sprang from early attempts to play the ophicleide with a clarinet mouthpiece. His developmental work continued when he moved to Paris in 1842 to set up his own workshop, and in 1846 he was granted patents for the saxophone family. His original design had two separate octave keys, which are now replaced by a single one; apart from this the saxophone remains virtually unchanged to this day. Figure 3.10 compares an early alto saxophone having two octave keys to a modern instrument with a single one.

It is interesting to note that the innovations of Adolphe Sax were not all welcomed by the other instrument makers in Paris, who constantly harassed him and subjected him to vindictive attacks in the press. Numerous legal proceedings which were instituted against him eventually drove him into bankruptcy.

3.3 REED WOODWIND FAMILIES

There are four main groups of reed woodwinds in common use today: clarinets, oboes, bassoons, and saxophones. Clarinets have an essentially cylindrical bore and use a single reed, while both oboes and bassoons are conical bored with a double reed. The saxophone has a conical bore and uses a single reed.

Clarinet

The range of different clarinets that have been produced over the ages is remarkable, but the only ones used extensively today are the following: (a) the E♭ (range G_3 to C_7, notated a minor third lower than sounding); (b) the B♭ (range D_3 to $B^\flat_6$, notated a tone higher than sounding); (c) the A (range $C^\sharp_3$ to A_6 notated a minor third higher than sounding); (d) the alto, pitched an octave lower than the E♭ (range G_2 to F_6, notated a major sixth higher than sounding; (e) the bass, an octave lower than the standard B♭ clarinet (range $D^\flat_2$ to C_6, notated a ninth above sounding pitch; and (f) the contrabass, an octave below the bass clarinet (range $D^\flat_1$ to C_5).

The clarinet in A is virtually identical to its twin sister in B♭ except for the semitone difference, its primary use being to simplify the playing of difficult passages in sharp keys. Orchestral players normally have a B♭ and A pair and use the same mouthpiece for both; this cannot be used on a C clarinet though, a fact that speeded this instrument's decline.

Despite its name, the basset horn is a clarinet pitched in F, a fourth below the ordinary B♭ model. It is normally constructed with four extra 'basset' keys which extend the lower range down to written C. It is similar in appearance to the bass clarinet but smaller in size, often with a single bend like the alto saxophone. A few compositions, notably the Mozart clarinet concerto, call for a basset clarinet. This is usually pitched in A and, like the basset horn, has extra keys to extend the bass range.

Clarinets are generally constructed in five separate sections: mouthpiece, barrel, upper joint, lower joint, and bell. The sections are connected together by socket and tenon joints. The main body, which comprises the upper and lower joints, carries the keywork; on smaller models this is sometimes made in one single piece. Tuning is accomplished by pulling out the mouthpiece or barrel a short way and many players carry two barrels of slightly different length to facilitate a greater range of tuning adjustment. On the standard B♭ clarinet the bore diameter is slightly less than 15 mm, and the total length is 67 cm to the tip of the mouthpiece.

Good-quality instruments are usually made from African Blackwood, but in recent years there has been an increasing tendency for student models to be made from plastic. The material of construction, however, is not the reason for its characteristically 'woody' sound; this is due to the bore shape and the acoustical end conditions imposed by the mouthpiece. In fact metal clarinets are not uncommon, especially in America and Italy, and were being made before 1850. Contrabass clarinets are frequently made of metal. Figure 3.9 shows B♭ clarinets made from wood and metal for comparison.

The lowest note on the standard Boehm clarinet is written E_3 (sounding D_3 on a B♭ instrument) although occasionally one finds an instrument, known as a 'full Boehm', which has an extension down to written $E^{\flat}_3$ and can thus play the compass of the A clarinet. From E_3 up to $A^{\sharp}_4$ the notes are produced by progressively shortening the tube length by opening holes in turn. The notes E_3 to G_4, are referred to as the chalumeau register, since this was approximately the range covered by the older chalumeau. Above these are three notes ($G^{\sharp}_4$, A_4, and $A^{\sharp}_4$) which link the clarinet register to the overblown notes above; these are collectively referred to as the throat register, and sometimes the individual notes are called throat tones. The middle range from B_4 up to $B^{\flat}_5$ is produced by overblowing the notes in the chalumeau register, raising their pitch by a twelfth; this is called the clarinet register. Above this, the clarion (or altissimo) register extends up to C_7 or thereabouts, the fingerings here being based on higher harmonics of the chalumeau register notes.

The mouthpiece on a clarinet is arguably the most important component in determining the overall tone quality. The extent to which higher harmonics are present in the sound, often referred to as the amount of 'edge', is governed largely by the shape of the internal cavity inside the mouthpiece, called the tone chamber. An open and smoothly curved tone chamber tends to give a rounder sound with few upper harmonics, whereas a more restricted shape with sharp edged cutaway sections tends to give more upper harmonics and a correspondingly brighter sound. A seemingly infinite variety of tone chamber designs are available on the market.

The base of the reed is clamped to the flat table on the underside of the mouthpiece using either a metal ligature or a binding of twine or fabric. Towards the tip, which is placed in the player's mouth, the surface curves away from the reed to allow it to vibrate. The shape of this curved section, known as the lay, is the other most important feature of a mouthpiece. A wide lay tends to produce a louder sound but is difficult to control, whereas a narrower one limits the power but allows the player more control over dynamics. Generally speaking, with a wider lay it is necessary to use a softer reed, otherwise the lip muscles become quickly fatigued and it is difficult to play pianissimo.

Oboe

The standard modern oboe, sometimes referred to as the soprano or treble oboe, is pitched in C. It has a range of $B^\flat_3$ to A_6 and is notated at sounding pitch. The resonating tube is made from hardwood or plastic, and is constructed in three sections: the upper and lower body sections and the bell. As with the clarinet, these are connected by socket and tenon joints. Although the oboe has a similar length to the B♭ clarinet it sounds higher because its internal bore is essentially conical, rather than cylindrical.

Fingering on the oboe is somewhat similar to the flute, since both overblow to the octave. The fundamental tones are essentially repeated at the octave, whereas fingerings in the top register are derived from higher harmonics. The thumb-plate, conservatoire, and conservatoire system Gillet models are all in common use today; the essential difference between these is in the fingering of the B♭ and C in the middle and upper registers. There is little to choose between them for ease of fingering, different passages being simpler or more difficult on one or other of the models. It is generally thought that the beginner can master the thumb-plate system most easily whereas the conservatoire systems offer advantages for the more experienced player.

Three different systems of octave levers are also in common use. The first of these is referred to as the simple system (sometimes called single-acting or non-automatic) and is standard on most student models in Great Britain. This has two separate octave keys, one used for the notes E to G♯ and the other for the notes A to C. The second is referred to as the semi-automatic system and is the one preferred by a high proportion of professional players. This is standard on the Gillet model and most student models in the USA. With this arrangement the first octave key (worked by the left-hand thumb) may be held open while the second one is in use. The mechanical coupling involved is quite uncomplicated and there are definite advantages over the simple system in fingering many passages. The third system is known as the automatic (sometimes called fully automatic or double-acting). In this case either octave key may be used for all of the notes E to C, or the instrument may be fitted with just a single octave key.

The reed on an oboe is in the form of two strips of cane, bound on to a metal tube (the staple). The staple may be made of brass, silver, copper or alloy. It is conical in shape and about 47 mm long, the lower part being covered with cork so that it makes an airtight fit in the end of the main barrel. Oboists normally carry a number of reeds. The cane strips lie face to face and are hollowed out on the inside and scraped down at the ends in such a way that there is an approximately elliptic aperture at the tip for blowing through. When a note is sounded the aperture opens and closes periodically, allowing through the puffs of air which maintain the resonance in the tube.

In addition to the oboe in C there are three deeper pitched members of the oboe family: the oboe d'amore, the cor anglais, and the bass oboe. Of these the cor anglais is the most common; this is pitched in F, a fifth below the standard oboe, and is usually notated a fifth higher than sounding. The oboe d'amore is pitched in A, a minor third below the standard oboe, and is notated a minor third higher than sounding. The bass oboe, and the wider-bored Heckelphone, are both pitched an octave below the standard oboe, and are notated either at sounding pitch or an octave higher.

In general all of the deeper-pitched models of oboe are constructed with a pear-shaped bell terminating in a constricted opening. The bell shape varies considerably between manufacturers, but the acoustical significance is not as great as is commonly supposed; the effect is confined largely to the lowest notes.

Bassoon

The bassoon family consists of only two members: the bassoon proper, with range $B^\flat_1$ to E_5, and the contrabassoon (or double bassoon), with range $B^\flat_0$ to $C^\sharp_4$. The difference between the two instruments can be seen in Figures 3.7 and 3.8. The great size of the contrabassoon makes it a very expensive instrument, and its use is largely confined to orchestral performances.

As we saw in the previous section, two distinct bassoon designs have evolved, the German and the French. Since the German is the one in more common use, it is the one described here.

As shown in Figure 3.11, the construction of a bassoon is in five parts: (1) the crook (or bocal) in the form of a curved length of metal tube, about 4 mm in diameter at the small end; (2) the wing joint (so named because its flattened shape

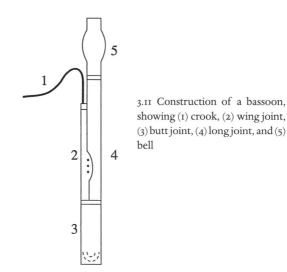

3.11 Construction of a bassoon, showing (1) crook, (2) wing joint, (3) butt joint, (4) long joint, and (5) bell

resembles a bird's wing); (3) the butt joint (or boot), in the form of two conical sections joined at the base by a metal U-section and protected by a metal cap; this is fitted with a hand support known as a crutch; (4) the long joint (or bass joint), which runs adjacent to the wing joint; and (5) the bell, which has a diameter of about 4 cm at the open end; this often has a bulge midway along its length primarily for strengthening purposes. The instrument may be supported either by a sling or by an adjustable spike fitted near the base.

The contrabassoon is generally made out of wood in two or three sections, with the folded back tubular lengths permanently attached to each other. Only the bocal, and sometimes the bell, can be detached. The fingering is significantly different from that of the bassoon.

Bassoons are generally made of maple although some of the French models use Brazilian rosewood. In order to protect the wood against the effects of condensation the wing joint and the narrower of the two tubes in the butt joint are normally lined with rubber or plastic. A few instruments for military use have been produced in ebonite, and plastic is occasionally used for student models. There have also been bassoons made in metal, but these have not achieved any degree of popularity.

The key system for the bassoon is the most primitive of all the woodwinds, and complicated fork fingerings are required for many of the notes. Both left- and right-hand thumbs are used in playing, and the left thumb is required to operate no fewer than nine different keys. Three of the tone holes are without any mechanism, two of these being in the wing joint. Here the holes are drilled at a slanting angle in order that they can be reached by the fingers of the left hand; if they were drilled at right angles to the surface they would be far too widely spaced. Since the bore of the bassoon is conical it overblows to the octave like the oboe, so the fingerings in the lowest register are essentially repeated in the next register.

The reed on the bassoon, like the oboe, is a double one. It is made so that it slides directly over the end of the crook, rather than being bound to a staple. It is larger than the oboe reed, and the sides generally fan out at a greater angle, making the playing tip broader in relation to the base. At various stages through the history of the instrument single-reed mouthpieces, like miniaturized versions of those used on clarinets, have been tried, but the double reed remains the standard bassoon reed.

Saxophone

The original patent for the saxophone covers fourteen instruments, seven military and seven orchestral; each has a nominal range of two and a half octaves, written B_3 to F_6. In descending order of pitch these are sopranino, soprano, alto, tenor, baritone, bass, and contrabass. In the military group the sopranino, alto, baritone, and contrabass are pitched in E♭, the other three being in B♭. For the orchestral group the corresponding pitches are F and C. The orchestral group has never really established itself and the only member which is encountered occasionally today is the tenor in C, more commonly called the 'C melody'. Of the military group the soprano (sounding $A^\flat_3$ to $E^\flat_6$), alto (sounding $D^\flat_3$ to $A^\flat_5$), tenor (sounding $A^\flat_2$ to $E^\flat_5$), and baritone (sounding $D^\flat_2$ to $A^\flat_4$) are all quite common; the sopranino and contrabass are very rare.

On the saxophone the written notes D to C form the basic scale which is repeated at the octave when the octave key is applied. There are two separate tiny speaker holes, the lower one for the notes D to G and the upper one for the notes A to C. On the modern saxophone these are both operated by a single octave key, the mechanism being devised in such a way that the appropriate one for the note being fingered is automatically opened.

In the lowest octave four separate keys are used to take the range down to B♭ and on some baritone saxophones there is an extra one for a low A. In Sax's original design the lowest note was B, but virtually all instruments nowadays have at least a B♭. In the top register three separate keys operated by the side of the left hand are used for the notes up to F. These notes are actually second harmonics played with the octave key depressed, but the keys can in fact be used to play fundamental tones in the mid-range of the instrument. Generally the fundamentals are only used for trill notes. A good many instruments are fitted with an additional key for F♯ operated by the right hand, but in fact most experienced players can obtain this note and higher ones using harmonic fingerings.

The standard material for construction of saxophones is brass, which can either be plated or lacquered to give a lustrous finish. Lacquered instruments are generally the more popular with jazz and dance band players whereas plating is most frequently used on instruments to be used in military bands. The greater durability of plating is a definite advantage when an instrument is to be used out of doors, such as in marching bands. Shortly after the Second World War the plastic saxophone was introduced, with a main body of plastic and metal keys and mountings. Although plastic saxophones achieved some popularity, their quality was rather poor and they were never seen as serious rivals to the more traditionally made brass instruments.

The saxophone mouthpiece (Figure 3.12) is very similar to that of a clarinet, as is the reed. On the saxophone the mouthpiece slides over the end of the crook, which is corked to provide an airtight fit. Tuning is then accomplished by sliding the mouthpiece on to a greater or lesser extent. This contrasts with the clarinet, where the internal bore of the mouthpiece matches that of the barrel at the point of connection, making a smooth join. Some saxophones, particularly early Conn models, have a screw arrangement for altering the length of the crook so that the mouthpiece itself does not have to be moved when tuning. The slot on the lower side of the mouthpiece, which is covered by the reed, is somewhat wider on the saxophone than on the clarinet, and is generally rounded at the end furthest from the tip, as shown in Figure 3.12(b); on the clarinet this edge is cut off straight.

On the saxophone, an even greater variety of tone chamber shapes seem to have been produced than on the clarinet, mainly to cater for the needs of the jazz and dance band musician. In some cases the interior of the chamber is completely smooth whereas on others it is machined to give sharp-edged ledges. The original saxophone mouthpieces were made of wood but this is not used at all now. As with the clarinet, ebonite is now the favourite material for mouthpieces, although metal is almost as popular. Metal mouthpieces have an inset piece of ebonite or

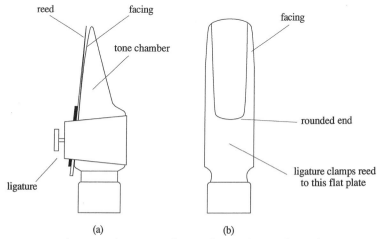

3.12 Saxophone mouthpiece: (a) side view, (b) view from underneath

similar material on the upper surface for the teeth to rest on; resting the teeth directly on the metal surface would be very uncomfortable for the player. Various types of plastics are also quite common in mouthpiece construction and occasionally unusual materials such as glass have been tried.

3.4 MAKING THE INSTRUMENT AND THE REED

Despite the enormous advances in manufacturing techniques which have taken place since the start of the industrial revolution, the manufacture of high-quality woodwind instruments remains to a certain extent a handcraft industry. This is particularly so in the case of the reed woodwinds because all of these, except for the saxophone, are generally made of wood. The variations and inconsistencies associated with a naturally occurring material then make the skills of the craftsman indispensable. For the production of student-quality instruments this has been overcome to some extent by the use of plastics, but even with these instruments a great deal of handwork is required, for example in the padding and regulation stages.

Within a large musical instrument factory there is considerable specialization, and many of the tasks are performed by semi-skilled labour. This contrasts with the small workshop of the craftsman instrument maker, where every stage of the production may be carried out by one person.

The body and keywork

The wood for making the different joints is imported as logs, usually from Africa, and is well seasoned before any working begins. The logs are split and sawn to produce billets, about 4 cm square in the case of clarinet joints, and a little longer than finally required. Blanks for the bell sections are often pyramid-shaped. The billets are rough bored with a small hole and turned to give the overall shape. This is followed by a further period of seasoning, usually in a drying kiln, to stabilize the moisture content at about 10 per cent. At this stage the air is free to pass through the centre of the tube, so the wood reaches a stable condition quite quickly.

The billets are then turned to shape and the bore opened out to its correct size; the tenons on each end are also turned. Forming the main shape of the body and bell and squaring off the ends is often carried out using a grinding process. This produces good results when the wood used is very hard and has a high silica content. The tone-holes and the holes for the pillars need to be positioned very precisely and a purpose-made 'setting out' tool is employed for this operation. Using a high-speed drilling head with a pneumatic chuck, this locates the hole position and chooses the appropriate cutter and drilling depth automatically. The tone-holes, counter bores, and pillar holes are drilled to a high degree of precision in the prescribed sequence set up on the machine. The complete set of holes on a particular joint is usually drilled in a matter of two or three minutes. Before the days of full mechanization, this would have taken a skilled turner at least one or two hours. When the wooden joint has finally been shaped it is further seasoned with oil or some form of synthetic resin. This can be done by prolonged immersion in a bath, pressure impregnation, or simple coating with a brush. When a joint has been completed, it is stored until required by the assembly shop.

The keywork is held to the wooden barrel by pillars screwed into the wood. Before these are screwed in, the holes must be threaded by another machine. This process, known as 'tapping', requires great precision, since the amount of wood left between the bottom of the hole and the inner bore is only about a millimetre. Too deep a tap would cause an indentation in the inner bore, or the hole might even break right through.

The keys on most woodwind instruments are made in nickel silver, although many other materials have been used. Although precious metals such as silver are frequently used for flutes they are not so common on the other woodwinds, possibly because the larger sizes make their use uneconomic. The keys can be produced either by forging or casting. Forging consists of hammering the metal into the appropriate shape, using dies where necessary. When this is done without heating it is known as cold forging. Forged parts are normally used where strength is required, e.g. in the connecting arms, since the hammering process strengthens the metal. In mass production lines keys are frequently produced by a process of drop forging and machining. This involves first cutting a blank from a strip of nickel silver and then cold forging it using a drop hammer or screw press. There may be two or three separate operations, in between which annealing takes place. The annealing process, in which the key is heated and cooled, softens it and relieves internal stresses. The shaping of the key is finished by machining.

An alternative to forging is to cast the key. Castings are usually made by the traditional lost-wax process, in which the required shape is first formed in wax. This is then covered by a substance which hardens and can withstand heat. On heating, the wax melts away leaving a cavity which can be filled with the molten metal. When this has hardened the covering is broken away to leave the metal casting of the original wax shape. Modern musical instrument factories employ various sophisticated versions of this basic idea, making use of plastics for the mouldings and vacuum techniques for removing air bubbles. Parts made by casting are often not very strong, unless subsequent heat treatments are used.

The component parts are soldered together and the completed keywork is buffed to give a good finish. After assembling, certain of the keys have to be pinned to their steels (the rods running inside the sections of tubing to which the keys are attached). The springs also have to be fitted. A variety of metals may be used for these, stainless steel and phosphor bronze being very popular. The strength of the spring depends to some extent on whether the key is an open or closed one. For closed-hole keys, which are held closed by the pressure of the spring in their rest position, a heavier gauge spring may be used.

Saxophone body

Because of the great popularity of the saxophone in the second quarter of the last century, the production of the instrument has become highly mechanized. It is said that in 1930 over one million saxophones were produced in the world. There does not seem to be the substantial market for individually handcrafted instruments that exists for the other woodwinds.

The body of the saxophone is generally made from thin-walled brass. The various parts of the conical tubing are made separately in sections and then joined together with ferrules. For example, on the alto and tenor the main body is in three sections: a straight part, a bell, and a U section which joins the other two together. On early saxophones traditional methods of tube drawing and hammering were used to produce the raw tube into which the holes were cut. The chimneys, which form the seating for the pads, were then soldered over the holes. This technique is still used in handmade flutes. In modern production methods the collars are drawn from the metal of the main tube, thus eliminating the join. Hydraulic devices are used to form the bell section and the various bends. In some early second-grade instruments these were produced by soldering together two half-sections face to face.

Pads

Good padding is absolutely crucial in woodwind manufacture, since even the tiniest leak can spoil the response of an instrument. A modest-quality instrument which is well padded will often blow better than a superior one which is poorly padded. The traditional materials for making pads are fishskin (sometimes known as gold-beater's skin) and leather. Fishskin actually does not come from fish, as the name suggests, but is the lining of a cow's intestine. However, as new synthetic materials improve in quality these are becoming increasingly popular on student models. Synthetic materials lend themselves better to mass-production processes because of their uniformity of composition.

There is a great variety of padding techniques in use for the various instruments, each with its own relative merits. Oboes are commonly padded in cork, although pads covered in fishskin or another material may be used for the larger holes. Generally clarinets and flutes use fishskin pads; the techniques used for padding with this material will be discussed in the next chapter. Saxophones use leather pads, often covered with a metal reflecting disc in the centre, for the purpose of minimizing sound absorption. On the bassoon a white pigskin is the most common.

Much of the art of padding centres around fixing the pad inside its cup. It is important that the pad closes flush against the tone hole rim in order that complete sealing is achieved without undue pressure being applied on the key. Pads may be either glued in position using shellac or other cement or they may be screwed to the key, depending on their size and type.

Reeds

Reeds for all the woodwind instruments are made from a tall plant, known as Arundo Donax (or Arundo Sativa), which is akin to bamboo. It is generally referred to as cane, although strictly speaking this term is inaccurate. It can sometimes be seen growing wild in warm climates, but for reed-making purposes it is cultivated, notably in southern France in the region known as Var between Marseilles and Nice. Being a natural material, it exhibits great variability in texture and consistency, influenced by factors such as soil, climate, and the time of cutting. As with wine, there are good and bad years for reed quality and there may be significant variations from one field to another in the same area.

The cane is harvested before it is fully ripe. It is then preferably left to mature in the open air for a period of three years, although nowadays this natural maturing is frequently replaced by kiln drying. Poorly matured reeds have a greenish colour, whereas a dark brown colour indicates that they have been excessively seasoned. The sticks are then sawn into lengths of about 10 to 20 cm, corresponding to the distance between joints on the Arundo Donax plant. The diameters vary considerably, but for oboe reeds they need to be typically 1 cm; for bassoon reeds diameters of more than twice this are required. Each stick is then split into three or four slices to form the blanks for the reed maker.

Clarinets and saxophones use almost identical single reeds (Figure 3.13); only the dimensions are different. The clarinet reed is slightly narrower. To make the single reed the blank is first planed down flat on the inner concave side. About half of the outer side is then thinned down progressively towards the tip which is very thin and forms the vibrating element. Different reed manufacturers have their own techniques for performing the thinning process, which are frequently kept as guarded secrets. The precise shape of the thinned section is of paramount importance in determining the playing characteristics of the reed. A thicker section is left in the centre of the reed, as shown in Figure 3.13; this is sometimes referred to as the reed heart.

Because of the variability in the material from which reeds are made, players

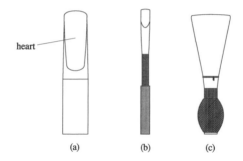

heart

(a)   (b)   (c)

3.13 Shapes of woodwind reeds: (a) clarinet or saxophone; (b) oboe; (c) bassoon

frequently need to tailor them to meet their own requirements. Many players prefer to buy a reed which they know is a little on the hard side and then to thin this down by scraping with a sharp knife or razor blade until it is of just the right strength. When doing this it should be remembered that new reeds have a tendency to be hard and will soften after being used for some time. When a reed is being scraped the heart generally should not be touched; material should only be taken from the tip and the sides. If the heart is scraped down then the reed loses all its resilience and the resulting sound is thin and spineless. An alternative way of softening a reed is to thin down the flat back on a sheet of very fine abrasive paper. The reed tip is so thin, however, that this has to be done with extreme care or else the reed will be ruined; usually one or two light wipes over a fine glass paper is sufficient.

Altering a reed which is too soft involves removing a very small strip of material from the thin end. This leaves the tip thicker and gives the reed more resistance to blowing. The results are usually only satisfactory if a very small change in hardness is required; reeds which are significantly too soft often have to be discarded. There are two ways of removing the tip. The simplest is to use a commercially produced reed cutter; this does not always give a clean cut when the amount being removed is very small. Because of this many players prefer to use the technique of burning the ends. Two coins of suitable size are placed one on either side of the reed so that just a small amount of cane protrudes beyond their edges. The tip can then easily be burnt off using a lighted match, controlling the amount removed by the position of the coins.

With a double reed instrument there is no mouthpiece, and the characteristics of the reed itself become even more important. The double reed is made from a strip of cane which is just a little more than twice the length of the finished reed. This is gouged out on one side and then folded over in two with the gouged part on the inside. The cane is then clamped into a device known as a shaper, which allows the edges to be cut around a template to form the overall shape. In the case of the oboe the free ends are then bound with twine to the staple; with the bassoon there is no staple, the free ends of the cane being bound with twine and wire on to a mandrel which is later removed. The tip of the reed is thinned by scraping and the folded end is cut off to give a clean edge. Before the cane is worked at each stage it is normally soaked in warm water for a period of half an hour or so to make it more pliable. The finished reed has an approximately elliptic aperture at its tip, which opens and closes as the reed is blown. Oboe and bassoon reeds can be compared in Figure 3.13.

The staple on an oboe reed is reusable a few times once the cane has exhausted its useful life; many players prefer to bind new canes onto the staple themselves. Alternatively staples can be recaned by a professional reed maker. In any event the player will normally have to make fine adjustments by scraping in order to bring the reed into a satisfactory playing condition. The precise amounts of thinning in the various regions are vitally important; as with the single reed, there is a heart which must not be scraped excessively. With a double reed the form of the whole scraped area is referred to as the scrape or lay. Individual forms of scrape have their own name: in the classic French scrape, for example, the lay tapers gradually and evenly from base to tip, while in the American scrape the lay has a thin tip backed by a distinct hump. Other players prefer to talk about U, V, and W scrapes.

The larger sizes of double reeds, for example on the cor anglais or bassoon, are normally wired, that is bound with a few turns of wire at a position just above the top of the thread binding. On the oboe, wiring is sometimes used, sometimes not. There are players who maintain that wiring chokes the natural vibrations of the reed and throttles the tone whereas others say that there are no adverse effects. The advantage of wiring is that it allows the opening of the elliptic aperture to be varied to suit the player's preference. Squeezing the wire slightly on the flat face of the cane closes the aperture, whereas squeezing on the sides will open it up. The effects of a wide or narrow aperture opening on playing characteristics are related to those of a wide or narrow mouthpiece lay on a single reed instrument. If the aperture is too open then the reed feels hard and the embouchure muscles tire quickly; the tone tends to be hard and the high notes difficult to play. Too narrow an aperture offers insufficient resistance to the air stream and the reed feels soft; this makes forte passages difficult and the reed may close completely in piano passages.

3.5 PERFORMANCE PRACTICE

Clarinet

Mention has already been made of the different registers on the clarinet and their respective tonal qualities, governed by fundamental acoustical properties of the instrument. In the chalumeau register the odd harmonics are predominant giving rise to the characteristic woody sound. Above this is the throat register which is the least resonant part of the instrument due to the short barrel length utilized; here the sound is very breathy. The clarinet register, above this, has a complete spectrum of harmonics and a correspondingly full sound. Higher still is the clarion register in which the fundamental is dominant; here the sound is more penetrating but lacks fullness.

Matching the different registers in a musically acceptable way is one of the most difficult skills that the clarinettist has to master. This is not made any easier by the fact that the clarinet is eminently capable of wide leaps, and these are used frequently by the majority of composers.

3.14 Excerpt from the clarinet part of Brahms's F minor Sonata for clarinet and piano. Jack Brymer points out the difficulties of playing this seemingly simple passage

The virtuoso clarinettist Jack Brymer, in his book *The Clarinet*, points out the difficulties encountered in performing even such a seemingly innocuous passage as the one shown in Figure 3.14, from the Brahms F minor Sonata, Op. 120 No. 1. The first note, written D_5, is in the clarinet register, with its full spectrum of harmonics. It is immediately followed by $B^\flat_4$ at the top of the throat register; this is the weakest note on the clarinet, with a very breathy sound. The G_4 in the second bar is similarly weak, and this is immediately followed by the very bright $B^\flat_5$ on an upbeat. Most clarinettists nowadays prefer not to talk about the different registers when teaching the instrument, since the objective is to produce as wide a variety of tone colours as possible over the entire range of the instrument.

Pitch control is as important as tone quality, and can also present problems for the clarinettist. There are certain notes which, even on a craftsman-made instrument, tend to be either sharp or flat. It is generally the case that the twelfth between written C_4 and G_5 is correctly in tune. Twelfths further up the instrument have a tendency to be too wide, whereas twelfths lower down are usually too narrow. Compromises then have to be made by the instrument maker in order to bring as many notes as possible close to their correct pitch. The result of this is that notes just below C_4 are sharp whilst notes just above C_4 are flat. Experienced players will automatically correct for these small deviations using embouchure control or sometimes using alternative fingerings in exposed passages. Pitch changes are most easily accomplished in the throat register where the tube length is short and hence has a less dominant role in pitch determination. Tightening the embouchure has the effect of raising the pitch, whereas slackening the embouchure lowers it. Most good players use a fairly tight embouchure and therefore find it easier to bring the pitch down rather than up. Using a hard reed has the effect of sharpening the pitch. A point to note is that the pitch depends on a complex coupling between the instrument, reed, and player and so different players using the same instrument and reed will sometimes sound notes at a different pitch.

In modern clarinet performance the reed is always used below the mouthpiece, resting against the lower lip although, as we have already noted, this was not always the case; during the first hundred years or so of the clarinet's development the reed was used uppermost. There are two distinct embouchure techniques in current use. In both cases the lower lip rests on the front teeth for support with the reed in contact with the lip. Most players then place the upper teeth directly on the top of the mouthpiece; this is sometimes referred to as a single embouchure. With the alternative double embouchure the upper lip is tucked in between the teeth and the mouthpiece so that there is no direct contact between teeth and mouthpiece.

The choice of single or double embouchure is a matter of personal preference and does not seem to have any dramatic effect on the tone quality. Most players find the single embouchure more comfortable and opt for this. Advocates of the double embouchure say that the sound appears smoother to the player because vibrations that would otherwise be transmitted to the player's head through the mouthpiece and upper teeth are dampened by the upper lip. A second advantage is that the mouth is slightly more open with the double embouchure which leads to a larger resonant cavity. The size of the oral cavity is an important factor in tone production and players often strive for a large cavity to produce a full sound. However, this can usually best be done by shaping the mouth for a suitable vowel sound such as 'oh'. A sound such as 'ee' has the opposite effect of closing the cavity, leading to a more shrill sound. Puffing out the cheeks is not generally thought to be good practice because this leads to the firmness of the mouth muscles being lost, although a few jazz players use this technique.

The question of vibrato is one which arouses much discussion and disagreement amongst clarinettists. With the other reed woodwinds vibrato is accepted as being part of the normal tonal characteristics of the instrument but with the clarinet there are differing opinions as to whether it should be used or not. Some purists, particularly those from the German school of playing, argue that the sound quality of the clarinet is so rich that it is only ruined by vibrato and that all works should be performed *senza vibrato*. At the other end of the scale are the jazz clarinettists such as Sidney Bechet, Benny Goodman, and Artie Shaw, whose tone is characterized by a wide and flexible vibrato. The modern approach is tending towards a general acceptance of vibrato when used with discretion. Leaving aside wobbles of the instrument and the like, vibrato can be produced in two ways: either by repetitive tightening and slackening of the lips or by periodic pulsations of the diaphragm. Most jazz and dance band players opt for the former, sometimes accompanied by movements of the jaw; in classical circles a combination of both is the norm, since this produces controlled and unobtrusive fluctuations which integrate with the overall sound.

Two of the earliest clarinettists to reach international fame as virtuoso performers were Joseph Beer and Franz Tausch. Beer was born in Bohemia in 1744 but

3.15 Excerpt from the Clarinet Concerto by Joseph Beer, showing his use of the low register, wide leaps, and arpeggios

spent the prime of his life in Paris where he founded the French School of clarinet playing. As well as performing extensively he composed a good deal of clarinet music and taught many pupils who went on to become leading players of the time. Beer himself was particularly fond of the chalumeau register and his compositions mostly contain lengthy low-register passages abounding in wide leaps and arpeggios. An example is the excerpt from his clarinet concerto shown in Figure 3.15. The French school became centred around the Paris Conservatoire when it opened in 1795; here the clarinet department was the largest in the institution, with nineteen professors and just over a hundred pupils. Its playing style was characterized by florid and brilliant passagework and the French players were renowned for their facility. Some authorities claim that a weakness in the early French school was that it produced players all to a set pattern, with little individuality.

Franz Tausch was born in 1762 in Heidelberg and was a child prodigy on the clarinet. He spent much of his early years giving concert tours in Austria and Germany but later moved to Berlin, where he had many pupils and established a series of weekly chamber-music meetings in his own house. In 1805 he founded a Conservatorium for wind players which soon established an international reputation and at one time had ninety pupils. His sound was said to have had an exceptional richness of timbre and expressiveness; this was to become the characteristic of the German school of playing. Many eminent clarinettists were taught by Tausch at the Conservatorium, including Heinrich Baermann, arguably the greatest clarinet player of all time.

The types of clarinet used in France and Germany had an important influence in the development of the characteristic styles of the two schools. In France, as we have seen, the Boehm system developed by Klosé and Buffet was adopted at the Conservatoire, whereas in Germany it was the Müller system that was in use. In 1812 Müller tried to get his instrument accepted by the Paris Conservatoire, and put it up for examination by the Commission. To his great disappointment, it was turned down, although the Müller clarinet did go on to become quite widely used in France. The bore of the French-style clarinet was significantly smaller than that of its German counterpart and the mouthpiece had a correspondingly shallower tone chamber. The French mouthpiece also had a shorter lay and was used with a softer reed, giving a very immediate response to articulation and an interesting sound spectrum. The heavier reed and longer lay gave the German instrument a much higher resistance but a very pure sound, particularly beautiful in legato passages, although its response to articulation was slower.

Of the avant-garde techniques which are available on the clarinet, perhaps the most convincing is the glissando which can be particularly good in the high register. Multiphonics, in which two or more notes are sounded simultaneously, are also very effective, but tend to be slow to speak.

Oboe

The embouchure on the oboe is formed by folding the lips round the teeth and holding the reed by the supported lips, only a millimetre or two of reed being left to vibrate inside the mouth without lip contact. It is the lower lip which exerts primary control over the reed and the position on the reed on the lower lip is therefore of paramount importance. The size of the reed and the aperture through which the air passes are small in relation to the other reed woodwinds, and this can put a considerable strain on the lip and facial muscles.

Despite the fact that the air pressure in the player's mouth is relatively high, the volume rate of air flow through the instrument is quite low. It is thus possible to play very long passages without the need for a breath, and in fact the player rarely exhausts all the air from the lungs in playing any given passage. This has been taken advantage of by composers; for example Figure 3.16 shows part of an oboe passage from Schubert's 'Unfinished' Symphony which lasts about forty seconds, depending on the speed taken by the conductor. Whereas it is possible for an oboist to play this in a single breath, a clarinettist would probably have needed two or three breaths. The small amounts of air being blown through the instrument can cause performance problems, since it means that there is a tendency for the breathing to be shallow and for stale unoxygenated air to be left in the lungs. Much emphasis is therefore placed on good breathing practices in oboe technique.

3.16 Part of the oboe solo in the second movement of Schubert's 'Unfinished' Symphony

The small air flows make circular breathing techniques particularly effective. Circular breathing involves inhaling through the nose to fill the lungs at the same time as one is blowing air out through the instrument using pressure from the cheeks. At first sight this seems impossible, but in fact many players find that it is not difficult to master; the Swiss virtuoso oboist Heinz Holliger has done much to further this technique. The main difficulty is that the player is continually changing from abdominal support to mouth pressure and this also necessitates movements in the palate which can easily lead to fluctuations in pitch and loss of tone colour. It is in fact virtually impossible to perform some modern compositions without using circular breathing or, alternatively, some form of mechanical aid.

Such an aid is Samuels's aerophor, which is called for in Richard Strauss's *Alpensin-fonie* and *Festliches Präludium*. The aerophor, now just regarded as a novelty, is essentially a pair of small foot-operated bellows which expel air through a narrow tube placed in the corner of the player's mouth. This was intended to be used to top up the human air reservoir at times when exceptionally long notes were encountered.

The tone quality of the oboe is usually considered to be at its best in the mid-range, where it is possible to obtain a wide range of dynamics; composers normally concentrate on this region. The lowest notes are very difficult to play softly, and when played by a beginner they often sound rather nasal; however a good performer can obtain an attractively warm and rich sound in this register. The very highest notes can sound somewhat piercing unless controlled carefully. To obtain these some players hold the reed directly between the teeth rather than the lips. Vibrato is now universally accepted on the oboe and this is produced from the diaphragm, possibly with the addition of a minimal amount of lip movement on slow melodies. Muting is used quite commonly and is most frequently accomplished by inserting some soft material, such as a handkerchief or cotton wool, into the bell.

Being a double-reed instrument, the oboe excels in multiphonics. There are numerous examples throughout the range which are quite stable and have a variety of tonal characters. There are also a number of good third harmonic notes which are not normally used but can be introduced for special effects.

Because the oboe can only be tuned within narrow limits it is generally used for giving the pitch to the orchestra. This tradition dates back to the Baroque orchestra where it was the only woodwind that was always incorporated. Sliding the staple further in or out of the upper joint sharpens or flattens the note but the changes are very small due to the narrowness of the tube at this point.

Distinctive national schools of oboe playing do not seem to have emerged to the same extent as they have done with the flute and clarinet, but the Paris Conservatoire was a dominant force in the development of playing technique. Its list of oboe professors includes such famous names as Charles Triébert and Georges Gillet, both of whom made important contributions to the development of the instrument in addition to being virtuoso performers. If there is a recognizable characteristic of French playing it is probably its rather light brilliant style, contrasting with the heavier woody sound which was developed in Austria and Germany and which one often associates with early recordings made in America.

Bassoon

What has been said about the oboe carries over to a large extent to the bassoon. Its tone quality, however, varies considerably in different parts of the range, mainly due to the rather peculiar and piecemeal way in which it is constructed. The characteristic melancholy and sonorous bassoon sound is associated with notes in the lowest octave and this quality is retained down to the very lowest notes, although it is extremely difficult to play these pianissimo. Indeed the dynamic range of the bassoon is generally rather small, although it can be extended a little by using a mute as in the case of the oboe. The notes D_3 to $F\sharp_3$ have a nasal quality and sound very much like the oboe, whereas just above these (G_3 to D_4) the tone is very much as in the lower register. From $E\flat_4$ upwards the sound becomes darker and more unearthly.

Like the oboe, the bassoon is generally played with a predominantly diaphragm-generated vibrato. Since the reed is much larger than on the oboe the air flow is correspondingly greater, so it is not possible to play such extended passages without taking a breath. Even so, the bassoon can play considerably more extended notes than counterparts of the same pitch in the brass family, which require much more air. Circular breathing can be used in the middle and upper registers, but it is not normally used for the lowest notes, which require too much breath. The range of multiphonics is similar to that available on the oboe.

The contrabassoon has a unique organ-like quality which is particularly effective in the low register. An essential feature, which must be taken into account in performance, is its slowness to speak. This is due to its great tube length; since it has a conical bore it is essentially twice as long as the contrabass clarinet, although its pitch is similar. Thus the standing wave patterns take a significantly longer time to become fully established. Partly because of this, the contrabass clarinet tends to be favoured over the contrabassoon as a general-purpose contrabass woodwind instrument.

Saxophone

The saxophone is sometimes mistakenly thought to be an easy instrument to play because its rather straightforward fingering system allows a beginner to reach the stage of playing a simple tune on it in a matter of hours. In reality, mastery of the instrument is as demanding as on any of the other woodwinds, development of a good tone and embouchure control being the most difficult aspects. Many classical players are clarinettists who double on saxophone.

The saxophone has never played a major role in the orchestra, its use being restricted to a few compositions such as Ravel's *Bolero*, Prokofiev's *Romeo and Juliet* and *Lieutenant Kije*, and Britten's opera *Billy Budd*. Since its invention it has always had a prominent place in the military band, and for the first fifty years or so of its life this was its only role. With the dance band boom which started about 1910, the saxophone became highly popular; it was the mainstay of many famous bands such as those of Guy Lombardo, Henry Hall, Glen Miller, and Joe Loss.

It is in the field of jazz, however, that the main innovations in style and technique have taken place. In the early days of jazz the trumpet and cornet were the dominant instruments, but their role was challenged in the early 1930s by the saxophone, particularly the tenor saxophone. Most of the early jazz saxophonists were American whites, such as Jimmy Dorsey and Bud Freeman, and the saxophone tradition has to a large extent been influenced by their concepts of jazz. The two black saxophonists Coleman Hawkins and Lester Young, who soon came to reign supreme, used as their models the early white saxophonists.

Hawkins developed a very big sound and was an innovator in the use of chord progressions for improvisation; earlier jazz exponents had improvised around a melody line. This contrasted with the light airy style of Young, who played long melodic lines with the minimum of vibrato. Charlie Parker, who later emerged as the undisputed master of the alto saxophone followed more in the style of Hawkins, using a hard reed and wide lay to produce an enormously powerful and biting sound.

One of the attractions of the saxophone for jazz playing has been its great expressiveness and almost human quality, with a timbre that is consistent over the complete range on the instrument. Another factor is its power; it is the only woodwind which can compete with the brass without electronic amplification. The embouchure on the saxophone is generally more relaxed than on the clarinet and the volume of air flow is considerably greater. Despite the amount of wind required some jazz saxophonists, notably Roland Kirk, have been able to master playing indefinitely long phrases using circular breathing. Vibrato is generally regarded as an integral part of the saxophone sound and in fact mastery of a flexible and controlled vibrato is one of the key elements in producing a good tone.

The dynamic range of the saxophone is very considerable in the middle and upper registers but on the lowest notes it is nearly impossible to play pianissimo. The written $B\flat_3$ tends to come out as rather more of a honk than a controlled tone. Mutes are produced for saxophones, designed to be placed in the bell, but these are not very effective and are rarely used. There are many alternative fingerings for notes in the altissimo register above top F and these notes are used quite frequently even though they can be quite difficult to play. Multiphonics are very unsatisfactory and are not generally used. Jazz players such as John Coltrane and Albert Ayler have explored a whole range of effects on the saxophone using higher harmonics and various distortions.

4

The Flute Family

4.1 ACOUSTICAL PRINCIPLES

A flute is a woodwind instrument whose air column resonances are excited by the oscillations of an air jet. This may seem a rather dry and technical description of one of the most flexible and expressive of musical instruments, but the essential character of the flute family arises from the way in which the thin sliver of flowing air which we call the air jet interacts with the natural vibration modes of the air column inside the instrument. In the following section we explore some aspects of this interaction.

Basic acoustics

In Chapter 2 we discussed the properties of an idealized flute behaving like a cylindrical tube open at both ends. We saw that the natural mode frequencies of the air column in such a flute would form a complete harmonic series, and that a periodic oscillation of the air jet could simultaneously feed energy into a large number of modes. In return, the air currents generated by the modes would stabilize the air jet oscillation and control its frequency.

The behaviour of a real flute differs in some important respects from this idealized picture. For a start, no real flute has a perfectly cylindrical tube. Although the Renaissance flute (Figure 4.1(a)) was usually a pipe of approximately constant diameter, the typical Baroque design (Figure 4.2(c)) tapers down towards the lower end, while the modern flute (Figure 4.2(a)) narrows towards the upper end. Nor is it realistic to treat both ends of the tube as completely open. The embouchure hole, across which the air jet blows, is usually considerably smaller in area than the cross section of the tube; on a transverse flute the embouchure hole is some distance below the upper end. We saw in Chapter 3 that the opening of side holes introduces a further complication at the lower end of the tube, while even the closed holes contribute small additional volumes under the fingers or pads.

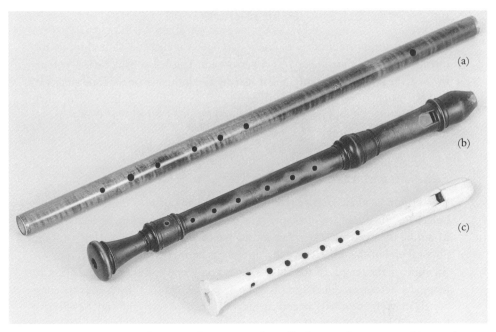

4.1 (a) Renaissance-type tenor flute (reproduction: Wood, Bradford c.1980); (b) Baroque treble recorder (van Heerde, Amsterdam, c.1720); (c) Renaissance descant recorder (Haka, Amsterdam c.1680)

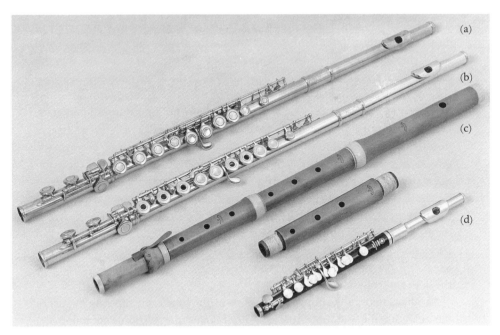

4.2 From top to bottom: (a): modern closed-hole Yamaha flute; (b): modern open-hole Sankyo flute; (c): boxwood one-key conical bore jointed flute with alternative upper joint (Collier, London c.1775); (d): modern Yamaha piccolo

The most important effect of these differences is that the natural mode frequencies of a real flute are not exact harmonics. This has considerable repercussions on the playing technique, and is also a major influence on the tone quality of the instrument. It is therefore worth examining in more detail the ways in which the end conditions and the tapering of the tube affect the tuning of the various modes of the air column.

End conditions on flutes

It was remarked in Chapter 2 that in a tube with an open end the standing wave bulges slightly out of the open end. The position of the pressure node at the end of a tube of diameter D is in fact a distance of approximately $0.3D$ beyond the physical end of the tube. This extra distance is known as the 'end correction' for the tube. If the length of the tube is L, and only one end is open, the effective length for acoustical calculations is given by $L_{eff} = L + 0.3D$. If both ends are completely open, there will be an end correction of $0.3D$ at each end, and the effective length will be $L_{eff} = L + 0.6D$.

The end corrections have the effect of lowering the frequencies of the natural modes by increasing the apparent length of the tube and therefore the wavelengths of the standing waves. The formula above is strictly only valid for low frequencies; as the frequency rises the end correction gets smaller. For tubes of dimensions similar to those of a flute, and for frequencies up to a few thousand hertz, the frequency dependence is small, so it is reasonable to assume that the correction to the sounding length of a flute due to the lower open end (when all the side holes are closed) is given by the first of the two formulae above.

In contrast, the end correction at the embouchure hole of a flute is different for each mode, since it depends on the frequency of the sound wave. On a transverse flute this dependence is strongly influenced by the effect of the cavity between the embouchure hole and the cork which seals the upper end of the tube. The low-frequency end correction for a typical flute embouchure is around 40 mm, and is not much affected by the cork position. With the cork placed so that its end face blocks the tube just above the embouchure hole, the end correction at 1,000 Hz is reduced to around 35 mm, while if the cork is moved up the tube by 30 mm the end correction at 1,000 Hz is increased to nearly 50 mm. Moving the cork thus has the effect of expanding or contracting the frequency ratios of the first few modes of the flute's air column.

Another important feature of the design of the flute is the tapering of part of the tube. In the Baroque flute the head joint (the section containing the embouchure hole) is approximately cylindrical, but the rest of the instrument gradually narrows towards the lower end. On the modern flute the lower part of the bore is essentially cylindrical, but the head joint narrows towards the upper end. These two modifications have the same effect of widening the intervals between the air column modes. On the modern flute the tapering of the bore and the placement of the cork (usually about 18 mm from the centre of the embouchure hole) combine to provide the desired intervals between the modes. Interestingly, on a well-made flute with the cork properly adjusted it is found that the second and third mode frequencies are not exactly two and three times the first mode frequency, as might be expected. Instead, the frequency ratios are slightly expanded.

Blowing and overblowing on the flute

Why has the flute evolved a design which results in the second and third modes being too sharp for true harmonics? The answer to this question is still not entirely clear, but part of the reason seems to relate to the way in which a player overblows on the instrument. In Chapter 3 we explained how an oboe player can raise the pitch of the sounding note by encouraging the reed vibration to jump from the first mode frequency to the second mode frequency. This is the process known as overblowing. Similarly, the flute player can raise the pitch by making the air jet vibrate at the frequency of the second mode instead of the first. In both the flute and the oboe, the first two modes are roughly an octave apart, so overblowing raises the pitch by about an octave.

For musical purposes, of course, 'about' an octave is not good enough: the overblowing technique must produce a true octave (at least, to within a few cents). Some problems arise, however, from the way in which the player encourages a flute to overblow. From the discussion of the air jet in Chapter 2, it is clear that there are two ways to increase the vibration frequency of the air jet: the jet speed can be increased, or the distance from slit to edge can be decreased. On the transverse flute both these methods are used. The slit in this case is the gap between the player's lips, while the edge is the far side of the embouchure hole. By moving the lips forward the edge-slit distance is reduced (see Figure 4.3); together with an increase in blowing pressure, this is enough to make the flute overblow into the upper register.

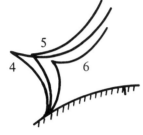

4.3 Lip positions of a flautist playing three notes F_4, F_5, and F_6, labelled 4, 5, and 6 in diagram, illustrating variation in lip coverage of the embouchure hole with increasing pitch

The problem is that moving the lips forward increases the extent to which the lower lip covers the embouchure hole. This increase in lip cover makes the end correction larger, flattening the overblown note. We can now see an advantage in the tapered head joint, which makes the second mode too sharp: by a suitable choice of taper this sharpening can be made to compensate for the flattening due to the increased lip cover, and the flute will overblow a true octave.

The stretching of the octave between first and second modes of the flute seems to be desirable also for another reason: it improves the strength and timbre of the notes of the lowest register. Using a specially constructed flute on which the degree of stretch could be varied by adjusting a stopper in a side tube, the American acoustician John Coltman found that the total power radiated was a maximum for an octave stretch of about 25 cents; this maximum was about 30 per cent greater than the power obtained with no stretching.

Finger-holes

The opening of finger-holes to shorten the effective length of the tube follows the principles already explained in our discussion of the reed woodwinds in Chapter 3. In that discussion the cut-off frequency of a woodwind instrument was defined, and it was noted that an instrument with large finger-holes will have a higher cut-off frequency than a similar instrument with smaller holes.

Flutes with relatively small finger-holes, such as the recorder and the Baroque transverse flute, have a more limited set of strong internal modes than the large-holed instruments such as the penny whistle and the modern transverse flute. As a consequence the modern flute has a brighter sound than its Baroque predecessor.

The size of the finger-holes also determines the effectiveness of cross-fingering. On an instrument with large holes and a high cut-off frequency, the first mode has a pressure node very close to the highest open hole. Since the standing wave in the air column is almost entirely confined to the region above this hole, closing other holes further down the tube has little effect on the pitch of notes in the low register. If the instrument has relatively small holes, the first mode frequency is closer to the cut-off, and the standing wave penetrates some distance beyond the highest open hole. Closing holes lower down the tube can then significantly lower the pitch. On Baroque instruments with relatively small holes and few keys, cross-fingering is used to supply many chromatic notes.

In the high register, the note played may be so high that the fundamental frequency is above the cut-off. In that case, the standing wave extends over the whole length of the tube. Cross-fingering can then either raise or lower the pitch of the note, depending on which part of the standing wave lies under the lower closed hole.

4.2 HISTORICAL DEVELOPMENT

The term 'flute' is used to describe a broad range of instruments from the modern orchestral woodwind to vessel flutes and folk instruments of many different types. As we have already seen, the essential feature of a flute is the use of an air jet to excite the enclosed air into vibration. In the transverse flute, the air column is excited by an air jet formed by the player's lips alone. This method of excitation is sometimes referred to as the free air reed. In contrast to instruments of this type are the duct or 'fipple' flutes, in which the air jet is formed by a channel in the mouthpiece. We begin our brief historical survey with the duct flute family, of which the most familiar modern examples are the recorder and the penny whistle.

Recorder

Duct flutes made from animal bones, having typically just three holes, were already in use in the iron age. The earliest surviving instrument which can be identified as a recorder dates from the fourteenth century; it has an approximately cylindrical bore, eight finger-holes at the front (including a duplicated lowest hole) and a thumb-hole at the back. These features are characteristic of recorders which have survived from the Middle Ages.

By the sixteenth century the instrument had developed the form generally described as the Renaissance recorder: normally turned from a single piece of wood, its bore was tapered down gradually from the mouthpiece towards the lower end. Renaissance recorders were made in a wide range of pitches, from sopranino to contrabass, and writers such as Michael Praetorius praised the effect of a consort of different sizes playing together. The larger models used keys to open and close holes which could not be reached by the span of the fingers. As with the Renaissance reed instruments, the lowest key was frequently protected by a perforated fontanelle.

In the mid-seventeenth century the recorder was remodelled by the group of French instrument makers which was also responsible for the development of the oboe. In its new form, known today as the Baroque recorder, the instrument was made in three separate sections: the head section, the main body, and the foot section. The head section, containing the duct, was of approximately cylindrical bore; the main body tapered down towards the foot to a greater extent than the Renaissance instrument and was also somewhat narrower. The Renaissance and Baroque designs may be compared in Figure 4.1.

The Baroque recorder had a greater range than its Renaissance counterpart, although it lacked some of the latter's fullness of tone in the bass. In the form perfected by Hotteterre and his successors it remained an important solo woodwind instrument throughout the Baroque period; the term 'flauto' on musical scores of this time normally refers to the recorder rather than the transverse flute. During the classical period the exploitation of the greater tonal variations and range that the transverse flute could offer led to the decline of the recorder. By the nineteenth century it had fallen into virtual disuse, although in the twentieth century it underwent a spectacular revival.

Flageolet and penny whistle

The instrument that came to be known as the flageolet originated in France in the late sixteenth century. It was high-pitched, with a length sometimes as short as 120 mm, and it was end blown through a duct mouthpiece like the recorder. The bore was conical, slightly tapered towards the lower end, and it had six finger-holes. Four of these were on the front; the other two, at the back, were closed by the left- and right-hand thumbs. The instrument was so tiny that if all the holes had been at the front it would have been difficult for an adult to cover them with the fingers. Flageolets became very popular with amateurs.

Just after 1800 William Bainbridge started making the so-called English flageolet in London. This had a different arrangement of finger-holes: six in front, and one at the back for the thumb. He also made double flageolets, comprising two

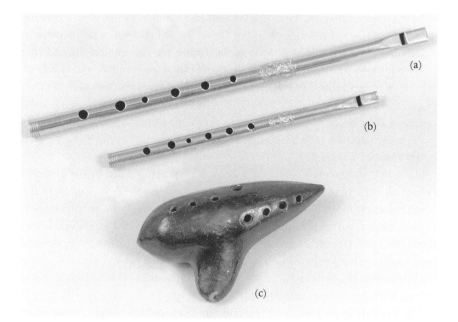

4.4 (a) whistle in B♭ (probably Hudson, London *c.*1855); (b) whistle in F (probably Hudson, London *c.*1855); (c) ocarina (Austria *c.*1900). Note the different sizes of finger-holes on the whistles

separate resonating tubes with a single mouthpiece. This allowed two melodies to be played simultaneously, with the difference tones sounding in the bass.

Nowadays the word flageolet is also sometimes applied to a rather different type of duct flute, more usually known as the penny whistle. This has six holes along the front, and no thumb hole. It is generally made from alloy tubing, with a moulded plastic mouthpiece, although earlier versions were constructed from tin plate (hence the alternative term 'tin whistle'), brass or celluloid. The tubing is thin-walled, giving the tone holes virtually no depth. Figure 4.4 shows penny whistles pitched in B♭ and F, dating from circa 1855.

End-blown flutes and panpipes

On an end-blown flute the upper end of the tube is cut off leaving a sharp rim across which the player blows. Instead of being cut off straight, the blowing end may be cut off on the slant or in a cupped shape; alternatively a notch may be cut into the rim. End-blown flutes made of bamboo or bone, with two or three side holes, are among the simplest and most primitive of the wind instruments; on the other hand, the traditional Japanese shakuhachi is an example of a sophisticated end blown flute with an unrivalled expressive range and a virtuoso repertoire.

In 1888 Carlo Giorgi invented a keyless end-blown flute which had a lip plate, similar to that on a modern transverse flute but positioned on the end of the tube. The instrument was held in front of the player's body, in the manner of a recorder. Giorgi's flute won a number of accolades but never caught on with flute players.

Panpipes belong to the family of end blown flutes, consisting as they do of a row of tubes of different length normally stopped at the lower end. The name was given by the ancient Greeks, who attributed their invention to the god Pan. Panpipes have inspired many works for the modern flute, perhaps the best-known example being the flute solo *Syrinx* by Claude Debussy, written for Louis Fleury.

An important feature of the panpipes is that each note on the scale has its own separate tube, as on a pipe organ, so it is possible to choose the optimum tube diameter for that particular pitch. This contrasts with the other woodwinds, such as the orchestral flute, where a compromise tube diameter has to be chosen to cover the complete playing range. There are two important consequences of the tube being closed at one end. First, a relatively short tube length is required for a given pitch of note. Secondly, the odd-numbered harmonics are predominant, giving the characteristically hollow tone.

Many different arrangements are used for grouping the tubes in panpipes, the most common being to have the longest at one end with a gradual reduction in length down to the shortest tube at the other end, as shown in Figure 4.5. A common alternative is to have adjacent pipes sounding thirds so that melodies may be played in consecutive thirds.

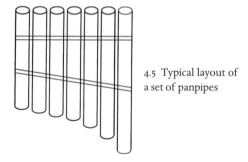

4.5 Typical layout of
a set of panpipes

Vessel flutes

In a vessel flute the resonator is a hollow cavity, rather than a narrow tube. It operates on the Helmholtz resonance principle, the pitch of the note being determined by the volume of the cavity and the total area of the open holes. Increasing the volume of the cavity lowers the pitch, whereas increasing the area of the holes raises the pitch. There are two important types of vessel flute, the ocarina and the gemshorn.

The ocarina probably dates back almost to the Stone Age. It has been found all over the world at various levels of sophistication, particularly in Africa, China, and Mexico. In its traditional form it is roughly egg-shaped, with a small number of finger-holes; it is blown either like a recorder through a duct mouthpiece or like a transverse flute across a large open hole. The usual material of construction is clay, and it is often made in the form of a highly decorated goose or other bird, hence its name which means 'little goose' in Italian.

A more elaborate version of the ocarina originated in Italy in the late nineteenth century. It is torpedo-shaped and is blown like a whistle; Figure 4.4 shows an ocarina dating from *c*.1900. There are ten tone holes, one to be covered by each finger or thumb. A further refinement sometimes incorporated is a plunger for making tuning adjustments. The holes are graded in size and are opened in succession to form the scale, as on the flageolet. However, since it is only the total area of opened holes which determines the pitch, it is possible to play the same note with different fingerings. In the 1940s the ocarina had a revival and was sold under the name 'hot potato', mainly for use in dance bands.

The gemshorn is similar in its acoustical principle to the ocarina, but is made from animal horn. The wide end of the horn is closed by a wooden plug containing a duct. Gemshorns appear in several illustrations from the fifteenth and sixteenth centuries, but very few instruments have survived, and there is some controversy over the number of finger-holes which were commonly used. Modern reproductions have a sound of remarkable sweetness and purity; as with the ocarina, the single Helmholtz resonance of the cavity gives a frequency spectrum particularly strong in fundamental and weak in upper harmonics.

Early and Renaissance transverse flutes

It is thought that the earliest form of transverse flute was the Chinese chi dating from about the ninth century BCE. Some Roman works of art depict instruments which could be transverse flutes, but could also be side-blown reed instruments. Firm evidence for the existence of the transverse flute in Western Europe is not available until around the eleventh century. The transverse flute first came to the Germanic countries and later, about the fourteenth century, to Spain and France. By the early sixteenth century it was well established throughout Europe. A good deal of information on the variety of flutes available in England during the sixteenth century has been obtained from King Henry VIII's inventory, made on his death in 1547: this listed seventy-two flutes.

Numerous flutes from the sixteenth century have survived and are to be found in the major instrument collections. They are essentially cylindrical tubes in one piece with an embouchure hole and six finger-holes for the basic scale, usually spaced in two groups of three. Chromatic notes could only be produced by cross-fingerings. Pictorial evidence indicates that earlier instruments were constructed in much the same way. The cylindrical bore instrument has become known as the Renaissance flute; a reproduction is shown in Figure 4.1.

In the Middle Ages and Renaissance small cylindrical transverse flutes known as fifes were commonly used by foot soldiers. The British flute band, which consists of flutes and drums, also contains a small flute commonly described as a fife. This instrument, a six-keyed flute pitched in B♭ a sixth above the concert flute, is significantly different from the Renaissance fife, however, since it has a narrow conical bore. The other members of the flute band are instruments of different sizes with a similar bore, giving a relatively shrill sound well suited to outdoor performance.

The Baroque transverse flute

In the seventeenth century the flute found it difficult to compete with other instruments in meeting the demands of the new expressive style of playing. In the upper octave especially it was difficult to keep in tune and play with even timbre. Instrument makers therefore sought to bring about improvements in design to meet the demands for refinement in tone quality and extended range.

The transformation took place in France and one of the leading figures in bringing about these changes was Jacques Hotteterre (1674–1763), a member of the distinguished French family of instrument makers. The new Baroque flute that emerged was made in three sections, which aided precise drilling of the tube. The main body was tapered down towards the lower end whilst the head joint, which slid over a tenon on the body, could be pulled in or out for tuning purposes. The conical bore had a flattening effect which allowed the finger-holes to be brought closer together, making it more manageable for the player. The short foot joint section was tapered (either contracting or expanding towards the end) or was cylindrical, dependent on the particular model.

The new flute was pitched in D, in the sense that raising the fingers in turn from the bottom gave the scale of D major. Aside from the conical bore the other main feature was that there was a seventh hole for the purpose of playing D♯ and its harmonics. Previously this could only be obtained by half-covering the lowest hole since cross-fingering is not available here. The additional hole was opened and closed by a key, operated by the right-hand little finger, which was held closed with a spring in its rest position. This addition now made the flute fully chromatic.

The basic range of Hotteterre's new flute was from D_4 to D_6 although several higher notes could be obtained with some difficulty. Notes above E_6 had to be forced and could not naturally be included in compositions. The tone was more consistent throughout the range than the Renaissance flute and more pure in quality. In the upper range it responded more readily to nuances although in the fundamental octave it was somewhat weaker.

An important design feature introduced later (about 1720) was known as the *corps de rechange*. The flute was divided into four sections: head joint, upper-body section, lower-body section and foot joint. Several upper-body sections of different lengths were supplied, to be chosen according to the pitch required. This arrangement allowed wider pitch variations to be accommodated without introducing mistunings across the instrument. Figure 4.2(c) shows a Baroque flute with an alternative upper section.

Once established, the one-keyed flute maintained its position as the standard instrument throughout most of the eighteenth century. Gradually, however, further keys were added to eliminate the necessity for cross-fingerings; first the four-keyed flute in about 1760, then the six-keyed, and finally the eight-keyed by the end of the century. In the first half of the nineteenth century there was no one model which could be considered as standard, since the one-keyed version continued to be made and used alongside the four-, six- and eight-keyed versions.

The most commonly used material for flute construction in the Baroque period was boxwood, although ivory was also used. Boxwood suffers from the disadvantage that it tends to absorb condensation, causing the wood to swell with adverse effect on the intonation. During the nineteenth century flutes were manufactured from many other materials, including cocus wood, ebony, and glass.

The Boehm flute

The beginning of the nineteenth century coincided with great changes in the musical life of Western Europe, marked by a move from the drawing room into the concert hall. Consequently the flute found itself competing with the volume of the brass in the symphony orchestra. Theobald Boehm (1794–1881), a renowned flautist and goldsmith in Munich, recognized the tonal deficiencies of the Baroque instrument and set about experimenting with radical changes in design to combat them. Boehm was impressed by the powerful sound of the virtuoso flautist Charles Nicholson, and inspection of his instrument convinced him that an important factor in determining the volume was the size of the tone-holes. Nicholson's hands were apparently large, and he had had the size of his tone-holes enlarged. However the intonation of his instrument was such that it could only be handled by a player of the calibre of Nicholson. Boehm began experiments to redesign the flute, with the twin aims of increasing its power and improving its intonation.

In 1832 Boehm came up with a design based on a greatly improved mechanism utilizing ring keys, similar to those which are used on the modern clarinet. It also had the holes placed in acoustically more correct positions, so the intonation was improved. Despite its more powerful sound and better tuning, his 1832 flute did not gain immediate acclaim, although gradually a number of leading players began to recognize its merits. By 1838 it had become officially introduced into the Paris Conservatoire. Boehm's aspirations, however, were not yet fulfilled, and in 1846 he returned to the design problem. This time he decided to make a careful study of acoustics, which he did under the direction of Dr Carl von Schafhäutl at the University of Munich. Applying the results of this collaboration led to his revolutionary 1847 design, which is in essence the concert flute used today.

Boehm reverted to the cylindrical body which had characterized the Renaissance instrument. His original design was for a 20 mm diameter bore, but this was eventually changed to 19 mm in order to improve the response in the upper register. The strength of the standing waves formed in the tube and the volume of transmitted sound depend on the amount of sound which is reflected back into the tube from the open end, which in turn is dependent on the ratio of the wavelength to the tube diameter. Wider tubes therefore produce more sound for the longer wavelengths in the low register but at the expense of the upper register. One would expect Boehm's 5 per cent change in bore diameter to have increased the range in the treble by about a tone, all other factors remaining equal, since the total range of the flute is three octaves; this was paid for by a poorer response on the lowest notes.

His experiments showed that with a cylindrical head joint it was extremely difficult to blow the upper register notes in tune; they always sounded flat, for reasons discussed earlier in this chapter. He found that this fault could be overcome by tapering the head joint down to 17 mm diameter at the cork.

Boehm was able to maximize the tone hole size, and hence the power, by having every hole covered by a pad and he devised an intricate mechanism for closing these. He also constructed a diagram, called a 'schema', for determining the positions of the holes, which can be used for instruments of different pitch, using a simple graphical construction.

Another important contribution that Boehm made was to the cutting of the embouchure hole. The embouchure hole on earlier flutes had generally been round or oval in shape and very small. Boehm adopted a much larger hole, approximately oblong in overall shape, with rounded corners.

The flute after Boehm

The modern flute is essentially the same as the original Boehm 1847 instrument. The only person subsequently to add a new key which is still in use today was the great Italian flautist Giulio Briccialdi. He developed a key to be operated by the left-hand thumb for producing B♭. On Boehm's original model there was only one thumb key (for B♮), so the first finger of the right hand had to be depressed to produce B♭. With the Briccialdi key it is possible to produce both B♮ and B♭ with the left-hand thumb, greatly simplifying the fingering of many passages.

One significant feature of the modern flute, which is a departure from the Boehm design, relates to the hole sizes. Boehm recommended only two hole sizes, one small one for the C♯ and trill keys and another larger for all the other holes. However, manufacturers have gradually deviated from this and it is quite common now to see flutes with four, five, or six different hole sizes. The object of this is to improve the homogeneity of sound throughout the range. There are many other minor deviations from the Boehm design, some of which will be discussed later in this chapter in connection with the range of designs that are available (Section 4.3).

Since the time of Boehm there have been many attempts to bring out radically new designs, but none has survived. Amongst the best known are the Rockstro, the Carte 1867 system, the Radcliff system, and the more recent Murray flute. The search for perfection still goes on, making use of new materials and computer-aided design.

Many improvements and minor modifications have been introduced by the leading flute makers, starting with Louis Lot in France, often thought of as the Stradivari of flute makers. He developed the open-hole design (to be discussed later). In England, the Rudall Carte company established a tradition of high-quality flute manufacture and innovation which has been followed up by individual craftsmen such as Albert Cooper. Cooper is responsible for the Cooper Scale, which in essence is a recalculated set of hole positions. In America the Haynes and Powell companies incorporated design features such as drawn tone holes and the 'gizmo' key, both of which will be described later in this chapter. Japan has taken a leading role in flute manufacture in recent years, with companies such as Muramatsu and Yamaha helping to bring down the price of high-quality flutes through the application of advanced manufacturing techniques.

Range of designs

Although the Boehm design is now standard for the concert flute, manufacturers offer a range of features to meet the tastes of different players. This can make the purchase of a new flute a difficult task for the beginner, especially since there are differing views about the relative merits of the various designs.

New wooden flutes are extremely rare, metal having taken over as the preferred material for manufacture. There are, however, still a significant number of older wooden instruments in use by both amateur and professional musicians. Wood seems to have maintained its popularity for longest in Germany and Britain. The majority of evidence indicates that the material of construction in itself does not significantly affect the tone quality. However, in the case of wood and metal there can be important differences in the internal shape of the resonating tube. For example, on flutes where both the body and head joint are made from wood there may be a sudden expansion in bore where the two are joined by socket and tenon. There are also differences in shape at the tone holes. Probably more important, however, is the variability in wood as a construction material which makes precision crafting difficult, particularly on a mass-production basis. Some players feel that wooden flutes tend to be unresponsive in the low register.

One of the most important choices that has to be made when purchasing a flute is between the open-hole or closed-hole models. This only applies to concert flutes because piccolos, alto flutes, and bass flutes are only made with closed holes. In the closed-hole, or plateau, model the pads cover the holes completely on all of the keys. With the open hole, or French, version five of the keys, namely the A, G, F, E, and D keys, have a hole in the centre which must be covered by the finger. The purpose of the perforations is to increase the venting, i.e. to minimize the influence of the open key on the sound wave propagation through the tone hole, although there seems to be little acoustical advantage in this. Figure 4.2 shows modern open- and closed-hole flutes for comparison. One problem from the manufacturer's point of view is that the hole positions are strictly speaking slightly different on the two models, since the flattening effect of a full pad at a given distance from the hole is greater than a perforated one. According to Albert Cooper some manufacturers have used the same hole positions for both models. In his opinion, closed-hole flutes generally tend to be better in tune than open-hole ones.

The use of open holes clearly introduces a further technical difficulty for the player since the notes will not sound properly unless the holes are perfectly covered by the fingers. Despite this, open-hole models are highly popular with professional performers. One point in their favour is that they allow more scope for fine tuning adjustments and the playing of microtones by partial covering. Beginners generally tend to prefer closed-hole models because of the difficulties associated with covering. People with small hands frequently find it impossible to cope with the open-hole version; sets of corks can be obtained to stop the perforations if necessary. Teachers sometimes prefer students to learn using open-hole instruments because this forces them to adopt better finger and hand positions.

Virtually all conventional Boehm flutes now use the closed G♯ system, although this was not the one originally favoured by Boehm. He preferred an open G♯ mechanism which treated the G♯ key in the same way as the others. This required the player to operate the G♯ key with the fourth finger of the left hand, using the little (fifth) finger for the G. Whilst Boehm's arrangement was simpler in its logic, it was widely thought to be awkward, requiring too frequent use of the little finger. With a closed G♯, the G key is operated with the fourth finger, making a direct progression down the C major scale from B to D as the fingers are lowered in turn. The G♯ is then operated with the left-hand little finger. This requires two G♯ tone holes, one of which remains closed until the G♯ key is depressed. There are a few professional performers who use the open G♯ arrangement and quite a number of such instruments are on the market.

The G key on a flute (and the tone-hole below) may be either in line with the other keys or offset. This is of no great acoustical significance. Players with small hands find the offset version more comfortable, so this arrangement is usually preferred for children. Many professional players, on the other hand, prefer the aesthetic simplicity of the in-line version. Also, it is sometimes considered that this arrangement is more conducive to good hand positions.

A problem arises with the conventional Boehm flute in playing E_6, since (in contrast with the original open G♯ mechanism) it is impossible to obtain the correct venting. The resulting note is both sharp and difficult to sound. The split E mechanism overcomes this difficulty by automatically closing the correct combination of holes when the standard E_6 is fingered. An earlier non-mechanized version of this was the split G; this was available from some manufacturers until quite recently. Split E mechanisms are fairly common on student flutes, but some professional players do not recommend them. The reason given for this is that $F^{\sharp}_6$ also blows sharp, and use of the split E tends to accentuate the difficulty of blowing this note in tune.

A variety of additional trill keys are possible, the most common being the C♯ trill. This is operated by an extra key adjacent to the standard B♭ shake and allows easy trilling between B and C♯.

The lowest note on the standard concert flute is C_4, whereas there is an increasing number of compositions which call for the semitone below, examples being Bartók's *Concerto for Orchestra* and Prokofiev's 'Classical' Symphony. This can be accommodated if a B foot joint carrying an additional tone-hole and key is employed; this option is now offered on most high-quality flutes. Some flautists claim that a B foot joint improves the quality of sound in the low register due to the greater length of tube which it gives below the highest open hole. There does not seem any real justification for this, however, and there is the disadvantage of the added weight which tends to spoil the mechanical balance of the instrument.

For flutes with a B foot joint a useful and inexpensive addition is the 'high C facilitator' or 'gizmo'. This allows the bottom B key to be closed independently, which improves the response of the top C.

The international pitch standard of $A_4 = 440$ Hz was adopted in 1939, and this is the standard of tuning for most orchestras and keyboard instruments. However, many modern flutes are tuned to $A_4 = 442$ Hz, on the basis that this gives greater flexibility of tuning adjustment; without this it can be difficult to bring an instrument up to pitch on a cold day. Another consideration is that in some areas of Europe a tuning standard of 442 Hz or even 444 Hz is preferred. Flutes can be retuned over a range of about 4 or 5 hertz without any significant distortion of tuning over the scale.

The special significance of the head joint of a flute was discussed earlier in the chapter. Although most flute makers provide head joints with their instruments, many advanced players prefer to purchase one separately to meet their personal preferences. There are many craftsmen who specialize in head joint design, meeting the demands of the perfectionist always in search of an improvement in response. The two most important features of a head joint are the taper and the shape of the embouchure hole. The taper is a primary factor in the tuning of an instrument whereas the embouchure hole mainly affects tone quality, although it must be stressed that the tone and tuning are interrelated.

It is possible to buy a head joint for the concert flute which is bent back on itself in a U shape, like a bass flute head joint. This is mainly for use by small children. It reduces the distance between the embouchure hole and the first key by at least 15 cm and brings the keys within easy reach of even quite young children. It also helps to increase the player's finger span a little, as the arms now lie more nearly perpendicular to the flute axis. In two well-known versions by Armstrong and Emerson the curved head joint is in two sections, a straight part incorporating the embouchure hole and a bent part in the form of a U. One objection to the U-shaped head joint is that there may be a tendency for the flute to rotate about its axis, upsetting the delicate balance of the instrument. Since no sling is used with the flute and the lip plate simply rests against the lower lip, a proper balance is crucial if the finger movements are to be uninhibited.

The piccolo is a small flute which plays an octave higher than the standard flute. An interesting point about the piccolo is that, unlike the flute, there are two bore shapes in common usage today. One has the body tapered down towards the bottom end, with a cylindrical head joint, much the same as the pre-Boehm flutes.

The other design uses a cylindrical body and a tapered head joint, as with the modern flute. The tapered body design seems the most popular with orchestral players because its tone is more mellow. The cylindrical body version is popular for military bands but tends to have a rather shrill tone. A conical bore piccolo is shown in Figure 4.2.

4.3 INSTRUMENT CONSTRUCTION

The first step in the process of making a flute is the formation of the tube which is the main body of the instrument. After this has been made the tone holes are added and then the sockets and tenons, which hold the sections together, are fitted. Next comes making and fixing of the keywork, then the padding and final regulation. Construction of the head joint can be considered as an independent operation.

Materials

In the case of the flute, manufacturers and players alike seem to attach more importance to the material of construction than with other wind instruments, despite the lack of evidence for any significant acoustical differences. We will only concern ourselves for the time being with metals, since wood and other materials are hardly ever used now, except for the reproduction of period instruments. The flute, being relatively small in size, lends itself to manufacture in some of the more expensive metals, which would prove prohibitively expensive on a larger instrument.

The most common metal nowadays for flute construction is nickel silver, and most student flutes are made from this. Nickel silver is an alloy of copper, nickel, and zinc and actually contains no silver at all. It is sometimes referred to as German silver, although white brass would probably be a more accurate name. This alloy is somewhat harder than brass and quite resistant to tarnish.

Brass is another metal frequently used for student flutes. As well as being relatively inexpensive, it is easy to machine. It is an alloy of copper and zinc and has a yellowish colour.

Nickel silver and brass flutes are nearly always plated, either with nickel or silver, to give them a bright finish. Silver-plating is generally preferred, not only for its appearance, but because it is less slippery, although it tarnishes more easily than nickel. Any tendency for the fingers to slip can impair the players' technique. Lacquering is not common on flutes, as it is with brass instruments, probably because it wears quickly. This would be a particular problem on the flute because of the extent of contact between the hands and the instrument body.

Professional quality and custom-built flutes are usually made from one of the noble metals, silver being by far the most popular. Silver is particularly favoured by craftsmen because of the ease with which it can be worked. This is a most important factor because it is primarily the quality of the craftsmanship which determines the playing characteristics. Silver also has a very high thermal conductivity and warms up quickly. Together with its low slip qualities, this makes it pleasant to feel. In its pure form silver is very soft, so it is used as an alloy with small quantities of copper. The purity of silver is normally marked on the barrel of the instrument: a mark of 900 would indicate an alloy of 90 per cent silver and 10 per cent copper, called coin silver. Sterling silver is 92.5 per cent silver and 7.5 per cent copper; this is quite soft, and flutes made from sterling silver are easily dented. On the other hand, silver flutes can generally be repaired relatively easily.

Nowadays there are quite a number of professional players who use gold flutes, although the general consensus of opinion is that this offers little advantage over silver, and in fact many players prefer silver. Like silver, pure gold is very soft and is always used in alloy form, usually mixed with silver and copper. The purity is measured in carat, 24 carat being pure gold. The most commonly used carat ratings are 9, 14, and 18; 9 carat gold, for example is 37.5 per cent gold, 31.25 per cent silver, and 31.25 per cent copper, whereas 18 carat gold is 75 per cent gold, 12.5 per cent silver, and 12.5 per cent copper. One great advantage of gold is that it is highly resistant to tarnish, since it is almost inert.

Occasionally one sees flutes made from platinum, a metal which looks similar to silver but is slightly greyer and less lustrous. It can be even more expensive than gold. This metal is also very resistant to tarnish but its use for flute-making does not seem to have aroused much enthusiasm amongst craftsmen. Another precious metal used on rare occasions is palladium. This closely resembles platinum in appearance but is substantially lighter.

It is quite usual to see flutes where the tube and keywork are made from different metals. A very common combination is silver-plated nickel silver keywork on a solid silver tube. This construction is a good deal cheaper than solid silver throughout. Often the head joint is purchased separately and made from a different material to the body e.g. a gold head joint may be combined with a silver body.

Tube and tone holes

The standard internal diameter for a concert flute tube is 19 mm, although slight variations are to be found from one model to another. A variety of wall thicknesses are used, ranging from about one quarter to a half of a millimetre. The acoustical evidence available indicates that this does not significantly affect the tone quality, although some flautists claim a preference for either a thick- or thin-walled tube (usually the latter). The added weight of a thick-walled tube may be a contributing factor in how the player perceives the instrument.

Tubes on most modern flutes are drawn: the tube starts out as a flat plate, which is drawn through a large circular die by pulling the centre with great force. Once the cylindrical shape has been formed it is drawn through successively smaller dies in order to bring the diameter down to the required dimension. In the drawing process the metal becomes work-hardened and must be annealed by heating to bring it back to its original softness (see Section 5.4). The drawing process requires specialist heavy machinery, so most flute manufacturers buy standard lengths of tube to work with.

Before drawn tubing became readily available, flute makers produced their own tubing using a seaming process. In this, a flat sheet of metal is bent round a cylindrical form, known as a mandrel, and the join is made by soldering. Some modern craftsmen still prefer to use this traditional technique.

On most modern mass-produced instruments the tone-hole chimneys are drawn from the tube wall in much the same way in which the tube itself is made from a plane sheet. The metal is drawn through a die which has been positioned on the outside of the tube at an appropriate location for a tone-hole. This is in contrast to the traditional technique of soldering the chimneys, in which the short lengths of cylindrical tubing making up the tone-hole chimneys are made separately using a lathe and are soldered into position at the appropriate positions. The holes are then drilled through the tube and are finished by reaming and scraping. Lead solder is normally used on silver and nickel silver flutes and silver solder on gold ones, the melting point of the solder having to be less than that of the metal being joined.

The metal in a drawn tone-hole tends to be thin since the original tube has had its walls stretched in the drawing process. This is good from the point of view of saving weight but the tone-hole chimneys may lack strength. Soldered ones have a greater thickness of metal and are generally far stronger. In the event of damage the soldered version is easier to repair, since there is more metal to work with. It is very difficult to draw tone-hole chimneys from a thin walled tube, because of the lack of metal available. Thin-walled flutes tend to have their tone-hole chimneys soldered. The greater metal thickness of a soldered chimney allows the face that meets the pad to be machined on a lathe, rather than the edge being lapped over; this gives a flatter face for the pad to seat against.

The height of a tone-hole chimney is generally kept as low as possible, for two reasons. Firstly, the cavity inside the tube when the pad is closed means that the internal dimensions differ from that of an ideal smooth tube, which affects the resonance frequencies of the tube. Secondly, it is thought that acoustic losses are likely to be minimized with a smooth internal bore. Experimental smooth-bore flutes have been constructed using curved pads made from synthetic materials but it is not clear whether this type of design actually gives an improved performance. The main problem in making comparisons between the different designs is the technical difficulty of making a smooth-bore instrument where the pads close perfectly without leaks.

Mechanism

When the tube and tone-holes have been completed the sockets and tenons are fitted. The sockets are usually just short lengths of tubing which telescope over the ends of the body and foot section. The tenons slide into these to make the joint. Often the tenon is just an extended section of the main tube with a narrow ring attached on the outside to act as a stop. The sockets and tenons need not necessarily be of the same metal as the tubing. In fact on the less expensive silver flutes the socket barrels may well be made of brass, silver-plated for appearance.

The keywork on a flute is attached to 'ribs' which run along the length of the tube. These are thin strips of metal which are stamped out of a sheet and soldered to the tube, forming a base to which the upright 'posts' can be fixed. The posts are short machined lengths of rod which support the 'steels' on which the key tubing rotates. One end of each post is soldered to a rib whilst the other end is drilled and threaded to accept the steels.

The remaining keywork consists mainly of various spatulas and trills, together with their connecting arms. These are produced by either forging or casting; the two processes and their relative merits have been described in the previous chapter. The component parts are soldered together and the completed keywork is buffed to give a good finish. After assembling, certain of the keys have to be pinned to their steels. The springs, commonly of steel or phosphor bronze, are then fitted. White gold alloy springs are sometimes used on high-quality flutes, these being very resistant to breaking. The large pads used for the G♯ and D♯ keys (on a closed G♯ model) are held in the closed position by the pressure of the spring, rather than the finger, so the springs need to be particularly strong; a heavier gauge spring may be used here.

Pads

The importance of good padding on a woodwind instrument has been discussed in the previous chapter. Although pads made from synthetic materials are sometimes found on student flutes, fishskin pads are the accepted norm on all good-quality flutes. The complete pad is made up of three layers, a cardboard backing, a layer of felt, of slightly larger diameter, and the outer layer of fishskin which wraps around the felt and is glued to the cardboard at the back to keep it in place.

A water-soluble vegetable glue is preferably used to fix the felt and fishskin to the cardboard. The fishskin is normally employed in double layers; its purpose is to create a hermetic seal with the tone-hole chimney. It is essential that the piece being used does not contain any tiny fissures or pinholes, otherwise the final seal will not be completely airtight. The purpose of the supporting felt is to take up any small geometrical irregularities when the pad is pressed against the tone-hole.

There are three different types of pad found on flutes: the large closed-hole pads, the large perforated pads found on open-hole flutes and the small pads used for the C# and trill keys. The small pads are simply glued into their cups with shellac. Large closed-hole pads are held in with a screw fixing through their centre, or alternatively a snap-on plastic or nylon stud. In the case of small pads the shellac used for gluing them is melted by heating the cup, and the pad is floated into position as the key is carefully depressed whilst the shellac hardens. Large pads are more difficult to align. Use is made of paper shims of various thicknesses which are inserted below the pad to raise points which are too low.

Once pads have been correctly set in their cups any small wrinkles are removed by ironing. This involves wetting the skin with water and then using a heated strip of metal, known as a slick, to iron the wrinkles out. The final process is to seat the pad. This involves lightly wetting the pad and then heating the cup over an alcohol flame. While this is being done the key is depressed so that the tone-hole chimney forms an indentation on the pad.

The final process in making a flute is the fixing of the corks and felts and the regulation, i.e. the adjustments of key openings and couplings. When the player opens a pad the resulting venting of the tube reduces its effective length. The amount of venting can be altered in the regulation process by adjusting the amount that each key opens when released. As far as the lowest octave is concerned, the pitch of any particular note (other than the lowest) will be sensitive to the key rise on the first open hole. If the key rise is increased then so is the venting and the pitch of that note will rise slightly. Thus choosing the correct key rise on each key is crucial to the overall tuning of the instrument. On open-hole flutes, the additional venting offered by a perforated key makes it less prone to pitch changes. Changing the key rise on a covered hole produces a greater pitch change than the corresponding change on a perforated key.

Head joints

Because of the great importance of the head joint in determining the playing characteristics, much attention is frequently lavished on its manufacture. One of the difficult aspects of making a head joint is creating a satisfactory taper. Many craftsmen base their taper shape directly on the dimensions given by Dayton Miller in his translation of Boehm's book (published in 1922). These measurements were taken from an excellent specimen of a Boehm and Mendler flute. (Carl Mendler worked in Boehm's shop from 1854 and was made a partner in 1867.)

The dimensions are reproduced in Figure 4.6, which is a facsimile of Miller's graph showing how the tube diameter varies along its length. At the slide the tube diameter is 19 mm and is of necessity cylindrical, but the diameter tapers down gradually to 17.1 mm at the cork. The diameter of the tube at the centre of the embouchure hole should be 17.35 mm. For comparison, a straight taper is also shown. With this, the tube changes suddenly from being cylindrical to being conical, whereas with the Boehm taper there is a gradual transition. Boehm termed the shape 'parabolic', and indeed the curve shown in Figure 4.6 does show some resemblance to one half of a parabola with vertex at the point where the slide starts. Boehm's mathematical description, however, should not be taken too literally.

Some student flutes have been made with a straight taper (that is, a tube of conical bore) on the head joint instead of the Boehm taper, presumably for ease of manufacture in a production line. Experiments have shown that this does affect the resonances of the instrument, although not

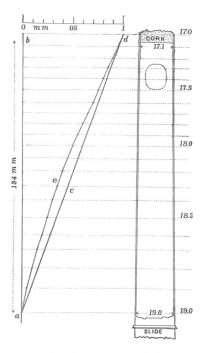

4.6 Boehm's 'parabolic' head joint. The figures to the right on the dotted lines are the diameters of the various sections, measured in millimetres. To the left is an exaggerated diagram of the actual contraction. Line *aed* represents the parabolic contraction. If the tube had been cylindrical, one side of it would have been represented by the line *ab*. If it had been a straight taper (conical) it would have been represented by *acd*

very significantly. The practice seems to have been most widespread on early mass-production models from Japan and is now encountered less frequently.

As with the main body of the flute, the most popular material for professional quality head joints is silver, although a whole range of other metals may be used, including nickel silver, bronze, brass, phosphor bronze, gold, platinum, and palladium. The usual starting point is a length of drawn cylindrical tube. Some craftsmen, however, prefer the traditional seamed tubing, in which case the starting point is normally a length of straight tapered tube, made by bending a sheet of metal around a straight tapered mandrel and then soldering along the butt joint. The Boehm taper shape is produced using a hardened steed mandrel, machined to the correct dimensions. The tubing is forced over the mandrel by squeezing it through a lead block with a hole in it, so that the metal is deformed to take up the mandrel shape.

When the tube has been made the embouchure hole must be cut in it and the chimney, which connects the lip plate to the tube, soldered in position. The lip plate is important because it is the main point of contact with the player and it determines the exact shape of the embouchure hole at the blowing end. In essence it is just a piece of metal sheet bent round to form a segment of a cylinder, with the edges lapped over and the embouchure hole punched in it. Some designs, however, are bowed upwards or downwards towards the hole. In practice, a great deal of effort may go into producing a lip plate, and on older flutes fine engravings are sometimes found as embellishments.

Two shapes of embouchure hole are commonly used, an oval and an oblong with rounded corners. The size of the embouchure hole is very important; one leading flute maker has proposed that optimum dimensions are a length of 11.9 mm and a width of between 10.3 mm and 10.4 mm, measured at the narrowest points, with a chimney depth of 5 mm. The far wall of the chimney is usually undercut by about 7°, i.e. it slopes away such that the chimney increases in size towards the bottom. The other walls may be slightly curved. Another point which is often considered to be important is the sharpness of the far corner against which the air stream strikes. Is is generally thought that a razor sharp corner gives a little more edge to the tone, providing greater attack on articulated notes.

The head joint is completed by the insertion of a cork to block off the end. Traditionally the crown, which moves the cork position when rotated, is ornamented, and many head joint makers have developed individual designs as distinguishing marks.

Maintenance

In order to preserve the pads and mechanism the instrument must be kept clean and dry. After playing, the tube should be swabbed through, preferably using an absorbent cotton handkerchief on a wooden swab stick. The metal cleaning sticks provided with many flutes can easily scratch the inside, especially of a silver flute. Excessive moisture on the instrument when it is stored in the case can damage the pads and may even induce rust to form on the steels. Sweat from the player's fingers can corrode the silver-plating of keys. The same applies to the other woodwind instruments. The joints should also be kept meticulously clean so that they fit together smoothly. Dirt will eventually cause wear and the fixings will become slack.

It is generally inadvisable to lubricate the mechanism after assembly, since the oil may eventually find its way onto the pads. A sluggish action usually indicates that the oil has become gummy, which means that the mechanism will have to be dismantled and cleaned before relubricating.

Another common cause of damage is the use of metal polish. If applied to an assembled flute this can easily get on to the pads and damage them, as well as clogging the mechanism. The correct time to polish the instrument is when it is dismantled. This is usually best done using a silversmith's cleaning cloth.

4.4 PERFORMANCE PRACTICE

Recorder

Reproductions of Renaissance and Baroque recorders are now easily available, and are widely used in the performance of music from the appropriate periods. The pioneering work of Arnold Dolmetsch in the 1920s used a Baroque model, and it is this type of instrument which has become enormously popular as an introduction to woodwind playing for schoolchildren. The Baroque instrument has also developed a twentieth-century repertoire; when a modern score specifies 'recorder' without qualification, it is the Baroque instrument which is intended.

Figure 4.1 shows a comparison between the Renaissance and Baroque designs. The Baroque instrument is generally made in three sections: the head joint containing the duct, the main body, and a short foot joint. The cheaper school models often combine the foot joint with the body. The bore is tapered down towards the foot to a greater extent than in the Renaissance instrument and is also somewhat narrower. The Baroque recorder has a greater range than its Renaissance counterpart but the tone is not as full in the bass.

The Baroque treble (alto) recorder shown in Figure 4.1(b) has eight holes, seven on the front and one at the back for the thumb, with the lower two holes on the front divided by drilling them as two separate small holes. By opening only one of the small holes a rise of a semitone can be produced. Renaissance instruments, such as the descant (soprano) recorder shown in Figure 4.1(c), do not always have the lower hole divided, so partial closure of the hole with the finger is required on some notes. For higher chromatic notes cross-fingerings are used. The recorder probably played a leading part in developing the system of cross-fingering which was used for producing semitones before woodwind key mechanisms were invented. Cross-fingerings are particularly effective on a recorder, primarily due to the fact that the holes are relatively small compared to the tube diameter and their depth is also relatively great. On instruments with larger holes and thin tube walls, such as the penny whistle, opening a single hole effectively truncates the tube at that position, so that the opening and closing of holes below this point has little effect on the pitch of the note.

Recorders overblow to the octave. The thumb-hole acts as a register vent for the upper range, where it is normally half-covered by pinching the thumb so that the nail divides the hole. The fingerings in the second octave are similar although not identical to those in the lowest register. Cross-fingerings are required on many of the notes. For example, C_5 is fingered on the treble recorder by closing all the left hand holes; to lower this a semitone to B_4, the next hole must remain open but one or two holes immediately below this are closed. The very limited dynamic range of the recorder can be considerably increased by the judicious use of alternative fingerings: a fingering which would render a given note too sharp at normal blowing pressure can be used to play the same note very quietly and in tune at reduced pressure.

The recorder has a pitch range of only about two octaves. Baroque-style recorders in common use, together with their ranges are the sopranino (F_5–G_7, notated an octave lower), descant or soprano (C_5–D_7, notated an octave lower), treble or alto (F_4–G_6), tenor (C_4–D_6), and bass (F_3–D_5, notated an octave lower and written in the bass clef). Reproductions of Renaissance recorders are also readily available and frequently played, including great bass and contrabass recorders descending as low as C_2 and a tiny garklein ascending as high as A_7.

The Baroque transverse flute

The eighteenth century is often said to have been the golden age of the flute, so great was the resurgence in its popularity. The growth in the repertoire was matched by the number of virtuoso players. As well as being the standard for professional players, the new conical bore instrument became fashionable with a multitude of amateur players. Their interest was catered for by a number of instruction books on flute-playing which laid the foundation for modern technique. Today these manuals give us invaluable insight into the playing style of the times. One of the most notable is the book *On Playing the Flute* by Johann Joachim Quantz, published in 1752.

The main features of technique and style of the Baroque transverse flute are closely related to the mechanics of the instrument. Although this had tonal advantages over its Renaissance predecessor and was easier to handle, it still only had one or two keys, and relied predominantly on cross-fingerings for the chromatic notes. By changing the cross-fingerings it was possible to make small modifications to the pitches of notes. The basic assumptions concerning intonation were different during this period from what they are today, particularly for instruments such as the flute, where the player had control over small changes in pitch. It was normal practice to differentiate between enharmonic notes; thus in Quantz's chart for the flute, different fingerings are given for C# and D♭, and for all the other enharmonically equivalent notes.

The notion of different pitches for enharmonic notes is bound up with the idea, discussed in Chapter 1, that the important musical intervals should be as close as possible to the intervals between the lower members of a set of harmonics. One possible way of approaching this ideal on a conventional keyboard is the tuning system known as mean-tone temperament. Within this framework, a semitone interval between two notes with the same letter name, such as F to F♯ or B to B♭, for example, should be close to 76 cents. The interval in this case is known as a minor semitone or chromatic semitone. On the other hand, the semitone interval F♯ to G or A to B♭ should have a width of 117 cents, known as a major semitone or diatonic semitone. The discrepancy between a diatonic semitone and a chromatic semitone is 41 cents (almost half an equal-tempered semitone); this is easily detectable if the wrong fingering is used.

In mean-tone temperament all the sharps are relatively low in pitch and all the flats correspondingly high. The reverse is true in Pythagorean temperament, which concentrates attention on the tuning of true perfect fifths. The reverse is also true in modern practice, in which sharps tend to be raised and flats lowered in order to enhance the function of leading notes. For the lowest sharps and flats on the flute, D♯ and E♭, it is not possible to use a cross-fingering, so on Quantz's flute two separate keys are used, one for each of these notes. Quantz recognized that this subtlety raised some problems when playing with a keyboard instrument whose notes must be tuned to a tempered scale.

The fingering schemes used in Baroque playing are clearly very complex and are made even more so by the fact that many notes have alternative fingerings. The best one to use in any given circumstance depends on the adjacent notes and the speed of the passage. In his book, Quantz gives a number of examples. Figure 4.7 shows his fingerings for notes in the lowest octave.

Setting the overall pitch of the flute for a performance was a fairly major problem in these times, since in the eighteenth century there was no such thing as standard pitch. Pitch varied from city to city, and even at the same place performers

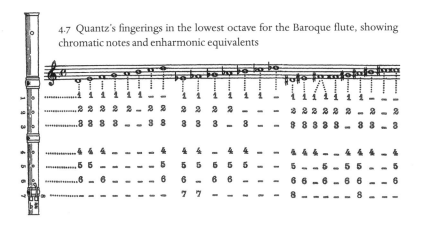

4.7 Quantz's fingerings in the lowest octave for the Baroque flute, showing chromatic notes and enharmonic equivalents

could find the harpsichord tuned higher or lower, depending on the particular tuner. The pitch could vary by more than a tone from one performance to another. We have already seen that to accommodate this, flutes generally had interchangeable middle sections of different length, known as *corps de rechange*, and Quantz himself also invented a type of tuning slide that allowed one to alter the length of the head joint section. Once the correct centre pieces had been chosen and the head joint adjusted, resetting of the head joint cork position was also advocated, drawing it back further from the mouth-hole for each shorter middle section and pressing it closer to the mouth-hole for each longer piece. The precise setting could be tested by sounding the low D against the middle and highest D; if these octaves were true then the setting was correct. If the high D was too high in relation to the low one then the cork had to be drawn back; if the high D was too low then it had to be pressed further in. Quantz suggests tuning the flute a little lower for an Allegro, where there is a tendency for a predominance of forte passages, and correspondingly higher for the softer Adagio. This compensates for the fact that the flute tends to drop in pitch when blown softly and is sharper when blown strongly. He also recommends tuning the flute a little lower when playing in the keys of E♭ or A♭, since the fingerings for the flattened notes give pitches a little sharper than the fingerings for the corresponding sharps.

The most striking feature of Baroque flute performance technique, in comparison with today's, is that there was great reliance on ornamentation and extemporisation. The flute of the time had a rather weak sound, particularly on the cross-fingered notes, and it was not customary to use any vibrato to enrich this. Instead, the sound was kept alive by the addition of copious embellishments, many of which were not written in by the composer. In order to master the flute, therefore, much attention had to be paid to the way in which these could be introduced to best effect.

Exactly where to insert appoggiaturas, shakes, and other variations was only learnt through experience and attentive listening, although certain general rules were sometimes cited. For example, if a long note follows one or more short notes on the downbeat or upbeat and remains in a constant harmony then an appoggiatura may be placed before the long note. Appoggiaturas were generally placed before notes which had quicker notes either before or after them and were also generally required in shakes. Shakes were always executed between notes a tone or semitone apart, rather than a third, as was sometimes the case in earlier times. In the case of a semitone shake the full tone fingering was frequently used but with the finger only partly raised to produce a half tone. Because of the speed, small imperfections in tuning went unnoticed. The speed of a shake was determined to a great extent by the mood of the piece, gay pieces requiring more rapid shakes than melancholy ones.

The extent to which ornaments could be added to a composition depended largely on its country of origin. Pieces written in France at this time generally had all the ornaments written in, leaving little room for the performer to add more. In Italian-style music much more was left to the imagination of the performer, to an extent that his or her contribution could be almost as great as that of the composer. The slow metre of an Adagio usually offered the greatest scope for embellishment, although ornaments and variations were not ruled out in an Allegro or even Presto. The accepted procedure was to play the principal subject at the beginning, just as written, and then to ornament it on the repeat. Ornamentation on the first playing could obscure the principal notes.

Cadenzas probably offered the player the greatest scope for improvisation and became particularly popular in flute music because of the flowing passagework that the instrument could produce. It seems to have been about 1700 that the cadenza became fashionable among the Italians and it was subsequently imitated by the Germans and others, although it was not taken up to any extent by the French. No rules were prescribed for cadenzas, and regular metre was seldom observed; they simply consisted of detached ideas put together in an impromptu manner by the player, allowing him to show off both his technique and personal emotions. Two-part as well as solo cadenzas were also quite common although these required preparation and were less arbitrary than their solo counterparts. In France a tradition of improvised preludes, played before the performance of a written piece, was important in the early eighteenth century; this improvisatory technique was described by Hotteterre in 1719 in a treatise entitled *L'Art de Preluder*.

Vibrato, as we know it today, is a continuous pulsation or modulation in the sound which forms an integral part of the player's sound quality. In flute-playing this originated in the late nineteenth century in Paris. However, before this time performers did sometimes make use of oscillations somewhat akin to modern vibrato, although this was generally reserved for special effects. There are references to the use of tremolo and vibrato produced by the breath as early as the seventeenth century. Also finger vibrato effects were commonly used since small oscillations in pitch could be produced easily on pre-Boehm flutes. This is referred to by Hotteterre as 'flattement'. Quantz also describes what the Italians call 'messa di voce', which is a swell in the sound towards the middle of a sustained note whilst executing a vibrato with the finger.

During the Baroque era the main ideas of flute technique were developed to a high degree of sophistication. Quantz describes in detail the basic principles of embouchure control and lip cover. He gives, for example, a diagram showing the extent to which the embouchure hole should be covered by the lips when playing in different registers. In the low register only a small amount of the hole is covered, whereas for the higher notes the lips come progressively further forward (see Figure 4.3). He also explains the flattening effect of increased lip cover and the corresponding sharpening associated with drawing the lips back. The basic tuning on pre-Boehm flutes was usually poor, so a flexible embouchure was essential to bring certain notes into tune as well as to compensate for pitch variations due to differing dynamics.

The French school

With the advent of the Boehm flute an enormously prestigious school of players and teachers emerged in France, centred around the Paris Conservatoire. The Conservatoire dominated musical education in France and admission to its classes was highly competitive. Amongst the legendary names who studied flute there and emerged as First Prize winners were Taffanel, Gaubert, Moyse, and Rampal. The word 'Prize' here referred to a particular standard which had been reached rather than to the result of a competition between students: the acquisition of a First Prize was an almost indispensable prerequisite for a successful musical career in France. The French school has set international standards for flute performance, and virtuosi throughout the world have accepted and developed the French style.

Boehm's design innovations were taken on board quickly in France, particularly by Louis Dorus, flautist in the Opéra and in the Societé des Concerts, a professional orchestra attached to the Conservatoire. Dorus became Professor at the Conservatoire in 1860; he introduced the new instrument to his pupils with enthusiasm, although his predecessor Jean-Louis Tulou bitterly opposed this right up to his death. Amongst Dorus's pupils was the young Paul Taffanel, soon to become the most renowned flautist and teacher in Europe. Taffanel led the revival of the flute and justly deserves the title 'father of modern flute-playing' so often accorded to him.

The essential characteristic of the French school of playing is the emphasis placed on tone development achieved by control of the breath and flexibility of the lips. Exponents of the French style advocate using a relaxed embouchure since this allows sensitive control of tone colouring, even if this is at the expense of power. A beautiful tone and a full palette of colours are the striking quality shared by all of the flautists who built up the French school, from Taffanel onwards. In addition to this, they produced an unsurpassed homogeneity of sound across the complete compass of the instrument. Taffanel and his successors constantly stressed the importance of a well-supported sound, even in the practice of simple technical exercises.

Another important aspect of the French school of playing is the emphasis placed on articulation and phrasing. This may have its origin in the French language, in which the tongue is frequently placed far forward in the mouth: compare for example the English and French pronunciations of the word 'flute'.

Traditional French tonguing technique also generally requires that the tongue is forward in the mouth so that the tonguing takes place effectively between the teeth. This produces rapid and clear articulation.

Philippe Gaubert was sent for lessons to Taffanel's father at the age of 7 and he proved so promising a pupil that four years later Paul Taffanel himself took him on. At the age of 15 he gained First Prize for flute at the Paris Conservatoire. Although Gaubert divided his attentions between flute-playing, conducting, and composing, he became professor of the Conservatoire flute class in 1919 where he expounded and developed the ideas taught him by Taffanel. Gaubert wrote many compositions for flute. Perhaps one of the best known to amateur flautists is his *Madrigal*, written in 1908. The *17 Big Daily Finger Exercises for the Flute*, by Taffanel and Gaubert (1923), will be familiar to nearly everyone learning the instrument.

The person who has probably done most for promoting the French school of playing is Marcel Moyse. Moyse had lessons from both Taffanel and Gaubert and also was a First Prize winner at the Conservatoire. He succeeded Gaubert as professor there in 1932, but in later life emigrated to America, following in the footsteps of a number of Gaubert's other students. Right up to his last years he gave frequent master classes in Europe and Japan. He also published numerous studies and exercises which are now basic material for both amateur and professional flautists alike. Moyse made recordings showing how some of these should be practised, which are an invaluable record of the teaching techniques of the French school. Another influential teaching work published by Moyse is his *Tone Development through Interpretation*, which he says is for the study of expression, vibrato, colour, suppleness, and their application to different styles. This gives some indication of the priorities he attached to tone development.

Mention has already been made of the fact that prior to the late nineteenth century vibrato was used principally as a special effect. This changed with the French school of playing, in which vibrato was considered an integral part of the player's tone. Nevertheless, Taffanel and his followers often warned against using excessive vibrato. Moyse said that he was never impressed by the wide and continuous vibrato used by trumpet and trombone jazz players, nor on the other hand by the very close and nervous vibrato of certain violinists interpreting Mozart. Moyse was reluctant to specify pulsation rates or even to explain how the vibrato was produced, preferring to rely on comparisons with sentiments and expressions in the human voice. This approach was also the one taken by Jean-Pierre Rampal, one of the twentieth century's greatest flautists, who was also a First Prize winner and later professor at the Paris Conservatoire. 'It is very difficult to speak about vibrato', said Rampal, 'because vibrato is something that should be natural. If you practise it, it is unnatural.' This view is not the one held by many teachers, however, who advocate the use of specific exercises for vibrato development.

The French school of playing is often associated with the silver flute, in particular the open-hole model, and many people have attributed some of the main characteristics of the French sound to this instrument. Scientific evidence tells us that the material of construction is of only secondary importance, and indeed some later exponents such as Rampal played on gold flutes. What was certainly of importance was that the French movement started with the introduction of the Boehm instrument, which was radically different from its earlier conical-bored counterpart.

English and American styles

The Boehm instrument did not become established as quickly in Britain and other parts of Europe, and in Britain a different style of playing developed at the same time as the French school was evolving in Paris. This was a denser, more forceful sound with harder attack, produced by a tighter embouchure pressed hard against the lip plate. The emphasis was on sound intensity and technical agility, rather than tone colouring. In England there was the tradition of Charles Nicholson, who had inspired Boehm's redesign. Players strove to reproduce his powerful reedy clarinet-like sound, particularly in the low register. In Vienna the conservative Franz Doppler was professor at the Conservatory until 1867 and he remained faithful to the old-system flute throughout his life. Here it was not until the early twentieth century that the Boehm flute gained acceptance.

With the emigration of many of the French school to the New World at the beginning of the twentieth century, much of the focus switched to America. A distinctive American style of playing began to appear, championed by William Kincaid, first flute in the Philadelphia Symphony Orchestra and distinguished soloist and teacher. This combined the French virtues of tone quality with a more virile quality, with stress on blending rather than contrasting colours. His ideas are well documented in the book *Kincaidiana*, essentially the reproduction of notes taken by one of his students, John Krell, from his classes at the Curtis Institute of Music in Philadelphia.

4.5 AVANT-GARDE TECHNIQUES

In the latter part of this century a new dimension of flute technique has emerged to satisfy the demands of contemporary composers. The vocabulary of sounds required from the flautist has now expanded to incorporate numerous special effects. Mastery of these unusual techniques is required in many modern works, of which we can mention but a few. For example, as early as 1936 André Jolivet calls for extended flutter tongue passages in his *Cinq Incantations*. *Le Merle Noir* (1951) is the only composition that Olivier Messiaen wrote for flute and this also uses flutter tongue to imitate bird sounds. In his composition *Sequenza* (1958) Luciano Berio makes the first known use of multiphonics on the flute. In some more recent pieces such as *Sunflowers* (1981) by Harvey Sollberger, all manner of effects such as key clicks and simultaneous playing and singing are demanded.

As well as being indispensable for the performance of many modern works, a study of the full vocabulary of the instrument is generally considered to be a useful vehicle for improving technique. The value of being fluent in playing harmonics (unconventional fingerings) was recognized even before Boehm's time; Charles Nicholson frequently used harmonics as a means of facilitating awkward upper-register passages. They are also used as non-discretionary special effects in many early works written by flautists, for example *Fantasie Pastorale Hongroise* by Franz Doppler. In his book *The Other Flute* Robert Dick (1975) gives copious exercises based on harmonic fingerings for the purpose of developing embouchure position and flexibility of the lips.

Multiphonics, the art of playing more than one pitch simultaneously, is one of the richest new fields for the flautist. There are literally thousands of pitch combinations which can be achieved with up to five notes sounding simultaneously. Extensive sets of fingerings are given by Robert Dick (1975) and Stokes and Condon in *Special Effects for Flute* (1976) although often the best fingering for a particular note combination can be found by experiment. This is not usually the normal fingering that would be used for either of the notes individually. The production of a multiphonic involves maintaining two or more oscillation frequencies simultaneously and the acoustic mechanism by which this is achieved is not always fully understood. In practice the technique for playing multiphonics is similar to that for harmonics except that the airstream is broadened out vertically to reach the target area of each individual pitch. When learning to play a 'double stop', for example, the player first masters blowing the individual notes with the multiphonic fingering and then holds the lower one whilst gradually introducing the upper by a slight adjustment of the airstream.

One of the most commonly used special effects on the flute is 'flutter-tonguing'. There are two ways in which this can be executed, the preferred one being to roll the tongue against the roof of the mouth creating a rapid tremolo. The alternative is to sound a guttural R in which the uvula is vibrated against the back of the throat, in a similar manner to gargling. Flutter-tonguing is particularly effective on the flute, hence it has become very popular with composers. It is frequently used by jazz and dance band flautists.

Microtones, i.e. pitch changes of less than a semitone, are most readily achieved on the open-hole model Boehm flute, although they are also possible on the plateau version. Quarter-tones are the ones most commonly used and fingerings are available (e.g. Robert Dick, 1975) for the full quarter-tone scale. Microtones are frequently combined in the form of microtonal segments, which are short scalar passages executed whilst leaving one of the upper holes open. The glissando might be thought of as an extension of this idea. On the open-hole flute the gradual pitch variation is achieved by successively sliding the fingers off the open holes and then lifting the rims. This technique is almost impossible to achieve on the plateau model flute. Going under the older name of 'glide', it dates back to the early nineteenth century, and was a favourite special effect of Charles Nicholson. On the pre-Boehm flutes the fingers covered most of the holes directly so the effect was easier to achieve. The technique became so popular that a mechanical sliding key device was patented by William Henry Potter in 1808.

A very interesting special effect, peculiar to the flute, is that of 'whistle tones', sometimes called 'whisper tones'. Both terms are quite descriptive because the sound is very faint and resembles that of someone whistling. Whistle tones are produced by blowing very lightly over the embouchure hole. The sound tends to jump between harmonics in a dancing fashion and it is only with great care that individual tones can be isolated. The harmonic series of the whistles is the same as that of the fundamental note fingered. The advent of electronic amplification has made the whistle tone a practically useful effect and it has frequently been used in recordings. Without amplification the sounds cannot be heard clearly at distances of more than 10 metres or so. William Kincaid is credited with pioneering whistle tones as a warm-up exercise for embouchure control, although their existence must have been known from the times of the earliest flutes.

Singing and playing simultaneously produces another useful effect on the flute; this idea has been used most extensively by jazz performers, for example Herbie Mann and the virtuoso saxophonist and flautist Roland Kirk. It is possible for the played and sung lines to move either together or independently and sometimes a falsetto voice is used.

There are many other flute-playing techniques which have occasionally been utilized, and doubtless the full range of possibilities has not yet been exhausted. Blowing the flute like a trumpet gives an interesting sound. This lowers the pitch of the fingered note because the tube now behaves as a cylinder closed at one end, as in the clarinet. The pitch is not lowered by as much as an octave, as might be expected, because the end correction at the embouchure hole is now smaller. The actual pitch change is something closer to a minor seventh. Another way of extending the range downwards is to block off the end of the tube with a cork or the side of the knee. These low notes are very difficult to produce, however, and weak in strength. Sometimes non-standard fingerings are used to produce notes of a hollow non-resonant quality, reminiscent of some primitive instruments. Occasionally composers have also called for sounds produced by tapping the keys or by using various unusual forms of accents and articulations.

5

Bugles and Horns

5.1 ACOUSTICAL PRINCIPLES

Basic acoustics

The brass instrument family is a sprawling one, encompassing many bizarre wonders of the plumber's art. The essential feature common to all members of the family is not the material from which the tube is constructed (which might be copper, silver, wood, or plastic), but rather the method by which it is sounded. The player's lips are stretched across an opening at one end of the tube in such a way that when a stream of air is blown into the tube the air flow is modulated by the vibration of the lips. The similarity between this behaviour and that of a woodwind double reed justifies our use of the term 'lip-reed aerophones' to describe members of the brass family.

We have seen that a woodwind instrument can be classified as either cylindrical or conical, depending on whether the tube has essentially the same diameter throughout its length or whether it tapers steadily from one end to the other. Brass instruments are difficult to classify since the many different bore profiles found cannot all be reliably distinguished by simple criteria. In the next chapter we will discuss trumpets and trombones, for which a large part of the tubing is cylindrical. In this present chapter we consider the other broad class of bugles and horns, characterized by a substantial section of 'conical' bore near the blown end of the instrument.

In Chapter 2 we saw that an exactly conical tube has a set of natural mode frequencies forming a complete harmonic series. Some members of the brass instrument family approach this simple idealized case: the alphorn (Figure 5.1) and the bugle taper fairly steadily from the mouthpiece to the bell, and the tubes are not interrupted by side holes or valves. The resulting set of nearly harmonically related resonances exerts a strong influence on the lips of the player, guiding the lip vibration towards one of the natural mode frequencies.

It is possible for the player to resist the lure of the air column resonances, and to force the lips to vibrate at a frequency which is between two of the natural modes.

5.1 Traditional Swiss alphorn in 11-foot G

But apart from requiring a high degree of lip control, this exercise does not usually result in a note with a satisfactory timbre. The problem is that the vibration of
the lips generates a set of harmonics in the air flow at the mouthpiece of the
instrument; if the fundamental of this set is not in tune with an air column mode,
it is likely that few of the upper harmonics will coincide with tube resonances. In
contrast, when one of the natural notes of the instrument is being sounded, each
mouthpiece harmonic finds itself close to an air column resonance. The resulting
interaction between lips and air column is known as a cooperative regime of oscillation, giving a sound with a high degree of pitch stability and a rich timbre.

It is still possible to set up a cooperative regime of oscillation, even if the lip frequency is not close to one of the air column modes, provided that several of the
low harmonics introduced by the lip vibration find resonant amplification in the
air column. Such a note is called a 'privileged' note; it is usually much harder to
sound than a natural note, for which the fundamental of the lip excitation also
finds an amplifying air column mode.

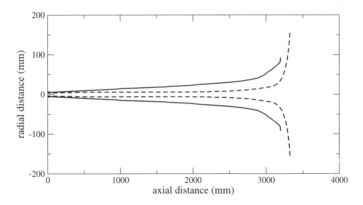

5.2 Comparison of bore profiles of alphorn in G (solid lines) and french horn in F (dashed lines)

In Figure 5.2 the bore of an alphorn in G is compared with that of a natural
(valveless) french horn in F. The instruments are approximately the same overall
length, although of course the french horn tube is normally coiled round several
times to make it easier to handle. Both instruments also start with an expanding,
approximately conical bore; the french horn at first expands more slowly than the
alphorn, but then starts to flare out rapidly, ending in a bell almost twice as wide
as that of the alphorn.

The effect of a flaring section on the air column resonances of a tube was discussed in Chapter 2. The rapidity of the flare and the diameter of the bell between
them determine the characteristic cut-off frequency of the instrument. Below the
cut-off frequency most of the sound energy is reflected back into the instrument,

giving strong air column modes. Above the cut-off, most of the sound energy is radiated out, and the internal resonances are much smaller.

Without the flare, the relatively narrow-bored tube of the french horn would end with an opening which would be too small to radiate efficiently. The carefully designed flare provides a much larger sound radiator; it also lowers the cut-off frequency while maintaining to a reasonable approximation the harmonic relationship between the modes.

The mouthpiece

In almost all brass instruments, the first part of the tube is a detachable segment known as the mouthpiece. It is possible for the player to sound the instrument without the mouthpiece by pressing the lips against the opening into which it normally fits. This exercise immediately reveals two of the important functions of the mouthpiece. Firstly, it is very uncomfortable to press the lips against the sharp rim of a narrow tube; the mouthpiece provides a smooth and normally rounded support for the lips. Secondly, it is much more difficult to achieve good intonation and tone quality without the mouthpiece.

The influence of the mouthpiece on tuning and timbre depends on its ability to alter both the pitches and the strengths of the air column resonances of the instrument. This ability in turn depends on the size and shape of the mouthpiece. The cross sections of some cornet and french horn mouthpieces can be compared in Figure 5.3(b, c, f, g). In each case the section next to the player's lips, known as the cup, is relatively wide; the tube then narrows down, reaching its minimum diameter at the throat; it then widens again in the section known as the backbore, so that at the point at which it opens into the main tube of the instrument the two diameters match.

Mouthpieces of cornets and bugles usually have a rounded cup with a pronounced throat, while those used with french horns have a smoother variation of profile. The two most important features of a mouthpiece are the volume of the cup and the diameter of the throat. The cup volume has a direct influence on the relative tuning of the natural modes of the instrument. Increasing the cup volume lowers the frequencies of the upper modes more than the lower modes; as a consequence, notes in the upper register of the instrument are flattened relative to those in the lower register. Correspondingly, reducing the volume of the mouthpiece cup preferentially sharpens the higher notes of the instrument.

For a given cup volume, the diameter and shape of the throat determine the Helmholtz resonance frequency of the mouthpiece. This parameter is a very important property of a mouthpiece, since resonances of the instrument's air column with frequencies close to the Helmholtz resonance are greatly strengthened by the addition of the mouthpiece.

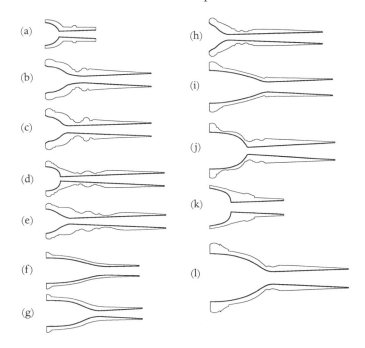

5.3 Some typical mouthpiece bore profiles. Left top to bottom: (a) cornett; (b) cornet, older pattern; (c) cornet, modern; (d) trumpet, older pattern; (e) trumpet, modern; (f) french horn, older pattern; (g) french horn, modern pattern; Right top to bottom: (h) bugle; (i) trombone, nineteenth-century French pattern; (j) trombone, modern; (k) serpent and (l) tuba

For the particular shape of mouthpiece used with the french horn, the boosting of the air column resonances occurs somewhat below the Helmholtz resonance of the mouthpiece. This strengthening of the low-frequency modes of the instrument is very important, because in a simple conical tube the lowest modes are naturally weak. Without the boost from the mouthpiece, the sound of the instrument would lack the rounded fullness contributed by the lower harmonics.

The hand in the bell

The player of a french horn normally has the right hand partially inserted into the bell of the instrument, with the fingers extended. This technique has the effect of raising the cut-off frequency, reducing the radiation of some of the higher frequencies and giving the sound a characteristically veiled quality. The higher cut-off also has the effect of providing a few more internal resonance peaks, which are valuable in securing the intonation of high notes.

The insertion of the hand in the bell also has the effect of lowering the frequencies of the natural modes of the air column in the horn. As a result, the pitch of each natural note is slightly lower than it would be if the hand were removed. By altering the angle and position of the hand the player can subtly control the intonation of the instrument.

When the hand is curved and the wrist pushed forward, the bell opening can be almost totally covered. A note produced with this technique is described as 'stopped'. There has been a long-standing debate as to whether the hand is effectively lengthening or shortening the air column when a stopped note is sounded. Recent acoustical experiments have shown unambiguously that, as the bell is progressively closed, the frequency of each natural mode goes steadily down—that is, the effective length of the air column is increased.

The confusion over the production of stopped notes on the horn has arisen because, when the bell of a horn in F has been almost completely closed, many of the modes have dropped in pitch until they are almost exactly a semitone above the next lowest mode of the open horn. Thus if the bell closure is accompanied by a slight increase in lip tension and breath pressure, the lip vibration will not follow the original mode downwards, but will jump to the next highest mode. The stopped note will therefore sound a semitone higher than the original unstopped note.

Side holes on bugles and horns

The natural notes of a bugle or a valveless horn are a close approximation to a harmonic series. A splendid repertoire of traditional alphorn music has developed using only the natural notes from the second harmonic to the sixteenth; we have seen how the player of the natural horn can supplement this rather meagre diet of notes by hand-stopping.

On woodwind instruments the repertoire of available notes is further extended by opening side holes in the tube. A thin-walled conical tube with a large open hole in the wall behaves to a first approximation as though the tube had been cut off at the opening. The shortened air column has a set of (almost) harmonic mode frequencies, similar to that of the complete air column but with a higher fundamental frequency. Six suitably spaced holes allow a diatonic scale to be played from the lowest natural note upwards.

The system of side holes has also been successfully used with conical bored members of the brass family. One instrument in particular—the cornett or cornetto—combined the flexibility of the lip reed with the dexterity of fingered side holes to become the most important virtuoso wind instrument of the early Baroque. In the first half of the nineteenth century the newly invented keyed bugle was an important member of many military and civilian bands.

To maintain the harmonic relationship between modes when a hole is opened, it is necessary that the diameter of the hole should not be much less than that of the tube at the position of the hole. An interesting illustration of what happens when this criterion is violated is provided by the serpent, a large-bore conical instrument invented at the end of the sixteenth century. The size of the basic six holes is limited by the fact that they must be covered by the fingers. The trouble is that the cut-off frequency for such a small hole in a large tube is low enough to fall among the first few modes, so that opening the hole has a different effect on each mode. Notes obtained with all holes closed are therefore much more stable than those requiring open holes. This problem was solved in the nineteenth-century ophicleide by increasing the hole diameter and using a system of keys and pads to effect closure.

Crooks and valves

The mainstream development of brasswind has bypassed the use of side holes to shorten the tube, evolving instead a variety of methods by which the basic tube length can be increased. The simplest method provides the player with a choice of crooks. These are alternative sections of tubing which can be inserted between the mouthpiece and the main tube of the instrument. A natural horn with some of its crooks is illustrated in Figure 5.4(b). When the F crook is employed, the overall tube length gives a set of natural notes close to harmonics of F; by changing to the longer D crook the player can obtain instead a set of harmonics of D.

5.4 (a) trompe de chasse in D (Le Brun, Paris, 1721); (b) horn fitted with D crook (Kretzschmann, Strasbourg, *c*.1830), with alternative crooks for B♭ alto and C basso and coupler for B♭ basso

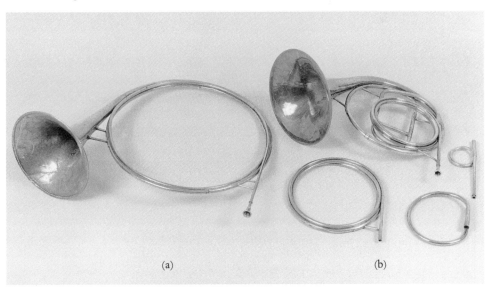

(a)   (b)

A completely chromatic compass requires twelve crooks, one for each semi-tone in the bottom octave of the instrument. In the higher registers the same note can be obtained using several different crooks: A₃, for example, can be played as the sixth harmonic of a horn in D or as the fifth harmonic of a horn in F.

The main problem with the crooking system is the time taken to remove one crook and replace it by another. Until the middle of the nineteenth century the standard orchestral horn was a natural instrument with crooks, of the type shown in Figure 5.4(b). If the music modulated so rapidly that there was insufficient time to change crooks, it was necessary to employ two players with instruments crooked in different keys. Composers had to exercise some ingenuity in working within this limitation: Figure 5.5 shows Beethoven finding notes for tonic and dominant seventh chords in D♭ major and B♭ minor from pairs of horns in F and E♭. The written F for the E♭ horn (sounding A♭) is the eleventh mode note, which would be too sharp if it were a true eleventh harmonic; the player is expected to flatten it by increasing the degree of hand coverage of the bell.

5.5 Excerpt from Beethoven's Overture to *Egmont*, from bar 269, illustrating the use of natural horns in keys remote from those in which they are crooked

The nineteenth century saw the development of valves, which allowed the almost instantaneous insertion of additional tubing into the horn. Early valved horns were supplied with two pistons, operated by the first and second fingers of the left hand. Depressing one piston added enough extra tubing to lower the pitch of each natural note by a semitone; depressing the other lowered each note by a tone. Later, a third valve lowering each note by a minor third was added, and this complement of three valves is now standard on most brass instruments.

Two types of valve are in common use in modern brass instruments. In both types, the diversion of the sound wave through an additional length of tubing is accomplished by the movement of a cylinder within the valve casing. In the piston valve the cylinder is displaced along its axis, while in the rotary valve it is rotated about its axis.

The three valves used separately are capable of chromatically filling all the gaps in the harmonic series down to the third harmonic except the (written) A♭s. On a french horn in F, for example, the basic tube length gives a harmonic series with fundamental F_1 and the fifth harmonic is A_3. Depressing the second-finger valve lowers all the pitches by a semitone, so that the fifth harmonic is now $A^\flat_3$. Depressing instead the first-finger valve lowers the fifth harmonic to G_3, while the third finger valve lowers it to $F^\sharp_3$. The next semitone down, F_3, can be obtained as the fourth harmonic of the basic tube with no valves depressed.

Proceeding further down the chromatic scale, however, we find that it is impossible to obtain $D^\flat_3$ (written $A^\flat_3$), which is four semitones below the fourth harmonic of the basic tube, using only one of the three valves. Simultaneously depressing the second- and third-finger valves, which separately lower the pitch by one and three semitones respectively, is the answer. Further combinations of valves bridge the gaps in the harmonic series down to the second harmonic, although the five semitones above the fundamental remain unplayable.

The obvious advantages of the valve system have not been achieved without some cost. Whenever a sound wave travelling down a tube meets a sudden change in the wall which confines it, part of the sound energy is reflected back up the tube. Many years of development went into refining the design of valves to minimize the disruption of the smooth tube bore, and on modern instruments this is not a serious problem. More intractable are the intonation difficulties caused by the use of valve combinations. Following the simple theory outlined in Chapter 2, we would expect a semitone valve to increase the length of an ideal conical instrument by just under 6 per cent. If the length of additional tubing is chosen to be 6 per cent of the basic tube length, however, it will obviously be less than 6 per cent of the longer tube produced by depressing one or both of the other two valves. We would therefore expect notes produced by valve combinations to be too sharp.

On valved bugles and horns this sharpening effect is indeed noticeable, and the tuning of the individual valve sections has to be adjusted to give the best compromise. The effect is, however, more complex than the straightforward calculation of percentages would suggest. The important factor which we have so far ignored is the disturbance of the conical bore introduced by the valve section. Since the additional tubing must start and finish with the same diameter, it is almost inevitably of cylindrical bore. The natural mode frequencies of a conical tube with a cylindrical part in the middle are no longer expected to be members of a harmonic series. When we consider a french horn, with its extensive flaring section, it is clear that the tuning of a particular note produced using a given valve combination is dependent on many factors. The art of the horn designer lies in balancing these factors to minimize the amount of humouring required from the player.

5.2 HISTORICAL DEVELOPMENT

The bugle and signalling horns

The use of animal horns and large sea shells to produce horn calls for signalling purposes has continued from prehistory to the present day. When blown with a lipped embouchure at a suitable opening cut at one end or into the side, a series of three or four pitches can be sounded, depending on the tube length and the skill of the players. The sounds produced are clearly recognizable and carry for considerable distances. Tests carried out for the British Royal Marine Artillery in 1854 on Woolwich Common found that copper bugles could be heard clearly two miles off.

Among the forms used in Europe have been the oliphant, made from an elephant's tusk, elaborately carved and recognized as a mark of status, the hunting horn, and the military bugle. Although such instruments may be regarded as signalling devices rather than as musical instruments, several have evolved into forms which are indubitably musical, and the signal calls have been used by composers and arrangers wishing to create military, hunting, or ceremonial allusions.

The common characteristic of horns of natural origin is an approximately conical-bore profile. When 'conical'-bore profile instruments are made of metal such as brass or copper, not only can they be made to any desired length, but portions of cylindrical or near-cylindrical tubing can be introduced. For the comfort of the player, a mouthpiece somewhat similar to that of a trumpet or a trombone (but with the cup usually more conical) is generally built in or provided as a detachable part of the instrument.

Conical metal horns have ranged in size from the English hunting horn, which is between 200 mm and 250 mm long and is not used for notes above its fundamental, through various sizes of coach horn, to the bugle, which is between 1,200 mm and 1,500 mm long, coiled once or twice, and sounds five notes. In the late eighteenth century, horn bands were formed in Russia using a complete spectrum of up to sixty such instruments, each tuned to a different single pitch, giving a chromatic compass of up to five octaves. Each horn had its player, who sounded his instrument when and for as long as the composer or arranger required his note.

The cornett

The idea of converting a signalling horn into a melodic musical instrument by introducing woodwind-type finger-holes can be dated back at least as far as the tenth century. To be successful, such an instrument requires a conical-bore profile, since the effect of the bell flare of a basically cylindrical-bore instrument is reduced when finger-holes are uncovered. The cone cannot be too wide, since too large a discrepancy between the bore diameter and the diameter of tone-holes easily covered by the fingertip would give an uneven tone quality.

The cornett was one of the most important melodic instruments of the Renaissance and Baroque periods, and its use continued into the eighteenth and even the early nineteenth centuries. It has six holes for the fingers and one for a thumb, with fingering similar to that of a recorder. It is played with a small cupped mouthpiece with a narrow rim, often likened to an acorn cup (Figure 5.3(a)). The most common (treble) size has as its lowest note with all finger-holes covered A_3, though a couple of semitones lower are possible with a slackened embouchure. Upwards from this a complete chromatic compass of well over two octaves is available. The instrument is normally gently curved (Figure 5.6(b)), ameliorating the wide stretch required of the fingers, although straight cornetts were also made and played. Quite often cornett players would choose to place the mouthpiece well to one side of the centre of the lips.

Cornetts were made in different sizes. With the rarer cornettino, pitched a fourth or less commonly a fifth above the treble cornett, there was no significant upper register that could not be obtained on the cornett, but the stretch of the fingers was less. The tenor and bass cornetts did not have the clear pungent voice of the treble, and their use was more infrequent.

The serpent, bass horn, and Russian bassoon

The serpent is often wrongly thought of as a bass cornett: it has the cornett's six finger-holes, but no thumb-hole, and the bore is much wider. There are surviving bass cornetts: the difference is marked. The sinuous shape of the serpent serves to bring the finger-holes within reach. It was nearly always made of wood (often wal-

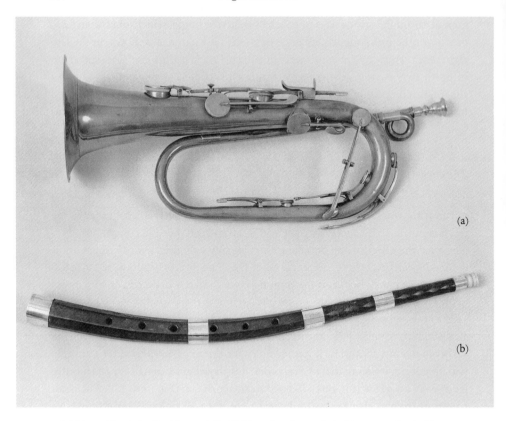

5.6 (a) keyed bugle in C with crook for B♭ (Pace, London *c.*1845); (b) cornett (probably seventeenth-century Italian)

nut) with leather binding; the crook was of brass and the mouthpiece of brass or ivory, rarely larger in volume than a euphonium mouthpiece, but with a cup shape approximating to a hemisphere (Figure 5.3(k)).

The inventor is invariably cited as Edmé Guillaume, a canon of Auxerre, France, and the date of invention 1590; research has not produced other contenders for this credit. Its role as a support for vocal music in churches continued through to the nineteenth century. Certainly the serpent was described by Mersenne (1636–7), at which time it was known only in France. James Talbot (1695) described the instrument in Britain, and by the mid-eighteenth century it was being used in march music in Germany.

The fact that the finger-holes are grouped in two sets of three to suit the human hand rather than spaced out along the tube as on a cornett, for instance, means that the fingering cannot define the pitch of the tone that is being played very precisely—the player has to pitch the notes by lip-power to a large extent. Often two

notes a semitone apart are fingered exactly the same way, and most notes can be 'bent' up or down by the player to a greater extent than on any other brass instrument. This lack of pitch centring is related to the fact that the hole diameters are small in comparison to the diameter of the main bore, as explained earlier in the chapter.

The serpent was most commonly built in 8-foot C. (For an explanation of the 'footage' notation as applied to brass instruments see Appendix 3.) The compass extends downwards only to C_2, but the serpent in a group of instruments can give the impression of an instrument an octave lower. It is not a loud instrument, but it can add a telling effect of depth. As with other brass instruments, there is no upper limit, but from C_4 to C_5 the tone loses character.

There are two basic ways of holding the serpent—the right hand can reach its three finger-holes from above or below, the latter giving reversed fingering compared with most woodwinds. The chromatic notes were originally obtained by half-holing, later by forked fingering. Towards the end of the eighteenth century three or more keys were sometimes added. In its most developed form, it had fourteen keys with all the holes covered and placed to best effect. This was not necessarily a better instrument for either player or listener, and the serpent finally yielded as a popular instrument to the ophicleide and the valved brass basses.

Several modified versions were made and favoured in different countries, generally easier to carry and of a narrower bore than the serpent. The 'bass horn' enjoyed a certain popularity in Britain alongside the serpent. It was invented in the 1790s by a French exile in London Louis Alexander Frichot and is of brass or copper in the form of a V with a large curving crook. The 'Serpent Forveille' with the body mostly of wood and a brass crook, was of comparable importance in France, as was the 'basson Russe' (neither Russian nor a bassoon) in which the crook and the bell fitted into a wooden butt section like that of a bassoon. The nomenclature is confused: a German 'Russisches Fagott' or 'chromatisches Basshorn' or an Italian 'cimbasso' might have designated any of these types. In general, these variants have three or four keys, retaining the six finger-holes in widely spaced groups of three, and the serpent's rather unfocused tone colour. They were usually pitched in C, and were not much made after 1835.

As a band instrument, the serpent was played more widely in its old age than in its youth. It was used considerably in France, Britain, Germany, and Italy. The most renowned solo player of the serpent, André, retired about 1840.

The trompe de chasse and orchestral horns

The french horn or modern orchestral horn is conventionally classed as one of the conical-bore profile brass instruments, though the modern instrument can have more cylindrical tubing than tapering. Even with the horns made at the time of the instrument's transition from the hunting field to the orchestra, many were made with successive lengths of cylindrical tubing, each section of wider bore than the previous, giving a terraced bore profile. How, then, do we define a horn—which are the features essential for an instrument that will sound to the listener and respond to the player like a horn?

The first requirement is a mouthpiece with a funnel-shaped cup of small diameter (Figure 5.3(d)) with the sides extending without interruption into the bore of the instrument, which is narrow at the mouthpipe end (the narrowest bore of any of the currently used brass instruments). This then increases gently through a combination of tapering and cylindrical sections (or a terraced profile bore) to a section where the expansion gets more and more pronounced, followed by a wide bell. The trompe de chasse (Figure 5.4(a)) is generally pitched in 14-foot D; hand-horns were regularly provided with crooks that allowed any pitch from 8-foot C or 9-foot B♭ down to 18-foot B♭; modern orchestral horns are basically in 9-foot B♭ with either 12-foot F or 6-foot F (or both) available by valve.

The natural horn, long used for hunting signals, found a distinctive role in orchestral and band music early in the eighteenth century. Players commanded a wide compass: in the higher part of the range, diatonic melodies were possible, but the lower part was limited to the notes of a bugle call. To enable the instrument to play in a variety of keys, changeable crooks of different length were supplied. The introduction of horn crooks has been credited to the maker Leichamschneider of Vienna around the year 1700. With one system of crooking, the 'master crook and coupler' type, a single tapering looped tube, the master crook, carried the mouthpiece at one end and fitted into one of a set of couplers at the other. The couplers were basically cylindrical-bore profile sections, used singly or in combination, that were interposed between the master crook and the body of the instrument. With the other system of crooking, terminal crooks, a distinct crook was provided for each desired pitch, each crook being capable of receiving the mouthpiece. Many instruments were equipped with a hybrid crooking system. Figure 5.4(b) shows a horn with three of its terminal crooks and one coupler.

'Hand-horn' is a term used to denote the playing technique explained in Section 5.1. A wider selection of notes could be played than was possible on the natural horn, forming the basis of the hand-horn tradition used during the period when the horn became popular as a solo instrument and entered the orchestra. It was found that with the overall bore profile described above, and for an instrument pitched not much above or below 12-foot F, the natural series of notes could be lowered by a semitone by partial occlusion of the bell, and by a whole tone with greater occlusion of the bell, as explained in 5.1 above. Thus a completely chromatic scale was available for much of the compass, though considerable skill was required to produce a consistent tone quality for open and stopped notes. The traditional layout of the tubing of the horn, with the axis of the bell approximately at right angles to the axis of the mouthpiece, helped to bring about this discovery: the hand-horn was then made with a more compact layout bringing the bell within easy reach of the hand.

With the natural horn and the early hand-horn, the whole instrument could be lowered slightly in pitch to bring it into tune with other instruments by inserting a small piece of tubing, a 'tuning bit', between the mouthpiece and the instrument or crook. From the mid-eighteenth century, it became more common to provide a 'tuning slide', with the tubing formed into two short parallel sections connected by a moving slide not far from the centre of the instrument. One version of the hand-horn, the 'Inventionshorn', dispensed with most or all of the crooks and was instead equipped with tuning slides of differing tube length. A further refinement, the 'Cor Solo', always had a fixed mouthpipe and was provided with tuning slides for the common keys for horn solos (G, F, E♭, and D). The advantage of these models was that by dispensing with crooks and couplers, the mouthpiece was more rigidly connected with the body of the instrument which was then always at the same distance from the player's lips.

Orchestral horns were most usually employed in pairs or, as orchestras grew, in fours. In the latter case, the first and third horns parts were generally higher than the second and fourth, and were often taken by players specializing in the higher part of the compass. Occasionally horns used by the players of the lower parts would be of wider bore. As with other orchestral wind instruments, distinct national styles evolved in the eighteenth century and lasted until the mid-twentieth century. The French and British preference was for a narrower-bore instrument with a lighter tone, full of character; 'Périnet' or piston valves were preferred. The 'Vienna horn' of the Austrian empire had a wider bore, especially in the final section of tubing before the bell, and the use of double piston valves persisted. The German horn had a wider bore than the French and rotary valves became standard: it is the German model which has evolved into the modern instrument.

The posthorn

Although little used today, the posthorn has an interesting history and is important as the forerunner of the most widely played brass instrument of all, the cornet.

The bore profile of the posthorn—and the cornet—is characterized by a narrower bore than the bugle; the second quarter of the tube length is of negligible taper or actually cylindrical. The profile is close to that of the french horn, but without the very narrow-bore at the mouthpipe and the wide bell. The tube length varies from the 'Posthorn Galop' novelty instrument in 2½-foot A♭ through the 5-foot A 'Posthorn Serenade' natural posthorn, down to 6-foot F or 6½-foot E♭ for the traditional coiled posthorn of continental Europe, the origin of the familiar symbol of postal services worldwide.

The mouthpiece cup shape of the posthorn is intermediate between the funnel of the french horn and the pronounced bowl of the trumpet, but usually closer to the former. The resulting tone quality, therefore, is bright yet warm; not as brilliant as that of the trumpet nor as mellow as that of the french horn.

The posthorn was limited to its natural series of notes but sometimes equipped with crooks for use in concerted music. Since it is shorter than the french horn, a player could not command much if any of the diatonic section of the natural series and the bell was too small for effective hand-stopping. It was, however, common in German-speaking countries to provide a single tone hole at about two-thirds of the tube length: it was placed so that the instrument could be held and the finger-hole controlled with a single hand (Figure 5.7(a)). With a posthorn in F,

5.7 (a) posthorn (Schürrlein, Nuremberg, late nineteenth century); (b) cornet (Courtois, Paris, *c.*1870). This illustration shows the coiled posthorn with a single finger-hole and the cornet in its mature state

such a tone-hole provided the notes lacking from the scale of B♭. Similarly, a posthorn in E♭ with a finger-hole would play melodies in the key of A♭.

Keyed bugles and the ophicleide

The keyed bugle was invented and patented in 1810 in Ireland by a militia band-master, Joseph Haliday (born in Baildon, Yorkshire in 1774) and gained immediate acceptance: it was a flexible and versatile instrument, the only soprano brass instrument of agility that was fully chromatic. Although the keyed trumpet was already in use in continental Europe, the keyed bugle appears to have been an independent (and an immediately successful) invention. The conical-bore and the large, well-spaced tone-holes (Figure 5.6(a)) proved satisfactory acoustically: the disparity in tone quality between notes with the keys closed and those with the keys open can be reduced with practice to be as negligible as on woodwind instruments. The most widely used size was the 4-foot C or 4½-foot B♭—in Britain bugles were generally built in C, frequently played with a short looped crook to give a B♭ instrument. The smaller E♭ bugle (similarly playable in D♭) was used less frequently in Britain than in the United States.

An early (perhaps the original) maker of the keyed bugle in Dublin was Matthew Pace: his move to London in 1816 no doubt furthered the popularity of the bugle in England. Although used alongside cornets, its popularity waned after 1840 and bugle tone colour was later supplied in bands by the flugelhorn.

The keyed bugle's popularity was matched—and outlived—by that of the ophicleide, invented by 1817 in Paris by the maker Halari and patented by him in 1821. After the Battle of Waterloo (the story goes), the English trumpet and keyed bugle virtuoso John Distin impressed Grand Duke Constantine of Russia at a military review in France, and was asked by the Duke for a copy of his keyed bugle. This was ordered from Halari, who went on to adapt the concept to a bass instrument. Actually, the ophicleide was conceived as the bass member of a family of three sizes. The 'quinticlave', lying in pitch between the ophicleide and the keyed bugle, had less success, and was replaced by valved instruments when that became possible. Halari deserves credit not only for developing the ophicleide (from the Greek *ophis* = serpent, *kleis* = cover or stopper) but also for producing it in a form which required little modification in its fifty or more years of popularity.

The distinguishing features of the ophicleide are its almost perfectly conical-bore and its relatively large tone-holes, all of which are covered by keys (Figure 5.8(a)). Most ophicleides have either nine or eleven keys—with the latter, each semitone in the lowest octave has its own key, but two fingers of the right hand have two keys to operate; with the nine-key instrument each finger (except the left-hand little finger) has one key to operate, but two notes in the lowest octave have to be produced by accurate lipping of the rather uncentred pitches produced

(a)   (b)

5.8 (a) (left): ophicleide in B♭ (France ? *c.*1860); (b) (right): tuba in F (Wolff, Oldenburg *c.*1900). Note the contrast in bore profiles

by forked fingerings. Ophicleides are pitched in 8-foot C or 9-foot B♭. The original idea was to use different crooks on one instrument in the manner of the B♭ crook for the C keyed bugle, but separate instruments were soon found to be preferable. Like serpents, but unlike later valved basses, ophicleides make regular use of all the fundamentals: their compass is three octaves and more from B_1 and A_1 respectively. The sound is firm and clear, with some of the mellowness of the euphonium and some of the reediness of the saxophone.

The invention of the valve and new instruments made possible

Through the eighteenth century and the early years of the nineteenth, both the trumpet and the horn were increasingly used in orchestral and band music. Despite the widespread use of hand-stopping in horn-playing and the rarer use of slide trumpets or keyed trumpets, composers and arrangers were very restricted in the kind of music they could write for brass instruments. Makers had to provide sets of crooks—up to four or five for the keys commonly used for trumpet music and ten or eleven for horns. Parts written for these instruments were closely related to the natural series of notes; if the music moved into a different key, time had to be allowed for the players to change crooks.

These limitations prompted the invention of the valve, which had the effect of an instantaneous change of crook. One of the first inventions (whose workings were not fully explained in contemporary writings) was by an Irishman, Charles Clagget, in 1788. The first successful valve was that of the musicians Heinrich Stölzel and Friedrich Blühmel in Prussia in 1814, though there may have been usable valves a little earlier. This pattern, latterly known as the Stölzel valve, was widely used in instruments made over the subsequent 100 years. Other designs followed; these achieved a similar effect by different mechanisms.

It was very soon realized that valves, when mechanically capable of being operated with sufficient speed, could be used not merely to change crook simply and rapidly, but also to play tunes and ensemble parts with great facility—more evenly and easily than by hand-stopping a horn and with greater rapidity than with the slide of a trombone or slide trumpet. From the 1820s on, valved horns and valved trumpets improved in the efficiency of their mechanisms and gained in popularity in bands and orchestras. Although there was continued resistance from traditionalists throughout the remainder of the century, by the early years of the twentieth century valved instruments were universally used both for the old hand-horn and natural trumpet repertoires and for the new repertoire for which valves were essential.

Not only did the invention of valves revolutionize horn and trumpet technique, but it also permitted the development of new kinds of brass instrument. The use of a slide in a trombone or in a trumpet necessitated a bore profile that included considerable lengths of cylindrical tubing. The use of finger-holes or keys for the cornett, serpent, keyed bugle, and ophicleide was most satisfactory for instruments with an almost purely conical-bore profile. The use of hand-stopping was only effective with instruments of the bore profile of the french horn—narrow at the mouthpipe, wide at the bell throat, and pitched not too far from 12-foot F. With valves, however, instrument makers had complete freedom to introduce instruments with any bore profile that resulted in an instrument that was acceptably in tune with itself.

Within a few years of the invention of the Stölzel valve, instruments in various sizes and shapes were being produced, particularly in Germany, with names such as 'bass Trompete' or 'chromatisches Basshorn' which do not correspond to present-day usage. They were, however, the forerunners of the cornet, the tuba, and all valved brasswind with bore profile intermediate between 'conical' and 'cylindrical', such as the saxhorns.

The cornet à pistons

It is not known who made the first cornet (it may well have been the Paris maker Halari) but it was invented *circa* 1825. It was a valved version of the posthorn. The cornet ('cornet à pistons' in France, 'cornopean' in Britain) was soon equipped with three valves (Figure 5.7(b)), which gave it a chromatic compass of over two octaves. The instrument was built in two basic sizes: the E♭ soprano which could be crooked into D, D♭, or C and the B♭ (the more common) which could be crooked into A, A♭, G, F, or low E♭. The cornet was played with a deep conical mouthpiece (Figure 5.3(b)) which, especially with the longer crooks, gave it a tone quality more akin to that of the french horn.

The cornet's success was immediate, especially in Britain and France: vast numbers were made in these countries or imported from Germany. It met the need for a melodic brass instrument capable of expressive playing which was robust, affordable, and not too difficult to learn. With the keyed bugle it was the main brass voice in the wind and brass bands which were becoming very popular in the mid-nineteenth century. The cornet has evolved to become more like the smaller valved trumpets—the mouthpiece now has a more pronounced cup (Figure 5.3(c)), and the crooks have been abandoned. To some extent this has been due to virtuoso players such as Jean Baptiste Arban, who emphasized the brilliance of the instrument at the expense of some of its characteristic sweetness.

Intermediate-bore instruments

Among the French derivatives of the German valved brass instruments of the 1820s were Guichard's 'valved ophicleide' (1832) and the 'Clavicor' (Figure 5.9(a)) patented in 1838. These were instruments of alto or tenor tessitura, more suited to marching bands than valved french horns which were just beginning to be used. The clavicor (or 'althorn') was latterly made in Britain also and was used by a significant number of bands in the 1840s and 1850s. Many other makers, including Sax, produced brass instruments of intermediate bore profile and played with a mouthpiece about halfway between the cup of the trumpet mouthpiece and the funnel of the horn mouthpiece.

Adolphe Sax, the Belgian-born inventor and maker of wind instruments, met

5.9 (a) clavicor in D (Jean, France, *c.*1840); (b) baritone in B♭ (Higham, Manchester, *c.*1890); (c) euphonium in B♭, compensating (Besson, London, *c.*1927). The wide bore of the bass saxhorn (euphonium) can be compared with the baritone saxhorn in the same key and with the fore-runner of the saxhorn (clavicor)

with considerable opposition from rival makers when he patented his 'saxhorns', and became embroiled in ruinous litigation in defending the patent. He can be given credit for producing well-made instruments with consistent fingerings and for a uniform notation system, but the members of the family were not new in themselves: instruments of comparable bore profile had been in use in Germany and elsewhere for several years. Excluding the extreme sizes, rarely used, the saxhorn family consisted of a soprano in 3-foot F or 3¼-foot E♭, a contralto in 4-foot C or 4½-foot B♭, a tenor in 6-foot F or 6½-foot E♭, a baritone in 8-foot C or 9-foot B♭, a bass in 8-foot C or 9-foot B♭, and contrabasses in 12-foot F or 13-foot E♭ (later also in 18-foot B♭). The bass (Figure 5.9(c)) was distinguished from the baritone (Figure 5.9(b)) by its larger bore. The tenor differed little from the instruments already known variously as clavicors or althorns, a source of confusion in nomenclature that has persisted to this day. The contralto was somewhere between the relatively narrow-bored cornet and the wider-bore valved bugle (flugelhorn).

Saxhorns were very rapidly adopted by the growing brass band movement in Britain as well as the military and other wind bands of France. The tenor horns and baritones of the present-day brass band are tenor and baritone saxhorns. The bass saxhorn was replaced by the virtually identical euphonium; the contrabasses became known as bombardons in bands and tubas in orchestras.

The tuba

Stölzel, extending the application of the valve from existing to completely new instruments, developed 12-foot F bass valve instruments from the 1820s. Parallel developments took place elsewhere: in Paris, for example the valved ophicleide. The name 'bombardon' was given in German-speaking countries to some of these early valved basses. In Berlin, the enterprising bandmaster Wilhelm Wieprecht had already introduced valved instruments into Prussian military bands when, in 1835 he developed a wider-bore bass in conjunction with the maker, Carl Wilhelm Moritz, with the name 'Baß-Tuba'. The wider bore was accompanied by a new design of piston-valve, now known as 'Berliner Pumpen'.

The term 'bass saxhorn' or 'Bb bass' gave way to the Austrian name, 'euphonium', for virtually the same instrument which had been developed by F. Sommer in 1843. This is probably because the role played by the instrument, like that of the ophicleide latterly, was not primarily to play the bass line in harmony but to provide an independent melodic line at tenor pitch. Like the ophicleide, the euphonium (Figure 5.9(c)) has a wide compass and is capable of virtuoso performance.

As an orchestral instrument, the bass tuba met the need for a deeper and fuller brass bass sound than that of the bass trombone, and was widely (and rapidly for such a conservative institution as the orchestra) adopted from the mid-1840s. Although the nature of the tuba's role was fairly clear cut, the size of instrument varied widely from one place to another. The original Wieprecht-Moritz Baß-tuba was pitched in 12-foot F and this was the pitch of many tubas in Germany (Figure 5.8b), Austria, and Britain. The tendency for bands to use instruments pitched in the 'flat' keys of Bb, Eb, Ab, and Db led to the use of the slightly larger Eb tuba; the desire for greater sonority led to the use of even larger instruments, and many tuba players have used tubas in low C or Bb, especially in America and Russia. In France, however, a small tuba in 8-foot C at euphonium pitch was for long the norm.

5.3 INSTRUMENTS IN MODERN USE

French horns and Wagner tubas

The modern orchestral horn is based on the German model as developed by Kruspe about 1898 and later made by Alexander of Mainz of such a quality that it

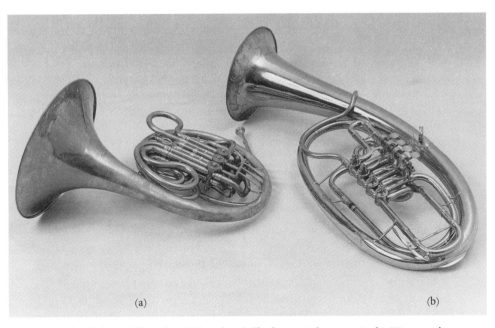

5.10 (a) french horn (Alexander, Mainz, first half of twentieth century); (b) Wagner tuba (Alexander, Mainz, 1935). The 'full double' horn in F + B♭ is shown together with the smaller of the two sizes of Wagner tuba (B♭)

was sought after by players worldwide (Figure 5.10(a)). This 'double horn' has a fixed mouthpiece leading to a valve operated by the left thumb; this valve selects one of two separate sets of tubing leading through the usual three rotary valves and back through the thumb valve to the bell. One set of tubing gives an instrument pitched in 12-foot F, the other gives 9-foot B♭. The valve rotors have two separate sets of windway passages, and each 'side' of the horn has its own tuning slides.

When the double horn was introduced, most players used a horn in 12-foot F, and may have used crooks for E♭ and D. The double horn would have given the opportunity of playing high passages with greater security by changing to the B♭ side. Modern practice, however, is to play most of the time with the horn in B♭, using the F side only for notes so low that it is unavoidable, or in passages where it simplifies the fingering. This trend to the use of smaller brass instruments to achieve greater reliability in pitching has continued, and some modern horns are built as double horns in 6-foot F and 9-foot B♭ or even triple horns in high F, B♭, and low F.

Some horns have a fifth valve. The most common function of this is to add enough tubing to compensate for the effect of hand-stopping: when the hand is pushed right into the bell, a characteristic menacing, nasal tone quality is produced, and the pitch appears to be raised (though see Section 5.1). The use of the fifth valve helps the player to play stopped passages without altering the usual fingering.

Wagner, to create a particular sound, specified a quartet of 'tubas'; today specially designed instruments known as 'Wagner tubas' are used, which take the mouthpiece of the horn, but have tubing of a wider bore towards the bell. The wide, upright bell precludes hand-stopping (Figure 5.10(b)). Wagner and other composers using these instruments call for two tenors in 9-foot B♭ and two basses in 12-foot F.

The cornet

Around the end of the nineteenth century, the cornet was widely used as an orchestral instrument, playing not only parts written for it by composers and arrangers, but also trumpet parts. To cope with these parts, players could manage with the instrument crooked into either B♭ or A, like clarinet players using instruments in B♭ and A for music in flat and sharp keys respectively. Far more cornets were in use in bands, but here music was no longer being written for cornets crooked in A♭ or lower keys—for the last century, all band parts have been for cornets in B♭. As a result, makers in the first half of the twentieth century supplied cornets in B♭ alone, or with shanks for B♭ and A. Sometimes the facility of changing between B♭ and A has been built in, either by an extra slide adding the length of tubing needed for a semitone transposition, or by an extra valve (usually rotary) called a 'quick-change' valve.

The cornet has now dispensed (quite recently) with terminal shanks and is currently made in two sizes, E♭ and B♭. Mouthpipes are fixed, except for some sopranos which have a sliding mouthpipe and restraining screw for tuning instead of a tuning slide. The mouthpiece has a more pronounced cup (Figure 5.3(c)) than the old cornet mouthpieces.

Saxhorns and other intermediate instruments

Of the family of narrower-bore saxhorns, only two remain in use: the 6¼-foot E♭ and the 9-foot B♭. The nomenclature is confused: as used in the British-style brass band, and following Sax, they are the 'tenor horn' and the 'baritone' respectively. In America and elsewhere they are 'althorn' and 'tenorhorn', which reflects better their role in band scoring. These instruments, rather bland in character, rarely feature as solo instruments. They are part of the traditional brass band instrumentation, and intermittent moves to replace them with french horns do not make much headway. In fact, their sober quality provides a very useful contrast in an all-brass group to the more colourful cornets, flugelhorn, and trombones.

The flugelhorn

The keyed bugle was more rapidly replaced by valved bugles in German-speaking countries than in Britain. The desire for an alternative tone colour at the pitch of the principal melody line led to the adoption of the 'flugelhorn' (the name prevalent in Austria), rather than the contralto saxhorn. It has had more importance in Austrian bands than British or French.

The flugelhorn has not enjoyed quite the popularity of the keyed bugle in its day. It is used singly in all-brass (British tradition) brass bands, and as an alternative instrument with a distinctive 'voice' of its own for trumpet players in jazz bands. There is also a very small orchestral repertoire requiring a flugelhorn.

Euphoniums and tubas

The euphonium (Figure 5.9(c)) proved such a valuable member of brass and wind bands that experimentation with its use as an orchestral instrument was inevitable. Compared with the bass tuba, however, the 'tenor tuba' has remained an orchestral rarity. When it does appear as an orchestral instrument, it is more usually played by a trombone player than a bass tuba player.

Orchestral bass tuba parts are played on perhaps a greater variety of instrument than any other orchestral part. In Britain today, the E♭ tuba is the most common, probably as a result of the high standards of manufacture of, and performance on, this instrument in British brass bands. Other instruments in regular use include the F, low C, and low B♭, but no longer with any pronounced geographical associations. Some players will use a 16-foot C tuba for the whole repertoire, others appear on the platform with more than one instrument in programmes with pieces of diverging tessitura. In order to cope with the international repertoire, F and E♭ tubas need to have four or five valves; the small French tubas in 8-foot C (now generally reserved for the highest lying parts) have six.

Revival of natural horns, cornetts, etc.

The movement to revive obsolete instruments such as the viol, the harpsichord, the recorder, and the cornett as more appropriate means of performing and bringing to life 'early music' gathered pace from the late nineteenth century onwards. By the 1960s, a number of makers were able to specialize in historical models, and brass instruments such as cornetts and natural horns were being offered.

There is obviously the opportunity for modern composers to write new music for these 'old' instruments. This has not happened to any great extent, despite skilled performers being available. The lower dynamic level of older instruments is, perhaps, one reason why they have not been much integrated with modern.

5.4 INSTRUMENT CONSTRUCTION

Materials

Bugles, horns, and other 'brass' instruments have been made from a variety of materials, most commonly from yellow brass, which is an alloy of 70 per cent copper, 30 per cent zinc with traces of lead and other elements. The material chosen has not only to produce a robust instrument which can make an attractive quality of sound for the listener and give a rewarding level of response to the player; it must also permit the manufacture of the instrument with economical workshop techniques.

Copper has been used, extensively so in Britain in the early nineteenth century, when it was regularly used with brass embellishments for natural and keyed bugles, though not for french horns or ophicleides. This tradition survives in the army regulation bugle, still made of copper.

Silver has been the choice for presentation and ceremonial instruments over the centuries. It is now economically feasible to use silver for the bell sections of orchestral instruments: some makers have offered this choice, but there is no clear musical advantage and it remains a rarity.

Other alloys have been tried. 'German silver' ('white bronze', 'Neusilber', or 'maillechort') is an alloy of copper, nickel, and zinc developed in the nineteenth century and has been widely used for whole instruments. It is now generally used for the 'garnishings' (embellishments) such as ferrules, mouthpipe sheaths, and garlands on instruments of brass. The formula for brass can, of course, be varied. An alloy of 80 per cent or more of copper with zinc ('gold brass') is today frequently used for orchestral instruments.

Where wood is used for the instruments considered in this chapter—for instruments or sections of instruments with finger-holes—the materials and techniques are to a large extent those of woodwind instrument manufacture. Modern materials have very little application. Fibreglass is used for the larger sections of some sousaphones to reduce the weight for marching band players; some cheaper serpents are also made in fibreglass.

The literature of wind instruments is littered with conflicting statements about the relative importance of the choice of material. In general, writers approaching the subject from an acoustical standpoint have minimized—or completely denied—the influence of material; practical musicians have emphasized its importance and have been prepared to pay makers substantial premiums for instruments of 'superior' materials. An objective examination shows that the vibration of the walls of a wind instrument has usually no measurable effect on the spectrum of the sound heard by a listener, the shape of the bore profile of the instrument and the oral cavities of the player being the predominant factors determining tone quality. In practice, concert audiences have listened to orchestras which have changed from wooden to metal flutes, or from yellow to gold brass french horn bells, without being aware of any difference. The styles of different players are quite apparent, and discriminating listeners will have noticed wide-bore trombones replacing narrow and German bassoons replacing French. The professional player, however, spends a working lifetime practising, performing, and teaching, and develops not only an acute ear but also a very physical sensitivity to instruments. All instruments have some notes which are more difficult than others for the player to produce, or to control the intonation and tone quality. It is in these finest aspects of the response of the instrument to the player, rather than in readily audible or measurable effects, that the choice of material becomes significant. The audiences benefit from listening to more confident players.

The wall thickness of a brass instrument is similarly not of critical importance, and is only a factor of significance to the more discriminating player. In general terms, it is the shape of the bore profile which determines whether a particular instrument is a flugelhorn, a french horn, or a saxhorn, and how readily it can be played in tune. There are, of course, other practical considerations: if the tubing is too thick, the instrument is unnecessarily heavy, while if it is too thin, the instrument is vulnerable to damage.

The shape and the final wall thickness of the sections of tubing which make up a brass instrument are traditionally produced by beating sheet brass over a shaped anvil or mandrel. The act of beating affects the crystalline structure of the metal, producing a state known as work-hardening. In the course of manufacture, each workpiece requires frequent annealing (heating and gradual cooling) to relieve stress in the metal and restore workability. Finished instruments often deliberately contain work-hardened sections, which are believed to add brilliance to the tone quality.

Work-hardened areas in a finished instrument make the brass vulnerable in the long term to 'stress corrosion cracking'. Surface contamination, some brass polishes, and atmospheric impurities act as catalysts for inter-granular corrosion, where the brass 'pulls itself apart' with disastrous results. The granular structure of brass is too fine to be seen by the naked eye, but stress-corrosion cracks can be clearly visible. In extreme cases (usually in thinly beaten sections of tube) whole coin-sized areas of brass fall out. A related problem, more common with factory-made instruments than hand-made, is brass dezincification. Internal moisture and external handling leach out the zinc, leaving patches of weak, porous copper. In both cases, the phenomenon spreads through the wall of the tubing.

Sections of tubing are joined by brazing with spelter (a brass alloy of slightly lower melting-point than the workpiece) and borax flux, by hard or silver soldering (requiring a moderate temperature), or by soft or tin soldering at a lower temperature. In general, seams running along the tubing are brazed; joints between one section of tubing and the next are soldered and protected by ferrules. Inevitably, the joints made later in the assembly process have to be done at a lower temperature to preserve joints previously made.

Shaping a tube

The tubing of all brass instruments has been traditionally made by cutting sheet brass to a template or pattern, shaping the pieces over first an anvil, then over a mandrel of hard steel, beating by hammer until the edges meet. A maker's collection of templates and mandrels, the physical embodiment of his instrument designs, is one of his most precious assets. The bell flare is produced by splaying with a pegging hammer on a shaped wooden block. In the case of widely flaring bells such as those of french horns and tubas, one or more inserted segments or gussets are needed to complete the bell. The work-hardening produced by this hammering has to be relieved by annealing: this is repeated many times between each successive stage of manufacture.

The joint in each section of tubing is seamed: on gently expanding sections, the workpiece is held in place with wire. On flared sections, one edge is tapered; the opposing edge is cut at intervals to form teeth, which are hammered over to grip the tapered edge. The traces of these teeth can be seen on close examination of bells of unplated instruments. The joints are then brazed, and pickled in dilute sulphuric acid to remove remnants of borax flux. Some makers prefer not to dip in a chemical bath and instead carefully scrape off any residues. The seamed joints are then planished: hammered on a 'stake' or anvil until they are beaten to a uniform thickness.

Gently expanding sections are then placed over a mandrel and forcibly drawn through a perforated lead plate, starting with the narrow end. This 'swaging' ensures that the sections conform exactly to the shapes of the mandrels and have smooth surfaces.

The bell flare is put over its mandrel on a lathe and burnished, smoothing it to a uniform thickness. The flare is worked while being turned ('spun') to conform to the shape of the mandrel and the end cut to size, turned over, and a wire inserted. The wire is soft-soldered in. Some bell flares are now in fact spun from flat sheet and brazed to the bell stem ('cross-seam welded') rather than being gusseted and seamed. Next the tubing is bent to the curves required in the instrument. The interior of each section is lined with a protective coating or 'whitening' and filled with lead. Very large parts are filled with a lighter low-melting-point alloy, pitch, or resin. Some makers actually use weak soap solution, which is then deep frozen: the part is worked while filled with ice. A stout bar is set into the filler to facilitate handling. When filled, each section is gripped at one end, bent to shape with the

bar around pegs in the workbench or around a form. Any wrinkles on the insides of the bends are smoothed out by hammering. Narrower parts are reduced to size by forcibly pulling through successively smaller holes in a perforated steel plate when filled with lead or on a mandrel. Filled sections are usually externally cleaned and polished before being emptied by gentle heating.

When brass instruments are factory-made, some of the traditional hand methods described above are replaced by mechanized processes. Small tubular sections can be formed from sheet metal by 'deep drawing' in presses. The sheet is forced between one pair of steel dies to the shape of a saucer. Further pairs of dies press the workpiece via a cup shape into an exactly formed section of seamless tube, which has to be cut to length at both ends. As with hand methods, workpieces have to be annealed after each stage. The bell flares of some smaller instruments are made by drawing; these are then cross-seam welded to the bell stem.

Brass tubing can, of course, be purchased ready-made in standard sizes. Sections of standard tube, or deep-drawn pieces are, in some larger factories, placed between pairs of steel dies and expanded by hydraulic pressure to the exact size and shape required.

The cost of setting up and making the dies for these mechanized processes is considerable, but they do enable large numbers of identical instruments to be produced economically. It is maintained that the quality of the product, given a good original design, can be as high as that produced by craft techniques, and some of the finest modern instruments are indeed produced by such methods. Others maintain that the fine control over wall thickness exercised in hand-beating is not matched by mechanical means, and that this justifies the labour and cost for professional-quality instruments.

Mechanisms

The production of valves requires great precision. The small connecting pieces ('knuckles') which lead from valve casings to the main tubing or to the tuning slides are produced by one of the methods described above. The valve cases themselves are turned and machined to size, then drilled to take the knuckles. The whole assembly of casings, connections, and knuckles is wired together and hard soldered at one time.

The rotors of rotary valves can be cut from a solid piece of brass or bronze, but piston valves must be as light as possible for speed and ease of playing, and so require a hollow construction. The body of the piston is produced, often by deep drawing, and drilled. The internal passages or 'coquilles' are bent pieces of tubing which are inserted through the drilled holes and silver-soldered to the piston. The protruding parts are then removed, and the pistons fitted by successively reaming the case, grinding the piston, and lapping. The rotors on some of the more expensive models of rotary valve instruments are in fact of hollow construction and are made comparably.

To prevent the piston rotating in use, a lug or 'key' projects from the piston body. It runs in a slot or 'keyway' cut in the inside wall of the case. The springs for piston valves are more usually mounted above the piston body ('top-sprung') in valves for small instruments, and placed beneath the pistons in valves for large instruments. In nearly all piston valves, compression springs are used.

In rotary valve instruments, the operating mechanism is all outside the valve case. Formerly, the springs were spiral leaves of steel wound inside drums ('clock-springs') but helical wire springs are now standard.

Keys for bugles and ophicleides do not differ from those for woodwind such as saxophones, though leaf springs are more common on such period instruments than helical or needle springs.

Assembly, finishing, and the mouthpiece

Parts are cleaned before the instrument is assembled. Small pressed parts have to be de-burred manually or in a vibrating bath. An instrument is assembled starting with the bell (or next largest section) and working through to the mouthpipe. Straight sections ('branches'), U-bends ('bows') and other shaped sections of tubing are joined by soldering and the joints protected by sleeves ('ferrules'). The valve tuning slides are soldered to the knuckles on the valve assembly. Stays are fixed between the branches and the valve tuning slides for rigidity. On larger instruments, vulnerable external curves are given a protective sheath or 'bow guard'. Particularly in German-speaking countries, a ring of sheet metal called a 'garland' is applied to the outside of the widest portion of the bell; it is secured at the rim and hammered down over most of its area.

The instrument is finished off with emery cloth, buffing, and hand polishing (traditionally with oil and rottenstone powder). Any inscriptions or decoration are engraved, and it is checked for leaks and intonation.

After polishing to produce a clean and attractive surface, all but the cheapest instruments are given some form of external protection. Electroplating, regularly offered by makers of brass instruments since the 1870s, gives a handsome, easily cleaned surface. The thickness of metal added has negligible effect on the performance characteristics. Usually silver is chosen, although silver-plating is expensive, even now. Nickel, chromium, or gold-plating have occasionally been used. Spraying with tinted or clear lacquer became popular in the twentieth century, giving virtually maintenance-free surfaces. Although cheaper than plating, lacquer is less durable, and deteriorates after a few years.

The mouthpiece supplied with an instrument may be made by the same maker, or by a specialist. For any given instrument, different players will prefer a variety of mouthpieces; few advanced players will use the mouthpiece originally supplied with an instrument. There is now a degree of standardization in the taper of the mouthpiece shank and receiver: products of different makers can usually, but not always, be interchanged. Precision in mouthpiece making is as important as it is in making violin bows or bassoon crooks—the part nearest and most directly under the control of the player is the most critical in the whole instrument.

In the past, mouthpieces have been made from various materials—brass, silver, ivory, perspex, etc. Before the advent of electroplating, the best brass mouthpieces had a silver sheet applied to the rim, since naked brass can upset lip tissue. Now nearly all mouthpieces are silver- or gold-plated.

5.5 PERFORMANCE PRACTICE

Ceremonial and signalling instruments

The technique of playing the natural bugle consists of elements common to all types of brass instrument. Only five notes are regularly used on the bugle, however, though more can be obtained with increasing difficulty.

The player determines the pitch of the note sounded by controlling the tension of the lip muscles, which is increased for higher notes, and by directing the stream of air through the lips: straight through the mouthpiece for low notes, downwards into the mouthpiece cup for higher notes. Pressing the mouthpiece hard against the lips can temporarily help produce higher notes, but teachers of all brass instruments warn that this reduces blood supply to the lips and causes rapid fatigue.

The volume of tone produced depends on the flow rate of air through the instrument, and is controlled by the player's lungs. The quality of tone, discussed below, also affects the perceived volume.

A note can be initiated simply by blowing: the muscle just below the lungs is tightened to give a sharp puff of air, as in blowing out a candle. The exact moment that the instrument sounds is difficult to control, however, and for all practical purposes brass players superimpose a stroke of the tongue on the puff from the lungs. A variety of 'tonguings' are used, depending on circumstance and on style. They are conventionally indicated in instruction books by consonants: 'du, tu, ku, gu' etc. If one note follows another without a break ('slurring'), it may require a different tonguing from the first note ('lu' or 'ru'), or none at all. Notes are terminated when desired by simply ceasing to blow, or by the action of the tongue preparing to play the next note.

Tone quality is not thought of as being a critical factor in bugle-playing, perhaps, though in practice the audibility of an instrument over a distance is dependent on the frequency spectrum of the sound produced. The player's control of tone is a matter of great skill, and depends in a subtle way on many factors, principally the shape of the air column inside the player: the mouth, larynx, trachea, and lungs. Teachers exhort pupils to adopt an upright body posture, relax the muscles of the throat, and to think in terms of producing tone by 'diaphragm support'. It is in this area that instrumental playing has most in common with singing.

Bugles in different countries are made to play at different pitches: B♭ in Britain, C in many European countries, low F in the United States (though the American bugle is not a simple conical instrument, being more like a trumpet). Early bugle horns were commonly in 3¼-foot D. The notation is transposed so that the player always reads the notes in Figure 5.11(a) although the sounds produced are actually those in Figure 5.11(b). Transposition, which we have already met in connection with the clarinet and other woodwind instruments, is a convention used in writing parts for most brass instruments.

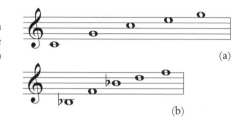

5.11 The notes of a bugle in B♭: (a) as written using the normal transposition and (b) as they sound

The repertoire for bugle necessarily includes terse motifs of three or four bars for calls such as 'Charge', 'Alarm', 'Half-left', or 'Commence firing'. Others, such as 'Reveille' and 'Tattoo' (the 'Last Post') are more extended.

Natural and hand-horn technique

The earliest horns used as signalling instruments in hunting were small instruments, the calls probably restricted to rhythmic patterns on a single tone. However, by 1680, in France and elsewhere, larger 'trompes de chasse' were capable of a more elaborate signals, and several codes were drawn up, the most important by the Marquis de Dampierre in 1723.

Horns were occasionally introduced into orchestral music from 1700 or so, initially as special effects and later for their intrinsic musical value. If not played by hunt servants, they were played by trumpeters, who used their clarino technique (see Section 6.5) to take the horn (usually in 14-foot D) up to its 16th or even 24th harmonic.

In the era of hand-horn playing (1750 to 1850), the horn became a virtuoso solo instrument, and at the same time an indispensable orchestral and wind band instrument. The principles of hand technique were codified, if not invented, by

Anton Joseph Hampel *circa* 1760. The instrument was no longer played with the bell pointing upwards or sideways in the air, but held down at the player's side with the hand kept in the bell of the instrument the whole time, serving to refine the bright sound of the natural horn. As described in Section 5.1, the back of the hand (usually the right hand) is placed against the far wall of the bell with the thumb pointing into the instrument, opposing the fingers. If the hand is flexed so that the ball of the palm comes towards the near wall of the bell, the pitched is lowered by a semitone. Further flexing lowers the pitch by two semitones. With skill, the tone quality of the stopped notes is compatible with the open notes, and a complete chromatic compass is possible in the middle and upper registers.

Hand-horn players were divided by aptitude into two classes: first-horn ('cor alto') players who specialized in the range C_4 to C_6 (written) and second-horn ('cor basse') players who specialized in the range G_2 to G_5. The latter were in no way inferior or less skilled: many soloists including virtuosi such as Punto were cor basse players. If music called for four horns, the third would be a cor alto player and the fourth a cor basse. Later, some soloists tended to occupy the middle ground as 'cor mixte' players.

The hand-horn technique was effective with the whole range of crooks from B♭ basso (18-foot tube length) to B♭ alto (9-foot) or C alto (8-foot). These crooks give a corresponding range of tone colour from dark and rich up to bright and brassy. The most popular crooks for soloists were F, E, E♭, and D.

When valves were first added to the horn, they were seen in France as a rapid and convenient means of changing crook. Two valves were sufficient and full hand-horn technique was used. Notable proponents of the early valved horn were Meifred, Kail, and E.-C. and J.-R. Lewy. From the 1840s, three-valved horns became more common, and the repertoire began to demand a fully chromatic valve technique, like that of the cornet. Schumann and Wagner wrote significant parts for 'pumpenhorn'. The role of the hand in the bell diminished, but to the present day the hand continues to give the player subtle control of tone and intonation.

Parts written for horns with crooks were always transposed (except treble-clef parts for horn in 8-foot C or bass clef parts for horn in 16-foot C). The crook to be used was stated at the beginning of a piece, and any changes in the course of the music indicated in advance. Thus, all horn parts were based on the written notes in Figure 5.12 with intermediate pitches obtained by hand-stopping or valves. If the horn was crooked into B♭ alto, the treble-clef notes sounded a tone lower than written; with the F crook they sounded a perfect fifth lower, and similarly for the other crooks. The bass-clef notes, however, were transposed an octave lower, so that with the F crook they sounded a perfect fourth higher than written. Since a hand-horn would most commonly be crooked in the same key as the music, written parts would then be 'in C'. Later, when valved horns were no longer necessar-

5.12 The notes of the natural horn as written, up to the 16th harmonic, showing how the higher notes are close enough for the gaps to be filled by hand-stopping

ily crooked in the same key as the music, horn parts often continued to be devoid of any key signatures and players became adept at reading parts with each note being given an accidental as required.

French horn technique

The English-language term 'french' here is a survival from the late seventeenth century, when the horn was a novelty introduced to England from France. It is not usually used in orchestral circles, where 'horn' is unambiguous, but serves in the wider world to distinguish the concert instrument (played with the right hand in the bell and the left on the valves) from saxhorns, flugelhorns, and others.

In orchestral music, the role of the horn developed from picturesque 'hunting' fanfares to become integral to the full orchestral sound, emphasizing the harmonic structure. This function continued alongside the truly melodic capabilities of the hand-horn and valved horn. The military and other wind bands, which became widely cultivated in the late eighteenth century, regularly included horns; the much larger nineteenth-century wind bands continued, readily using valved instruments when they became available. Present-day military and 'concert' bands now call on the full range of orchestral horn technique. As a soloist's instrument, the horn fell in importance from the mid-nineteenth century to the mid-twentieth, when Dennis Brain re-established its solo status.

Later nineteenth-century horn parts, such as those in the music of Richard Strauss, fully stretched technique and stamina. This led to the use the four-valve double horn, which allowed taxing high passages to be played on a horn in high B♭ while retaining the horn in F for passages where tone quality was important.

Modern horn technique continues many of the traditions of the hand-horn era. Parts are now written for horn in F, though usually without the anomalous octave discrepancy in the bass clef, and often without key signatures. Players use instruments in F, B♭, high F, or occasionally high B♭ as they think fit, and mentally transpose as necessary.

Additional effects employed in the Romantic era include stopped notes with the hand nearly closing the bell (see Section 5.1) notated '+', playing in a loud, blaring manner ('cuivré or 'schmetternd'), trills, glissandi, and double or triple tonguing.

Until the mid- to late-twentieth century, one could hear quite noticeable region-
al characteristics of instrument design and playing styles. German instruments
had a wider bore and a broad sound, whereas the French preferred a narrow-bore
and a more highly coloured tone. The stress of playing the traditional Viennese
horn, in F with a wide bell mouth and a much-admired rich tone quality, was reck-
oned to reduce a professional performer's active life by ten years. The Russian
sound was characterized by a pronounced vibrato. British style, intermediate
between French and German, followed more the former until the Second World
War and changed to the latter after. This was most distinctly indicated when in
1951 Dennis Brain changed from the French F model to a F + Bb Alexander.

Brass and wind band instruments

In general, playing valved horns such as the cornet, the flugelhorn, the saxhorns,
and the tuba is more straightforward than playing the french horn. There is no
hand-in-bell technique, and the range of most of the music is between the 2nd and
8th natural notes. The player of any one instrument will usually read music using
a single conventional transposition (in many types of band, treble clef is used with
the 2nd harmonic of the open tube written C_4). Figure 5.13 shows the fingerings
for a three-valve instrument in C or a transposing instrument such as a cornet,
flugelhorn, or saxhorn. The fingering for other valved instruments normally follows a similar pattern. A typical British brass band score is illustrated in Figure 5.14.

On the other hand, considerable dexterity in valve technique is frequently
called for. Cornet players in brass bands cope with minimally simplified violin
parts in transcriptions of orchestral music and with very demanding original compositions. Rapid passages are sometimes double- or triple-tongued, a technique
involving the repeated alternation of the tongue striking the front and back of the
palate. A further technique, called for on occasion for all orchestral and band
brass, is 'flutter-tonguing', in which notes are played while the tongue vibrates as
in a rolled 'r'.

Many band players have to play 'on the march'. Simultaneously marching in the
right direction at the right speed, holding the instrument in playing position and

5.13 The fingering for a three-valve instrument either an instrument in C or a transposing
instrument such as a cornet, flugelhorn, or saxhorn. o indicates no valves operated. Some alternative fingerings are shown; 3 is always an alternative to 12

5.14 Excerpt from *Journey into Freedom* (Eric Ball, 1967) showing transposition of instruments in Britis brass band scoring—only the bass trombone and timpani are written at concert pitch. In this example th melody is played by four 'solo' cornets and tenor trombone, the counter-melody is played by flugel horr 2nd E♭ tenor horn, 1st B♭ baritone and euphonium, the other instruments play chordal accompaniment (Copyright 1967 by Boosey & Hawkes Music Publishers Ltd)

reading from a march card precariously mounted on the instrument in a 'lyre', the bandsman then has to exercise adequate control of breathing and embouchure to produce stirring music.

The orchestral bass tuba player is not as frequently called upon to play solo passages as the other wind instruments, but may have to cope with very deep parts such as occur in Russian music (written for tuba in low C or B♭) and equally with high parts such as those written for the French tuba in high C.

The tuba player has less direct control over intonation than does the player of a smaller instrument—'lipping' up or down by altering the configuration and tension of the lips and the mouth and throat cavities has relatively less effect. For this reason, many tubas (especially in Britain) are fitted with compensating valves, which provide the player with a close approximation to the correct tube length for all fingerings. Other tubas are equipped with five or six valves, such as the six-valve Vienna model: these give the player many alternative fingerings and allow adjustment of each of the valve tuning slides to give a satisfactory tube length for all notes. Some tubas, including most rotary valve models, are arranged so that the main tuning slide can be adjusted while playing by the left hand, the right being given four valves to finger.

Mutes

This topic will be dealt with more fully in Chapter 6, since both the variety and the importance of mutes are greater for trumpets and trombones than they are for bugles and horns.

Mutes for french horns were known in the eighteenth century, and 'con sordini' indications were given in some of Beethoven's and Weber's horn parts. Quite what was intended is unclear, since hand-horn technique is required to play these parts, and this is precluded by the insertion of a common mute into the bell. It was only with valved horns that it became possible to play a muted french horn with fluency. Even so, timbre modification was easier and more controllable with hand-stopping than by muting, and the effect on pitch of any one mute will be different for different crookings of the horn. French horn mutes currently in use are usually 'straight' mutes, used when the part indicates 'con sordino', and 'stopping' mutes, which can be used instead of hand stopping when 'gestopft' is indicated. These raise the pitch by one semitone on a horn in F, and well over one semitone on horns in B♭ and descant horns in high F. Horns are often equipped with a valve to correct the effect of muting on pitch and to allow the player the use of normal fingering in muted passages.

Mutes (usually straight) are frequently used for cornets in brass band compositions, and more rarely for the other brass band instruments. The use of a straight mute in the orchestral tuba produces a dry, empty tone of little attraction, but is required by twentieth-century composers when the tuba has to play with other muted brass.

Avant-garde techniques

For a long time, playing chords on a single horn was regarded as a freak effect, but producing 'multiphonics' is now the staple of avant-garde brass technique. One standard method of playing a multiphonic is to sing at the same time as a producing a lipped sound on the instrument. If the two pitches produced lie close together, beats can be heard. If the pitches are more widely spaced—perhaps by a third or a fourth—the resultant difference tone gives the impression of a bass note and the effect of a chord. Clearly, there are different possibilities for men and women.

Avant-garde music for brass instruments exploits all conceivable elaborations of this technique, including the addition of consonants and other body sounds.

Further techniques also applicable to horns will be mentioned in the next chapter.

6

Trumpets and Trombones

6.1 ACOUSTICAL PRINCIPLES

Basic acoustics

Trumpets and trombones are lip-reed aerophones, like the horns and bugles discussed in the preceding chapter. It has already been noted that brass instruments have been designed with almost every conceivable type of tube, and it is difficult to draw clear boundaries between different sub-groups. Nevertheless, trumpets and trombones share the important characteristic that half or more of the basic tube length is of approximately cylindrical bore (Figure 6.1). This predominance of tubing with little or no expansion has important consequences for the musical performance of the instruments.

The natural notes of a trumpet or trombone are close to being a complete harmonic series. Indeed, the entire repertoire of fanfares for natural trumpets is built on the use of the notes of the harmonic series. The association between trumpets and harmonics is so close that the Renaissance stringed instrument using only harmonics was called the tromba marina, or trumpet marine.

It can therefore come as a surprise to realize that if the whole length of the trumpet were of cylindrical bore a complete harmonic series would be unobtain-

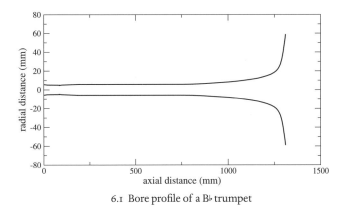

6.1 Bore profile of a B♭ trumpet

able. Since the lips provide an effective closure of one end of the tube, a cylindrical trumpet would, like a clarinet, have mode frequencies corresponding to only the odd-numbered harmonics. In Chapter 2 it was pointed out that the flaring section behaves acoustically as though it were shorter at low frequencies than at high frequencies. Adding the flaring section therefore lowers the pitch of the low modes less than it does the high modes; by a careful design of flare, the mode frequencies are brought close to a complete harmonic series.

A practical experiment with a trombone can illustrate the role of the flare in converting the odd-members-only harmonic series of a cylindrical tube into the all-members harmonic series of the complete instrument. A tenor trombone is usually packed in its case in three sections: the mouthpiece, the slide section, and the flaring section. The slide section includes most of the cylindrical tubing in the instrument. Applying the lips to the entrance of this section alone (where the mouthpiece normally fits), a skilled brass player can sound around eight of the natural notes. With the slide in its closed (i.e unextended) position, the natural notes obtained are approximately those shown as black notes in Figure 6.2. As we would expect, they are close to an odd-members-only harmonic series, in this case with a fundamental pitch of A_1.

Adding the mouthpiece to the slide section lowers each natural note by about a semitone, with the flattening effect growing as the mode number increases. The natural notes are further lowered by the addition of the flaring section; the set of natural notes of the complete instrument is shown by the white notes in Figure 6.2.

6.2 The white notes give the pitches of the first ten natural notes of a B♭ trombone. The black notes give the pitches of the corresponding natural notes obtained from the slide section only

The interval between each pair of black and white notes in Figure 6.2 shows (to the nearest semitone) the drop in pitch when the flaring section and mouthpiece are added to the slide section. The drop is greater for high-numbered modes than it is for the lower modes: the second mode falls by a little under six semitones, whereas the eighth mode falls by more than nine. As a consequence, the white notes from the second upwards are very close to being members of a complete harmonic series with fundamental $B^\flat_1$.

Pedal notes

What about the first natural mode of the complete trombone? We have shown its pitch ($E^\flat_1$) in brackets in Figure 6.2 because it is difficult to determine by playing the instrument. It can, however, be measured using acoustical test equipment. It is seven semitones too flat to be the fundamental of the $B^\flat_1$ harmonic series. The problem is inherent in the relative proportions of cylindrical and flaring sections: the cylindrical portion of the tube tends to give intervals which are too wide, and the flaring section does not occupy a sufficient fraction of the total length to completely override this tendency.

Nevertheless, a note of pitch $B^\flat_1$ can be played on the tenor trombone. This is called a pedal note. In order to understand what is going on when a pedal note is being sounded, we must recall that if the player's lips are vibrating with frequency 58 hertz (corresponding to the pitch $B^\flat_1$), the airflow in the mouthpiece will contain components at all the harmonic multiples of this frequency. The second, third, fourth, and higher components of the mouthpiece airflow will all find near-

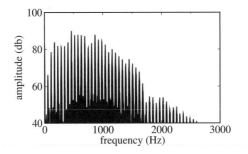

6.3 Frequency spectrum of the pedal note $B^\flat_1$ played on a B♭ tenor trombone

by air column resonances, and this is sufficient for a cooperative regime of oscillation to develop. The fundamental component, with pitch $B^\flat_1$, remains relatively undeveloped, since there is no air column resonance close enough to be useful. The absence of a fundamental resonance makes the pedal note an example of the class of 'privileged notes' described in Section 5.1.

In the light of this discussion, we can understand why a pedal note has a particular spectral character, with a weak fundamental and strong upper harmonics (Figure 6.3). Pedal notes are occasionally called for on the trombone, either for their special timbre or to supply an otherwise unavailable note. On the trumpet they are more difficult to play in tune, and are not normally used.

Cut-off frequency

As with the bugles and horns, the acoustical behaviour of the trumpets and trombones depends to a considerable extent on the parameter known as the 'cut-off frequency'. When a sound wave whose frequency lies below this limit travels from the mouthpiece end and approaches the bell, a large fraction of its sound

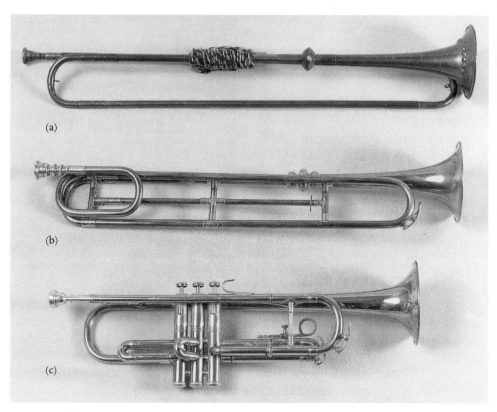

6.4 (a) natural trumpet in D (Huschauer, Vienna, 1794); (b) slide trumpet with D crook (Higham, Manchester, c.1865); (c) Valved trumpet in B♭ (Vega, USA, modern)

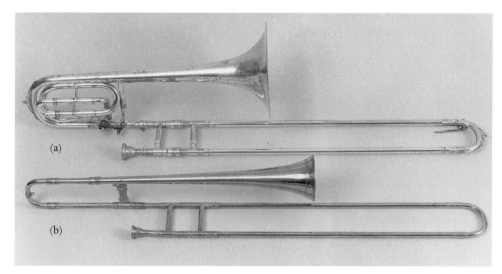

6.5 (a) B♭ + F trombone (Germany, modern); (b) tenor trombone (sackbut) in B♭ (Anton Schnitzer, Nuremberg, 1594)

energy is reflected back towards the mouthpiece, and a strong internal standing wave is set up. If the frequency is above the cut-off, most of the sound energy passes on out of the bell, and the internal standing wave is much weaker.

The cut-off frequency is determined by the shape of the flaring section and the diameter of the bell. On a modern B♭ trumpet, the cut-off frequency is typically around 1,500 hertz; on the modern tenor trombone it is around 700 hertz. In each case this corresponds roughly to the frequency of the sixteenth mode. Some virtuoso players of the trumpet and trombone venture higher than the sixteenth natural note, but in this region there are no significant air column resonances to assist the vibration of the lips.

In the Baroque era, trumpets and trombones were made with a different type of flare, terminating in a much smaller bell than that typical of a modern instrument (see Figures 6.4 and 6.5). Instruments of the Baroque pattern are once again being manufactured and played, and it is interesting to compare the acoustical properties of the two designs. The cut-off frequency of the Baroque instrument is usually higher, which means that a few more air column modes are strong enough to join in supporting and guiding the lip vibrations. This helps to make high notes more secure and easily sounded. On the other hand, the fact that more high-frequency sound is trapped within the instrument obviously implies that less is radiated, and the Baroque instrument lacks some of the brassy brilliance of the modern equivalent.

Mouthpieces on trumpets and trombones

A trumpet mouthpiece performs broadly the same function as a horn mouthpiece in acting as a support against which the player's lips can be pressed. It also serves the important acoustical purpose of strengthening some of the natural modes of the trumpet's air column. In Chapter 5 we saw that on the horn, with its long initial section of conical tubing, the lowest modes were weak, and the horn mouthpiece was adapted to strengthen these low modes. In contrast, the first few modes of the trumpet are normally strong enough to need little assistance. A typical trumpet mouthpiece (Figure 5.3(e)) is designed to boost the fifth, sixth and seventh modes, whose frequencies are close to its own Helmholtz resonance frequency of around 700 Hz. The spectrum of a trumpet sound thus usually contains powerful components in this frequency range.

Similar considerations apply to the trombone mouthpiece. A tenor trombone in B♭ has a set of natural notes an octave below that of a B♭ trumpet; we might therefore expect the trombone mouthpiece to have a Helmholtz resonance frequency half that of the trumpet, at about 350 Hz. In fact, a typical tenor trombone mouthpiece (Figure 5.3(j)) has a Helmholtz resonance at around 500 Hz. The design of the mouthpiece is such, however, that the boosting effect occurs a little below the resonance frequency, and it is again normally the fifth, sixth, and seventh modes which benefit.

The strengthening of modes around the sixth has an important effect on the timbre of the trumpet and trombone. The characteristic firm, rounded sound of these instruments in the middle of their range arises from the power of the lower harmonics. On a tenor trombone, for example, the sixth mode has a pitch of F_4. When the note $B^\flat_2$ is played, its third harmonic coincides with the sixth mode; when the note F_3 is played, it is the second harmonic which is strengthened by the sixth mode.

Crooks, valves, and slides

The system of interchangeable crooks, which was described in Chapter 5 in connection with the natural horn, was also used with trumpets and trombones as early as the sixteenth century. Although Stölzel's valve system was introduced on the horn in 1814, valved trumpets using essentially the same mechanism were not being manufactured and played until the early 1820s.

The slide system found on the modern trombone, on the other hand, is by its nature confined to instruments with a large proportion of cylindrical bore. (With some trombones, the two legs of the slide are of slightly differing diameters, but this has little effect on the sound produced.) Trombones with workable slides were developed in the fifteenth century, and the system has not changed significantly since that time. The essential idea is that of a telescopic crook, which can be lengthened or shortened while the instrument is being played.

The 'double slide' principle is illustrated in Figure 6.6. When the slide is extended by a distance L the total tube length is increased by $2L$. The greatest virtue of the system is that the tube length can be changed continuously, rather than in the discrete steps provided by valves, allowing the player to make subtle adjustments of intonation. Seven 'positions' of the slide provide the starting points for such

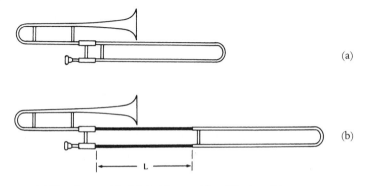

(a)

(b)

6.6 Trombone with slide in (a) 1st position; (b) 7th position adjustments. In the first, or closed, position the slide is unextended. A B♭ tenor trombone in first position has a total air column length (from mouthpiece to bell) of about 275 cm, and its natural notes correspond to harmonics of B♭$_2$. Extending the slide by approximately 8 cm puts the instrument into second position. Since each leg of the slide is 8 cm longer, the overall air column length is increased by 16 cm, which is enough to lower each natural note by a semitone. Moving the slide from first to second position is therefore equivalent to pressing down the semitone valve in a valved instrument.

Extending the slide step by step through the remaining positions lowers the set of natural notes by successive semitones. Since each semitone step reduces the frequency of a particular natural note by about 6 per cent, we might expect it to increase the length of the air column by the same percentage. This expectation is largely fulfilled, although the tuning of the lower natural notes is affected by the fact that, when the slide is fully extended, the proportion of cylindrical to flaring tubing is much greater than on the unextended instrument.

If the change in length between adjacent positions is a constant percentage, the actual distance between positions must increase as the slide is moved out. A slide movement of 8 cm suffices to go from first to second position, but to go from sixth to seventh requires a movement of more than 11 cm. We came across the same effect in the discussion of valve combinations in Chapter 5. On a valve trombone both these semitone steps would be provided by depressing the same valve, so that the fact that two different additional lengths are required poses a problem. With a slide, it is merely necessary for the player to learn the correct positions.

The problem of valve combinations is in fact less serious for trumpets and valve trombones than it is for the bugles and horns. This is because the proportion of cylindrical to flaring tubing, already large in trumpets and trombones, is considerably increased when valves are used in combination. This increase has the effect of flattening the pitches of the lower natural notes of the extended air column, partially compensating for the sharpening effect of the combination. The flattening is only significant in the bottom register of the instrument, but higher notes can usually be played without employing the more damaging valve combinations.

6.2 HISTORICAL DEVELOPMENT

The natural trumpet

As we have seen above, the natural trumpet is not a simple instrument. Any tube approximating to a cone is likely to be able to produce a series of notes bearing a usable semblance to the harmonic series, and primitive signalling instruments have generally been such cones, perhaps in the form of animal horns. An instrument with a sizeable proportion of its tube length a cylinder, however, requires an appropriate mouthpiece and a carefully proportioned expanding bell section in order to be able to produce a series of notes tolerably conforming to the harmonic series. Such trumpets seem to have been developed in the late Middle Ages.

Natural trumpets (as in Figure 6.4(a)) can have as small a tube length as 4-foot C (some cavalry trumpets) or as long as 9-foot B♭; common keys for the Baroque trumpet were 6¼-foot E♭, 7-foot D, and 8-foot C. The archetypal mouthpiece cup shape is a hemisphere, with an abrupt angle between the cup and the backbore (Figure 5.3(d)), though modern trumpet mouthpieces have a gentler shape with rounded edges (Figure 5.3(e)).

The sound of the natural trumpet is arresting and brilliant, though the Baroque trumpet is not as forceful as the modern instrument and balances well with stringed instruments and the woodwind of the period.

There is reliable evidence of the use of trumpets to sound music based on the notes of the harmonic series in the fifteenth century. Before this, trumpet-like instruments sounded signalling calls probably based on one or two pitches, not necessarily a true interval. The instrument's commanding presence led to its association with pageantry, ceremony, and the nobility. For centuries (up to the early nineteenth in some places) its use was restricted by law and codified by the guild system. The trumpet's role in royal, civic, military, and judicial ceremony is a tradition that continues. Its military use is associated with the cavalry, for which codes of signals have been devised comparable to the standard bugle calls of the infantry.

As a musical instrument, the trumpet has frequently been used in operas and other works to evoke pageantry and ceremony. Its use as a solo instrument and as a voice in polyphonic compositions relied on the use of the upper, or 'clarino', register—that part of the harmonic series which comes close to a diatonic scale. With the mouthpiece of the time, fine control of intonation could be exercised by the lips, though even for a good player the use of the clarino register was difficult and tiring. The best-known clarino trumpet parts are those in the music of Bach and Handel. From the mid-eighteenth century into the Classical period, the structure of music came to rely more on harmony, and the lower and middle register of the trumpet was used to fill out the harmonies and accentuate cadences.

The slide trumpet

The slide trumpet of the Renaissance had a single slide: the mouthpiece was attached to a straight tube which could slide inside one of the 'yards' forming the body of the instrument. In performance, of course, the mouthpiece was held against the lips and the main body of the instrument was moved as necessary.

Such a slide could lower any of the notes of the series sounded by the instrument by one, two, or three semitones only. This was enough to extend the diatonic compass of the instrument down to written A_3, and allow a complete chromatic scale from A_4 upwards. The degree to which slide trumpets were used is uncertain. No early slide trumpets have survived, but numerous pictures show trumpets being played with one hand holding the mouthpiece to the lips—a posture only really necessary for the slide trumpet.

The 'flat trumpet' of the time of Purcell seems to have been a revival of the slide trumpet. The last flourish of the slide trumpet was in English orchestral music of the nineteenth century, especially in oratorio. The instrument in this case had a double slide (Figure 6.4(b)). Unlike the trombone, the slide was on a proximal rather than a distal bow, and drew towards the player—or rather, past the player's left ear. This model, hardly known on the continent, retained the F, E♭, D, or C tuning of the natural trumpet and the true trumpet tone quality, and was only replaced in England (by the low F valve trumpet) at the very end of the century.

The sackbut and trombone

The Renaissance slide trumpet, described above, had one main design fault: the moving part of the instrument was heavy, the stationary part light. This was overcome by the double slide of the trombone (Figure 6.5), which had the added advantage that a given lowering of pitch could be achieved with half the distance of slide movement compared with a single slide instrument. In nearly all trombones, in fact, the length of cylindrical tubing is such a large proportion of the whole that the slide will accommodate seven positions, i.e. the pitch of any note playable with the slide in can be lowered by up to six semitones. This allows a continuous chromatic compass of over two octaves (on a B♭ tenor trombone, from E_2 to $B^{\flat}_4$ or higher, the upper limit depending on the skill of the player).

Trombones have been made in many sizes: those in 6-foot F or 6½-foot E♭ are termed altos, those in 8-foot C or 9-foot B♭ are termed tenors, and those in 11-foot G, 12-foot F, or 13-foot E♭, basses. The trombone mouthpiece has exhibited a great variety of cup shape: some early instruments appear to have had hemispherical mouthpiece cups with a sharp angle at the opening to the backbore, rather like large versions of contemporary trumpet mouthpieces; many French narrow-bore trombones in the late nineteenth and early twentieth century had funnel-shaped cups like large versions of horn mouthpieces (Figure 5.3(i)). Today an intermediate shape is used (Figure 5.3(j)), and one suspects that this shape has been used in one place or another for a long time.

Given the variety of mouthpiece models used for both trumpets and trombones, it is hard to lay down acoustic criteria for distinguishing an F trumpet from an F alto trombone, or a B♭ bass trumpet from a B♭ tenor trombone. One would have to point to very fine differences in bore profile, bore size, and mouthpiece cup shape. Nevertheless, the difference is usually apparent to the player and, with conventional performance techniques, to the listener also.

The trombone had been developed by the early fifteenth century. Its concept was so simple, and its early form so satisfactory, that its development has been in matters of detail such as bore size and the interior profile of the mouthpiece. The tuning slide was added in the nineteenth century: even as late at 1889, some cheaper models lacked this useful feature. Although the tenor size (in the nineteenth century often pitched in C but now generally in B♭) has been the most widely used, the classic complement was a set of alto, tenor, and bass—either disposed in F, C, and G or in E♭, B♭, and F or a mixture of these.

The trombone had virtually disappeared in Britain for most of the eighteenth century, but in the first quarter of the nineteenth century it returned to fashion as an instrument popular in bands and used orchestrally. The name 'sackbut' or a variant was used in Britain before its disappearance; the instrument returned with its Italian name. Today players use the word sackbut to refer to an early instrument (characterized by a small bell diameter as in Figure 6.5(b)), or a reconstruction used for playing early music.

The trombone has been played frequently with a very forceful style which gave it associations only now being thrown off, but no doubt appealing to many bandsmen and bandmasters. Through the nineteenth century there was a trend to use 9-foot B♭ instruments for alto and bass parts as well as tenor, the latter requiring a trombone with a valve. The alto, capable of less volume than the tenor and bass, and not as full in tone as valved horns, was less popular in bands, and appears to have been used only orchestrally after the 1860s. The bass in G, more manageable than the F bass (but with the outer slide still controlled by means of a handle), had a particular appeal in Britain, however; they were as numerous in early bands as tenor trombones and became the standard bass trombone in the orchestra as well as brass and military bands until the mid-twentieth century.

The keyed trumpet

As we saw in Chapter 5, towards the end of the eighteenth century players of the french horn learnt to fill in many of the gaps between the notes of the natural series of the instrument by opening and closing the fist inside the bell. This added considerably to the versatility of the instrument. It was at this time that the slide trumpet began to take on a new lease of life in Britain. On the continent, some trumpets were made coiled, or in a curved shape known as the 'demi-lune' model, bringing the bell within reach of the hand for stopping. It is difficult to gauge the success of this measure: the stopped notes must have had a muted quality in some degree, but quite a number of demi-lune trumpets were made.

A more radical approach to the problem was to introduce tone holes covered by keys, something after the manner of a woodwind instrument. The keyed trumpet appears to have originated in the second half of the eighteenth century, and to have been developed by Weidinger of Vienna (for whom Haydn wrote his Trumpet Concerto) *circa* 1795. As with the stopped trumpet, there is an inescapable discrepancy in tone quality between notes of the natural series of the trumpet with all tone holes covered and the intermediate notes obtained with the keys, but with practice this can be minimized, especially in the upper register. A considerable number of keyed trumpets were made, mostly with four or five keys. Many were pitched in 5½-foot G, a popular key for trumpets at that time, and equipped with crooks for F, E♭, D, etc. This however gave rise to a serious problem: the relative position of the tone holes along the tube length depended on the length of tubing added by the crook, and the fingering of the keys therefore varied depending on the crook being used. For these reasons, the keyed trumpet never replaced the natural trumpet, and gave way before very long to the valved trumpet.

Valve trumpets and trombones

We saw in the previous chapter how valves were first applied to the horn and the trumpet. For orchestral use, trumpets continued to be made with five or so crooks in addition to valves. Most of the early valve trumpets were in F. This is the instrument written for by Wagner, Bruckner, Sibelius, and Elgar. Once the valve trumpet was accepted, however, players found that they could obtain nearly the whole compass of trumpets in F, E♭, D, and C using a much smaller instrument, such as a valve trumpet in 4½-foot B♭ (Figure 6.4(c)). Using a smaller instrument increases the gap between the notes of the natural series at any given pitch, and as a result any passage (and especially high passages) can be played with reduced risk of sounding wrong notes. This gain in security outweighed the loss of the superior tone quality of the low F trumpet—an imponderable consideration—and the sacrifice of notes below E_3. From Richard Strauss onwards, composers and arrangers wrote with the expectation that trumpet parts would be played on a high B♭ trumpet.

This smaller instrument is much closer to a cornet than is a larger trumpet. In fact, in many places orchestral trumpet parts were regularly played on cornets in the late nineteenth and early twentieth centuries: Sullivan was merely being realistic in scoring for cornets rather than trumpets in the Savoy operas. The distinction was not lost, however, and from the 1920s onwards the B♭ trumpet (at one time with a quick-change valve to put the instrument in A) has been the instrument most frequently used to play parts scored for any contemporary or historical trumpet. Players simply learnt to transpose at sight parts for trumpets in F, E♭, D, C, etc.

Soon after valves were invented, they were applied to the trombone. They add to the facility with which trills and certain passages can be played, but this gain has not generally been held to outweigh the loss of the superior tonal qualities of the slide trombone. Nevertheless, the valve trombone has continued to exist in the shadow of the slide, being used in cramped theatre pits, for cavalry bands, and as a doubling instrument for trumpet players.

6.3 INSTRUMENTS IN MODERN USE

Trumpets of different sizes

We have seen that the adoption of valved trumpets led to the widespread use by the middle of the twentieth century of the small B♭ trumpet (Figure 6.4(c)) for playing both the older natural trumpet repertoire and contemporary music. This was the trumpet of the dance band era; it is also the instrument taught in schools today. Orchestral players have continued the trend to smaller instruments, and many Baroque and Classical parts are played on instruments of half the tube length of the trumpets they were written for. Instruments which can be played in either E♭ or D are very common, those in C are widely used, those in G or F less so. For playing the high parts of the clarino repertoire, a piccolo trumpet in 2¼-foot B♭ (generally with four valves) is used. At the same time, these small trumpets have attracted a repertoire of parts written specially for them.

The universal familiarity with recorded music has increased audiences' expectations of accuracy in performance. Professional brass players have had to put a greater premium on accuracy than on tone quality to secure their livelihoods, though the degree of sacrifice of quality that results from the use of small trumpets is a subjective matter. Another factor which has influenced the modern design of brass instruments has been the economic necessity for symphony orchestras to fill larger concert halls. This, coupled with a preference for greater volume in performance, has led to the use of instruments with considerably wider bore.

Apart from piccolo trumpets, the modern trumpet has three valves, lowering the notes of the main series by two, one, and three semitones respectively, as in other valved brass instruments. To enable the player to correct the intonation, especially when two or three valves are used in combination, the first and third valve tuning slides move freely, and are controlled by levers, or 'triggers', sprung to return to closed position. Usually the valves are operated by the first, second, and third fingers of the right hand, the triggers by the left hand.

The majority of trumpets have Périnet valves, but makers in German-speaking countries offer rotary-valved instruments for orchestral use. Since rotary-valved trumpets need both hands to play, they are less convenient for the manipulation of mutes; also, they cannot produce a glissando with the valve half-depressed. For these reasons, in countries where rotary valves are commonly used, trumpets with Périnet valves are also made as 'jazz trumpets'.

The trombones

The principal trombone has always been the tenor. Smaller instruments are light in tone and the slide positions, separated by smaller distances, are more difficult to judge. Larger instruments are more cumbersome: the slides are heavier and require a handle to reach the further positions. Execution is further slowed down by the longer distances between positions. The tendency throughout the nineteenth century was to replace the family of alto, tenor, and bass with three instruments of B♭ tenor pitch.

In France, and from the mid-nineteenth century Britain also, the favoured instrument was a narrow-bore model with a bright tone, tending to become strident if played too loudly. In Germany and Austria a wider bore was preferred, giving a sonorous tone quality in forte but tending to lack character in piano. It is this wide-bore instrument which is now universally used. In Britain it was adopted in the dance bands in the 1930s, the orchestras in the 1950s and brass and wind bands in the 1960s and 1970s. The change in the case of orchestras has been reinforced by the need to perform to large audiences in large halls, and the musical fashion of orchestral performances reaching massive volumes of sound at climaxes.

The design of the tenor trombone has been refined, particularly by American makers. The instrument has an even gradation of tone throughout the compass and throughout the dynamic range. The slide movement has been made remarkably free of friction, and the weight of the outer slide is now almost negligible.

The alto trombone disappeared from bands in Britain in the third quarter of the nineteenth century as the overall dynamic level increased. It has never completely disappeared from orchestral use: the staple part of the repertoire has been the music of the Classical and early Romantic periods, and parts written for the alto trombone by Beethoven, Schubert, Schumann, and Mendelssohn are taxing to play on the tenor. The orchestral alto trombone, in E♭, is now generally a wide-bore instrument to balance the rest of the brass section. For the repertoire from the mid-nineteenth century on, however, the standard complement in orchestras and bands has been two tenors and one bass trombone.

The bass trombone has changed radically. Following the invention of the valve, a single valve was added to the tenor trombone in Germany to extend the compass downwards and to increase flexibility by offering many more alternative slide positions for most notes—this was called the 'Tenorbass Posaune' because it allowed a single instrument to play the parts of both tenor and bass instruments

(Figure 6.5(a)). This is the instrument that was written for by Wagner in his later works, Richard Strauss, and subsequent German composers, replacing the F bass trombone and often the basic tenor also. The valve lowers the pitch of the instrument's natural series by a fourth, giving a trombone in B♭ and F. When built with a wide bore, this instrument is now called simply a 'bass trombone'. Frequently there are two valves, giving an uninterrupted chromatic compass down to F_1 or lower, depending on the skill of the player.

In France, the use of a bass trombone of any kind was largely discontinued, and much of the orchestral repertoire is for three tenors. In Britain, the bass in G (surviving from a period when altos were frequently in F, and tenors in C) was universally used until the mid twentieth century—it is the instrument written for by Elgar and Vaughan Williams. After briefly blossoming into a form with a single valve (G and D) it too was replaced by the wide-bore B♭ and F, orchestrally in the 1950s and a few years later in bands.

The contrabass trombone in C or B♭ (16-foot or 18-foot tube length respectively) is scored for occasionally, and versions with a double slide or with valves have been used. A B♭ and F bass trombone with the second valve can manage the compass of the true contrabass, and is sometimes used.

All the trombones in fact exist in valved versions: the small sizes rarely, the large more frequently. Many of the scores of Italian operas (such as those by Verdi) were written with the facility offered by valves in mind. The tone quality is not acceptable for orchestral purposes, but the instrument survives in bands in many places.

Revival of natural trumpets and sackbuts

The movement to revive obsolete instruments such as the viol, the harpsichord, the recorder, and the cornett, as more appropriate means of performing and bringing to life 'early music', gathered pace from the late nineteenth century onwards. By the 1960s, a number of makers were able to specialize in historical models, and brass instruments such as natural trumpets and early trombones were being offered. The trumpets, although resembling surviving Baroque and earlier models, were in fact often equipped with vent-holes, normally covered by the fingertips of the right hand. Opening the appropriate vent-hole stabilizes and helps tune one or more of the natural notes and inhibits some of the other natural notes, assisting accuracy in the high part of the compass where the difference in terms of lip tension between adjacent notes of the series is very small.

Today, instruments more closely following historical models are available: slide and keyed trumpets are being reproduced as well as natural instruments. Early models of trombone are also made: altos, tenors in B♭ and basses in F or E♭.

Degrees of authenticity vary: some reproductions are made with approximately the right proportions but with present-day techniques, others are made using historical metal-working tools and practices, with tubing made from sheet brass, bell pipes thinly beaten, and joints waxed rather than soldered.

6.4 INSTRUMENT CONSTRUCTION

Slides

The construction of trumpets and trombones employs the same techniques as that of bugles and horns, described in Section 5.4. The requirements for trombone slides, however, introduce new factors. The outer slide must be as light as possible and must move as freely as possible over the inner slide, yet the area of contact must remain airtight. The design of trombones has improved considerably in meeting these requirements. Since the middle of the nineteenth century, only a short section at the foot of the inner slides (the 'stocking') approaches the internal diameter of the outer slide: the upper part is slightly narrower in external diameter. This reduces the sliding contact area and allows a tighter fit.

Friction is lower between dissimilar metals. Early in the twentieth century, phosphor bronze was used for at least the stockings of the inner slides of better-quality instruments. It is standard practice today for the whole inner slide to be chromium-plated. (Phosphor bronze was also used instead of the usual copper-plate for the sliding surface of some valve pistons; these too are now usually chromium-plated.) More recently, it has become possible to make the whole outer slide of thinner, lighter material. This has made practicable the very wide bore trombones in use today.

Historical techniques for sackbuts and trumpets

Accompanying the increased use in the performance of 'early music' of historically appropriate models of instrument has been an interest in the revival of historical technology to produce these instruments. This is particularly apparent in the case of trumpets and trombones.

The early forms of these instruments not only had a narrower bore and reduced bell flare compared with the modern, but there seems to have been an emphasis on a loose, unsoldered construction. The straight sections ('yards') of trumpets were not soldered in position, but were separated with a wooden block and wrapped round with cord or spaced by an ornamental ball or 'pommel'. The bow furthest from the player was loosely fastened to the bell with a wire ring. Similarly, sackbuts were constructed with the parallel sections not connected with soldered stays but kept correctly spaced by loose stays with hinged clasps which lightly gripped the tube. It is thought that, originally, the joints between the straight sections and the bows were made airtight by wax rather than solder. To what extent this loose construction was intended to favour tone production is not known—it may have been to facilitate dismantling for storage and transport.

It also appears that the bells, although carrying substantial and heavily embellished garlands, were carefully beaten out and consequently thinned because large areas of sheet brass were not available or, later, to improve the response of the instrument. Makers often burnished bells and cylindrical sections by firmly drawing polished steel rods over the workpiece on its mandrel.

6.5 PERFORMANCE PRACTICE

Ceremonial and signalling instruments

The techniques of trumpet playing are basically the same as for bugle- and horn-playing. Exactly the same control of lips, diaphragm, and tongue is required. The traditional ceremonial natural trumpet is in D, cavalry trumpets and 'Fanfaren' are in E♭, and other trumpets are in F, G, or B♭. These are all written for as transposing instruments: thus the normal range of notes used as in Figure 6.7(a) will sound a tone higher on the D trumpet or a minor third higher on the E♭.

Many ceremonial trumpeters now play valved instruments, with the technique of orchestral trumpets described below. All, however, share one requirement: a nerve of steel to come in hitting the true note with complete confidence after any required period of silence.

Clarino trumpet technique

On a 7-foot D trumpet, a skilled performer can sound notes up to the 24th harmonic, as in Figure 6.7(b). Clearly, from the 8th harmonic upwards, it is possible to

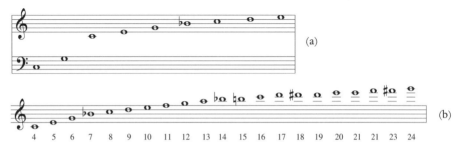

6.7 The notes of the natural trumpet as written: (a) up to the 10th harmonic, as used in signalling and ceremonial trumpet calls and (b) the clarino register up to the 24th harmonic

play diatonic melodies. This is the 'clarino' register of the trumpet, brilliantly exploited in the Baroque era. In a true harmonic series, the 7th, 11th, 13th, 14th, 21st, 22nd, 23rd harmonics are out of tune (more or less so depending on the temperament). The best Nuremberg trumpet makers of the eighteenth century did, however, manage to make instruments with usable 11th or 13th harmonics. The mouthpiece of the period, with a sharp edge between the cup and the bore, and the overall lower dynamic level of the Baroque trumpet facilitated control of these notes.

Orchestral trumpet parts rarely went above the 16th natural note (C_6) and the highest note in Bach's trumpet parts is E_6: the G_6 a minor third above occurs in trumpet concertos including those by Michael Haydn. These parts were written for trumpets in D or C.

It should also be added that horn music of the eighteenth century demanded a comparable technique, with parts going up to the 16th, 18th, 20th, and exceptionally the 24th natural note, though the sounds were, of course, an octave or so lower, depending on the crook being used.

This treacherously difficult trumpet- and horn-writing fell from fashion in the Classical period, the heyday of crooks and hand-stopping. Melodic trumpet parts returned in the Romantic era with the valved trumpet, mechanized to be fully chromatic.

Orchestral trumpet technique

The modern trumpet repertoire is largely written for valved trumpets in 4½-foot B♭ or 4-foot C. The orchestral player will generally also be equipped with smaller trumpets in D and E♭, in F and G, and a piccolo in 2¼-foot B♭. The most appropriate instrument is then chosen for each performance. Since orchestras with present-day instrumentation perform a great deal of nineteenth-century music, trumpet players, like horn players, become highly proficient at transposing at sight parts written for a wide variety of instruments and crooks.

Apart from this, actual performance practice is much the same as for the cornet (described in Section 5.5). Indeed, modern trumpet technique is probably derived in larger measure from cornet technique than from that of the classical trumpet.

Trombone technique

Without moving the slide, the tenor trombone can play the white notes shown in Figure 6.2. The slide is long enough to lower each of these by six semitones, thus giving a chromatic compass from E_2 upwards. The beginner is taught that there are seven positions of the slide, but this is only a first approximation applicable at an elementary level. In fact, the extension of the slide required to play, say, C_3 in tune on most trombones is not the same as that required to play an F_2 although both are nominally in 6th position. A large part of trombone technique is the mastery of exact slide placement to play in tune with the rest of the ensemble. Trombone slide movement and legato playing are not as simple as valve movement and legato on valved brass, although in the upper register (where there are alternative slide positions and less movement is required) technical facility is possible not far short of that of valved brass.

The trombone is not usually a transposing instrument. In the late eighteenth and early nineteenth centuries, the standard complement was alto, tenor, and bass trombone, with parts in the alto, tenor, and bass clefs. From the same time when the alto became less used, curiously the bass clef came to be used more, and is now standard except for high orchestral parts. Although orchestral players have to be fluent in the three clefs, band players will usually only have to read in one.

Mutes

Mutes for brass instruments are devices to modify the timbre or to reduce the volume. They extend the palette of sounds available to composers. They also alter the 'feeling' or response of the instrument to the player: designers of mutes attempt to reduce or at least make this effect consistent over the pitch and dynamic ranges. This is especially true of 'practice mutes' which are used where players need to consider their neighbours without inhibiting their technique. Composers have given players quite severe challenges—not only in finding mutes that work consistently over the required range, but also in the time allowed to insert or remove them.

Trumpet mutes date from the seventeenth century or earlier. Mersenne in 1636 described and illustrated hollow wooden mutes, and Monteverdi in 1607 discussed the transposition required if some passages in *Orfeo* were played using muted trumpets. More recently, Wagner, Debussy, Strauss, Stravinsky, and Bartók have exploited muted brass. Early jazz players used standard straight mutes and improvised others from sink plungers, hats, etc. Many of King Oliver's classic solos were recorded using muted cornet.

Mutes can be made from wood, card or fibre, metal, plastic, etc. Most mutes are inserted into the bell and are held in place by pieces of cork sheet, which also give the thin metal of the bell some protection. 'Straight' mutes (today often subtly curved rather than truncated cones) have no passage for air through them: they are positioned by small strips of cork with large gaps for the air to pass between mute and bell. Their sound is nasal in piano and hard in forte. This is the mute required when a part is marked 'con sordino' without further qualification. 'Cup' mutes are straight mutes with an attached cup approximately the same diameter as the bell of the instrument.

Other mutes are positioned by a complete ring of cork, and require an air passage through the mute. Practice mutes, 'stopped mutes' for french horn, and Harmon mutes are of this kind. The last, named after its inventor, T. Harmon, has a central narrow tube opening out to a hemisphere; by moving the hand over the mouth of this tube, the player can imitate the vowel sounds 'oo' and 'ah', leading to the alternative name 'wah-wah mute'. The Harmon was first scored for in Gershwin's *Rhapsody in Blue* (1924).

A similar effect is obtained by the hand-held plunger mute. Other mutes are fastened to the bell by clips ('bucket mutes') or fixed to a music stand ('derby' or 'hat' mutes). This offers considerable scope for composers, since it is possible to use two mutes simultaneously if one is placed in the bell and the other is attached to a stand.

All these are available for trumpets and trombones. Harmon and plunger mutes require a trombonist to support the instrument with the palm of one hand while operating the mute with the fingertips.

Avant-garde techniques

We discussed in the previous chapter the technique of vocalizing while playing and the effect of playing chords, which is equally applicable to the trombone (less so to the trumpet). Other devices which, while not new, are rare in written music are the glissando and trills. The former, easily produced on the trombone, can be made on a piston-valved instrument by half-depressing one or more valves: the ambiguous tube length will respond to the pitch imposed by the player's lips. Trills, while straightforward on valved instruments (though some more easily fingered than others) have to be produced by the lips alone on the trombone and are only available in the upper register. The trombone, like the violin family, is well suited to playing music using quarter-tones or other microtones.

A large part of the creative element of avant-garde music is in devising new effects, and a listing here would be soon dated. Some effects are idiomatic, such as the 'plopping' of suddenly removing a valve tuning slide or a trombone slide. Others are not, such as the percussive effects of hitting, scraping, or rubbing part of the instrument with a specified beater.

7

Percussion Instruments

7.1 ACOUSTICAL PRINCIPLES

Any instrument whose sound is created by striking or hammering can be described as a percussion instrument. The dulcimer, the cimbalom, and the piano, which employ hammered strings, are in this sense all members of the percussion family. In normal musical usage, however, the term is restricted to members of the idiophone and membranophone classes. As we saw in Chapter 2, the characteristic feature of an idiophone is that the sound is generated by a vibrating bar or plate; the membranophone is characterized by the fact that the sound emanates from a vibrating membrane. Occasionally, instruments from both these classes are excited by non-percussive means: a tambourine can be sounded by rubbing a moistened thumb along the skin, and some modern composers have asked for cymbals and vibraphone bars to be stroked with a violin or cello bow. Nevertheless, the instruments are still considered to be members of the percussion family, since the normal playing technique involves a percussive stroke.

Basic acoustics

Looking at the bewildering array of exotic objects assembled in the percussion section of a modern symphony orchestra, one might reasonably wonder whether they shared any common acoustical property. The obvious link between them is the percussive excitation: a closer examination of this will lead us to identify some important features which characterize all the instruments normally found in the orchestra's 'kitchen'.

The first point to note is that a single percussive stroke delivers energy to the instrument in one short burst. The energy is taken up by the various natural modes of the vibrator, each vibrating at its own mode frequency. The sound wave which radiates from the vibrating instrument carries away some of this energy; some of it is turned into heat by frictional processes. The energy stored in the natural modes thus steadily diminishes, and the sound dies away. The sudden start and gradual decay of the sound is one of the most characteristic features of the percussion instruments.

It is, of course, possible to replenish the stored vibration energy by a further percussive stroke. This is the technique used to provide a sustained drum roll; the player holds a stick in each hand, and a rapid alternation of right- and left-hand strokes supplies a regular series of bursts of energy to the drumskin. Provided that the rate of decay of sound after each stroke is not too great, this can give the illusion of a continuous sound. A similar technique is used on the xylophone and marimba, although the faster decay of the vibrations of the bars on these instruments means that the sound is perceived as a reiteration of separate notes.

Pitched and unpitched percussion

Another important feature of percussion instruments arises from the fact that the vibrating objects employed come from the idiophone and membranophone classes. We saw in Chapter 2 that the natural modes of such objects do not have harmonically related frequencies; the natural mode frequencies of drumskins and plates are more closely spaced than a harmonic series, while those of bars and tubes are much further apart.

After the percussive stroke, each of the natural modes of the instrument radiates sound at its own mode frequency. Remembering that the brain assigns a definite pitch to a sound only if it recognizes a set of harmonics in its frequency spectrum, we might conclude that the inharmonic mode frequencies of a percussion instrument would give a sound without a clear pitch. This is indeed true of many percussion instruments, such as the side drum and the cymbal.

In instruments of the tuned percussion category, on the other hand, the object which is struck does radiate a sound with definite pitch. There are various ways in which this sense of pitch is achieved, some of which were reviewed in Chapter 2. The vibrator can be mounted in such a way that all modes except the first are damped, as in the glockenspiel. The vibrator can be specially shaped to give some of its modes a harmonic relationship, as in the vibraphone. The dimensions of the vibrator can be so chosen that the mode frequencies lying within the dominant region for pitch perception have an approximately harmonic relationship, as in the tubular bell.

The fact that the natural mode frequencies of percussion instruments are usually inharmonic has a direct bearing on the importance of the point of striking. A glockenspiel bar is normally struck at the centre because this is an antinode for the crucial first mode, which gives the sense of pitch. The second mode frequency is not harmonically related to the first, and would disrupt the sense of pitch; but the second mode has a node at the centre, and is therefore not excited by striking at this point. On the timpani, as we saw in Chapter 2, the striking point emphasizes those modes which contribute to the sense of pitch, at the expense of those which do not. Thus the choice of striking point affects not only the timbre of the note, but also the clarity of its pitch.

Hammers

The weight and composition of the hammer, mallet, or stick with which the instrument is struck has an important bearing on the strength and timbre of the resulting sound. The amount of energy carried by a hammer head of mass m travelling with speed v is

$$E = \frac{1}{2}\, mv^2$$

Doubling the mass of the head will therefore double the amount of energy for a given speed of impact; doubling the speed will increase the energy carried by a factor of four.

The maximum practical mass of a percussion hammer head is set by the limitations of the human physique. The forces required to move the hammer from note to note, and to accelerate it to the desired speed, are supplied by the muscles of the player's arm and hand (sometimes aided and sometimes hindered by gravity). The heavier the hammer, the longer these processes will take. For a single stroke on a large tam-tam, the player may take several seconds to prepare and accelerate a large and massive mallet; on the other hand, the rapid reiterations required by a virtuoso xylophone solo can only be executed using alternating right- and left-hand strokes from sticks with relatively light heads.

The timbre of the sound is strongly affected by the composition of the hammer head. An important factor is the compliance of the striking area of the head, which is a measure of how readily the head deforms in response to an applied force. A soft rubber head has a high compliance, since even a small force can squash it considerably; a metal or hardwood head has a small compliance, since a very large force is needed to produce a noticeable deformation.

The time during which the hammer remains in contact with the struck object depends on the properties of the object and the hammer. To simplify the discussion, let us assume that the struck object is much harder and heavier than the hammer head. The contact time T_c is then determined primarily by the mass and compliance of the head. When the head first strikes the object, its momentum carries it forward, and it is squashed against the hard surface of the object. This deformation generates a force which slows the head down, stops it, and makes it rebound. The lower the compliance of the head, the greater will be the force generated by the deformation, and the faster will be the rebound. On the other hand, a more massive head carries greater momentum at a given speed; the deformation force will therefore take longer to slow and stop a heavy hammer than a light one.

We can thus see that a short contact time requires a light hammer of low compliance, whereas a long contact time requires a heavier, more compliant head.

The contact time directly affects the timbre of the sound, because the hammer blow is most efficient in transferring energy to the vibration modes of the object with frequencies close to

$$f = 1/2T_c$$

Thus if the contact time is 5 ms, the struck object will be preferentially excited into modes which radiate frequencies around 100 Hz. If a harder, lighter hammer reduces the contact time to 0.5 ms, frequencies around 1,000 Hz will be more prominent. In general, hard, light hammers give the bright, sharp sound associated with high-frequency components, and are therefore preferred for instruments such as the glockenspiel. Soft, heavy hammers generate low-frequency vibrations, and are normally used on bass drum and tam-tam. When the object struck is a drumskin the deformation of the skin is also important, and it is part of the skill of the player to choose the appropriate weight of stick for a particular instrument.

Energy transfer between modes

In the preceding discussion, we have assumed that the energy given to a particular mode by the percussive stroke remains associated with the vibration of that mode, until it is either radiated away as sound or turned into heat through internal friction in the vibrating object. In some instruments, particularly those in which the vibrating object is made from sheet metal, another process can occur: energy initially taken up by one mode can be gradually transferred to another mode. The musical significance of this process lies in the fact that each mode vibrates with its own characteristic mode frequency. A shift of energy from one mode to another therefore implies a change in the radiated frequency spectrum, and in the timbre of the sound.

A dramatic illustration of energy transfer between modes is provided by Figure 7.1, which shows two measurements of the frequency spectrum of the sound from an orchestral cymbal struck by a hard wooden stick. In the first measurement, taken just after the stroke, most of the sound energy is in the frequency region below 2,000 Hz. One second later, a major fraction of the energy is in the region above 3,000 Hz.

The late blossoming of the high frequencies provides a 'splash' which is highly characteristic of the undamped cymbal. A similar effect is found on the tam-tam, although the greater size of the plate and the use of a heavier, softer hammer mean that the whole process is transferred to a much lower frequency range. Because the initial vibrations are strongest at frequencies to which the ear is rela-

7.1 Frequency spectrum of the sound of a heavy orchestral cymbal struck by a hard stick (a) immediately after the stroke; (b) one second after the stroke

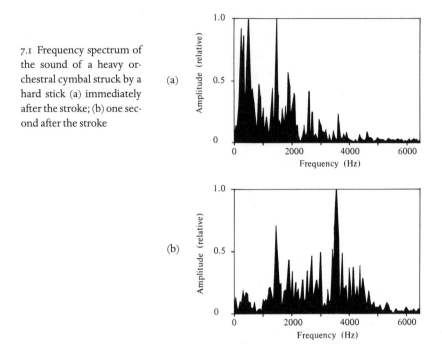

tively insensitive, the transfer of energy towards the region of the ear's maximum sensitivity can give the impression that the loudness of the tam-tam sound grows for several seconds after the stroke. This is a fact which the player has to bear in mind when judging the strength of the blow.

7.2 HISTORICAL DEVELOPMENT

Xylophones, glockenspiels, triangles, etc.

The xylophone had to wait until the 'percussion age' of the mid- to late-twentieth century before attracting much attention from composers and arrangers, though it has a long history of virtuoso performance. The idea of an array of bars tuned to the notes of a scale is ancient, and widespread geographically. The wooden-barred xylophone is an essential constituent of much African music. In Europe, it was noted by sixteenth- and seventeenth-century writers; at this time it was a single row of fifteen to twenty-five bars tuned to a diatonic scale. A second row with the five extra bars per octave required for a chromatic xylophone was added by the mid-nineteenth century. Orchestral parts for the xylophone started with Saint-Saëns in 1874; the instrument has now assumed a role as a versatile and flexible component of the percussion section of the modern orchestra and bands of many kinds. The marimba, taking its name from earlier native American instruments, was developed in the United States *circa* 1910 as a form of xylophone with lower compass.

The glockenspiel, in which a row of tuned metal bars is used to create the effect of small bells, offered the advantages of being easier to make and carry than the corresponding peal of bells. It does not seem to have been known in Europe before the seventeenth century. In the twentieth century it became an important tuned percussion instrument; it is used orchestrally and in other ensemble music for the sake of its own timbre, without necessarily conveying an association with bells. The vibraphone, discussed below, was developed from the glockenspiel by the Leedy Drum company in the United States *circa* 1920. The triangle has, unusually, evolved in historical times to become simpler. From medieval times up to the nineteenth century, triangles normally had a series of rings on the lower bar: the effect of a single note would be more of a 'zing' than the clean 'ting' of a note on the plain modern model. The rings derive from the ancient sistrum, an instrument with rings that was shaken rather than hit. The triangle has been used orchestrally since the early eighteenth century.

Cymbals, bells, and gongs

Cymbals have developed largely independently in oriental and Western cultures. In the Middle Ages (as also in Greek and Roman civilizations) they were of thicker gauge metal than that currently used; a pair would be held horizontally and played with a primarily vertical movement. From iconographical evidence they appear to have been 150 mm to 250 mm in diameter. Cymbals have been used in orchestral music since 1680, at first rarely, but from the mid-nineteenth century commonly. Their use in dance and military music has been frequent. Since the eighteenth century, they have been held vertically and played with a primarily (though never purely) horizontal movement. The size has increased, large orchestral cymbals now being some 500 mm in diameter, and the metal is thinner. In the twentieth century, there was a dramatic increase in the varieties available, as we see in the next section.

The use of a set of bells as a musical instrument (as opposed to a means of communication) goes back at least as far as the Middle Ages. Many pictures from the tenth to the fifteenth centuries show rows of bells being struck with hammers by one or two players; the bells were arranged by size, suspended at eye-level or mounted on a stand. Much later, sets of bells with leather handles and internally mounted clappers were used for handbell ringing: music-making with handbells (fully developed in the nineteenth century) usually requires a team of players and skilfully arranged part-writing. Gongs were developed in the Far East: considerable sophistication of timbre, requiring highly specialized manufacturing processes, is a long-established requirement. Tuned gongs reached their high-point in terms of musical function in the gamelan orchestras of Bali and Java. Tuned and untuned gongs are now made in Europe and America as well as in Asia.

Drums

The medieval tabor appears to have originated with the Arabs or the Saracens, and was brought to Europe in the thirteenth century by returning crusaders. The tabor had a small cylindrical shell, usually with two rope-tensioned heads and snares which could be on either head. Later tabors were larger, but continued to be played with a single stick. A common association was for the tabor to be played with one hand, accompanying a three-holed pipe played with the other (often to provide dance music). The heyday of the tabor was before the middle of the seventeenth century, though in some places use of the pipe and tabor continued into the nineteenth century. Tabors were also very widely used in outdoor court and civic music. At first, the heads were secured by rope laced through the skins. Later, the head was 'lapped' to a wooden hoop (flesh hoop); it was tensioned by a second hoop, with holes for the rope (counter-hoop), which pressed the flesh hoop down the outside of the shell.

A large tabor was used by Swiss mercenaries in the fifteenth century. It was rope-tensioned, with a snare on the upper (or batter) head, and was played with two sticks; this acquired important military functions in marching and signalling. Such a drum, played with two sticks in two hands, is now known as a side drum. With the snare on the lower head, the standard modern disposition, it appeared in the sixteenth century. It was significantly larger than the medieval tabor, some 600–750 mm in both diameter and depth. It takes its name from the fact that it is slung at the player's side, with the head at an angle suitable for two-handed playing.

The side (or snare) drum found occasional orchestral use in the eighteenth and nineteenth centuries to give a martial flavour: in the twentieth century, however, its use has developed to exploit its own musical characteristics rather than its associations.

From the early nineteenth century, the diameter, and sometimes the depth, were reduced; the shell was often made of brass rather than wood. In the middle of the nineteenth century, rod-tensioning was introduced as an alternative to rope. The transition from rope-tensioned drums 300 mm deep to shallower rod-tensioned drums has been very gradual; deeper drums have been retained for marching bands, while shallower drums have found favour for jazz and dance-band work. Orchestral snare drums are often intermediate in size.

The bass drum, with a wooden, cylindrical shell, heads of skin (usually at both ends), and no snares, was rare in Europe until the fashion for 'Janissary' music in the eighteenth century. The early bass drum was long, with smaller diameter heads than are now customary, and was rope-tensioned. This form was known as the long drum, particularly in the military band. From the early nineteenth century, there was a gradual change to a shorter drum with larger diameter heads. Screw-tensioning was applied to these bass drums with shorter shells and wider diameter heads by the middle of the century. Bass drums can survive many years of use, and the new and old patterns have coexisted for long periods. Single-headed bass drums ('gong drums') were used earlier this century in orchestras and dance bands: they can have a good tone but also have more of a tendency to give a sound with a definite pitch.

Small kettledrums, or nakers, probably brought to Europe with the returning crusaders, were known by the thirteenth century. Their main use was in dance music and military music, in the latter often associated with trumpets. Nakers were invariably used in pairs—the two bowls were of similar size, possibly with the heads differently tensioned to give sounds of high and low pitch. Larger kettledrums came from the Ottoman empire in the fifteenth century; the ceremonial use of pairs of kettledrums slung on either side of a horse ('cavalry drums') dates from the sixteenth century, and has continued to the present day (Figure 7.2(a)).

Pairs of kettledrums were of different sizes, and were originally laced round the bowl. Lapped heads and screw-tensioning (with a removable key rather than handles fixed to each screw) developed in Germany at the beginning of the sixteenth century. By the early seventeenth century, kettledrums were recognized as tuned instruments, rather than just 'high' and 'low', and a pair would most frequently be tuned to the interval of a perfect fourth or a perfect fifth.

Used with trumpets, a pair of kettledrums would generally reinforce the bass line of tonic and dominant played by the lowest trumpet. Like trumpet-playing, kettledrumming was protected by guilds, and the skills were passed from master to apprentice without written codification. The employment of kettledrummers was largely a prerogative of royalty and nobility.

Playing from written parts came with orchestral use in the late seventeenth century. At first, the music was restricted to the trumpet's usual keys of C and D. A pair of kettledrums would play the tonic and the dominant; if in D, they would be written for as a transposing instrument 'in D'. Occasionally, more ambitious pieces with five, six, or more drums were written.

The size of kettledrums was originally constrained by use on horseback, but increased when instruments were made for orchestral use. A Baroque period orchestral pair were typically 455 mm and 505 mm in diameter, with depths of 280 mm and 380 mm respectively. These would, in a small ensemble, produce the

(a)   (b)

7.2 (a) 22 ½ in. cavalry kettledrum (Potter, Aldershot, *c.*1850); (b) 25 in. pedal timpano (Premier, Wigston, *c.*1932)

notes G_3 (or A_3) and C_3 (or D_3). With both heads slacker, the pair would give the more common tuning to a perfect fourth, C_3 (or D_3) and G_2 (or A_2). By the end of the eighteenth century orchestral kettledrums sometimes reached diameters of 590 mm and 675 mm. French and English drums tended to be larger, German smaller. At this time, timpani were still beaten at the centre of the heads; the modern beating point, some 115 mm from the edge, was adopted in the second half of the eighteenth century.

Timpani sticks were formerly entirely of wood, some 200 mm–330 mm long, with a small knob at the beating end. These produced a loud, dry sound suitable for playing out of doors. From the mid-eighteenth century, sticks with knobs covered in leather or cloth (felt) provided a softer alternative. By 1800, covered sticks were the more common, with wood used on occasion. Various coverings were tried, such as chamois or flannel, and some heads were made of layers of disks of different materials. From *circa* 1825, sponge-covered heads were introduced in France, and their use was promoted by Berlioz. These used a variety of Mediterranean sponge, not as soft as bath sponge, but soft enough to allow very quiet timpani playing; this extended the musical scope of the instrument. From *circa* 1845, piano felt (in varying grades of hard and soft) was used for the core of the knob; this material now prevails.

It was Beethoven who most significantly developed the use of timpani as a musical voice separate from that of the trumpets. From his time, tuning was by T-handles, integral with the screws passing through the counter-hoop to brackets on the shell. These allowed more rapid retuning in the course of the music than the separate tap key applied to each screw head in turn. Beethoven introduced many other tunings for timpani. The use of three or more timpani came later in the nineteenth century.

The increased chromaticism and more frequent modulation in music of the mid-nineteenth century prompted many inventions aimed at mechanical devices to speed retuning. Some of these 'machine timpani' required tuning by a single master screw, connected by cables to pulleys on the counter-hoop; others involved rotating the drum bowl itself. Wagner composed his *Ring* cycle, starting in the 1850s, with timpani having a single tuning handle in mind. The idea of controlling the pitch by a pedal, leaving both hands free to play, dates from about 1840, but the first practicable model of pedal timp was the Dresden model of 1881 invented by Carl Pittrich. Later modifications of the pedal principle include the balanced action of Ludwig and Danly (1919–20), in which the tension in the head was balanced against the compression of a spring in the pedal mechanism, making control of pitch easier. Figure 7.2(b) shows a timp from the early 1930s with both pedal and T-handles for equalizing the tension around the head.

The tambourine, known in Britain as the timbrel until the late eighteenth century, can be traced as far back as the second century CE in Roman civilization. Henry VIII had four timbrel players amongst his seventy-nine musicians. The jingles were formerly of heavier gauge than the modern thin metal. Tambourines of previous centuries sometimes had small bells attached or, occasionally, snares.

The 'Janissary music' which became very fashionable in Europe in the eighteenth century derived from the percussion of the Ottoman Turks of the fourteenth century. The elements of the Janissary band included a large bass drum, one end beaten with a stick and the other with a bundle of twigs (a switch), kettledrums, cymbals, tambourines, triangle, and a percussion stick with jingles known as the 'Turkish crescent' or 'jingling Johnny'.

7.3 INSTRUMENTS IN MODERN USE

Trends in percussion

Before looking at individual instruments, it might be helpful to look at the situation of the percussion player today. Perhaps more than with other instruments, old models of instruments continue in use alongside new patterns. The general tendency for modern instruments to be made capable of being played at greater volume is equally true of orchestral and band percussion. Music traditions worldwide have their own particular instruments: these may actually change less as cultural traditions become more self-conscious. In contemporary music, whether composed concert music or pop, any instrument from any culture new or old can be called for; this is especially true in percussion, where playing techniques can, perhaps, be transferred more readily. Percussion players have to be able to handle a wide variety of instruments in any case (unlike, say, a violinist who could play one fiddle throughout a professional lifetime), and learning a new instrument is always easier when one has learnt a number already. The mid-twentieth-century

7.3 Drum kit as used in dance bands *c.*1940, mounted on console for easier mobility, including the following: drum console with trap table (Premier, Wigston, *c.*1930), bass drum (Ajax, *c.*1930), bass drum damper, pedal beater (Broadway), two tunable tom-toms, side drum with damper (Vere & Son), sizzle cymbal (suspended from swan-neck), crash cymbal (suspended from swan-neck), hi-hat cymbals on pedal stand (Ajax, *c.*1950), cowbell, pair of choke cymbals (mounted on trap table) and set of four temple blocks with pair of side drum-sticks (Premier, Wigston), pair of bass drum roller beaters, pair of wire brushes (Ludwig) and small wooden beater

7.4 Modern drum kit as used in pop groups, concert wind bands, and theatre pit bands, including the following: bass drum with tone patch, bass drum pedal, two tunable tom-toms mounted on bass drum, tom-tom floor-standing, side drum, side drum stand, ride cymbal, cymbal stand, hi-hat cymbals, pair of side drum-sticks

dance-band drum kit and the basic modern kit in Figures 7.3 and 7.4 show the variety of instruments commonly played by one person in a single session.

Percussion is now far more prominent than it used to be. In both concert and dance music, percussion used to be part of the 'backing'—now it is frequently the centre of attention. Composers, performers, and instrument makers have more scope for creating imaginative new effects with percussion than with any other class of non-electronic instrument.

Composers and others who wish to specify the sounds they have in mind must consider three elements: the instrument itself, the beater (which may be the player's fingers), and the beating spot. It was pointed out earlier in the chapter that a single instrument can sound quite different if hit in different places, even with the same stroke of the same beater. Notations have been devised to express these elements, though for most instruments there are conventional beaters and playing spots which a percussionist will use if not instructed otherwise. Precision in nota-

tion is important, as is the layout of the instruments on the platform, since inefficient scoring may lead to more players than are strictly necessary being called on
to perform a piece.

Instruments with vibrating bars

Most instruments with vibrating bars are used to sound notes of recognizable
pitch. All except those intended for young children (which sound only the notes of
a diatonic scale) are fully chromatic. Unless played from a keyboard (as in the
celeste), the bars are arranged in two unequal rows, corresponding to the white
and black notes respectively of a piano or organ. The player holds a beater (sometimes two) in each hand.

The xylophone has wooden bars, each lightly resonated with a tube of the
appropriate length (closed at the lower end) suspended beneath each bar. High-
quality rosewood is scarce, so synthetic materials are now often used. The bars
corresponding to 'black' notes are generally raised, slightly overhanging the
'white' bars. The width and spacing of the bars is uniform. A three-and-a-half-
octave range (F_4 to C_8) is common, though many have a four-octave range (C_4 to
C_8). The music is generally transposed, written an octave lower than it sounds.
The xylophone can dominate most ensembles, as its sound does not blend with
other instruments.

The marimba is similar to the xylophone, but sounds an octave lower (C_3 to C_7).
The lower notes have wider bars than the higher, and the resonators are more
substantial.

The vibraphone has the same basic layout as the xylophone, though generally
with the bars on one level. Its bars are of metal, generally an aluminium alloy.
Because the sound dies away relatively slowly, there are dampers, controlled by a
pedal. The player can damp individual notes with the fingers. The tops of the resonators are fitted with discs that can almost close each tube: these can rotate about
their diameters, alternately opening the resonating tubes beneath the bars and let-
ting the bars sound without resonators. The discs are coupled and driven by an
electric motor so that they open and close together, giving a vibrato effect to the
whole instrument at once. This vibrato is a fluctuation of volume, not pitch, and
the speed can be varied; the motor can also be turned off if no vibrato is required.
A three-octave range (F_3 to F_6) is general. Beaters with heads consisting of a hard
core wound with soft wool are used to produce the gentle sound characteristic of
the instrument, though plastic-headed beaters can be used for a harder sound.

The glockenspiel, with much smaller metal bars than the vibraphone, has no
dampers or resonators. The bars are of steel, and the two-row layout is usual. The
concert model, in a wooden case that is placed on a table or special stand for use,
generally has the rear row ('black notes') raised. The marching band model, some-

times called the bell lyra, has the bars in two vertical columns suspended between supports which mimic the horns of the ancient lyre. The clear bright sound of the glockenspiel is actually two octaves above the written notes: the range is normally two and a half octaves, written G_3 to C_6 and sounding G_5 to C_8.

A glockenspiel is generally played with hard beaters. Versions with hammer mechanisms played from a keyboard are called for by some composers. The advantages of being able to exploit the facility of keyboard technique are offset by a weaker sound. The celeste is a large keyboard glockenspiel with resonators; its range is normally five octaves, written C_2 to C_7 and sounding C_3 to C_8. The weak bottom octave is often omitted in modern instruments.

The glockenspiel can give the effect of small bells, but if the sound of large bells is required for concert purposes, a set of vertically suspended tubular bells in a frame is used. The full set is eighteen, written C_4 to F_5, arranged in two rows. The actual sound produced by a tubular bell consists of eight or so frequencies in the audible range. Because these are the natural mode frequencies of the tube, which are not related harmonically, the ear interprets the pitch of the sound as the fundamental whose harmonics are the best match to the audible frequencies. In fact, the nominal pitch of a tubular bell corresponds to a frequency that is not normally present in the sound. Because there is a dominant pitch region (a range of frequency preferred by the ear for pitch identification), it is practically impossible to make tubular bells sounding significantly higher or lower than the normal range of C_4 to F_5, however long or short the tubes are made. The tops of the tubes are closed with metal caps, and the instrument is played by striking these caps with a rawhide mallet.

Unlike the tubular bells, which are designed to give an impression of pitch, the triangle is made to minimize any effect of definite pitch. Although the ear generally matches the frequency components in the sound of a metal bar with the harmonics of a fundamental at the nominal pitch, the two bends which make a straight bar into a triangle alter the frequencies in the sound of a well-made instrument so that they do not match any harmonic series. Triangles are made in different sizes (sides of 150 mm to 250 mm are commonest), but larger triangles do not necessarily sound lower than smaller, and the choice will be of the most appropriate tone quality. Triangles are suspended from one or both of the closed corners and struck with a metal rod.

Instruments with vibrating plates

Most instruments with vibrating plates are used to produce sounds of indeterminate pitch. The simplest, however, are tuned. These are the metal rectangular plates used in various ways. Graded series of bronze keys, carefully tuned and mounted on wooden 'cases', are important melody instruments in gamelan orchestras. In Western music, shaped plates of steel or bronze are sometimes used as 'bell plates' in preference to tubular bells.

Gongs also are tuned. A tuned gong is made of heavy-gauge bronze, with a deep rim and often with a central boss or dome. A wide range of pitches can be made: anything between C_2 and C_6 is not regarded as extreme. As we saw earlier, a gong beater should be soft, but it also has to be heavy for the larger gongs to impart enough energy. A gong is struck gently on the boss or in the centre. The pitch of a gong can be lowered gradually by up to two octaves by lowering it into water (an effect actually called for in some modern scores).

Tam-tams are not entirely distinct from gongs—there is a middle ground—but the term is now reserved for instruments of indeterminate pitch. A tam-tam has a much shallower rim, never has a boss, and is at least 600 mm, often 900 mm in diameter. The beater is wool-covered wood, soft and heavy. Struck at the centre, a tam-tam is deep and clear; at the edge it is bright and splashy. The normal playing spot is just off-centre.

The most varied of the percussion families is perhaps that of the cymbals. In pairs they can be clashed or gently brought together in numerous ways; suspended singly they can be played with a wide range of hard beaters, soft beaters, and wire brushes. Unlike gongs and tam-tams, but like bells, all cymbals are held or suspended at their centres. The sizes in common use range from 200 mm to 600 mm diameter. Orchestral pairs, held by leather thongs, come in different gauges: heavy for Wagnerian music (the sound approaching a clang), medium for Austrian (zing), and light for French (swish). Single cymbals can be bought in seven or so gauges. Hi-hat cymbals are pairs mounted horizontally on a stand, brought together and released under the control of the player's foot on a pedal. Generally the upper cymbal is of thinner metal than the lower.

Crotales or finger cymbals are much smaller in diameter, though of heavier gauge. They can be made pitched or unpitched; when pitched, they are typically in the range C_5 to C_6. When played in pairs, they are held by leather thongs on the thumb and index finger. Pairs may be deliberately off-tuned as with castanets. Pitched crotales might be better regarded as small bells of flattened shape.

Bells, almost always pitched, are sounded at the rim either by striking with a beater or by an internally mounted clapper. With clapper bells, it is more common for the whole bell to be swung so that the rim hits the stationary clapper. The sound produced by a bell consists of a number of audible frequencies, which decay at different rates. The lowest, the 'hum tone', lasts longest, but is not the most prominent initially, and only provides the nominal pitch of very small bells. Where it is musically important to have the purest possible pitched sound, for example in a carillon, the first five modes of vibration are tuned in the bell foundry. The bells used for the most ambitious musical purpose are traditional handbells. A team of ringers stands behind tables bearing up to sixty bells with clappers and wooden handles, picking up and swinging the bells to play melodies with accompaniments in full harmony. The bells in drum kits, on the other hand, are regarded as unpitched, although they are used in different sizes. They are known as cowbells, and are played with drum sticks as beaters.

Bells are almost always made of metal. Some patterns do not have an open bell mouth, but are almost closed, apart from a slit. Wooden slit bells are known as temple blocks, and have their distinctive 'clock' sound, decaying quite quickly. A set of five may be tuned to a pentatonic scale. They are played with wooden sticks or soft beaters.

If the opening is reduced to a slit in a block of wood, we have the instrument known as the wood block. This is about 150 mm long, and is played with side-drum sticks to give an unpitched 'clack' sound.

Castanets, also of wood, have a shallow hollow in the surfaces which strike each other. Traditionally, players use two pairs, one in each hand, striking them rhythmically to produce an unpitched 'cleck' sound. Actually, the two shells in a pair are differently pitched, and pairs of pairs are again differently pitched. For orchestral use, castanets are not tied to the player's hands, but are fastened loosely (so that they spring open) to a wooden handle; either this handle is shaken, or the shells are played with the fingertips.

Steel pans, originating in the mid-twentieth century in Trinidad but now heard worldwide, are unusual in that a number of distinct pitches can be sounded from a single surface. Pans, which are made as trebles, altos, tenors, or basses, are made from the complete ends of oil drums, skilfully beaten concave, separated into discrete areas by grooves, heated, and tempered; finally the area for each note is beaten upwards until it is in tune. Treble pans can have as many as thirty-two notes; basses usually have four or less. Pans are played with rubber-tipped beaters.

Drums

Drums have a greater capacity to sound notes of determinate pitch than is commonly realized. With many drums, measures are taken to suppress the effect of pitch and thus the need to tune the drum to suit the tonality of the music. These measures include fitting snares or jingles, tuning two heads to different pitches, and choosing an appropriate beating spot.

The modern side drum, or snare drum, is cylindrical, some 350 mm in diameter. The depth of side drums varies considerably: the late eighteenth-century military drum shown in Figure 7.5 is 350 mm deep, the 'Guard's pattern' side drum used ceremonially is just under 300 mm, orchestral drums are 200 mm or less; the marching-band drum in Figure 7.5(b) is 150 mm, and drums as shallow as 80 mm have been used in drum kits. Although taking its name from being suspended at the player's side for marching, for concert use the side drum is placed on a stand.

(a)   (b)

7.5 (a) side drum (England, 1796), showing snare head; (b) shallow modern side drum (Boosey & Co., London, *c.*1925) showing batter head

The upper head, known as the batter head, is positioned and angled for the convenience of the player. The lower head carries the snares, which are gut, wire-wound silk, or coiled wire, usually between six and twelve in number. When the drum is being played, the snares are tensioned so that they rattle against the lower drum head, which vibrates in response to the upper. When the drum is not being played, they are slackened so that the rattle is not induced by vibrations picked up by the snare head from other instruments. On occasion, a composer may ask for the side drum to be played without snares, perhaps with the intention of producing the effect of the ancient tabor. Without snares, the side drum tends to produce a bright ringing sound with a definite pitch. The normal beaters for side drums are slender wooden sticks, with a pronounced bead turned in the wood at the playing end. Because of its long-standing use in military bands, composers sometimes use the side drum in opera or programme music to exploit its military associations. Civilian bands find the side drum indispensable, too, when playing on the march. Many bands, for instance Scottish pipe bands, prefer drums with a very light timbre, so that their drum corps can execute elaborate embellishments of the basic rhythmic pattern.

Tom-toms come in a wide variety of sizes. They are cylindrical drums without snares, and can be either single- or double-headed. They are generally of indefinite pitch, being described simply as 'high' or 'low' according to size. The heads are tuned to different pitches in the case of double-headed tom-toms. They can also be used as tuned drums, especially if single-headed: the range E_2 to $B^\flat_3$ is best.

Bongos are small single-headed drums, usually used in pairs of different sizes. The shells are conical, of wood, with the heads on the wide ends. They are not, however, normally regarded as being of definite pitch. Bongos are played with sticks or with the fingertips. Conga drums are large bongos, usually in the shape of an elongated barrel. Timbales, or timbales creoles, are intermediate in size and of metal.

The bass drum is used in a variety of forms. The basic instrument, used in marching bands, has two heads tuned to different pitches to minimize any impression of definite pitch. On the march, the bass drum is carried on the player's chest, supported by a carriage strap, with the heads vertical; it is played with a single beater, or with one in each hand. If the band is playing 'at the halt', the bass drum is placed on a stand, still vertical. Orchestral bass drums can be larger, perhaps 1 metre in diameter and 500 mm wide. They are always mounted on a stand, but may be horizontal or at an angle. Different kinds of beater are used, but the characteristic shudder of the bass drum is produced with a fairly heavy wool-covered beater. Jazz and dance-band bass drums, the central feature of any drum kit, are smaller and played with a pedal. They are often damped (with a small disc of felt sprung to press against one of the heads) to shorten the sound.

The tambourine is a single-headed drum with brass jingles set in the shell, which is always fairly narrow. There is usually also a hole in the shell for one of the player's fingers, so that the instrument can be held securely without touching the head; pairs of jingles are distributed around the rest of the shell. The most common methods of playing are shaking (only the jingles sound), beating with the knuckle or the palm, 'rolling' with a moistened thumb on the head, or using beaters with the instrument resting on a cushion.

Timpani (kettledrums) are constructed and played to give the clearest possible impression of pitch, as explained in Section 2.4. The playing spot, about one eighth of the drum's diameter from the rim, favours those modes of vibration which coincide best with the harmonic series of the nominal pitch. The principal determinants of tone are the size, tension, elasticity, and flexibility of the head. Calf-skin heads sound perceptibly mellower than plastic heads. The size and material used for the bowl, and the number of perforations in it, have less audible effect. Timpani are tuned by adjusting the tension of the head. Most commonly, the head is lapped onto a flesh hoop, placed over the bowl, and stretched by a counterhoop which presses down on the flesh hoop. The counterhoop is pulled down at six points (sometimes eight in large drums), equally spaced round the circumference. If the flesh hoop and counterhoop are of slightly larger diameter than the bowl, the drum is said to have a floating head.

The most common mechanisms for control of the tuning of timpani are hand screws and pedal action. Mechanisms involving a single handle or rotation of the bowl are rarer. Hand screws usually have fixed T-handles for all the screws except the one nearest to the player; a projecting handle here would be at risk from collision with the sticks in playing, so a detachable key or a hinged drop-handle is provided instead. Pedal action is much more rapid than the action of tightening or slackening six hand taps, and many modern compositions require machine drums. A drum with a good head can be tuned over an octave, but the best tone is given in the middle of the range. The range of best tone for common sizes of drum is given in Table 7.1.

Table 7.1 *Preferred pitch ranges for different drum sizes*

diameter in mm (and inches)	calf head	plastic head
565 (23 in.)	D_3 to $G_3^\sharp$	F_3 to $B_3^\flat$
615 (25 in.)	$B_2^\flat$ to F_3	C_3 to G_3
690 (28 in.)	F_2 to C_3	G_2 to D_3
740 (30 in.)	$E_2^\flat$ to A_2	F_2 to C_3
790 (32 in.)	$C_2^\sharp$ to $G_2^\sharp$	D_2 to A_2

Smaller drums are used occasionally, for example a piccolo timpano with range F_3 to C_4.

If a drum is over-tensioned, there is the risk of the head tearing; if it is too slack, the sound becomes weak and flabby. Like gut strings on stringed instruments, the tone quality of drum heads deteriorates with time and use. The pedal action on pedal timpani normally gives a range of a fifth; this can be chosen from the overall range of the drum by screw-tuning. Pedal actions giving larger ranges have been tried, but extending the range unacceptably reduces the accuracy of pitch control.

7.4 INSTRUMENT CONSTRUCTION

Percussion instruments and the techniques for making them are so varied, that even a superficial treatment is beyond the scope of this book. Instead, we have chosen to look at one or two of the more specialized processes.

Tuning glockenspiel and xylophone bars

As explained in Chapter 2, the first mode frequency of a long thin metal bar of length L and thickness T is given by the formula

$$f_1 = KT/L^2$$

where *K* is a constant characteristic of the material of the bar. Normally a glockenspiel is made from a set of bars cut from a strip of metal of constant thickness. The sounding pitch, which is determined by the first mode frequency, is thus dependent only on the length of the bar.

To achieve exact tuning of each bar, the bar can be cut slightly longer than the calculated length, which will make its pitch a little too low. Material can then be filed or milled from one or both ends until the pitch has been raised to the desired value.

If a bar is too sharp, its first mode frequency could be lowered by uniformly reducing its thickness. A much more convenient approach is to cut a shallow transverse groove in the underside of the bar at the centre. In the first mode of vibration, the centre is an antinode, which is the point of greatest flexure of the bar. Cutting a slot here has the effect of reducing the stiffness of the bar, without significantly reducing its mass; the consequence is a lowering of the mode frequency.

Although the xylophone bar has a non-uniform cross section, for reasons explained in Chapter 2, the same tuning procedures can be applied. Care must be taken to consider the effect of tuning adjustments on the second mode, which also contributes significantly to the xylophone sound. Additional grooves can be cut at the antinodes of the second mode to ensure that the pitch relationship between the first two modes is maintained.

Bell-founding

As with other metal percussion instruments, bell-making originated in the East. It has, however, been established longer in Western civilization than the techniques for making gongs and cymbals.

Small bells are cast using the traditional lost-wax process: the inside is modelled in clay and covered by wax to the thickness of the bell, then surrounded by more clay. The whole mould is then baked so that the wax melts and runs off, and the clay hardens.

Large bells are cast without the use of wax. On a cast-iron base plate an inner mould or core is made of brick and coke, covered with a loam of clayey sand, straw, and horse manure. The loam is shaped to the interior profile of the bell using a crook, a shaped tool which is turned round a vertical shaft on the axis of the bell. The core is dried at 150°C and sealed with graphite and whitener. An outer mould or cope is built on a cast-iron base, perforated to allow gases occurring in casting to escape. This is mounted bell-mouth up, coated with loam, and shaped to the exterior profile of the bell using a different crook. The two moulds are clamped together, carefully placed to be concentric, and mounted bell-mouth downwards, often in a pit. Bell metal is usually a bronze of 77 per cent copper and

23 per cent tin: an alloy with more copper is softer and gives a poorer tone, an alloy with more tin is harder and more liable to crack. The bell metal is heated in a furnace to some 1,200°C, then poled—stirred with a stick of willow to impart a trace of salicylic acid, which acts as a flux. The molten metal is poured into the mould through a header box and allowed to cool. The moulds then have to be broken out, and cannot be used for another bell. Excess metal is fettled off.

The cast bell is now turned down to its final size on a vertical lathe, mounted bell-mouth up on a face-plate. The skill of the bell founder lies in knowing how to remove small amounts of metal from different areas to tune the principal vibrational modes. For a bell of perceived pitch C_4, the principal tones would be the hum note C_3, the so-called fundamental C_4, the tierce $E^\flat_4$, the quint G_4, and the nominal C_5; occasionally bells have been tuned with the tierce a major third above the fundamental. The relative intensities of the principal tones give the characteristic sound of the bell.

The design of the clapper is important also for the tone of a bell: not only does the mass have to be appropriate, it also has to be distributed to give the best moment of inertia.

Preparation of drum heads

The traditional parchment-makers' technique was to take the skin of a calf, goat, sheep, or donkey and soak it in water for several days to remove dirt and blood. It would then be treated for a week or so in slaked lime solution. Hair would be removed by hand, the skin rubbed, and the inner side scraped with a knife to give an even thickness. When dried the resulting skin would be thick, opaque, and relatively stiff.

From the 1850s on to the present day, thinner skins have been produced. The hair is removed and the skin smoothed mechanically, then treated with alum and fixed with a vegetable tanner or mineral salts. The skin is then stretched on a frame.

Skin heads are lapped to a wooden flesh hoop by careful stretching and wrapping round the hoop when wet. For timpani to give their best tone, the playing spot on the head has to be carefully chosen. This is often close to, but not on, the line (clearly visible) on the skin which followed the animal's backbone. The head, lapped to the flesh hoop, then has to be placed on the drum so that the playing spot is correctly positioned relative to the drop-handle or loose-key tuning screw.

From *circa* 1950, plastic heads of polyethylene terephthalate have been used for many drums, including most orchestral timpani. They maintain tuning better when ambient humidity changes (an important consideration), but are less resonant than calf heads and give a drier, more metallic sound with a more rapid decay. Plastic heads are not lapped, but are fixed to metal hoops as a factory operation.

7.5 PERFORMANCE PRACTICE

Choice of beaters

In general, soft beaters have a larger contact area between instrument and beater and damp the higher overtones: they are more appropriate for instruments being used to convey a definite pitch. Vibrating plates such as gongs and cymbals can be made to produce a great variety of sounds with different beaters, whereas vibrating bars such as xylophones and triangles are less affected. With vibrating plates and membranes, the beating spot is also of critical importance.

Beaters are chosen for tone, attack, and volume; sometimes a balance must be struck between conflicting desiderata. The weight of a beater depends on the amount of energy that has to be transmitted to the instrument with each stroke. Beaters are named after their most common use, or after the instrument from which they elicit that instrument's most characteristic tone, but any beater can be used on any percussion instrument (that will not be damaged by it) if desired by the composer, arranger, or performer. A selection of beaters in common use is shown in Figures 7.6 and 7.7.

The most basic beater is, in fact, the fingertip. Some of the most intricate and subtle of all drumming, on the Indian tabla, is entirely done with the fingers. Finger-style playing is effective on small drums such as bongos, but not on large drums such as timpani.

Hard beaters are used for the side drum, the glockenspiel, the xylophone, and the triangle; they are also used for bells. Side drum beaters are wooden sticks with tapered shafts and a bead at the contact end. Since the motion of the stick is rotational (about a point near the middle), the distribution of mass along the stick is as important for the player's control as the total weight. Side drum sticks are also frequently used for the cymbals. Beaters (or mallets) for the glockenspiel and the xylophone are typically spheres of wood, hard rubber, or plastic, mounted on a wooden shaft. The triangle is played with a metal rod. Tubular bells are played with mallets having rawhide heads on wooden shafts.

Medium beaters are most common for the marimba, vibraphone, gongs, and timpani. The vibraphone is most characteristically played with beaters having wool-wound heads mounted on supple shafts. Timpani sticks vary more widely than most percussion beaters, but most have wooden shafts. The heads, approximately spherical, are of felt or are felt-covered.

Soft, large-headed heavy beaters wound with wool are used for the tam-tam and the bass drum. Wire brushes are used instead of sticks on the side drum and cymbals in much dance-band work.

With many percussion instruments, the basic technique is 'hand-to-hand' playing. One beater is held in each hand, the hands playing alternate notes. Some pas-

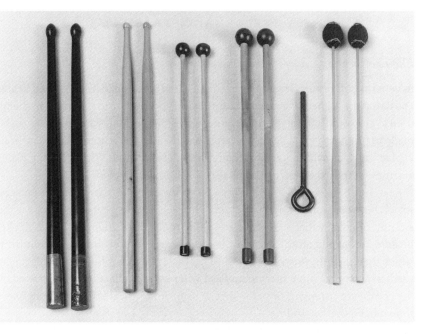

7.6 Beaters for percussion instruments (left to right): pair of side drum-sticks (nineteenth century), pair of side drum-sticks (Premier, Wigston, *c.*1975), pair of glockenspiel or xylophone beaters with wooden heads (Peachey, London, *c.*1970), pair of glockenspiel or xylophone beaters with rubber heads, triangle beater, pair of soft vibraphone beaters (Rose-Morris, London, modern)

sages may require one hand to play consecutive notes, or for one hand to cross over the other.

Side drum techniques and notation

The basics of side drum stick technique are known as the rudiments, the production of rhythmic elements from which drum parts are made. Techniques learnt on the side drum (in many ways the most demanding) are then used on other drums.

The single stroke roll, played hand-to-hand on adjacent playing spots, is the principal means of playing a sustained note on the timpani. The double stroke roll ('mammy-daddy') is the standard or rudimentary side drum roll: the stick in one hand strikes the head twice, bouncing back in between, then the stick in the other hand strikes the head twice, and so on. Either kind of roll can be played smoothly, or with accents on certain beats.

Individual side drum strokes can be embellished, usually by rapid strokes preceding the principal stroke, which is accented. A single decoration is called a

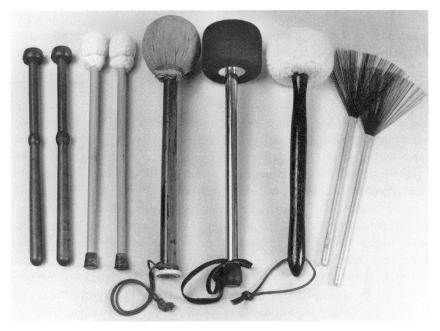

7.7 Beaters for percussion instruments (left to right): pair of timpani sticks with wooden heads (reconstruction: Tony Bingham, London, 1991), pair of timpani beaters with felt heads (James Blades, Cheam, *c.*1975), leather covered bass drum beater (nineteenth century), felt-covered bass drum or tam-tam beater (Japan, *c.*1980), lambswool-covered tam-tam or bass drum beater (Chalklin, 1991), pair of wire brushes (Ludwig, modern)

'flam', two decorative strokes a 'drag', three a 'ruff'. The 'paradiddle' is a departure from hand-to-hand playing that can be used to shape a phrase or to prepare one hand to move to a different instrument: it can be indicated:

LRLL RLRR

A 'rim-shot' is used to give a single note of different quality from, and often louder than, a normal stroke: one stick is placed with the tip on the centre of the drum and the shaft on the rim, then struck with the other stick. Alternatively, in the 'hoop crack', the skin and the rim are hit simultaneously with one stick. A side drum can be muffled or damped, either permanently with a felt disk pressed against one of the heads or temporarily, by placing a folded cloth or other object on the batter head.

Timpani technique

If the repertoire can be played on two timpani, a pair with diameters 615 mm and 690 mm is common; an average set of three drums for orchestral use might be 590 mm, 640 mm, and 725 mm, although the lowest could well be larger. The player can stand or sit, but the drums should be adjusted so that the lower arms and the sticks are horizontal when the beater heads touch the drumskins.

Tuning is a critical part of the timpanist's skill, particularly when it has to be changed rapidly in the course of the music (perhaps when the rest of the ensemble is playing in a key different from that of the timpani's next entry). In hand-tuning, the drum has to be in tune with itself right round the skin, requiring skilful adjustment. To change the pitch of a skin head does not necessarily mean the same number of turns on all the screws: skins are less elastic along the line of the backbone than across it. In lowering the pitch, after the screws are slackened, the head is pressed in the centre to ensure that it has slipped over the shell all round. Because the act of playing a loud note enlarges the surface area of the head, a loud note tends to sound flatter than a quiet note (the increase in tension caused by the stretching has less effect on the pitch). The timpanist may wish to anticipate this effect when tuning.

The normal action of the foot on pedal timpani is to disengage a clutch with the heel, move the whole pedal to its new position, and then re-engage the clutch with the heel. The Dresden action involves a sideways movement to engage or disengage the clutch. With the Ludwig balanced action the tension of the head is balanced by springs, so that the player simply raises the pitch with the toe and lowers it with the heel.

Since the pedal only gives a range of a fifth, it may be necessary to screw tune the drum in advance to give the right lower and upper notes. A player can only approximately control the pitch by the feel of the pedal, or by any pitch gauge attached to the pedal mechanism, so fine tuning (when there is preparation time) is by ear as with hand-tuned drums. Although players can with practice operate the pedals effectively while playing, the idiomatic use of the pedal is for quick retuning rather than to allow timpani to play tunes. This is in contrast to the use of valves on brass instruments, which were originally thought of as a mechanism for quickly changing crook, but which proved more than adequate for melodic playing. The pedal glissando is common in modern timpani writing: an upward glissando is the more effective on a single note, as a rapid slackening of the head hastens the decay of a sounding note.

Timpani sticks are most commonly rested across the index fingers of each hand, with the thumbs placed on top. The grip on the sticks is critically important for proper control of rhythm and tone. If the sticks are held too near to their heads, loud playing is impossible; if they are held too near the stick ends, control is impaired. The normal playing action takes its energy from the wrists and its control from the fingers—the arms and elbows are only involved in changing from one drum to another.

A beating point some 75–100 mm from the edge gives the best pitch definition over a wide dynamic range. For very quiet passages, the playing spot can be moved nearer the edge. In single strokes, the player cannot rely on bounce to return the sticks: good tone is obtained by skilfully controlled lifting of the sticks, giving a sensation of 'picking notes off' the drum. Beating is hand-to-hand unless the music requires double beats in one hand in order to have the hands in the right position for the following note. For a particularly emphatic sforzando, both hands can be used simultaneously on one drum. Rolls on the timpani have to be a great deal less rapid than on smaller drums to be effective, though more rapid strokes smooth a crescendo. In a sustained roll, the player will be aware of individual strokes, while in the audience only a continuous tone is perceived. This is partly because each stroke gives rise to surface noise, audible only at close quarters. In loud rolls, the player is helped by the bounce of the sticks from the skin.

An undamped timpani note is perceptible for some three seconds (depending on ambient sounds), so notes often have to be terminated by 'wiping them off' the drumskin with the middle, ring, and little fingers of one hand. This is essential for staccato playing.

In Baroque (and some Classical period) music, only the basic part was written; it was expected that this would be elaborated by the timpanist with various rolls and embellishments, especially to emphasize cadences. This embellishment ('Schlagmanieren') was extemporized, but drew on a repertoire of stock formulae.

Timpani can be muted by placing a small cloth on the drumskin (a small duster, for example, is sufficient), by touching the head with one hand, or by holding down the stick after sounding a note. A muted note is not strongly pitched, and musical requirements for quiet playing are usually met by the gentle use of soft-headed beaters near the edge of the drum.

It is quite possible to play chords on two or more timpani, especially if there is more than one player. Discords are not so effective, as the notes tend to sound unpitched.

8

Stringed Instruments Played with a Bow

8.1 ACOUSTICAL PRINCIPLES

There is an interesting paradox in the operation of a bowed stringed instrument. To produce a sustained sound, the player places the resined hair of the bow against the string and pulls it steadily across the string in one direction. Yet we know that the sound produced corresponds not to a movement in one direction, but rather to a rapid oscillation. Moving the bow smoothly across the open A string of a violin, for example, results in a listener's eardrum being pushed in and pulled out 440 times a second.

We found the same paradox in the behaviour of wind instruments: the player blows a stream of air through the instrument as smoothly as possible to create a steady note, but the note is in fact a rapid fluctuation in the rate of air flow.

In each case, the heart of the instrument contains a mechanism for converting a steady one-directional motion into a controlled oscillation. For wind instruments the mechanism takes various forms: the air jet of the flute, the cane reed of the clarinet or oboe, the lips of the trumpeter. For the bowed strings, the secret lies in the periodic sticking and slipping of the bow hair as it presses against the string.

In Chapter 2 it was explained that, under normal bowing conditions, the stick-slip cycle is synchronized with the fundamental mode of the string, so that the energy imparted by the bow helps to build up a strong periodic vibration of the string. We will return shortly to consider what is meant by 'normal bowing conditions'. It is worth pausing briefly, however, to note an important distinction between the ways in which wind and stringed instruments radiate sound.

The tube of a wind instrument has only one important acoustical function, which is to confine and shape the vibrating air column. When the instrument is played, musically useful sound energy is stored in the standing waves of the air column. This energy is radiated directly into the surrounding atmosphere through the openings in the tube. The strong pressure vibrations in the air column force the walls of the tube to vibrate in sympathy, but in a well-designed instrument these wall vibrations are too small to contribute significantly to the radiated sound.

The musical energy store in a stringed instrument is the vibrating string. Unlike the vibrating air column of the wind instrument, however, the string is very inefficient at communicating its energy directly to the surrounding air. Even if a violin string were bowed with maximum strength by a virtuoso player, it would be inaudible in a concert hall, but for the fact that the string vibrations are coupled through the bridge to the wooden body of the violin.

The body of a stringed instrument has its own natural resonances, and in a good instrument these are carefully designed to respond to the string vibrations in a way which gives a musically satisfactory sound. After discussing the ability of the player to modify the string motion by bowing technique, we shall return to consider the nature of the body resonances and their effect on the radiation of sound.

The bowing action

Stringed instruments played with a bow have for three centuries formed the foundation of the Western European orchestra, and the repertoire of virtuoso solo and chamber music is far larger than that of any other class of non-keyboard instrument. Part of the reason for this predominance lies in the remarkable degree of control which the player can exert by varying the action of the bow. Although we have insufficient space to explore all the subtleties of bowing technique, it is useful to identify the basic principles governing the relationship between bow motion and string vibration.

In Chapter 2 we saw that the motion of a bowed string follows a remarkably simple pattern. At any instant, the string has the kinked shape corresponding to two sides of a triangle, the third side being the line joining the fixed end points of the string. During the course of one cycle of vibration the kink forming the apex of this triangle moves along a curved path from one fixed point to the other and back to the first. Some of the shapes adopted by the string during the cycle are drawn in Figure 2.17.

The amplitude of the string motion, defined as the maximum displacement from the position of rest, is largest at the centre of the string. The player controls the loudness of a particular note primarily by varying the amplitude of the string vibration. To achieve the desired amplitude, the player can adjust three aspects of the bowing: the speed with which the bow is pulled across the string, the force with which it is pressed against the string, and the position on the string at which the bow makes contact. It is worth considering the role of each of these variables in turn.

Since the bow hair sticks to the string for a large part of the vibration cycle, it is fairly obvious that, if the position of bow contact on the string is kept unchanged, a greater amplitude of vibration must mean a faster bow speed. An important point to note is that the force between the bow and the string does not come directly into this argument. Pressing harder with the bow will not increase the amplitude of vibration if the other two variables are kept unchanged. The player must nevertheless maintain the bow force within certain limits in order to ensure that the stick–slip cycle remains synchronized with the fundamental mode of the string. If the force becomes too weak, the cycle may jump to one of the higher mode frequencies; if it becomes too strong, the stick–slip motion becomes irregular and the sound degenerates into a raucous squawk.

There is a way in which the player can increase the string amplitude without bowing faster. If the bowing point is moved closer to the bridge end of the string, a given displacement of the bowing point results in a larger amplitude at the centre of the string. In addition, a larger fraction of the cycle time is spent on the 'stick' part of the stick–slip cycle. Both of these effects increase the amplitude achievable with a fixed bowing speed. Thus a long note without a change of bow direction is more easily played close to the bridge.

Bowing near one end of the string does have dangers as well as advantages. The American scientist John Schelleng made a theoretical study of the bow–string interaction, and Figure 8.1 is based on some of his results. Although Schelleng made some simplifying assumptions in his calculations, the curves in Figure 8.1 show at least qualitatively why the player has to exercise careful control over bow force when changing the bowing point.

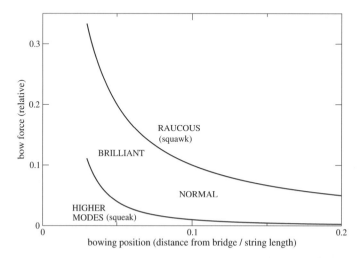

8.1 The maximum bow force (upper curve) and minimum bow force (lower curve) which result in a musically acceptable sound, shown as a function of the distance of the bowing point from the bridge. Based on a theoretical calculation by John Schelleng

The minimum bow force necessary to avoid jumping to a higher mode (which we can loosely call the 'squeak limit'), and the maximum force which maintains a stable vibration (the 'squawk limit'), both increase steeply as the contact point approaches the bridge. The range of acceptable forces between the two limits also increases, but, more significantly, the ratio of the squawk limit to the squeak limit decreases sharply as the distance of the bowing point from the end of the string is reduced. The diagram in Figure 8.1 suggests that when this distance is a fifth of the string length the maximum bow force is twenty times the minimum; when the distance is one twentieth of the string length both limits are higher, but the maximum force is only five times the minimum. In practice, this means that the inexperienced player finds it much more difficult to avoid either a squeak or a squawk when playing near the bridge. A skilful player, on the other hand, can generate a much louder note near the bridge without quickly running out of bow.

Two other aspects of bowing technique demand at least a brief mention. The foregoing discussion has implied that a change in bow speed, force, or position will alter the amplitude of the string vibration without otherwise changing its pattern. If this were really the whole story, we would expect that altering the bow position would not noticeably change the timbre of the sound. It is a fact of musical experience, however, that bowing nearer to the bridge tends to increase the relative strength of high-frequency components in the sound. More careful study of the bowing process shows that our picture of string motion is oversimplified: a real string excited by a bow of finite width does not have the abrupt kink shown in Figure 2.17. The apex of the triangle is rounded off, to an extent which depends on the bowing position and which in turn affects the timbre of the sound.

We have concentrated our discussion on the steady part of a bowed note, but we cannot leave the topic of bowing technique without remarking on the wide variety of ways in which the player can choose to initiate the sound. The stable vibration patterns shown in Figure 2.17 do not spring into life fully formed, even when the correct combination of bow force, speed, and position have been chosen. For a short time (typically around a fiftieth of a second) various processes compete for control of the string, giving rise to a rich mixture of harmonic and inharmonic frequency components in the attack transient. One of these processes involves the excitation of a set of string modes quite different from the transverse modes which we have previously discussed. These are torsional modes, in which the string rotates around its axis. Recent research has shown that torsional modes can play an important role in the transient behaviour of bowed strings.

The function of the bridge

If the fixed ends which determine the vibrating length of the string were completely unyielding, waves travelling along the string would be totally reflected at the ends. Powerful standing waves would be set up on the string; these standing waves would have little musical significance, however, since the unyielding supports would be incapable of transmitting any sound energy to the body of the instrument and hence to the ears of the listeners.

On the other hand, we have seen that the kink which travels along the string from the bowing point must be strongly reflected at each end if the stick–slip cycle is to be properly stabilized. Too efficient a transfer of energy from string to body could weaken the reflection of the kink to such an extent that it would be impossible to play a steady note.

In the many different designs of stringed instruments, these competing demands are satisfied in different ways. In the violin, for example, the bridge has two feet which rest on a thin, flexible top plate (Figure 8.2). A slender cylinder of wood called the soundpost is wedged between the top plate and the back plate of the instrument. The top of the soundpost is usually placed just behind the bridge foot at the high-pitch side of the violin. The exact placing of the soundpost has a profound effect on the way in which the instrument plays, to the extent that the French describe this little wooden stick as the 'soul' of the violin.

The proximity of the soundpost to one foot of the bridge means that that side of the bridge is relatively unyielding. The other foot of the bridge, under the low-pitch strings, is more flexibly supported, although the degree of flexibility is mod-

8.2 Violin with back removed to show bass bar and soundpost. Note that the soundpost is here glued to the underside of the top plate to illustrate its normal position; in the complete instrument is is usually wedged between top and back plates

ified by the supporting strut known as the bass bar which runs under the top plate parallel to the string direction. This asymmetry in the support of the bridge means that much of the energy transfer from the string to the violin body takes place through a rocking motion of the bridge, which is effectively pivoting on its treble foot.

Body resonances in stringed instruments

The labours of generations of musical inventors have resulted in a wide variety of body shapes for stringed instruments. The long, thin box of triangular cross section on the tromba marina, the flaring horn projecting from the strohviol: all serve the same basic function, which is to convert the vibrations of the bowed string into a radiated sound wave.

It is sometimes stated that a resonating body amplifies the sound generated by the string. Certainly the sound would be much quieter without the resonator. There is, however, an important distinction to be drawn between the action of a resonating body and that of an electrical pickup and amplifier. The sound output power of an electrically amplified violin can be hundreds of times greater than the maximum power which the bow is capable of feeding to the string: the extra power comes from the electrical supply to the amplifier. There is no source of energy in the wooden body of the violin, and without electrical amplification the power supplied by the bow sets an upper limit to the possible radiated power. The resonating body draws energy rapidly from the string; only if the player is capable of feeding energy into the string at a comparable rate will the potential benefit of the resonance be realized in a louder sound.

Unfortunately, radiation of sound is not the only process which draws energy from the string. Whenever any kind of motion is initiated, frictional forces come into play which dissipate some of the energy of motion. The energy does not disappear completely, but is converted into heat. Friction within the string itself, and in the bridge and body of the instrument, is constantly draining energy from the string vibration, and the bowing process must make up this deficit as well as supplying the sound energy. A good instrument feels easier to play than an unresponsive one partly because a greater proportion of the bow energy goes into sound.

We talk, somewhat loosely, about the 'resonance' of a violin body. In fact, the body of a stringed instrument has many different natural modes of vibration, each mode contributing a resonance with its own characteristic frequency. The first few resonances of the violin body occur at fairly widely separated pitches. Does this mean that only notes at these pitches will be effectively radiated? Fortunately not: the natural modes of the body are broad resonances, in the sense that the response of each extends over a pitch range of several semitones. One of the secrets of designing a good instrument lies in choosing the strength and placing of the body resonances so that they overlap to give the desired response over the whole frequency range of the instrument.

Even an instrument of the highest quality does not respond uniformly at all frequencies. Indeed, much of the individual character of the instrument comes from this very lack of uniformity. This point is illustrated by Figure 8.3, which shows the results of loudness curve measurements on three very different violins. The loudness curve is obtained by bowing the instrument at semitone intervals over its complete playing range; at each pitch, the highest sound level at which the player can produce a sustained note of good tone quality is measured by a sound level meter.

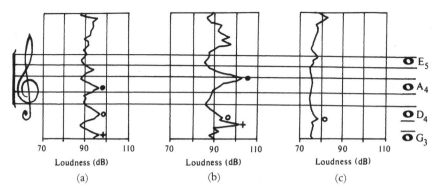

8.3 Loudness curves for three different violins: (a) a Stradivari; (b) an eighteenth-century instrument of second quality; (c) a poor-quality modern instrument. Open circle: 'main air resonance' (MAR); filled circle: 'main wood resonance' (MWR); cross: 'wood prime'. Notes on right show open string pitches. Adapted from Carleen Hutchins

It can come as a considerable surprise to violinists to realize that even an excellent Stradivari can show variations of more than 6 decibels in the loudness curve (Figure 8.3(a)). When playing normally, rather than in a scientific test, the experienced player compensates automatically for such variations. This compensation would be considerably more difficult to achieve on the violin whose loudness curve is shown in Figure 8.3(b), however; in the test, the maximum sound output for the note E_4 was 15 decibels lower than could be achieved at the pitch B_4.

The loudness curve for the Stradivari shows three peaks in sound output at pitches corresponding roughly to those of the three lowest open strings (A_4, D_4, and G_3). The peak near to D_4 is related to the lowest-frequency resonance of the air contained within the cavity of the violin, which is sometimes described as the 'main air resonance'; its frequency is controlled by the volume of the cavity, the flexibility of the walls, and the size of the f-holes cut in the top plate. The pitch of the air resonance can be estimated by blowing across one of the f-holes.

There is a resonance of the wooden body of the violin near in frequency to the first air resonance. Some makers claim that constructing the violin in such a way that this body resonance coincides in frequency with the first air resonance improves the playing properties of the instrument.

There is another important resonance of the wooden body of the violin, sometimes described as the 'main wood resonance', at around 500 Hz. The second air resonance is normally a little lower in frequency. These two resonances combine to give the broad resonance peak around the frequency of the A string (440 Hz).

The third major peak in the loudness curve, known as the 'wood prime', is different in character from the other two, since it does not occur at the pitch of a resonance in the instrument. It is in fact exactly one octave below the wood–air resonance described in the previous paragraph. To understand the origin of the wood prime, we must recall that, when a particular note is played on the violin, the vibration transmitted from the string to the body through the bridge contains not just a single frequency component, but a whole harmonic series of such components. If the note played is A_3, for example, these components will have pitches A_3, A_4, E_5, A_5, and so on. There is no body resonance at the pitch A_3, so the 1st harmonic will not be strongly radiated. The 2nd harmonic, whose pitch is A_4, is however well placed to take advantage of the body resonance at around 440 Hz. As a result, the lowest notes on the violin are strong, with a special timbre characterized by a powerful 2nd harmonic and a relatively weak fundamental.

Although we have used the violin as an example when discussing the role of body resonances, similar principles apply to most other types of acoustically amplified stringed instruments. Without strong body resonances, the energy imparted by the player would remain trapped on the string. A somewhat quirky instrument of the type illustrated by Figure 8.3(b) is still more rewarding to play than the uniform mediocrity of an instrument with no strong resonances, such as that recorded in Figure 8.3(c).

Sound radiation from stringed instruments

The body of a violin or cello does not radiate sound energy with uniform efficiency in all directions. The directional pattern depends on the frequency of the sound; there is no noticeable directionality at low frequencies, while at high frequencies there is a general tendency for sound to be preferentially radiated outwards from the top plate.

When interpreting the musical significance of the directional nature of sound radiation, it is important to bear in mind that a single note played on the violin has many frequency components. Thus when the violinist plays the note A_3, the first two harmonic components have frequencies of 220 Hz and 440 Hz respectively; these will sound as strong behind the player as in front. The 5th harmonic, whose frequency is 1,100 Hz, will in contrast be radiated considerably more strongly in the forward direction. The timbre of the violin therefore sounds brighter to a listener in front of the player.

The situation is more complicated in a normal room, since much of the sound energy reaches the listener after multiple reflections from the walls. Nevertheless, it has been argued that the radiation patterns of the bowed strings should be carefully considered when arranging an orchestra on the concert platform.

8.2 HISTORICAL DEVELOPMENT

The earliest bowed strings

Musical instruments of the chordophone family, based on the vibrations of stretched strings, are known to have existed as early as the third millennium BCE. These were not bowed instruments, however, but lyres belonging to the family of plucked strings to be discussed in the next chapter. Some writers have claimed that the technique of bowing was also introduced in the third millennium BCE, but modern scholars discount this view. In fact, the idea of sounding a string by drawing a bow across it does not seem to have become widespread until the tenth century CE. Probably originating in central Asia, the use of the bow spread through the Byzantine empire and the Arab world, until by the end of the eleventh century bowed instruments were common throughout Western Europe.

Manuscript illuminations and carvings from this period show instruments of various shapes, sometimes with one string, sometimes with several. The bows are also very varied in shape, some with almost straight sticks, others with sticks strongly curved outwards in the form of a letter C. There is no evidence that concave bows, with the stick curving inwards towards the hair, were used in this early period.

Rebec

The names used to describe instruments in medieval literature are very varied, and there is often confusion as to which type of instrument is indicated by a particular writer's use of a given name. The term rabab was used to describe a range of bowed instruments of Moorish origin, and from this word evolved a bewildering array of different terms such as rubebe, rebecq, rubible, and rabel.

To bring order to this confusion, modern writers have tended to select the term rebec to describe an important family of instruments, characterized by a body with a pear-shaped back merging smoothly into a neck carved from the same piece of wood (Figure 8.4(a)). The top of the body was covered either by a

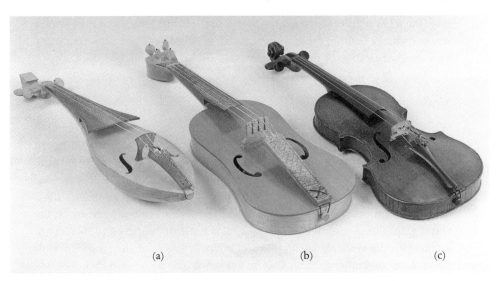

(a)   (b)   (c)

8.4 (a) alto rebec (Ellis, *c.*1980); (b) reconstruction of a late medieval fiddle (Ellis, *c.*1980); (c) violin (Tononi, Bologna, *c.*1700). Note that the original medieval fiddle on which the reconstruction (b) was based had five strings

stretched skin or by a wooden plate. Some scholars claim that the term 'rebec' was used only to describe instruments with wooden soundboards, and certainly this is the type of instrument which became firmly established in Europe.

Although it is not possible to be certain of the internal construction of instruments in illustrations, and no early rebecs have survived, it is unlikely that a soundpost was used. The number of strings, made from twisted sheep gut or silk, varied from one to four or more, although most illustrations show either two or three strings. Some illustrations show loops of gut, called frets, tied round the neck to guide the placing of the left-hand fingers.

There was no standardization of playing position or bowing technique in the Middle Ages. Sometimes the instrument is shown held vertically, with the body resting on the player's lap; sometimes it is held with the body under the player's chin and the neck almost vertically downwards; sometimes it is held horizontally across the player's chest. The bow may be held at one end or near the middle, with an overhand or underhand grip. It was clearly a period of experimentation and development.

By the fifteenth century the rebec had become one of the standard instruments used by the minstrel bands attached to noble households. Modern reconstructions of rebecs usually have a powerful nasal sound, especially on the upper strings, and this characteristic also fitted the instrument for use by the groups of itinerant musicians who played for dancing in marketplace and tavern. By this stage the rebec commonly had three strings tuned in fifths; the sixteenth-century writer Agricola describes four different sizes of rebec—discant, alto, tenor, and bass—with the strings of the discant tuned to G_3, D_4, and A_4.

Medieval fiddle

While the pear-shaped rebecs were developing in northern Europe in the eleventh century, musicians in southern Europe seemed to have favoured a rather different design of bowed instrument. This had a body in the shape of an elongated oval, often thinning to a waist in the middle. The back was flat, and the neck was made from a separate piece of wood jointed to the body. Illustrations frequently show the instrument being played with the neck vertical and the body resting on the player's lap. The description 'medieval viol' is sometimes applied to this instrument, since the vertical playing position is characteristic of the family of viols which developed four centuries later. It seems unlikely, however, that there is any direct line of descent from the eleventh-century instrument to its fifteenth-century successor, and most writers prefer the more neutral term 'fiddle'. Indeed, some scholars extend the category of medieval fiddle to include the early pear-shaped instruments which we have called 'rebecs'. Here we will maintain the common distinction that a bowed instrument with a flat back and a separate neck is a fiddle, while one with a pear-shaped back and integral neck is a rebec.

Like the rebecs, fiddles are shown in illustrations with different numbers of strings. The early instruments often had five strings, sometimes with one lying off the fingerboard and therefore available only as a drone of constant pitch. There is considerable uncertainty about the nature of the bridges which would have been fitted to these fiddles: a flat bridge allows all the strings to be sounded simultaneously, implying extensive use of drone harmonization, while a curved bridge allows each string to be sounded singly. Probably both techniques were employed. Jerome of Moravia, writing at about the middle of the thirteenth century, suggested that a five-string fiddle could be strung G_2–D_3–G_3–D_4–G_4, which certainly suggests a drone accompaniment in open fifths.

The fiddle was established as a favourite instrument of the twelfth-century troubadors. In the thirteenth century it was frequently referred to in literature as an instrument capable both of virtuoso display and artistic refinement. Throughout the Middle Ages and the early Renaissance, groups of fiddlers were part of the retinue of royal households. Figure 8.4(b) illustrates a modern reproduction of a fiddle shown in the fifteenth-century painting *The Coronation of the Virgin*, although with four strings rather than the five of the original. In 1545 Henry VIII's battleship *Mary Rose* carried two fiddles basically of the medieval pattern, and it seems likely that the fiddles which played (along with rebecs) for Mary Queen of Scots in Edinburgh in 1561 were also of this type. By the middle of the sixteenth century, however, a further development had taken place in northern Italy, which was soon to sweep both rebec and medieval fiddle from the musical scene.

Emergence of the violin family

A variant of the medieval fiddle, known as the lira da braccio, had established an independent existence in Italy by the end of the fifteenth century. The lira da braccio had seven strings, two of which were drones lying to the side of the fingerboard. The bridge was flat enough to allow several strings to be played simultaneously, and one of the principal uses of the instrument was to provide a chordal accompaniment for singing.

Illustrations show that the lira da braccio was made with a variety of body shapes, but in the early years of the sixteenth century a version evolved which differed from the traditional medieval fiddle in several important respects. The belly and back were arched outwards, rather than flat; belly and back overhung the side ribs by a few millimetres; the C-shaped holes in the belly were replaced by f-shaped holes; and the inward-curving waist of the body became divided from the outward-curving upper and lower sections by sharply defined corners.

It is now generally accepted that the earliest true violin emerged in the first quarter of the sixteenth century, when an unknown Italian maker combined the body shape of the lira da braccio with the stringing arrangement of the rebec. The result was a three-stringed instrument which combined some of the best features of both its parents: the sophisticated construction of the body contributed volume and depth of tone, while the reduced number of strings and the tuning in fifths provided for agility and flexibility of bowing over the whole range of the instrument.

The first evidence for the existence of the violin comes from northern Italian fresco painters. In decorating the walls of the Palazzo di Ludovico il Moro in Ferrara, between 1505 and 1508, the painter Garofalo or one of his pupils provided us with the earliest-known illustration of a musician holding a violin. About thirty years later, Gaudenzio Ferrari painted a family of violins (treble, alto or tenor, and bass) in the cupola of Saronna Cathedral. Although some of the detail is obscure (and iconographical evidence must always be treated with caution), these and other wall paintings provide strong evidence that instruments recognizable as early versions of the violin, viola, and cello were in common use in northern Italy in the first half of the sixteenth century.

Like the rebecs from which they derived their system of tuning, the new violins initially had three strings. By about 1550 a fourth string had been added, at a higher pitch than the original three, in order to increase the upward compass of the instrument. Philibert Jambe de Fer, in a treatise published in Lyons in 1556, gives details of the tuning of the members of the violin family in use at that time. The 'dessus' was tuned G_3–D_4–A_4–E_5, like the modern violin; the 'hautecontre-taille' was tuned C_3–G_3–D_4–A_4, as is the modern viola; the 'bas' was tuned $B^\flat_1$–F_2–C_3–G_3, a tone lower than the modern cello.

The birth of the violin family was such an important event in the history of music that it is hardly surprising that numerous myths have grown up around it. It has been claimed that the first member of the family to emerge was the viola rather than the violin, but the available evidence suggests that the three sizes described by Jambe de Fer came into existence at essentially the same time. Part of the confusion which surrounds this question arises from the fact that the Italian term 'viola' was at this time a very general one, encompassing all members of the violin and viol families. The description 'viola da braccia' (literally 'arm viola') specified a member of the violin family, the smaller of which were held on the arm, while 'viola da gamba' ('leg viola') distinguished a member of the viol family, all of which were supported between the legs. The violin was thus a treble viola da braccio.

Attempts have also been made to identify the 'inventor' of the violin, although it is most likely that several makers working in Brescia in the early years of the sixteenth century must share the credit. Andrea Amati, born in Cremona some time before 1511, is the earliest maker to whom surviving instruments can be attributed. While there is no evidence that Amati actually invented the violin, the craftsmanship and quality of his instruments must be important factors in explaining the enthusiasm with which the new family was accepted into musical life throughout Europe. Towards the end of his life, Amati is reported to have supplied a complete string orchestra of thirty-eight instruments (violins, violas, and basses) to the French court of Charles IX.

Development of the Baroque violin

In the sixteenth century northern Italy maintained an unchallenged dominance in the field of violin-making. The two great centres were Cremona and Brescia. The Cremonese school founded by Andrea Amati was continued by his sons Antonio and Girolamo, while the Brescian school was led by Gasparo da Salo and his pupil Maggini. Instruments by these famous makers were exported all over Europe, and commanded very high prices: a single instrument by Gasparo da Salo was sold for more than 50 lire (several times the annual wage of a servant at the time).

It was not until the beginning of the seventeenth century that composers started to write music which exploited the particular properties of the violin family. In the sixteenth century the string bands were used to double the sung parts in vocal music, or to provide dance music for courtly festivities. The orchestration of a given piece of music was to a large extent dependent on the particular forces available on the occasion. This casual attitude to instrumentation is evident on the title page of Anthony Holborne's 1599 collection of dance music, described as 'suitable for violins, viols, and other musicall wind instruments'.

Claudio Monteverdi was one of the first major composers to make use of the expressive qualities offered by the violins. In the opera *Orfeo*, written in 1607, for example, it is an enchanting piece of imitative music for two violins which lulls the boatman Charon to sleep, allowing Orfeo to cross the river Styx and enter the Underworld.

At the same time, Italian composers such as Giovanni Paulo Cima, Giovanni Fontana, Biagio Marini, and Dario Castello were experimenting with works for one or two solo instruments with continuo accompaniment. The continuo might be a bowed instrument such as a bass viol or bass violin, a plucked instrument such as a harp or chitarrone, or a keyboard instrument such as a harpsichord or organ. Many of the solo parts in these early pieces of chamber music are equally suitable for wind or stringed instruments—indeed, they are often inscribed 'for violin or cornetto'. But some of them make use of wide leaps and arpeggiated figures which are clear harbingers of a developing violin idiom. From time to time there are double-stoppings (simultaneous playing on two strings), or instructions such as 'tremolo with the bow' or 'pizzicato' which make sense only on the violin. By the middle of the century composers such as Marco Uccellini had further developed the potential of the violin family in chamber music, while its scope for virtuoso display in solo music was dramatically demonstrated by the Bohemian composer Heinrich Biber in his 'Mystery' Sonatas, published around 1674.

The basic form of the violin, as developed by Andrea Amati and his contemporaries in the sixteenth century, proved equal to the increasing demands of seventeenth-century composers and performers. One musical development which had significant implications for the design of the violin was the increase in its playing range. The upward compass of the violin was extended by the use of higher positions (that is, by moving the hand further down the fingerboard), and the fingerboards were lengthened accordingly.

By the time that Maggini died, in about 1632, the Cremonese had established an unchallenged supremacy among Italian violin makers. Nicolo Amati, the son of Girolamo, carried the refinement of design and craftsmanship to a new level of perfection, although his work was rivalled by that of Jacob Stainer in Austria. Stainer and Amati produced violins of a broadly similar pattern, with a relatively highly arched belly and back. For a century or more, these instruments were prized above all others; among the famous musicians who owned Stainer violins in the eighteenth century were Leopold Mozart and J. S. Bach.

Nicolo Amati occupies a special place in the history of violin-making, not only because of the quality of his own instruments, but also because he taught most of the important makers of the next generation. Among his pupils was Andrea Guarneri, the first of the famous family of five makers of that surname. The last member of the family, Andrea's grandson Joseph del Gesu, made some of the finest instruments of any period.

Another of Nicolo Amati's pupils was Antonio Stradivari. The evidence that Stradivari learned his craft from Amati is actually quite tenuous, amounting only to the inscriptions on two violin labels. There is no doubt, however, that Stradivari's early instruments were strongly influenced by those of Amati—so much so, that those produced before about 1690 are sometimes described as 'Amatise'.

Even in his apprenticeship, however, Stradivari was experimenting with modifications to the currently accepted model of violin. In the middle of the century Amati had constructed some instruments in which the volume of the body was increased by widening the upper and lower sections. This was presumably with a view to increasing the loudness and carrying power of the instrument; Amati seems not to have been entirely content with the result, since his later instruments reverted to the smaller pattern. Around 1690 Stradivari also explored the advantages of a larger body, this time by increasing its length by about 3 per cent. Again, the result left something to be desired, and by the beginning of the eighteenth century Stradivari had returned to the classic body length (about 355 mm) used by Amati.

The quest for a more penetrating violin sound was fuelled by the development of the concerto form. First in the concerti grossi of Corelli, then in the violin concertos of Albinoni and Torelli, the soloist was required to project the sound in a musical context in which many other instruments might be playing simultaneously. In the instrument which he made in 1704 (now known as the 'Betts'), Stradivari arrived at a model which became the prototype, not only for most of his own extensive output, but for the majority of subsequent makers up to the present time.

The principal structural modification which distinguished the classic Stradivari instrument from the Amati design was a substantial reduction in the arching of the belly and back, giving the violin a noticeably slimmer profile. This flattening, together with other more subtle changes, permitted Stradivari to create violins with a rich yet powerful sound, which were eagerly taken up by the virtuosi of the time. It is worth noting, however, that many major players throughout the eighteenth century continued to prefer the sweetness of the Amati and Stainer violins for chamber music, in which strength of sound was not of paramount importance.

Viola and cello in the Baroque period

The discussion above has concentrated on the development of the soprano member of the violin family, since in the Baroque era the major advances (both musical and technical) were focused on the violin proper rather than on its larger siblings. Nevertheless, most of the major violin makers also produced violas and cellos. Stradivari in particular devoted considerable attention in the latter part of his long working life to experimenting with the overall size and relative proportions of the cello; as with the violin, he established a model which has served as an example to makers ever since.

The development of the viola was complicated by the fact that the acoustical requirements on this alto or tenor member of the violin family are partly at odds with the scale of the normal human frame. If it is to be held on the arm, as is the violin, it cannot have a body length greater than about 450 mm; even this size is difficult to manage for a player with an average length of arm. Yet this is considerably shorter than the instrument should be if it is scaled acoustically according to its pitch, a fifth below the violin.

The viola played an important role in the string bands of the sixteenth and early seventeenth centuries, since much of the repertoire was in five parts and violas were expected to play the three inner parts. For this purpose, violas of different sizes were made, although they were customarily all tuned in the same way $(C_3-G_3-D_4-A_4)$; the larger instruments played the lower parts, the smaller instruments the upper. This diversity of size has continued to characterize the viola up to the present time.

Michael Praetorius, in the second volume of his encyclopedic *Syntagma Musicum* published in 1619, gives the tuning $(F_2-C_3-G_3-D_4)$ of an instrument intermediate between the cello and the viola. This 'tenor violin' must have been played cello-style, rather than on the arm, and did not survive to become a standard part of the seventeenth-century string orchestra.

The Tourte bow

Up to the middle of the eighteenth century, the bows used on stringed instruments were far from standardized. The sticks varied in length, depending on the type of music being played. In France, where dance music was of great importance, players favoured a relatively short bow, whereas the legato phrasing and refinement of expression characteristic of the Italian sonata demanded a much longer bow. The sticks were tapered towards the tip, and were either straight or outward curving. By the early eighteenth century the tip of the bow had developed a noticeable 'head', which supported the hair away from the stick and allowed the full length of the hair to be used in playing. Figure 8.5(b) illustrates an eighteenth-century bow which, although made for a bass viol, is typical of the general nature of the bows used on violins and viols in the first half of the eighteenth century.

By the end of the eighteenth century the violin bow had undergone a major transformation, from which it emerged in the form which has remained standard

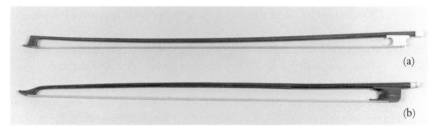

8.5 (a) violin bow (Dodd, England, eighteenth century); (b) bass viol bow (Germany, mid-eighteenth century)

in its essential details from that time to the present. The credit for this development, which had far-reaching effects on the construction of violins and the evolution of playing technique, is usually given to one man: François Tourte. Tourte was the younger son in a family firm of Parisian bow makers. He did not invent the modern bow, as is sometimes claimed; but he synthesized a number of trends and innovations with the skill of a master craftsman.

The major change was in the curvature of the bow. While almost all previous violin bows had had sticks which were either straight or of convex curvature (that is, curving away from the hair), Tourte settled on a concave curvature, which was obtained by repeated heating and bending. The stick was thinned smoothly towards the tip, but then widened gracefully into a pronounced head. The extra weight introduced by the enlargement of the head was counterbalanced by metal inlays in the 'frog' (the end under the player's hand). The amount of hair was increased, and a metal ferrule at the frog ensured that the hair lay in a flat ribbon. Finally, Tourte standardized the violin bow length at about 750 mm. An example of the new style of bow, by the London maker John Dodd, is illustrated in Figure 8.5(a).

The concave curvature of the Tourte bow allowed the player to apply a stronger and more uniform pressure to the string over the whole length of the bow than was possible with a straight stick. It was thus ideally suited to the type of sustained cantabile playing at fairly high volume which was required by the classical violin concerto. At the same time, the change in balance caused by the increase and redistribution of weight in the bow permitted the introduction of new types of articulation, while restricting the accessibility of others. The rapid and almost complete acceptance of the Tourte bow had a major impact on the way in which violin-playing evolved in the nineteenth century.

The nineteenth-century violin family

The adoption of the Tourte bow was only one of a series of changes which revolutionized the nature of violin manufacture and performance in the late eighteenth and early nineteenth centuries. By this time the focus of innovation had shifted from Italy to France, and French makers such as Nicholas Lupot responded to the continuing demand for a violin with a more powerful sound by introducing various structural modifications to achieve this end. The strings were made longer and heavier, with a consequent increase in their tension. The height of the bridge was also increased. These changes combined to put a much greater downward force on the belly of the violin, and to increase the force tending to bend the neck away from the body. It was therefore necessary to strengthen the internal structure of the body by thickening the soundpost, and by thickening and lengthening the bass bar. The neck was mortized into the body in order to strengthen this joint, and tilted backwards in order to reduce the twisting effect of the string tension on the joint. The length of the neck was also increased to accommodate the greater string length.

With these changes, the violin was equipped to meet the new challenges of the Romantic concerto and the pyrotechnic solo performances of virtuosi such as Nicolò Paganini. Comparable modifications were also made in the design of violas and cellos. By this stage, the violin family had essentially arrived at its modern state, although various further innovations, such as the chin rest on the violin and viola and the spike on the cello, were adopted in the course of the nineteenth and early twentieth centuries. The most significant of these later changes was the replacement of gut strings by overwound and pure metal strings. Already in the eighteenth century, the G string on the violin was normally a gut core with a spun overlayer of metal. Gradually the use of overwound D and A strings became customary, although it was not until the twentieth century that the gut E string was replaced by a single steel strand.

And what of the wonderful instruments of the past, the violins by Amati, Stainer, Stradivari, and Guarneri which had been treasured by eighteenth-century players? Most of these were taken apart and rebuilt in the modern style, the neck tilted and lengthened, the fingerboard lengthened, the bridge raised and the internal structure strengthened. The flatter instruments of the Stradivari pattern responded to this modernizing process much more satisfactorily than did the highly arched Amatis, and a remodelled Stradivari became the most highly sought after of all violins. Indeed, although around 650 violins made by Stradivari are still in existence, not one is known to have survived without modification.

The Renaissance viol family

The viola da gamba, a fretted, stringed instrument held with its body supported by the legs and bowed underarm, emerged in the fifteenth century and, within a century, became one of the most important court instruments. The gamba developed in parallel with and distinct from the violin family. Although illustrations of waisted, bowed string instruments are known from the twelfth to the fourteenth centuries these appear to have a separate evolution and are perhaps closer to medieval fiddles rather than true medieval viols. The revived use of a gamba rather than a braccia playing position for a waisted stringed instrument in Europe appears to have first emerged in Aragon. Thurston Dart, in Baines (1961), related the basic shape and construction of fifteenth-century viols to the flat-backed, stringed vihuela de mano or plucked guitar, developed in Spain, and used the term 'bowed guitar' to describe the first true viol. Ian Woodfield argued that the Moorish rabab, a small, stringed instrument held downwards and bowed, was an earlier structural influence on the development of the Valencian viol. Illustrations of instruments from the fifteenth century show a remarkable variety in the sizes, structure, number of strings, and playing practice. They suggest a rich period of experiment and change in response to influences from Italy and Spain. These prototype viols, usually with straight bridges, may have been bowed as a drone, as the angel musician appears to be doing in the altarpiece of *c.*1500, Sardinian school, in the Museo Nazionale, Cagliari. Other illustrations of the viol from the quarter-century between 1485 and 1510 commonly depict a tall, slender instrument with a tenor-scaled body, ribs about the width of its long neck and from three to six long strings. Together with other Spanish cultural features, the viol spread eastwards into Naples and the papal states and achieved instant success. In Mantua, Isabella d'Este was one of many patrons of the arts who ordered several viols of varied sizes. Most Italian viols had fretted fingerboards and a slightly arched bridge which allowed individual strings to be bowed. This important ability to sustain a melodic line endowed the viol with a versatility which immediately opened up a much wider range of musical possibilities.

The repertoire considered particularly suitable for the earliest Renaissance viols is difficult to determine, but after the development of the arched bridge the viol was probably useful in a wide range of secular chansons and dances as well as religious music. Northern composers working in Italy wrote appropriate part settings of songs for viols and by *c.*1518 the viol or 'grosse Geige' was so popular in German-speaking Europe that it appeared in Hans Burgkmair's engravings of courtly instruments celebrating the Triumph of Maximilian I. Instruction manuals for amateur viol players were produced which reveal that German instruments might have either five or six strings and a variable number of frets. Treatises by Judenkünig (1518), Gerle (1532), and Agricola (1545) indicate that players used lute tablature and commonly played in consorts of large viols or duets with a lute or voice. By 1530 the viol had developed much deeper ribs which necessitated a bend in the back to meet the neck. Sloping shoulders and a pegbox with a flat-sided scroll with a spiral groove became characteristic of Venetian viols. The earliest surviving viol of this type is thought to be in the Kunsthistorisches Museum, Vienna, labelled 'Fransiscus Linarolus Bergomensis Benetiis Faciebat'. Francesco and his son Ventura together with Hainrich Ebert and Antonio and Battista Ciciliano perfected and popularized this form of the viol in the mid-sixteenth century although fashion dictated some temporary variations in form. A large-scale viol like a double bass developed in Italy and Germany, bringing the number of identifiable regular sizes of viols to six—large bass, small bass, tenor, alto, discant, and small discant.

In addition to the use of viols in large-scale ensembles or viol consorts solo viol-playing developed in sixteenth-century Italy. Sylvestro di Ganassi, himself a virtuoso player, wrote an exhaustive manual (*Regola Rubertina* 1552) advocating expressive playing and describing techniques of playing with the goal of a perfect performance. Diego Ortiz in his *Trattado de glosas* of 1553 and Francesco Rognoni in *Selva di varii passagge* of 1620 extended the virtuosic possibilities of the solo viol.

The Baroque viol

By the seventeenth century, the viol had settled into a more standard instrument of exceptionally light construction, with a thin, arched belly, deep ribs glued flush with the front and back plates, and internal structural supports including a bass bar and soundpost. The bridge was higher than that common on Renaissance viols, and the wide neck sloped backwards in order to accommodate the resulting angle between the strings and the belly. The seven gut frets, tied at semitone intervals, could be individually fine tuned. Six (occasionally five or seven) gut strings, the lower three often overwound, were attached to a tailpiece which was in turn hooked to a wooden post at the lower extremity of the belly. Sound-holes positioned at the waist of the belly were usually C-shaped.

The viol bow tended to be less arched than those of the Renaissance, but was differently weighted from the contemporary cello bow; it was played with an underhand grip (palm upwards). Snakewood seems to have been the material most prized for bow construction.

In the seventeenth century the viol blossomed into one of the most important of chamber-music instruments, with an extensive repertoire of music for consorts of up to eight viols as well as a large number of pieces for solo bass viol. The bright, ringing sound characteristic of an open string is obtainable on all the notes of the viol, since the string is stopped by the fret rather than the finger, and this clarity of sound was particularly valued in polyphonic consort music. The characteristic shaping of viol notes, and the expressive quality of sound obtainable over an extensive dynamic range, were considered in the seventeenth century to allow the viol to approach the human voice in flexibility.

The first printed music explicitly for viol is contained in the *Regola Rubertina* of Ganassi. It includes a piece for voice accompanied by viol. Ganassi's exercises, like those of Ortiz, emphasize the importance of the complex string-crossing necessary to play in the improvisatory style popular in the sixteenth century. In the seventeenth century, virtuosity reached its zenith with the compositions of Sainte-Colombe (who is generally credited with the addition of the seventh string to the bass viol) and his pupil Marin Marais.

Marais occupied an important position at the French court, and his music displays a brilliant command of melodic line, harmony, and ornamentation. Nevertheless, by far the greatest corpus of music for viols is that of the English consort composers. Music for between three and seven viols by Tomkins, Coprario, Ferrabosco, Gibbons, Jenkins, Lawes, Locke, and above all Byrd, exploited the capacity of a matched set of instruments to blend their sounds into an entrancing and intricate web of polyphony. These compositions were known all over Europe in the seventeenth century, and are still the heart of the viol repertoire today.

In the eighteenth century, the viols were gradually overpowered by the louder sonorities of the violin family. The bass retained a role as a continuo instrument, although a few composers, including J. S. Bach, wrote music for solo bass viol with continuo accompaniment. The last virtuoso performer and composer in the eighteenth century was Carl Abel; when he died in London in 1787, viol-playing in Europe effectively came to an end.

Revival of viol playing in the twentieth century

The viol was among the first of the 'historical' instruments to be revived in modern times. The second half of the nineteenth century saw several short-lived performing groups and gamba societies, but it was Arnold Dolmetsch who initiated serious research into the construction and repertoire of Baroque instruments. With his family and pupils he formed a performing group in London in the early twentieth century, which revived the viol music of such composers as Ferrabosco and Marais. The formation of the Viola da Gamba Society helped to foster interest in viol music and to encourage makers and players. An equally vigorous movement developed in Germany.

Many of the early revivalist makers were over-influenced by contemporary techniques in cello construction, and tended to produce powerful but over-heavy viols with thick strings, high bridges, and incorrectly angled necks. Dietrich Kessler investigated carefully the constructional techniques of early makers, making use of his own extensive collection of original viols. From these studies he evolved a series of models of lighter construction. Subsequently, many of the most respected makers, such as David Rubio and Michael Heale, have concentrated on faithful reproductions of carefully researched original instruments by master craftsmen like John Rose and Henry Jaye.

In recent years there has been a proliferation of courses on the making, restoration, and playing of viols. A small but growing group of makers and players now specializes in the Renaissance viol and its music. Modern viol tutors designed for amateur players are readily available, and composers such as Peter Maxwell Davies have written for the instrument. The popularity of the soundtrack of the 1991 film *Tous les Matins du Monde*, consisting largely of the viol music of Sainte-Colombe and Marais played by Jordi Savall, reflected the continuing momentum of the revival of interest in the viol.

8.3 INSTRUMENTS IN MODERN USE

Violin

The violin is by far the most versatile member of its family. It not only provides the most characteristic voice of the symphony orchestra, but it has an unrivalled repertoire of solo and chamber music. Under its more informal alias of 'fiddle', it is equally at home in a wide range of folk-music styles from Shetland reels to Appalachian bluegrass. With some electronic assistance, it has carved an important niche in jazz and popular music.

Nearly all modern violins conform closely to the body outline established by Stradivari, with the nineteenth-century modifications already discussed. The body length is typically 355 mm. The four strings are tuned G_3–D_4–A_4–E_5; the typical sounding length (from the 'nut' at the top of the fingerboard to the bridge) is around 325 mm. The E string is normally of unwound steel; the lower three may be gutwound with aluminium or silver, or may have a nylon or steel core wrapped by a steel ribbon.

Above the fingerboard nut, each string is wound over a wooden peg, inserted laterally through two holes in the hollow pegbox at the top of the neck. The tension of the string is adjusted by turning the peg, relying on the friction between the wooden surfaces to prevent the string slackening after adjustment. The other end of the string is secured to a tapering tailpiece mounted below the bridge. Fine tuning of the top string is usually assisted by a metal screw adjuster, fitted at the point where the lower end of the string joins the tailpiece.

The violin is usually played with the neck approximately horizontal and the lower end gripped under the chin, although some folk fiddlers are highly inventive in discovering unorthodox playing positions. A chin rest is usually fitted to the left-hand side of the tailpiece (as the player sees it). Most players also use a detachable shoulder rest or pad between the back of the instrument and the shoulder.

The violin bow used with a modern violin is similar in its general outline to the model of Tourte, with a typical overall length of about 740 mm, although there is considerable variety in the weight, balance, and degree of taper of the bows favoured by different players. The tension of the hair is adjusted by a screw in the frog; when the bow is not in use, the tension is reduced to minimize the risk of distortion of the bow stick.

Scaled-down versions of the violin are made for young children to practise on; these instruments are usually strung and played in the same way as a full-sized instrument.

It should also be noted that the majority of players who specialize in Baroque music have now come to realize that the modern violin is not the most appropriate instrument for this repertoire. To satisfy the demand for authentic 'Baroque' violins and bows, many makers have returned to the techniques and patterns of the great makers of the seventeenth and eighteenth centuries. Indeed, some have gone even further, constructing replicas of the instruments used in the sixteenth-century string bands. While these historical reconstructions will certainly never replace the modern instrument with all its power and flexibility, they offer fascinating insights into the way in which the music of the past might have sounded to contemporary listeners.

Viola

As was already noted, the viola has in some ways suffered from an uncertainty as to whether its relationship to the (treble) violin was that of alto or tenor. Indeed, the old English term for the viola was 'tenor'; while the French formerly used the same word, the viola is now called the 'alto' in French. This dichotomy is reflected in the relative lack of standardization in the size of the instrument: violas in use at the present time range in body length from under 400 mm to 450 mm or more, with an average length of about 420 mm.

The four strings of the viola are tuned C_3–G_3–D_4–A_4, and are normally of either overwound gut or steel. Each string is a perfect fifth lower than the corresponding string on the violin, which means that the frequency of each string is reduced by a factor of 2 : 3 in comparison with the violin. It is sometimes stated that, if the viola were a perfectly scaled-up violin, its body length would be increased by a factor of 3 : 2, the inverse of the frequency ratio quoted above. However, such a scaling would not only produce an unmanageable body length of 533 mm; it would significantly alter the relationship between the frequencies of the body resonances and those of the open strings. Carleen Hutchins, the American physicist and violin maker, has designed a viola whose principal body resonances are in the same relative positions as those of the violin, but even this instrument has a body length of 510 mm, rather long to hold on the arm.

It is clear, then, that the conventional viola must be considered on its own terms, not as a scaled up violin. And on its own terms it has an individual voice which has won it a place, not only as an invaluable 'filler' in the middle register of orchestral string texture, but as a poignant soloist in chamber music and concerto.

Violoncello

The violoncello, commonly described simply as the cello, is the bass member of the violin family. In fact, in the sixteenth and early seventeenth centuries it was described as a bass violin, the term violoncello being first recorded in 1665. In the general pattern of its construction it resembles the violin and viola, although the ribs are proportionately much deeper than those of the violin. The four strings are tuned C_2–G_2–D_3–A_3, an octave below the viola. They are frequently of gut over-spun with metal, although nylon and steel cores are also used.

The lowest string on the cello has a vibration frequency which is one third that of the corresponding string on the violin. A simple linear scaling of the violin using the inverse of this factor would give an instrument with a body length of 1,065 mm; even a more modest scaling preserving the relative pitches of the body resonances would require a body length of around 860 mm. Although cellos with body lengths greater than 800 mm were constructed in the seventeenth century, Stradivari's small model with a body length of about 755 mm has become the standard pattern for modern instruments. The success of the small-scale cello is partly due to the extra depth of the ribs; the consequent increase in the volume of the internal cavity places the pitch of the air resonance close to that of the second lowest string, as it is on the violin.

The principal practical difference between the cello and the higher-pitched members of the family is dictated by the size of the human frame. The cello is much too large to be held on the arm, and is always played with the neck uppermost and the body sloping down between the player's legs. In the seventeenth century, the lower end of the instrument was often rested on the ground between the player's feet; in the eighteenth century, the smaller instrument was supported on the calves. Modern reproductions of historic cellos are still played in this way, but the true modern cello is invariably fitted with an endpin, or spike, which rests on the floor. The virtuoso Paul Tortelier pioneered the use of a long endpin, which was bent so as to tilt the cello closer to the horizontal.

The sounding length of the strings on the cello is typically around 690 mm, rather more than twice that typical of the violin. The cello bow, like that used on the viola, is somewhat shorter and heavier than the violin bow. As with the violin, smaller-scale cellos and bows are manufactured for children.

Double bass

The contrabass member of the violin family, known in English as the double bass, is less standardized in scale and shape than the other members of the family. This is partly for historical reasons—the earliest stringed instrument playing at contra-bass pitch was the large viol known as the violone, and many modern double bass-es still retain the sloping shoulders and flat back characteristic of the viol family. For a very large instrument like the double bass, the viol shape also has some prac-tical advantages in comparison with the other popular pattern based on the violin outline: it is simpler and more economical to construct, and allows the player more unrestricted access to high positions on the fingerboard.

The average body length of an orchestral double bass is around 1,150 mm. This size of instrument is sometimes known as a three-quarter bass, since much larger instruments, with body lengths up to 1,400 mm, are also to be found. The double bass rests on the floor, the player either standing or sitting on a high stool behind the instrument.

The string length also varies considerably from instrument to instrument, although most orchestral basses have a string length of about 1,050 mm. The stringing and tuning of the double bass is again less standardized than in the other orchestral stringed instruments. The most common model at present has four strings, tuned E_1–A_1–D_2–G_2. The tuning in fourths, rather than the fifths found on all the other members of the violin family, is another relic of the contrabass viol, but it is also dictated by the large string length. Stopping on the fingerboard two notes a tone apart requires nearly twice as great a stretch of the fingers on the dou-ble bass as it does on the cello; tuning the strings closer in pitch reduces the neces-sity for the left hand to stretch or jump large distances on one string.

The double bass plays a vital role in the symphony orchestra, providing a solid foundation for the string texture. Frequently the double-bass section is given the same music as the cellos, but an octave lower. In fact, double-bass parts are nor-mally written an octave higher than they sound; cellos and basses are then playing the same written notes, but the sound is of octave doubling. From time to time, of course, the individual voice of the double-bass section is heard on its own, usual-ly to mysterious or menacing effect.

Not infrequently, orchestral double-bass parts call for notes below E_1. Some instruments have a fifth string, normally tuned to B_0, on which these notes can be played. Four-stringed instruments can be fitted with a mechanical extension to the pegbox, which when activated allows the pitch of the E_1 string to be lowered in semitone steps to C_1. If neither of these recourses is available, the player must sim-ply transpose the unplayable notes up an octave.

Two types of bow are in common use on the double bass. The French type has the same general form as the cello bow, but is shorter, heavier, and more strongly curved. The German type has a much wider frog, which is grasped end-on by the player's right hand, like a saw. The pizzicato technique is especially important on the double bass; in jazz and dance music it is the standard method of playing, the bow being reserved for special effects.

The Hutchins violin octet

We have seen that the larger members of the violin family are far from being simply scaled-up violins. The viola and the cello are too small to play that role, while the double bass is not only too small but is usually constructed and strung quite differently from the violin. It is also evident that the modern violin family lacks a true tenor member, intermediate in size and pitch between the viola and the cello.

From time to time, makers have attempted to redesign the conventional instruments, or to construct a modern equivalent of the late Renaissance tenor violin, with a view to creating a more homogeneous violin band. By far the most significant and systematic of these attempts has been that of Carleen Hutchins in the mid-twentieth century. Basing her work on careful scientific analysis of the properties of violins, Hutchins devised a mathematical scaling technique which allowed her to design and construct a family of eight instruments which could with some confidence be described as scaled violins.

All the instruments of the Hutchins octet have four strings, and the characteristic violin body shape. The smallest, which she rather confusingly calls the treble, has a body length of 270 mm, and is tuned G_4–D_5–A_5–E_6, an octave above the conventional violin. The soprano, with a length of 300 mm, is tuned C_4–G_4–D_5–A_5. The violin and viola have their conventional tunings; the violin is of the normal size, but the viola has a body 510 mm long, and is played vertically like a small cello. The octet has a true tenor member, with a body length of 660 mm; it is tuned G_2–D_3–A_3–E_4, an octave below the violin. The baritone has the tuning of the cello, but its body length of 860 mm is about 14 per cent greater than that of a conventional cello.

The octet is completed by two basses. The small bass has a body length of 1,040 mm, slightly less than a conventional three-quarter double bass, but is tuned A_1–D_2–G_2–C_3, a fourth higher than the normal orchestral instrument. The large bass has a massive body 1,300 mm long, and has the conventional bass tuning E_1–A_1–D_2–G_2.

The fundamental design principle behind all of these scaled violins is that the body resonances should be at the same relative pitches on each instrument. For example, the main wood resonance of the violin is close to the second highest string pitch of A_4; on the treble, this resonance is close to A_5, which is again the pitch of the second highest string. On the baritone, the second highest string pitch is D_3, and the instrument is scaled to put the main wood resonance at that pitch.

Hutchins has made several sets of scaled violins. Individual instruments have been highly praised by major players, but as yet the new family has failed to win a significant place in the mainstream of musical life. Heard as an ensemble, the violin octet certainly does produce a remarkably strong and integrated sound, quite different from that of an ensemble of conventional strings; it remains to be seen whether it will develop a sufficiently interesting repertoire to reward players for the effort involved in mastering the technical demands of the new instruments.

The viol family

The most common use of the viol at the present time is in amateur consort-playing. Instruments based on the models of Henry Jaye are typical of the viols used by modern consort players. The smallest instrument in normal use is the treble or soprano in D, with its six strings tuned D_3–G_3–C_4–E_4–A_4–D_5. Two larger instruments are both described as tenor viols: the tenor in A, tuned A_2–D_3–G_3–B_3–E_4–A_4, and the more common tenor in G, tuned a tone lower to G_2–C_3–F_3–A_3–D_4–G_4. The standard bass is in D, an octave below the treble (D_2–G_2–C_3–E_3–A_3–D_4).

Players specializing in the Renaissance repertoire of the viol now have access to reproductions of sixteenth-century instruments by makers such as Linarol and Ciciliano. In this period the sonority of low-pitched consorts was particularly cultivated, and a Renaissance viol quartet might consist of a tenor in A, two basses in D, and an extra large bass in A (a fourth lower than the standard bass). These instruments, with their lighter construction and unwound bass strings, generate much less sound energy than the viols modelled on later originals, but the characteristic reedy timbre has surprising carrying power.

For the virtuoso music of the seventeenth and eighteenth centuries, a suitable instrument would be one based on the models left by French masters such as Bertrand. Many of the pieces by Sainte-Colombe, Marais, and Forqueray require a seventh string, which is normally tuned to A_1. Occasionally a small six-string bass is used to perform the elaborately ornamented sets of variations (or divisions) in which the English viol composers excelled; such an instrument is known as a division viol.

The violone is in essence a double-bass viol. Like the double bass of the violin family, its tuning is rather less standard than that of the other instruments in the family, but it is commonly tuned an octave below the standard bass in D.

8.4 INSTRUMENT CONSTRUCTION

The construction of bowed stringed instruments has traditionally been considered to be the preserve of the master craftsman. Although factory-built instruments became common in the nineteenth century, and a flood of mediocre instruments has resulted from the application of mass-production techniques in the twentieth century, the best instruments continue to be produced by individual makers, often working in relative isolation and using idiosyncratic techniques.

Rather than attempting a survey of the many different methods used to manufacture the various bowed instruments in modern use, we will concentrate on the materials and techniques most commonly found in violin construction. Much of this discussion is also applicable to the construction of the other members of the violin family; a few remarks about the major differences in viol construction are appended.

Materials used in violin construction

Although enthusiastic inventors have experimented with violin bodies of leather, tin, bakelite, and papier mâché, only instruments made of carefully selected woods have been found to be musically acceptable. It is hardly surprising that the material of which the body is made should be crucial to the sound of the instrument. The vibrating string on its own radiates a negligible amount of sound energy; what the listener hears is the sound radiated by the vibrating body. The resonances of the body determine the rate at which the vibration energy of the string is converted into sound, and shape the frequency spectrum which establishes the timbre.

Since woodwind instruments with metal and plastic bodies have been highly successful, it is perhaps worth recalling here that the function of the body of a woodwind instrument is totally different from that of a stringed instrument. In the former case, body resonances are normally insignificant, since the sound radiated by the body is negligible in comparison with the sound radiated directly by the air column. It would be unwise to state categorically that no material other than wood will ever make a successful violin body; but any such material will have to display the same resonant properties as the woods currently used. So far, no such alternative material has established itself.

For the top plate of the instrument, a soft wood such as pine or spruce is normally chosen. Trees from high altitudes in northern countries are ideal, since the slow rate of growth gives a close-grained texture with the optimum acoustical properties for this vital component of the violin. The back and ribs are made from a harder wood, usually maple or sycamore. For best results, the trees are not sawn longitudinally into planks, but cut radially with an axe (a process known as 'quartering'). The thin wedges of wood which are cleaved in this way are left to dry or season for several years; they are then ready for use in violin construction.

The neck and pegbox are usually made from the same maple or sycamore used in the back plate. The fingerboard is traditionally ebony, a particularly hard wood which stands up well to the constant abrasion of steel strings. The bridge is made from particularly close-grained maple. The soundpost and bass bar are normally spruce or pine, while the other internal structural elements (blocks and liners) may be spruce, pine, or willow. The pegs are made from a hardwood such as rosewood or ebony.

The glues used in violin construction are usually animal glues, which when dry provide more flexibility than resin glues. A joint made using water-soluble animal glue can also be relatively easily disassembled; this is an important point, since it may at some time be necessary to remove the top or back plate to carry out internal repair work.

Mystical qualities have often been attributed to the varnishes used by the great Cremonese violin makers. While these varnishes undoubtedly contributed greatly to the visual beauty of the instruments, the idea that the wonderful sound of a Stradivari derives from some lost secret in the recipe for the varnish has no historical or scientific foundation. A good varnish must seal and preserve the wood, covering the exterior with a thin skin which is flexible rather than hard and brittle. Oil-based varnishes satisfy these conditions better than spirit-based varnishes, although the much longer drying time of the oil-based varnish is a practical disadvantage.

Technique of violin construction

The constructional technique used by most modern violin makers is very similar to that employed by Stradivari, except that some of the labour is relieved by the use of power tools. The first stage in the construction involves the preparation of a solid mould, around which the body is assembled. A professional maker will have several such moulds ready for use; a collection of moulds used by Stradivari in his Cremona workshop is preserved in the Stradivarius Museum there.

In discussing the way in which the violin is assembled, it is helpful to refer again to Figure 8.2, which shows a violin with the back plate removed. The ribs, which form the sides of the body, are cut in the form of flat strips, and planed to a thickness a little under 2 mm. They are then dampened and bent over a heated iron former, a careful and laborious process which is continued until the strips have acquired the necessary curvature.

The rounded blocks at the neck and tailpiece ends of the internal cavity, and the smaller triangular blocks at the four corners, are held in position by the mould, and the ribs are glued onto these blocks. The thin strips of rectangular section known as liners are then glued around the inside edge of the ribs to provide a seating for the back plate.

If a sufficiently large wedge of wood is available, the back plate may be made from a single piece; otherwise, the wide ends of two wedges are glued together. There appears to be little to choose acoustically between a single and a two-piece back, but a two-piece back using adjacent wedges from the same tree can display a pleasing visual symmetry, especially when the wood is highly figured maple. The outline of the back plate is cut out using a saw, with the grain of the wood parallel to the long axis of the plate. The arched profile of the outside surface of the plate is arrived at by lengthy gouging and scraping. The sculpting of the plate is guided by the frequent application of templates, into which the profiles of several representative cross sections of the plate have been cut.

Once the outside surface of the back has been established, the plate is thinned down by drilling, planing, and scraping the inner surface. A finished plate might typically be about 4.5 mm thick at the centre of the waist, but only 2.5 mm thick in the middle of the upper and lower sections. The exact final dimensions of the plate will vary from one example to another, since the ideal resonant properties depend also on the quality and treatment of the particular sample of wood.

Before the back plate is fixed to the ribs, the purfling is inserted. This is a laminated strip about 1.5 mm wide, consisting of a layer of light-coloured wood (poplar or maple) sandwiched between two layers of very dark wood (ebony or black dyed pear). The purfling is glued into a channel cut round the perimeter of the plate. Its function is primarily decorative, although it has been suggested that the freedom of vibration of the plate may improve with age as a result of the glue in the purfling drying and cracking.

After the back plate is glued to the ribs, the body structure can be removed from the mould. Another set of liners is then glued around the upper inside edges of the ribs. The body is then ready for the fitting of the neck and the top plate.

The top plate is cut and shaped in the same fashion as the back plate; for acoustical reasons, it is practically always made from two jointed sections. A typical top plate might have a thickness varying between 2.4 mm and 3.4 mm. The two f-holes are cut into the plate, and the long supporting strut known as the bass bar is glued along the underside.

In controlling the final thinning of the top and back plates, the maker can estimate the pitch of the principal resonance of each plate by holding it lightly at the edges and tapping it. The resulting sound is known as a 'tap tone'. Some makers prefer to excite the tap tone by bowing the edge of the plate with a violin bow, or by using a signal generator and loudspeaker. Carleen Hutchins has suggested that the tap tones of the separate top and back plates should differ by at least a semitone if the completed violin is to have the correct overall response.

The neck, scroll, and pegbox are sculpted from a single piece of wood by a combination of sawing, drilling, chiselling, and gouging. The neck is dovetail-jointed into the block at the neck end of the body. The top plate is then glued down to the ribs, and the instrument is ready for varnishing. Many coats are applied, with each coat being carefully rubbed down after drying to ensure a uniformity of colouring and a silky finish. If oil-based varnishes are used, this process can last for several weeks.

After varnishing is completed, the fingerboard is glued to the neck and the tuning pegs fitted into the pegbox. Other fitments, such as the nut and the tailpiece, are added. The bridge, which is typically about 33 mm high, is placed in line with the transverse notches in the f-holes; it is not glued in position, but is held down by the pressure of the strings. The feet of the bridge are carefully shaved to ensure that it is properly seated on the curved top plate.

One of the most sensitive stages in the construction of the violin is also one of the last: the fitting of the soundpost. This is a cylindrical stick, usually between 6 mm and 7 mm in diameter. Although the soundpost is attached to the top plate in Figure 8.2 in order to illustrate its normal position, it is not in practice glued in place, but wedged between top and back plates. The optimum position for the soundpost is usually found to be about 6 mm behind the foot of the bridge which lies under the E string. Small changes in the location of the soundpost can have a profound effect on the strength and timbre of the sound of the violin, since these changes alter not only the ability of the bridge to communicate sound energy to the body, but also the nature of the body resonances. The final adjustment of the soundpost is therefore made after the violin is strung, using a special tool inserted through one of the f-holes.

Viol construction

The techniques used by modern viol makers are in general very similar to those already described for violin-making. Apart from the obvious differences in number of strings and body outline (see Figure 8.6), the Baroque viol shares most of its constructional features with the violin family, including the carved upward arching top plate, the bass bar, and the soundpost. The back of the viol is not, however, arched; it is made from a flat plate, bent towards the top to meet the back of the neck.

The most striking difference between the structure of a viol and that of the corresponding member of the violin family is that the plates and supports are generally much thinner and lighter in the viol. This lightness of construction is made possible by the relatively low string tension, which reduces the downward force on the bridge and belly. The back is so thin that it is incapable of sustaining the force transmitted by the soundpost; the latter rests on a transverse bar glued to the inside of the back plate.

The construction of historically accurate reproductions of Renaissance viols presents some additional problems to the modern maker. On instruments following the pattern of the early Venetian viols of Francesco Linarol, the top plate is not carved into its arched form, but bent from a flat plate, using the technique described above for the ribs. The curved plate is supported on two transverse struts, whose upper profiles are shaped to fit the curvature of the plate. The bending of the top plate is complicated by the fact that the curvature is greater at the neck end than at the tailpiece end.

Early Renaissance viols appear to have had neither soundpost nor bass bar. However, the sixteenth century was a period of experiment and development in stringed instrument construction, and many variations in internal construction

(a)   (b)

8.6 (a) bass viol (Kaiser, Düsseldorf, *c.*1700); (b) violoncello (Dewar, Scotland, late eighteenth or early nineteenth century). Note the difference in body size between two instruments of comparable tessitura

are found in surviving examples. A few specialist makers are at present exploring this area, and several musically successful but highly differentiated models of Renaissance viol are now available.

String materials and manufacture

Gut strings are made from the intestines of sheep. The intestines are cleaned using various types of solvent, cut into strips, soaked in water and stretched to form long thin filaments. While still wet, the filaments are twisted together under tension; after drying, the surface is polished smooth to give a plain gut string. A gut violin E string will typically contain about half a dozen filaments, whereas the bottom string of a double bass might require more than a hundred.

The nature of the lower strings used on Renaissance and early Baroque viols is still a matter of debate. Single gut strings are not satisfactory at low pitches, since they have to be made so thick that they respond sluggishly and have a dull sound. Several modern string makers have experimented with techniques for overcoming this problem. One approach is to make a thick but flexible string by tightly twisting several wet gut strings together to form a rope; such a string is known as a 'catline'. Another method is to impregnate a thinner single gut string with a metal salt solution which increases its density. Both methods give musically satisfactory bass strings, although it is an open question whether either method was used in the sixteenth century.

For instruments from the mid-seventeenth century and later, low-pitched gut strings usually had a tightly coiled spiral of wire wound round the gut core. Such overwound strings have a much smaller diameter than a plain gut string of the same pitch, and a greater flexibility which improves the response of the string. Gut strings on modern-style instruments are now almost invariably overwound, often with very fine metal ribbon which provides a smoother surface than cylindrical wire.

Gut strings with the degree of uniformity necessary to ensure good intonation and timbre are inevitably expensive, and various synthetic materials have been tried in the quest to find a satisfactory but cheaper alternative. Many high-quality strings are now made by winding aluminium strip on to a core of nylon or similar plastic.

Although Michael Praetorius in the early seventeenth century expressed the view that metal violin strings gave a better sound than gut, it was not until the twentieth century that all-metal stringing of members of the violin family became commonplace. The basic principle of wire manufacture has not changed since the early Middle Ages, although it is now highly automated. The metal is formed into a long cylinder by rolling or extrusion. After the cylindrical surface has been cleaned and lubricated, the rod is pulled through a hole in a block known as a draw-plate. Since the hole diameter is smaller than that of the original cylinder, the rod is thinned and narrowed. If necessary, several stages of reduction are employed to achieve the desired length and diameter of wire. Appropriate heat treatments in the course of the drawing process are important in giving the wire the necessary properties of strength and elasticity.

A steel core wrapped with aluminium strip now provides the basis for many brands of violin family strings. The better-quality strings use a multi-stranded rope metal core for the larger diameters, giving the advantages arising from improved flexibility which were outlined in the earlier discussion of gut catlines.

Bows

Without a good bow, the best viol or violin must remain an unfulfilled musical promise. Bow manufacture is a specialized craft, and the best bow makers command very high prices for their products. The major element in the bow is, of course, the stick, since it is the weight and elasticity of this which primarily determines how the bow responds to the player's demands. Snakewood, Brazilwood, and ebony were found by Baroque makers to have the right combination of properties for a bow stick; the best bows for modern instruments are almost invariably made from the variety of Brazilwood known as Pernambuco.

The bow stick is shaped to the desired profile, and given the appropriate degree of curvature by heating and bending. Sometimes fluting is carved into part of the stick, but usually the cross section is either round or octagonal.

Although the 'catgut' used in violin strings is actually sheep gut, the 'horsehair' on the bow does come normally from the tails of horses. Black horsehair is used, especially on double bass bows, but white hair tends to be finer and is preferred by most players. A modern violin bow requires around two hundred individual hairs, spread out into a flat ribbon some 10 mm wide; a Baroque bow, with a considerably narrower ribbon, might have only half this number of hairs.

One end of the ribbon of hair is pressed into a slot cut in the lower face of the head of the stick, where it is held by a small wooden wedge. The other end is similarly fixed on the bottom of the frog, which is normally made of ebony. The frog is attached to the stick through a metal screw mechanism mounted in the hollowed-out end of the stick; when the nut which protrudes from the end is rotated clockwise, the screw pulls the frog away from the tip, tightening the hair.

Not all horses grow the quality of hair required for bow-making. Even with the right horse, only a few per cent of the hairs in the tail will be sufficiently long and homogeneous. The inevitable limitations in the supply of good-quality horsehair have led some manufacturers to experiment with synthetic substitutes, and bows 'haired' with nylon are now fairly widely used. Most players, however, still prefer the traditional white horsehair.

8.5 PERFORMANCE PRACTICE

From their emergence in the thirteenth century to the present time, instruments with bowed strings have played a vital role in the development of Western European instrumental music, and have gathered an immense repertoire encompassing almost every genre and style. There is no space here to survey even a fraction of this rich heritage; the following section can only provide an introduction to the basic features of the playing techniques of the violin and viol families, with some passing references to the major composers and performers associated with them.

Bowing technique on the violin family

The first important rule in bowing any stringed instrument is that the hair of the bow should be pulled across the string at least approximately at right angles to the string. If this rule is violated, the hair will slide along the string, reducing the efficiency of the stroke and risking the high-pitched squeals arising from the excitation of longitudinal string modes.

The normal method of holding the modern violin bow is at the frog, which is pressed between the thumb and the second and third fingers of the right hand. The first finger rests on the bow stick, and plays an important role in determining the pressure exerted by the bow on the string. The little finger is not normally in constant contact with the stick, but can be used to provide a stabilizing force when playing near the heel of the bow.

This 'Franco-Belgian' grip allows the full length of the hair to be used in playing, and is firm enough to support even the heaviest strokes required in modern playing technique. In earlier periods, a lighter grip was often employed, with the hand further up the bow. The frontispiece to Francesco Veracini's *Sonate Accademiche*, published in 1744, is an engraving of the composer playing a violin; his right hand is holding the bow above the frog, with the thumb on the underside of the stick and the first three fingers on the upper side. Michel Corrette, in *L'École d'Orphée* (1738), describes a similar grip, a quarter of the way up the bow, as typically Italian. Numerous other paintings and engravings from the Baroque period show this style of grip, which is frequently employed by present-day players of the Baroque violin. It would be wrong to assume, however, that this was the only type of grip used in the eighteenth century. Corrette also describes a typical French grip near the frog, with the thumb under the hair, while Leopold Mozart's highly influential treatise *Versuch einer grundlichen Violinschule* (1756) illustrates a bow being held at the frog in a manner quite similar to the modern grip.

All of the grips described in the previous paragraph are overhand grips, in the sense that the back of the hand is uppermost. Similar grips are used on the viola

8.7 Two excerpts from the violin part of Stravinsky's Suite from *L'Histoire du soldat*, illustrating bowing instructions. Upper: the symbol above the first note indicates an up-bow; the symbol above the last note indicates a down-bow. Lower: phrases to be played with jété strokes (© 1987, 1992 for all countries Chester Music Ltd, London. All rights reserved. Reproduced by permission)

and cello. With the overhand grip, it is easiest to exert a strong force on the string at the heel (the frog end of the bow). A stroke which starts at the heel (called a 'down-bow') thus tends to be more strongly accented than one which starts at the tip (an 'up-bow'). The distinction between down-bow and up-bow is of fundamental importance in the phrasing of a piece of violin music, and the appropriate bowing is often indicated on the music (see Figure 8.7). An orchestral string section can only produce a unified sound if all its members use the same bowings, and it is usually the responsibility of the leader (the principal first violin) to ensure that the string parts are appropriately marked.

A passage of consecutive notes is usually played using alternating up- and down-bows, unless a contrary indication is marked in the music, as in Figure 8.7. The use of separate bows for each note is described as 'détaché' bowing.

A variant of détaché bowing is sometimes described as 'sprung détaché'. In this, the bow pressure is released just before the bow stops, and reapplied just after the change of direction. The effect is that of a rapid diminuendo at the end of one note, merging almost imperceptibly into a quick crescendo at the start of the next. The more yielding Baroque bow lends itself very readily to this stroke, and the crisp but smooth articulation which it produces in rapid playing is much valued in Baroque style. It is probably what Leopold Mozart had in mind when he wrote that 'every note . . . has a small though barely audible softness at the start of the stroke', adding that 'the same softness must also be heard at the end of every stroke'.

In the 'martelé' bow stroke, there is a strong though momentary increase in bow pressure at the start of each note; the bow is also stopped on the string for a perceptible interval between successive notes. It gives an emphatic articulation, and is most successful in the upper half of the bow. The speed with which martelé strokes can be repeated is limited by the elastic properties of the bow hair.

A slur, which is a curved line over or under a group of notes, is usually in modern bowed string music an instruction that the entire group of notes is to be played with a single stroke of the bow. Unmodified by any other indication, a slur implies the most legato type of playing, in which only the change of finger or string marks the transition from note to note. When staccato marks (dots) are found between the note heads and the slur, however, the intention is that the notes are played as a series of martelé strokes using a single bow stroke.

The bowings which have been described so far have all been 'on the string', which means that the bow remains in contact with the string throughout the stroke. Many of the most spectacular effects are achieved by bowings which are 'off the string': at some point, the bow hair either rebounds from the string or is deliberately lifted from it. The most gentle off-the-string bowing is the 'sautillé', in which the bow is allowed to bounce a short distance above the string between notes; it is most effective where the bow is most springy, at the centre. When the hand and arm muscles are also used to lift the bow between strokes, the bowing is described as 'spiccato'; this is more effective nearer the heel. The reader should be warned that earlier writers sometimes used these terms with different shades of meaning: Geminiani, for example, in *The Art of Playing on the Violin* (1751), seems to be describing spiccato bowing when he refers to 'a Staccato, where the bow is taken off the Strings at every Note'.

The most dramatic off-the-string bowing is the 'jeté' or 'ricochet' stroke (Figure 8.7), in which the bow is thrown at the string with such force that it rebounds several times. On each rebound a different note can be sounded; by altering the height of the hand during the stroke, it is possible to make the bow bounce from string to string.

Apart from the rich variety of bow strokes available, there are other aspects of bowing technique which can greatly affect the sound of the instrument. Moving the bowing point closer to the bridge requires greater bow pressure, but gives a stronger sound with lower bow speed. This ceases to be true when the bowing point is within a centimetre or so of the bridge; the pressure required for normal excitation of the string is impossible to achieve, and instead an eerie combination of upper partials is obtained. Sometimes required as a special effect, this type of bowing is indicated by the instruction 'sul ponticello' (literally 'on the bridge'). The converse technique, in which the bowing point is moved up to the end of the fingerboard to give a gentle, rather featureless sound, is described as 'sul tasto' ('on the fingerboard').

The bow is generally tilted towards the player so that only a relatively narrow band of the hair comes into contact with the string. Rotating the bow to increase the width of the active hair ribbon increases the strength of the sound, but the timbre is changed by the increased damping of the high string modes. Sometimes the player is explicitly instructed to use the full width of the bow hair.

The tremolo is a bowing technique which is used to great effect in orchestral string music. It consists of a rapid reiteration of the same note as quickly as possible, using very short alternating strokes at the tip of the bow. It cannot be played loudly because of the shortness of the bow stroke employed, but it powerfully conjures up an atmosphere of mystery or magic. It should not be confused with two other bowing techniques which have been described by the same term. Monteverdi, in *Il Combattimento di Tancredi e Clorinda* (1624), used rapidly repeated semiquavers to evoke the excitement of battle, and later described this technique as tremolo. But the notes are played in strict time, and this effect is now usually described as measured tremolo to distinguish it from the unmetrical repetition of the modern tremolo. Even earlier, in 1617, Biagio Marini in *Affetti musicali* asked violin players to 'tremolo con l'arco'. But Stewart Carter (1991) has argued convincingly that this type of tremolo, which appears in various other Italian works around this time, was in fact a gentle pulsation introduced by a rocking motion of the right hand, imitating the sound of an organ tremulant stop. A similar technique, which gives slight emphasis to the start of each note in a slurred legato phrase, is practised by modern players under the title of 'portato' bowing.

Fingering technique on the violin family

When one of the fingers of the left hand presses a string against the fingerboard of a violin, the sounding length of the string is shortened, and the pitch rises. The fixed nut at the upper end of the fingerboard has effectively been replaced by the finger. This is the basic principle behind the left-hand fingering technique of all the members of the violin family.

The detailed application of this simple principle varies considerably among the different members of the family, largely because of differences in size. On the violin and viola, two adjacent fingers of the average hand can comfortably stretch the distance required to change the pitch of a note by a whole tone at the upper end of the fingerboard. The basic position of the hand is such that the first finger can stop each of the four strings to raise the pitch by a tone; pressing down the second finger raises it by a further tone. The spacing between second and third fingers is closer than that between first and second, and corresponds to a semitone; while the fourth finger adds a further tone, raising the pitch of the unstopped string by a fifth. The number of the stopping finger is sometimes indicated on the music.

This location of the fingers is known as first position. It is clearly based on the diatonic scale, the first five degrees of which are obtained by successively pressing down fingers 1, 2, 3, and 4. The intervening chromatic notes can be obtained by moving the appropriate finger up or down the fingerboard, without changing the basic position of the hand. Alternatively, the entire hand can be shifted up the fingerboard by a distance equivalent to one semitone; it is then described as being in half position.

8.8 The standard method of holding and playing the bass viol (from *The Division Violist* by Christopher Simpson, revised edition 1665)

To play notes higher than a fifth above the top string, it is necessary to move the hand up the fingerboard. Such a shift must be accompanied by a contraction of the spacing between the fingers, since the semitones become closer as the string length is reduced. Although in principle any arbitrary extent of shift is possible, in practice certain specific higher positions are normally employed. These correspond to the different steps of the diatonic scale. Thus, in the second position, the first finger is a tone higher than in first; in third position it is a major third higher; in fourth position it is a perfect fourth higher; and so on.

The use of positions up to the seventh was already required by such seventeenth-century virtuoso composers as Biber, and some of the earliest paintings of the violin family appear to illustrate playing in positions higher than first. By the eighteenth century, the different tone quality obtainable by playing in high positions on the lower strings was valued as an expressive device, and in the nineteenth century Paganini delighted and amazed his audiences with pieces, ranging over two octaves, played entirely on the G string of the violin.

On the cello, the whole-tone interval between second and third fingers is an uncomfortably large stretch for most players, except in higher positions. In the basic first position, the four fingers give successive semitone intervals; in the extended first position, the second, third, and fourth fingers are all moved down the fingerboard by a semitone, so that the fingers span a major rather than a minor third. Shifts to higher positions are accomplished in the same manner as on the violin, although for positions above the fourth a violin-style finger spacing can be adopted. Access to the end of the fingerboard (and even beyond) is achieved by unhooking the thumb from its normal position behind the neck, and using it as a movable stop on the fingerboard.

The problem of finger spacing is even more acute on the double bass. Two systems are in common use. In one, a semitone interval separates first and second fingers, and also second and fourth fingers; the third finger is not used as a stop except in high positions. In the other system, the finger spacing is extended so that the four fingers span three semitones.

Bowing and fingering on the viol

The standard method of holding the viol and bow is that illustrated by Christopher Simpson in *The Division Violist* of 1659 (Figure 8.8). The feet are placed flat on the ground; the player supports the viol vertically on the thighs or between the knees in such a way that bowing about four fingers' width from the bridge is not impeded by the knees. The arms remain in a relaxed position, with the left hand curved gracefully over the fingerboard and the thumb behind the second finger to allow maximum flexibility and extension. In first position the index finger lies on the second fret, and the subsequent fingers are placed at semitone intervals above.

For the virtuoso repertoire high positions must be used to avoid flurries of position-changing and string-crossing. Positions above the frets are commonly employed, although there is of course a subtle change in timbre when the string is stopped by the finger instead of by a fret.

Much of the expression possible in viol-playing lies in the sophisticated movement of the bow. Unlike the cello, the viol bow is held underhand, with the index finger lightly resting along the wooden stick and the thumb supporting the side of the wood nearest to the hair. Pictures of viol players in the mid-sixteenth century show a bow grip with the second and third fingers also resting on the stick, but by the end of the century it was customary to exercise fine control of the bow force on the string by pressing with the second finger on the bow hair.

The push or forward stroke is the naturally strong stroke in viol-playing, and the pull or backward stroke tends to be weaker. The volume of sound can be increased by bowing nearer the bridge with increased pressure, or by increasing the speed of the bow; correspondingly, a diminuendo can be achieved by a reduction in bow speed or a retreat from the bridge and reduction in bow pressure.

Instruction manuals from the seventeenth century concentrate on the variety of distinct sound qualities which can be achieved by shaping notes with bow control. The treatises of Danoville (1687), Loulie (*c.*1696), Rousseau (1687), and Marais (1725) offer an invaluable resource of information on all aspects of viol-playing, ranging from the most basic advice on body posture and tuning to descriptions of subtle bowing techniques such as the the *coup d'archet* and the *coup de poignet*. Since this information is now readily available through facsimile publications and scholarly translations, it is possible for the modern player to learn how to reproduce the most delicate and expressive sounds of the viol, including the judicious use of those ornaments which provide the 'salt which seasons the melody'.

Multiple-stopping

The simultaneous playing of more than one string is described as multiple-stopping. The simplest version of this technique is double-stopping, in which two adjacent strings are bowed together. When one of the strings is open (unfingered), the technique is equivalent to the sounding of a constant pitch drone string, which was one of the earliest features of bowed string-playing. The fingering of both strings offers the player the opportunity to play two part music. By the seventeenth century, Italian composers such as Biagio Marini expected violinists to cope with such technical demands as passages of consecutive thirds; similar virtuosity was demanded on the viol by the French composer Sainte-Colombe. In the Romantic era, double-stopping became an important means of achieving greater power and dramatic effect, especially in concerto-playing (Figure 8.9).

Simultaneous playing on more than two strings is rendered almost impossible

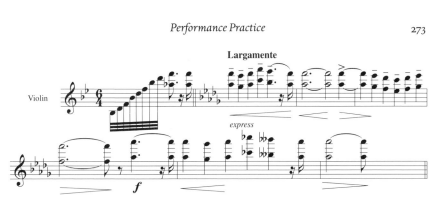

8.9 Excerpt from the solo part of Sibelius's Violin Concerto, illustrating the use of double-stopping (© 1905 Robert Lienau Musikverlag, Frankfurt am Main, Germany. Reprinted by permission)

by the curvature of the bridge on modern instruments. Nevertheless, the repertoires of both violin and viol families contain many examples of music in which the player is presented with a chord containing three, four, or even (in the case of the viol) six notes. Probably the most famous piece of triple and quadruple stopping in the violin repertoire is the opening of the Ciaccona from J. S. Bach's Second Partita for unaccompanied violin (1720) (Figure 8.10). Strongly conflicting opinions on the correct way of playing this and similar passages have been vigorously expressed by different players over the years. The mid-twentieth century

8.10 Facsimile of the opening bars of the *Ciaccona* from the Second Partita for unaccompanied violin by J. S. Bach, illustrating triple- and quadruple-stopping (facsimile of autograph manuscript)

even saw the brief appearance of a so-called 'Bach bow', the hair of which could be slackened so as to allow all four strings to be played at once. There is no evidence at all that such a bow existed in the eighteenth century. It is now generally accepted that the historically appropriate technique is to play the notes in the chord as a rapid arpeggio, usually from bottom to top, the highest one or two notes being sustained for the length of the written chord.

Arpeggiated chords are even more idiomatic on the viols, the family of 'bowed guitars'. The virtuoso performer-composers of the seventeenth and eighteenth centuries, including the French Sainte-Colombe and Marais and the English Hume and Simpson, delighted in the rich sonorities of multiple-stopped chords on the bass viol; the effect is even more luscious when two viols perform multiple-stops simultaneously (Figure 8.11).

It is, in fact, possible to sound a three-note chord on the violin or viol, by moving the bowing point much further from the bridge than normal and bowing with great firmness. The effect is inevitably strident, but it is occasionally called for as a dramatic gesture. The instruction that the chord should not be arpeggiated is given explicitly in the part.

8.11 Closing bars of Concert XLVIII *Le Raporté* for two viols by Sainte-Colombe, illustrating simultaneous multiple-stopping

Vibrato

On a member of the violin family, the sounding length of a stopped string is fixed by the bridge at one end, and the stopping finger of the left hand at the other. By rocking the stopping finger periodically in a direction parallel to the string, without actually sliding it along the string, the player can cause a slight fluctuation in the sounding length, and therefore the pitch, of the string. This effect is known as vibrato.

Although vibrato primarily introduces a pitch modulation, it also influences the perceived loudness and timbre of the sound. These secondary effects arise because an instrument such as the violin has a large number of body resonances closely spaced in frequency throughout the upper part of its playing compass. As the basic pitch rises and falls during the vibrato cycle, the frequency of each of the harmonic components generated by the string also rises and falls. At one point in the cycle, the tenth harmonic may be boosted by a particular body resonance; a little later in the vibrato cycle, the pitch may have risen so that instead it is the ninth harmonic which receives this boost from the fixed-frequency body resonance. Thus as the pitch rises and falls, the harmonic structure is also modulated, introducing a subtle but significant variation in the timbre of the sound.

The constant changes in pitch and timbre of a note played with vibrato have an interesting effect on the perceived loudness of the sound. The perceptual mechanisms of the human brain is much more sensitive to varying stimuli than to stimuli which remain static; in consequence, although vibrato does not normally increase the energy output of the instrument, it can make the sound seem louder.

The extent to which vibrato is employed, and the magnitude and frequency of the pitch modulation, are to a large extent matters of personal taste. Practically all players of the modern violin family use a continuous vibrato, with a typical pitch variation of around 15 cents above and below the mean pitch, and a modulation frequency of about 5 Hz. This application of a fairly strong vibrato as an indispensable aspect of tone production appears to date from the late nineteenth century, although there is continuing controversy about the extent to which earlier players used vibrato. Certainly, writers from the seventeenth century on refer to the technique; there is no doubt that it was used for ornamentation, and as a special effect, throughout the Baroque and Classical eras. Modern specialists in Baroque playing frequently use a very gentle vibrato, reserving the large amplitude fluctuation for ornaments.

Vibrato is also occasionally used on the viol, although the application of the technique has to take into account the fretting of the fingerboard. Rocking the finger does not change the string length, as it does on a violin or cello; it does, however, cause a small fluctuation in the string tension, as the finger rolls towards the fret and away from it. An ornament using this technique is described by Marais as a 'plainte'; a similar effect is recommended by the sixteenth-century writer Ganassi for music 'particularly sad and afflicted'. A more dramatic vibrato, the 'flattement' or 'close-shake', is introduced by tapping the string with a second finger just on the bridge side of the stopping finger. Christopher Simpson states that this should be done 'as close and and near the sounding note as possible may be', and the resulting variation of pitch is much less than a semitone.

Unconventional and virtuoso playing techniques

From the time that the troubadors delighted the courts of medieval Europe with displays of virtuoso fiddling, the bowed stringed instruments have attracted performers eager to explore and extend the limits of contemporary technique. The dazzling feats of one generation tend to be absorbed into the standard repertoire of the next, so that the limits of the avant-garde are constantly changing. Here we have space to list only a few of the more specialized playing techniques in use in modern music for bowed strings.

(i) *Unconventional bowing*

Instead of pulling the string across the bow in the usual way, the player may drum on the string with the hair, allowing the bow to bounce without sliding along the string. A variant of this technique is the 'col legno', in which the player turns the bow upside down and strikes the string with the wooden stick. Occasionally the player may even be instructed to stroke the string with the wooden part of the bow, although this is likely to scrape the varnish if performed on metal-covered strings.

(ii) *Pizzicato*

The normal pizzicato is performed by plucking the string with one or two fingers of the right hand, usually while it continues to hold the bow. Left-hand pizzicato involves plucking the string with a left hand finger, which must obviously be nearer the bridge than the stopping point on the string. The use of the left hand in this way allows the player to bow one string while simultaneously playing pizzicato on another, or to rapidly alternate pizzicato and arco passages. This technique is particularly associated with the nineteenth-century violinist Paganini.

The composer Bartók called for various innovative pizzicato techniques, including one which is often described simply as a 'Bartók pizzicato'. This involves plucking the string strongly in the direction perpendicular to the fingerboard, so that the string rebounds from the fingerboard with a loud snapping sound. Another technique particularly associated with Bartók is the pizzicato glissando, in which the stopping finger slides up or down the fingerboard after the string has been plucked.

(iii) *Harmonics*

If a string is touched lightly with a left-hand finger, at a point which is $1 : n$ th of the string length from the nut, bowing or plucking gives a sound whose pitch is the n th harmonic of the open string. Thus, for example, the player may touch the A string of the cello at a point a quarter of the way from the nut to the bridge; the resulting sound does not have pitch D_4, as it would if the finger were firmly pressed on the fingerboard, but A_5, the fourth harmonic of the open string (pitch A_3). This note is described as a 'natural harmonic'.

The acoustical principles underlying the technique of playing harmonics were outlined in Section 2.3. When the string is touched a quarter of the way along its sounding length, a displacement node is enforced at that point. Only vibrational modes with a node at that point can then be sounded; these include the 4th, 8th,

12th ... etc. Thus the sound is not in fact the sine wave tone of a single harmonic, but a harmonic spectrum whose fundamental is the 4th mode frequency of the open string. The high-frequency components are usually fairly strongly damped, giving a characteristically thin timbre to the natural harmonic.

Natural harmonics were introduced in the eighteenth century, and soon became part of the virtuoso's armoury of special effects. To these were added 'artificial harmonics', created by stopping the string normally with one finger and touching lightly with another. Entire pieces were composed using only harmonics. The remarkable instrument known as the 'tromba marina' or 'trumpet marine', essentially a one-stringed bass with a narrow triangular body, developed an extensive repertoire in the late seventeenth and early eighteenth centuries based solely on the notes obtainable as natural harmonics of its single string. The bridge of the tromba marina is mounted asymmetrically, so that one foot rattles against the soundboard as the string vibrates; this ensures that even harmonics as high as the sixteenth are produced with a strident, metallic timbre.

Harmonics are used in violin technique not only for virtuoso effects, but also to avoid the use of very high positions or particularly awkward fingerings. The disadvantage of interspersing harmonics and normally played notes is that it is difficult to disguise the characteristic difference in timbre between the two techniques.

(iv) *Scordatura*

The tuning of the strings of an instrument to a set of pitches other than those considered standard is described as 'scordatura'. Sometimes this technique is used to obtain notes not otherwise playable on the instrument; for example, the bottom string of a bass viol may be lowered from D_2 to C_2 if this particular note is required in a piece. The mechanism sometimes used on a double bass to lower the pitch of the bottom string is in fact a scordatura device. The disadvantage of this adjustment of the usual pitch of a string is that abnormal fingerings have to be used for all the other notes on the string.

Scordatura has been employed for various reasons at different periods. The seventeenth-century virtuoso violinist Biber prescribed highly unusual tunings for many of his violin sonatas to enable otherwise unplayable intervals and passages to be performed. In folk music, scordatura is frequently adopted to allow a drone accompaniment to be played on open strings. Retuning tends to alter the characteristic timbre of the instrument: Mahler asks for a solo violin to be tuned a tone higher than normal in the scherzo of his Fourth Symphony, to give a harder, more wiry sound. In the *Firebird* Suite, Stravinsky asks the first violins to tune their top strings down a tone, so that by running a left-hand finger lightly up and down the string, an arpeggio of natural harmonics of D_5 can be played. Scordatura has also been employed in the performance of microtonal music.

9

Plucked and Hammered Stringed Instruments

This chapter is concerned with instruments in which a string is set into vibration by a sudden impulse. On harps, lutes, and guitars the impulse is provided by a pluck from the player's finger or thumb or from a plectrum held in the player's hand; on the dulcimer and cimbalom it is imparted by a blow from one of a pair of hand-held hammers. Much of the following discussion applies equally to instruments in which the transfer of the impulse is mediated by a keyboard mechanism, but the clavichord, harpsichord, and piano are of sufficient importance to merit separate treatment in the succeeding two chapters.

Basic acoustics

There are many similarities between the plucked stringed instruments discussed here and the bowed stringed instruments covered by the previous chapter. Indeed, the pizzicato technique, in which the strings are plucked by the fingers or thumb of the hand which normally holds the bow, is important on all members of the violin family, and is the normal method of playing the double bass in jazz ensembles. Whether the string is bowed, plucked, or struck, there must still be a bridge to transmit the vibratory energy of the string to a body which is capable of radiating an audible sound wave.

It is unnecessary to repeat here the general principles governing the design of the body and bridge of a stringed instrument, which were surveyed in Section 8.1 and will be further explored in Chapters 10 and 11. Instead we shall concentrate on some points which are of particular significance in the behaviour of plucked and struck strings.

At the outset, we recall that the impulsive excitation of a string leaves it vibrating simultaneously in many of its natural modes. These modes have frequencies which deviate slightly from an exact harmonic series because of the stiffness of the string. The coupling of the string to the resonating body of the instrument can also affect the tuning of the natural mode frequencies. Usually the inharmonicity is sufficiently small that the listener hears a single fused tone with a well-defined pitch. Each mode decays and radiates at a different rate, which depends on the strength of coupling through the bridge and the resonant properties of the body at the relevant frequency. A change in timbre, sometimes accompanied by a slight change in pitch, can be heard as the sound dies away; this is due to the fact that different groups of frequency components dominate at different stages of the decay.

Choosing the point of attack

In our discussion of plucked and hammered chordophones in Chapter 2, we noted that varying the position of plucking or hammering can strongly affect the timbre of the resulting sound. It is worth examining the nature of this sensitivity in a little more detail, since the resulting control of tone quality is an important part of the playing technique of instruments such as the guitar.

Immediately after the string has been excited, each of its natural modes has a certain amplitude. The variation of timbre is achieved by varying the relative sizes of these amplitudes (although we must remember that the frequency spectrum of the radiated sound also depends strongly on the properties of the instrument body).

To find out whether a particular mode will be strongly or weakly excited, we need to make use of two rules. The first rule applies both to plucked and hammered strings, and is most simply formulated in terms of the standing wave pattern for the mode in question. Standing wave patterns for the first six modes of a stretched string were shown in Figure 2.14, in which it can be seen that each pattern is outlined by a curve (in fact a sine curve). The first rule states that the efficiency of the excitation is proportional to the height of this curve at the point of plucking or striking.

To bring out the meaning of this rather formal statement, let us consider a string plucked at two different places. First it is plucked at the centre of the string; then it is plucked a quarter of the way from one end.

For the first mode, the curve has its maximum height at the centre, which is an antinode; let us call this height 100 per cent. A quarter of the way from one end the height is reduced to 71 per cent. According to the first rule, then, a given strength of pluck will be most efficient at exciting the first mode if it is applied at the centre; the same pluck applied a quarter of the way along the string will give a first mode amplitude reduced to 71 per cent of that obtained at the centre.

For the second mode, the situation is quite different. The centre is now a node, so the height of the curve is zero. Plucking at the centre will totally fail to excite the second mode. A quarter of the way along the string, on the other hand, is an antinode; the height of the curve is 100 per cent, and the efficiency will be the maximum possible. We see here examples of the general principle that, when a string is excited at a particular point, modes with antinodes at the exciting point will be strong and modes with nodes at the exciting point will be absent.

It should be noted here that the rules which we are discussing strictly apply only to excitation at a point. A fingertip, plectrum, or hammer will act over a small but not infinitesimal length of the string, so the rules must be treated as approximations in a realistic musical case. Nevertheless, for a hard, narrow plectrum or hammer we should expect that excitation a quarter of the way along the string would give a very weak 4th harmonic, while excitation at the centre would leave all even harmonics weak.

The first rule mentioned above gives only the relative efficiencies with which a particular mode can be excited at different points. To compare the amplitudes of different modes excited at a fixed point we need to invoke a second rule, which takes two different forms for the plucking and hammering cases.

For a hammered string, the second rule relates the amplitude of a particular string mode to the mode number. In fact, there is not one simple rule for hammered strings—the dependence of the amplitude on the mode number depends on the details of the mass and hardness of the hammer head, and on the nature of the struck string. Nevertheless, there are two cases in which a useful approximation is available. If the mass of the hammer is very much less than the mass of the string, the second rule tells us that the amplitude of the mode is roughly independent of mode number. Of course, this rule has to be applied along with the first: if the string is struck by a very light hammer at the centre, for example, all the even harmonics should be very small (in theory absent) and all the even harmonics equal in amplitude. This may be approximately valid for the bass strings on a piano.

If the hammer is heavier, but still somewhat lighter than the string, the amplitudes are independent of mode number up to a certain frequency, then fall off inversely with mode number. The twentieth mode, for example, might have only half the amplitude of the tenth mode if the striking position was an antinode for both modes.

For a plucked string, the second rule has a more drastic effect, since it states that the mode amplitude is inversely proportional to the square of the mode number. In consequence, the mode amplitudes fall off much more rapidly with increasing mode number than for the hammered string.

It would be unwise to conclude this discussion without a reminder that the shape and hardness of the plucking or striking object can also greatly influence the relative strengths of the string modes. Nevertheless, it is both interesting and significant that the hammering and plucking processes have characteristically different effects on the timbre of the resulting sound.

The feel of a string

The action of plucking a string involves pulling the string sideways and then releasing it. The properties of the string have to be carefully chosen if it is to respond properly to plucking by the player's fingertip, as is the case on the harp, lute, and classical guitar. The nature of the problem can be experienced by reaching into a piano and attempting to pluck the strings (with the sustaining pedal depressed to raise the dampers). The piano strings have not been optimized for finger-plucking, although this technique is occasionally demanded in modern compositions. It is relatively easy to pluck one of the three C_4 (middle C) strings, but much harder (and more painful) to elicit a reasonable sound from the C_7 string three octaves higher.

The difficulty in plucking the C_7 piano string arises because it does not yield sufficiently to the force applied by the relatively soft fingertip. The C_7 string on a concert harp moves much more readily in response to fingertip pressure. The difference between the two strings is sometimes described by saying that the harp string has a greater 'feel' than the piano string. Feel in this context is a technical term, defined as the distance (d) moved by the string divided by the force (F) applied by the fingertip:

$$\text{feel} = \frac{d}{F}$$

The feel depends on the length of the string L, and on the tension T. It also varies with the point of plucking; the string is much more yielding at the centre than it is near one end. Consider first the case in which the string is plucked at the centre. The force which resists the plucking movement arises because, on both sides of the plucking point, the tension force has a component attempting to pull the string back into its undeflected position. Some elementary trigonometry shows that the total restoring force is given by

$$F = \frac{4Td}{L}$$

thus, for the case of plucking at the centre, we find that

$$feel = \frac{d}{F} = \frac{L}{4T}$$

When the same string is plucked one tenth of the way along the situation is rather different. Most of the restoring force comes from the shorter string segment. The total restoring force generated by the same plucking amplitude is now considerably greater:

$$F = \text{II.I} \ \frac{Td}{L}$$

In consequence, the feel of the string, given by

$$feel = \frac{d}{F} = \frac{L}{\text{II.I}T}$$

is reduced to about a third of the value that it has when the string is plucked at the centre.

The decrease in feel as the plucking point moves further from the string centre has significant consequences for the playing techniques of harp and guitar. It is also important to ensure that the different strings on a finger-plucked instrument do not vary too much in feel.

Pitch-bending

Pulling a string away from its equilibrium position increases its length slightly, and this stretching is accompanied by an increase in tension. For the string displacements which are practicable on a musical instrument, the tension is unlikely to change by more than a few per cent, but such a change will have a significant effect on the pitch of the note.

We will come across several examples of this type of pitch variation in the course of the present chapter. To clarify the nature of the effect, we consider here the pitch-bending technique which is a staple feature of electric guitar-playing; similar techniques are important in the playing of the Indian sitar and Chinese pipa. The fingerboard of the guitar is crossed by a series of metal frets, which have the same function as the gut frets on the viol. With a finger of the left hand, the player presses the string against the fingerboard. The finger contacts the string just on the upper side of one of the frets, and the sounding length of the string is determined by the distance from that fret to the bridge. In pitch-bending, the finger is moved parallel to the fret, pulling (or pushing) the string away from its undeflected line as shown in Figure 9.1.

The pitch change which results from a given sideways displacement depends on

9.1 Geometry of a guitar string pulled sideways on a fret to give pitch-bending

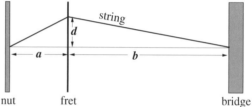

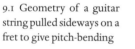

the properties of the string, and in particular on the Young's modulus Y of the string material. This property determines the tension resulting from a given amount of stretching (strictly, it is the tensile stress divided by the fractional increase in length). If the bending increases the total string length L (measured from nut to bridge) by an amount x, the fundamental frequency of the played note will change from f to f', where

$$\frac{f'}{f} = 1 + \left(\frac{Y}{8\rho L^3 f^2}\right) x$$

The increase in length which is obtained by pushing the string a distance d along the fret can be worked out from the geometry of Figure 9.1:

$$x = \left(\frac{1}{a} + \frac{1}{b}\right) \frac{d^2}{2}$$

It should be noted that these formulae are both approximations, which are close to the truth for normal musical instrument strings. Combining the two formulae, and substituting typical values for a steel guitar string stopped at the third fret ($Y = 2 \times 10^{11}$ pascals, $\rho = 7.8 \times 10^3$ kilogrammes per cubic metre, $L = 0.63$ metres, $a = 0.1$ metres, $b = 0.53$ metres), we find that

$$\frac{f'}{f} = 77 \frac{d^2}{f^2}$$

with d measured in millimetres and f, f' in hertz.

Several conclusions of musical importance can be drawn from this burst of mathematics. Firstly, we should note that the string diameter has not come into the calculation: changing from a thick, tight string to a thinner slacker one will not alter the sensitivity to pitch-bending if the string is tuned to the same basic frequency in each case. Secondly, we can see that the fractional change in frequency is proportional, not to the distance the string is pushed along the fret, but to the square of this distance. This means that the pitch change produced by a small displacement is much greater if the string has already been pushed some distance to the side.

Finally, it is interesting to observe that the top three strings on an electric guitar are normally the same material (unwound steel) and total length; a given displacement on the third fret will produce a much bigger pitch bend on the third string (basic frequency 233 Hz) than on the first string (basic frequency 392 Hz), since the pitch bend formula contains an inverse dependence on the square of the basic frequency. Pulling the top string along the fret by 10 mm will, according to the formula, increase the frequency by 5 per cent, giving a pitch bend of 85 cents; the same displacement will bend the pitches of the second and third strings by 149 cents and 227 cents respectively.

9.2 HISTORICAL DEVELOPMENT

Plucked instruments in antiquity

The idea of plucking a stretched string to make music has a history stretching back through many thousands of years. Carvings, pottery decorations, and surviving instruments show that by the third millennium BCE the culture of Mesopotamia had developed several types of plucked stringed instruments. Although their shapes and sizes varied greatly, they shared the two essential features of all stringed instruments: a frame to support the strings under tension, and a body or resonator to radiate an audible sound wave when driven by the string vibration. Depending on the way in which these two features were provided, the Mesopotamian instruments are now described as either 'lyres', 'harps', or 'lutes'.

The lyre had a resonating body in the form of a bowl or box, covered by a soundboard. Two arms extended in the plane of the soundboard, and were joined at their extremities by a bar known as the yoke. The strings were tied to the yoke at one end, stretched over a bridge on the soundboard and fastened at the lower end of the body. The number of strings depicted varies from three or four to as many as eleven (on the Ur standard, from about 2600 BCE). Because of the symmetrical design of the instrument, the strings were all the same length.

In Ancient Greece the lyre was an important instrument for music-making on a relatively intimate scale. The resonating body was traditionally a tortoise shell, the extending arms being antelope horns. A larger instrument of the same general design, with a wooden body, was used for more public and ceremonial purposes; this was known as the 'kithara'. Both of the Greek instruments were normally provided with seven strings. Illustrations show the player plucking the strings, sometimes with a finger and sometimes with a short stick (or plectrum).

On the lyre, the strings lie in a plane parallel to and just above the soundboard. The harp, in contrast, is characterized by the fact that the strings lie approximately in a plane at right angles to the soundboard. A bar known as the neck protrudes from the soundboard in the plane of the strings, which are fixed to the neck at one end and to the soundboard at the other. In most later harps, the far end of the neck is also joined to the soundboard by a supporting strut called the fore-pillar, but this feature is absent in the harps of Mesopotamia, Egypt, and the classical world. Mesopotamian harps are shown with up to six strings, but Egyptian paintings illustrate more elaborate instruments with up to twenty strings. The harp was also a popular instrument in Greek and Roman music-making.

Towards the end of the third millennium BCE, Mesopotamian illustrations start to show the third type of plucked stringed instrument, the lute. In the Hornbostel-Sachs classification system, the term lute is a very general one: the lyre is classified as a 'yoke lute', and the violin as a 'necked box lute'. In normal musical usage, however, the lute is a plucked instrument with a resonating body (usually pear-shaped) and a neck whose upper surface lies more or less in the plane of the soundboard. The strings lie along the neck and parallel to the soundboard; one end of each string is wound round a tuning peg in the neck, the other end being fixed on the body.

The lutes shown in Mesopotamian and Egyptian carvings and paintings are of the long-necked type, with a fairly small resonator and a thin neck several times the length of the body. The instruments are usually shown with two strings, and appear to have been played with a plectrum. The short-necked lute, with a larger resonator and a neck typically shorter than the body length, first appears in the art of classical Greece, and is also shown in some carvings from north-west India in the first century CE. These instruments have four or five strings, and again are shown being plucked by a plectrum.

Medieval plucked strings

Very few stringed instruments have survived from the period before 1500, and those still in existence have usually been subjected to drastic modifications during the intervening centuries. Pictorial records provide a fascinating but uncertain guide, since a depiction of a player with an instrument may be a literal transcription of a contemporary scene or a fanciful allegory. Many medieval literary works contain references to stringed instruments, but it is not at all obvious how the instrumental names used by writers such as Chaucer and Machaut should be matched up with the instruments shown in paintings and sculpture. After a period of considerable confusion, medieval scholars are now in broad agreement as to how the major medieval plucked instruments should be described, and it is this consensus which is summarized here. It should be noted, however, that most books written before 1980 use different names for several of the instruments discussed in this section.

The plucked instruments of the Middle Ages can be usefully divided into two broad categories: those without a fingerboard, including the lyre, harp, and psaltery, and those with a fingerboard, including the lute, citole, and gittern.

Of the instruments without fingerboard, the lyre survived from the Roman era into the early Middle Ages in the Germanic tribes of northern Europe (including England). An instrument clearly related to the Greek kithara, is shown in miniatures from the eighth to the twelfth centuries, often played by King David in Old Testament illustrations. Typically with six strings, and a yoke which was an integral part of the body, the lyre was described at this period by the names 'rotte', 'kithara' and (confusingly) 'hearpe'. By the thirteenth century its use appears to have declined, although a bowed version (the 'crwth') survived much later, especially in Wales.

From the ninth century onwards, King David is very often shown playing a harp. This early medieval instrument was of a basically triangular shape, frequently with the neck curved towards the soundbox and a fore-pillar curved outwards. In the thirteenth century, around twelve strings are normally shown, although in the following century the number of strings had doubled. A poem by Guillaume de Machaut, the fourteenth-century writer, composer, and diplomat, specifically refers to a harp with twenty-five strings. These strings would normally have been gut, although there are contemporary references to the use of wire harp strings, plucked by the nails. The tuning of the medieval harp was essentially diatonic; twenty-five strings thus allowed for a span of a little over three octaves, with the possibility that an additional string may sometimes have been used to supply chromatic alternatives (such as B♭ : B♮).

The instrument known from the eleventh century onwards as the 'psaltery' was a box zither, with a set of parallel strings running across the top of a box-shaped resonator. Illustrations show psalteries with triangular, trapezoidal, and 'pig snout'-shaped resonating boxes. The strings were frequently metal, and although some depictions show finger-plucking the use of a plectrum seems to have been preferred.

The plucked instruments with fingerboards which were played in medieval Europe can all be viewed as different members of the short-necked lute family. The word 'lute' appears to have been first used in France in the thirteenth century; it derives from the Arab word 'ud, which described a large short-necked lute popular throughout the countries of the Middle East from the eighth century onwards. The deep pear-shaped body was constructed from several tapered strips of wood which were bent over a mould and glued together. In the thirteenth century this instrument was introduced into Moorish Spain, from which it spread to other parts of Europe. Like its Arab progenitor, the neck of the lute was normally unfretted, and it was played using a plectrum. By the mid-fifteenth century, the European instrument had gut frets tied around the neck, and its four or five double courses of gut strings were plucked by the fingers.

The tuning of the lute depended on its size; the general rule was to tune the top string as high as it would go without breaking. As we saw in Chapter 8, for a given string material the highest obtainable pitch depends only on the string length, and not on its thickness. A typical string length on a medium-sized fifteenth-century lute was about 600 mm, allowing a gut string to be tuned to around G_4. The two middle courses of the four-course instrument were most commonly a major third apart with a perfect fourth above and below, while the five-course instrument had an additional course tuned a fourth higher still. A common tuning for the four-course lute in the fifteenth century would probably thus be around F_3–$B^\flat_3$–D_4–G_4, while a five-course lute of the same string length might be tuned C_3–F_3–A_3–D_4–G_4.

Smaller plucked instruments playing at a higher pitch were very popular in the thirteenth and fourteenth centuries. The 'citole' seems to have originated in southern Europe in the late twelfth century, and its use spread through France to England and Germany in the course of the thirteenth century. The back of the body was not arched, as on the lute, but flat or only slightly convex; body and neck were carved from one solid piece of wood, covered by a flat soundboard. The outline of the body shape was varied: some citoles closely resembled the medieval fiddle, with an oval or slightly waisted outline, some were spade-shaped (often with upswept wings), some had a holly-leaf outline. The neck was fretted, sometimes with wooden bars. Citoles are usually depicted with four strings, and the player is normally using a plectrum. By the late fourteenth century the citole had fallen out of use except in Spain, where it continued in popularity into the fifteenth century.

The 'gittern' was essentially a small treble lute, with a characteristic pear-shaped body merging into a short neck. It was known in Europe by the second half of the thirteenth century. At this stage the body of the gittern was not built up from wooden strips as on the lute but carved from a solid block like the rebec; the neck was carved from the same piece of wood. Later versions of the gittern used the built-up construction of the larger lute, but retained the smooth taper of the junction between body and neck. Some gitterns are shown fretted, others have an unfretted neck. The instrument achieved the peak of its popularity in the fourteenth century, although instruments of much the same type remained in use for many centuries throughout Europe. To avoid confusion, it should perhaps be noted here that the Spanish term for gittern was 'guitarra'; this term was transferred in the fifteenth century to the instrument with a waisted body which was the predecessor of the modern guitar.

Renaissance and Baroque harps

In the fifteenth century, the desire for a downward extension of the pitch range of the harp led to the development of an instrument with a longer resonating box and a neck which swept substantially upwards towards the pillar. A typical instrument of this period might stand about one metre high. Agricola, writing in 1529, described a harp with twenty-six strings tuned diatonically from F_2 to C_6. No chromatic strings were provided on the harp described by Agricola, although a note could be sharpened by a semitone by pinching the string near one end, or by pressing it against the neck or soundboard. The strings were usually of gut, and were plucked by the fingertips, although the Irish were known for their tradition of wire-strung harp-playing.

One interesting feature of the fifteenth-century harp was the frequent use of 'brays'. These were pins used to fasten the strings to the soundboard, and were shaped in such a way that a plucked string vibrated against the bray, giving a characteristic buzz to the sound. The brays could often be rotated to introduce or remove this effect at will.

By the mid-sixteenth century, the inability of the harp to play chromatic music fluently had become a serious problem, and in Spain and Italy the double harp was introduced. This had two rows of strings, one the usual diatonic rank, the other providing chromatic alternatives (and some unisons with the diatonic rank). The player was required to reach between the diatonic strings to pluck those of the chromatic rank. The Italian 'arpa a due ordini' had the two ranks parallel, while the Spanish equivalent, the 'arpa de dos ordenes', had the two ranks crossing at an angle. The range of both versions was usually four octaves, typically from C_2 to C_6.

Not long after the introduction of the double harp, the 'triple harp' made its appearance in Italy. This was basically a double harp with an extra diatonic rank, the chromatic rank being sandwiched between the two diatonic ranks. The triple harp had the advantage that the diatonic strings could be reached easily by both hands over the full compass of the instrument; the greater number of strings also offered greater power and resonance.

The double and triple chromatic harps established themselves as important continuo instruments in the early Baroque period, with an extension of the downward compass to G_1. Composers like Monteverdi wrote specifically for the 'arpa doppia': this term could refer to either the double or triple harp, the adjective 'doppia' (double) relating to the downward pitch extension (as in double bass) rather than the stringing arrangement. By the late seventeenth or early eighteenth century the triple harp had become the standard form of harp in Wales, a position it retained until the twentieth century. Gut stringing was almost universally employed on double and triple harps, although it has recently been argued that the consorts written by the seventeenth-century English composer William Lawes for violin, theorbo, bass viol, and harp were originally played on a metal-strung Irish chromatic double harp.

Development of the pedal harp

Despite the many advantages of the triple harp, the large number of strings presented significant problems of tuning and maintenance, while the diatonic basis of the tuning system made it difficult to play in remote keys. In the seventeenth century there were various experiments using mechanical devices to sharpen or flatten particular strings on an otherwise diatonically tuned harp. The simplest system made use of a blade or hook fixed to the neck a little below each tuning pin. When this blade was turned, it pressed against the string, shortening its sounding length and raising the pitch by a semitone.

This simple blade system is surprisingly effective, and is still used on many types of small diatonic harp. It has the obvious disadvantage, however, that the player has to stop playing with one hand in order to rotate a blade. By the late seventeenth or early eighteenth century, in southern Germany, a system of pedal-operated levers had been evolved which permitted the player to rotate the blades by using the feet. In the course of the eighteenth century this pedal mechanism became highly sophisticated, with a set of seven pedals (one for each degree of the diatonic scale) mounted at the base of the pillar. The control rods ran inside the pillar, and the upper part of the lever system was housed in the hollowed-out neck.

The centre of development of the harp in the eighteenth century was Paris, and the noted French piano manufacturer Sebastien Érard made several major contributions to the evolution of the pedal harp. In 1792 he introduced the 'fork' system, which used two short rods mounted on a disc to stop each string; this gave a much more secure termination to the stopped string than the devices employed up to that time.

In 1810 Érard made an even more significant advance in harp design with the introduction of the double action. Two discs were mounted beneath each tuning pin, and each of the seven pedals could be located in one of three positions. In the upper position, the unstopped length of the string sounded. In the middle position, the upper disc rotated so that its fork stopped the string, raising its pitch by a semitone; the lower fork remained disengaged. When the pedal was moved to its lowest position, a further rotation brought the lower fork into contact with the string, raising the pitch by a further semitone. Although the playing of passages involving rapid modulations can entail some very vigorous footwork, the double-action pedal harp has proved equal to almost all the challenges of the nineteenth and twentieth centuries, and remains the standard concert harp at the present time.

Renaissance and Baroque lutes

The transition from plectrum technique to finger-plucking, which occurred in the second half of the fifteenth century, ensured for the lute a position of major importance in the art music of the next two centuries, since it gave the instrument a capacity for the playing of elaborate polyphony. The technical development of the lute during this period consisted chiefly in a continuing quest for deeper sonorities by the introduction of lower-pitched strings. Around 1500 the five-course lute gave way to a six-course instrument. The standard tuning of the six-course Renaissance lute was G_2–C_3–F_3–A_3–D_4–G_4, although the absolute pitch level was much less standardized than the relative tuning of the courses and a tuning with each string a tone higher was also common.

As we have seen, an instrument with a top gut string tuned to G_4 must have a string length of the order of 600 mm. The sixth course of the lute required a string of the same length tuned two octaves lower, necessitating the use of a much thicker gut tuned well below its breaking point. Such strings had a rather dull sound, and to add brightness it was customary to use a double course in which only one of the two strings (the 'bourdon') was actually tuned to the nominal pitch; the second string was of thinner gut, and was tuned an octave higher, thus reinforcing the upper harmonics of the bourdon. Doubling at the octave was frequently used on the three lowest courses of the lute, especially on larger instruments such as the bass lute, tuned a fourth lower than the pitches given above. Towards the end of the sixteenth century, improvements in string manufacture provided much more satisfactory bass strings; octave doubling was then no longer necessary, and it became possible to add even deeper strings. An early seventeenth-century lute with nine courses is shown in Figure 9.2(b). By this stage the ten-course lute was in widespread use. This had the usual set of six courses doubled at the unison, with four further single 'diapasons'. The diapasons were not intended to be stopped on the fingerboard, and indeed some of them normally lay too far to the bass side for this to be possible; they were tuned to the notes required in a particular piece (typically C_2–D_2–E_2–F_2).

Despite the advances arising from better string materials, makers continued to experiment with other methods of improving the bass response of the lute. One obvious solution to the problem of the shortness of the bass strings was to make them longer. The invention of one of the most spectacular versions of this solu-

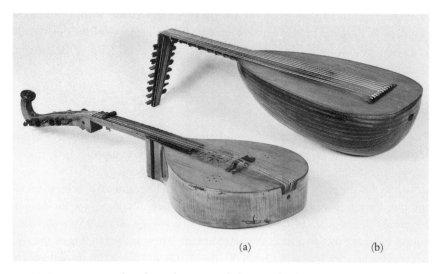

(a)   (b)

9.2 (a) cittern (anon., early eighteenth century); (b) lute (Buchenberg, Rome, early seventeenth century). Note fastening for wire strings on the cittern and tie-bridge on the lute

tion, the 'archlute', was claimed by the Paduan maker Piccinini. This instrument had six conventional lute courses, tuned and played in the normal way, but an extension to the neck ended in a second pegbox carrying eight further diapason strings. The extension of the neck was at a slight angle to the main neck, so that the diapason strings ran off to one side of the fingerboard. The diapasons were between one and a half and two times the length of the stopped strings, giving them great power and richness of sound.

A similar development, which also appears to have originated in north Italy at the end of the sixteenth century, was that of the 'chitarrone' or 'theorbo'. Like the archlute, the chitarrone had an extended neck, a second pegbox and a set of unstopped diapason strings. The critical difference was that the stopped strings were considerably longer on the chitarrone than on the normal lute, which meant that the top string could not be tuned to the normal lute pitch (G_4 or A_4). Instead, it was tuned an octave lower. Frequently, the same was true of the second course, making the third course the highest in pitch. Thus Michael Praetorius gives the following tuning for the chitarrone: F_1–G_1–A_1–B_1–C_2–D_2–E_2–F_2–G_2–C_3–F_3–A_3–D_3–G_3.

The re-entrant tuning (with the pitch of the strings not rising steadily across the instrument) makes the instrument relatively intractable for solo music; however, the large body and long strings provide a wonderfully rich timbre in ensemble and continuo-playing. Praetorius drew a distinction between the larger 'Roman' chitarrone and the smaller 'Paduan' theorbo, but almost all other writers of the period use the two terms interchangeably. Under one or other title, the instrument played a leading role in the accompaniment of vocal music into the eighteenth century.

In France, the development of the lute in the seventeenth century took a rather different route. In the early part of the century, a two-headed instrument resembling the theorbo was popular, although instead of all the diapasons going to a single second pegbox, each diapason on the French two-headed lute had its own nut and peg. This allowed the lengths of the diapasons to increase steadily, avoiding the drastic discontinuity in sound sometimes heard on the theorbo between the sixth stopped course and the first diapason. Eleven and twelve courses were commonly provided on French lutes at this time, and this type of instrument was also very popular in England. Although the Italians had broadly retained the tuning pattern of the classic Renaissance lute for the top six courses of the Baroque instruments, the French introduced a wide variety of alternative possible tunings.

Later in the century, the whole question of the stringing of bass courses was transformed by the introduction of overwound strings, which gave a bright powerful sound at a much shorter length than unwound gut. The French makers then largely returned to a single-headed model with eleven courses; in the eighteenth century German manufacturers further extended the single-headed lute to thirteen courses, with a mechanism which allowed some extension of the lowest strings.

Mandore, cittern, and guitar

The small gut-strung treble lute, which had been one of the most popular plucked instruments of the Middle Ages, continued to flourish in the Renaissance. The medieval names for this instrument, such as 'guitarra' and 'gittern', were used increasingly from the fifteenth century onwards to describe the waisted-bodied predecessor of the modern guitar, and from about 1570 French writers referred to the high-pitch lute as the 'mandore'. About this time the traditional form of construction, with a body and neck carved from an single piece of wood, gave way to a method of construction similar to the larger lutes, in which the back was built up from tapered ribs.

Mandores were built with four, five, or six courses; single stringing was normal, although some courses might be double on a seventeenth-century instrument. Various sizes of mandore were available, and the tuning was adjusted to suit the size of the instrument. The conventional tuning pattern used fourths and fifths; a small four-course mandore, with a string length of around 300 mm, might be strung C_4–G_4–C_5–G_5, whilst a typical tuning for a larger five-course instrument, with a string length of 450 mm, would be C_3–F_3–C_4–F_4–C_5. Occasionally a tuning pattern with the major third characteristic of the larger lute was employed: the Scottish Skene manuscript, from about 1630, describes a mandore tuning with the same relative pitch intervals as the top five courses of the Renaissance lute. On an instrument with a string length about half that of the lute, the actual pitches would be about an octave higher.

The strings of the mandore were practically always gut, although James Talbot, writing at the end of the seventeenth century, states that wire was sometimes used. The strings were plucked either by the fingertips or by a quill plectrum: several writers refer to the practice of plucking the mandore with a piece of quill tied to one of the fingers of the right hand.

In Italy the mandore was known as the 'mandola'. Italian players preferred the smaller type of instrument, with a string length around 300 mm, and by the eighteenth century the diminutive form 'mandolino' had become the standard name. The Italians also adopted a different type of tuning, mostly in fourths. A characteristic Italian mandolino in the early eighteenth century would have six paired courses, with a tuning G_3–B_3–E_4–A_4–D_5–G_5. About the middle of the eighteenth century, a quite distinct variant developed in the area around Naples: this 'Neapolitan mandolino' had a much deeper body than the older instrument, and four pairs of metal or overwound strings tuned in fifths like a violin. For a time the six-course instrument co-existed with the Neapolitan mandolino, but during the nineteenth century the Neapolitan instrument achieved wide popularity, and in Italy and elsewhere the gut-strung instruments disappeared.

Another type of wire-strung plucked instrument had, however, been in wide-spread use since the fifteenth century. This was the 'cittern', which was a development from (perhaps even a conscious revival of) the medieval citole. Like the citole, the early citterns had a body, neck, and pegbox carved from one block, although by the end of the sixteenth century citterns were being manufactured by violin makers using similar techniques of construction to those of the violin. The outline of the cittern was roughly pear-shaped in plan view, but its body was shallow, with a flat or slightly convex back. The sides typically tapered so that the box was shallower at its base than at the junction with the neck; at this junction there were frequently small scrolls, which have been seen as relics of the upswept wings of the citole.

The neck of the cittern was fretted. Fifteenth-century illustrations show five or six frets, which were probably of wood, but later eighteen or nineteen brass frets were fitted. The instrument was wire-strung, and was normally played with a plectrum. In Italy, the country in which the cittern appears to have originated, the fully developed instrument had six double courses, with a typical tuning of D_3–F_3–B_3–G_3–D_4–E_4 (a re-entrant tuning). The string length of such a cittern would be around 500 mm, although instruments varied considerably in size. In England the cittern was a very popular instrument; the favourite type had four courses, tuned B_3–G_3–D_4–E_4 like the top four courses of the Italian instrument. In France a four-course cittern was also preferred, but the lowest course was normally tuned a tone lower than on the English cittern. French instruments also frequently had a third string on each of the two lowest courses, tuned an octave higher than the nominal pitch to add brightness to the sound.

The close tuning of the cittern made it well adapted for chordal accompaniment of singing, and it was one of the most widely played instruments in seventeenth-century Europe. It was traditionally the instrument found in barbers' shops: it was assumed that the waiting customer could while away the time strumming a popular air or dance tune. The cittern also acquired a significant repertoire of solo art music, and featured in several of the mixed consort groups popular in England in the early seventeenth century.

By the end of the seventeenth century the use of the cittern had declined. An instrument dating from the early eighteenth century is illustrated in Figure 9.2(a). During the following century, various related wire-strung instruments evolved. Among these was the 'English guitar' or 'guittar'. Despite its name, this instrument was not a guitar, but a member of the cittern family: it had a deeper body than the Renaissance cittern, and six courses of metal strings tuned C_3–E_3–G_3–C_4–E_4–G_4. The top four courses were double, the lower two single, and the playing technique involved plucking the strings with the fingertips. The instrument had a brief but extensive popularity in Britain in the second half of the eighteenth century.

The term 'guitar' is one of the most confusing in the history of musical instruments. We have seen that it was used in the Middle Ages to describe a small lute with a pear-shaped outline and arched back. The characteristic shape of the modern guitar, with its smoothly in-curving waist, absence of corners, and flat back, was already present, at least in embryo, in some of the stringed instruments of the medieval period; but, as far as can now be ascertained, these were bowed fiddles. By the fifteenth century, however, a Spanish instrument had evolved which united the waisted, flat backed, body shape to the finger-plucking technique and tuning system of the lute. This instrument was known as the 'vihuela da mano'. In the course of the sixteenth century the vihuela developed a virtuoso repertoire, almost completely displacing the lute in its country of origin. Only one instrument is known to have survived from the sixteenth century; this has a string length of 730 mm, considerably longer than the average lute of the time. This instrument is probably atypical, however, since instruments illustrated in early vihuela tutors appear to be of the same general size and string length as contemporary lutes. Vihuelas were typically fitted with six or seven double courses of gut strings. Although the vihuela was very much a Spanish speciality, a similar instrument was also known in Italy by the title of 'viola da mano'.

Another fifteenth-century development was a four-course plucked instrument, with the same body shape as the vihuela but built on a much smaller scale. This instrument came to be known as the guitar. Various tunings were used on the four-course guitar, including G_3–C_4–E_4–A_4; frequently the lowest course consisted of a bourdon string at the nominal pitch and a thinner string an octave higher. The neck of the instrument carried eight or ten gut frets. In the sixteenth century the four-course guitar was popular in Italy, France, and England, with a substantial published repertoire of dance music, fantasias, and song accompaniments. Although the finger-plucking technique of the lute was used on the guitar, the strumming of chords by raking the thumb or first finger across all four strings was considered to be the most characteristic idiom of the instrument.

Larger five- and six-course guitars appeared in the sixteenth century. By the early seventeenth century, the five-course guitar was firmly established, with a string length of around 650 mm (similar to that of the lute). A five-course guitar by the important maker Matteo Sellas is shown in Figure 9.3(a). The normal tuning was A_2–D_3–G_3–B_3–E_4, the lowest two courses being doubled at the octave. Frequently the bourdon strings on the lowest courses were replaced by strings an octave higher, giving the re-entrant tuning A_3–D_4–G_3–B_3–E_4; the fourth and fifth strings were then used melodically rather than providing a bass to the upper strings. The strumming technique, described as *rasgueado*, was much employed, and from about 1600 special chord symbols were provided in song accompani-

9.3 (a) guitar, five-course, ten-string (Matteo Sellas, Venice, 1613); (b) guitar, six-string (C. F. Martin, New York, nineteenth century); (c) electric guitar, Les Paul model (Gibson, *c.*1970)

ments. In the later seventeenth century, lute-style plucking, described as *punteado*, was also employed, although without bourdons on the fifth and sixth courses the guitar was essentially a treble instrument, and a complete continuo accompaniment required the addition of a theorbo or viol to provide the bass line.

In the course of the eighteenth century the guitar developed into a self-contained instrument capable of supplying its own bass. The six-course guitar became standard, with a tuning E_2–A_2–D_3–G_3–B_3–E_4. Improvements in string manufacture, including the introduction of overwound bass strings, led to the use of single strings on all the courses. In the early years of the nineteenth century various structural improvements were made, including the provision of a separate fingerboard, fixed metal frets, and machine heads for tuning. Around the middle of the century the body dimensions and outline of the classic guitar were established, and have remained largely unaltered since; a typical example is the Martin guitar shown in Figure 9.3(b).

Dulcimer and cimbalom

The dulcimer, like the psaltery, is technically a box zither: a number of strings are stretched across a soundboard, with a shallow box acting as a resonating chamber below. It is possible either to pluck the strings of the dulcimer or to strike them with hammers, but hammering of the strings is the normal and distinctive method of playing the dulcimer.

There is no firm evidence of the existence of hammered dulcimers before the twelfth century, when a Byzantine ivory book cover illustrates an instrument of trapezoidal shape, apparently strung and clearly being played with two hammers. Although there are numerous depictions of plucked psalteries in the centuries which followed, it is only after the mid-fifteenth century that further illustrations are known which unambiguously show the hammering technique which identifies the dulcimer. These fifteenth-century illustrations appear to be of instruments with one string for each note, and between six and nine strings in total. Some instruments have the strings passing over bridges, while others do not.

In the sixteenth century the instrument showed a more developed form, with between eight and twelve double courses (two unison strings for each note) passing over bridges. Commonly a bridge divided at least some of the strings in the length ratio of 2:3, with both ends of the string being playable; this gave two notes a perfect fifth apart. Some illustrations from this period show a feature that became characteristic of the dulcimer: the strings are not all in the same plane. Two bridges run almost directly away from the player; one double-string course passes over the right-hand bridge and through a hole in the underside of the left-hand bridge, while the neighbouring course passes under the right-hand bridge and over the left-hand bridge. This means that alternating courses decrease in height above the soundboard to the right and to the left.

In the Baroque period it became normal to have four unison strings in each course, with between eighteen and twenty-five courses. The instrument was popular in many parts of Europe, especially in the German-speaking areas where it was known as the 'Hackbrett'. In the last years of the seventeenth century the German musician Pantaleon Hebenstreit developed a large dulcimer with 185 double strings of gut and metal; this instrument was named the 'pantaleon', apparently on the instructions of the French king Louis XIV who admired it.

During the eighteenth and nineteenth centuries further refinements were introduced, including extensions to the box to incorporate longer bass strings and multiple bridges to make the instrument more chromatic. These developments culminated in the introduction in the 1870s of a large concert dulcimer by the Schunda family of instrument makers in Budapest. This has come to be known as the 'cimbalom', which is the Hungarian word for dulcimer. The concert cimbalom stands on a solid wooden frame, and has pedal-operated dampers for the strings; it can be played chromatically over four octaves and has a wide dynamic range. The cimbalom has been included in orchestral scores by several important composers, including Liszt, Bartók, and Stravinsky.

9.3 INSTRUMENTS IN MODERN USE

Harps

The pedal harp is the only purely plucked stringed instrument to have found a permanent place in the modern symphony orchestra. The orchestral instrument is usually described as the concert harp. A typical present-day concert harp has a hollow fore-pillar about 1.8 m high; at its base is a pedal box, from which emerge seven double-action pedals. The resonator has a rounded back, and the soundboard is tapered so that it increases in width towards the lower end. The strings emerge through holes in the soundboard and rise to the neck, where they pass over bridge pins and are wound round metal tuning pegs. The strings are traditionally gut, with the lowest octave overwound, although nylon and metal-cored strings are now also in use.

The pedal system is in essence that introduced by Érard: rods and levers mounted inside the fore-pillar and in a hollowed-out slot within the neck connect the pedals to pairs of disc-mounted forks below the tuning pegs. The harp normally has forty-six or forty-seven strings, depending on whether the lowest nominal pitch is C_1 or D_1; the strings are tuned diatonically, the highest nominal pitch being G_7. With each of the seven pedals in its middle position, the diatonic scale of C major is obtained. Raising the B pedal to its highest position flattens all the strings with pitch name B to B♭, giving the diatonic scale of F major. Raising all the pedals puts the harp into C♭ major. Conversely, depressing a pedal to its lowest position sharpens all the corresponding strings; with all the pedals fully depressed, the harp plays in C♯ major.

Small harps without pedals are widely played, notably in Ireland and Scotland. An early nineteenth-century small harp developed by the Irish maker John Egan was a conscious attempt to revive and perpetuate the ancient native tradition of harp-playing, but Egan's design borrowed many features from the contemporary concert harp. Among these was a finger-operated version of the concert harp's pedal mechanism, which could sharpen simultaneously by a semitone all strings with the same pitch name. The modern clarsach has typically between twenty-four and thirty-four gut or nylon strings, tuned diatonically. A system of hand-operated rotating blades allows each individual string to be sharpened by a semitone, so that it is possible, for example, to have a C♮ in one octave and a C♯ in another. The clarsach has developed its own solo literature, and is widely used in the performance of traditional Irish and Scottish instrumental and vocal music.

Many other types of harp are in current use. With the growth of interest in the use of historical instruments in the performance of early music, reconstructions of medieval, Renaissance, and Baroque harps are now available. The triple harp of the seventeenth century is a standard continuo instrument in many early Baroque ensembles; a similar instrument was in widespread use in Wales throughout the eighteenth and nineteenth centuries, and this too has been revived. Finally, the important tradition of harp-playing in Latin America must be mentioned. Most Latin American countries have their own characteristic version of the diatonic harp, and the splendidly vigorous virtuoso playing tradition derives at least in part from the Baroque techniques imported from Spain in the sixteenth and seventeenth centuries.

Lutes

Reconstructions of various types of historic lute are used in modern performance of the lute repertoire. For the music of the sixteenth century a six-course lute is appropriate; although no unaltered instrument has survived from this period, lutes made by Laux Maler in Bologna around 1530 were greatly prized at the time, and despite subsequent modifications his instruments still provide a basis for reconstructions.

Lute music of the seventeenth and eighteenth centuries usually requires an instrument with more than six courses. For the rich English repertoire of the early seventeenth century, a ten-course lute is frequently employed, while the later French composers require an instrument with eleven courses. German eighteenth-century lute music calls for a thirteen- or fourteen-course lute. All of these types of lute are now again being manufactured, together with reconstructions of archlutes and chitarroni.

Mandolins

The mandolin is the most popular small plucked instrument in use in present-day Europe. Modern mandolins are direct descendants of the Neapolitan mandolino, with four unison pairs of strings and the violin tuning G_3–D_4–A_4–E_5. The strings are about 300 mm long, and are steel, the lower courses being overwound. As on the modern guitar, the tuning pegs are fitted with machine heads.

The body shape of the instrument has two different forms. In the traditional design, based on the Neapolitan mandolin, the resonator has a very deep arched back, and the soundboard tilts downwards from the bridge to the string fixing. In the alternative design, which achieved wide popularity in the twentieth century, the body is shallow and flat-backed; the belly may be slightly convex, and f-holes frequently replace the central circular sound-hole of the traditional mandolin.

Guitars

The standard classical guitar of the present day is based on a model developed in the late nineteenth century by the Spanish maker Torres. It has six single strings; the upper three are nylon, the lower three silk or nylon wound with metal. The tuning is normally E_2–A_2–D_3–G_3–B_3–E_4, although the bottom string is frequently lowered a tone or more as required by the music. The strings pass through holes bored in a bridge glued to the soundboard, and are fixed on the bridge; at the top of the fingerboard they pass over a nut and are wrapped round tuning barrels with machine head adjustment. The belly and the back are flat, and the fingerboard has nineteen fixed metal frets (see Figure 9.3(b)). The Flamenco guitar used in traditional Spanish dance music has a similar design, but with lighter construction.

Steel-strung guitars are now of immense popularity in folk and popular music. In the early part of the twentieth century the greater volume obtainable from metal strings, especially when played using a plectrum, was a major advantage; with the advent of electrical amplification, the use of magnetic pickups on steel strings introduced a whole new family of electric guitars. Instruments without electrical amplification are often described as acoustic guitars.

One common type of steel-strung acoustic guitar has the same general shape as the classical guitar, but with a wider, deeper body and a neck reinforced by a steel rod to cope with the added string tension. Usually the neck is longer and the fingerboard narrower than on the classical instrument, with fourteen frets before the neck joins the body instead of the twelve on the classical guitar. A variant of this type is the twelve-string guitar, with six double courses; normally the lowest three courses each have a string at the nominal pitch doubled by another an octave above, as on the sixteenth-century guitar. Both six- and twelve-string acoustic guitars may be played with the fingers, but the use of a plectrum or plastic picks fitted to the fingers is more common.

The cello-style acoustic guitar is distinguished by the convex arching of the belly and back, and the use of f-holes instead of a circular soundhole. First made by the Gibson company in the 1920s, it became the standard jazz guitar. Various other experiments have been made with the shape of the resonating box of the guitar; one development which has been widely accepted was the introduction by the Ovation company in the 1970s of a rounded back made from a synthetic material resembling fibreglass.

All of the steel-strung guitars described above can be fitted with magnetic pickups. However, the use of electrical amplification removes the necessity for a resonating body, and the second half of the twentieth century has seen the solid-bodied electric guitar gain a firm footing, not only in the field of popular music, but also in the works of several mainstream composers. A classic type of solid guitar, the Gibson 'Les Paul', with two separate sets of magnetic pickups mounted underneath the strings, is shown in Figure 9.3(c). The electric bass guitar, with four strings tuned E_1–A_1–D_2–G_2 as on the double bass, has also achieved wide popularity.

9.4 CONSTRUCTIONAL TECHNIQUES

The basic methods of construction of plucked stringed instruments with wooden bodies are essentially the same as those used to manufacture the bowed stringed instruments described in the previous chapter. However, each individual instrument has its own technical requirements and traditional features. In this section we consider a few of the constructional techniques used on the lute and the modern classical guitar.

Lute

The characteristic pear-shaped vaulted body of the lute is formed by building it up from a number of narrow strips of wood, called 'ribs'. The ribs are tapered almost to a point at each end, and are bent over a mould and glued together to form the back. The resulting shell is typically less than 1 mm thick. The early sixteenth-century lutes were made from nine or eleven relatively wide ribs of sycamore; later instruments were made from yew or maple, and as many as fifty ribs might be used. At the upper end of the body, the ribs are gathered together round a softwood block which is joined to the neck. Normally the neck is fixed to the block by a mortised joint, although the historically authentic technique is to hammer nails through the block into the end of the neck. At the other end of the body, the junction of the ribs is protected by a capping strip.

The upper surface of the body is formed by a flat soundboard, usually made of two or more strips of a softwood such as pine. To protect the join between soundboard and body a thin strip of parchment or cloth may be glued around it; this is known as the 'lace'. The soundboard has a central soundhole, traditionally filled by an elaborately carved fretwork design called the 'rose'. The underside of the soundboard is strengthened by a number of transverse wooden bars. The neck is made from a harder wood such as beech. On relatively early lutes the neck is quite thick, and has eight gut frets tied around it; later instruments have a longer, thinner, and wider neck, with ten frets. Early instruments may have several wooden frets glued to the soundboard to continue the pattern of the gut frets. On most modern lutes the traditional gut strings have been replaced by plain and over-wound nylon.

The arched shape of the lute body is inherently strong, and the walls need not be thick or heavily braced. The strings of the lute are also fairly thin, and under only moderate tension. These factors combine to make the lute a light but highly responsive instrument, lacking depth of tone but with a bright sound which carries well.

Guitar

The construction of the guitar is quite closely related to that of the viol (see Section 8.4); this is hardly surprising, since the two different types of instrument have a common parent in the Spanish vihuela. The body is much heavier than that of the lute; the soundboard is commonly up to 2.5 mm thick, and is made from two symmetrical sections of close-grained spruce or similar softwood. Traditionally an elaborate system of spruce bars glued under the soundboard helps to provide the required combination of strength and resonance. Different makers have their own patterns of bracing, although 'fan-strutting', in which the struts radiate outwards from the underside of the bridge towards the bottom of the soundboard, is very widely employed.

The flat back is also usually made in two sections; maple and rosewood are popular materials for the back and the sides of the guitar. The ebony fingerboard is usually fitted with nineteen nickel silver frets. The hardwood bridge and string holder is glued to the upper surface of the soundboard. The position of the bridge is determined by the positioning of the frets on the neck; if the bridge is not in exactly the right position it will be impossible to play the instrument in tune. The height of the bridge, and of the nut at the upper end of the fingerboard, must also be adjusted carefully to ensure that the height of the strings above the frets (the 'action') is correct.

The thickness of the soundboard and the positioning of the supporting struts are vital in determining the resonant properties of the instrument. A well-made guitar is more responsive than a lute at low frequencies, but less so at high frequencies. This gives the guitar its characteristic warm and rounded sound, contrasting with the pearly clarity of the lute.

9.5 PERFORMANCE PRACTICE

Harp

The conventional playing technique of the harp uses the thumb and the first three fingers of each hand to pluck the strings, the little finger being considered too weak to serve a useful function. The position at which the string is plucked depends on the type of sound required. If the plucking point is at the centre of the string, the lower string modes are predominantly excited, and the sound is full and rounded. Plucking near to the soundboard, on the other hand, gives more energy to the higher string partials, and the sound becomes harder and more sharply etched. We saw earlier that the feel of a string, which is a measure of how easily the string may be displaced by the finger, is greatest at the centre; the resistance of the string to the plucking motion increases as the plucking point approaches the soundboard, and very close to the end of the string it is impossible to play with any volume.

The use of harmonics, which was discussed in the previous chapter in relation to the bowed strings, is a technique which has been much employed in harp music. For notes played with the left hand, the side of the palm is rested lightly at the point halfway along the string. This damps the odd string modes; when the upper section of the string is plucked by the thumb or one of the fingers, the octave above the basic string pitch is sounded. Since the side of the palm can touch several adjacent strings simultaneously, it is possible to play two- or three-note chords with the left hand, using only octave harmonics. With the right hand, the first joint of the index finger is used to damp the odd modes, the string being plucked by the thumb; only one harmonic at a time can be played by the right hand. As on the violin, higher harmonics can be played by moving the damping point to the appropriate string node. Thus, for example, by touching the string one third of the way along, the third harmonic is available, a twelfth above the basic string pitch.

The playing of scales and arpeggios is a staple of the technique of every type of harp. There is no mechanical damping mechanism on the harp; it is therefore sometimes necessary to damp the strings with the flat of the hand to avoid undesirable clashes of harmony. On the other hand, the way in which one arpeggiated chord can dissolve into another is an idiomatic feature much exploited in harp music.

Certain technical effects depend on the pedal mechanism. One of these is the use of 'synonyms', which are strings with a different pitch name tuned to the same pitch by the manipulation of the pedals. For example, the C pedal fully depressed sharpens the C_4 string to $C^{\#}_4$, while the D pedal fully raised flattens the D_4 string to $D^{\flat}_4$. Since the instrument is tuned to equal temperament, these two notes have the same pitch. A very rapid reiteration of the same pitch may then be performed by alternately plucking these two strings; this is a technique also available on the diatonic notes of the triple harp. On the pedal harp, all notes except D♮, G♮, and A♮ have synonyms.

Another very important use of synonyms is in the playing of chordal glissandi. By appropriate pedalling, it can be arranged that all the strings of the harp are tuned to the notes of certain chords; the chordal glissando is then performed by sweeping the second finger upwards or the thumb downwards across the strings, depending on the direction of the glissando. Although this effect has become something of a cliché of harp music, it gives a striking and dramatic effect.

Lute

The classic lute technique of the late Renaissance and early Baroque is described in several contemporary treatises. The left hand is held with the thumb behind the neck of the lute, and the palm arched so that the fingers come down almost vertically on the fingerboard. The string is pressed against the fingerboard just behind the fret which is to determine its sounding length. The positions of the frets can be adjusted, since they are tied loops of gut, and minute alterations in the temperament of the instrument can be achieved by subtle adjustment of the frets. As on the viol, small pitch changes can also be made by pulling the string sideways along the fret, thus altering its tension.

The first three fingers and thumb of the right hand are used to pluck the strings. Pictures of lute players sometimes show the little finger of the right hand in the air, but several instruction books emphasize the advantage of pressing it against the fingerboard near the treble end of the bridge to provide a point of support and stability. The fleshy part of the finger or thumb is used to pluck the two strings of a course simultaneously; the nails are not used. The difference in timbre obtain-

9.4 *Pavanne ou tombeau de Mr Raquette*, by Denis Gaultier (*c*.1670) (facsimile of original French lute tablature)

able by moving the plucking point from the rose towards the bridge is recognized and exploited.

Renaissance and Baroque music was written in 'tablature', and most modern players continue to use this system. Tablature is a method of explaining to the player where on the fingerboard to put each of the required fingers. French, German, and Italian musicians each had their own systems of tablature; Figure 9.4 shows a piece of lute music in French tablature. The letters *a*, *b*, *c* . . . describe the first, second, third . . . frets (the nut counting as the first fret). An *a* written above the top line indicates that the top string should be plucked without stopping; a *b* above the second line indicates that a finger should stop the second string at the first fret; a gap above the third string indicates that this string should not be plucked; and so on. Of course, it is vital that the lute should be tuned the way that the composer expected; otherwise, the tablature instructions will not give the desired pitches. In the seventeenth century it was customary for French lute music to specify the required tuning, since many variants were in common use.

Guitar

In many ways, the technique used on the modern classical guitar is similar to that of the lute. The position of the left-hand, and the placing of the left hand fingers behind the frets, is in essence the same. One difference which is immediately noticeable to the listener is the use of vibrato. A rocking motion of the finger generates a pitch variation due to the change in tension, as on the viol; this effect is used as a subtle ornament in lute-playing, but is a major feature of the timbre of many guitarists.

The right-hand technique of the guitar is substantially different from that of the lute, with a much greater variety in the types of plucking action used. Two basic strokes are identified as *apuyando*, in which the finger plucks a string and comes to rest against the adjacent string, and *tirando*, in which the finger rises freely after plucking. Most modern guitarists also use the nails rather than the flesh of the fingertip, to produce a more ringing sound. The contrast between the brilliant sound obtained near the bridge and the mellower timbre obtained over the sound-hole is exploited as it is on the lute (see Figure 2.16).

It is possible to sound notes on the guitar using only the left hand. If one left-hand finger stops the string at a fret, a second left-hand finger can be used to pluck the string just on the bridge side of the stopped fret. Another technique involves pressing the string percussively against a fret, using the energy of collision to excite the string; this technique, described as 'hammering on', is used in some American folk guitar and banjo styles.

Harmonics are readily obtained on the guitar, and are an important feature in many compositions. Natural harmonics are played by touching the open string at one of its nodal points rather than pressing the string against the fingerboard. Artificial harmonics are also employed; these require the player to stop the string with one finger, while touching it lightly with another finger at a nodal point of the stopped string. Scale passages, chords, and even entire pieces can be played using only harmonics.

The most characteristic sound of the Renaissance and Baroque guitar was the *rasgueado* strumming technique. In the nineteenth century this aspect of guitar technique was neglected, while guitar players and composers cultivated the *punteado* finger-plucking style hitherto considered more typical of the lute. The *rasgueado* style survived in traditional Flamenco playing, and in the great upsurge of interest in writing for the guitar which has taken place in the twentieth century, many composers have reintegrated these two sides of the guitar's personality in their music.

10

Clavichord and Harpsichord

10.1 ACOUSTICAL PRINCIPLES

The modern keyboard is such an integral feature of musical life that its character-istic pattern of black and white stripes is in itself a potent symbol of music. The idea of using pivoted levers to control a set of pre-tuned musical resonators is at least as old as the organs of the classical Roman period, although it was only in the early fifteenth century that the currently accepted layout of seven naturals and five accidentals per octave was standardized.

A solo keyboard performer can weave an intricate web of polyphony, or create a massive chordal structure, with a facility impossible on any other type of instru-ment. Yet this facility has its price: the player is separated from the source of sound by the key mechanism, which imposes constraints both on the design of the instrument and on the available range of dynamics and expression.

In this chapter we discuss the clavichord and the harpsichord, two radically dif-ferent solutions to the problem of applying a keyboard mechanism to a stringed instrument. In the following chapter we turn to a third solution—the piano-forte—which was developed several centuries later than the clavichord and harp-sichord, but has come to dominate the family of keyboard strings.

Basic acoustics

In their essential acoustical features, the keyboard stringed instruments are no dif-ferent from the plucked and struck strings which we discussed in Chapter 9. Again we find a string excited by a sudden impulse, vibrating with a set of natural modes whose frequencies are slightly inharmonic; again we require a resonant body, cou-pled to the string through a bridge, to ensure that the energy of the string vibra-tion is radiated efficiently as a sound wave.

One characteristic feature of the keyboard instruments is the wide range of pitches covered. The highest and lowest strings on a harpsichord with multiple registers can have a total pitch span of six or even seven octaves. If such an instrument is to sound well over its entire compass, much attention must be devoted to choosing suitable string materials and dimensions, and to designing a soundboard with a wide range of overlapping resonances and a careful gradation of physical properties from treble to bass regions. We first discuss these problems of stringing and soundboard design, then turn to a brief examination of the different methods of exciting the string which characterize the clavichord and the harpsichord.

Stringing of clavichords and harpsichords

For reasons of strength and stability of tuning, metal strings are almost always used on keyboard instruments. Early instruments were normally strung with brass or iron wire; there are occasional references to the use of silver and even gold strings when expense was not a limitation. Harpsichords built in the twentieth century have frequently been strung with steel wire, but in recent years makers of historically accurate reproduction instruments have returned to the traditional string materials.

The designer of a clavichord or harpsichord has several choices to make when considering the stringing of the instrument. The pitch of a given string is determined by the string material, the length and diameter of the string, and the tension to which it is subjected. These various parameters are related by the equation (see Section 2.3)

$$f_1 = (1/2L) \sqrt{T/m}$$

where f_1 is the fundamental frequency of the string vibration, L the string length, T the tension, and m the mass per unit length of the string. If the string has a diameter D, and is made of material with density ρ,

$$m = \pi \rho D^2 / 4$$

so that

$$f_1 = (1/LD) \sqrt{T/\pi \rho}$$

It appears at first sight that the designer of a clavichord or harpsichord has complete freedom in choosing the string lengths, since a given string length can be made to sound at any pitch by a suitable choice of diameter, tension, and density. In practice, however, there is a limit to the tension which a string can sustain; this limit is set by the physical properties of the string material. A useful parameter in this context is the tensile stress, defined as the tension force divided by the cross-sectional area of the string. The area of a string of diameter D is $\pi D^2/4$, so that the tensile stress can be written as

$$S = 4T/\pi D^2$$

The fundamental frequency of a string can be expressed in terms of the tensile stress as

$$f_1 = (1/2L) \sqrt{S/\rho}$$

One interesting point about this equation is that it contains neither the string diameter nor the tension. Any combination of these variables which gives the same tensile stress will give the same pitch to a string of given length and density.

When a string is tightened too far, it breaks. The maximum tensile stress which a string can sustain before breaking is a characteristic of the string material, called the ultimate strength (U). It is found that the best sound is obtained from a string when its tensile stress is close to the breaking point; part of the reason for this is that the natural modes of the string become increasingly inharmonic as the tension is reduced. In practice, the stress on a harpsichord string tuned up to playing pitch is never more than about 92 per cent of the ultimate strength. The 8 per cent margin of safety is equivalent to a pitch difference of about 150 cents, so that the string is liable to break if it is tuned much more than a semitone above its normal pitch.

If we require, then, that $S = 0.92U$, we find that the fundamental frequency of the string is given by

$$f = (1/2L) \sqrt{0.92U/\rho}$$

Since U and ρ are both characteristic properties of the string material, we see now that the freedom of choice of string length has almost entirely evaporated: once the string material has been chosen, a particular pitch or frequency requires a specific string length L to give the desired stress.

The brass alloys commonly used in the sixteenth and seventeenth centuries have values of density and ultimate strength such that the ideal length of a string tuned to the pitch C_5 is about 270 mm (assuming an A_4 at 440 Hz). For iron, with its greater ultimate strength, the corresponding string should be about 330 mm long. These lengths pose no problem to the designer of a keyboard instrument. If the formula were followed rigorously, however, the string length would be doubled for each octave drop in pitch, so that the string length for C_2 would be a little over 2 m in brass and more than 2.5 m in iron. An instrument with such long strings would be cumbersome; in practice, makers have compromised by making the bass strings shorter than their ideal lengths.

If the entire instrument were strung with wire of the same material and diameter, this relative shortening of the bass strings could only be achieved by reducing the tension, with a consequent loss of volume and tonal purity. To maintain the tension in a string of reduced length without altering the pitch, it is necessary to increase the mass per unit length: this can be done in several ways. The most obvious is to increase the string diameter, using thicker gauges of wire in the bass than in the treble. The disadvantage of this approach is that the thicker strings have greater stiffness, and the natural modes are more inharmonic. An alternative method, which we already observed in our discussion of bowed and plucked

10.1 Clavichord viewed from above, showing parchment rose and overwinding of bass strings

strings in Chapters 8 and 9, is to overwind the basic string with a spiral of heavy wire such as copper or silver, as shown in Figure 10.1; this increases the mass per unit length without adding greatly to the stiffness. A third possibility is to use wires of different materials. Since the optimum length for a given pitch is less in brass than in iron, an instrument whose upper and middle registers were iron-strung might have strings in the bass of yellow and red brass.

Soundboards

In all of the instruments discussed in the present chapter, namely the clavichord, virginals, spinet, and harpsichord, the strings pass over a bridge mounted on a resonating soundboard. The bridge defines one end of the sounding length of the string, and transmits some of the string's vibrational energy to the soundboard. The relative rigidity of string and soundboard, known technically as the 'imped-ance ratio', determines the efficiency with which this energy is transmitted. As with the stringed instruments discussed in the previous chapters, if the sound-board is too rigid, nearly all the energy will be reflected back onto the string, and hardly any sound will emerge; if the soundboard is too responsive, the energy will be radiated away very quickly, giving a note with a powerful attack but little sustained aftersound.

The size of the soundboard also affects its ability to radiate sound. The small soundboards found in clavichords, virginals, and spinets are not very effective at radiating low frequencies. The depth of tone characteristic of a large harpsichord is principally due to the large area of the soundboard. Recent measurements have shown that the acoustical performance of harpsichord soundboards is dominated by a series of resonances below 400 Hz.

The harpsichord and the other instruments discussed above also display the equivalent of the air resonance in a violin, the air cavity being formed by the space between the soundboard and the floor of the case. Although the resonance of this volume of air does not directly contribute much to the radiated sound, it has a significant effect on the apparent stiffness of the soundboard, and therefore indirectly influences the way in which the soundboard radiates. The rose hole cut in most soundboards, or the substantial opening behind the keyboard in instruments made by the Ruckers family, will thus affect the sound of the instrument by modifying the resonance frequency of the internal volume.

Clavichord action

The mechanical system which converts the motion of the player's finger into the sounding of a note is called the 'action' of the instrument. The clavichord action provides the simplest possible mechanism for impulsively exciting a string. As in all keyboard instruments, the basis is a set of levers, or 'keys', normally made of wood. One key is supplied for each note in the compass of the instrument; the keys are pivoted on a common axis, and in their state of rest are approximately horizontal.

Near the end furthest from the player, the key carries a metal blade known as the 'tangent'. On the clavichord, each note is usually sounded by a pair of unison strings, and in its rest state the tangent lies a few millimetres below the appropriate string pair. To sound the note, the player presses the key downwards with a finger, causing the tangent to rise and strike the strings from below.

After the initial stroke, the key is held down for as long as the note is required to sound. The tangent remains in contact with the strings, and the sounding length of each string is determined by the distance from the tangent to the bridge. The impulse given by the tangent stroke sends waves travelling not only towards the bridge, but also in the opposite direction, towards the 'hitch pins'. A strip of felt known as 'listing' is woven between the strings near the hitch pins to damp out unwanted sounds from the sections of string between tangent and hitch pin.

One great advantage of the clavichord action is that it allows the player to control the loudness of the note. If the key is pressed down gently, the tangent contacts the string at a low speed, setting up vibrations with very small amplitude; with a firmer stroke, the tangent velocity is greater and the string vibration correspondingly more vigorous. On a well-made instrument, great subtlety of dynamic shading is possible.

The major disadvantage of the tangent excitation principle is that it is acoustically inefficient. The tangent should ideally provide the fixed point at one end of the string; in fact it is attached to the key lever, and some of the string vibration energy is dissipated in the key mechanism or absorbed by the player's finger. The tangent also supplies less energy to the thin treble strings than to the thicker bass strings; one of the major problems of the clavichord builder is the difficulty of making the treble end of the compass strong enough to match the bass. Increasing the speed at which the tangent hits the string (by increasing the leverage of the key, or simply by pressing harder on it) introduces an unacceptable pitch bend by pushing the string too far from its equilibrium position. For these reasons, the clavichord is essentially limited to music on a domestic scale.

Harpsichord action

The way in which a clavichord string is excited is closely related to the 'hammering-on' technique used in guitar-playing (see Section 9.5). The action of the harpsichord family is a mechanized version of the normal plucking stroke. The plucking finger is replaced by a thin bar called the jack, mounted vertically near the end of the key lever. The upper parts of three sets of jacks can be seen in the photograph of part of a harpsichord in Figure 10.2; Figure 10.3 shows two harpsichord jacks removed from their instrument. The upper end of the jack carries a pivoted tongue from which protrudes a short plectrum or 'quill'. In the state of rest, the plectrum lies just below the string; when the key is pressed down, the jack rises and the plectrum plucks the string.

The pivoted tongue is necessary to ensure that, when the key is released, the plectrum does not pluck the string again as the jack falls. Because of the pivoting arrangement, the tongue tilts backwards on the down stroke, and the plectrum slides almost silently over the string. The residual sound is quickly damped by a piece of felt protruding from the top of the jack.

The most important point to note about the harpsichord action is that the amount of energy imparted to the string is almost entirely determined by how far the string is pulled before it slides off the plectrum. This in turn depends on the stiffness of the plectrum. The speed with which the plectrum pushes past the string has very little effect on the strength of the pluck; in consequence, the player has only a very limited ability to alter the loudness of the note by varying the speed of the key stroke.

The touch sensitivity of the clavichord gives it one major advantage over the harpsichord. On the other hand, the sounding length of the harpsichord string is determined by the nut at one end and the bridge at the other, and the designer of the instrument is free to choose plucking points which are capable of imparting energy efficiently to many of the string modes. The string is released by the plectrum before the sound begins, so the problem of pitch bend is limited to a short transient effect at the start of the note. The harpsichord can therefore be made to

10.2 Harpsichord by Gould of Glasgow *c.*1980, showing 4-foot wrest pins, nut, and jacks

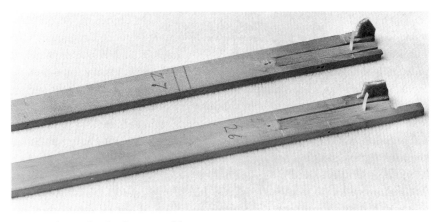

10.3 Two harpsichord jacks removed from instrument

produce a far greater volume of sound than is possible on the clavichord. Dynamic variation on the harpsichord can be provided by having several sets of strings, each plucked by its own rank of jacks and a system of stop levers determining which ranks are active. Tonal variety is provided by choosing different plucking points for the different sets of strings, or by fitting different ranks of jacks with harder or softer plectra.

10.2 HISTORICAL DEVELOPMENT

Clavichords and harpsichords came into prominence in Western Europe during the sixteenth century. Their precise origins are a matter of debate, although it is known that they existed in the fifteenth century; there are clear references to both instruments in literature of that period. They remained popular until the beginning of the nineteenth century, by which time they had been almost completely superseded by the piano. The last pre-revival clavichords and harpsichords were built just after 1800; the Kirckman factory produced harpsichords until 1809 and clavichords were made in Germany and Sweden until about 1820. By this time, however, virtually all of the manufacturing companies had either turned to making pianos or gone out of business.

We have seen that the principles of sound production in the clavichord and harpsichord are quite different; correspondingly, the instruments served different functions within the musical community. The simplicity of the clavichord mechanism made it relatively cheap to produce. Clavichords made before about 1750 were generally light and portable, usually constructed so that they could stand on a table. However, because of their tiny sound, they were used principally in the home. Harpsichord players and organists found it convenient to have a clavichord on which to practise keyboard technique; it could also be used in the accompaniment of solo singers and instrumentalists. The eighteenth-century harpsichord was a much larger instrument, comparable in size with a small modern grand piano. The mechanism was also quite complex, making the instrument relatively expensive. The harpsichord was the keyboard instrument used for public performance in theatres and concert halls, although it was also to be found in the houses of the wealthy middle classes and the aristocracy.

The more modest home might boast a 'virginal' or a 'spinet'. These were small versions of the harpsichord; they had almost invariably a single keyboard, with only one set of strings and jacks. The distinctive feature of the virginal is that its strings run parallel to the keyboard rather than being perpendicular to it as in the case with the harpsichord or the modern grand piano. The term spinet is used for instruments where the strings run at an oblique angle to the keyboard. The relatively small sound and limited tonal capabilities of these instruments rendered them most suitable for domestic purposes.

The clavichord

The earliest references to clavichords, at the beginning of the fifteenth century, describe instruments which had a number of strings all of the same length and tuned to the same pitch. The tangents were arranged to strike the strings at positions which subdivided the string into its appropriate segments to give the required pitch; for example if the octave above the open string pitch was required then the tangent would strike the string at its centre. Segments of strings that were not required to sound had their vibrations damped by cloth wound between them. These early clavichords had their origin in the monochord, and were thus referred to as 'monochordia'. The monochord was an ancient instrument making use of a single string stretched over fixed bridges; a movable bridge was placed under the string to subdivide its length into two segments, thus producing the different pitches.

Early clavichords generally had three or four notes using the same string or pair of strings; such instruments are referred to as fretted. Clearly if more than one note used the same string then these notes could not be played simultaneously; if they were, then the highest note played would be the only one to sound. The different notes using the same string were chosen such that they always formed dissonant or infrequently used intervals; in this way all the commonly used consonant chords could be played. The method of having all the strings of equal length and tuned to the same pitch presented problems for the overall layout of the instrument; in particular the keys had to be sharply bent in order to bring the ends holding the tangents into the correct striking positions. The effect of this was to limit the playing range to about three octaves. However, the simplicity of the monochord concept also had its attractive features, notably the simplicity of tuning. In order to tune the clavichord the felt listing could be removed, and the tensions of the strings adjusted until each string sounded the same pitch when plucked. The pitch interval between two different notes obtained by striking the same string was fixed, although it could easily be reset by bending the tangents slightly.

By the end of the fifteenth century a new generation of clavichords had emerged in which the concept of tuning every string to the same pitch had been abandoned. These later instruments had an extended range, typically four octaves, and were generally more compact than their predecessors, with the keys less sharply bent. They maintained the idea of fretting, and typically used two different metals for the strings, brass in the bass and steel in the treble. The earliest surviving clavichord is actually hexagonal in shape, with the keyboard along the longest side and the shortest side at the back; it is Italian and dates from 1543. The hexagonal shape can be achieved because the bass strings are at the front of the instrument, as in the virginal. The keyboard on this instrument protrudes from the case and is positioned off-centre to the left. Sixteenth-century instruments were not all hexagonal, however; a rectangular shape with protruding keyboard was very common.

The clavichord was popular all over Europe during the sixteenth century. Fretting patterns were devised which produced different groupings of notes in successive octaves; this allowed the instrument to be tuned entirely in octaves, without recourse to the use of fifths or other intervals which an amateur player might find more difficult to tune. In the seventeenth century, however, the popularity of the clavichord declined in most of Europe. This decline was particularly marked in Flanders, where the harpsichord started to take precedence. In Germany, however, the clavichord still maintained a high profile. By now it was becoming the norm to have the keyboard inset within a rectangular box so that there was no projection outside, giving the instrument a much neater and more compact appearance. With this layout the soundboard could be made larger, enhancing the resonances, and also the strings could follow a diagonal line, rather than being perpendicular to the keys. A major advantage of diagonal stringing was that the line of the tangents could be made to run more nearly parallel to the keyboard; the keys could then be made of similar length, improving the uniformity of the touch. The bridges were now being made in a curved shape, rather than being segmented as was often the case on earlier instruments.

The harpsichord

The earlier harpsichords can probably best be considered as mechanized forms of the psaltery, with simple keyboard-operated mechanisms added to perform the plucking action. A treatise by Arnaut of Zwolle, dating from about 1440, describes such a mechanism in considerable detail. These early instruments were quite short, generally with only one string per note. They did not use dampers, so that the strings were free to vibrate after sounding, as in the psaltery.

Later instruments, from around the sixteenth century, tended to use multiple stringing; usually one set of strings was tuned to the written pitch, while a second set was tuned an octave higher. A string which sounds at the written pitch is commonly described as an '8-foot string', and a string tuned to sound an octave higher than written pitch is called a '4-foot string'. It is important to note that the terms '8-foot' and '4-foot' do not indicate the actual string lengths employed, but reflect a terminology borrowed from the pipe organ (see Chapter 12). We can thus say that the sixteenth-century harpsichord typically employed a set of 8-foot strings and a set of 4-foot strings. The mechanism also developed considerably more sophistication in the course of the sixteenth century, with the introduction of dampers. By the seventeenth century it became the norm to have both strings at 8-foot pitch, with an optional third set at 4-foot pitch. During the eighteenth century elaborate instruments incorporating 16-foot and even 2-foot registers were occasionally built and, in a few cases, three keyboards. The various registers were brought into action by moving the jacks with slides operated by stops; these either projected through the sides of the case or through the board above the keys. In the latter case a lever mechanism was necessary.

The development of the harpsichord was very much associated with national schools of construction, amongst which the Italians and Flemish were predominant.

The Italian harpsichord

The Italians were a major influence in the development of the harpsichord, although they generally maintained simple designs. They completely dominated the market during the sixteenth century, exporting their instruments throughout Western Europe. In fact they continued successfully with this trade for three hundred years; all over the continent Italian harpsichords could be found in theatres, churches, drawing rooms, in fact almost anywhere where music was played. Notable amongst the distinguished workshops were those of the Trasuntino family working in Venice and Naples. The Italian harpsichord played a crucial role in the development of the music of this period.

In comparing different designs of harpsichord, it is useful to have a method of summarizing information on the lengths of the strings in a particular design. Frequently two parameters are quoted: the length of the C_5 string (described as the 'scale'), and the length ratio of two strings an octave apart (known as the 'stringing ratio'). The scale is determined by the material of which the string is made, and by the actual pitch at which the C_5 key is intended to sound, as we saw in the previous section. Italian harpsichords generally had shorter scales than Flemish instruments, with a brass C_5 string length of 270 mm as typical. The stringing ratio was normally very close to two, implying that the string length doubled for each drop in pitch of one octave. From our earlier discussion we can infer that the ratio of string tension to mass per unit length ($T : m$) must have been nearly constant throughout the instrument; thicker strings in the bass must therefore have been at higher tension.

Sixteenth-century Italian instruments had quite thin cases, typically 4 mm or 5 mm thick; cypress wood was used, or less often maple, with mouldings round the edges and internal bracing for strength. The complete instrument was housed in a much more substantial outer case with a lid, hence the name 'inner-outer harpsichord'. The outer case was usually decorated with paintings or covered with leather, and was supported on a stand. The large stringing ratio meant that the bentside was quite deeply curved in order to accommodate the required lengths of string. Soundboards were usually made of cypress or spruce, with one or more circular holes decorated by roses made from wood veneer or layers of parchment. The normal disposition of string registers was 2 × 8-foot (two sets of strings tuned in unison), but some were 1 × 8-foot and 1 × 4-foot (one set of strings tuned an octave above the other). Usually the range was four octaves, although this was sometimes extended by four or five semitones.

Later Italian harpsichords were mostly made with a single thick-walled case, but by clever use of mouldings and veneer these were made to look like the earlier inner-outer instruments; they are usually referred to as 'false inner-outer'. By the eighteenth century virtually all instruments were of this type.

It was common with early instruments to use 'short-octave tuning'. This was a device used to increase the compass of an instrument in the bass register without actually adding more strings and associated keys. A few notes at the bottom of the compass were retuned to lower pitches in such a way that diatonic notes could be played whereas accidentals such as C♯ and E♭ were left out. In the most usual arrangement the octave was compressed into the nine notes normally sounding E to C, as shown in Figure 10.4. The six white notes (or black ones if the normal convention has been reversed) then sounded C, F, G, A, B, and C, the missing D and E being sounded by the two lowest black notes. The only available accidental was then B♭, which was sounded by the third black note from the bottom. It is seen that the four notes C♯, E♭, F♯, and G♯ are missing. However, it is worth remembering that any of the notes could be retuned for particular instrumental pieces which required one of the missing notes. On some instruments the bottom two black notes were split cross-ways with the front halves playing the notes assigned to the short octave tuning; the back halves then played the normal accidental.

A useful feature of the short-octave tuning was that it brought the playing of some wide intervals easily within the span of the left hand, thus increasing the possibilities for enhanced bass sonorities. The tenth C to E for example was reduced to an octave span, and this was often written in the music.

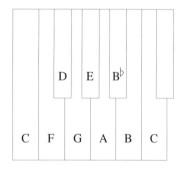

10.4 (right) Short-octave tuning used on some early instruments

Harpsichords from northern Europe

In the middle of the sixteenth century harpsichord workshops were starting to appear in Flanders; by the end of the century this region became a major centre for harpsichord-making, completely dominating the scene in northern Europe. Greatest amongst the early Flemish makers were members of the Ruckers family, headed by Hans Ruckers, who set up shop in Antwerp in about 1570. The tradition that he established was followed by his sons Joannes and Andreas, and later his grandson Andreas. The Ruckers family was a foremost influence in the perfection of the harpsichord.

The cases of the Flemish instruments were typically made of softwood about 10 mm thick, usually poplar or lime, and were braced for added strength. This rather heavy construction contrasted with their more graceful Italian counterparts. The length of the C_5 string was typically about 350 mm, considerably longer than the Italian instrument. This increase in scale reflected the Flemish preference for iron strings, although in the lower part of the compass brass was still used to avoid the necessity for excessively long strings in the bass. The result of this foreshortening in the bass was that the shape of the bentside on a Flemish harpsichord differed significantly from its Italian counterpart. The shapes of the two designs are compared in Figure 10.5; it will be seen that the Flemish bentside has a much smaller degree of curvature, approaching more nearly a straight edge.

Flemish harpsichords were usually covered completely with decoration both inside and out. The soundboards were typically painted with motifs such as flowers, fruit, and birds, whilst the inside of the case and lid were covered with block-printed paper and then decorated. The outside was often marbled. This gave the Flemish and Italian harpsichords distinctly different appearances; the Italian makers relied principally on the mouldings, carvings, and mother-of-pearl and ivory inlays for embellishment, saving more elaborate decoration for the outer case, which was probably produced by another class of craftsman.

Comparing the sounds of the Flemish and Italian instruments, the Flemish tended to have greater sustaining power, primarily associated with heavier and more rigid bridges. The sound on the Italian instrument had a characteristic immediacy and marked attack.

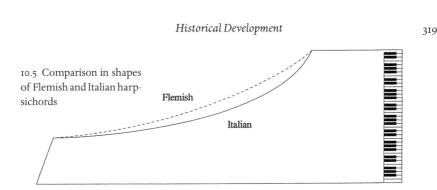

10.5 Comparison in shapes
of Flemish and Italian harpsichords

Flemish

Italian

In the seventeenth century France also produced harpsichords. Early instruments tended to be rather light in construction and bore a greater resemblance to
the Italian model than to the Flemish. Later French harpsichords from workshops
such as the Blanchet family were, however, modelled on the Ruckers designs. The
French are probably more famous for their modifications (*ravalements*) of earlier
Ruckers instruments. A *ravalement* often involved a major reconstruction; extra
keys with the necessary strings and jacks were added to expand the range or to fill
in missing chromatic notes, and the instrument was frequently redecorated in
contemporary style. In some cases this meant that the whole case had to be
rebuilt. The reconstructed Ruckers harpsichords were greatly prized, and frequently commanded twice the price of a new instrument.

Some harpsichords underwent *ravalement* several times. The high price also led
to a market in forgeries, with new instruments having old wood grafted on and
counterfeit roses fitted to give the impression of an old instrument which had
undergone reconstruction. Some harpsichords were produced in England during
the seventeenth and eighteenth centuries, notably by the Haward and Hitchcock
families in London. An extant two-manual harpsichord made about 1725 by
Thomas Hitchcock is now in the Victoria and Albert Museum. Features of this
instrument are its double curved bentside and fine veneering on some of the inner
facings. During the eighteenth century a major influence in establishing the reputation of harpsichord-making in England was Hermann Tabel, a craftsman from
Antwerp who emigrated to London about 1700. He trained both Shudi and Kirckman, who between them subsequently dominated the market. The typical English harpsichord of this period had a thick-sided strongly braced case, often
veneered in mahogany. The bentside was straight for much of its length, finishing
in a gentle curve. In the eighteenth century there were about ninety harpsichord
builders in London, but the majority of these seem to have confined their activi-
ties to the construction of bentside spinets, leaving the production of harpsichords proper to Shudi, Kirckman, and a few others.

In Germany, clavichord and harpsichord construction developed in a number of
leading cities such as Berlin, Dresden, and Freiberg. The most notable centre was
Hamburg, where the Hass family and Christian Zell established their own style of

construction and produced instruments noted for their clarity and brilliance of tone. Hass harpsichords often featured unusual and impressive specifications, and were elaborately decorated.

The virginal and spinet

During the sixteenth and seventeenth centuries virginals were constructed extensively in the major harpsichord centres of Italy and Flanders and, to a lesser extent, in England. They were almost certainly much more common than harpsichords, principally because of their simplicity and quite modest price. The relative smallness in size of virginals as compared to harpsichords and the limitations of their single set of strings placed severe restrictions on their tonal capabilities; nevertheless, virginals had a distinctive quality of their own and could be used for the performance of virtually the whole of the contemporary repertoire. They undoubtedly played an important role in the development of keyboard music during this period.

We have already noted that the strings on a virginal run parallel to the keyboard; another distinguishing feature is that the longer bass strings are at the front, giving the possibility of a wide variety of shapes. Many virginals were rectangular and bore a superficial resemblance to a clavichord, whilst others were polygonal, either with the keyboard inset into the longest side or protruding from it. The method of construction of these different-shaped instruments tended to be quite similar, although the rectangular ones frequently had a superior tone, especially in the bass, due to the greater area of soundboard around the bridge.

The row of jacks on a virginal normally ran diagonally from the front left to the back right, making the key levers short in the bass and correspondingly long in the treble. The 'touch ratio' of the levers, defining the relative motion of the jacks and the keys, was maintained approximately constant by angling the balance rail on which the keys were pivoted. The jacks themselves were arranged in pairs which plucked in opposite directions, each pair being separated by a pair of strings.

On most Italian virginals the keyboard was placed in the centre of the long side, whereas Flemish builders sometimes used the alternative arrangement of placing the keyboard either to the left or to the right. With the keyboard central or to the left, the jacks ran quite close to the left-hand bridge, as shown in Figure 10.6(a). This had the effect that the plucking position was near the centre of the string for the top notes but was proportionately closer to the end for the low notes. The timbre was therefore relatively strong in fundamental mode in the treble; the bass was more strident, with stronger upper modes giving a timbre resembling that of the harpsichord. With the keyboard to the right, the plucking position was much closer to the centre of the strings over the whole range (Figure 10.6(b)). As explained in Section 9.1, plucking at the centre of a string gives a timbre charac-

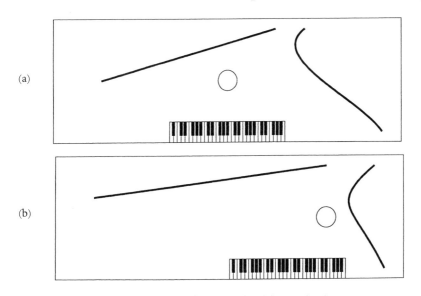

10.6 Comparison of (a) virginal and (b) muselar shapes

terized by a weakness of even harmonics. Virginals with their keyboards placed to the right had such a distinctive sound that they were given their own name of 'muselar'. Flemish muselars were frequently fitted with a stop called the 'arpichordum', which produced a buzzing sound in the tenor and bass by causing the strings to vibrate against metal hooks or wires; these were the only virginals which had any means of changing their timbre. The effect of the arpichordum is to enrich the timbre by reintroducing the missing partials.

Virginals and muselars were sometimes made in pairs, combining the standard instrument sounding at 8-foot pitch with a much smaller one at 4-foot pitch. These pairs were known as 'mother and child'. In the 'mother' instrument was a compartment in which the 'child' was housed. The child could be taken out and played separately, or the two instruments could be coupled by placing the child on top of the mother with her jack rail removed. In the latter case, when notes were played on the mother both instruments sounded simultaneously.

Like the virginal, the spinet had a single set of strings and one keyboard, but in the case of the spinet the bass strings were at the back. When these were shorter than the length of the keyboard, the instrument was generally trapezoidal in shape. The more common and elegant 'bentside spinet' was a larger instrument in which the bass strings were longer than the keyboard; the typical shape of this type of instrument is shown diagrammatically in Figure 10.7. The great advantage of the spinet was its compactness; because of the oblique stringing it was considerably smaller than a harpsichord of equivalent compass.

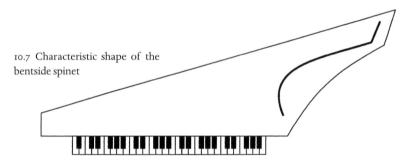

10.7 Characteristic shape of the bentside spinet

The spinet was developed in the early seventeenth century and gradually took over from the virginal, particularly in England where it became the standard domestic instrument by the end of the century. In Italy, where some of the earliest examples of spinets originated, the virginal maintained its popularity for longer.

Twentieth-century harpsichords

The last Kirckman harpsichord was built in 1809; in all probability regular production had stopped well before this date. During the greater part of the nineteenth century harpsichord-making remained in abeyance; it was not revived until the Paris Exposition of 1889, at which the Pleyel and Érard companies separately exhibited new harpsichords. Both of these were loosely based on an instrument by Pascal Taskin dating from 1769, now in the Russell Collection at Edinburgh. The new Pleyel and Érard harpsichords, however, were built very much along the lines of a grand piano, with much heavier framing, strings and bridges than traditional eighteenth-century instruments. They had two manuals with a five-octave compass, disposed as 2 × 8-foot, 1 × 4-foot, and their keyboards were very similar in both appearance and touch to the piano. In London Arnold Dolmetsch also produced his own harpsichord, a single-manual instrument, which he displayed at the Arts and Crafts Exhibition in 1896. 'Revival harpsichords' also appeared in Germany, frequently using the so-called 'Bach disposition' which put a 16-foot and one 8-foot on the lower manual and a 4-foot with another 8-foot on the upper. This appears to have been based on a harpsichord in a Berlin collection which had been altered, was incorrectly associated with Bach, and later became discredited.

In 1912 the Pleyel company demonstrated their new 'Landowska' model in Germany. This was inspired by Wanda Landowska, the first of the revival generation of internationally renowned harpsichord virtuosi. The Landowska model bore an even greater resemblance to the modern grand piano, and was later given an iron frame. It had thick strings and a sophisticated fine-tuning system with keyboards of the same size and similar touch to the piano. The case was of natural wood veneer with the grain running vertically like the modern grand piano, with the sides of the keyboard well cut away to make the hands of the player more visible to the audience. The disposition was 16-foot, 8-foot and 4-foot on the lower manual and 8-foot on the upper, register changes being accomplished with a set of seven foot pedals. Landowska was Professor of Harpsichord at the Berlin Hochschule für Musik from 1913 to 1919, and played on this instrument until her death in 1959. Her fame was crucial in establishing the Pleyel instrument, which in turn influenced other makers in Germany. Despite their sophisticated construction the early revival harpsichords are generally now considered to have a somewhat thin and dull sound.

In the early 1950s a revival in harpsichord-making based on traditional construction techniques started, particularly in America. This trend gradually spread internationally although it took longer to establish itself in Germany where the revival harpsichord had taken a strong hold. Nowadays the traditionalist approach is firmly established and virtually all new harpsichords are constructed on these lines.

10.3 THE CLAVICHORD AND HARPSICHORD TODAY

We have already seen that modern harpsichord makers base their designs almost exclusively on traditional instruments; the same is true for the clavichord. Thus most new harpsichords and clavichords are essentially reproductions of seventeenth- or eighteenth-century instruments. Compared to the piano, the number of new instruments produced is extremely small, although it is steadily rising. Usually the makers are individual craftsmen, working alone or with one or two assistants in a small workshop. Because of this the range of designs is enormous, particularly in the case of the harpsichord, where a bewildering variety of registrations, ranges, and national styles is available. Despite this, the construction of modern clavichords and harpsichords has developed some degree of uniformity based on demand, price, and fashion. Reproductions of historic instruments based on a late stage of development from around the mid-eighteenth century are now considered as standard. It is the basic construction of such reproductions that will be described here, keeping in mind that many variations are possible.

How the clavichord works

The essential feature of the clavichord, as we have already said, is that the strings are struck by metal tangents. The pressure of the tangent against the string also sets the speaking length and hence the pitch of the note.

In construction the clavichord is usually rectangular in shape. Its case is typically something over a metre in length, a third of this in width and about 10 cm deep. Often, though not always, the keyboard is inset into the longer side. A modern reproduction instrument is shown in Figure 10.8. The whole instrument is normally quite light and portable, weighing about 20 kg, and has the appearance of a large suitcase when the lid is closed.

When played it can be rested either on a table or on a purpose-built stand. Usually the opened lid serves as a music desk. With the lid closed the appearance of the clavichord is very similar to the virginal. With the lid open, however, the simple clavichord mechanism means that the key levers are visible immediately below the strings. The physical depth of the clavichord is usually less than the virginal since the top of the keys are only fractionally below the level of the strings. On the virginal, this distance has to be greater to allow for the more complex mechanism.

Figure 10.9 shows the clavichord mechanism schematically. The strings are arranged in pairs, two strings for each note, with the bass strings nearest to the keyboard. The strings usually run at a slight angle to the keyboard, with the bass end further from the keys, in order to reduce the discrepancy between the lengths of the treble and bass key levers. At their left-hand end the strings are fixed to the hitch pins, set into the hitch-pin block. The right-hand ends are wound round the

10.8 Fretted clavichord by John Barnes and Darryl Martin, Edinburgh 1990; copy of Friederici, Gera, 1765

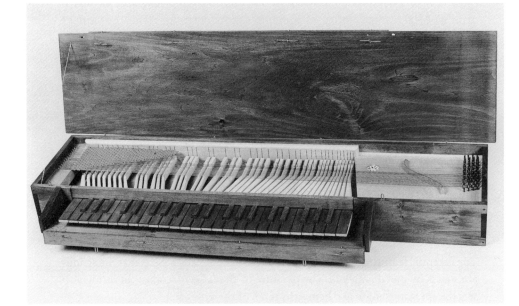

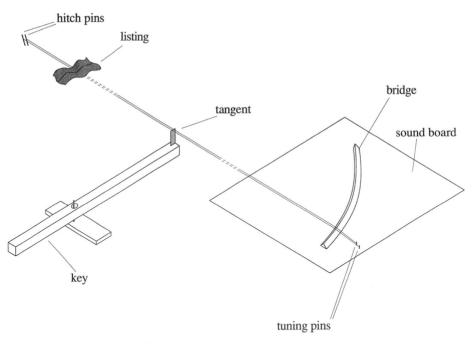

10.9 Diagram illustrating clavichord mechanism

tuning pins, set into the wrest-pin block. To the right of the keyboard the strings pass over the bridge, which is fixed to the top of the soundboard.

The keys rest on a balance rail which acts as a pivot point for the lever mechanism. Metal pins are set into the rail to hold the keys in place. These pass through slots in the keys at their pivot points, positioned somewhat closer to the front for the longer naturals than for the shorter sharps. Each key extends back to the full depth of the instrument. To locate its position at the far end a small slip of metal, whale-bone, or other appropriate material is let into the end of the key; this protrusion runs in a slotted rail, sometimes called a 'diapason', fixed inside the back wall of the case. Set vertically into each key near its far end is the small metal tangent, usually made of brass. As the key is depressed the tangent rises up to strike the lower side of the pair of strings, simultaneously forming the sounding length and initiating the vibrations. The left-hand end of the strings are interwoven with cloth listing in order to dampen the vibrations of the section between the tangent and the hitch pin when the note is sounding. When the key is released the listing dampens the vibrations in the full length of string between the hitch pin and the bridge, thus stopping the note sounding. In order to obtain the correct striking positions the majority of the keys need to be bent in shape. In the front playing section the keys are straight but they then spread out at different angles, either to the right or left, depending on the particular striking point required.

Strings on a clavichord are normally made of either brass or iron. Frequently the bass is strung with brass and the middle and upper registers with iron, it being felt that the brass gives a fuller and rounder sound and iron gives a greater clarity. The bass strings are often overwound, as seen in Figure 10.1. The use of two strings per note gives increased volume and also enhances the tone quality, since the two strings are tuned to very slightly different frequencies.

Almost all clavichords were fretted until about 1740, after which fretted and unfretted instruments coexisted; the unfretted instruments became more popular, until by 1790 nearly all were unfretted. Modern clavichords were almost all unfretted until about 1970, when the practice of copying old instruments came into vogue. Nowadays both fretted and unfretted instruments are produced. Double fretting, in which no more than two adjacent notes share the same string, is usual, since this does not seriously limit the playing repertoire. The lowest notes cannot be fretted because the difference in striking position between two adjacent semitones on long strings is too great.

The soundboard on a clavichord is relatively small. It runs at a level fractionally above the top of the keys and essentially occupies the space to the right of the keyboard, which amounts to about a third, or even as little as a quarter, of the inside space. Since the bottom of the case is enclosed, the soundboard is in effect the top surface of a box. As we noted in the earlier discussion of acoustical principles, the resonances of the air cavity inside this box affect the motion of the soundboard, and hence the radiated sound. An opening is incorporated to allow free movement of the air from inside to outside of the box; the rose on a guitar and f-holes on a violin have a similar function. The opening on the clavichord can be a rose set in the soundboard, often finely decorated with parchment, as seen in Figure 10.1, or some other material. Alternatively, it may be an opening in the box on the side facing the keys, sometimes referred to as a 'mouse hole'.

The soundboard itself may be either plain or reinforced on the underside with one or more ribs. The smallness in size of the clavichord soundboard is one factor limiting the loudness of the instrument, although we have seen that the nature of the action sets a more fundamental limitation.

The bridge is made of wood, of the order of a square centimetre in cross-section but narrowed at the top; it usually runs in an S shape from the left-hand back corner to the right-hand front corner, to allow for the fact that the treble strings at the back are shorter than the bass strings at the front. It has been found that the vibrational characteristics of the soundboard are improved if the bridge does not extend right to the soundboard edge. Bridge pins are fixed in the top side of the bridge to guide the strings laterally into their correct positions.

In contrast to the harpsichord, special devices are found only rarely on the clavichord. This is probably because the primary attractions of the clavichord are its inherent simplicity and portability, both of which are lost if the mechanism is made too complicated. Also its tiny sound does not lend itself to a wide range of modifications. Nevertheless, certain special features are occasionally incorporated. For example, triple-stringing may be used, possibly with the third strings in the bass tuned an octave higher and occupying their own bridge.

The compass of a modern clavichord is normally a little over four octaves, typically from C_2 to E_6 or F_6. This is adequate for the performance of the music of most composers from the Baroque period.

Because of the relatively small number of strings, tuning the clavichord is not an enormous task, and can usually be carried out by the experienced player. However, the procedure is complicated somewhat by the fact that the pitch of any particular note depends to a certain extent on the pressure applied to the key. Pressing a key down hard stretches the string by a small amount and hence increases the tension. This results in a rise in pitch, since the effect of the tension increase far exceeds the fall in pitch due to the increased string length. When carrying out the tuning it is therefore vital that an even touch is used. In much the same way as with the modern piano, a single string from each pair is first brought into tune, in accordance with the particular temperament being used, while the other is damped out using a tuning wedge. The second string in each pair is then brought into unison with the first.

The relative tuning of the two strings within a pair is particularly crucial on a clavichord, since the mechanical coupling between them through the raised tangent is very strong. If the two pitches are matched extremely closely then the strings vibrate together in phase for a very short period of time as though they were a single string, producing a sound which dies away very rapidly. The main sound, which is heard after this short initial transient, has a long sustain time but is very weak and insipid. It has been postulated that the reason for the weakness of the aftersound is that after a few cycles the string vibrations have reached a stable state in which they are moving in anti-phase, i.e. in opposite directions. In this state they effectively work in opposition to each other in transferring energy to the bridge. The locking of the two strings in anti-phase can be avoided by increasing the frequency difference, although this can obviously not be carried to the stage at which a beat becomes obtrusive. In practice the relative settings can readily be judged by the quality of the sound when they are struck together.

How the harpsichord works

In appearance, the harpsichord is not dissimilar to a medium-sized grand piano, although it is considerably lighter in construction and more ornately decorated, and sometimes has two manuals. The sides of the case are not generally cut away around the keyboards to expose the players hands, like the piano; the part of the case enclosing the keyboards is referred to as the 'key well'. It is common to have a stand with four legs, rather than the three customary on the piano. There are usually hand stops or pedals to control the registrations and special effects; a modern instrument will typically have up to four hand stops. With the lid raised, the mechanism can be seen to be quite different from that of the piano; the strings are relatively light and mounted on a wooden frame, as opposed to the heavy strings and massive iron frame of a modern piano.

The layout of the harpsichord mechanism for a double-manual instrument with two 8-foot registers and one 4-foot register is shown schematically in Figure 10.10, and several details can be seen in the photograph of the treble end of an instrument of this type reproduced in Figure 10.2. Each string is attached at the keyboard end to a tuning pin, fixed into the wrest plank, and at its far end to a hitch pin. Attached to the top of the wrest plank is the nut, over which the string passes. At its other end the string passes over the bridge fixed to the top of the sound-board, the speaking length being the distance between the nut and the bridge. In the case of the piano or clavichord a single hammer or tangent is used to strike more than one string, but with the harpsichord each string needs to be plucked separately with its own quill. To accommodate this, pairs of strings tuned to the same pitch are separated, with the jacks running between them and the quills for their respective strings facing outwards. This means that the closely spaced strings are tuned to different pitches.

The keys pivot on a balance rail with their far ends under the jacks, which run vertically in slotted bars known as 'jack slides'. These slides can be moved sideways by a small amount, sometimes by using a lever mechanism, in order to bring the various sets of jacks and quills into their plucking position. In this way, either one, two, or more strings can be plucked simultaneously, depending on the vol-

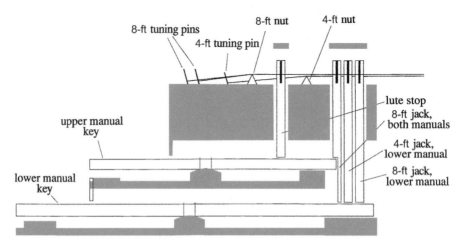

10.10 Diagram illustrating harpsichord mechanism

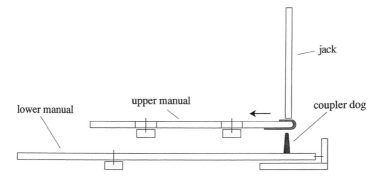

10.11 Diagram illustrating French harpsichord keyboard coupler

ume and tone quality required. Directly over the jacks, and extending over the full width of the instrument, is a 'jack rail' which stops the jacks from jumping out of their slides. In some instruments the jack rail also serves to limit the total amount of movement when the key is depressed, called the 'key dip'.

Each jack generally rests on a single key. Thus in Figure 10.10 the 8-foot jack furthest from the keyboard is operated only by the lower manual, while the lute jack is operated only by the upper manual. An exception is the 'dogleg jack', which rests on both upper and lower manual keys simultaneously and operates under the action of either. The 'keyboard coupler', found in instruments of French design, is an alternative approach to the dogleg. This allows jacks on the upper manual to be activated from the lower manual when the coupler is engaged but keeps the manuals independent on disengagement. Figure 10.11 shows the principle of operation. The whole upper manual can slide in or out by a small amount, typically about 7 mm. For the coupler to be engaged, the upper manual must be pushed in; as a consequence, the mechanism is given the expressive title of 'shove coupler'. To disengage the coupler the upper manual is pulled out so that the vertical projection on the end of the key bypasses the lower surface of the key above. When this type of coupler is engaged, both key and jack on the upper manual move in response to a key movement on the lower manual.

An alternative less common arrangement, found on German instruments, combines both coupler and dogleg. Figure 10.12 shows this mechanism. Here the lower manual moves in and out. A block sits on top of the lower key lever which activates the dogleg when in the engaged position. To disengage the coupling the lower manual is pulled out so that the block bypasses the dogleg. An

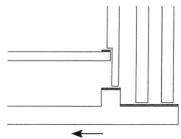

10.12 Diagram illustrating German harpsichord keyboard coupler

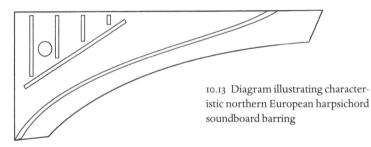

10.13 Diagram illustrating characteristic northern European harpsichord soundboard barring

advantage of this design is that the coupler only activates the jack on the upper manual, rather than the jack and the key, so the action is lighter.

The strings on a harpsichord are generally of plain wire and are not overspun in the bass except on very short instruments. Strings may be of either iron or brass, and range in diameter from approximately 0.2 mm in the treble to 0.6 mm in the bass; these diameters are much smaller than those of piano strings of comparable pitch. On a full-size harpsichord the lowest pitch string might typically have a length of 170 cm. Lengthening the strings tends to increase the volume of sound, since longer strings have greater mass and therefore greater vibrational energy. Harpsichords with excessively short strings tend to have a sound which has virtually no fundamental in the bass; the upper mode frequencies also deviate somewhat from true harmonics, making the sound confused and uncertain in pitch, although this effect is not nearly so important as on the piano because the strings are much thinner. The position of the plucking point in the treble is constrained considerably by the physical size of the jack and is usually about one third to one half of the way along the string. In the bass, the length of the key restricts the plucking position to being about one tenth of the way along the string.

The soundboard on a harpsichord is usually made from spruce. It is much thinner than a piano soundboard, varying in thickness from about 2.5 mm in the treble to 3.5 mm or 4 mm in the bass. Beyond the ends of the bridge, it is thinned down to about 2 mm to counteract the proximity of the case. Underneath it is strengthened by ribs; a typical barring which might be found on an instrument from northern Europe is shown in Figure 10.13. There is one long rib, known as the cut-off bar, running approximately parallel to the bridge, which essentially subdivides the soundboard into two separate sections. There are no braces under the section which supports the bridge, but the bridge itself acts as a stiffening member here. The section on the bass side is divided into a number of panels, usually four or five, by ribs running parallel to the keyboard. There may also be a 4-foot hitch-pin rail, known as a 'boudin'. On instruments from southern Europe the alternative arrangement known as 'cross-barring' is more usual; this is shown in Figure 10.14.

The bottom of the harpsichord case is enclosed. As we saw earlier, this means

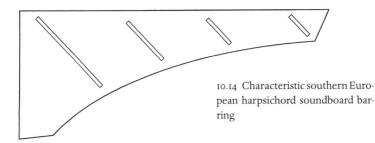

10.14 Characteristic southern European harpsichord soundboard barring

that the soundboard forms the top plate of a resonating box. For this reason harpsichord soundboards are frequently provided with a sound-hole, made in one of the small panel sections; often there is an internal opening into the key well. The sound-hole is fitted with an ornamental rose, sometimes cast in a tin-lead mixture and showing an angel playing a harp with the initials of the maker.

A single bridge for each pitch of string is standard on the harpsichord, as opposed to the separate treble and bass bridges on the piano. Thus an 8-foot, 4-foot disposition would have two bridges and a 16-foot, 8-foot, 4-foot would have three. Each bridge is gently curved in an inverted S shape and is fitted with bridge pins which control the spacing between the strings and provide a precise cut-off point for the sounding length.

As pointed out in the section on acoustical principles, a major factor in determining the persistence of the sound once a key has been depressed is the impedance ratio between the strings and the soundboard. On the harpsichord the strings are lighter than on the piano but the soundboard is also much less rigid, leading to a string-to-soundboard impedance ratio which is rather higher. Consequently the sound dies more rapidly than on the piano. This decay is made even more rapid by the effect of air-damping on the light strings.

As a key is depressed, the quill rises and strikes the underside of the string in much the same manner as a clavichord tangent. It then remains in contact for a short period, during which time vibrations are set up along the two segments of string from the quill to the bridge and the nut respectively. Thus the sound starts with a very brief impulsive buzz; it settles to the true pitch of note once the quill has released the string and allowed it to vibrate along its full sounding length. An additional tapping sound also arises at the end of a note as the quill slips past the string. Finally the damper on a harpsichord tends to be relatively firm and narrow which again produces a clavichord-like sound as it falls back onto the top of the string at the note end. Overall the harpsichord sound contains more upper-mode frequencies than the piano, but the effect of air-damping is to deaden these more quickly than the lower modes.

Harpsichords generally have one or more optional devices for tone colouring, brought into operation either by hand stops or pedals. The most common are the 'harp stop' (alternatively termed 'buff stop') and the 'lute stop'. The harp stop brings into operation a damping mechanism in the form of a batten of wood located near the nut. This has pads of buff leather or felt attached to it which touch on the strings when the stop is engaged, so damping the upper harmonics. The result is a muted sound which dies very rapidly; it is much less bright than the normal tone, and dominated by the percussive attack. The lute stop, on the other hand, simply brings another set of jacks into play which pluck one of the 8-foot sets of strings near to the nut, producing a strident sul ponticello effect. Much more rarely found is the 'peau de buffe' stop, which brings into operation a set of jacks fitted with leather quills designed to tone down the attack noise.

The compass of a harpsichord is typically five octaves, from F_1 to F_6 at 8-foot pitch. On two manual models, the lower manual may well have three ranks of strings at 8-foot, 8-foot, and 4-foot pitches, which can be combined in different combinations to produce a range of dynamic levels and timbres. The upper manual usually has a single 8-foot rank, with the harp and lute stops and a coupler mechanism for combining its sounds with those from the lower manual. Single manual instruments frequently have just two 8-foot ranks with a harp stop.

Virginal and spinet

The virginal and spinet, being essentially smaller and simpler forms of the harpsichord, have mechanisms which are much the same. Both normally have just a single keyboard with one 8-foot set of strings and a corresponding single set of jacks. Their range may be four to five octaves. Traditionally neither the virginal or spinet have had any means of varying the tone colour. Some modern spinets have a harp stop and also a piano stop, which allows the jacks to be partly withdrawn from the strings; these are not found on historic instruments, and are no longer in fashion. On the spinet the longest strings are at the back of the soundboard; on the virginal they are at the front, like the clavichord.

10.4 CONSTRUCTION AND TUNING OF HARPSICHORDS AND CLAVICHORDS

Most of the specific repertoire of the harpsichord and clavichord dates from the seventeenth and eighteenth centuries, and is often highly idiomatic in terms of the contemporary instrument. At the present time there is much interest in performing this historic repertoire on instruments characteristic of the relevant period, rather than on keyboards of modern design with entirely different mechanical and acoustical characteristics. Thus the modern versions of these instruments tend to be reproductions of early designs, although often incorporating features which take full advantage of modern materials and manufacturing techniques. The primary goal of the instrument maker is the production of a keyboard which preserves both the action and the tonal characteristics of the earlier period; this is achieved either by copying a particular extant original or, more frequently, by combining features of a number of early examples.

Surviving historic instruments are widely dispersed, and access to them is often restricted. It is impractical for each individual maker to take measurements from every old instrument of interest; even if a maker has access to a suitable original, the making of drawings is a highly skilled and specialist task, comparable with the production of an Urtext edition from original musical manuscripts. Old instruments may have to be partly dismantled in order to generate detailed drawings. They are rarely in perfect condition and have usually suffered distortions and undergone modifications. Drawing up detailed plans therefore involves an element of subjective judgement based on a knowledge of the original crafting processes.

This problem has been addressed by early keyboard specialists, such as John Barnes at Edinburgh University, who have produced detailed sets of drawings of a range of early instruments which can be used as benchmarks by amateurs and professionals alike. Some professional builders work closely to the original drawings; others incorporate their own special features, such as the inclusion of additional notes at the extremes of the range to allow the instrument to cover an extended playing repertoire.

Historic instrument collections, such as the Russell Collection at Edinburgh University and the collection of the Smithsonian Institution in Washington, act as foci for scholars studying the design of early keyboards. Keepers of such collections usually discourage the use of their instruments in actual performances, except under the most carefully controlled conditions. The reason is that continual movement under varying environmental conditions, and occasional heavy-handed use by players, can cause irreversible damage to unique and irreplaceable items. Also a good deal of repair is often required in order to bring a historic instrument up to full concert standard; this could involve the replacement of parts which would compromise its authenticity. The preferred approach is to use these historic examples for study, employing modern reproductions in performance.

The popularity of the harpsichord and clavichord has increased greatly in recent years, as has interest in the techniques of their manufacture. This is due in no small way to the availability of these instruments in kit form. Kits were pioneered by the Zuckermann and Hubbard harpsichord companies in the early 1960s. Zuckermann's first kit was a five-foot long harpsichord with a straight, rather than bent, side, and a heavy frame with a piano-style keyboard. Hubbard's first kit instrument was far more sophisticated, but correspondingly more difficult to build. In the hands of the dedicated enthusiast, a modern kit can be turned into an instrument every bit as good as one constructed professionally; indeed, the parts which go into a kit are generally the same as those which go into a custom-built instrument.

In the late eighteenth century some of the larger workshops, for example those run by Kirckman and Shudi in London, would no doubt have employed techniques not dissimilar from the ones used nowadays by those companies producing kits. When making jacks, for example, sets of parts for batches of instruments would have been produced at the same time, so that they were available when required at the appropriate stage of construction of a particular instrument. Like modern mass-production techniques, this type of approach requires that each part is made with a high degree of precision, to ensure that it fits with the other parts chosen.

Smaller workshops making just a few instruments a year worked on a more individual basis. They were not in a position to obtain the high accuracy required for making all parts interchangeable, and so adopted the approach that each part was made to fit the previous ones rather than being made to some predetermined tolerance. Indeed, even the larger workshops followed this procedure for the production of keyboards. This construction philosophy is well summarized by the two rules given by John Barnes in his book on traditional methods of making a spinet. These are: (1) whenever possible, reduce the elements of a design to a series of linear measurements indented as graduations on a wooden ruler; (2) choose the order in which the parts are made and assembled so that the variations which

10.15 Spinet soundboard being held in position for gluing by go-bars

inevitably occur in making the earlier parts can be compensated in the later parts.

The central facility of a modern harpsichord or clavichord workshop is the assembly bench. This of necessity needs to be as large as the complete structure of the instrument. Generally the bench is made so that it can be raised to different heights; the appropriate height is set depending on which section is being worked on. Above the bench is a wooden ceiling area which allows 'go-bars' to be used to hold down parts, often while they are being glued. A go-bar is simply a length of springy wood which is bent into a bow shape and forced between the ceiling and the part to be held down. Figure 10.15 shows a spinet soundboard being held in position by go-bars for gluing.

Where possible most makers nowadays prefer to use traditional hand tools, an exception being the band saw which greatly simplifies many of the construction-al tasks.

Soundboard and frame

Wood for the soundboard on a harpsichord or clavichord generally comes from some variety of conifer tree, typically Swiss pine for an instrument constructed in Europe. The best trees are taken from regions high in the mountains. The wood must be quarter sawn; the planks are then cut radially outwards from the centre of the tree so that the grain runs along their length and is also perpendicular to the surface. The method of sawing is crucial in optimizing the resonance characteristics and also in giving the planks the required rigidity and strength. With quarter-sawn wood the layers between the growth rings in effect act as though the wood were laminated; this has a strengthening effect and gives resistance to cracking. The planks tend to have a pliability akin to that of corrugated cardboard; across the grain the wood is quite flexible but along the grain it is relatively stiff. In soundboard construction the grain is usually made to lie approximately in line with the strings, although on the spinet the grain was traditionally diagonal to the strings.

The complete soundboard, which is flat rather than bowed like that of the piano, is made by gluing together a number of planks, about 3 mm in thickness and typically about 100 mm wide. The planks are laid side by side and butt-jointed together. Traditionally a hot glue, made from animal skins, horses hooves, and the like, is used for all joints. This is kept hot in a glue pot, and brushed onto the parts to be joined after these have been warmed (nowadays generally with an electric radiant heater). Hot glue has the advantage that it gives a degree of adhesion immediately it is cool which allows the work on the next stage of construction to begin.

Full adhesion is not achieved until the glue is dry. Another major advantage is that joints can be freed by soaking in water; this is often a great help when repairs are needed. In some cases the glued soundboard must be planed in order to bring it down to the desired thickness. If a sound-hole is to be incorporated this may be cut out using a circle cutter, similar to that used for a guitar. Alternatively the circle is simply marked out and the wood cut with a sharp knife. Occasionally soundboards are laminated, gluing together two sets of planks with their grains set at an angle. This minimizes the likelihood of cracking and is particularly advantageous in countries where the climatic conditions are extreme.

Once the soundboard has been formed, and cut to the correct size to fit into the case, the bridge is glued on. The bridge is made from a dense hardwood such as maple, beach, or walnut. Ideally it should be cut from a single piece of wood, to avoid joints, and the grain should follow approximately the line of the bridge in the bass region. Some modern makers, however, prefer to build up the bridge by gluing together a number of laminations. This tends to be stronger, although the extra strength is not so necessary on a harpsichord or clavichord as on a piano.

The top sharp edges of the bridge are bevelled, and bridge pins are inserted in the sloping face by first drilling holes into the wood and then driving the pins home so that a few millimetres project above the surface. The bridge pins locate the strings, and also ensure that there is a metal-to-metal contact at the bridge end of each string. In a few designs the speaking length of the string is actually in contact with the wood of the bridge, but this is the exception rather than the rule.

The string location at the bridge may require one or two pins, depending on the angle between the string and the bridge at the particular point in question. With single-pinning, the segments of wire on either side of the pin must be angled to each other in order to generate the force required to hold the string firmly against the pin. This generates a sideways force on the bridge, referred to as side draft; the pin is angled in the opposite direction to the side draft. Care must be taken that the total side draft is not so great that the bridge is bent over or broken off the soundboard. With double-pinning, the wire snakes between two pins set into the bridge a short distance apart and at opposing angles, in which case the segments of wire on either side can be in line. With double-pinning there is no sideways force tending to tilt the bridge. Figure 10.16 shows a section of a harpsichord bridge illustrating both single- and double-pinning.

Once the bridge and pins have been fitted, the soundboard is braced underneath. This is done by gluing strips of wood such as spruce or poplar to the soundboard surface. In the case of the clavichord there is typically only one bar, running approximately at right angles to the line of the bridge. Directly under the bridge the bar may be cut away so that it does not make contact with the underside of the soundboard at that point. The completed soundboard, with its bridge and bars fitted, is then glued onto the case to form the top surface of the sound box. Around the sides of the case it lies on liners, and on the keyboard side it is supported on the belly-rail.

10.16 Part of 8-foot bridge on harpsichord by Dulcken *c.*1740, with double-pinning for bass strings and single-pinning for treble strings

Keyboard

The technique used for constructing the keyboard is very elementary; it is designed to economize on material and to ensure that all the keys fit perfectly together. Firstly a keyboard panel is made up by gluing together several boards of spruce, or possibly lime, using butt joints and with the grain of the wood running along the length of the keys. A keyboard ruler, marked out with the sizes of the sharps and naturals, is then used to score lines on the wood where the breaks come between the keys. Cuts are then made along these lines with a band saw and the keys are finally separated using a chisel. Often there is no attempt to make the joints in the keyboard panel coincide with the saw lines, so some of the keys have joins in them. The clearance between the keys is automatically formed by the width of the saw cut. It is quite common for the natural keys to be black and the accidentals white, the reverse colouring to the modern piano; usually the black keys are veneered with ebony.

It has been known at least since the sixteenth century that strings perform best when they are tensioned close to their breaking point. Different string materials have different breaking strengths: brass breaks before iron, for example, and iron breaks before steel. The wrought-iron wire used on many early instruments before the middle of the nineteenth century had a relatively low breaking strength compared to the modern high-tensile steel wire (known as 'music wire') used for pianos. Modern clavichords and harpsichords whose designs are based on traditional instruments do not perform at their best when strung with steel strings, since the tensions which can be safely applied are well below breaking point. For this reason manufacturers now produce iron wire for stringing purposes, which has a tensile strength similar to the wire used prior to the nineteenth century. It is interesting to note that knowledge about the type of wire used has been a useful guide to researchers trying to decide at which pitch levels various early instruments were tuned.

On clavichords it is common to use overwinding in the low register. The overwinding is usually taken right up to each end of the string, and is frequently of the open type in which the outer wire only partially covers the inner core. The winding is close for the lowest bass strings, and more open for the higher ones, as seen in Figure 10.1.

Quilling

On a harpsichord, the quill is a crucial component in determining the tone quality, and thus requires special attention from the maker. Raven or vulture feathers are considered best for quill-making, but crows feathers are acceptable and more readily available. The largest six or eight feathers from the adult crow are the ones that are used, a single feather being sufficient for three or four plectra. The feather is cut on a wooden block with a sharp knife at about ten degrees to the surface, to form a shape similar to a pen nib. The soft white part of the feather is held uppermost while cutting, the hard black part being in contact with the block. Most of the white part is removed by the cut; it is the hard black part which actually plucks the string, and this is uppermost when the quill is held in the jack.

Once all of the quills have been fixed into the jacks, the complete set is voiced by shaving away small amounts of material from the undersides. This thins the tips in much the same way as a reed is scraped. The process continues until adjacent notes match in strength and there is a satisfactory balance between treble and bass. Quills are sometimes lubricated with olive oil, although they work perfectly well without this treatment.

Although most players would claim that the traditional crow or raven's feather quill gives the best sound, this material has some practical disadvantages. Feather plectra wear quite quickly and need continual replacement, and they are also sensitive to changes in humidity. For these reasons some harpsichord makers prefer to go for a synthetic material for their quills despite the fact that this involves sacrificing a degree of authenticity. The commonly used plastic is 'delrin'. When properly voiced, delrin is almost indistinguishable in sound and feel from bird feather. It does, however, last three or four times longer and is not significantly affected by the atmospheric conditions. A disadvantage is that it tends to fail suddenly, presumably due to fatigue, whereas bird feather quills fail gradually.

Historic temperaments

Traditionally a good deal of emphasis has been placed on tuning the harpsichord and clavichord, to the extent that people learning to play these instrument might have been expected to have at least some degree of proficiency in tuning their own instruments. There are two reasons for this. Unlike the piano, harpsichords and clavichords tend to go out of tune very quickly, and frequent retuning is required. Thus being solely reliant on a professional tuner becomes impractical. Secondly, the keyboard music of the seventeenth and eighteenth centuries was not written to be played on instruments tuned to equal temperament. In equal temperament the pitch ratio for any particular interval is the same no matter where it is played on the keyboard; each tonality (key) thus sounds essentially the same except for its pitch level. In other temperaments this is not the case, the result being that the different keys have their own individual characters. Indeed, it may be impossible to play in certain keys because they sound intolerably out of tune. Thus some knowledge of the way in which the instrument has been tuned is essential for the performer.

We have already seen that all temperaments are compromises, in the sense that it is impossible to devise one in which all of the intervals are pure (see Section 1.3). Many different tuning schemes have been tried over the ages; here we have space only to outline the major features of some of the temperaments most commonly used on harpsichords and clavichords.

Within a temperament, fifths and thirds make opposing demands: if the fifths are pure then the thirds are too wide, whereas pure thirds make the fifths too narrow. In the Middle Ages the favoured scheme was to keep the largest number of possible fifths pure at the expense of the thirds. This criterion is satisfied by Pythagorean temperament, which is best illustrated by drawing a circle of fifths (Figure 10.17). The intervals between all of the fifths in the circle (C to G, G to D, etc.) are pure, as indicated by the os between these notes, except for the interval G♯ to E♭ which is one comma (24 cents) too narrow. The G♯–E♭ interval is known as the 'wolf', since it sounds so badly out of tune; it arises because twelve pure fifths exceed seven octaves by one comma.

Pythagorean tuning provides four approximately pure major thirds, namely B to D♯, F♯ to A♯, D♭ to F, and A♭ to C. All the remaining thirds are one comma too wide; this arises because the interval of four perfect fifths is one comma wider than a pure major third plus two octaves. Unfortunately the thirds that are pure

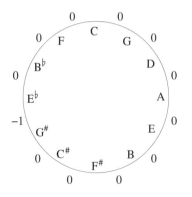

10.17 Pythagorean temperament showing deviations, in commas, from pure fifths

are ones that are not frequently used. It was suggested by Arnout van Zwolle in the fifteenth century, however, that the wolf could equally well be moved to the interval B to F♯ so that the pure thirds became the more useful set based on D, A, E, and B.

The polyphonic styles of the Renaissance brought about a demand for temperaments which had better thirds, and by the end of the fifteenth century mean-tone temperaments were in use. In the simplest form of mean-tone temperament, known as 'quarter comma mean-tone', all the usable major thirds are tuned pure by narrowing each fifth by a quarter comma, as shown in Figure 10.18. Like Pythagorean temperament, this is described as a regular temperament, since all the fifths in the circle are the same size except for the wolf.

The accidentals are most commonly tuned to F♯, C♯, G♯, E♭, and B♭. It is impossible to use one of these accidentals in place of its enharmonic equivalent, since the discrepancy in quarter comma mean-tone is 41 cents. Thus only keys using these particular accidentals may be used, namely the six major keys B♭, F, C, G, D, and A and the three minor keys G, D, and A. If a different set of keys is required, it is of course possible to retune one or more of the notes to its enharmonic equivalent: the E♭, for example, could be tuned down by 41 cents to turn it into a D♯, thus gaining the keys of E major and minor at the expense of B♭ major and G minor.

Other variants of mean-tone temperament were described by musical theoreticians, and some at least were also put into practice. 'Sixth comma mean-tone',

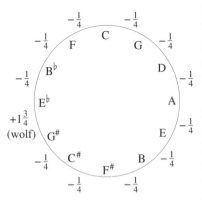

10.18 Quarter comma mean-tone temperament showing deviations, in commas, from pure fifths

in which each fifth is narrowed by 4 cents (a sixth of a comma), was favoured by some performers, possibly because it reduces the discrepancy between the two sizes of semitone in the scale.

In the Baroque period composers for the harpsichord and clavichord were not content to confine themselves to the narrow range of keys offered by mean-tone, and there was a move towards temperaments which allow all the keys to be used. This implies that the circle of fifths closes, so that no fifth which can be played on the keyboard is unacceptably out of tune; a temperament which satisfies this criterion is called a circular (or circulating) temperament. There is only one regular circular temperament: this is equal temperament, in which each fifth is narrowed by 2 cents. Equal temperament was well understood and described in the sixteenth century; it failed to satisfy most Baroque musicians, partly because of the lack of individual key colour which we already noted, and partly because the major thirds are very wide (14 cents greater than just intonation).

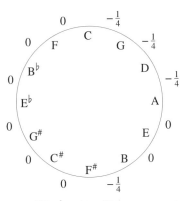

Rather than having all the major thirds equally out of tune, it is possible to devise temperaments in which the keys with fewest accidentals have almost pure thirds; the more remote keys must then have thirds even wider than equal temperament. Such temperaments are described as irregular. At the end of the seventeenth century Andreas Werckmeister, the German organist and theorist, devised a number of irregular circular temperaments. A well-known exam-

10.19 Werckmeister III temperament showing deviations, in commas, from pure fifths

ple is the 'Werckmeister III temperament' shown in Figure 10.19. In this scheme, four fifths are narrowed by a quarter comma (6 cents), while the others remain pure. This leads to major thirds which are widened by amounts ranging from 4 cents to 24 cents. Werckmeister III and similar irregular temperaments are widely used in the modern performance of the Baroque repertoire.

Tuning the harpsichord and clavichord

The procedure for tuning a harpsichord or clavichord is similar in principle to that of the piano, which is described in Chapter 11. Once the desired temperament has been decided on, a single octave is tuned and then the remainder of the range is set from this. Individual intervals are tuned by listening for beats between appropriate partials of the notes (Section 1.3). In tuning an octave, for example, one listens for beats between the fundamental of the higher note and the second partial of the lower; for a fifth, the beat to listen for is between the third and second partials of the lower and upper notes respectively.

Harpsichords and clavichords present their own individual difficulties as far as tuning is concerned. Harpsichords have only one string per jack, but usually have a number of registers. The standard procedure is to begin by setting one 8-foot register, and then to tune the others against this using unisons and octaves. In the case of the clavichord, the pitch is affected by the playing pressure, which must therefore be maintained consistent throughout the procedure. Ideally the touch should be firm but shallow when tuning. The relative tuning of the two unison strings on each clavichord note is very important, since the vibrations of one string are transferred to the neighbouring unison string via the tangent. This coupling is stronger on the clavichord than on a harpsichord or piano because of the lightness of the tangent–key combination and its relative lack of rigidity in comparison to the bridge–soundboard combination. When the two strings are tuned precisely to the same pitch they interact in such a way that the strength of the sound is lost; for a full sound they must be tuned to very slightly different frequencies.

10.5 PERFORMANCE PRACTICE

Performance techniques on the harpsichord and clavichord differ very considerably from those of the modern piano, and are strongly related to both historical developments and the acoustical and mechanical characteristics of these instruments. Neither instrument has the power of the piano; however, this is offset by their transparency of tone, allowing clarity in part-playing and a wealth of nuances. Both instruments have a relatively light touch compared to the piano although in practice the clavichord is quite strenuous to play since the key pressure has to be maintained throughout the full duration of each note in order to maintain the sound.

The actions in both cases are extremely simple, particularly on the clavichord where only one simple lever is involved on each key. This gives the player a degree of control which is not possible when more complicated mechanisms are involved. With the piano, for example, the hammer is thrown against the string, so player control is lost before the string is actually sounded, whereas with the harpsichord the player can feel the quill plucking the string. The ultimate degree of control is achieved with the clavichord, where the player can feel the string throughout the sounding of the note and can alter the sound after it has been initiated. Small changes of finger velocity create large changes of loudness (within the limited overall dynamic range), and variations of the pressure exerted on the string can also have a pronounced effect on the pitch. Successful clavichord-playing thus requires a the development of a high degree of finesse in finger control.

Principally because of the degree of control afforded by the clavichord, this little instrument became regarded in the Renaissance and Baroque periods as the ideal training and practice instrument for the whole range of keyboards then available. Indeed the clavichord was an almost indispensable workhorse for many of the great masters, both as an aid in composition and as a practice instrument when on concert tours. In 1763, for example, Johann Andreas Stein made a clavichord for the Mozart family which was taken round by the young Wolfgang on his concert tours in order that he could keep up his practice. Beethoven also used the clavichord extensively and is reported to have thought that amongst keyboard instruments it was the one which could best control tone and expression.

During the sixteenth and seventeenth centuries mention of the clavichord appears on a number of title pages of keyboard works, but usually as an alternative to the harpsichord or virginal. It was not until the eighteenth century that the characteristic qualities of the clavichord became fully recognized, and compositions appeared specifically written with this instrument in mind. The most important composer of clavichord music was C. P. E. Bach; he recommended that every keyboard player should possess both a harpsichord and a clavichord, and should play them interchangeably, the touch of one being beneficial to the quite different touch of the other. However, it was a widely held view of teachers of the time that if one learnt to play on the clavichord it was relatively easy to progress to the harpsichord; the reverse was not necessarily the case since the clavichord demanded more in the way of touch control.

Harpsichord technique

Perhaps the most important acoustical characteristic of the harpsichord which affects playing technique is its very limited dynamic range; without introducing registration changes the player has only a modicum of volume control, achieved by more or less aggressively attacking the keys. It is incorrect to say that the player has no dynamic control: the eminent performer and academic Peter Williams states firmly that '. . . despite widespread belief to the contrary, a good harpsichord and a good harpsichord player can distinguish between loud and soft'. Nevertheless, the relative uniformity of dynamic level means that musical expressiveness is highly dependent on fine variations in the timing of individual notes; indeed timing makes possible a wealth of expression.

Another important acoustical characteristic of this instrument is the rather rapid rate at which the note decays after the key is depressed. This makes legato passages difficult to execute at slow tempi, although legato can be very effective in andante passages.

As a key on the harpsichord is gradually depressed, the player can sense the moment of contact between plectrum and string, and also the moment at which the plectrum slips past the string. The precise nature of this reaction to key pressure depends to a considerable extent on the regulation of the instrument. It should be noted that the plucks associated with different stops are always arranged such that they occur in a predetermined order, rather than all simultaneously. Because of the nature of this action there is a tendency for players to place emphasis on use of the fingers in developing technique, rather than using weight from the shoulders, as is often the case with the piano.

Finger techniques have developed which differ from those used on the piano. Traditionally, three methods of key attack are distinguished: from just above the surface of the key; from the surface, with the fingers in contact with the key before depressing it; and with the key partially depressed before playing so that the plectrum is in contact with the string. The last approach gives a very immediate attack but is one which may appear foreign to players brought up on the piano. Whichever touch is employed, it is clearly essential that sufficient pressure is exerted by the player to force the quill past the string. A difficulty encountered here is that even on the most finely regulated instrument this force is bound to vary somewhat from key to key, since an element of human judgement is involved in thinning the quills. The speed of key release is important when playing the harpsichord, principally because it affects the rate at which the sound is damped. Also, since the quill retouches the string as the jack descends, small unwanted sounds can result through misjudgement of the release speed.

Dynamics and tone variation on the harpsichord are derived principally through the control of articulation and legato. Extended passages of sustained notes have the effect of building up sonority, while the opposite is the case for detached notes. Thus the overall levels of sound can be adjusted within certain limits by incorporating different degrees of detachment or overlap of successive notes. Producing a slight overlap of notes, known as 'overlap-legato', will generate an overall increase in volume; a slight detachment of the notes, on the other hand, will give a corresponding fall. The latter might be used, for example, in the accompaniment part to a melody. This technique is well known to organists, whose instrument has the same limitations. The detachment of notes is often more acceptable in playing environments which are fairly resonant, in which case the reverberation of the room helps with the illusion of legato. Use of different forms of legato and staccato for adjusting overall sound levels must be differentiated from the use of articulation used for accentuating individual notes and beats.

When notes of a chord are sounded precisely simultaneously on a harpsichord the tone tends to be strident and harsh. For this reason it is common practice, as with the harp, to spread chords slightly. The speed of arpeggiation affects the perceived dynamic level, a rapid speed sounding louder than a slower one. Chords struck without any arpeggiation tend to be used principally for sforzando effects. Many variations in shading can be achieved by using the spreading technique to different degrees in the available registers. On the clavichord, chord-spreading is not required for dynamic contrast so is not used so extensively. Even here though, loud chords are frequently arpeggiated in order to avoid an excessively percussive start to the sound. On the harpsichord it is not possible to colour chords by placing greater emphasis on certain notes, as it is with the clavichord and piano. Different textures and sonorities must therefore be achieved by fine adjustments in the striking and release times of the constituent notes.

Double-manual harpsichords became quite common by the late seventeenth century, offering the player scope for achieving both volume and tonal variations throughout the performance of a piece of music. Despite this, as with the organ, little music has been written requiring specific registration changes, probably because of the wide variety of registrations found on different instruments. Use of various string combinations and special effects such as the buff, harp, lute, and peau de buffe, add considerable tonal variety in a performance but should not be seen in any way as a substitute for the primary resources offered by articulation, different forms of legato, and timing.

Registration changes are frequently reserved for new movements or long repeats. However, changes of manual are sometimes called for in the course of an ongoing passage, and may be indicated in the score by forte and piano markings (forte for lower manual and piano for upper). An example is found in Bach's *Italian Concerto* (Figure 10.20), which, like his *Goldberg Variations* and *French Overture*, was specially written for two-manual harpsichord. In such cases the fingers are required to move smoothly between manuals in order to preserve continuity, a task that may be extremely difficult on some instruments of early design where the manuals are positioned a considerable distance apart.

Clavichord technique

Like the harpsichord, the clavichord appears to have a very light touch in comparison with the modern piano, but here the superficial resemblance between the

10.20 Excerpt from the *Italian Concerto* by J. S. Bach, third movement; the dynamic markings indicate interchange of hands between the two keyboards of a double-manual harpsichord

two instruments stops. With the clavichord the player not only has control of the dynamic levels of the individual notes and the balance between them, but is also responsible for the tone quality.

Most clavichordists tend to play with the fingers in close contact with the keys, leading to a sensation of pressing the strings into vibration, rather than striking them. Once a key has been depressed, the pressure must be maintained throughout the duration of the note. Since the tangent acts as an end support for the string and is connected directly to the finger by the key lever, it is essential that the finger is kept firm after striking the key. Key release should nearly always be rapid, otherwise the string will buzz against the tangent. This is particularly important in the low register, where the strings are relatively slack. A common playing fault is to allow the tangent to ricochet off the string, an effect known as 'blocking', 'chucking', or (most graphically) 'spitting'. This occurs when the strike of the key is not sufficiently firm; the result is a weak tone dominated by buzzing sounds similar to that heard when a guitar string is not adequately stopped at the fret. Blocking tends to occur on the treble strings and some instruments are more prone to it than others.

One of the attractive features of the clavichord, in comparison with other keyboard instruments, is that the player can make small pitch variations while the note is sounding. Increased pressure on the key stretches the string and raises the pitch, while a momentary slackening of key pressure will cause the pitch to drop. The player may simply make a single inflection in pitch after the note has been sounded or, more commonly, may incorporate *bebung*, where the pitch is modulated. This is implemented by applying a pulsating pressure to the key once it has been struck. *Bebung* is effectively equivalent to vibrato on a flute or violin and introduces life into the sound. Having become accustomed to hearing the flute and violin played with vibrato, most listeners would find their sounds rather bland if this was altogether eliminated; the same applies to the clavichord. C. P. E.

10.21 Markings to indicate *bebung* playing on a clavichord

Bach notated *bebung* into his scores by putting a slur over the note with a series of strokes below it, indicating the number of vibrations required (Figure 10.21). He recommended, however, that for the best effect the vibrations should not normally be started before half the value of the note had passed.

A fretted clavichord presents its own problems for the player. If two notes are fretted together on the same string then clearly it is impossible to play them simultaneously. If the notes are to be played consecutively then it is important that the first is released fully before the next is depressed, otherwise an unpleasant metallic noise will result. However, it is still possible to achieve a more or less unbroken legato line between fretted notes and even to trill between them.

Accompaniment

Both the harpsichord and the clavichord are inextricably associated with the role of accompaniment. Pictures of clavichordists from the sixteenth century invariably depict them accompanying a singer or solo instrumentalist. During the seventeenth century the growth of harmony based around the major and minor tonalities led to the emergence of the figured bass, with its implication that the supporting parts of the accompaniment were vertically, i.e. harmonically, related. A typical figured bass part is shown in Figure 10.22. This is made up of a melody, a bass line known as the 'basso continuo' or 'thorough bass', and the figures below which indicate the harmonies. From the figures the player is expected to impro-

10.22 Opening of Sonata IX by Corelli, showing figured bass

vise an accompaniment in much the same way as a keyboard player nowadays may improvise an accompaniment to a popular song using chord symbols. A fundamental difference between these two approaches, however, is that the figured bass can only be realized if the player has a basic knowledge of harmony, whereas the modern chord symbols give the notes of the chords directly without relationship to the key.

The harpsichord developed as the most important continuo instrument of the seventeenth and eighteenth centuries, and much performance technique is related to its use in this role. So universal was the use of the figured bass in ensemble music that this period is sometimes referred to as the 'thorough-bass period'. Three different styles of accompaniment may be identified: 'simple style', where three- or four-part chords are played in the right hand against the bass line in the left; 'natural style', where the mood of the soloist is followed using principally broken chords; and 'composite style', where the right hand plays contrapuntally against the solo part using both imitation and embellishment. In Italy a style of accompaniment developed which showed considerable technical display, making copious use of arpeggios and figurations. Contrasting with this was the French style, which was far less flamboyant.

Special effects

The harpsichord does not seem to lend itself readily to the production of special effects for avant-garde performance. If strings are plucked by hand, little sound results unless the key is depressed to raise the damper, which cannot easily be done silently. 'Preparing' a harpsichord may also be difficult because only the top rank of strings is accessible. On the other hand, tuning the harpsichord strings to unusual pitches is relatively easy compared to the piano, principally because each jack has only a single string to pluck; the piano has three strings per note over most of its range.

Clavichords are more amenable to playing in unusual manners. Friedrich Wilhelm Rust, for example, in his clavichord sonata published in 1939, requires the player to drum with the fingers on the strings to produce the effect of a kettle drum at a distance. He also utilizes a technique similar to playing harmonics on a harp, where the player touches the string halfway along its length with the finger of one hand whilst playing with the other hand.

II

The Pianoforte

II.I ACOUSTICAL PRINCIPLES

Basic acoustics

Like the clavichord and harpsichord discussed in the previous chapter, the piano consists essentially of a set of metal strings, stretched across a supporting frame and coupled through a bridge to a soundboard. The crucial feature which distinguishes the piano from the other keyboard stringed instruments is the way in which the string is set into motion. When a key is pressed, a hammer is thrown towards the string; the hammer head hits the string and rebounds, leaving the string in free vibration.

The piano is in fact a mechanized dulcimer. Although the first working pianos, constructed by Cristofori around 1700, were described in contemporary documents as 'harpsichords with loud and soft', the fundamental difference between the plucking action of the harpsichord and the hammering action of the piano made it inevitable that the new instrument would develop its own powerful and individual personality.

The principle of the piano action

The basic problem to be solved in the design of a successful piano action is that of allowing the hammer to rebound from the string. If the hammer were simply attached to the end of the key lever, it would remain in contact with the string after the stroke, like a clavichord tangent. For the hammer to be free to bounce off the string, it must be in free flight before the impact. All piano actions must therefore have some means by which the hammer is first pushed towards the string and then released by the pushing mechanism.

The simplest possible hammering action is illustrated schematically in Figure II.1. The hammer shank is attached to the solid frame of the instrument by a hinge, and supported from below by a rod mounted on the key lever. In the rest state, the hammer head lies underneath the string. When the key is pressed down,

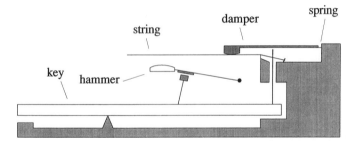

II.I Diagram illustrating simplified piano action, as used in the instruments by Johannes Zumpe

the rod rises, thrusting the hammer shank upwards and forcing the hammer to rotate about the hinge. The motion of the rod is halted when the key reaches its bed; provided that the hammer has gained sufficient momentum, it continues upwards until the head hits the string.

This elementary mechanism was used in some eighteenth-century pianos, but it suffers from several drawbacks. The most serious is the danger that, after striking the string, the hammer will fall back, rebound from the rod, and strike the string a second time. The earliest Italian pianos already had a more sophisticated action designed to solve the problem of double striking; later in this chapter we will review the many further refinements which were added to the basic hammering mechanism in the course of the eighteenth and nineteenth centuries. The action on a modern grand piano is a remarkably complex and sophisticated piece of mechanical engineering, but its basic purpose is the same as that of the simple action shown in Figure II.I: to throw the hammer towards the string, and to allow it to rebound.

Strings

The same general principles which govern the behaviour of clavichord and harpsichord strings apply to the piano string. After a hammer blow, the string is left with many of its natural modes vibrating simultaneously; each mode gradually decays, radiating its own characteristic mode frequency through the bridge and soundboard. The first mode frequency of the string, often called the fundamental, is determined (Section 2.3) by the length L, the tension T, and the mass per unit length m according to the equation

$$f_1 = (1/2L)\sqrt{T/m}$$

The higher mode frequencies deviate slightly from an exact harmonic series because of the stiffness of the string, and also because of effects associated with the coupling to the soundboard. To minimize the inharmonicity, it is desirable that the string tension should be as high as possible, within the limit set by the ultimate strength of the string material. As we saw in Chapter 10, this requirement essentially prescribes the ideal length for a string of given material and pitch, independently of its diameter. On a piano, the string tension is not generally taken as close to the breaking point as it is on a harpsichord; the tensile stress is typically about 50 per cent of the ultimate strength for a steel piano string. As a consequence, although the ultimate strength of steel is much higher than that of iron, the typical length of a C_5 piano string is about 34 cm, which is roughly the same as the corresponding string on an iron-strung harpsichord.

An important feature of the design of all stringed instruments is the scaling rule which determines the relative lengths of the different strings. According to the formula just quoted, if two notes an octave apart are sounded on strings of the same tension and mass per unit length, the lower-pitched string must be twice as long as the higher. In the previous chapter we saw that the 'octave-doubling' scaling law was usually modified on the harpsichord, since its adoption would lead to undesirably long bass strings. The problem is even more acute on the piano because of its greater compass: were the octave-doubling rule to be strictly followed, the highest treble string on a modern grand piano (C_8) would be 4 cm long, whereas the lowest bass string (A_0) would have a length of nearly 5 metres.

In the design of a practical piano, the scaling rule is usually modified in a way which slightly increases the lengths of the highest strings while drastically reducing the lengths of the lowest strings. In order to achieve this without unacceptably large variations in string tension, the mass per unit length of the strings is increased in going from treble to bass. The strings in the middle and upper ranges of the piano's compass are single strands of steel, with a diameter which increases in several steps in going from treble to tenor; the bass strings consist of steel cores overwound with spirals of copper. As we saw when discussing other members of the string family, the overwound string has a much lower degree of inharmonicity than a single strand string with the same mass per unit length.

Over most of the piano's compass, the pressing of a key causes a hammer to strike either two or three strings simultaneously. The strings which are struck by a particular hammer are tuned to an almost perfect unison. In order to understand why this multiple-stringing is required, and why it is desirable to avoid tuning the strings within a group to exactly the same frequency, we need to look at the way in which the string energy is transferred to the soundboard.

Bridge and soundboard

We recall from our discussion in Chapter 8 that the efficiency with which energy is transmitted from a vibrating string through a bridge to a soundboard depends on the relative impedances of string and bridge. In this context, the impedance is defined as the applied force divided by the velocity. For a string with mass per unit length m, under tension T, the impedance is given by

$$Z = \sqrt{Tm}$$

The impedance of the bridge depends on the details of the instrument's construction. A heavy bridge mounted on a strongly braced soundboard will have a very high impedance, since a large force will produce only a small motion of the bridge; a light bridge mounted on a thin and flexible soundboard will respond to the same force with a much more vigorous motion, so the impedance will be much lower.

The important principle determining the transfer of energy is that of 'impedance matching'. If the bridge had the same impedance as the string (that is, if they were exactly matched), then the energy carried along the string by a travelling wave would be totally transmitted through the bridge; none would be reflected back onto the string. This would not be a desirable situation musically, since the result of a hammer striking the string would be a very loud sound lasting only a few thousandths of a second. If the bridge impedance were either very much greater or very much less than the string impedance (that is, if the impedances were strongly mismatched), then nearly all the energy reaching the bridge would be reflected back along the string. Strong standing waves would be set up on the string; these would decay away very slowly, since only a tiny amount of the string energy would be leaking out through the bridge. This extreme would be equally undesirable musically, since the result would be a very long but almost inaudible note.

Clearly the piano designer must find a compromise, in which the impedances are sufficiently mismatched to trap energy on the string for at least several seconds, but sufficiently close to give an adequate loudness of radiated sound. In practice, the bridge impedance is always larger than the string impedance. A typical unwrapped steel piano string with a diameter of 1 mm will have an impedance only about one thousandth of the impedance of the bridge across which it passes. This mismatch helps to sustain the sound for around 20 seconds after the hammer has struck, but provides a rather inadequate loudness. Increasing the diameter would increase the string impedance and decrease the mismatch, but the resulting increase in loudness would be obtained at the cost of a reduction in the length of decay and an increase in inharmonicity.

Multiple-stringing provides the solution to this dilemma. A triplet of strings supplies three times as much energy to the bridge, without the increased inharmonicity which would result from a single thicker string. To avoid a reduction in the decay time of the sound, however, it is necessary that the strings are not tuned exactly in unison. We can understand this requirement by considering the behaviour of three strings in perfect unison. The hammer blow will drive all three strings upwards at the same instant; since they have exactly the same natural mode frequencies they will continue to move up and down in phase with one another. As far as the interaction with the bridge is concerned, it would make no difference if the three separate strands were fused together into a single thicker wire.

Another way of looking at this problem is to consider the resistance experienced by one of the strings as it tries to push the bridge downwards. If the bridge is simultaneously being pushed down by the other two strings, it will appear to yield more readily. That is, each individual string of the triplet will find the effective impedance of the bridge reduced by the action of the other two strings. The net effect is to lessen the impedance mismatch between strings and bridge. The musical consequence is that when the three strings of the triplet are tuned in exact unison the decay time of the sound is much shorter than it would be were only one string excited.

This phenomenon is eliminated by leaving tuning discrepancies of a few cents between the strings. As the strings drift in and out of phase with one another, each individual string finds the other two sometimes helping and sometimes hindering its efforts to move the bridge; on average it experiences the same bridge impedance that it would if it were the only string present, and the long decay time is preserved. In addition, the slow beating between the strings of the triplet is usually felt to add a desirable warmth to the piano tone.

The mass per unit length of the lowest strings is greatly increased by the copper overwinding, and this in turn increases the string impedance. In order to maintain the correct impedance ratio, the bridge impedance for the bass strings must be correspondingly increased. Normally a separate, heavier bridge is used for the overwound strings (see Figure 11.2).

Hammers

The hammers of a piano are graduated in size, with small, light heads in the treble and larger, heavier heads in the bass. The correct choice of hammer head properties is of vital importance in achieving the desired tone quality in each part of the piano's compass (Section 2.3). If the head is too light, it will rebound from the string without transferring a significant amount of energy, and the resulting sound will be weak. If the head is too heavy, it will remain in contact with the string too long, and will tend to damp out the string vibrations.

When one of the bass strings on a modern piano is struck by the hammer with a force corresponding to a mezzo-forte note, the hammer head remains in contact with the string for around 4 milliseconds. This contact time is only a small fraction of the period of vibration of the first string mode, and the resulting sound is rich in high-frequency components. In the treble, the string and hammer remain in contact for only about half a millisecond, but since this corresponds to several periods of the fundamental vibration the higher modes are much weakened by the damping due to hammer head contact. This gradation of timbre from richness in the bass to simplicity in the treble is an important characteristic of the piano sound.

Another feature of the piano which depends on the nature of the hammer heads is the dependence of the timbre on dynamic level. The head of the hammer is constructed in such a way that it effectively becomes harder as the dynamic level is increased. As a consequence, the hammer–string contact time is shorter for a loud note than it is for the same note played quietly, and the spectrum is much richer in high-frequency components. This coupling between dynamics and timbre is determined by the properties of the hammer head and the string, and it is

II.2 A modern Steinway concert grand, photographed from above to show details of frame and action. Note the separate bridges for treble and bass strings

impossible for the player to change the loudness of a note without altering its tone quality.

Touch

How much can a player vary the sound of a single note by the way in which the key is depressed? Bearing in mind that the piano action detaches the hammer from the key before the impact with the string, we can see that key manipulation can affect only two features of the impact: the exact instant at which it happens, and the speed of the hammer head as it meets the string. Niceties of timing are of crucial importance in the playing of several notes, either sequentially in a melody or simultaneously in a chord. For a single, isolated note, however, only the hammer speed is important. A fast, forceful motion of the finger will accelerate the hammer rapidly, while a smoother, sustained pressure on the key will cause the hammer to accelerate more gradually; if the final speed of the hammer is the same in both cases, the resulting string motions will be identical.

There are two additional ways in which touch might influence the sound of a note. Firstly, the pitchless thumps generated by the finger hitting the key and the key hitting its bed can make significant contributions to the sound, and both the strength of the thumps and their timings relative to the string impact will depend on the type of touch employed. Secondly, the rapid acceleration of the hammer in a staccato attack can excite resonances in the hammer. Transverse standing waves similar to those in a tubular bell can be set up on the hammer shank; it has been suggested by some researchers in piano technology that these might influence the interaction between the hammer head and the string. However, studies of the behaviour of realistic hammers show that such an effect is most unlikely to play a significant role in the sound of the piano.

11.2 HISTORICAL DEVELOPMENT

Limitations of the harpsichord and clavichord

From the beginning of the sixteenth century onwards both the harpsichord and clavichord performed important roles in both domestic and professional musical life. However, by the early eighteenth century new musical needs were arising; composers were making increased use of lyrical melodies demanding dynamic inflection, and public performances to larger audiences called for instruments with greater volume. The clavichord fulfilled the needs for dynamic contrast and expressiveness, but was so soft that it was basically restricted to solo use and accompaniment of songs in the home. The harpsichord, on the other hand, had the greater volume required for public performance or use in instrumental ensembles, but was limited in its ability to interpret a melodic line by its lack of facility for gradual dynamic variations within the scale.

What was sought was a keyboard instrument which could produce a substantial sound level while allowing the player direct control of volume from one note to the next. Various attempts were made at producing harpsichords with swell mechanisms. A knee- or foot-operated lever was used to control the opening of part of the lid, or shutters set in a frame above the soundboard, thus allowing out varying amounts of sound. However, these afterthoughts were very cumbersome in use and could not produce the subtle variations required in melodic interpretation. There were also several attempts at producing an instrument which generated a continuous sound by bowing the strings, normally using rotating rosined wheels; none of them attained any degree of success, although C. P. E. Bach did write a sonata for Hohlfeld's 'Bogenklavier', patented in 1754.

Cristofori's invention

It was Bartolomeo Cristofori, a harpsichord maker and keeper of instruments at the Medici court in Florence, who first came up with the radically new design which could fulfil the musical requirements. It appears that Cristofori first began work to implement his new ideas in the 1690s and completed his first instrument in 1700. It was referred to at the time as 'gravicembalo col piano e forte'. Cristofori's design incorporated solutions to all of the fundamental problems encountered in producing an instrument working on the hammer principle; in particular it had escapement, dampers, and check. Unfortunately this resulted in a mechanism which was considerably more complicated than the conventional harpsichord, and this deterred manufacturers from putting his ideas into production. Most early piano makers used simplified mechanisms, and the next century or so saw what was in effect a reinvention of Cristofori's original design.

Perhaps the most innovative feature that Cristofori introduced was the 'escapement'; this was a solution to the basic problem in piano design that we already noted earlier in this chapter. Immediately after the hammer has struck the string it must be free to rebound; if it remains pressed against the string, the main vibrations will be damped, and new pitches will be introduced corresponding to the vibrations set up between the hammer and the end supports. The hammer, in effect, must be thrown freely against the string, and therefore its motion needs to be freed from that of the key itself at some time before striking actually takes place. This means that the player loses direct control of the hammer in the final part of its motion. It is thus imperative that the hammer is not released too early, otherwise the player will not have complete control of the hammer speed and hence the volume of the note. On the other hand, if the hammer is released at a position very close to the string it will rebound from the key and restrike the string, possibly a number of times. Cristofori solved this problem by devising an ingenious mechanism which kept the hammer in direct contact with the key up to a position close to the string and then allowed the hammer to fall right back once the string had been struck, even when the key remained depressed.

Another important feature of Cristofori's mechanism was that it incorporated a multiple lever arrangement which made the hammer velocity eight times that of the key; as a consequence of this the key had a far greater resistance. He also provided a 'back check' for catching the hammer on its fall; this completely eliminated the possibility of rebound, even in fortissimo playing. His instruments also had 'dampers', which were raised when the key was depressed and fell back on the strings after key release to dampen the vibrations. The strings themselves were thicker and heavier than on the harpsichord, and held at greater tension, although they were still thin in comparison to those of the modern piano. Combined with the fact that the hammers were relatively hard and light, this gave the instrument a sound which was much closer to that of the harpsichord than is the sound of the modern piano. In fact a criticism at the time was that the volume was smaller than that of the harpsichord. There was also an 'una corda' device for shifting the keyboard sideways so that the hammers only struck a single string.

Cristofori was not the only craftsman of that period who was intrigued by the possibility of producing a percussive stringed keyboard instrument. Jean Marius and Christoph Gottlieb Schröter were amongst those who worked on the development of a competing idea known as the tangent piano. This was much more similar to the harpsichord than Cristofori's instrument. Instead of employing a hinged hammer to strike the string it used a thin strip of wood, somewhat similar to a harpsichord jack, which was free to move vertically within guides. This was thrown up to strike the string when the key was depressed. Despite its pleasing sound the tangent piano failed to gain favour with musicians of the time. It is also now accepted that Cristofori made his first piano well before these other developments took place, so his claim to be the inventor of the piano seems justified.

Cristofori's invention was not immediately taken up by other keyboard manufacturers in Italy. In fact it was Gottfried Silbermann in Germany who was to follow through his ideas. About the time of Cristofori's death in 1731, Silbermann started making experiments of his own. Silbermann's pianos were virtually identical to those of Cristofori except that they included hand stops for lifting the treble and bass dampers; all the essential features of the modern piano were now incorporated, including sustaining and una corda devices. Being able to sustain the bass or treble registers separately had musical advantages, especially when playing a melody in the right hand against an accompaniment in the left. Silbermann's later pianos gained recognition from J. S. Bach, to the extent that the composer effectively acted as his agent.

Viennese and English actions

In the German-speaking world Silbermann seems to have been almost alone in his enthusiasm for the Cristofori design, which gradually fell into oblivion. Other makers went for a different approach, known as the *prellmechanik*, which bore more resemblance to the clavichord than to the harpsichord. The essential feature of the *prellmechanik* action is that the hammer is mounted on one end of a pivot which is attached to the key. The simplest design does not have an escapement mechanism. When the key is depressed the fulcrum rises but the other end of the pivot is held down by a fixed bar, forcing the hammer to rise towards the string. Since the distance of the bar from the fulcrum is less than that of the hammer, a velocity advantage results.

Around 1770 Johann Andreas Stein, one of the foremost makers of the time, devised a rather simple and ingenious escapement for the *prellmechanik* action. Other leading makers, particularly Anton Walter, helped to refine this, and the resulting mechanism became more or less standard for all pianos produced in the

11.3 Photograph of *Prellmechanik* action with escapement, often known as the 'Viennese action'. Several keys have been removed to reveal the escapement mechanism

German-speaking world. It later became known as the 'Viennese action', on account of the fact that in the first half of the nineteenth century Vienna had developed into the leading centre for producing this type of piano. The *prellmechanik* action with escapement (Viennese action) is shown in Figure 11.3. In place of the stationary rail, each key has its own escapement block held by a spring. The short arm (or 'beak') of the lever on which the hammer is mounted is lodged under a narrow ledge at the top of the block. As the key is gradually depressed, the ledge holds down the beak, and the hammer at the other end of the lever is forced to rise. Because the end of the key is moving through an arc of a circle, a point is reached when the beak slips from under the ledge; this position is set to be when the hammer is close to the string. Once the hammer has struck the string it is free to fall clear and return to its rest. When the key is released, the beak forces its way past the sprung escapement block back to its original position.

Like the harpsichord, the Viennese piano often had one or more hand-, knee- or pedal-operated stops to vary the tone colour. An example is the 'moderator', which introduced a strip of cloth between the hammers and the strings; this became almost a standard feature from the early 1790s. In the 1780s the moderator was generally engaged by a hand stop, but this was superseded by a knee lever about 1790. Other stops such as the 'bassoon', where a strip of parchment was brought in contact with the strings to produce a buzzing sound, were brought in by Viennese makers after about 1800, but these were essentially gimmicks. Pedals became common after 1810, gradually replacing hand stops and levers. The Viennese-action piano had a brilliant and clear tone, particularly in the upper register, and was undoubtedly a superb vehicle for the expressive styles of the period. However, the search for greater power, demanded by public concerts in large halls and with full orchestras, eventually led to its demise in favour of the 'English-style' actions.

The opposing school of piano construction which emerged in England was based more directly on the concepts originated by Cristofori. The Seven Years War (1756–63) and other conflicts of the mid-eighteenth century had driven many German craftsmen to England, amongst these being Johannes Zumpe, a former pupil of Gottfried Silbermann. On arrival in London he worked for the famous Swiss-born harpsichord maker Burkat Shudi, but later set up shop for himself. Zumpe's first pianos, although based on the Cristofori concept of the hammer being mounted independently from the key, were of a radically simplified design, essentially that shown in Figure 11.1. In fact they had no escapement or even back check to stop the key from rebounding. The entire mechanism had just three levers, one for the hammer, one for the key and a third for the damper. When the key was depressed a short metal rod with a padded end stop, attached to the other side, came into contact with the hammer lever and forced the hammer upwards towards the string. The end of the key also pushed up a wooden rod, known as the sticker, which raised the damper to allow the string to vibrate freely. When the key was released the hammer returned under the action of gravity, but a spring was used to assist the return of the damper.

Zumpe pianos were housed in an oblong case and had the general appearance of clavichords, although they were significantly louder; they were referred to as 'square pianos'. When John Christian Bach came to Britain he used a piano in his concerts, which undoubtedly helped the instrument gain acceptance in this country. There is some doubt as to whether J. C. Bach actually used a Zumpe square piano; in any case, pianos made by Zumpe became enormously popular, so much so that demand outpaced production capacity and the assistance of other makers had to be sought in order to fulfil the orders.

The original Zumpe action was eventually superseded by a more sophisticated double action incorporating back check and escapement, developed by John Geib; by about 1812 this had been incorporated as standard by all leading English manufacturers. Probably the best-known maker to take up the manufacture of square pianos was John Broadwood, who completely remodelled the Zumpe design. Broadwood had married Burkat Shudi's daughter, and became his partner in 1770; the company became famous for its square pianos at a time when London makers were regarded as amongst the finest in Europe. Figure 11.4 shows the essential elements of what is generally referred to as the 'English action'.

In 1771 Americus Backers exhibited in London a 'Forte Piano' whose design incorporated many innovative features. The action was similar to that invented by Cristofori in that it included a check to improve repetition, but it eliminated Cristofori's intermediate lever. The jack operated directly against the butt of the hammer, and the escapement was regulated by an adjusting screw. Two pedals were provided at the front of the instrument: the left pedal operated as an una corda, reducing the number of unison strings struck by the hammer, while the right pedal was the earliest known sustaining pedal, raising all the dampers simultaneously. This type of instrument, which became known as the 'English grand piano', is the direct antecedent of the modern grand piano.

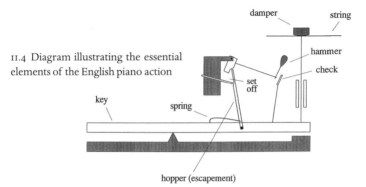

11.4 Diagram illustrating the essential elements of the English piano action

After the death of Backers in 1778 John Broadwood worked on the development of the English grand piano in collaboration with Robert Stodart. Broadwood made improvements to the sound quality by producing a more even distribution of string tensions across the range; he also optimized the striking position of the hammers on the strings, choosing a striking point about one ninth of a string length from the end. The Broadwood company was by far the largest of the London manufacturers, and in 1800 was producing about 400 pianos a year.

The range of very early grands, both English and Viennese, was typically five octaves, and this compass was retained until the early 1790s. By 1800, five and a half octaves had become standard, extending to six octaves (F_1 to F_7) by about 1820 and six and a half octaves (C_1 to F_7) by 1827; this was Chopin's compass. However, there was a lack of uniformity between leading makers, and some well-publicized individual instruments were built with a compass that was larger than the norm.

Developments in the nineteenth and twentieth centuries

In Paris, during the latter part of the eighteenth century, Sébastien Érard had been successfully manufacturing his own version of the Zumpe square piano and a combined harpsichord and piano known as the 'clavecin mécanique'. During the years of terror in the French Revolution he was forced to spend a period in London, where he continued his experiments aimed at improving the English action. By 1808 he had produced the first version of his 'double escapement action', which was to become the blueprint for the modern grand action. With this arrangement the hammer falls back to an intermediate position after striking, rather than returning directly to its rest position; this permits rapid repetition of the note. With the older single escapement the hammer fell right back to its check every time the tone had been sounded; this gave an adequate response time with light hammers, but was too sluggish with the heavier hammers in use by the beginning of the nineteenth century.

American technology had a major impact on piano design in the nineteenth century. Alpheus Babcock, a Boston piano manufacturer, obtained a patent in 1825 for a one-piece metal frame, which he incorporated in his square pianos; he later worked with Jonas Chickering, who in 1843 patented a one-piece metal frame for a grand piano. The metal frame gradually became indispensable for supporting the increasing string tensions demanded by the quest for greater power, and the Chickering firm developed into one of the largest American piano manufacturers. The firm of Steinway was established in New York in 1853; in 1859 Henry Steinway obtained a patent for a metal framed overstrung grand, although the overstringing technique is thought to have been used as early as 1835 by other makers.

The square piano maintained a prominent profile in musical life until the middle of the nineteenth century, after which the manufacture of this form of piano declined; the last Steinway square piano was made in 1888. Its place was primarily taken by the upright piano. Around 1800, John Isaac Hawkins in Philadelphia made a major advance by implementing the English action on an upright instrument with the tuning pins at the top and the longest strings extending to the ground. In 1811 the London maker Robert Wornum succeeded in producing an upright which was only a little over a metre high; this modern design became known in some quarters as the 'cottage piano'. Wornum also developed the 'tape-check action' which is used in nearly all modern uprights; this is shown in Figure 11.5. The tape helps the hammer to return to the check.

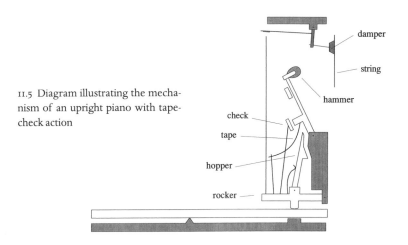

11.5 Diagram illustrating the mechanism of an upright piano with tape-check action

Both pianists and composers who had been schooled in the Austrian keyboard tradition remained faithful to the Viennese action throughout the first half of the nineteenth century, praising its expressive capabilities. However, amid calls for actions with greater power and more rapid response, the Viennese action was unable to compete with the Érard action; by 1900 it had become virtually obsolete.

The twentieth century saw few advances in the design of conventional pianos (as opposed to electronic substitutes). The early part of the century was a peak time for the piano industry, with practically every other household in Europe and America being the owner of an instrument. However, the bottom fell out of the market in the 1930s depression, and a large number of manufacturers went out of business. For the next twenty years or so, many of the surviving firms concentrated their efforts on producing very small pianos for the modern home; the baby grand and the miniature upright became popular. Both instruments had a tendency to be musically unsatisfactory because of their inadequate string length, often allied to an inferior action. By the 1970s the focus of world piano production had shifted to Japan, centred around the giant Yamaha Corporation, who now produce high-quality pianos of traditional design utilizing the latest techniques in production technology.

11.3 THE PIANO TODAY

Grands and uprights

It is generally accepted that grand pianos are superior to uprights, and for this reason their use for concert performance is almost universal. The upright is basically designed to save space, and has its place primarily in the home or practice studio. The more expansive layout of the grand provides the space required for an adequate length of string; its action is also superior, since the hammers and dampers fall directly under the action of gravity without reliance on springs. The fact that the soundboard is horizontal, rather than vertical, is also an advantage. A second-rate grand, on the other hand, may well be musically inferior to a high-quality upright.

Grand pianos come in a wide range of sizes, from less than 150 cm in length to nearly nearly twice this. Steinway, for example, offer sizes ranging from their 'baby grand' at 155 cm to a 'concert grand' at 274 cm; Bösendorfer go a step further with their 'Imperial' model, which is all of 290 cm in length. At the other extreme, a grand in the Kemble range is only 136 cm long. The standard concert grand, found on most concert platforms, is about 275 cm long; this is close to nine feet in imperial measure, and such an instrument is often called a 'nine-foot grand'. The smaller 'six-foot' instrument is sometimes referred to as a 'boudoir grand'. The term 'baby grand' is normally associated with an instrument of five foot or less. Small grand pianos are sometimes fitted with a simplified action, which has the drawback that it can require a significant amount of maintenance to keep it in good order. Another problem with very small baby grands is that the reduced key length can adversely affect the touch.

The usual pitch range of the grand piano is 7 ¼ octaves, from A_0 to C_8, a total of eighty-eight notes in all. Some pianos, notably the Bösendorfer, have an extended range in the bass, taking the pitch right down to C_0; Bösendorfer produce grands with ranges of 7 ¼, 7 ¾, or 8 octaves. This enormous pitch range is almost matched by the wide dynamic range which can be produced. A full concert grand can hold its own in forte passages with a full symphony orchestra, but is also capable of the most delicate pianissimos.

Upright (sometimes called 'vertical') pianos range in size from the 'full upright', standing at 130 cm or more, down to the miniaturized 'spinet' model, which may not be taller than 85 cm. As with the grands, the smallest upright models tend to have an inadequate string length, which makes for a poor sound quality. The smallest sizes also have their action set below the level of the keyboard, which makes them mechanically unsatisfactory.

Strings

Throughout the middle and upper ranges of the piano, typically from B_2 upwards, it is standard practice to have three plain steel strings for each note. A single octave below this ($B^{\flat}_1$ to $B^{\flat}_2$) is then double-strung with 'overspun' (overwound) strings; the lowest have single overspun strings. On a grand piano the strings are held at the end furthest from the keyboard by hitch pins fixed to the iron frame, and at the end nearest the keyboard by wrest pins (or tuning pins). In the treble and tenor, a single length of plain wire and a single hitch pin usually serve for two adjacent strings, the wire simply being looped around the pin. Since there are three strings per note in these ranges, this means that some of the lengths of wire serve for two separate notes tuned a semitone apart. However, since the string tensions on adjacent notes are nearly equal this does not cause any tendency for slippage round the hitch pin. In the bass, each string normally has its own individual length of wire and hitch pin, the wire being twisted into a loop at the end to place over the pin. The wrest pins are made of hardened steel, and are usually roughened or finely threaded at one end; the roughened end is driven into the 'wrest plank' (or 'pin-block'), which is supported by the iron frame. The upper end of the pin is given a square or similar cross section to fit a standard tuning key. The wrest plank is made of wood specially chosen to withstand the high stresses encountered and also to resist rotational slippage of the pins. A laminated construction using maple wood is preferred. Steinway, for example, advertize their use of a 'hexagrip pinblock', built from six maple layers set at $45°$ to one another.

The speaking length of the string is set at the end furthest from the keyboard by the bridge. At the keyboard end, the strings above D_5 or so pass under a bar, known as the 'capo tasto bar' (or 'capo d'astro bar'); strings lower down the scale pass through a metal stud known as an 'agraffe' (patented by Sébastien Érard in

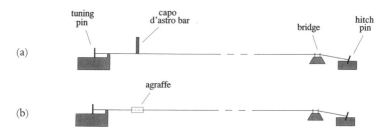

11.6 The two commonly used methods of string support on pianos: (a) capo d'astro bar; (b) agraffe

1808), each note having a single agraffe. The two methods of string support are shown in Figure 11.6.

Steinway utilize a system of stringing referred to as 'duplex scaling' in order to enhance the sound of notes in the treble. This relies on the principle of 'sympathetic vibration', whereby if two undamped strings are tuned to harmonically related frequencies then exciting one will induce vibrations in the other. The vibrational energy is transferred from one string to the other through the bridge and the surrounding air. In a conventionally strung piano the short sections of string adjacent to the supports at either end, which do not form part of the sounding length, are damped out by intertwining strips of felt between the wires. With duplex scaling these short segments are left free to vibrate, their lengths having been chosen so that their frequencies of vibration coincide with upper modes from the main sounding length. In this way the higher mode frequencies in the sound are strengthened.

Duplex scaling was patented by Steinway in 1872, although the principle had been anticipated a half century earlier by the German piano maker Wilhelm Leberecht Petzoldt. He produced a piano with a small bridge behind the main one, with the same idea in mind, but the instrument was found to be difficult to tune and was finally abandoned.

Blüthner pianos use a rather similar, albeit more complicated, scheme known as 'aliquot scaling', patented in 1873 by Julius Blüthner. With this arrangement, each of the notes which are normally triple-strung has an additional fourth string; this is not struck and remains undamped, so that it vibates in sympathy with the three struck strings. For the notes in the treble, the additional aliquot string is tuned in unison with the other strings, whereas in the tenor range it is tuned an octave higher in order to support preferentially the higher modes. The aliquot strings in the tenor have a separate bridge from the struck notes. The effect of the aliquot strings is very small, and the technique is not used on some of the latest Blüthner models.

Pedals and dampers

The standard grand or upright has either two or three pedals; the left-hand one is the una corda pedal (sometimes called the 'soft pedal'), and the right-hand one is the sustaining pedal (sometimes inappropriately called the 'loud pedal'). If there is a third one, it is placed between the other two and is called the 'sostenuto' pedal.

On the grand piano, depressing the una corda has the effect of moving the whole action and keyboard to the right, so that in the triple-strung upper register only two of the three strings are struck by the hammer. In the double-strung part of the bass register only one of the two strings is struck. The resulting sound is both quieter and less brilliant in timbre than a normal note; these effects arise from a combination of the facts that one string is not being struck and that a less compacted part of the hammer is striking the wire.

In practice, the horizontal shift of the action may not be quite sufficient to bring the hammers completely clear of the strings in question, so a major part of the effect is due to the change in hammer hardness. For the very lowest notes, with only one string, the change is entirely due to this. On an upright, the soft pedal does not move the keyboard; instead, it brings the hammers closer to the strings, reducing their impact velocity and diminishing the volume. An alternative arrangement, used on some uprights, is that a strip of thick felt, known as a 'céleste', is introduced between hammers and strings.

The sustaining pedal raises the dampers from all the strings simultaneously. Its name describes its most obvious function: to sustain notes even after the player has released the keys. It also performs the more subtle role of allowing the strings which have not been struck to act as sympathetic resonators. The sostenuto pedal is used to catch the dampers that are already raised when the pedal is depressed. If a note or chord is played, and the keys are held down until the sostenuto pedal has been depressed, the sound will continue after the keys are released; the player is then free to use the sustaining pedal on the other notes in the normal way.

Dampers are not used on the uppermost notes on the piano; usually the highest note having a damper is around F_6. Above this, the natural decay rate of the sound is so rapid that a damper is unnecessary. The decay rate on the lower notes is much slower, and efficient damping becomes of paramount importance. Thus the dampers are much larger and heavier in the bass than in the treble.

Action and touch

Virtually all modern grands employ the 'roller double escapement action'. The key acts as a lever, pivoted about a central support, and the non-playing end of this has a capstan screw, known as the pilot, fixed to it. When the key is depressed the pilot pushes up an intermediate lever, which in turn acts on the jack and ultimately the hammer via a roller. The jack is shaped so that it comes in contact with a set-off button before the hammer has risen fully up to the string; this sets the escapement mechanism into action, allowing the hammer to continue its flight to the string and then to fall back to an intermediate position, where it is held by the check and the repetition lever. If the key is then partially raised, the check (which is attached to the end of the key lever) releases the hammer; depressing the key once more throws the hammer back towards the string, through the action of the repetition lever. In this way, rapid reiterations of the note can be achieved.

The term 'touch', when used to describe the instrument rather than the player, generally denotes the force which has to be applied to the tip of a key in order to depress it; this is normally measured with the damper raised, since the resistance of the damper is only felt when the hammer is already in motion and is therefore of secondary importance. Typically piano touch is about 0.5 newtons (equivalent to placing a mass of around 50 gm on the key), but it is heavier in the bass than in the treble; the variation across the keyboard is of the order of 20 per cent, depending on the particular model. Since the black notes are shorter than the white ones, their pivot point has to be placed further from the player, otherwise their touch would be very much greater.

The actual feel of the note to the player also depends on the detailed mechanics of the action. As the key is gradually depressed, a change of feel occurs at the set-off point, where the hammer leaves the jack. Some pianists like this change to be as small as possible, whereas others like to sense it positively on the grounds that this gives them more control at the actual instant of hammer release.

Smoothness and consistency of touch across the keyboard are of paramount importance. This tends to be better on full-size grands, which have a greater key length. The variability of touch across the keyboard can be affected by the weight of the dampers, since the lower notes have more massive dampers than the higher ones. A noticeable difference in feel may also be experienced at the point on the keyboard where the dampers stop.

Hammers are always covered with felt and are of a larger size in the bass than in the treble, which is a contributing factor in making the bass touch heavier. New hammers tend to give a rather muffled sound due to the softness of the felt striking the string, whereas more worn hammers are harder and produce a brighter sound.

Bridges and soundboard

Modern pianos, almost without exception, have two separate bridges and are 'overstrung'; that is, the strings on each bridge lie in separate horizontal planes, one above the other. Both of these features can be seen in Figure 11.2. The longer treble bridge normally serves for all the triple-strung notes and extends more or less the full width of the soundboard. The short bass bridge carries the overspun strings and is located at the back of the soundboard, behind the treble bridge on a grand or below the treble bridge and close to the floor on an upright. Overstringing has two separate advantages over stringing in a single plane. Firstly, it allows a greater length of string to be used for a given frame size. Secondly, it means that the bridges are more centrally placed on the soundboard, thus making better use of its resonance characteristics.

The soundboard of a grand is constructed slightly convex in shape (bulging upwards), so that the ribs, which run along the underside, act as arches of very low curvature to support the great downward pressure exerted by the strings on the bridges. A typical soundboard is 9.5 mm thick in the treble, thinning down to 6.5

mm in the bass, although Steinway use a diaphragmatic design in which the thickness tapers from 8 mm at the centre down to 5 mm at the edges.

Soundboards can easily become cracked, especially if housed in rooms with powerful central heating, and this can seriously affect the sound of the piano. Deformation of the soundboard is one of the factors which cause pianos to deteriorate with age; the great pressure of the strings over many years tends to flatten out the soundboard, upsetting the delicate balance between the resistances offered by the strings and soundboard. Other common reasons for a piano deteriorating are that the mechanism wears and the strings become rusted, or that the instrument becomes infested with moths, beetles, or rodents.

Frame and casing

All modern pianos have a metal main frame (usually cast iron) to withstand the enormous forces exerted by the stretched strings. Each string has a tension of about 700 newtons, making the total force on the frame about 150,000 newtons; this is equivalent to the force that would be produced by supporting the frame at the bridge end and hanging a mass of 15,000 kg from the wrest plank. A force of this magnitude would destroy the older type of wooden frame completely. The actual case of the piano acts as a solid foundation for mounting the interior parts; as such, its rigidity is also important to the overall acoustics of the instrument.

11.4 MAKING AND TUNING A PIANO

Strings

Above any other technological advances, it is the development of modern high-tensile steel wire which has made possible the modern piano. The early fortepianos used iron wire for the middle and upper registers and copper and brass for the bass; all of these materials are extremely soft and unable to sustain high tensions. A string under high tension requires a great deal more force to displace it by a given amount than does a string under low tension; consequently the vibrational energy it can store and eventually transfer to the soundboard is much greater. The volume that could be obtained from the early instruments was thus severely limited. It must be borne in mind, however, that most of the instruments of the classical orchestra were quieter than the orchestral instruments of today; modern experience with orchestras of reproduction instruments has verified that the fortepiano of Mozart and Beethoven was quite capable of holding its own in a concerto.

Apart from the question of volume, the use of high-tensile steel wire across the whole range of the instrument has helped to overcome problems of tuning stability. Early instruments with wooden frames required continuous retuning, a task that was time-consuming and difficult for the amateur to perform. The problem was made worse by the fact that temperature changes put the treble out of tune with the bass, since different metals were used for the strings in these ranges. Modern pianos, on the other hand, retain their tuning adequately for domestic purposes over periods of six months or so because they are strung with steel wire on a metal frame.

The breakthrough in steel wire manufacture came round about 1820, when techniques were developed for drawing wire through holes in diamonds and rubies; this allowed much harder metal to be treated. The tensile strength of a wire is due partly to the material used and partly to the drawing process. The steel billet is first formed into a circular rod by passing it a number of times through rolling mills. It is then drawn through a series of holes of decreasing size until the required gauge is obtained; at various stages it is annealed by heating and then cooling again. Changes in the molecular structure take place during the drawing process, increasing the tensile strength of the wire to around 2.5×10^9 pascals (newtons per square metre). The extent to which the wire stretches under tension is also reduced. Modern wire-drawing techniques allow strings of considerable consistency and roundness to be produced. If strings are not perfectly round the upper mode patterns may be upset thus affecting the tone quality, a fault known as 'falseness'. This may become particularly apparent if a string is oval in shape and is then twisted along its length.

We saw in the previous section that the length of the C_5 string on a modern piano is normally between 33 cm and 34 cm. Scaling the string lengths by a factor of two on each octave would then make the top C string 4 cm in length. Such a short string would not be very practical, primarily for two reasons. First the diameter to length ratio would be so large that it would be more like a rigid bar than a flexible string, and the inharmonicity would become a real problem. Secondly the bridge would be drawn very close to the edge of the soundboard, with a resulting loss of tone quality.

Increasing the lengths of the upper strings is not, however, without its problems. Too great a string length would bring the tension on the top string dangerously near to the breaking point. It has also been found from experience that the string tension should not vary by too great an amount over the instrument, otherwise temperature changes will cause it to go out of tune. Thus an increase in tension on the top notes should ideally be matched by similar increases on the tenor and bass strings; a substantial overall increase in tension would require an even more massive frame, with undesirable implications for both the weight and the cost of the instrument. In practice, a string length slightly in excess of 5 cm is deemed to be optimum for C_8: Wolfenden recommends a length of 54 mm, with a string diameter of 0.8 mm (English Gauge Number 13½), giving a tension requirement of 785 newtons.

A practical advantage of the fact that strings on a piano are not as close to their breaking point as are strings on a harpsichord is that the piano strings last longer. Many old pianos still have their original strings; this is quite rare with harpsichords, particularly for the left-hand strings on any particular note, since these are longer and consequently stretched nearer to breaking.

It has already been pointed out that a doubling of string length with each octave would result in an instrument of massive size. A further practical implication is that the feel would be excessively large for the lower strings: feel (which was defined in Chapter 9 as the transverse string displacement per unit force) is proportional to the string length for a fixed string tension. The hammer would see the string as a very weak spring, rather than a stiff one, and the contact time on striking would be so long as to impair the tone quality. For extreme lengths, the transverse excursions of the strings could be so large that adjacent strings would collide with each other.

The solution normally reached is that, for each octave step towards the bass, the length of the string increases by a factor of 1.9, while the thickness increases by 1.06 (or a whole gauge number on the English scale). This implies a tension increase of about 1.5 per cent per octave towards the bass. Below C_4, there needs to be a further foreshortening and corresponding diameter increase, the precise values used being very much dependent on the model size and the preference of a particular manufacturer.

The increase in diameter of the plain steel wire strings cannot be continued further down than about B_2 because the strings would become too stiff. For these lower notes there are very many higher mode frequencies falling within the audio range and if the string is too stiff these become unacceptably sharp. The solution adopted is to use overspun strings for the very lowest notes. In the region of overspun strings, bichords are used for the upper notes and single strings for the lowest ones, in order to match dynamic levels. Despite the use of trichords in the treble and single strings in the bass, some critics claim that the piano is bass heavy.

It is impracticable to make the core of the highest overspun string as thick as the lowest trichord and, since there is a change from three to two strings at this point, the hammers would encounter a sudden reduction in stiffness if this were not corrected by increasing the tension on the overspun wires. In fact most designers introduce an increase in tension of about 15 per cent at this point. It is worth noting here that on the lower notes the strength of the string is not a great problem, since the cross-sectional area of the strings increases much more rapidly from treble to bass than does the tension; it is thus the shortest string that is nearest to its breaking strain.

Spun strings are usually made by specialist string makers, rather than by piano manufacturers. In Europe, the steel core is overspun with copper; in America, iron coverings have frequently been used, usually coated with tin in order to inhibit rusting. Even when coated with tin, however, iron coverings have a tendency to rust in a damp climate. Strings may be overspun with either a single or double covering, the double coverings being used on the lowest strings. The covering does not extend to the full speaking length of the string; a couple of centimetres is left uncovered at each end. The steel core is generally a little softer than an uncovered string, which allows twisted eyes to be made at the end of each string for fixing purposes.

Various techniques are employed to ensure that the covering does not slip on the core. The traditional one was to score each core along its length by drawing it between two files, but it is now more common to 'swage' the core at each end of the covering. An alternative approach, used extensively in Germany, has been to use a hexagonal core. In this case the covering is so soft, compared to the core, that the final covered string is to all intents and purposes circular, so falseness does not result.

The position at which the hammers strike the strings is very important in determining the tone quality. It is known that if a string is excited at a nodal position for any particular mode then this particular modal frequency will be suppressed. Since the 7th harmonic of any fundamental note is badly out of tune relative to the minor seventh in the equal-tempered scale, and the 9th harmonic forms a discord (e.g. the 9th harmonic of C_2 is D_5), it has been suggested that a striking distance between a seventh and a ninth of the way along the string could be tonally advantageous. The usual striking distance for bass and tenor notes is about one eighth of the speaking length from the end. In reality the situation is complicated by the fact that the hammer remains in contact with the string for a finite length of time, which allows standing waves to be set up in the short length of string between the hammer and the end support; this tends to reintroduce some of the suppressed components. However, it is still evident in the measured sound spectrum from the piano that if the string is struck at a distance one eighth from the end, the modal frequencies around this, that is the seventh, eighth, and ninth, are partially suppressed (see Section 2.3).

In the upper range, the higher modal frequencies become smaller and smaller in magnitude, so the need for their suppression is obviated, and other considerations become more important. It has been found that striking the string closer to the end, where it is less compliant, gives the hammer a more positive rebound and correspondingly improves the tone. This also reduces the thud of direct impact which tends to be heard in the top octave. As a result, the proportionate striking distance is gradually reduced from about one eighth at middle C to about one fourteenth for the top note.

Frame and soundboard

As a first step in the creation of an iron frame for a piano, a pattern is constructed out of wood. From this a permanent iron pattern is cast which, in turn, is used to produce a whole batch of finished frames. Iron has a very small shrinkage rate on cooling (about 1 per cent) but, even so, careful account must be taken of this in making the drawings for the original pattern. Since there are two casting processes where shrinkage takes place, the wooden pattern must be made 2 per cent larger than the finished frame size. Internal corners are rounded off to eliminate weakness points, and all parts are made with a small taper in order that the sand mould is not destroyed when the pattern is removed.

Soundboards are typically made from spruce, *picea abies* (popularly known as Norway spruce) being the most highly favoured. This wood is exceedingly light and elastic, making it highly responsive to vibrational excitation. As with all woods, the rate of propagation of sound waves along the grain is much greater (about four times) than across the grain. Underneath the soundboard, the ribs (or bars) are also generally made of spruce, but other woods such as pine may also be used. The ribs are set at right angles to the grain in order to increase the propagation velocity of vibrations in that direction, so making the distribution across the soundboard more homogeneous. Different manufacturers have their own preference as to how the grain should be aligned in relation to the bridges. It is also not uncommon for makers to use a laminated construction for the soundboard. It is important that soundboards are varnished, in order to seal the surface; otherwise the natural resins in the wood tend to evaporate over a period of time, causing the resonance characteristics of the board to deteriorate.

The manner is which the ribs are glued to the board is important. This needs to be done in such a way that the board is in a permanent state of compression, so that it can assist the ribs in supporting the downward force exerted by the strings. The ribs themselves are arched on one side with a very gentle curvature. The board may then be heated and bent on a frame, which is hollowed out to a curvature just greater than the one used for the ribs. When the ribs are then glued down on to the board, and the pressure is released, the ribs have a tendency to spring back to their original shape and in doing so put the board in a state of compression.

Because of its great rigidity, beech is generally used for the construction of bridges, although not necessarily over the full height. Spruce or maple may be used for the lower part and beech for the top strip which holds the pins. This improves the resonance characteristics, since the speed at which vibrations are carried in beech is relatively low. As far as possible, the direction of the grain should run along the length of the bridge. This can be accomplished by making the bridge is sections, cut with the grain and lap-joined together. An alternative approach sometimes used is to laminate the bridge with strips of maple, or other similar wood, running perpendicular to the surface of the soundboard and topped with beech. The problem here is that there is a possibility of the glued joints opening under adverse climatic conditions.

The moving parts

Actions tend to be made by specialist manufacturers, and only a few of the largest piano companies make their own. The keys themselves are frequently made of Norway spruce. These rock on a felt circle placed over a central balance pin. The choice of felt is important. This must be firm enough to ensure a minimal loss of motion in the lever action, but sufficiently soft to make the motion silent. The choice of wood for the shanks, which hold the hammers, is very important. This should not exhibit too high a degree of flexibility, otherwise the shank will bend and the hammer will remain in contact with the string too long, causing a damping effect. Hickory and maple have admirable properties for this purpose. In the past, high-quality pianos often had their white keys veneered with ivory and their black ones with ebony; neither of these is used nowadays because of the high cost of ebony and the conservation restrictions on the use of ivory. Both substances have been replaced by modern plastics.

A number of companies have made piano actions either partly or wholly from synthetic plastics and light alloys. This allows the manufacturing process to be automated, reducing the costs and permitting the use of modern quality-control techniques. Wholly synthetic actions have only been partially successful, and the traditional wooden-constructed actions are still used in all high-quality pianos. The use of synthetic materials for the bearings has however brought about real improvements, and these are used extensively in place of the older metal pins and cloth bushes.

A considerable amount of attention has been lavished on the manufacture of the hammer, because this single component has a dramatic effect on the tone. Like the actions, hammers are most frequently produced by specialist companies. Piano hammers are made of wood, covered with either a single or a double layer of carefully selected felt. The felt used for the covering starts off as a roof-shaped strip, thicker for the bass hammers and thinner for the treble ones. With the noses of the hammers facing downwards and placed in contact with the vertex, the other two corners of the roof are bent upwards using a machine and glued around the wood, as shown in Figure 11.7. The hammers are then separated by making vertical cuts in the felt. In this way the outer felt layer of the hammer, which was originally the horizontal base of the roof, is brought into a state of tension, whereas the inner felt, which was originally the vertex, is highly compressed. A hammer made in this way is hard on the inside and relatively soft on the outside; this gives

11.7 Felt covering on a piano hammer: (a) the felt starts out roof-shaped; (b) it is then forced over the hammer and glued in position

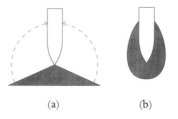

(a)   (b)

the best tone quality. Finishing is carried out using fine glass paper. Usually the flat striking face of each hammer is rounded slightly to make it convex shaped.

Ideally a hammer, when originally made, should be just a little harder than is finally desirable. This leaves room for a final adjustment to be made by the 'voicer'. The highly skilled job of voicing is carried out by inserting needles into the felt to soften it. In this way fine adjustments to the tone quality of each note can be made, although it is impossible to disguise fundamental faults by voicing. If the softening process is taken too far, it can be partially reversed by pressing the felt surface with a hot iron. However, this procedure is not entirely satisfactory, because it creates a hardened skin on the surface, reversing the desired reduction of hardness from centre to outside.

Dampers are made from felt similar to that used for the hammers. The amount of damping required for the heavy bass strings is much greater than for the light treble strings. For this reason the damper felt used on the single overspun bass strings is normally cut in a V-shaped clip which falls over the string, thus maximizing the string–felt contact. For an overspun bichord, used higher up in the bass, the felt may be cut either as a single wedge to fall between the strings or as a double clip; the clips are used for the lower bichords because of their greater damping efficiency. In the tenor and treble ranges, the felts are cut with a plane contact face, since the damping power required here is not so great. In this way the power of the dampers is varied gradually across the keyboard range, from a maximum in the bass to zero for the top undamped strings.

Tuning

Tuning is probably the most important single factor that affects the tone quality of a piano. Even a mediocre instrument can sound musically acceptable when well tuned, whereas the sound of the finest concert grand can be ruined by bad tuning. Like all keyboard instruments, pianos must be tuned to a tempered scale. In the case of the modern piano this is almost always equal temperament.

Individual notes are set by listening for beats (pulsations in loudness, explained in Section 1.3) between notes sounded at different intervals. As an example, on the standard pitch equally tempered scale with A_4 at 440 Hz, the first mode of the C_4 string has a frequency of 261.63 Hz. If we assume for the moment that the mode frequencies of the string are exact harmonics, the third mode frequency is three times this at 784.89 Hz. The corresponding frequency for G_4, an equally tempered perfect fifth above, is 392.00 Hz, and the 2nd harmonic of G_4 is twice this frequency at 784.00 Hz. Once C_4 has been set, G_4 can be tuned against it by playing both notes simultaneously and listening for beats. If the relative tuning is correct, the second harmonic of the G should beat against the third harmonic of the C with a beat rate of 784.89−784.00 = 0.89 Hz, or just under one beat per second. One way of adjusting this accurately would be to use a stopwatch, and to check that there are nine beats in ten seconds. If two pitches have exactly the same frequency then the beats between them become infinitely slow and effectively disappear.

The procedure for tuning a piano is first to set the pitch of one string near the centre of the keyboard against a tuning standard, with the other two strings of the trichord damped by felt wedges. The tension of the undamped string is adjusted until the beats between the string sound and the standard disappear. Once the single string has been tuned correctly, the other two are brought into tune with it, again by listening for beats. The optimum setting is when the three strings are very slightly mistuned relative to one another; as was explained in Section 11.1, exact matching of the three string frequencies leads to the sound having an excessively fast decay rate.

From this one note a complete octave is then tuned using intervals of a fourth, fifth, and octave, with other intervals such as the major third and major sixth being used as checks. This process is known as 'laying the bearings'. This one octave then forms the base against which all the other octaves are tuned.

It was pointed out in Section 11.1 that the mode frequencies of a piano string are not strictly members of a harmonic series: because of the stiffness of the metal strings, the upper mode frequencies are always sharp compared to true harmonics. Consequently, the process of tuning by beats leads to the high notes on a piano being sharp and the low ones being correspondingly flat as compared to the calculated equal temperament pitches. This is referred to as 'octave-stretching'. Correctly tuned pianos always have stretched octaves. If a piano were to be tuned with all the notes matching the calculated equal temperament pitches precisely then the treble would sound flat and the bass correspondingly sharp, a defect which is noticeable on early electronic pianos.

Modern pianos, with their massive cast-iron frames, have a very high degree of tuning stability. Nevertheless, small variations do occur, particularly under concert conditions, where the piano may be subjected to the full power demands of the solo performer and also moved a good deal. Most concert grands are therefore retuned before each major performance. Loose wrest pins are often a cause of a piano going rapidly out of tune, but generally this only occurs on older pianos. The manner in which the pins are handled by the tuner is also an important factor; hence the title 'firm tuner' earned by some technicians. The reason for this appears to be that a wrest pin is held in a state of torsion along the embedded length in the wrest plank, and acts something like a very stiff coiled spring. By applying the appropriate amount of back pressure before the tuning crank is removed from the pin, the experienced tuner can even out the frictional force along the length of the embedded section and reduce the tendency for the pin to unwind.

The tuning process can also leave a difference in string tension between the speaking length and the short section between the pressure bar and the wrest pin, due to the friction at the pressure bar. Again, the experienced tuner can minimize this by judicious application of forward and reverse pressures on the crank, interspersed with a few heavy blows on the keys, to ensure that subsequent slippage does not take place.

11.5 PERFORMANCE PRACTICE

Tone control

The enormous popularity of the piano, now sustained over nearly three centuries, is due in large measure to its great versatility. Only in recent years has its superiority in this respect been challenged by electronic keyboards, but even here the degree of control offered by the acoustic piano remains unmatched. The piano has the virtues of being both polyphonic and touch sensitive, with a vast range both in pitch and dynamics. However, it remains principally a percussive instrument and, even with the assistance of the pedal, its sustaining power is very limited.

The tone quality of a single note on the piano cannot be altered in the same way as it can be on say the flute or the violin. On these instruments, once the note has been initiated it can be sustained, and its characteristics can be altered as it continues to sound. For example, vibrato can be introduced, or variations in tone quality can be brought in by varying the blowing or bowing technique. Such variations are not possible on the piano, because at the moment when the hammer strikes the string it is in free flight, and the player has no control over its motion. The manner in which the key is released, however, is of considerable importance, because it affects the finishing transient of the note. Unless the sustaining pedal is depressed, a rapid release of the key brings down the damper abruptly and causes a sharp finishing transient. Even when the damper has fallen back on the string the sound does not stop instantaneously; the low notes in particular have a tendency to ring on.

The sound produced when the key is struck by the finger, known as upper-key noise, can be quite audible. Upper-key noise tends to be particularly significant in staccato playing, where the the fingers strike the keys in a percussive manner; in this case it may be used to enhance the articulation. In legato cantabile passages the fingers have more of a stroking action on the keys, and the upper-key noise is negligible.

In producing a beautiful singing melody or a sonorous chord the pianist relies on the precise timing and relative volume of the individual notes. Thus, although a single note sounded by a virtuoso concert pianist sounds essentially the same as that note played by a beginner, it is when a series of notes are sounded that the skill of the expert shows up. This is in stark contrast to an instrument like the flute, where the sound of a single note gives the listener an immediate indication of the skill of the player. In a melodic line it is physically impossible to match the intensity at the start of a note with the finish of a previous one, since the sound dies very rapidly once it has been initiated. The player has to judge the peak intensities so that they follow a smooth variation, thus creating the illusion of an even legato. Many teachers feel that mastering the technique of legato playing is one of the most difficult aspects of piano-playing.

In the case of chord-playing, the relative strength of the different notes is a crucial factor. The distribution of strengths depends on the particular context, but a very common situation is when the top notes in a sequence of chords form a melody, as in the Chopin C minor Prelude (Figure 11.8). Extra weight is then usually given to the top notes, in this case the outer side of the right hand, in order to make them stand out. Individual notes within a chord can also be made to stand

11.8 Start of the Prelude Op. 28 No. 20 by Chopin

out by fractionally adjusting the time at which they are sounded in relation to the other notes.

Early development of piano styles

For the first century or so of its development, the piano coexisted with the harpsichord and clavichord, so it is not surprising that piano-writing and technique were both dominated in the early years by the legacies handed down by players of these earlier instruments. The result of this was that emphasis was placed on non-legato passagework, agility and fluency of the fingers, rather than on legato playing and strength of tone. In Mozart's day a short detached manner of playing seems to have been the norm. Practice of scale passages and technical exercises, typified by the ones in Clementi's *Gradus ad Parnassum*, became the basic diet of the piano student. Clementi's pupils were instructed to hold their hands and arms in a horizontal position and to avoid all unnecessary movements; much practice was advocated to strengthen weak fingers and develop evenness of tone. The emphasis on fingerwork in *Gradus ad Parnassum* was later to be parodied by Debussy in his piano composition with the same name, but it is worth pointing out that Clementi also showed foresight into new styles which were to emerge later.

Beethoven was one of the first to realize the full potential of the piano and to place emphasis on tone quality rather than fluency. His early sonatas could be played on either the harpsichord or the piano, but his later works, such as the 'Hammerklavier' Sonata, transcend the resources of the earlier instrument, particularly in terms of dynamic contrast. It must be remembered though that the pianos used by Beethoven still did not have either the volume or the sustaining power of the modern instrument.

Beethoven paid particular attention to legato technique, thus breaking from the earlier traditions. His own playing was noted for its tremendous power, and he was constantly searching for instruments with greater range, more brilliant treble, and more sonorous bass. His first piano was an Érard (now in the Kunsthistorisches Museum in Vienna); later he acquired an 1817 Broadwood (now in the Hungarian National Museum) and finally a Viennese Graf (now in the Beethovenhaus, Bonn). Apparently none of these fully met his demands in terms of sonority and robustness.

Amongst the pupils of Beethoven was Carl Czerny, famous today for the many studies that he wrote. Czerny laid emphasis on fluency, smoothness, and brilliance and formed what came to be known as the 'School of Velocity'. He was teacher to many of the most important pianists of the nineteenth century, to whom he must have passed on many of the techniques learnt from Beethoven, particularly with regard to fingering, movements of the thumb, and hand and finger positions.

Great pianists of the nineteenth century

The nineteenth century saw the rise of the concert virtuosi; the greatest of all of these was Franz Liszt, who was a pupil of Czerny. Liszt developed an incredible technique, bringing into play the full use of the wrist, arm, and shoulder; in fact, he used the complete upper part of his body to achieve control of the keyboard. This contrasted with earlier schools of thought which concentrated almost entirely on finger movement. In this way Liszt was able to develop tonal shades of almost orchestral proportions, which he was able to display to the full in the performance of his own piano transcriptions. On one well-known occasion the 'March to the Scaffold' from *Symphonie Fantastique* by Berlioz was being conducted by the composer. After the performance Liszt played his own transcription on piano; the effect surpassed even that of the full orchestra, causing a furore in the audience. Liszt created a new concept in piano-playing, which has inspired successive generations of piano virtuosi.

Frédéric Chopin was a contemporary of Liszt and a rival virtuoso pianist, although, in comparison, he gave few concerts. As much as Liszt, he was responsible for revolutionizing the concepts of piano-playing. He dismissed many of the traditional rules of fingering, and the idea of trying to equalize the strength of each finger. Instead, he emphasized the individuality of the fingers and the importance of taking advantage of the shape of the keyboard layout and the purchase offered by the black notes. It is typical of him that he started his pupils on the scale of B major, in which the long fingers lie comfortably over the black notes, rather than on C major, which he thought was the most difficult to play because of the lack of reference points for the fingers to locate. Chopin realized that the spontaneity of music could be ruined by excessive emphasis on technique. He established a new romantic style making extensive use of rubato to give a singing quality to melodic lines. Rubato is a subtle give and take of the time values allocated to individual notes and chords which delays or accelerates the flow momentarily without altering the overall tempo. Many players since have over-sentimentalized and spoiled some of Chopin's music by the use of excessive rubato.

The best-known piano teacher in Europe during the nineteenth century was Theodor Leschetizky. Like Liszt, Leschetizky was a pupil of Czerny. Numbered among his pupils were many of the greatest pianists of the time, including Paderewski and Schnabel. A number of books have been written describing the so-called 'Leschetizky method', although he himself emphasized the importance of instruction being geared towards the individual pupil. In essence, Leschetizky's concepts were similar to those of both Liszt and Chopin, the emphasis being on the production of singing tone rather than flamboyant technique.

It is worth noting that the ability to make the piano 'sing' a melody, which was evidently very striking in the playing of Chopin and Liszt, was considerably aided by the relatively light damping of the piano of the time, which allowed notes to linger for a significant time after the key was released. Different articulation and pedalling must be employed to obtain a similar effect on the modern piano.

National schools

During the nineteenth century schools of piano-playing became established in Russia, Germany, and France, each with their own characteristic styles.

The Russian school became centred around the St Petersburg Conservatory, founded in 1861 by Anton Rubinstein, and later also the Moscow Conservatory, founded by his brother Nikolai. Great pianists such as Sergei Rachmaninov and Josef Hofmann emerged from it. A characteristic of the Russians was their colourful and rather extrovert approach, held within a rigid rhythmical framework. Little use was made of rubato, but tempo changes were frequently employed to bring out highlights or emphasize structural elements in the music.

The German School emerged a little later, mainly in Berlin, Frankfurt, Stuttgart, and Leipzig. It contrasted with the Russians by taking a more serious and academic approach, frowning on the light-hearted and the colourful. Bach's *Well Tempered Clavier* was the foundation training for all of its pupils. An early exponent of the German style was Clara Schumann, wife of the composer. Being the daughter of the piano teacher Friedrich Wieck, she was brought up on a diet of Beethoven and the classics. A more eccentric example was Ferruccio Busoni, an addict of Bach's music who was acknowledged for his masterful interpretation of the later works of Beethoven. Busoni taught for many years in Berlin.

Artur Schnabel, Wilhelm Backhaus, and Claudio Arrau were also regarded as exponents of the German school. Schnabel pioneered a scholarly approach to performance by researching the origins of the music he played through the study of first editions and early manuscripts. He did much to authenticate the performance of music by the great composers, particularly Bach, Mozart, Beethoven, and Schubert.

Schnabel, however, still retained the romantic roots passed down to him through his teacher Leschetizky. Backhaus was more strongly in the German tradition, with his emphasis on structure and eloquence of execution. Born in Chile but trained in Germany, Arrau was the last of the great masters from the German school, with a broader repertoire and more general approach than his predecessors.

A school of playing also developed in France, centred at the Paris Conservatoire, but this did not achieve the strength of its Russian and German counterparts. The French playing technique was light and elegant with an emphaisis on fluency, as exemplified by Henri Hertz, a famous salon pianist who also taught at the Conservatoire. The French pianists generally failed to achieve depth of tone and musical feeling. One exception was Alfred Cortot, who was a teacher at the Conservatoire. He became the best known of all French pianists, particularly through his large number of recordings and also through his piano transcriptions. A well-known example of the latter is his solo version of the *Dolly Suite*, originally written by Gabriel Fauré for two pianos.

In England, although no real school of playing developed, the teacher Tobias Matthay had a great influence on the development of piano technique. His 'relaxation methods' were aimed at economy of effort. An example is the avoidance of what is sometimes referred to as 'key bedding', in which considerable force is maintained on the key after the note has sounded; this is unnecessary, since once the hammer has gone into free flight no further pressure from the finger can affect the tone. Matthay also paid much attention to the understanding and mastery of forearm rotation, as illustrated by the exercise reproduced in Figure 11.9.

Matthay put so much emphasis on relaxation, possibly in reaction to the more muscular approach of the German school, that his ideas have often been misinterpreted. Otto Ortmann clarified some of the concepts by making use of more detailed physiological studies; Ortmann explained the interrelationship between tension and relaxation in his book *The Physiological Mechanics of Piano Technique*

11.9 A forearm rotation exercise by Tobias Matthay. In his instructions Matthay writes: 'Play a broken octave scale, accenting all the outer notes when the passage travels in the direction away from the body; and accenting all the inner notes when the passage travels towards the body. These accents are to be given by means of the Rotary process; and they are to be given (1) purely by rotary exertion, and (2) by weight-lapse in conjunction with it—as required in brilliant passages and in cantabile passages respectively.'

(1929). Ambrose Coviello was also prompted to write a book entitled *What Matthay Meant* (1948).

Use of the pedal

It has already been noted that the early piano had nothing like the sustaining power of the modern instrument. During the classical period the pedal was used primarily for special effects; when it was applied, it might be kept down throughout whole passages. The advent of the Romantic movement at the beginning of the nineteenth century saw the pedal taking on a much more important role. Chopin, in his compositions, gave precise instructions on how it should be applied, and Liszt attached so much importance to its use that he is reported to have said that 'without the pedal the piano is just a dulcimer'.

There are two principal ways in which the pedal can be applied. The technique now known as 'rhythmic pedalling', where the dampers are raised at the moment of striking the note or chord, was for a long time considered to be the normal method. When the pedal is applied in this manner the complete set of strings are free to resonate with sympathetic vibrations at the moment of striking. On early pianos, with less sustaining power, this method can be applied quite freely with good effect, but on the modern instrument it tends to create a cavernous sound and can only be used with economy.

The most common method of pedalling is now 'legato pedalling' (or 'syncopated pedalling'), which is primarily aimed at creating a legato line between a series of notes or chords. The pedal is changed on each new note or harmonic progression, with the dampers being lowered momentarily when each new one is played in order to damp out the previous sound. Precise timing is required in order that there are neither undesirable overlaps of sound nor detectable gaps between the notes.

Debussy created a new concept in the use of the pedal for tone colouring. He frequently asks for the pedal to be applied before the striking of a series of chords; a wash of tone colour is thus created, a resonant background on which the main sonorities are floated. In this way he builds up tone pictures in the same spirit as the great Impressionist painters of his time. A typical example is the excerpt from his Prelude No. 3 Book 2, shown in Figure 11.10, where the Habañera bass is set against the wash of colour above.

A technique used quite extensively on pianos with only two pedals is that of 'half-pedalling'. This is used when a bass line needs to be sustained against a more rapidly moving melody in the treble, and relies on the fact that the strings in the bass take much longer to damp than the ones in the treble. The legato pedalling principle is used for the melody line in the treble, but the dampers are only lowered for a very short instant of time on each change of note and are barely allowed

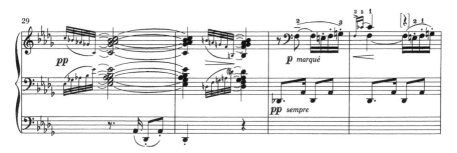

11.10 Excerpt from the Prelude Book 2 No. 2 by Debussy (by courtesy of United Music Publishers)

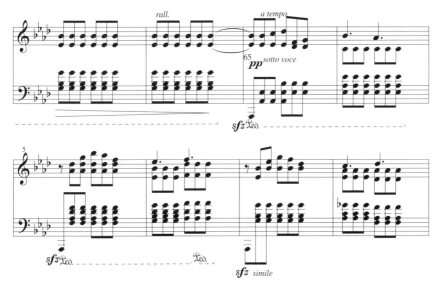

11.11 Part of the Prelude Op. 28 No. 17 by Chopin, showing a typical use of half-pedalling which allows the low Ab in bar 65 to be prolonged into bar 66

to touch the strings. This touch is sufficient to dampen the upper strings, but allows the bass ones to ring on and maintain the line of the accompaniment. An example where this technique might be used is in the passage from the Chopin Prelude shown in Figure 11.11; here the A♭ in the bass could be sustained by half-pedalling. When a sostenuto pedal is available the technique becomes redundant, because the third pedal can be used to sustain the bass while the melody is pedalled in the usual way using the sustaining pedal.

Contemporary trends

The tonal capabilities of the piano explored by Debussy form the cornerstone of the development of piano style in the twentieth century. His ideas were taken up and developed by composers such as Arnold Schoenberg and Bela Bartók, who made use of techniques such as the silent depression of prescribed keys in order to enhance the sonorities of other notes. An example of this is seen in the Passacaglia on DSCH by Ronald Stevenson, shown in Figure 11.12. Bartók also had his own innovative ideas, and was a pioneer in a new neo-classical approach which exploited the percussive capabilities of the instrument to the full. Students from the complete beginner to the most advanced can study his playing techniques in all their aspects through the six volumes of his *Microkosmos*. These are a masterly set of studies written as a complete course of instruction, dealing with every difficulty

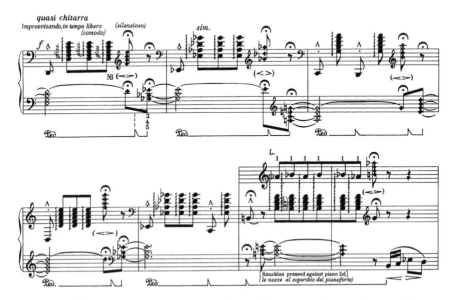

11.12 Part of the *Passacaglia on DSCH* (1960–2) by Ronald Stevenson, showing the use of silently held notes (indicated by diamonds) to enhance sonorities (by permission of the composer)

TONE	MATERIAL	STRINGS (L→R)	DISTANCE FROM DAMPER (INCHES)	MATERIAL	STRINGS (L→R)	DISTANCE FROM DAMPER (INCHES)	MATERIAL	STRINGS (L→R)	DISTANCE FROM DAMPER (INCHES)	TONE
				SCREW	2-3	1 1/4*				A
				MED. BOLT	2-3	1 3/8*				G
				SCREW	2-3	1 5/8*				F
				SCREW	2-3	1 3/16*				E
				SCREW	2-3	1 3/4*				Eb
				SM. BOLT	2-3	2*				D
				SCREW	2-3	1 7/16*				C#
				FURNITURE BOLT	2-3	2 3/16*				C
16va				SCREW	2-3	2 1/2*				B
				SCREW	2-3	1 7/8*				Bb
				MED. BOLT	2-3	2 7/8*				A
				SCREW	2-3	2 1/4*				Ab
				SCREW	2-3	3 3/4*				G
				SCREW	2-3	2 5/16*				F#
	SCREW	1-2	3/4*	FURN. BOLT + 2 NUTS	2-3	2 3/8*	SCREW + 2 NUTS	2-3	3 1/4*	F
				SCREW	2-3	1 7/8*				E
				FURNITURE BOLT	2-3	1 7/8				Eb
				SCREW	2-3	1 5/16				C#
				SCREW	2-3	1 1/16				C
	(DAMPER TO BRIDGE = 14 7/8; ADJUST ACCORDINGLY)			MED. BOLT	2-3	3 3/4				B
				SCREW	2-3	4 3/16				A
8va	RUBBER	1-2-3	4 1/2	FURNITURE BOLT	2-3	1 1/4				G#
				SCREW	2-3	1 3/4				F#
				SCREW	2-3	2 5/16				F
	RUBBER	1-2-3	5 3/4							E
	RUBBER	1-2-3	6 1/2	FURN. BOLT + NUT	2-3	6 7/8				Eb
				FURNITURE BOLT	2-3	2 9/16				D
	RUBBER	1-2-3	3 5/8							Db
				BOLT	2-3	7 7/8				C
				BOLT	2-3	2				B
	SCREW	1-2	10	SCREW	2-3	1	RUBBER	1-2-3	8 1/4	Bb
	(PLASTIC (5 & G))	1-2-3	2 5/16				RUBBER	1-2-3	4 1/2	G#
	PLASTIC (OVER L-UNDER 2-3)	1-2-3	2 7/8				RUBBER	1-2-3	10 1/8	G
	(PLASTIC (5 & D))	1-2-3	4 1/4				RUBBER	1-2-3	5 1/16	D#
	PLASTIC (OVER L-UNDER 2-3)	1-2-3	4 1/8				RUBBER	1-2-3	9 3/4	D
	BOLT	1-2	15 1/2	BOLT	2-3	1 1/16	RUBBER	1-2-3	14 1/8	Db
	BOLT	1-2	14 1/2	BOLT	2-3	7/8	RUBBER	1-2-3	6 1/2	C
	BOLT	1-2	14 3/4	BOLT	2-3	9/16	RUBBER	1-2-3	14	B
	RUBBER	1-2-3	9 1/2	MED. BOLT	2-3	10 7/8				Bb
	SCREW	1-2	5 7/8	LG. BOLT	2-3	5 7/8	SCREW + NUTS	1-2	1	A
	BOLT	1-2	7 7/8	MED. BOLT	2-3	2 1/4	RUBBER	1-2-3	4 1/8	Ab
	LONG BOLT	1-2	8 3/4	LG. BOLT	2-3	3 1/4				G
				BOLT	2-3	1 1/16				D
8va ba	SCREW + RUBBER	1-2	4 7/16							D
16va ba	ERASER (OVER D UNDER C + E)	1	6 3/4							D
	AM. PENCIL CO. #366									

*MEASURE FROM BRIDGE.

11.13 Some of Cage's instructions for his Prepared Piano in *Sonatas and Interludes*. From Edition Peters No. 6755 © 1960 by Henmar Press Inc., New York. Reprinted by permission of Peters Edition Limited, London

that the modern pianist is likely to encounter. He put much emphasis on the independence of the hands and employed unfamiliar rhythms, often inspired by the traditional folk songs which he collected over a period of years.

Over the last few decades, with the increase in travel and international exchange, national schools of playing have effectively disappeared. The charisma and showmanship of concert pianists in the tradition of Liszt has given way to a new breed of virtuosi, with a tendency towards a uniformity of style conditioned by the precision called for in the recording studio. The Canadian Glenn Gould is an example of one who devoted a large part of his career to making recordings, in his case principally of the works of Bach. Recent exponents of the international school, such as Maurizio Pollini, display flawless technique and execute authentic and literal interpretations of compositions from a broad repertoire, including the avant-garde.

Avant-garde playing involves all manner of unconventional playing techniques, such as the playing of cluster chords with the back of the hand or a length of wood, placing weights on the keys to keep them depressed, plucking the strings with the finger or a plectrum, and striking the strings with hand-held hammers or other objects. John Cage introduced the concept of the 'prepared piano', and many others have followed up his ideas. The piano is prepared by inserting a variety of objects between the strings, such as spoons, bolts, and wedges, which have the effect of changing both timbre and pitch. Figure 11.13 shows some of his instructions for preparing a piano for the performance of his composition *Sonatas and Interludes*. Other avant-garde composers have used drawing pins inserted into the hammers, so that the strings are struck by the metal heads of the pins. It has to be borne in mind, of course, that such 'preparations' may permanently change the properties of the instrument.

It goes without saying that jazz has left its mark on both piano composition and playing style, as it has done with other instruments. A common approach of ragtime, boogie-woogie, and early dance-band pianists was to maintain a rhythmic bass, often in octaves or tenths, against which ornamented melodies were played in the right hand, making use of syncopation and cross-rhythms. This type of playing calls for a very strong left-hand technique and rhythmic independence of the hands. In more modern jazz groups the rhythmic bass is often provided by double bass and drums, allowing the pianist greater freedom to improvize.

12

The Pipe Organ

12.1 ACOUSTICAL PRINCIPLES

A pipe organ is essentially a set of mechanically blown aerophones controlled by a keyboard. The basic acoustical principles of aerophones were discussed in Chapter 2; in Chapters 3 and 4 we saw how these principles were exemplified in members of the orchestral woodwind families. Much of this earlier discussion is directly relevant to the behaviour of organ pipes. In particular, the basic distinction between instruments excited by an air jet (flutes, whistles, panpipes) and those excited by a vibrating reed (oboes, clarinets, bassoons) is paralleled by the major subdivision of organ pipes into two classes: 'flue' pipes and 'reed' pipes.

Flue pipes

A pipe which is excited by an air jet is described as a flue pipe. A large organ will contain many different types of flue pipes, including those classified as flutes, principals, and strings. The distinctions between these varieties will be explained later in the chapter, but in each the sounding mechanism is identical in principle to that of the recorder or whistle.

Figure 12.1(a) is a schematic diagram of the lower part of a typical flue organ pipe. Air is admitted under pressure into a volume at the base of the pipe, known as the 'foot'. At the top of the foot the air escapes through a slit in the form of a thin flat jet. This jet travels across an opening in the side of the pipe called the 'mouth'; the interaction with the 'upper lip' at the top of the mouth induces a wiggling motion of the jet. The resonances of the air column strongly influence the frequency at which the jet wiggle stabilizes, as explained in Chapter 2. If the air pressure and the distance from slit to upper lip (the 'cut-up') are properly chosen, strong standing waves are set up in the pipe, at frequencies very close to the natural frequencies of the air column. Usually the pitch at which the pipe sounds is that of the fundamental mode, although it is possible to make a pipe overblow by increasing the air pressure or reducing the cut-up.

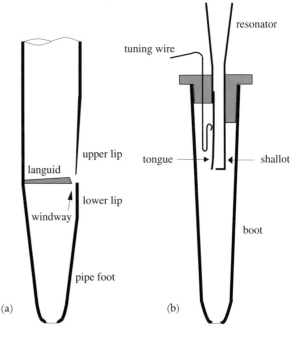

12.1 Diagrams illustrating (a): the lower part of a typical organ flue pipe; (b) the lower part of a typical organ reed pipe

In the interaction between an air column and an air jet, the air column is the dominant partner. The tuning of an organ flue pipe is thus accomplished by adjusting the effective length of the resonating section; the air jet obediently adapts to the new resonant frequency. The effective length of a pipe open at the upper end can be altered by moving a sliding section, or by opening or closing a side slot at the top of the pipe. If the upper end is closed, the plug which closes it may be moved up or down to alter the effective length.

Another method of tuning a flue pipe can be employed if the pipe is fitted with 'ears'. These are vanes fitted at either side of the mouth of the pipe, whose primary purpose is to assist in the formation and direction of the air jet. Figure 12.2 shows a photograph of the mouth of a flue organ pipe with ears. Angling the two ears inwards reduces the effective area of the mouth aperture, and lowers the resonance frequency of the pipe; angling them outwards has the opposite effect. Adjustment of the ears is equivalent to the control of intonation by variation of lip cover in a flute embouchure (see Chapter 4). However, repeated bending of the ears is liable to make them break off, so this is not employed as a regular tuning technique.

Reed pipes

We have noted the similarity between the sound generator of an organ flue pipe and that of a recorder. Although reed pipes are given the names of many orches-

12.2 Photograph of the mouth of a metal flue pipe with ears

tral instruments—including oboe, trumpet, and bassoon—the basic sounding mechanism on all reed pipes has a strong resemblance to the single reed mouthpiece of the clarinet or saxophone.

A schematic diagram of the base of an organ reed pipe is shown in Figure 12.1(b). As in a flue pipe, air under pressure is admitted into an approximately conical chamber (called in this case the 'boot') through a small hole at the tip. The upper surface of the boot is a solid block, through which the main resonating tube of the pipe penetrates. The part of the resonator within the boot is known as the 'shallot'; it is closed at the lower end, but has a rectangular slit cut into the side. This slit is equivalent to the lay of a saxophone mouthpiece (see Figure 3.12). As on the saxophone, the aperture is almost closed by a reed which is clamped to the tube wall at one end but free to vibrate at the other. The reed in an organ pipe is usually described as the 'tongue' of the pipe.

The crucial difference between the sound generator on an organ reed pipe and that on a single-reed woodwind is the nature of the material from which the reed is made. On the saxophone or clarinet, the reed is a flexible strip of cane, thinned down towards the tip to make it soft and yielding. In the interaction with the resonating air column the reed is very much the junior partner, willing to take advice from the more powerful air column when it comes to choosing the optimum sounding frequency. This is of course essential for a woodwind instrument, since the opening of side finger-holes changes the resonance frequency of the air column over a wide pitch range: the reed must be willing to follow. The fact that the player's soft upper lip is pressed against the saxophone or clarinet reed also helps to make the reed more complaisant by damping its own resonances.

An organ-pipe tongue, in contrast, is a springy strip of metal (normally brass). In place of the upper lip of a woodwind player, we find the bent end of a metal wire pressed firmly against the tongue near its upper end. Figure 12.3 is a photograph of a disassembled organ reed pipe, in which it can be seen that the other end of the bent wire passes through the block and emerges at the side of the resonating tube. This wire is used to tune the reed pipe: pulling it upwards (away from the foot) lowers the pitch of the note, while pushing it downwards raises the pitch. The pipe can be tuned in this way because the reed is strong enough to dominate the air column; the choice of sounding frequency is basically made by the reed, and the air column must follow. When the tuning wire is pulled out, the vibrating length of the tongue is increased and its natural frequency is lowered.

Needless to say, the natural frequencies of the resonating pipe are still of great importance. The vibrating tongue admits a modulated flow of air to the pipe, corresponding to a set of frequency components which are harmonics of the natural frequency of the tongue. If some of these components match resonances of the pipe they will set up strong standing waves in the pipe, and will contribute strongly to the radiated sound. After the tongue frequency has been adjusted, it is therefore necessary to tune the resonator to optimize the loudness and timbre of the pipe. The variations of pressure caused by the standing wave at the lower end of the resonator can also help to strengthen and stabilize the vibration of the tongue; if the length of the pipe is maladjusted so that its resonances hinder rather than help, the tongue may stop vibrating completely.

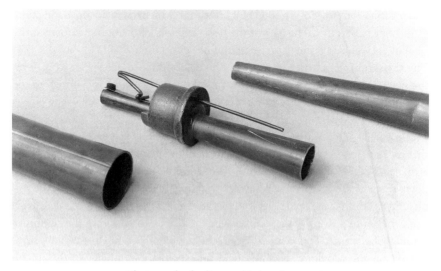

12.3 Photograph of a disassembled reed organ pipe

The reed shown in Figure 12.3 is a 'beating reed': this means that the width of the tongue is slightly greater than that of the shallot. A high pressure in the boot forces the tongue against the shallot, closing the aperture and stopping the flow of air. The entrance to the resonator can remain closed for a significant fraction of the period of vibration, giving a jerky, pulsating type of excitation rich in upper harmonics. Very occasionally organ reed pipes are given 'free reeds', so called because the tongue is slightly narrower than the slit and is free to pass through it. Clearly this type of reed will give a more smoothly varying air flow into the resonator, with a weaker retinue of upper harmonics. Free reeds are found principally in harmoniums, accordions, and mouth organs.

Shapes of resonator

From the discussion of resonating air columns in Chapter 2 we can understand why nearly all resonators in flue or reed organ pipes are either cylindrical or conical. These are just the shapes of air columns which have harmonically related resonance frequencies, able to react with the harmonics of the flow generated by the air jet or the reed to create a rich and powerful sound.

The nature of the resonances in a pipe depends on whether the ends are open or closed. An open flute is a cylindrical flue pipe with an open upper end; like all flue pipes, the lower end of the resonator is also open at the mouth. The pipe will therefore have a complete set of harmonic resonances, and a relatively rich sound. A stopped flute, in contrast, has a cylindrical resonator with its upper end closed and its lower end open; in this case the odd-numbered harmonics are much more powerful than the even ones. The effect of the closed upper end is sometimes modified by piercing it with a short tube much narrower than the main bore; the even harmonics are then partially restored, and additional resonances appear at high frequencies determined by the length of the narrow tube.

In Chapter 4 we discussed the end corrections which have to be added to the physical length of an orchestral flute to account for the acoustical properties of the embouchure hole and the opening at the lower end. Similar corrections have to be made for the organ pipe: the effective acoustic length is always greater than the physical length from the lower lip of the mouth to the top of the pipe. We also saw in Chapter 4 that the end corrections depend to some extent on the frequency of the sound wave in the tube. Thus it was a slight oversimplification to describe the modes of a flute pipe as 'harmonics'; a wide short pipe with substantial end corrections can have mode frequencies which deviate noticeably from a harmonic series. When such a pipe is blown, only the lowest modes contribute significantly to the sound, which is therefore strong in fundamental and weak in upper harmonics.

The lower end of the resonator in a reed pipe behaves acoustically as a closed end; it is therefore not practicable to have a resonator with its upper end stopped, since there would be no aperture through which the sound could be radiated. A cylindrical resonator on a reed pipe gives a clarinet-like sound with weak even harmonics; a conical tube gives a complete harmonic spectrum. Sometimes a pipe is constructed from several cones with different degrees of taper, in order to emphasize particular components of the frequency spectrum of the reed.

Scaling of pipes

A set of organ pipes of a particular type is known as a 'rank'. A modern organ, with a keyboard spanning five octaves from C_2 to C_7, requires sixty-one pipes for a rank, one for each note in the compass. If the pipes are open flutes, the longest is about 8 feet (2.4 m); this has given rise to the convention that any rank which sounds at written pitch is described as 8-foot (or 8'). The shortest pipe in the open flute rank is 7.5 cm long. The question then arises of how the diameter of the pipe should be related to its length to give the best tonal effect across the whole rank.

The simplest procedure would be to make all the pipes the same diameter. This would be unsatisfactory because the tone quality of the pipes would then vary drastically within the rank: the low notes would have a pungent sound rich in upper harmonics, while the high notes would have a bland timbre with only one or two low harmonics contributing to the sound. One reason for this is the effect of frequency-dependent end corrections mentioned above. Another reason is that a cylindrical pipe open at one end can only support a strong standing wave if the wavelength in question is significantly greater than the diameter of the tube. If this criterion is not satisfied, the wave travelling down the tube is not diffracted at the open end (see Section 2.2), and the sound energy leaks out instead of returning to reinforce the standing wave.

For a cylindrical tube open at both ends, with an effective length L and a diameter D, the wavelength of the nth mode is given by $\lambda = 2L : n$. The standing waves will be weakened by diffraction if λ is less than about $2D$. We can thus expect strong modes up to $n = L : D$. If we made all the pipes in an open flute rank of diameter 3 cm, the value of $L : D$ would be 80 for the C_2 pipe and 2.5 for the C_7 pipe: the longest pipe could sustain up to eighty modes, while the shortest could only manage two.

In the light of the foregoing discussion, it might seem obvious that the way to get a uniform timbre in the rank would be to choose the diameter of each pipe to be a fixed proportion of its length. The value of $L : D$ would then be the same for each pipe, which would have the same number of strong modes. We saw in Chapter 1, however, that the perception of timbre is a complex matter which depends on more than merely the number of strong frequency components in the spectrum. A high-pitch pipe with many strong harmonics can sound shrill and harsh, while a low-pitch pipe with exactly the same number and strength of harmonics sounds attractively rich and reedy.

The way in which the diameter of the pipe depends on its length is known as the 'scaling law'. In practice, it has been found that the best tonal balance within a rank is obtained by a scaling law which reduces the diameter of the pipes a little more slowly than the length. The long low-pitch pipes then have a larger $L : D$ ratio, and a richer harmonic spectrum, than the short high-pitch pipes. A flute rank might have an $L : D$ ratio of 10 for the longest pipes, reducing to around 4 for the shortest pipes.

Pipes in combination

All but the very simplest of pipe organs have many different ranks of pipes. Each rank is linked to a 'stop' which the player can manipulate; the different ways in which the stop control mechanism can operate are described in Section 12.3. A large organ will have several keyboards ('manuals') and a pedal board, each with its own set of stops. Drawing the '8-foot Flute' stop on a particular manual means that the keys of this manual will sound pipes from the 8-foot Flute rank.

If several stops are drawn simultaneously, a single key will sound the corresponding pipes from each selected rank in combination. Much of the art of the organist lies in choosing interesting and appropriate timbres for a given piece of music by the selecting and combining of stops, a process described as 'registration'.

Some of the ranks are designed to sound an octave higher than written pitch; such a rank is described as '4-foot', since the pipe sounded by a given key is half the length of the pipe sounded by the same key in an 8-foot rank. A stop which controls a 4-foot rank of pipes is described as a '4-foot' stop. Since the basic frequency of the 4-foot pipe is twice that of the 8-foot pipe, the addition of a 4-foot stop gives a sound with strengthened 2nd harmonic; multiples of this harmonic are also strengthened, resulting in a brightening of the timbre. Similarly, a 2-foot stop sounds two octaves higher than written pitch on its own, and in combination strengthens the 4th harmonic (and multiples) of the basic 8-foot sound.

Ranks are frequently provided which contribute odd upper harmonics to the combination: the corresponding stops are known as 'mutation stops'. Examples are the 2⅔-foot stop (3rd harmonic, sounding a twelfth higher than written), and the 1⅗-foot stop (5th harmonic, sounding two octaves and a major third higher than written). A 'mixture stop' adds a selected combination of upper harmonic ranks to give further spice to the sound.

12.2 HISTORICAL DEVELOPMENT

The hydraulis

The organ originated in Greece around the third century BCE. Manuscripts by Athenaeus and Vitruvius from the first and second centuries CE attribute its invention to an Alexandrian engineer named Ctesibius. An account of the organ of this period, referred to as a 'hydraulic organ' or 'hydraulis', is given by the Alexandrian mathematician Neron, and further details are known from later manuscripts and from surviving terracotta models. The hydraulis had all the basic elements of the modern organ: a means of generating and regulating the air supply, a set of pipes for producing the sounds, and a series of valves operated by the player to direct the wind into the required pipes.

From the earliest times the organ has exerted a particular fascination, not only because of the combination of technology and art involved in its construction, but also because the potentially enormous power and vast capabilities of the instrument are normally under the control of a single player. Indeed the hydraulis appears to have been revered primarily as a great engineering achievement, rather than as a musical instrument; it was probably used mainly at large gatherings such as circuses, theatres, and games.

The principle of the hydraulis is quite sophisticated. Air pressure is generated by a piston attached to a lever arrangement; in some later versions there were two separate pistons, requiring two people to operate the pumps. When the piston is lowered, air is sucked in through the inlet valve which closes on the upward stroke. Air is then forced through a non-return valve into the hemispherical air chamber, known as the 'pnigeus'. The pnigeus is housed in a tank which is partly filled with water; an increase in air pressure then forces water out of the pnigeus into the tank, generating a pressure head equal to the difference in the two water levels. The pressurized air is used to feed a number of pipes which are individually activated by engaging hand-operated slider valves, returned by spring action.

The distinguishing feature of the hydraulic organ was the stabilization of the air pressure by the water head, which allowed a continuous air flow to be maintained. The immense weight of the water made the instrument extremely heavy and cumbersome, and the operation of the sliders required considerable strength. Normally there would have been one or two people to engage the sliders and a further one or two to operate the pumps, depending on the particular design. The fact that there was so much water around also caused major mechanical problems due to rusting of ironwork and warping of wood. Hydraulic organs were made until the eleventh century, but were gradually superseded by purely pneumatic systems which were already well known in the fourth century.

Early developments in Europe

In the eleventh century many monastic churches throughout Western Europe had organs; they were used on ceremonial occasions, and may also have been played during Mass. By the end of the fourteenth century virtually every church of importance in Western Europe had at least one organ. The beginning of an epoch of rapid development of the organ had begun. Improvements were made in the keys, making them smaller and lighter so that they could be operated by the fingers. Chromatic notes were added to the diatonic ones, and the range of the keyboard increased to between two and three octaves.

By the end of the fifteenth century many of the features of the modern organ had been invented. Amongst the major advances which had come about were the slider and spring chests which allowed certain groups of pipes to be inactivated by the operation of stops, thereby allowing a range of tonal variations. Multiple keyboards and pedal boards were also introduced, and bellows design was improved. The roller device had been incorporated into the action, enabling the builder to place the pipes in essentially any desired arrangement rather than constraining him to order them chromatically. The technique of pipe scaling, by which the diameter of each pipe was matched to its length in order to produce the optimum tone quality, had replaced the earlier practice of making each pipe the same diameter.

Small portable organs were widely used in the medieval and Renaissance periods. Three distinct types can be distinguished: the 'positive', the 'portative', and the 'regal'. The positive was an organ of moderate size, played with both hands and blown by a second person operating one or two pairs of bellows. The bellows were usually weighted to give pressure regulation. There would typically be two rows of open metal flue pipes forming a single rank. Positives were too large to be carried by the player, but portable enough to be moved by a couple of people; they could thus be used in different parts of a church, or transported readily from one church to another.

The portative was an altogether smaller instrument; it could be placed on the lap or on a table and could easily be carried in a procession. Usually the player pumped the bellows with the left hand, leaving the right hand free for playing melodies on the keyboard. A typical portative might have a single rank of wooden or metal flute pipes, with a range of two octaves from C_4 upwards.

The regal was distinguished by the fact that the sound was produced, not by flue pipes, but by a set of beating reeds with only the most vestigial of air column resonators. Since the instrument did not require long pipes it could be made in a very compact and portable form. The characteristic nasal timbre was widely utilized in the sixteenth century in religious, ceremonial, and theatrical music, although the stability of tuning of the regal was notoriously uncertain.

From the fourteenth to the sixteenth century the art of organ-building was dominated by Germany and the Netherlands, where most of the new developments were pioneered. There were also important instruments constructed in France, Spain, Italy, and elsewhere in Europe, although some of the early examples in these countries were of German manufacture. In England, most of the early organs appear to have been built by monks or priests; with a few exceptions, these were small in size with a single manual and without pedals.

In the seventeenth century, many fine organs were constructed throughout the Western world. The organ at St Gervais in Paris, which many members of the Couperin family played regularly, was typical of a large organ of this period. It had four manuals plus pedal board; two full-size manuals operated major sections of the organ described as 'Positif' and 'Grand Orgue', and two short manuals controlled smaller sections called 'Echo' and 'Cornet Séparé'. This last manual was restricted to a single Cornet chest used solely for right-hand solo purposes. Various new stops were introduced during this period, such as the Vox Humana which was available on the Grand Orgue at St Gervais, and improvements in tone were accomplished through attention to voicing. There was a tendency for makers to lavish resources on the external embellishments and, as a result, many organs from this time were extravagantly ornate. Front pipes were often gilded and embossed with ornamental patterns and their lips formed to look like animal jaws, while the case was ornamented with foliage, animals, or angels playing trumpets.

As organs are both expensive and long-lasting, and cannot easily be changed in pitch, it has happened from time to time that organs built to the standard pitch of a particular period continue in use when a different orchestral pitch has been adopted. When such an organ is used together with orchestral instruments, the music for one or the other has to be transposed. For example, in Germany in Bach's time almost all the organs had been built when the orchestral pitch was about A460 (known as 'Chorton' or 'choir pitch'). The oboes and bassoons which had recently been introduced into the orchestra were made at the French pitch, which was one tone lower (known as 'Cammerton' or 'chamber pitch') or sometimes a minor third lower (known as 'Tief Cammerton'). At Weimar, Bach transposed the woodwind parts, while choir, trumpets, and strings tuned to the organ; at Leipzig, the choir and strings tuned to the woodwind and he transposed the organ and trumpet parts. In the course of time, new organs were built to the Cammerton pitch, although many organs at Chorton pitch survived. A similar situation occurred in England at the end of the nineteenth century, when the standard orchestral pitch was lowered. Some Victorian organs are still at their original high pitch, more than a century later.

The practice of tempering the tuning of organs has also varied over the years. The question of temperament is particularly significant for the organ, whose sustaining power, steady pitch, and clear sound accentuate the roughness of intervals which are not in just intonation. When it was possible, organs were tuned to as harmonious a temperament as possible; the general adoption of equal temperament was resisted until the middle of the nineteenth century. Even in the sixteenth century, however, Arnolt Schlick noted the problems arising when an organist was forced to play in remote keys. Bach's organists at Leipzig, transposing down a tone, had to play in keys with two flats more than the orchestra; when Bach wrote in E♭ major or C minor, for example, the organist was playing chords in five flats. Clearly these organs must have been 'well tempered' (close to equal temperament).

In the latter part of the eighteenth century interest in organ composition underwent a decline from the peak it had reached in the works of J. S. Bach. Indeed, both Haydn and Mozart wrote barely a handful of works for organ. Nevertheless, considerable activity in organ-building continued throughout this period. One important innovation was the 'swell', whereby sets of pipes were enclosed in a shuttered box whose opening and closing was under the control of the player. As well as allowing the organist the possibility of introducing rapid crescendo and diminuendo effects, this gave additional control over the overall dynamic level. Abraham Jordan, who built the organ at St Magnus, London Bridge in 1712, claimed the invention as his, although in fact the idea had been used previously in Spain for at least half a century for solo stops. By 1730 virtually every new organ had a swell, and eventually it became accepted as the main second manual.

The Romantic influence

The Romantic movement which dominated nineteenth-century music did not in general find the organ an ideal vehicle for expression. Many composers of the time avoided it completely or composed for it rather unsuccessfully. However, organ builders took full advantage of the technical achievements of the industrial revolution, and the organ became more sophisticated mechanically and more powerful. More and more stops and couplers were introduced, together with expressive devices which allowed the organ more closely to resemble the orchestra.

A builder of great influence in this period was Aristide Cavaillé-Coll. He revolutionized the French Classical organ along orchestral lines, while maintaining elements of Classical tradition such as the slider chest. Cavaillé-Coll was the first to utilize the Barker lever action, which employed pneumatic devices to couple the keys to the pallet valves opening the airways to the pipes. He normally reserved this innovation for the Great Organ, maintaining direct mechanical action for the other sections. Among the many fine instruments which he constructed was the organ of St Clothilde in Paris, where César Franck was organist from 1859 to 1890.

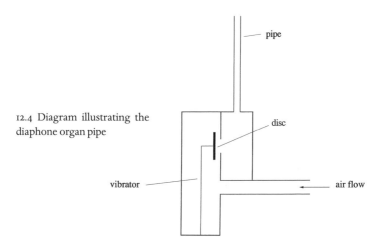

12.4 Diagram illustrating the diaphone organ pipe

The work of the electrical engineer and organ builder Robert Hope Jones took to the extreme the nineteenth-century tendencies for mechanical innovation and ever-increasing sonority. Hope Jones's organs, and even more so those of his imitators, are considered by many to display some of the worst features of organ design, but his inventiveness is beyond dispute. Fully electric actions were introduced, based on the use of small electromagnets. The electric coupling made it easy to borrow pipes from one rank for use in another, a concept which was to be taken to its ultimate conclusion in the theatre organ. In 1894 Hope Jones invented a new type of organ pipe known as a 'diaphone', in which the airway to the pipe is periodically cut off by a small valve attached to a vibrating arm, as shown in Figure 12.4. When the pipe is activated the plate is set into vibration, resulting in air entering the pipe in a periodic series of puffs matched in frequency to that of the pipe. The diaphone produced a very loud sound but an extremely strident tone quality. It has sometimes been likened to a fog horn, and indeed fog horns have been designed on this principle.

In the second half of the twentieth century there was a movement away from the excesses of the period around 1900, and a resurgence of interest in organ construction in the Baroque and Classical traditions. Emphasis was placed more on clarity of tone and sensitivity to player control, rather than on extremes of volume and mechanical sophistication.

Theatre and cinema organs

Although the history of the organ is primarily associated with the church, from the seventeenth century onwards parallel developments were taking place in theatres and, later on, cinemas.

By the beginning of the seventeenth century small positives, portatives, and regals were already being used in entertainments such as Monteverdi's opera *Orfeo*. In the course of the century larger instruments were installed in theatres such as the Drury Lane Theatre in London, for use in concerts, theatrical productions, and operas. During the eighteenth century it was not uncommon for theatres in London to put on concerts by famous showman organists, for example 'Mr Clint of Barnet'. Organ concertos acting as interludes between acts of oratorios also became the vogue at Covent Garden and elsewhere, and esteemed musicians such as Handel became associated with these.

In the early 1900s, the heyday of silent films, organs were designed specifically for use in the cinema. These were a direct development of the ideas of Hope Jones; indeed, the original cinema organ was designed by the Wurlitzer Company in America (about 1925) in collaboration with Hope Jones, under the title of the Wurlitzer Hope Jones Unit Orchestra. Other companies such as Compton followed with similar designs. The 'unification principle' (sometimes referred to as the 'unit organ principle') was applied to these instruments: each pipe was given its own unit chest to stand on, and these could be coupled together in any desired configuration by the electrical linkage. In this way it was possible to use a single pipe for a number of ranks. A pipe of 2-foot nominal length, for example, could serve as C_4 in the 8-foot register, C_3 in the 4-foot register, F_2 in the $2\frac{2}{3}$-foot register and C_2 in the 2-foot register. To allow this, the 8-foot rank had to have additional pipes to encompass the extended range (the 'extension principle'), although overall the scheme produced a great economy of pipework and saving in cost. It was not without its problems, however. Because the pipes need to be tuned to a tempered scale, correct tuning of mutations becomes impossible. In the example just given, C_4 would not be precisely the 3rd harmonic of F_2 in equal temperament so the note F_2 in the $2\frac{2}{3}$-foot register would be out of tune.

The whole sound-generating system of the cinema organ was normally housed in a room built adjacent to or above the screen. It was connected to the main auditorium by a shuttered wall, in which the shutters could be opened and closed under control of the swell pedal. The so-called 'organ chamber' was in effect one large swell box. Occasionally the organ chamber was housed under the stage or was split in two halves, one on either side of the screen. If there were two swell boxes, pipes of different tone qualities were often segregated between them, so that by opening one box and closing another at the same time the organist could dissolve one colour into another while playing. The swell shutters were ingeniously arranged to open one at a time by means of electrical contacts attached to the swell pedal; for soft passages only one or two shutters would be open, whereas with the swell pedal fully depressed all shutters would be open. The organ chamber had to be easily accessible for maintenance; the complexity was such that minor faults could easily develop and might even need fixing during a performance. A common occurrence was that a tiny particle of dust or a splinter would find its way into the wind mechanism and lodge in one of the valves, causing the pipe to continue sounding after the key was released. This was referred to as a 'cypher'. To cater for this eventuality most organs in Britain were fitted with 'ventils'; these allowed the organist to shut off the wind supply to a part of the organ affected by a cypher, so that the whole performance would not be ruined.

In addition to the more conventional organ tone colours, new distinctive sounds were introduced, the most characteristic of the cinema organ being the Tibia Clausa, a stopped pipe introduced by Hope Jones. Pitched percussion instruments such as xylophone, chimes, glockenspiel, sleigh bells, vibraphone, harp, and even piano were incorporated . Tunes could be played on all of these from the keyboards. There were also unpitched percussion sounds such as gong, tambourine, sand block, triangle, and the like. Special effects such as door bell, siren, steamboat whistle, police whistle, thunder, pistol shot, crockery smash, and many others helped the organist in the accompaniment of silent films, which was the original purpose of the cinema organ. Typically the organ console was on a lift which raised the organist into view for solo playing and lowered the console for film accompaniment. The console itself normally had two or more manuals and a pedal board and the different tones were activated by tabs set on a curved facia. Special effects were sometimes activated by separate foot-operated pistons.

The cinema organ, though very popular in its day, had a very short lifespan. With the advent of talking pictures its original role disappeared. Many cinemas maintained their organs for a number of years, using them for musical entertainment in the interludes between films. This practice eventually declined, however, due to the high cost of maintaining the organs and the difficulty of finding sufficiently accomplished players to handle these extremely complex instruments. A few cinemas were able to retain their organs; the Capitol Cinema in Aberdeen, for example, still had its original Compton Organ in full working order in the 1990s. Some other cinema organs were bought up by societies of organ enthusiasts and restored to their original glory in different surroundings. Many masters of the cinema organ, such as Sandy McPherson, Reginald Foort, and Robin Richmond, became household names, and a new generation of cinema organists is now emerging through the organ club circuits.

12.3 HOW THE ORGAN WORKS

In the space available here, any description of the "King of Instruments" can only be an outline sketch. The most striking feature of a large pipe organ is its mechanical complexity; indeed, this very sophistication is sometimes held to be a fault on the grounds that the audience can become more interested in the instrument than the player, thus weakening the emotional bond between performer and listener. Another complication is that virtually every organ is unique in its mechanical construction, in contrast to an instrument like the violin, examples of which all conform to the same basic specification. Organs in different countries have also differed considerably over the ages, to the extent that it has sometimes been impossible to play music from one country on an instrument in another. For example, before 1800 much German organ music could not be performed in England because English instruments lacked a pedal board.

On pre-nineteenth-century organs each pallet valve, which emitted air into the pipes, was linked directly with its corresponding key by a simple mechanical linkage ('tracker action'). The player thus had a considerable degree of control over the starting and finishing transients of the notes. This important characteristic was lost with the introduction of more sophisticated mechanisms: first the pneumatic systems, and later the full electrical arrangements in which the organist essentially activated a series of switches as the various notes were played. As we have already seen, there has been a return this century to more traditional designs, restoring to the player the element of direct control and emphasizing tone quality rather than extravagant specification. The mechanism by which different ranks of pipes are coupled together has undergone a corresponding evolution, with the eventual return to the simple slider action.

Slider chest

The most basic layout for an organ is the 'slider chest', shown in Figure 12.5. This was introduced about the fifteenth century, and forms the building block for many

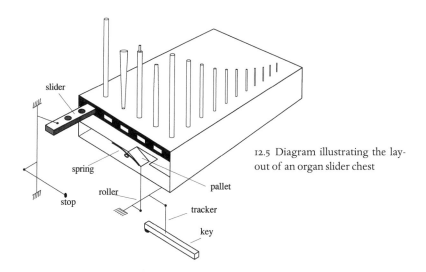

12.5 Diagram illustrating the layout of an organ slider chest

modern instruments based on traditional concepts. There are a number of ranks of pipes, each separate rank having its own tonal characteristic. For example there might be several ranks of flue pipes of pitch 8-foot, 4-foot, 2-foot, etc. and other ranks of reed pipes, each rank being made up of similar pipes appropriately scaled throughout the pitch range. Pressure-stabilized air is supplied from the blower to a chamber known as the 'pallet box'. When a single note is played on the keyboard, air is emitted from the pallet box through a 'pallet valve' into a narrow channel (or 'groove'). The groove runs transverse to the line of each rank of pipes, such that one pipe from each rank, corresponding to the pitch of the played note, can sound. This airway channel is sometimes referred to as a 'tone channel'. Normally not all of the ranks will be activated simultaneously. Whether a particular rank sounds or not is determined by the position of its 'slider', a narrow strip of wood drilled with holes which align themselves with the pipe inlet holes when the slider is drawn to the 'on' position. When the slider is pushed in, the two sets of holes do not align; no air can pass to the pipes, and that particular rank will not sound. Thus in Figure 12.5 a particular pipe will sound only if it lies at the junction of a tone channel for which the key has been depressed and a slider (sometimes described as the 'stop channel') which has been drawn to the 'on' position. On modern instruments the sliders are sometimes moved by electrically activated solenoids which can achieve a smooth and almost silent motion.

There are two other types of chest which bear a close resemblance to the slider chest. The medieval 'block chest' is essentially the same but without the sliders, making it impossible to separate the different ranks; when a key is depressed every rank with that tone channel will sound. In a slightly more sophisticated version of this, the chest is divided into two 'half chests'; each has its own pallet valve, both pallets opening when the appropriate key is depressed. A valve is then used to direct wind from the bellows to either a single half chest or both of them together. With the 'spring chest', there is a small pallet or groove valve, placed in the tone channel under every pipe. Each groove valve belonging to a single rank is operated by a guide rail such that, when the rail is moved by drawing its stop knob, the valves are all opened. The groove valves are fitted with springs so that they close once the stop knob has been returned.

The stop mechanism on the spring chest is considerably more complex than the slider, and takes up more room. Also it is much heavier in its operation, since the pressure of fifty or so pallet springs must be overcome when drawing a stop. When the stop knob is drawn it needs to be secured in a notch, since it is under tension, and when it is released the springs tend to snap back into their original position. The slider action too has its disadvantages, although the fact that it has better withstood the test of time seems to indicate that these are not so great. Warping of the wood from which the slider is made tends to be the principal problem, because this leads to leakage and stops the slide from gliding smoothly. Nowadays sliders may be made from synthetic material to overcome this problem, and slider seals may be used to ensure a wind-tight and secure movement.

The mechanisms by which the pallet valves and sliders are operated are also shown in Figure 12.5. The key is pivoted at its end point, and a 'tracker rod' is attached part way along its length. The other end of this cannot normally be fixed directly onto the pallet, since the width of the wind chest will exceed the length of the keyboard. This difficulty is overcome by means of a 'roller', to which the tracker from both the key and pallet are attached, the various rollers all being mounted on 'roller boards'. Using rollers, it is possible to achieve a symmetry and balance in the overall structure, rather than having all the weight of the large pipes concentrated at the bass end. The arrangement shown in Figure 12.5, with end-pivoting for the keys, is known as a 'suspended action'. An alternative scheme, in which the key is pivoted centrally, is referred to as a 'balanced action'. Sliders may also be fairly remote from their stop knobs, so a heavier-duty mechanical linkage is used.

Cone valve chest

The 'cone valve chest' originated between about 1775 and 1785, and is found principally in German organs from the nineteenth century. Unlike the slider chest, the cone valve chest has no grooves, but each pipe belonging to a particular rank is mounted on a stop channel through which air flows when the relevant stop is drawn. The pipes are connected to the stop channels by cone-shaped pallets which are held closed by the combined action of their weight and the wind pressure when a stop has been drawn (Figure 12.6). On depression of a key, each valve corresponding to that particular tone is forced open, allowing air to flow to the pipes. Note that valves will open regardless of whether or not there is wind in a particular stop channel. This requires additional effort from the player, and also makes the system rather noisy. When a single soft stop is played, the 'accompaniment' supplied by the opening and closing of all the other stops can be annoying. On the

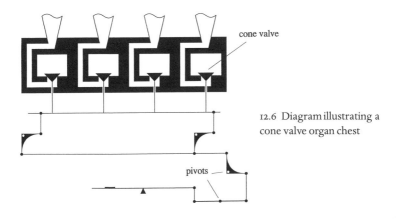

cone valve

12.6 Diagram illustrating a cone valve organ chest

pivots

other hand, cone valves have the advantage that they are relatively simple to construct and virtually eliminate problems of leakage.

Many organists and organ builders believe that eliminating the grooves has an adverse effect on tone quality. In the traditional slider chest, all the pipes which sound simultaneously when a key is depressed are fed from the same groove; the pipes are therefore coupled together by way of the air supply. It should be noted that all these pipes will have harmonically related pitches. Protagonists of the slider-chest system claim that this coupling affects the pipe resonances and aids in the blending of the sounds; this would appear to be possible, although there does not seem to be any scientific evidence in support of the hypothesis. Probably more important than such acoustic coupling is the fact that with the slider chest the pipes which sound simultaneously are all activated by a single pallet valve; they thus sound at the same instant and with the same attack, giving the player better control over the starting transient.

Pneumatic and electric actions

In very large organs, where the pipework may be a considerable distance from the keyboard, direct mechanical action becomes unwieldy and the keyboard touch unresponsive; this is particularly troublesome with the cone-chest system, in which valves have to be opened even though the pipe to which they were connected is not sounding. The problem may be addressed by introducing some form of subsidiary mechanism.

The 'Barker lever action' (patented in 1839) offers a means of lightening the playing touch. This is illustrated in Figure 12.7. The primary pallet on the wind

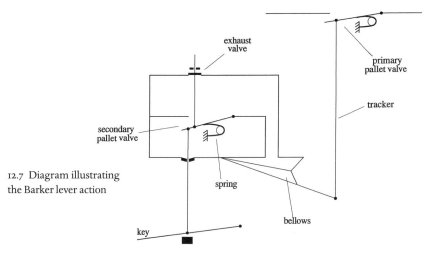

12.7 Diagram illustrating the Barker lever action

chest is regulated by a secondary bellows which is controlled by a relay valve, activated by the key. When the key is depressed, air is admitted through the secondary pallet valve to inflate the small bellows. The motion of the bellows draws down the tracker which is connected to the wind-chest pallet. On release of the key the bellows deflates, the air being emitted through the exhaust valve. The mechanism is placed as near as possible to the keyboard, at a position where the tracker is still in alignment with the keys. In this way a number of keyboards may be coupled together without increasing the key pressure.

With 'tubular pneumatic action' the keys are linked to the wind chest by lengths of thin tubing (traditionally lead), and thus restrictions on the relative positioning of keyboards and pipes are virtually eliminated. There are two relays in the wind chest, known as the 'primary motor' and 'secondary motor', the latter operating the main pallets which control the flow of air to the pipes. Two different arrangements are possible, known as 'pressure' and 'exhaust' systems.

In the pressure system, the key moves a pallet valve housed in what is known as the 'touch box'. On depression of the key, air under pressure in the touch box flows into the keyboard end of the pneumatic tubing, activating the primary motor at the other end. The primary motor is only required to operate a small valve, which in turn allows air to flow to and from the secondary motor. In this way the air flow through the pneumatic tubing is kept to a minimum and the pipe diameters can be correspondingly small. In the alternative exhaust system, depression of the key opens a pallet which allows pressurized air in the pneumatic tube to escape. The fall in pressure at the other end then activates the primary and secondary motors. Exhaust pneumatic systems are more reliable since the motors are internal; this protects them from dust and also makes them less noisy.

The commonly found 'membrane chest' uses cone valves operated by a pressure pneumatic system. A small pouch of leather or other membrane is placed below each valve pin. When a key is depressed, pressurized air in the pneumatic tubing opens a membrane-operated relay valve which allows air to flow to the membranes operating the main cone valves. All the valves associated with a particular note then open simultaneously in much the same way as with the Barker lever action. The relay valve is double-acting: when it closes off the incoming air, it simultaneously opens an exhaust channel to release the pressurized air in the membranes. Like the cone chest, the pressure-operated membrane chest just described suffers the disadvantage that on depression of a key all of the valves governed by that particular note are opened, regardless of whether or not their stop has been drawn.

'Electro-pneumatic action' goes one step further in removing the player from direct contact with the main pallets in the wind chest. In this case the primary and secondary pneumatic motors are retained, but the valve which controls the motion of the primary is moved by an electromagnet. Each key is fitted with a contact switch which completes an electrical circuit when the key is depressed and thus activates its own electromagnet.

In some modern organs registration changes are made with the aid of electrically driven solenoids, or pneumatic bellows activated by solenoids, even though the key action may be completely mechanical. In a slider-chest organ, for example, each slider will be drawn in or out by a solenoid or bellows attached to its end, brought into action by electrical switches operated by the stops on the console. Some organists feel that mechanizing the action of the stops in this way does not lead to any significant loss of control. The advantage is that complex registration changes can be brought about very rapidly with the aid of pistons. These are controls which are located at convenient positions around the console, mainly below the manuals. They are linked up to various combinations of solenoids according to a prescribed pattern, which can be set up by the organist in advance of a performance. This kind of stop control can be noisy and not quite instantaneous, particularly with the older systems, and many organists prefer the direct mechanical action.

Air supply

On very early organs air was normally supplied by way of hand-operated bellows. These were typically wedge-shaped, with one side fixed to the floor and the other moving up and down, pivoted about a hinge at the lower end. They were connected directly to the wind chest, the air pressure being determined by the weight of the top half of the bellows; additional weights could be added in order to create a higher pressure. To ensure continuity of flow at least two pairs of bellows were required, connected by non-return valves and recharged in succession by the organ-blower. From about the end of the eighteenth century most organs made use of a 'reservoir', which was in effect a secondary set of weighted bellows included in the air line between the hand-operated feeder bellows and the organ itself. The reservoir stabilized the air pressure and also made it possible to use a single pair of feeder bellows. The customary placing of the reservoir as near as possible to the organ minimized the loss of pressure in the pipework between the reservoir and the instrument, an important consideration in performing passages which required large amounts of air.

Nowadays electrically driven blowers are universally used; these are normally powered by constant-speed AC motors. There may be separate reservoirs for each division, allowing for the possibility that different divisions could operate at different pressures.

In most modern organs the pressure is regulated by devices known as 'schwimmers'. In one common form of this system, the bottom of each wind chest is a movable board (the schwimmer board), attached to the sides by a flexible seal; in

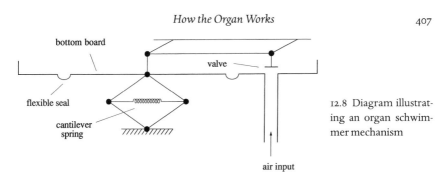

12.8 Diagram illustrating an organ schwimmer mechanism

effect the schwimmer board is the bottom plate of a bellows. Motion of the board operates a valve, so that when it rises air is allowed to flow into the chest. The board is held in position by springs, sometimes in a cantilever configuration as shown in Figure 12.8. When the air supply to the wind chest is switched on, the pressure inside forces down the board against the action of the spring, at the same time closing off the air-supply valve. When air is taken by the pipes, the pressure drops and the board rises under the action of the spring. This opens the valve, allowing air to flow into the chest, thus stabilizing the pressure and flow rate. A great advantage of this type of schwimmer mechanism is that it is located close to the pipes so its reaction is almost instantaneous. The alternative is for the schwimmers to be in the form of small separate wind chambers.

The pressure at which air is fed to a pipe is crucial in the determination of its tonal characteristics. Both voicing and pitch are radically affected by even small pressure changes. It is conventional to measure air pressures in an organ in millimetres of water. If a glass U-tube with one side connected to the air line is partly filled with water, the air pressure will force the water level in the connected side of the U-tube lower than the water level in the open side; the difference in heights of the water columns is then equal to the pressure (in millimetres of water). Organs of early design, and those with Spanish and Italian origins, often operate at pressures as low as 40 mm, giving them a gentle quality of tone; French and German organs tend to operate at rather higher pressures. Organs from the Romantic period are generally designed to generate much greater sound power, and typical air pressures are of the order of 100 mm or more. Hope Jones used a pressure of 140 mm for his diaphones, and in theatre organs the pressure may be 300 mm to 450 mm. The highest pressure in use in Britain today is probably the 1,270 mm on the Liverpool Cathedral Tuba Magna. In mechanical action organs the pressure must not be too high, or else the pallet valves will be difficult to open and the touch will be heavy.

Organ pipes and specification

As we have already seen in Section 12.1, organ pipes are of two types, flue pipes and reed pipes. Flue pipes are often classified as 'flute', 'principal', or 'string', depend-

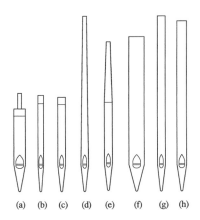

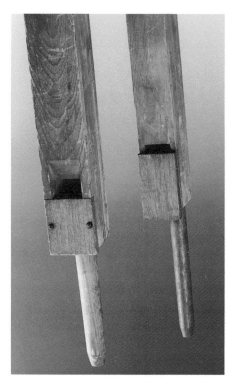

12.9 (Above) Relative dimensions of some common organ flue pipes. (a) rohrflöte; (b) quintadena; (c) gedackt; (d) spitzflöte; (e)spillflöte; (f) nachthorn; (g) salicet; (h) nomprinzipal

12.10 (Right) Photograph of the lower ends of two wooden organ flue pipes

ing on the ratio of pipe diameter to length. Flutes are the fattest pipes and have a correspondingly round sound, strong in fundamental. The strings are the thinnest, sounding with a much greater proportion of higher harmonics. Principals are of intermediate diameter, giving a fairly balanced distribution of harmonics, hence their generic name; these are the basic sound of the organ. Pipes may be either open or stopped, the stopped pipes being strong in odd-numbered harmonics like the clarinet and also half the length of an open pipe of the same pitch. In addition, there are tapered and chimneyed pipes. Tapered pipes open at the end (such as the Spitzflöte or Gemshorn) have similar characteristics to cylindrical open ones, the main difference being that the taper tends to strengthen the 2nd harmonic. If a chimney is fitted on the end, in the form of a cap with a narrow vent tube in it, then the pipe behaves like a closed cylindrical pipe, the main differences being that resonances of the vent tube can enhance higher harmonics of the main pipe, and the tendency for odd harmonics to be strong is lessened. There are many other possible pipe shapes; the Spillflöte, for example, has a cylindrical lower section and tapered top. Figure 12.9 shows some of the most commonly used flue pipes, scaled in size so that they all sound the same pitch. The majority of pipes are made of metal, but wooden ones are also quite common; Figure 12.10 shows two wooden flute pipes.

The Open Diapason, Principal, Twelfth, and Fifteenth are all normally open metal pipes of moderate scale, as are the mixtures; these produce a characteristic organ tone of which the ear does not tire. The Stopped Diapason is most commonly of wood, although it can also be of metal. Flutes can be of wood or metal, either open or stopped. A chorus of these at 8-foot, 4-foot, 2⅔-foot, 2-foot, and 1⅗-foot gives a beautiful and rich sound, known in France as the 'Jeu de Tierce'; it is also the basis of the Solo Cornet stop. In the Rohrflöte or Chimney Flute the stopped end is pierced by a narrow chimney, giving a slightly brighter sound.

Reed pipes also come in a wide variety of forms, some of the most common being shown in Figure 12.11. As we have seen in Section 12.1, with reed pipes the fundamental pitch is determined primarily, although not totally, by the resonant frequency of the tongue. The resonator may be tuned either to the fundamental or to one of the higher harmonics; hence the pitch of the pipe is not immediately apparent from the length of its resonator. In Figure 12.11, for example, the 4-foot Clarion is considerably longer than the 8-foot Regal. Very short resonators reinforce the upper harmonics only and their tuning is not critical; they are sometimes referred to as 'untuned resonators'. Long resonators tuned to the fundamental or 2nd harmonic, however, have a profound influence on the sound. The tuning of these is critical, so they are referred to as 'tuned resonators'.

The most common reed stop is the Trumpet 8-foot. This can be used as a solo

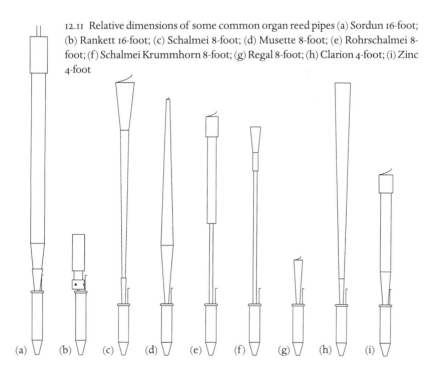

12.11 Relative dimensions of some common organ reed pipes (a) Sordun 16-foot; (b) Rankett 16-foot; (c) Schalmei 8-foot; (d) Musette 8-foot; (e) Rohrschalmei 8-foot; (f) Schalmei Krummhorn 8-foot; (g) Regal 8-foot; (h) Clarion 4-foot; (i) Zinc 4-foot

(a) (b) (c) (d) (e) (f) (g) (h) (i)

stop or, especially with its 4-foot counterpart the Clarion, for chords and full effects. The French Baroque masters played slow figures on these or other reed stops. Well-voiced rich and fiery Trumpets are one of the glories of organ sound. Another fine reed stop is the Crumhorn (or Cremona or Clarinet). This has half-length resonators and is placed on the Choir Organ; it is somewhat less powerful than the Trumpet. The reeds in the Swell Organ are typically a Trumpet and an Oboe 8-foot. The Vox Humana 8-foot, with quite short resonators, is another characteristic reed stop. The French place this stop on the Great Organ where it can be contrasted with the crumhorn on the Choir or the Oboe on the Swell.

As we have already seen, pipes of the same type are grouped together in ranks, normally sixty-one pipes for each rank, giving a five-octave span. These ranks can be played either separately or in combination with others. It is worth noting here that although the various ranks will be harmonically related (for example, a 4-foot rank could be added to an 8-foot rank since the pitch difference is exactly an octave), this is not quite the same as adding harmonics by pulling drawbars on a Hammond organ (see Chapter 13). In the case of the Hammond organ each of the constituent tones is a pure sine wave, whereas on the pipe organ each pipe within a given rank will generate its own complex pattern of harmonics. Thus adding the 4-foot rank to the 8-foot will have the effect of reinforcing not only the second harmonic, but also the fourth and other even harmonics of the 8-foot pipe.

It is not practicable to have separate ranks of pipes for very high harmonics, the upper limit being normally a 1-foot stop. The problem of adding brightness to the sound is addressed by having mixture stops, controlling several ranks of harmonically related pipes simultaneously. For example, the lowest note (C_2) on the keyboard might sound pipes of pitch G_4, C_5, and G_5 with a mixture stop. A point is soon reached in a mixture where the pipe lengths for the top notes are too short to be of any practical use. For example the open pipe length corresponding to the highest note on the keyboard (C_7) in the 1-foot register is less than 10 mm, with a pitch at the top of the audible range. To overcome this difficulty, a system known as 'breaking back' is adopted, in which at appropriate points in the register the smallest rank disappears and a larger one takes its place.

Stops which sound at a pitch designated by a different letter to that of the key being depressed on the keyboard are called 'mutations' (see Section 12.1). The primary mutations are the 3rd and 5th harmonics of the 8-foot pipes, designated 2⅔-foot and 1⅗-foot, sounding G_3 and E_4 respectively when the lowest note C_2 on the keyboard is played. These blend in with the 8-foot and 4-foot stops because of the harmonic relationship. A 2⅔-foot stop may sometimes be referred to as a Quint since it sounds at an octave plus a fifth above the written pitch. Likewise a 1⅗-foot stop may be referred to as a Tierce, since it sounds at the interval of two octaves plus a third, although this stop name is usually reserved for a flute-toned stop of this pitch.

The group of ranks controlled by one single manual is called a 'division', or occasionally an 'organ'; this latter name derives from the concept that a complete instrument is made up by combining a number of smaller organs. Each of the separately named divisions has its own wind chest. Two-manual organs normally have Pedal, Great, and Swell divisions. The Pedal division is controlled by the pedal board, laid out just like a normal keyboard but controlled by the player's feet. The Great is the chief division of the organ and contains the main principals. Ranks from the Swell division are contained within a shuttered box. Opening and closing of the shutters, which produces corresponding changes in dynamic level, is controlled by a swell pedal.

Larger organs may have more than two manuals. The third manual will typically be called the Choir; fourth and fifth manuals may be called Solo, Bombarde, or Echo. A Bombarde division, as the name implies, will consist of very powerful ranks, contrasting with the Echo, which has predominantly delicate tones. The solo ranks are principally designed for the playing of single-line melodies. Choir divisions generally have a relatively subdued sound. Confusion often arises between the terms 'Choir Organ' and 'Chair Organ', since the words are so similar. The Chair Organ, corresponding to the Positif in France and the Rückpositiv in Germany, originates from the idea of an "organ behind the bench", the pipework being behind the player. The Choir Organ is usually thought of as an organ for accompanying the choir. Nowadays the two terms are often taken as being synonymous.

The 'tremulant' is a device which causes fluctuations in wind pressure and gives a vibrato to the particular division of the organ on which it operates. Many different devices have been developed over the last four centuries. The most satisfactory ones generally make use of a small bellows which oscillates under the control of a weighted spring and delivers pulsations of air to the wind chest. The tremulant is normally incorporated into the Swell division and can be brought into action or turned off using a stop. French organs were frequently supplied with two tremulant stops, a mild one and a stronger one. On modern organs there may be controls for varying the amplitude and frequency of the tremulant.

It is clear from several explicit indications in early seventeenth-century Italian music that the tremulant was used as an expressive device in this period with a much slower rate of pulsation than that which became popular in the Romantic era. In the first half of the twentieth century forceful and very fast tremulants became associated with the cinema organ. The almost continuous use of this effect, combined with loud and reedy stop combinations, gave the most characteristic sound to that instrument; partly as a reaction, it fell out of favour amongst church organists. Nowadays, better acquaintance with the design of the early organ has led to a revival of more traditional designs which can give beautiful effects, especially with flutey and quieter combinations.

12.4 HOW AN ORGAN IS CONSTRUCTED

There have been several schools of organ-building, and the pipe organs of different European countries have their own characteristics. Rather than describe these
styles of organ with the brevity imposed by the length of a single chapter, we here
discuss in some detail the nineteenth-century English model, with occasional references to other traditions. This will give an impression of the factors which need
to be taken into consideration in designing a pipe organ.

By the very nature and size of the organ, the concepts involved in its construction are quite different from those which concern the maker of a flute or a violin.
Most organs, even those of modest size, are individually designed and built to fit
their permanent homes in churches, concert halls, or conservatoires. An organ
will represent an enormous investment for its owners, and several years of plan-
ning and design are not uncommon. Even as far back as the early 1800s a modest
three-manual parish church organ would have cost in the order of £500. Nowadays a similar instrument will cost around £100,000.

Positioning of the organ

Since organs are normally associated with either places of worship or prestigious
concert halls, their external design and positioning is of prime importance.
Indeed the organ is often considered to be a major architectural feature of the hall
or church in which it is placed.

Within a concert hall the positioning of the organ is not normally a problem. In
most cases it can be placed at the front of the room, behind and slightly above the
seats of the orchestra and chorus. The large blowing mechanism associated with
older organs is frequently housed beneath the stage area where the orchestra sits
or, if there is a basement, lower down in the building. With electromagnetic
action the console may be designed so that it is movable, although this trend has
now gone out of fashion.

The size and position of a church organ are related not only to the architecture
of the building but also to the function of the instrument in the liturgy; the overall acoustical effect in relation both to the choir and to the congregation requires
careful consideration. In the Middle Ages positioning was less of a problem
because the organs were small in size and indeed often portable. Cathedral
builders in the Middle Ages would not have anticipated that organs could reach
the enormous size we are accustomed to today, and therefore did not make any
substantive provision for the organ in their architectural layout.

In the sixteenth century in English parish churches, a small organ used for alternating with plainsong or accompanying the choir in an anthem was often placed

in the rood loft over the screen separating the chancel from the nave. In the eighteenth century, when the organ accompanied hearty congregational metrical psalm-singing and played spectacular voluntaries on several manuals, it was much larger, and usually placed in a west gallery. It should be noted here that early churches in England and on the continent were traditionally built facing east, nominally towards Jerusalem, so the altar was at the east end. In cathedrals and college chapels (such as Kings College, Cambridge) in the seventeenth and eighteenth centuries the organ was normally placed on the large screen between the choir and nave; it had two fronts facing east and west, and commonly had enough large pipes for two Open Diapasons on the Great. The principal front with its Chair Organ faced east into the choir.

In Germany, where there was frequently a sizeable orchestra as well as a choir, the organ was normally in a large west gallery. With this arrangement the sound has an unobstructed path into the main body of the church, although it reaches the congregation from behind. Some churches, particularly those of Gothic design, have a large window at the west end, which causes an architectural problem if the organ is to be sited here. This problem can sometimes be overcome by splitting the organ so that the two halves lie on either side of the window. It is still possible to use tracker action in this situation, but electro-pneumatic action gives a much simpler solution.

Clearly there is no single solution to the problem of organ location, and the position chosen must always be specific to the particular church or concert hall in question. It is important that the air supply should always come from the interior of the church or concert hall. If air is drawn in from the outside then temperature and humidity changes will cause problems. Air intakes are usually fitted with filter units; these were particularly important features of the early cinema organs, which often had to operate in smoke-filled auditoria.

Layout and mechanism

With the advent of electro-pneumatic action the organ designer was confronted with an almost limitless number of design possibilities. This led to organs of extravagant specification and elaborate layout. Designers often went for a totally open or semi-cased arrangement of the pipes; an example is the Royal Festival Hall organ, built in 1954, where the pipes span the complete width of the auditorium. As we have seen, modern organ designers have returned to mechanical action which favours a simple compact layout.

In a mechanical-action organ the design and construction of the action is extremely important since this, to a large extent, determines the responsiveness of the overall mechanism. In order to keep the touch light and its response rapid, rollers need to be as light as possible; they are now usually made from aluminium

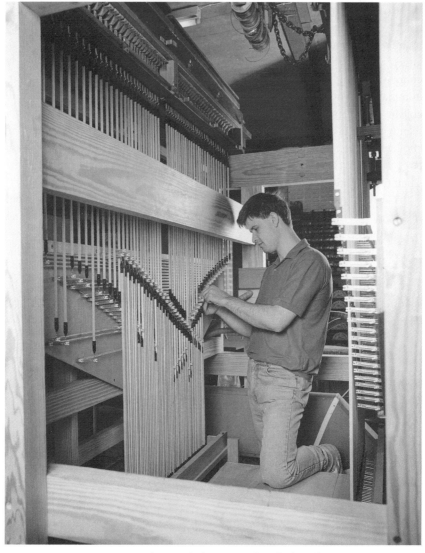

12.12 Final stage of adjustment of a roller board

or aluminium alloy. A differential leverage of typically 3 : 2 is incorporated into the roller mechanism. Rollers rotate on bearings which are screwed to the roller board; the use of modern synthetic materials for the bearings allows friction losses to be kept low without the need for lubrication. The roller board, on which all the roller mechanism is mounted, must be made from a wood that will not warp, otherwise the mechanism can become stressed. Plywood satisfies this requirement. Figure 12.12 shows the final stage of adjustment of a roller board.

A typical layout for a modestly sized church organ is shown in Figure 12.13. In this example there are two manuals operating the Great and Swell divisions, plus the Pedal division. The pipes of the Great division occupy the central position and are displayed to the congregation with the Pedal pipes at the side. In this case the Swell division is behind the Great with the movable shutters at the front, out of view of the listener; a commonly used alternative is to have the Swell in an elevated position above the Great.

The casing of the pipework and the spacing of the pipes inside is important for optimum tone quality. Generally speaking organs sound best when they are encased at the back, rather than being open on all sides, since the case helps to project the sound to the listeners. Having a stone wall behind the organ is considered good. Within the casing the pipes themselves should not be placed too close together, otherwise interference effects can spoil the sound. Such interference can arise either from the strong local sound fields around the pipes or from interactions between the air flows to adjacent pipes.

It is common practice to arrange pipes on a chest so that the largest ones are shared between the two ends. This halves the weight on one end of the wind chest. The arrangement of pipes at the front of the organ is also important to the overall appearance of the instrument. Some classical ways of arranging the front

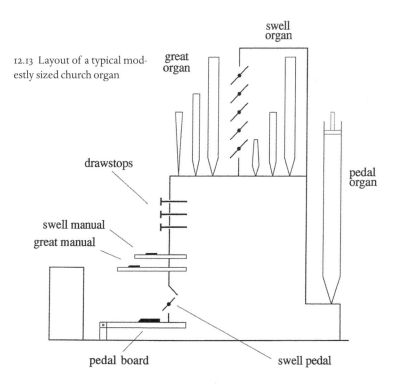

12.13 Layout of a typical modestly sized church organ

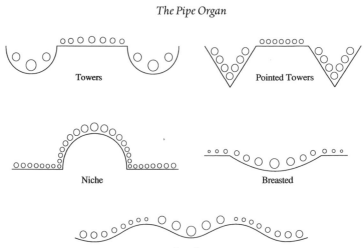

12.14 Some classical ways of arranging the front pipes on an organ

pipes are shown in Figure 12.14. The front pipes are normally ordered in succession in each half of the case. Thus, if the pipes on the left-hand side are C, D, E, etc. respectively, the pipes in the corresponding positions on the right-hand side would be C♯, D♯, F, and so forth. Pipes of only a semitone difference in pitch have very similar lengths and so the overall appearance is one of symmetry. Sometimes the symmetry is strengthened by making corresponding pipes on either side (for example the C and C♯) of precisely the same length. The longer pipe is then brought to the correct pitch by cutting an opening in the back at the top of the pipe, which effectively shortens its length.

Making and voicing organ pipes

Over the course of history a remarkable variety of materials has been used in the construction of organ pipes, including glass, porcelain, and even paper. Nowadays it is standard to use either metal or wood. By far the most common organ pipe metal is a mixture of tin and lead. The tin content varies considerably, from about 30 per cent to 90 per cent. If the tin content is above 75 per cent the alloy is generally referred to as 'tin'. This is the most highly prized metal for organ pipes, but can not always be used because of the high cost of pure tin. Tin is very ductile, and stands up to being bent many times over the years in the tuning process without cracking. It is relatively inert and resistant to attack by chemicals in the air, so it retains its lustrous appearance over long periods although, when placed in oak rackboards, tin pipes will eventually be eaten away by acid in the wood.

'Metal' is a technical term used by organ builders for a mixture of tin and lead, and is generally used to signify an alloy with approximately equal amounts of the two metals. In England especially, so-called 'spotted metal' is commonly used; this is a lead–tin alloy with about 30 per cent tin content. Sheets of spotted metal have a mottled pattern on the surface which comes about naturally in the casting process as the molten metal cools. Lead by itself is hardly ever used because its extreme softness would mean that very thick metal gauge would be required, making the pipes excessively heavy. Zinc is sometimes used for the largest pipes, being cheaper than the lead–tin alloys, but the tone quality is often considered inferior.

Metal organ pipes are generally made from seamed sheets. The first step in the construction process is the casting of the sheets. Once cast, lead–tin alloy sheets may be thinned down to the prescribed thickness by scraping, a process referred to as 'planing', before being cut into their required shapes; it should be remembered here that these metals are quite soft and can easily be cut with a sharp steel knife. Each cut sheet is then worked around a mandrel to give it its final shape, and the edges are soldered together. The soldering requires considerable skill because it is very easy to fuse the metal in the process, particularly if the tin content is high. Pipes are generally made slightly longer than required so that the voicer has room for adjustment. This also applies to the upper lip, which will have to be cut away in the voicing process.

Well-made wooden pipes may last longer and give better service than inferior metal ones. Whereas metal pipes are often made by specialist firms, wooden pipes are usually made by the organ builder himself. The construction techniques and tools employed are essentially those of conventional joinery, but considerable care has to be taken in the precision of the cutting and the choice of wood. Canadian pine is a common choice of wood, but others such as oak, cedar, deal, or even mahogany may be used. Proper seasoning is of great importance since even slight cracking or warping, causing glued seams to open, will prevent the pipe from sounding.

Before being incorporated into the organ each pipe needs to be individually 'voiced', an art which requires considerable experience and skill. An organ builder will generally have a bench set up for this task, with an appropriate wind supply to which the pipes can be connected. The process of voicing involves fine adjustments to the pipe mouth and foot hole to ensure that the pipe speaks readily and with the required timbre. Voicing is particularly important on the larger pipes; these may not produce a note at all when unvoiced.

On a metal pipe, the first task of the voicer is to open or close the hole in the foot to achieve the desired rate of air flow through the pipe. The next step is to set the correct distance between the upper and lower lips, which is done by cutting back the upper lip to the required level with a sharp knife. Typically 'one fifth cut-up' is used, meaning that the distance between the lips is one fifth of the pipe diameter. This is set using a pair of proportional dividers; one end of the dividers is set to the pipe diameter whilst the other end is used to scribe a line on the upper lip, indicating where the cut must be made. Fine adjustments to the lips are then carried out by bending the metal with a purpose-made voicing tool; the languid (see Figure 12.1) may also be bent slightly in order to redirect the air stream. Throughout the process the pipe is repeatedly sounded and adjustments made until it speaks to the voicer's satisfaction. Final adjustments may need to be made when the pipe is installed on the actual organ; Figure 12.15 shows this task being carried out. Wooden pipes do not generally require extensive voicing because they can be made fairly precisely to the optimum shape, but fine adjustments can be made using sandpaper.

The manner in which a pipe is voiced affects the sound quality to a degree that is immediately apparent to the listener. Over the last three centuries or so the practice of 'nicking' the languid has become common practice. Nicking involves cutting notches along the edge of the languid and in some cases along the inside of the lower lip. This stabilizes the jet and has the effect of making the pipe speak more predictably; it also reduces the strength of upper harmonics. The severity with which pipes are nicked varies considerably but generally it is heaviest on the larger pipes. Heavy nicking of the languid is seen on the pipe pictured in Figure 12.2.

12.15 Voicing an organ flue pipe

On early organs the pipes were not nicked, with the result that the sound started with a characteristic transient, rich in upper harmonics, giving an interesting and musical attack to the note. The revival of Classical concepts of organ design during the middle part of the twentieth century brought about a demand for Classical voicing without nicking; it was felt by many organists that nicked pipes had an uninteresting sound. However, nowadays a compromise stance is often taken in which only the lightest of nicking is used. Even five or six very light nicks on the languid can, however, significantly alter the sound. On wooden pipes the nicking process involves scribing notches into the block. When the sound starts with an overemphatic 'chiff' or 'cough' it is usually a sign of poor voicing.

Room acoustics

With any musical instrument, the sound heard by both the listener and the player depends to a large extent on the acoustics of the room or auditorium. In the case of the organ this is particularly relevant since the instrument is normally permanently installed within the architectural environment. An examination of the room acoustics is in fact the first task of the organ builder. For a detailed examination of this topic the reader is referred to *The Musicians Guide to Acoustics* by Campbell and Greated. Here we will just discuss briefly the most important parameter describing the acoustical response of a room: the reverberation time.

Enter an empty church or hall and clap your hands. The clapping motion is completed in a small fraction of a second, but the sound rings on for a time which depends on the acoustical properties of the room. The reverberation time is defined as the time it takes for the sound intensity to diminish from its peak value by a factor of one million (i.e. for the sound pressure level to fall by 60 db). A rough guide to the value of the reverberation time in a particular hall can be obtained by creating a loud sound and estimating the time taken for it to die into inaudibility. Electronic instruments are available which can measure the decay rate and give an accurate measure of this parameter; it can also be calculated from the architectural specifications of the hall. A large concert hall or church can have a reverberation time of several seconds, so it can be seen that the effect on the performance of a piece of music is very significant.

Concerning the impact of room acoustics on organ construction there are a few points worth noting. First of all the sound intensity in a room varies in direct proportion to the reverberation time divided by the room volume. An organ will therefore sound loudest in a small but very reverberant room and softest in a large acoustically dead room. In the latter case it would be necessary to install an organ with a large number of ranks, or alternatively operate at high wind pressure, in order to achieve an acceptable level of sound. The value of the reverberation time depends on the amount of absorbent material in the room and covering the walls, floor, and ceiling. Certain types of material preferentially absorb particular frequency bands: heavy carpet on a hard floor tends to absorb the high frequencies most, whereas large glass windows and wood-panelling are more absorbent at low frequencies. The effect of this is that reverberation time varies with frequency. The McEwan Hall in Edinburgh, which houses a Hope Jones organ, may be taken as an example. This is a large and very resonant hall with a high domed roof and wooden seating. Measured reverberation times with the hall empty are as follows: 2.4 s at 125 Hz, 2.7 s at 250 Hz, 3.9 s at 500 Hz, 4.8 s at 1,000 Hz and 4.4 s at 2,000 Hz. The fact that there are expansive areas of wood-panelling on the walls is probably the major factor here which causes the low-frequency reverberation times to be less than the high-frequency ones.

Changes in reverberation time with frequency must be borne in mind when balancing the power of the pipes in the different registers. Another factor of great significance is the effect of the audience in adding to the sound absorption in the hall. An occupied room will generally have a considerably lower reverberation time than an empty one. This problem has been partly overcome in many new concert halls by the use of padded seats which absorb essentially the same amount of sound whether they are occupied or not. Finally, in very large rooms such as cathedrals the absorption of the air itself can be significant. Air preferentially absorbs sound at the high-frequency end of the spectrum, causing a reduction in reverberation time in this region. Because air absorption is proportional to the volume of the hall, while the other causes of absorption are related to the internal surface area, it is only for the largest spaces that air absorption becomes important.

12.5 TECHNIQUES OF ORGAN-PLAYING

Playing characteristics of the organ

The most important characteristic of the pipe organ, from the point of view of playing technique, is that it can sustain a sound indefinitely, and at constant volume, whilst a key is depressed. Once the key is released, however, the sound dies almost immediately. In fact it will ring on for a fraction of a second after the air has stopped, in much the same way that a harpsichord string will continue to sound for a short while after it has been damped, but this effect is only significant on the lower-pitched pipes. This may be contrasted with the electronic organ or piano, where the sound can be made to sustain for a considerable time after the finger has been taken off the key. The lack of sustaining power of the organ, after key release, has important implications for fingering. A newcomer to the organ who has been used to the piano is often surprised at the number of times it is necessary to change fingers on the same note in order to produce a smooth melodic line. A commonly encountered example where finger substitution may be required is in the playing of consecutive thirds. It goes without saying that attention must be paid to the room acoustics in deciding how much detachment there should be between notes. This applies to any instrument but is particularly relevant to the organ since many organs are installed in rooms with very long reverberation times.

The organ may also be likened to the harpsichord in the way that its dynamic levels are 'terraced'. Unlike the piano, on which the loudness is touch-sensitive, the organ sounds at the same volume regardless of how vigorously the keys are struck. The volume can only be altered by changing the registration or by using the swell pedal. On the organ it is possible to achieve an almost perfect legato, provided that appropriate fingerings are available; in this respect it differs markedly from the stringed keyboard instruments. Since the sound of a note does not die away after the key has been struck, the volume at the start can be almost exactly matched to the volume at the end of the previous note. In judging the timing of notes the player has to be aware of the three separate phases in the sounding of a pipe: the starting transient, the steady sound, and the decay transient. Sometimes the steady sound is referred to as the 'vowel', in analogy with the speech sound of this name which is produced by the unimpeded passage of air through the vocal tract. The starting transient is then referred to as the 'consonant'. On a mechanical action organ both the first and last phases can be controlled to a certain extent by the player, who can allow the pallet valves to open or close more or less slowly under the action of the key. However, the length of the starting transient is also highly dependent on the pipe design and voicing, and a good player adjusts his touch accordingly. In general, large pipes have a longer starting transient.

Because the organ is not touch-sensitive to loudness, the player has to shape phrases through a subtle use of the time dimension. On stringed keyboard instruments the natural dying of each note gives fresh impetus to the sound of the following note. Thus the stringed instrument has an advantage over the organ when it comes to the projection of fast passages and arpeggios. These can be particularly troublesome on an organ in a very reverberant room. The organist frequently makes use of miniscule silences between notes in order to allow the three phases of the pipe sound to come through cleanly; this type of touch is referred to as 'détaché'. 'Staccato', where the key is released immediately the vowel sound is established, is in effect the most extreme form of détaché playing. In staccato playing care must be taken that the vowel sound has time to establish itself before it is cut off, otherwise only the starting transient will be heard.

A unique feature of the organ is that a number of parts can be played at the same time, each having its own independent tonal characteristic. This immediately raises the question of independence of the hands and feet, one of the most difficult parts of organ technique to master. It is quite common for the organist to be required to play three separate melodies simultaneously, one in the left hand, one in the right, and a third on the pedals. This arises, for example, in the Trio Sonatas by J. S. Bach (Figure 12.16).

12.16 Excerpt from Trio Sonata No. 1 by J. S. Bach

Registration

Registration (the selection and manipulation of stops) is an important aspect of organ technique. Generally speaking, registration is not altered on a division whilst it is being sounded, since this would lead to notes with poorly defined timing. Music will be played on one manual whilst the registration is being changed on another; in this way the start or end of a note is always governed by the depression or release of a key, as opposed to the drawing or return of a stop. Modern organs often have pistons operated either by the foot or the thumb which will allow the organist to implement certain prescribed combinations of stops with a single movement.

Before the eighteenth century it was not common for any registration marks to be given on organ music. Early registration markings were usually of a very general nature, for example 'Organo Pleno' ('Plein Jeu' in French), or 'Full Organ'. It was not until about the middle of the nineteenth century that more specific instructions became commonplace. Today, composers have differing views on the extent to which detailed registrations should be marked on the score. Some composers, who are often organists themselves, will mark in every stop in detail; a difficulty here is that organs differ greatly in their stop specifications. Other composers prefer to leave the player the freedom to choose appropriate stops. Registrations used on early hand-blown organs were limited to some extent by the availability of wind; it would usually have been impossible, for example, to have had all the stops sounding together.

In order to obtain the most satisfactory registrations, the organist must be familiar with the sounds and strengths of all the various stops and how they combine. The number of different stops, however, is vast, ranging from the very soft Vox Angelica to the chorus reeds at the other end of the dynamic scale. It is possible, however, to group together stops which have similar sounds. Some basic groupings are as follows:

Foundation: These are the medium-bore flue pipes, either open or stopped, which form the basic sound of the organ and are of unison (8-foot) pitch. They are sometimes referred to as diapasons.

Chorus: Chorus stops are open metal pipes of normal or principal scale which are added to the diapasons to increase power and build up to Full Organ.

Flutes: These are wide-bore (large scale) open flue pipes, with titles such as Blockflöte and Spitzflöte. They have a wide range of dynamics, and their spectra are characterized by a strong fundamental component.

Stopped flutes: Gedeckt, Bourdon, and other stopped flutes are relatively soft, never sounding louder than forte.

Half-stopped flutes: Flutes whose upper ends have stoppers pierced by chimneys, such as the Rohrflöte, have a dynamic level normally below mezzoforte, and a timbre more coloured than the completely stopped flutes.

Strings: These are narrow-bore (small-scale) flue pipes, and are less common than the flutes or diapasons. Apart from the Salicional, they are nearly all named after string instruments. They have a very bright tone and cover a wide dynamic range.

Chorus reeds: These loud reed pipes are all named after brass instruments, except for Bombarde.

Semichorus reeds: These are reed pipes with short resonators, mostly rather soft and never louder than forte.

Imitative reeds: These are designed to imitate instruments from the orchestra, the most common examples being Oboe, Bassoon, and Clarinet.

Céleste: This is usually formed from a combination of two string ranks tuned to very slightly different frequencies; the resultant beating gives a gentle vibrato.

Mixtures: Mixture stops select combinations of ranks giving a balanced cluster of high partials. They are used in combination with other stops to generate a bright festive tone colour.

The basic stop combination, which is the foundation for most other combinations, is the Open Diapason 8-foot together with the Stopped Diapason 8-foot. This full warm sound can be used on its own for slow, fairly soft pieces and for accompaniment. For successively louder effects the two diapasons can be augmented by the Principal 4-foot; the Twelfth 2⅔-foot and Fifteenth 2-foot Mixture; the Sharp Mixture; the Cymbal; and finally the Double Open Diapason and/or the Bourdon 16-foot.

Pedalling

Organ pedal boards vary considerably. On old organs the pedals were often simply a set of short parallel levers protruding from the bottom of the case; on modern organs they are much longer. In most Western European countries the parallel layout of pedals has been retained; in Britain and the United States, on the other hand, the standard pedal board is concave, and the pedals radiate outwards from an imaginary centre behind the player. The disposition of the pedal levers is similar to that of a keyboard; Figure 12.17 shows the layout of a modern British pedal board. Notice that the spacing between each of the adjacent pedals is the same, in contrast to the keyboard where the spacing between the black notes is larger than between the white ones. The result of this is that on the pedal board there are considerably larger gaps between the groups of accidentals, which helps the player in locating the foot position by feel. The normal range is two and a half octaves, from written C_2 to F_4 or G_4.

The first stage in learning pedal technique is to gain familiarity with the pedal board so that notes can be located entirely by feel, without reliance on sight. In the Baroque period the toes were used almost exclusively for the execution of pedal passages, the most common procedure being to alternate left and right feet. This type of procedure was well suited to the short parallel pedals of the period. Indeed on modern small electronic organs, with only one octave of pedals, all the notes

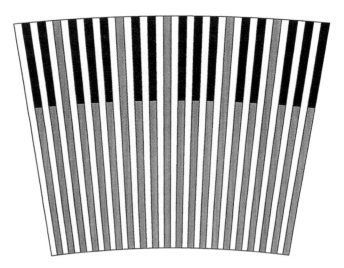

12.17 Layout of the modern British pedal board

are normally played with the toes of the left foot. In this case, however, maintaining a legato line is not a problem because a sustain facility is incorporated into the electronic circuitry. On modern pipe organs the pedals are played with both left and right foot toes and heels, although the heels do not play black notes. In scale passages it is normal to play a few notes alternating the toe and heel of one foot, and then to change to the other foot. In order to maintain a legato line it is sometimes necessary to substitute a heel for a toe, a toe for a heel, or one foot for another; it is also possible to slide with the toe from a black key to an adjacent black or white key. Two-note chords of a second or third can be played with a single foot. Thus quite complicated polyphony can be written for the pedals.

It is important for the organist to have suitable footwear. Relatively thin leather soles are considered ideal so that the feet can easily slide on the wooden pedals.

Notation

Organ music is normally written on three staves with the lowest stave representing the pedal part. The upper two staves are used for the parts played by the two hands in the same way as the piano. The two upper staves can also be used to signify separate manuals. Changes of manual are either represented by name or by Roman numerals, I being the lowest manual. Registration instructions are written above the staves which they affect, with + and – signs indicating that a stop has to be added or subtracted from an existing combination.

On the pedal board, use of the heel is occasionally indicated by U (or sometimes O) and the toe by the symbol ∧. When written above the stave or note these refer to the right foot and when written below they indicate the left foot. Substitution or sliding of the foot is indicated by the use of two symbols together, joined by a line or a slur. Thus ∧–U written above the line would mean substitute the right heel for the right toe, whereas U–∧ written below the line would mean substitute the left toe for the left heel. ∧–∧ indicates that the toe must slide from the first note to the second. When changes of foot are involved the two symbols are written at different levels with the right foot at the higher level. Thus ∧/∧ written below the stave would mean that the right toe is substituted for the left toe, whereas U//∧ written above the stave would mean that the left toe is substituted for the right heel. As an example of how the notation is used, Figure 12.18 shows the pedalling given by C. H. Trevor for a study by Heinrich Reimann.

Avant-garde techniques

Few avant-garde techniques have been developed for the organ. The most common one is the use of cluster tones either on the manuals or on the foot pedals. Quite large cluster tones can be played on the pedal board with a single foot.

12.18 Pedalling instructions given by C. H. Trevor for a study by Heinrich Reimann

An interesting effect can be obtained by turning off the blower during the course of a performance. When the air-flow rate drops below a certain value flue pipes will cease to speak normally, producing instead whistle tones. The overall effect is a gradual diminuendo combined with a downwards glissando, somewhat reminiscent of a bagpipe deflating, together with various extraneous sounds as the individual pipes cut out.

Cinema organ techniques

Playing technique on the cinema organ is essentially the same as for more traditional instruments, and indeed many cinema organists are accomplished performers on the church organ. However, there are some features which are special to the cinema, and which require a different approach. Most importantly it must be remembered that the cinema organ is designed to be a one-man orchestra, and the player in general strives to imitate the sounds of conventional acoustic instruments within the orchestra. This is not the case with the church organ. Thus the approach to the use of the tremulant, for example, is quite different. Orthodox church organists often entirely avoid the tremulant, whereas on the cinema organ it is a vital and integral part of the sound. Even small cinema organs will have at least two tremulants with a range of settings for frequency and amplitude. Large organs may have as many as ten tremulants, although generally only three or four would be used at any one time. A point worth noting here is that the reverberation time in a cinema auditorium is considerably less than in a church of similar size, because of the high absorption of padded seats, carpets, and curtains. Under these conditions the sound of an organ is considerably enlivened by the use of tremulants.

In taking on the role of the full orchestra the cinema organist has to be particularly adept at bringing about rapid changes in registration. To this end, cinema organs have tabs for bringing in the various sounds, rather than the more cumbersome stops which are characteristic of the church organ. Tabs are simply switches which are designed in such a way that they can be rapidly flicked down to the on position or brought back up by the touch of a finger. They are arranged in rows, and are normally coloured in order to aid location. Complicated combinations of tabs can be brought into action with pistons; the combinations are set in advance by a switchboard which is frequently set in the back of the console. Many organs are also fitted with a crescendo pedal which gradually adds in all the stops one by one until the full organ setting is reached. An indicator is usually provided on the console showing which stops have been brought in by the crescendo pedal.

One of the more interesting techniques used by the cinema organist is the glissando. This does not require any mechanical aids, but is executed purely by finger work. The performer plays up a chromatic scale rapidly with the tremulant on full amplitude; the listener hears this as a continuous portamento, the individual notes being undetectable. The glissando is only fully effective on the Tibia Clausa, or a stop combination where this tone is dominant. The tremulant is not as effective on other pipes so the pitches do not run together as well.

Finally, the organist must be at home with the mechanism known as second touch, since this is often required in order to play a melody and an accompaniment with one hand on a single manual. When normal pressure is exerted on a key it depresses to the first touch, sounding a prescribed stop combination. If heavier pressure is exerted the key overcomes a spring and depresses to the second touch, about 3 mm lower; this can be set to a different stop combination. In his book *The Cinema Organ* Reginald Foort cites 'In a Persian Market' as a piece in which he used this technique to good effect. Towards the end of the piece he would play both the tune and the accompaniment with the left hand, leaving the right hand free to add decorative chords on the glockenspiel on another manual.

13

Electroacoustic, Electromechanical, and Electronic Instruments

The electrophone class of musical instruments is now very large and multi-faceted, and the structure of this chapter is consequently somewhat different from those describing instruments in the other four major classes. Section 13.1 treats the acoustical principles associated with the electroacoustic sub-group: the electronic detection of sound waves and mechanical vibrations, the amplification and modification of these signals, and their subsequent conversion into sound through loudspeakers. Section 13.2 briefly surveys the explosive growth of electrically based instruments during the twentieth century, including the development of electromechanical and early electronic instruments. Section 13.3 deals with purely electronic techniques for generating musically useful signals, and reviews the different methods now available for sound synthesis. Section 13.4 is concerned with electronic music control techniques. Finally, Section 13.5 surveys the rapidly changing field of electronic music performance practice.

13.1 ELECTROACOUSTIC PRINCIPLES

Amplification of either the sound waves or the mechanical vibrations produced by a musical instrument requires three stages: transducer, amplifier, loudspeaker. Each of these three will be considered separately in this chapter. A transducer transforms mechanical or sound energy into electrical energy and in the musical context will be either a microphone or a pickup: a microphone responds to sound waves and a pickup responds to mechanical oscillations. The amplifier's purpose is to increase the power of an electrical signal, and in dealing with it we will take on board a range of devices which are frequently used for modifying the signal, for example reverberation and various special effects. The loudspeaker performs the inverse function to the microphone in that it converts electrical energy into sound waves. The characteristics of the loudspeaker can be of considerable significance and indeed a special purpose speaker, such as a Leslie speaker (to be discussed later in this section), may well form part of the instrument itself.

Microphones

Using a microphone-amplifier-loudspeaker system to increase the sound level from a standard acoustic instrument may well be the simplest means of obtaining high-quality reproduction. This is commonly referred to as a 'public address' (or PA) system. Although using a PA system is straightforward in principle, obtaining high-quality reproduction may be no simple matter.

There are two stages involved in the transformation of sound waves into an electrical signal. First, the pressure fluctuations in the air are made to move a very light diaphragm; secondly, the motions of the diaphragm are converted into an electrical signal. Considering the first of these, there are basically two different modes of operation. The diaphragm may be made as one side of a small box, so that it is exposed to the sound waves on only one side, the inner side being closed off by the other surfaces of the box. This is referred to as 'pressure operation', since the diaphragm moves with the pressure fluctuations on the outside of the box. The essential feature of the pressure microphone is that it is omnidirectional, responding equally to sound coming from any direction. The reason for this is that pressure is a scalar quantity, which means that its value is independent of direction.

In practice the directional characteristics of a pressure microphone are influenced by the shape of the casing. Low-frequency waves are unaffected but high-frequency ones will have wavelengths that are comparable in magnitude to the casing size, resulting in attenuation of waves coming from the back. Thus the microphone is omnidirectional for low frequencies but at high frequencies it is most sensitive to waves travelling directly towards the diaphragm. Typically, a microphone would be essentially omnidirectional at 1 kHz but significantly front-biased at 10 kHz. In the second type of microphone, known as a 'pressure gradient' or velocity microphone, the diaphragm is open to the sound waves on both sides. The difference in pressure between the two sides then determines the overall force on the diaphragm at any instant. This type of microphone is most sensitive to sound waves coming from either front or back and is referred to as bidirectional.

The sensitivity of a microphone to sound waves coming from different directions can be represented by a graph known as a 'polar sensitivity plot' (Figure 13.1). For an omnidirectional microphone the plot at low frequencies is a circle, whereas at higher frequencies it bulges in the direction perpendicular to the diaphragm, indicating increased sensitivity for high-pitched sound incident directly on the diaphragm. In the case of the bidirectional microphone the polar plot takes the form of a figure of eight, showing high sensitivity in two diametrically opposite directions perpendicular to the diaphragm but a theoretical zero sensitivity for sound arriving from the sides. Most microphones used for musical applications are designed so that they combine both omnidirectional and bidirectional characteristics. This can be done by suitable choice of case geometry and insertion of appropriate sound-absorbing pads. If the two are combined in equal proportions then the resulting polar diagram takes on a heart shape; such microphones are therefore referred to as 'cardioid'.

When a microphone is used at some distance from an instrument it will pick up reverberant sound coming from all directions, due to the reflections from the walls, in addition to the direct sound. The omnidirectional microphone picks up more reverberant sound because it is sensitive in all directions; it therefore needs to be placed nearer to the instrument than either the bi-directional or cardioid type to give a predetermined balance of direct and reverberant sound.

At very close distances (less than one wavelength) bidirectional and cardioid microphones tend to show a 'proximity effect', whereby the low frequencies are accentuated. Omnidirectional microphones do not show this to any extent and are therefore often recommended for close-up work.

Turning now to the methods of converting the diaphragm vibrations into electrical energy, we find two different principles of operation in common use: magnetic (sometimes termed dynamic) and electrostatic. There are two types of microphones operating on the magnetic principle: 'moving coil' and 'ribbon'. Electrostatic microphones are either of the 'condenser' or 'electret' type. Other principles of operation are also used, but not usually for high-quality music reproduction. For example, early telephone receivers used carbon granules packed behind the diaphragm, working on the principle that the electrical resistance var-

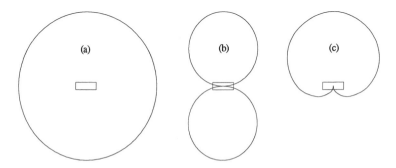

13.1 Polar sensitivity plots for microphones: (a)omnidirectional; (b) bidirectional; (c) cardioid. In each plot, the distance of the line from the centre of the microphone in a given direction represents the sensitivity in that direction

ied with contact pressure. Microphones used in cheap tape recorders frequently make use of the piezoelectric effect in crystals.

In the moving coil microphone a coil of wire is fixed to the back of the diaphragm and moves within an annular slot in a high field stationary permanent magnet. As the diaphragm moves, the coiled wire is made to move through the field lines of the magnet, inducing a current in the wire. Normally a transformer is included in the microphone in order to increase its impedance so that it matches the amplifier input. The voltage output of a moving coil microphone for a given sound level is quite low; on the other hand, it tends not to pick up a lot of mechanical noise, making it very suitable for general purpose use. In principle, moving coil microphones are pressure-operated and therefore omnidirectional, but several commercially available types have casing designs which result in unidirectional or cardioid characteristics.

Instead of the usual circular diaphragm, the ribbon microphone uses a thin strip of conducting metal foil held under tension within the field of a permanent magnet. The ribbon takes the place of both the coil of wire and the diaphragm in the moving coil microphone. It is so light that it gives very good frequency response, but tends to be prone to interference effects from mechanical vibrations. Ribbon microphones are normally open at both sides and are pressure-gradient operated, so they have a figure-of-eight response pattern. However, this is often modified to unidirectional by inserting pads on one side of the ribbon.

Condenser (or capacitor) microphones operate on the electrostatic principle. They tend to be expensive but are often of very high quality. The thin diaphragm forms one pole of a capacitor, the other being a rigid backplate placed a short distance away and arranged in such a way that the whole unit is in the form of a small capsule. The capacitor forms one component in an electrical circuit, which maintains a steady polarizing voltage across it. When the diaphragm vibrates the capacitance varies and a fluctuating output current is generated. Since the sensitivity is very low, a preamplifier is normally incorporated into the housing.

Some condenser microphones are constructed with effectively two capsules placed back-to-back. The sensitivity of a capsule is proportional to the polarizing voltage, so by switching appropriate voltages on the two capsules it is possible to obtain a range of directional characteristics.

A disadvantage of the condenser microphone is that it requires a power supply, both to generate the polarizing voltage and to power the preamplifier. This problem is overcome in the electret microphone, in which the diaphragm is made from a material (known as an electret) which can permanently sustain an electric charge. Electret microphones usually have a small battery-operated preamplifier built into the casing. They are often quite cheap and of good quality but their directional patterns cannot be altered by switching.

One of the major difficulties in using a microphone to amplify a musical instrument is avoiding 'acoustic feedback', the ear-piercing shriek often heard when the amateur is setting up a system. Feedback arises when sound from the loudspeakers is picked up by the microphone, producing a continuous amplification loop. It can usually be avoided by using a unidirectional or cardioid microphone. The most common arrangement is to have both the loudspeakers and microphones at the front of the stage with the speakers facing the audience and the microphones facing towards the stage. The microphones are then extremely insensitive to sound coming from the direction of the speakers. 'Monitor speakers', for feeding some of the amplified sound directly to the player, are then placed at the front of the stage facing in the same direction as the microphones. Sometimes a microphone is physically attached to the instrument, in order to allow the player freedom of movement over the stage. In this case feedback can be a particular problem because the directional properties of the microphone are upset by the proximity of the instrument. One way of minimizing feedback in wind instruments is to use a miniature microphone with a tube attached to it which is inserted into the headjoint or mouthpiece by drilling a hole. The sound levels inside the instrument are so high that the amplifier gain can be set very low and the feedback cycle does not become established.

Pickups

There are two forms of pickup nowadays in common use: the 'magnetic pickup', which responds to the vibrations of a metal string, and the 'contact microphone' or 'bug', which is fixed to the body of the instrument. Other types of pickup, for example the electrostatic transducer, have been used quite extensively in the past.

By far the most common use of magnetic pickups is on the electric guitar. The principle of operation is very similar to the moving coil and ribbon microphones, except that in the case of the magnetic pickup the conductor remains stationary. In its simplest form, a single coil of wire is wound round a frame inside which there are six metal polepieces, one for each string. These can be adjusted in height but are usually set to be about half a millimetre below the string. Underneath the polepieces is a strong permanent magnet which magnetizes them. As a string vibrates it changes the magnetic field through the coil and so a voltage is induced in it, which passes to the output socket via controls for adjusting the volume and tone. The magnetic pickup relies on the fact that the strings are made of steel, which is itself a magnetic material; it will not work with nylon or gut strings, even if they are overwound with a non-magnetic metal such as aluminium or silver.

A problem with the magnetic pickup in its simplest form is that it is also prone to picking up the alternating signal from nearby power cables, giving a characteristic 'electronic hum' at 50 Hz or 60 Hz (the frequency of the power supply). A more sophisticated design known as the 'humbucking pickup', invented by Seth

Lover in 1955, overcomes this to a large extent. It utilizes two separate coils connected in series and wound in opposite directions. These are positioned adjacent to each other, each one having its own set of six polepieces, magnetized in opposite directions by a single permanent magnet underneath. This has a noise-cancelling effect which improves the clarity of the sound, although there are disadvantages, the primary one being that the increased length of winding reduces the sensitivity to the highest frequency components. Compensation can be made for this, to a certain extent, by appropriate adjustment of the tone controls on the instrument or the associated amplifier. Most Gibson guitars use humbucking pickups; a Gibson 'Les Paul' electric guitar with two humbucking pickups is illustrated in Figure 9.3(c).

The position of the pickup along the length of the string is a crucial factor affecting the tone. The lower modes of vibration have smaller amplitudes of motion near to the ends of the strings (see Section 2.3); for example, the fundamental mode has its maximum amplitude halfway along the speaking length. Thus if the pickup is placed near to the bridge it accentuates the higher frequencies, whereas if it is placed nearer to the centre of the string it accentuates the lower modes. It is common for guitars to have two separate pickups, a treble one placed close to the bridge and a bass one placed at the lower end of the fingerboard. The outputs from the two pickups are combined in appropriate proportions using a mixer circuit. Some guitars, such as the Fender Stratocaster, have three pickups.

The bug is placed directly in contact with some vibrating part of the instrument. There are two types in common use. The magnetic bug is in effect a small moving coil microphone, where either the coil or the magnet is placed in contact with the moving part. The piezoelectric bug is made from a small crystal of piezoelectric material which generates a voltage when placed under stress. A whole range of different types of bug is available on the market, designed for varying applications. Most frequently bugs are clamped or glued to the body of the instrument, for example the top plate of a guitar or violin. The quality of reproduction is not usually as good as that obtained from a magnetic pickup placed under the strings, but the bug does not rely on the strings being magnetic; for this reason it is most frequently associated with the violin family, or with nylon or gut strung guitars. Bugs are sometimes attached to piano soundboards, and have also been used to good effect on the soundboards of harps. Piezoelectric versions can be extremely small and may sometimes be inserted into a small hole drilled, for example, into the bridge of a violin. There are also bugs for clarinets and saxophones which are clamped under the ligature so that they respond directly to the vibrations of the reed.

The main problem with bugs is that they are highly sensitive to the exact position on the instrument; even small changes in position can have dramatic effects on the sound. The reason for this is that soundboards and bridges have very complex vibrational patterns and it is difficult to find a single position which produces a uniform response across the playing frequency range. In practice a good deal of experimentation is required to find the best position for a bug on a stringed instrument. A bug placed under a woodwind instrument reed is less prone to positioning problems. Another problem when using a bug is that of feedback. The plate of a violin or guitar, for example, will act in effect like the diaphragm of a microphone and will respond to the sound waves generated by the loudspeaker, thus creating a feedback loop.

Amplifiers

Of the three elements in a sound amplification system (detector, amplifier, and loudspeaker) the amplifier is probably the one which causes the musician least concern. Modern electronics means that almost distortionless amplification can be achieved with equipment of only modest cost and the whole amplifier unit need only be considered as a 'black box'. However, a few points are worth mentioning.

Most amplifiers nowadays use transistors as the basic amplifying components. They are relatively compact and light compared to the older valve amplifiers, and are also very reliable. However, there are high-quality power amplifiers available which still use valves, and some musicians prefer these.

Perhaps the main decision that has to be made by the musician is what power is required. A typical power for general application is 100 watts. The important thing to remember here though is that the normal power rating of an amplifier describes the electrical power fed to the loudspeaker; the actual volume generated is dependent on the efficiency of the loudspeaker. The other point to remember is that the ear responds to power effectively in a logarithmic manner, which means that a change of volume corresponding to one step in dynamic level, say from *f* to *ff*, requires an increase in power by a factor of approximately 10 (see Section 1.4). Thus the difference in sound level between a 50 watt and a 100 watt amplifier is not very great. In musical applications amplifiers rarely operate at anything like their maximum rated levels. The main purpose of going for high power is to eliminate distortion on the occasional high-volume transient signal.

Some electric guitar players like to use distortion as a special effect, and for this reason guitar amplifiers are sometimes fitted with a control for limiting the peaks of the signal, often labelled 'valve distortion'. When distorted, the output is said to be related to the input in a 'non-linear' way. If a pure sine wave is amplified non-linearly then higher harmonics will be introduced; non-linear amplification of the sum of two sine waves can also introduce difference tones at a frequency lower than either of the two components. When operated within their rating levels, modern amplifiers frequently give a distortion of only 0.1 per cent or even less; this compares with typical distortion levels of 2 or 3 per cent for loudspeakers.

It is important that noise levels introduced by the electronic circuitry are not so high that they become audible. However, nowadays this will rarely be the case. Possibly of greater importance is the frequency response of the amplifier. Ideally an amplifier should have a flat frequency response; that is, it should give the same degree of amplification at all frequencies.

Amplifiers have electrical impedance ratings associated with both their inputs and outputs; typically there are separate inputs for high-impedance and low-impedance transducers and outputs for loudspeakers of rating 4, 8, and 16 ohm. It is important that the microphone, or other transducer, and the speaker are correctly matched to their appropriate connections. If the 'ohm' rating of the loudspeaker is not the same as the amplifier rating then a mismatch occurs, and a loss of power will result. If a high-impedance microphone is used in a low-impedance socket then a voltage drop at the input results and the volume will be reduced. Generally speaking a high impedance microphone can only be used with a relatively short lead; if the lead is too long then electronic noise may be picked up and the all-important signal-to-noise level will fall. If an extended length of cable has to be used then the microphone should be of the low-impedance type using a 'balanced line'.

Special effects

One of the main advantages of amplifying an instrument electronically is that devices can be incorporated to modify the signal and produce a whole range of effects. Special effects devices are most commonly associated with the electric guitar, but can be used with other instruments.

One of the most basic effects devices is that of 'delay', in which the output follows the input signal precisely, except that it is delayed in time by a prescribed amount. This is generally the basic component in some more complex device, for example the 'chorus' unit. The chorus effect is obtained by adding a delayed signal to the original one, using a mixer unit. For very long delays, in excess of 60 ms or so, the listener hears a distinct echo superimposed on top of the original sound, whereas in the normal operating range of between about 10 ms and 60 ms, the effect is that of two instruments playing in unison. A more realistic full chorus effect is obtained by continuously varying the delay time using an oscillator.

'Phasing' is similar to chorus in that a delayed signal is added to the original one but in this case the delay time is only a fraction of a cycle and is frequency-dependent. As with the chorus, an oscillator is used to continuously vary the amount of phase shift. When two signals are out of phase they will cancel, but they will reinforce each other when they are in phase. Phasing therefore produces peaks and troughs in the frequency response curve, which are continuously swept up and down by the action of the controlling oscillator. The effect to the listener tends to be less dramatic than chorus and is most marked when the signal has a wide-frequency range.

Another variation of the chorus effect is known as 'flanging'. Here the output from the delay line is fed back and mixed with the original signal to form the input for the delay line, thus creating a loop. The aural effect is much stronger than either chorus or phasing and the listener is aware of a distinct sweeping of the spectrum.

'Reverberation' and 'echo' units are further applications of the delay line, designed to simulate the natural effects of reflections from walls and other surfaces in a room. The delay line is tapped off at different stages to provide a number of signals delayed by different amounts. These are added in a mixer to form the output, which is also fed back to the input to produce a loop and additional echoes. The terms reverberation and echo are essentially used for the same thing, except that echo usually implies that only one or two delays are incorporated and that discrete echoes can be heard. The older type of echo unit used a continuous tape loop with a number of 'read' and 'write' heads to produce the delays. Nowadays echo units nearly all use digital electronics. Reverberation units, on the other hand, sometimes make use of a reverberation spring which has a number of transducers along its length. The signal is fed in at one end and then tapped off at the different positions, corresponding to different delay times. Reverberation units using the spring technique are frequently incorporated into ordinary PA amplifiers.

Loudspeakers

The type of loudspeaker used is of crucial importance in obtaining the desired sound quality. Practically all conventional loudspeakers operate on the moving coil principle and can be viewed as moving coil microphones in reverse. The diaphragm, which may be made of either paper or metal, has a coil of wire fixed at the back of it and this is free to move around the polepiece of a strong permanent magnet, fixed to the casing of the speaker. When an alternating current is passed through the coil a force is induced which pushes the diaphragm in and out, thus producing the sound waves.

Distortion levels for loudspeakers tend to be an order of magnitude higher than for amplifiers. The other factor of importance is the frequency response; small speakers only produce high frequencies efficiently and large speakers are only efficient at generating low frequencies. Ideally a loudspeaker should have a flat response over the range 20 Hz to 20 kHz. An approximation to this is usually obtained by using two or more speakers of different size mounted in the same cabinet. Bass speakers with a cone diameter of 20 cm or more are referred to as 'woofers'; 'tweeters' for the high-frequency ranges are 8 cm in diameter or less; other speakers are referred to as 'mid-range'. When more than one speaker is to be used, the driving signal must be filtered out into its constituent bands using a 'cross-over' circuit. If a cross-over is not used then distortion occurs, for example by the low-frequency components overloading the tweeter; power loss may also result.

Special loudspeakers have been designed for specific musical applications, probably the best example being the 'Leslie' speaker. This makes use of the Doppler principle to produce fluctuations in the frequency, akin to vibrato. For a treble-range Leslie speaker the sound is emitted through a horn which is rotated by an electric motor. Thus effectively the sound is propagating from a moving source. When the bell of the horn is moving towards the listener the frequency of the note is increased, whereas when it has rotated a half turn and is moving away from the listener the frequency drops. Most Leslie cabinets have both a rotating horn and a bass speaker with a rotating baffle; this operates on the same principle.

13.2 HISTORICAL DEVELOPMENT

Electrically powered instruments

Since the early nineteenth century, inventors and musicians alike have experimented with the use of electrical circuitry in the development of musical instruments. In the early days electricity was used simply as a means of powering certain functions normally performed manually in the operation of an otherwise acoustic instrument. Such electrically powered instruments are not members of the electrophone class, for which the final stage is the conversion of an electrical signal into sound by a loudspeaker or similar transducer. Nevertheless, the effective application of electricity in musical instrument technology was an important step towards the creation of true electrophonic instruments.

One of the earliest applications was the use of electromagnets for closing the valves on pipe organs, referred to as 'electric action' (see also Section 12.3). The first electric actions came out in France and Britain in the 1860s, although experiments had been conducted in Britain thirty years before this. Similar developments quickly followed in America and other parts of Europe. With the simplest 'direct electric action', depressing a key closed a switch in an electrical circuit, activating an electromagnet which closed a pallet valve and allowed air to flow into the tone chamber. All manner of more sophisticated electromechanical and electromagnetic relay systems were subsequently devised, but the important point was that whole series of pipes could now be brought into action with only minimal pressure on the key. A further advantage over mechanical actions was that the pipework could be remote from the playing manuals. Electromagnets were also brought in for activating the sliders and couplers, and electric fans were introduced for supplying the wind.

Electric actions were also successfully applied to the 'orchestrion', a type of sophisticated barrel organ, popular for home use in the nineteenth and twentieth centuries for the performance of classical and dance music. Orchestrions often had extremely complex mechanisms, with percussion, chimes, and other effects as well as organ pipes. Early versions were controlled from a pinned barrel, but later ones used sets of punched cards, joined together so that they could be stacked and automatically fed through the machine.

Electrically powered 'player pianos' were also introduced at the end of the nineteenth century. Many experiments were conducted, aimed at incorporating electric actions into the piano itself and also other instruments such as the bassoon, but these came to nothing.

Early electrophones

In the last quarter of the nineteenth century developments were taking place in the field of telegraphy which were to have important implications in the development of electronic musical instruments. In 1874 in Chicago, Elisha Gray invented a technique for simultaneously transmitting a number of Morse messages down the same telephone line, known as multiplexing: More sophisticated versions of this idea are used nowadays to send multiple telephone messages and computer data down the same line. Gray produced what was known as a 'musical telegraph'. Different pitched signals were generated using steel reeds, set in motion by electromagnets, rather like the conventional door-bell hammer. These could be controlled by a keyboard, of one octave in the first instance but later extended to two octaves. Gray produced a crude form of loudspeaker to receive the signal, made from a washbasin and an electromagnet. He showed that the difference in pitch between the signals could be used to separate them out at the receiving end and he demonstrated this by transmitting musical tunes over very long distances. Gray's ideas were not taken further at the time in the field of telecommunications because a few years later Alexander Graham Bell invented the telephone, making Morse Code largely redundant.

In the 1890s on the east coast of America, Thaddeus Cahill invented an electromechanical organ known as the 'telharmonium' (or 'dynamophone' as he preferred). This was based on the principle of the tone wheel, to which Cahill gave the name 'rheotone'. The rheotone was a large rotor, 40 cm or more in diameter, whose circumference was made in the form of alternate conducting and insulating strips. Conducting brushes were placed in contact with the rotor so that when it rotated there was an alternating make-and-break. When placed in a circuit, this gave rise to an alternating current, whose frequency was determined by the speed of rotation and the number of contact breaks. Transformers were used to smooth the square-shaped waveforms into something resembling sine waves and these were combined to give the final complex waveform. This was converted to sound by means of either loudspeakers made from piano soundboards or telephone receivers fitted with large horns. On later versions the rheotones were replaced by alternators consisting of toothed soft iron wheels rotating in a magnetic field which induced alternating currents in armature windings.

The telharmonium was played from a keyboard like a conventional organ but normally there were two players. For a short time it looked as though it might become quite successful: in 1906 one was installed in the Telharmonium Hall in New York and daily concerts were given, with the sound also being transmitted to subscribers through specially laid telephone lines. However, the quality of both the reproduction of sound and the technique of the performers was poor, and the whole operation became financially unviable after only a couple of years.

Amplified sounds

The era of electronics, and the new breed of musical instruments associated with this, really began in 1906 when Lee de Forest invented the triode vacuum tube, the basic component in the valve amplifier. However, it was not until the mid-1920s that amplifiers were produced commercially which were capable of amplifying tiny currents to a degree where a loudspeaker could be powered. About the same time the pickups described in the previous section were being developed. The main ingredients for an electroacoustic instrument were thus available, and by the 1930s all manner of these had come onto the market.

Amongst the earliest of the electroacoustic instruments was the electric guitar. Because of its importance this will be discussed separately later on in this section. Virtually all the other plucked strings followed suit and electric mandolins, banjos, and even harps were soon available.

Electric violins appeared about the same time as guitars; in these days, the violin was very popular in dance bands as well as orchestras. The familiar shaped body with its f-holes was now no longer required, since all the amplification was done by the electrical circuitry. Electric violins came in a variety of shapes, either with a solid body or in skeleton form like the early practice violins. Violas, cellos, and double basses soon followed. However, the quality of reproduction of all the bowed strings tended to be poor and they did not achieve the same early success as the electric guitar. String players who required amplification more frequently used a conventional acoustic instrument with a microphone.

Electric pianos had a more successful early history. One of the first and best-known instruments was the 'Neo-Bechstein Flügel' manufactured by the Bechstein company in Berlin for about ten years from 1931. It had the general appearance of a small grand piano, with a full eighty-eight note range, but there was a separate cabinet to house the loudspeaker system. The mechanism was similar to that of a normal piano, albeit much lighter in touch, but there was no soundboard. Treble and bass notes had single strings, while the middle range had two strings per note, with a separate pickup for each set of five notes. All the strings were shorter and much lighter than on an acoustic grand piano. Volume was controlled by the left-hand pedal, whilst the right-hand pedal operated a set of dampers in the normal way for sustaining the sound. In its time the Neo-Bechstein had some limited success and was used in a number of film scores, but it did not meet the exacting requirements of the serious pianist and the conventional acoustic grand had adequate volume to meet the demands of popular music of the day.

A number of other electric pianos soon appeared, for example the 'elektrochord', marketed in Germany by the August Förster Klavierfabrik company in 1936, which used electrostatic pickups. With an electrostatic pickup the string forms one pole of a capacitor, the other pole being a metal plate placed at a short distance from the string. The elektrochord used pickup plates positioned either horizontally above or below the string or vertically on the side. When a string is initially struck it vibrates predominantly in the vertical plane, so exciting the pickups above or below it. After a short instant the horizontal vibrations become more significant and so the pickups on the sides are activated. By using a number of pickups at different locations it was possible to vary the timbre, attack, and decay over a wide range. The elektrochord used two strings per note, except in the very lowest register, but only one was struck by the hammer; the purpose of the other was to enhance the sound through sympathetic vibrations (as with 'aliquot' strings on acoustic pianos). Another electric piano using electrostatic pickups was the 'dynatone', marketed in 1938 in America.

Over a period of years many other electric pianos appeared; the most successful was the 'Rhodes piano' (sometimes referred to as 'Fender-Rhodes' because of the collaboration between the two companies) which appeared in America in 1965. This used a mechanical element referred to as a 'tone bar', which operated in a similar manner to a tuning fork. Its vibrations were essentially sinusoidal, but the pickup was non-linear, with the effect that additional harmonics were generated; these were true harmonics in contrast to the Neo-Bechstein (see Section 13.1). Rhodes pianos had the great advantage of being small and relatively portable. A characteristic of their tone was the long sustain, similar to that on a vibrophone. The Fender-Rhodes sound is still used extensively, although the instruments themselves have now been superseded by purely electronic pianos, which are much lighter in weight but can produce almost the same timbre.

Various types of electronic keyboard instruments have also been invented which rely on the vibrations of a reed, either steel or steel-tipped. Typical of these was the 'orgatron', manufactured in America from 1934. This was designed primarily for church use and was the first electronic organ to be produced on a large scale. The reeds were housed in sound-proof chambers and excited by air suction, electrostatic pickups being used to convert the vibrations into electrical energy. A rotating blade was used in front of the loudspeakers to produce a tremolo effect, an idea which may have been an influence on the development of the Leslie speaker. In other keyboards the reeds were struck or plucked. An example was the 'clavier', manufactured in 1954 in America by the Acusti-Lectric Company; this used plucked steel reeds and electromagnetic pickups.

If one instrument can be said to stand out above all others in the development of early electronic instruments it must be the 'Hammond organ'. Invented in America by Laurens Hammond and John M. Hanert and patented in 1934, its success was such that by the end of the 1930s the Hammond Organ Company were making about fifty a week. The Hammond utilized the tone-wheel idea that had been used earlier on the telharmonium, the main difference being that the Hammond employed electronic valve amplifiers which meant that it could be produced on a much smaller scale. The tone wheels were all linked together by a system of gears and driven by a synchronous motor, which ensured that the notes remained perfectly in tune with each other, even if the overall pitch wandered very slightly. Tone quality was exceedingly good; in fact even to this day some players prefer the authentic sound of the original Hammond to that of its modern counterparts. The basic concept of the Hammond was that 'drawbars' were used to select different combinations of so-called 'upper harmonics' (not true harmonics as we will see later) in order to build up complex tones. The organs had two manuals and a pedal board and were normally operated in conjunction with a Leslie speaker.

About the same time as the Hammond, a number of other instruments came on the market using the tone-wheel principle, although none of these was anything like as successful. For example the 'Magneton', developed in Vienna, used tone wheels of different profile in order to produce a range of timbres; this was primarily intended for church use. The American-made 'Gnome' had the unusual feature that the keyboard was stationary: when the player touched a note a circuit was completed through his or her body which triggered the sound. Other organs, like the French 'Cellulophone', made use of the photoelectric effect by having a disc rotating in front of a light beam. Equidistant slits were cut round the disc so that the light was periodically interrupted, and the flashing beam which resulted was directed onto a photocell in order to produce an alternating current similar to that coming from a tone wheel. In England, the Compton Organ Company manufactured an organ known as the 'Electrone', which used electrostatic tone wheels consisting of pairs of flat insulating discs. One disc had a set of sinusoidal waveforms engraved on it which were filled with metal, representing the fundamental and the octaves. The other disc was used for holding a matching set of electrodes. There were twelve pairs of discs, one for each semitone, which were made to rotate at different speeds using a system of pulleys. A number of Compton organs were installed in cinemas around the country.

The concept of using a rotating wheel to interrupt a light beam was also used to produce the earliest electronic rhythm machine, constructed in Russia in 1931. This used a polyphonic keyboard where each note produced an upper harmonic of a fundamental tone sounded by the lowest note and repeated at a rate which increased with the pitch.

The demand for pickups on acoustic drums and other percussion was not great in the early days because the instruments normally had adequate volume in their own right. In any case early amplifiers could not deal with the high power levels necessary to make amplified percussion viable.

Electric guitar

The earliest electric guitars were of the 'Hawaiian', or 'steel', type in which the strings are stopped by a steel bar held in the left hand. The Rickenbacker A22 and A25 models produced in 1931 were of this type; they became known as 'Frying Pans', because of their shape. Electric guitars proper developed in two distinct forms, the 'semi-acoustic' hollow-bodied instruments and later the 'solid-bodied' ones. Solid-bodied instruments produce virtually no sound without electronic amplification but have the advantage that they can be constructed extremely rigidly. Semi-acoustic guitars produce a small amount of sound without any amplification, although not sufficient for actual performance.

The standard electric guitar has six strings tuned to E_2–A_2–D_3–G_3–B_3–E_4, exactly as its classical counterpart, but there are also twelve-string versions in which the top two strings are doubled at the unison and the others are doubled at the octave above. The 'bass guitar' has only four strings tuned to E_1–A_1–D_2–G_2, the same as the double bass.

In the mid-1930s the Gibson company introduced a semi-acoustic electric guitar with a hollow body. This had f-holes in place of the conventional circular rose and a pickup for detecting the string vibrations. It was not until 1948, however, that Leo Fender and George Fullerton brought out the first commercially produced solid-body guitar, known as the Fender Broadcaster. The body was made of solid ash with a cut-away to allow easy access to the high frets, whilst the neck was made of maple with the machine heads for adjusting string tensions placed all together on the lower side. It had two single-coil pickups, one by the bridge to accentuate the high-frequency modes and the other near the end of the fret board to accentuate the low frequencies. A switch allowed the player to select either of the pickups or the two together for different sound effects. In 1950 the Broadcaster was renamed the Telecaster.

In 1952 the Gibson company introduced their own solid-bodied electric guitar, the Les Paul model. This was made basically to the classical guitar shape but with a cut-away section for access to the high frets (Figure 9.3(c)). The machine heads were placed three on either side in traditional style. Originally it had two single-coil pickups like the Fender, but in the mid-1950s they were replaced by double-coil 'humbucking' pickups. The year 1954 saw the launch of another Fender solid-body instrument, the Stratocaster. This had three separate pickups; it also had a 'tremolo arm' which allowed the player to exert an extra tension on the strings by pressing against the arm, thus introducing vibrato effects.

Various other innovative guitar designs have come onto the market, for example the Gibson twin-necked guitar, one neck having six strings and the other twelve. However, the Telecaster, Les Paul, and Stratocaster have become classic designs which have been mimicked by many other manufacturers, particularly in Japan.

Electronic oscillators

The instruments discussed so far have all relied on some form of mechanical motion to produce the electrical signal which ultimately drives a loudspeaker. One of the great advances in the development of electronic instruments was the realization that controlled pitches could be produced purely electronically by using an oscillator circuit, a basic component required for radio transmission.

It was in 1920 that the first purely electronic instrument appeared before the public. The prototype was called the 'Etherophone' (sometimes spelt 'Aetherphon'); it was a further nine years before this was being manufactured for the market, now under the name of 'theremin' (after its Russian inventor Léon Thérémin). The theremin was controlled from two antennae, in the form of a vertical rod for the pitch and a loop for the volume, which responded to the proximity of the right and left hands respectively. The player did not actually touch the instrument. Moving the hands altered the capacitance between the body and the antennae and appropriate circuitry was used to produce a radio frequency signal from this. Mixing the signal with a fixed frequency sine wave then gave rise to a beat frequency within the audio range. A major problem with the theremin was that it had no points of reference, such as a keyboard, for the hands to work from; control was thus extremely difficult. It was also monophonic. Nevertheless, it was taken seriously enough for a number of major composers to write for it, including Percy Grainger and Bohuslav Martinů. In the 1930s a simplified form of theremin was sold in combination with an electric gramophone so that the user could play a melody against the recorded accompaniment.

The Frenchman Maurice Martenot met Theremin in 1923 and became interested in his new instrument. Five years later he came out with his own, known as the 'Ondes Martenot' ('Martenot Waves'). This was again a monophonic instrument, with a voice-like quality. Early versions used a pull wire to vary the pitch; the player wore a ring on one finger, attached to the end of the wire whilst the other hand operated controls for the volume and timbre.

On later models the pull wire was replaced by a ribbon with a dummy keyboard behind for gauging the pitch. Later still a normal keyboard was added to the ribbon controller; the keys were capable of a lateral movement which caused small pitch changes and allowed vibrato effects to be introduced. The Ondes Martenot established itself as a serious instrument, to the extent that composers of the calibre of Milhaud, Koechlin, Honegger, and Messiaen wrote works for it and classes were given on the Martenot at the Paris Conservatoire in the late 1940s. It was also used extensively in film music.

The first organ to use oscillators was the 'Coupleux-Givelet organ', developed in France between 1928 and 1930. However, the early oscillators did not have a high degree of frequency stability, and it was many years before purely electronic instruments made the electromechanical systems obsolete. The Hammond Organ Company, for example, did not replace their tone-wheel system with electronic oscillators until the late 1960s. Modern oscillators use crystals to create the high degree of stability required for music reproduction.

A milestone in electronic instrument development was the invention of the transistor in 1947. With this new miniaturized component it was possible to make instruments very much more portable and complex. A new breed of 'synthesizers' appeared, mainly in America, which were capable of producing a vast range of complex sounds; later versions often incorporated automatic rhythm units. In the 1970s American domination of the market was relinquished to the Japanese, who now make so many electronic keyboards that scarcely a week passes before a new one has come onto the market.

Impact of computers

Marketing of the first digital computers by the Remington Rand company in 1951 began a new era of electronics, and it was not long before experiments were being conducted on the digital synthesis of sounds. The principle was explained in Section 2.6: waveforms can be created, stored, and manipulated as series of numbers in a computer, and then finally converted into continuous signals for driving a loudspeaker using a device known as a 'digital-to-analogue converter'. Digital circuits are now capable of performing all the functions of the earlier analogue ones and can also be used to sample and hold sound waves of great complexity.

The first fully computerized organ to be available commercially was the 'Allen organ', patented in America in 1971. This produced all of its sounds from instructions stored in its computer memory, based on recorded spectra from pipe organs. It was popularized by concerts given on tour by the organ virtuoso Carlo Curley, using the organ in conjunction with more than three hundred loudspeakers. Digital technology has advanced so rapidly that similar techniques are now used on even some of the most modestly priced home instruments. The capabilities of a digital instrument can often be greatly enhanced by linking it to a microcomputer, now very common in the home.

As with the compact disc player, digital instruments are capable of giving a very high quality of reproduction, and the more sophisticated models offer a great deal of flexibility. For example the player can sample just a few sounds from an instrument and then replay melodies with the same voicing extended over the complete range of a keyboard. In the studio, complete performances of orchestral proportions can be built up with such realism that it is sometimes difficult to judge whether the music originates from a live performance or from a computer synthesis.

13.3 ELECTRONIC SOUND GENERATION

In order to generate electronically tones that resemble the sounds of acoustic instruments it is necessary to reproduce both the transient effect associated with the rise and fall of the sound level and the spectral content of the sound. For example, when a note is struck on the piano it takes a certain time for the sound level to build up to its maximum value; once this has been reached it dies quite rapidly even though the key remains depressed. On releasing the key the sound fades away very rapidly, but not instantaneously. These rise and fall times, and also the relative intensity levels at different time instants, are set on a synthesizer using a unit referred to as an 'envelope generator'. The waveform itself will have a complex structure reflecting the different frequency components in the spectrum at any given instant of time; there are a number of different techniques available for reproducing this, the most common being additive, subtractive, frequency modulation, and granular synthesis.

The standard envelope generator used with a keyboard synthesizer has four primary controls: 'attack', 'decay', 'sustain', and 'release', hence its name ADSR generator. When a key is depressed the ADSR generator is triggered; its output rises more or less rapidly, depending on the setting of the attack time. When the maximum has been reached the signal level falls back to a constant voltage, determined by the setting of the sustain level. The time for the signal to fall back to the sustain level is known as the decay time and is set by a separate control. On key release the

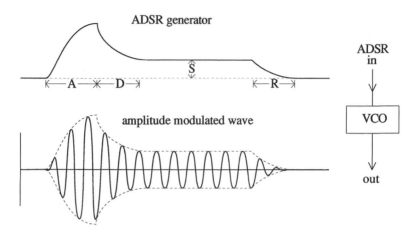

13.2 Amplitude modulation of a pure sine wave by an ADSR envelope generator

signal dies completely in a time determined by the setting of the release time. The overall shape of the envelope produced in this way is shown in Figure 13.2.

The primary function of the ADSR generator is the shaping of the envelope of the signal amplitude. This is done by passing the signal through a 'voltage controlled amplifier' (VCA) which has a second input, controlled by the ADSR generator. The signal to this second input determines the gain of the amplifier, and thus the signal becomes amplitude-modulated in a manner determined by the setting of the four parameters A, D, S, and R. This is shown for the simplest case of a pure tone in Figure 13.2. As we will see later, envelope generators can also be used for other control purposes, for example changing the spectrum shape.

The three most commonly used techniques for generating waveforms with specified spectral characteristics are additive synthesis, subtractive synthesis, and FM synthesis. These concepts were developed for generating tones in early electric organs and synthesizers, and are the basic building blocks used for modern computer-based systems.

Additive sound synthesis

The earliest attempts at synthesizing musical sounds electronically relied on the fact that complex waveforms could be generated by adding together certain simple frequency components. This technique, known as 'additive synthesis', remains one of the basic methods by which different tones may be produced. Central to this concept is the mathematical exactitude which tells us that any complex waveform, provided it is precisely repeatable, can be made up by adding together pure sine waves whose frequencies are the fundamental repetition frequency and the higher harmonics of this. The amplitudes and phases of the components must be appropriately chosen to match any particular complex waveform.

The principle is well illustrated by the drawbar electronic organ, exemplified by the classic Hammond organ. This uses a set of 'drawbars' to control the tone. The drawbars are labelled using a convention borrowed from the pipe organ, and described in Section 12.1. A pipe organ stop which plays at written pitch is described as '8-foot', one which plays an octave higher than written pitch is described as '4-foot', and so on. On some drawbar organs this convention is taken over directly, but more often the drawbar which plays at written pitch is described as '16-foot' rather than '8-foot'. Usually only six or seven drawbars are provided, typically 16-foot, 8-foot, 5⅓-foot, 4-foot, 2⅔-foot, 2-foot, 1-foot. If the 16-foot drawbar is considered to be the fundamental then the 8-foot drawbar represents the 2nd harmonic, the 5⅓-foot drawbar the 3rd harmonic, and so on. The proportion of each harmonic is determined by how far out the drawbar is pulled. By withdrawing different combinations of drawbars it is possible to obtain a whole variety of sounds all with the same fundamental pitch.

With the drawbar system there is no means of changing the relative phases of the different components. Variable phase is unnecessary since the ear is relatively insensitive to phase. Synthesizer units are available for use as acoustic demonstration, in which a whole range of harmonics can be added with adjustable phase; however, although changing the phase alters the shape of the waveform as displayed on an oscilloscope, it has virtually no audible effect.

In practice drawbars do not all generate tones which are true harmonics of the fundamental, since the waveforms are actually those of notes in the equally tempered scale. For example, suppose the 16-foot drawbar plays the note C_2. With the drawbar combination given above the higher harmonics are then obtained by adding in the tones for the notes C_3, G_3, C_4, G_4, C_5, and C_6. Four of these notes are higher octaves and will therefore be precisely in tune, but the frequencies of the notes G_3 and G_4 are not precise multiples of the frequency of C_2 in the equally tempered scale.

In the early days of electronic music development it was thought that the additive synthesis principle was the complete answer to the problem of reproducing the sounds of acoustic instruments since, in principle, waveforms of arbitrary complexity could be reconstructed by the addition of appropriate components. The only problem then seemed to be that each instrument should be characterized precisely by the appropriate frequency spectrum and the additive synthesis electronics should be adequate to reproduce this spectrum shape in detail. It soon became clear that this was a gross oversimplification of the problem; in fact, on the classic drawbar organ most of the sounds bore little resemblance to any acoustic instrument.

What then was the problem? The drawbar system can indeed give a reasonable representation of the frequency spectrum of any given instrument. One factor is that the ear is so sensitive that a very large number of component frequencies need to be included for a satisfactory reconstruction. Much more relevant though is the fact that the envelope of the signal, defining the way the signal starts and finishes, is of equal importance to the spectrum when it comes to characterizing an acoustic instrument. Thus even with an extremely large number of drawbars it would be impossible to reproduce realistic sounds without careful electronic processing to reproduce representative transients.

Subtractive synthesis

The problem of requiring a very large number of component frequencies in a realistic synthesis is partly overcome in the technique of 'subtractive synthesis'. The synthesizers developed and marketed by Robert Moog and by Korg in the 1960s used this technique. The idea is to start with a signal which has a large number of frequency components and then to subtract out, by means of electronic filters, the components that are not required. Signals having many frequency components can readily be generated by modern circuitry. For example, a signal in the form of a square wave can be generated by periodically switching between two preset voltage levels. With this approach, a tone with a complex spectrum can be generated with just a single electronic oscillator. An added advantage is that, since all the spectral components originate from the same waveform, they are constrained to be precisely in tune with one another.

As well as square waves, there are a number of other wave forms which are commonly used to produce the complex spectrum. Most common are the pulse, the sawtooth, and the triangular waveform. A square wave has all the odd harmonics, where the amplitude of each one drops in inverse proportion to the number of the harmonic; this compares to the pure sine wave which has only the fundamental frequency. The triangular waveform similarly has only odd harmonics, but in this case the amplitudes drop off more rapidly towards the higher frequencies in inverse proportion to the square of the mode number (i.e. the 3rd harmonic is one ninth the amplitude of the fundamental, and so on). Pulse signals, on the other hand, have components at all of the harmonic frequencies. As the pulses become narrower the amplitudes of the higher components become relatively higher compared to the fundamental until, when the pulses are extremely narrow, the amplitudes die off only very slowly towards the higher frequencies. Likewise the sawtooth waveform has all the harmonics present; their amplitudes in this case fall off in inverse proportion to the mode number, like the square wave.

Figure 13.3 compares the frequency spectra for the different waveforms where the period in each case is T, i.e. the frequency of the fundamental is 1 : T. For the pulse signal the width has been taken as 25 per cent of the period; this proportion is known as the 'duty cycle'. In displaying the spectral components the commonly used convention of making the height of the fundamental equal to unity has been adopted. It has also been assumed that the mean values of the different signals are all zero; otherwise a peak at zero frequency would have occurred.

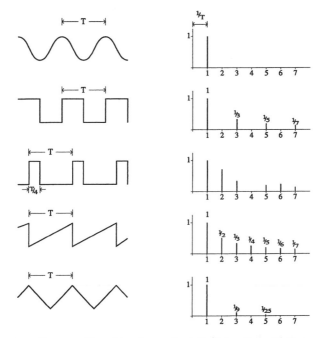

13.3 Different waveforms used for subtractive synthesis (left), together with their spectra (right)

Having generated the complex source waveform, the next stage is to filter out the unwanted components. Four types of filter are commonly used: 'high pass', 'low pass', 'band pass', and 'band reject'. A low-pass filter is the same as the single tone control on a radio. Frequencies up to a certain 'cut-off' value pass through the filter unaffected but above this there is a progressive attenuation as the frequency increases. The transition between the attenuated and unattenuated frequency bands is a gradual one but once this has been passed, the roll-off towards the high frequencies reaches a constant value. Different designs of filter have different roll-off rates, the most common being 24 db per octave. The decibel roll-off rate here refers to the power reduction in the signal as the pitch increases by an octave. For a 24 db roll-off the voltage is reduced by a factor of about 16 on each octave rise. Other filters with a lower roll-off rate (usually 12 db or 6 db per octave) or a sharper roll-off (36 db per octave) are sometimes used. The effect of low-pass filtering is to make the timbre more mellow.

A high-pass filter is the reverse of the low pass; in this case it is the low frequencies that are attenuated, with the high frequencies passing through the filter unaffected. High-pass filtering dampens the fundamental, so the resulting sound is thin and lacking in depth. Band-pass filters allow only frequencies within a set band of frequencies to pass. The effect of this is very much dependent on the band width of the filter as well as the setting of the centre frequency. As with the other filters, the attenuation rate changes gradually at the edges of the acceptance band, rather than the cut-off being sharply defined. As the name implies, a band reject (or notch) filter is the opposite of a band pass, all frequencies being passed except those within a prescribed band. Often the effect of notch filtering is rather small.

Some synthesizers have a 'resonance' control, normally to be used in conjunction with the low-pass filter. The effect of activating the resonance control is to produce a peak in the filter response curve at the cut-off frequency. In effect this transforms it into a band pass filter with a sharp roll-off at the high-frequency end and a small roll-off at low frequencies.

In the early generation of analogue synthesizers, such as the Moog and Korg instruments, the individual voltage-controlled components had their own input and output connectors arranged on a display panel. These could be connected by the player in any required arrangement using a set of short leads, a process known as 'patching'. This arrangement allowed a great deal of flexibility but was rather cumbersome, making this type of instrument only suitable for studio work. These instruments were often purchased along with a separate unit referred to as a sequencer. This took the form of a chain of voltage generators, whose levels could be individually adjusted with knobs. When set to run, each generator was turned on and then off in sequence, at a rate determined by the setting of the clock. The output of the sequencer was used to cycle through a pattern of notes, typically 8 or 16, on the synthesizer.

FM synthesis

FM synthesis, short for 'frequency modulation synthesis', is an alternative technique to subtractive synthesis by which sounds with complex spectra can be generated from only a few input parameters. The FM technique was pioneered by John Chowning at Stanford University, California and is the basis on which the Yamaha Corporation X series of synthesizers operate. The Yamaha DX7 is one of the best-known synthesizers that have come onto the market and is still used widely, although its technology has now been superseded.

The technique of frequency modulation is probably best known in connection with radio broadcasting; standard radio signals are transmitted and detected using either amplitude modulation (AM) or frequency modulation (FM). From the musical standpoint these concepts can probably best be understood by considering how tremolo and vibrato are produced. For a pure sine wave, both the amplitude and frequency are constant. When tremolo is added, the frequency remains constant but the amplitude varies periodically. An effect like this is heard if the swell pedal on an organ is moved up and down at a constant frequency. In electronics terminology, this is referred to as amplitude modulation. With vibrato, on the other hand, the amplitude remains constant but the frequency is varied periodically over a small range at a rate of a few cycles per second; we say that the frequency is being modulated at the given rate. Frequency variations of this type are generated by a violinist when the string length is periodically shortened and lengthened by vibrations of the hand on a stopped note. This is referred to as frequency modulation. Note that in practice, when a musician talks about producing vibrato on a note it is understood that there will probably be an element of both vibrato and tremolo.

When FM is used for synthesizing musical sounds of different texture the underlying principle is the same as that for the generation of vibrato, the only difference being that the modulating frequency is generally much higher. In order to explain the effect of this it will be useful for us at this stage to define some terms commonly used in FM analysis. The frequency of the tone before modulation is termed the 'carrier frequency'; we will use the symbol f_c to denote this. The frequency of the modulation is termed the 'modulating frequency' and will be denoted by the symbol f_m. In normal vibrato f_c is many times higher than f_m, typically 100 or 1,000 times higher. The ear then hears a clearly defined pitch which fluctuates up and down over a small range, the amplitude of this rise and fall being termed the 'frequency deviation', denoted by f_d. Thus the frequency will rise to $f_c + f_d$, fall back to $f_c - f_d$ and then rise again and so forth at a rate of f_m cycles per second. The ratio of modulating to carrier frequencies $f_m : f_c$ is referred to as the 'harmonicity ratio'. In FM synthesis f_m is generally in the audio range and f_c and f_m are usually chosen so that there is a simple integer relationship between them: for example, with f_c set at 1 kHz f_m might be set at 100 Hz or 2 kHz. At these high modulation frequencies the ear does not hear a pure tone wandering up and down in pitch; instead of this the aural sensation is that of a complex tone of constant pitch.

The frequency components (f) of the FM tone are given by the simple mathematical relationship

$$f = f_c + kf_m$$

where k is a positive or negative integer number ± 1, ± 2, ± 3, etc.

Let us see how this can be applied by considering an example. Suppose that f_c is 440 Hz, corresponding to A$_4$, and that this is modulated up and down within the range 275 Hz to 605 Hz at a rate of 110 Hz, i.e. $f_d = 165$ Hz and $f_m = 110$ Hz. The spectrum of the sound will then have a frequency component at 440 Hz (correspond-

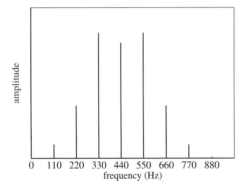

13.4 Spectrum of a frequency-modulated wave with carrier frequency 440 Hz, modulation frequency 110 Hz, and modulation index 1.5

ing to $k = 0$) and there will be lower side bands at 330 Hz ($k = -1$), 220 Hz ($k = -2$) etc. and upper side bands at 550 Hz ($k = 1$), 660 Hz ($k = 2$) etc. Notice that all of the spectral components are harmonics of a 110 Hz fundamental, so this is the pitch that the ear hears, i.e. A_2. In this case, then, the ear senses the pitch of the modulating frequency, rather than the carrier as would be the case with ordinary vibrato. The complete spectrum is shown in Figure 13.4. It can be seen that the spectral peaks are grouped around the central frequency of 440 kHz and that their heights are not all the same; in fact the central peak at the carrier frequency is not the highest.

Readers who are interested to know precisely how the heights of the spectral peaks can be calculated should refer to one of the standard texts on electronic music synthesis. In summary though, the heights are determined by a set of Bessel functions which can be found from a table for any given value of the modulation index I, which is the ratio of frequency deviation to modulating frequency $f_d : f_m$. These peaks may be positive or negative in amplitude. A peak with positive amplitude is said to be in phase whilst a negative peak is out of phase by half a cycle. The phase of a peak does not have an audible effect unless there are other peaks of the same frequency present, in which case the peaks either add or subtract from each other, depending on their relative phase. Applying the rules for calculating the frequency components in the spectrum, it will be seen that negative frequencies can easily arise. These are treated in exactly the same way as positive frequencies except that their phase is shifted by half a cycle.

The number of significant spectral components is determined by the size of the modulation index I. Only k values of magnitude up to $I + 1$, or the next highest integer, lead to peaks of significant height. This, of course, is only a rule of thumb estimate, but will suffice for most purposes. In our example, $I = 1.5$, so we take k values with magnitude up to 3, giving sidebands on either side of the carrier. Inspection of the spectrum will show that at $k = \pm 3$ the sidebands have become quite small; for k values of larger magnitude the spectral peaks are so small that they are insignificant.

It is instructive to examine the spectrum shown in Figure 13.4 a little more closely. There are nine spectral lines, symmetrically placed about the central peak, although the heights of the outer two peaks are insignificant. Their heights in fact can be calculated to be 0.02, 0.11, 0.42, 1, 0.92, 1, 0.42, 0.11, and 0.02, where the values have been scaled to make the highest one equal to unity. The first peak of height 0.02 is at zero frequency; it has no aural significance and is filtered out in the electronic circuitry in any case. The interesting point is that exactly the same sound could have been produced on a drawbar organ by playing the note A_2 and adding in seven upper harmonics by withdrawing the drawbars, each to a length corresponding to the appropriate spectral peak. This, however, would require the use of eight drawbars, whereas with the FM synthesis only three controls are required.

Negative frequencies are always encountered when the modulating frequency is greater than the carrier. Suppose for example that f_c = 100 Hz and f_m = 400 Hz. Then with k = –1, f_s = –300 Hz and with k = –2, f_s = –700 Hz etc. Thus the actual spectrum generated will have components at 100 Hz, 300 Hz, 500 Hz, 700 Hz, etc., i.e. all the odd harmonics. This produces a hollow sound like the chalumeau register on the clarinet. In this case the components arising from the negative and positive frequencies arise alternately in the spectrum. In other cases they can overlap; for example if f_c = 100 Hz and f_m = 200 Hz. Then with k = –1, f_s = –100 Hz and there is already a spectral component at 100 Hz due to the carrier. Similarly with k = –2 and 1 the corresponding frequency values are –300 Hz and 300 Hz, and so forth. This can be used to good effect by detuning either f_c or f_m by a small amount; in this case the corresponding positive and negative frequency components will beat together generating an amplitude modulation or tremolo.

It will be seen that the FM technique offers a very simple way of producing a whole range of spectra using just three input parameters. Clearly the player does not have the same degree of control over the spectrum shape as with the additive synthesis approach but, nevertheless, a wide variety of useful timbres can be generated. By varying the modulation index the player can introduce more or fewer upper harmonics; a high modulation index gives a large number of upper modes and a correspondingly bright sound. Voice-like sounds are particularly easy to generate using FM because the overall shape of the spectra can readily be made to resemble the voice's formant characteristics, with f_m set to the fundamental frequency of the note and f_c set to the centre of the formant peak associated with a particular vowel. The special case when f_m is equal to f_c is particularly useful for the generation of brass sounds; in this case all the harmonics are present.

In the Yamaha DX7 there are six 'operators' in the form of digitally controlled oscillators with their own envelope-shaping circuitry and input for controlling the frequency, which may come either directly from the keyboard or from the output of another operator. Operators are linked together in patterns known as 'algorithms' which can be set up by the player to produce the desired sound. As an example, the output from operator 1 may be used as the input to operator 2, causing frequency modulation; this complex frequency-modulated wave may then be used as input to operator 3 and so forth. In this way waves with extremely complex spectral characteristics may be generated. It is also possible to produce feedback loops in which the output of a specified operator is fed back as input to itself.

Inharmonic frequencies

In order to produce a precisely pitched sound the spectrum components need to be harmonically related; this requires that the harmonicity ratio should be an integer or an integer fraction. Although this is the most usual case of interest, spectral components which are not harmonically related are often required, particularly in the simulation of percussive sounds. Such sounds, and their corresponding frequency components are referred to as being 'inharmonic'. Already we have seen that a small amount of inharmonicity is desirable in the generation of piano tones, which have a percussive element. When simulating instruments such as tubular bells and gongs the spectral components will need to differ widely in frequency from those of a harmonic series.

Inharmonic sounds can in principle be generated by additive synthesis, provided that there are sufficient frequency components available. Generally speaking though, electronic organs can only generate spectral components which are harmonically related, since they utilize a single set of twelve oscillators for the highest octave; frequencies in the lower octaves are generated by a process of frequency division. In more sophisticated modern synthesizers it is possible to produce a set of arbitrary frequencies which can be added together. In the case of subtractive synthesis, all the frequency components in the spectrum must of necessity form a harmonic series. With FM synthesis, on the other hand, it is quite simple to produce inharmonic spectra, simply by choosing f_c and f_m values that do not have an integer relationship. In this way, very effective simulations of bells, gongs, and the like can be produced.

Ring modulation

Ring modulation is a non-linear technique in which one waveform is used to amplitude modulate another. It has been used extensively in early electronic music synthesis for the creation of chordal structures, e.g. by Jean-Claude Risset in his composition *Mutations*, 1987.

To be more specific, the original waveform, known as the 'carrier', is multiplied by a second waveform, known as the 'modulator'. This distorts the carrier wave and introduces additional components into the frequency spectrum. Both signals normally oscillate about zero, unlike conventional amplitude modulation (AM) used in radio transmission where the modulator fluctuates about a mean positive value. The simplest case of ring modulation is where both the carrier and the modulator are sinusoidal waves. If the frequencies of these two waves are f_c and f_m respectively, the spectrum of the resulting waveform has peaks at $f_c + f_m$ and $f_c - f_m$ i.e. sidebands are introduced on either side of the carrier but the carrier wave itself disappears. For example, if the carrier wave is at 880 Hz and the modulator is at 220 Hz then the resulting waveform will have components at 660 Hz and 1,100 Hz but there will be no components at either 880 Hz or 220 Hz. It is seen that ring modulation frequently results in a change of pitch; also the resulting components may not be harmonically related.

Ring modulation is frequently used to make the sound spectrum more dense. Multiplying two complex sounds generates a waveform that has spectral components that are the sum and difference between the frequencies of each component in the carrier and each component in the modulator. If the carrier has c spectral components and the modulator has m components then the resulting wave can have up to $2cm$ components. Fewer spectral peaks are generated when some of the original components are harmonically related because of sidebands overlapping.

Waveshaping

Waveshaping uses a non-linear transfer function to map an input signal onto an output signal, i.e. the input signal is distorted by the transfer function. A simple example of waveshaping is the distortion that occurs when an amplifier is overloaded. Careful choice of the transfer function, however, can produce useful spectra which change dynamically with the amplitude of the sound. The amount of distortion depends on the extent to which the transfer function deviates from a straight line. A straight line will produce no distortion whereas extreme deviation in the slope will generate many components in the spectrum. The transfer function is frequently specified mathematically as a polynomial equation but its values are stored in a table by the computer to achieve computational efficiency. The fact that waveshaping results in a spectrum that changes with the amplitude of the sound makes it very useful for the synthesis of real acoustic instruments, particularly brass sounds.

Granular synthesis

The concept of 'granular synthesis' originates from the work of Gabor in 1947. According to Gabor's theory, sound can be considered as a series of short sonic pulses, or 'grains'. This concept is very similar to the idea that light may be thought of as a series of short photon pulses, each with its own frequency content.

Individual grains are normally in the form of a waveform modulated by a short envelope in the form of a pulse, e.g. a bell-shaped or triangular amplitude envelope. Grains are typically between 5 ms and 50 ms in duration and they need to be generated in large numbers, typically several hundred per second, in order to produce useful results. The grain waveform can vary from simple sinusoids to complex waves and are normally generated electronically. They may also be in the form of sampled sounds, multiplied by short window waveforms which die to zero at the edges. The relative amplitudes of the individual grains may also be variable.

Because of the large number of grains involved it is important to implement a high-level strategy for manipulating them. There are several approaches to this and new ones are constantly being conceived. Xenakis, for example, proposed a scheme in 1971 whereby the time domain is divided into frames, analogous to the frames in a movie film. These are then played at a constant rate in order to produce continuous movement. This is sometimes referred to as 'synchronous' granular synthesis. In an alternative 'asynchronous' approach, developed by Curtis Roads in 1985, the grains are randomly spaced in time, within specified limits. This generates clouds of sound with specified temporal and spectral characteristics.

Physical modelling

In simulating a musical instrument with a technique such as FM or subtractive synthesis, the user tries to match the time-dependent characteristics of the spectrum to the actual sound. A fundamental problem here for the musician is that the input parameters—for example, the modulation index or harmonicity ratio—bear little or no relationship to control parameters used for playing an actual acoustic instrument, such as blowing pressure, lip pressure, or bow velocity. Thus even though the model may be operating in real time it is very difficult to control it in an expressive manner.

A 'physical model' simulates the actual physical process of sound production directly, e.g. the way in which sound waves are generated by a reed and resonate within the tube of a woodwind instrument. The algorithms for such models may be extremely complex and expensive in computer time but the recent advances in computer technology have opened the way to the construction of a number of commercial real time instruments.

The very simplest of algorithms for physical modelling are of the 'source-filter' type, in which the signal flows in one direction only, from the excitation source, through the resonator to the output. Models of this type have been used with some limited success to simulate both voice and percussion sounds. The implication here is that changing the characteristics of the resonator does not automatically change the nature of the excitation. This clearly could not be valid for an instrument such as the clarinet where the vibration frequency of the reed must be dependent on the resonant frequencies of the air column.

More sophisticated models incorporate a 'feed-back' mechanism whereby the output waveform is channelled back to the source. In fact the characteristics of the excitation waveform are normally highly complex and must be derived from a detailed knowledge of the physical mechanisms, e.g. the vibration mechanics of the reed, over a range of amplitude and phrasing variations. The most common technique for dealing with the resonator in a wind instrument is to model it as a series of 'wave guides', which are effectively filters that mimic the action of the changing bore of the tube. Wave-guide modelling techniques are also commonly used to model stringed and percussion instruments, although for these instruments other approaches such as 'finite element analysis' have also been applied successfully; in essence, the body of the instrument is divided into small physical elements and the motion and interaction of these elements is computed using the basic laws of mechanics.

The first commercial synthesizer that used physical modelling was the Yamaha VL1. It generates all its sounds completely from physical model algorithms without any sampled sounds or acoustic input. Because of the complexity of the computations involved it only supports two-voice polyphony and is really designed for solo performance. It is commonly used with a wind controller which roughly resembles a clarinet in overall shape, mouthpiece, and fingering but produces no sound itself. Alternatively one can input signals from a keyboard midi controller and some other control devices such as a breath-pressure controller. Other companies such as Korg and Roland have also produced physical modelling synthesizers specifically designed to model drums or guitar. The theory of physical modelling is advancing rapidly and the technique is being increasingly used in commercial synthesizers. Physical models are also now available as virtual instruments for software-based synthesizers.

Noise

Noise is the ultimate limiting case of an inharmonic sound, in that it has no discernible pitch or pattern. Nevertheless noise can play a crucial part in characterizing a musical sound. For example, the breathy attack of a note on the flute or panpipe can be a crucial and distinguishing feature which good electronic synthesis must seek to capture.

In terms of electronics, the basic noise signal is referred to as 'white noise'; this term is used in analogy to white light which has all the coloured components of the optical spectrum present. White noise has all frequency components in more-or-less equal proportion, that is its frequency spectrum is flat. In practice, white noise has to be band-limited: the frequency components only cover a limited range, normally the audio range in acoustic applications. When applied in different musical situations it is then filtered to produce the desired effect. Unfiltered white noise sounds much like the rushing sound of the wind or the background noise on a poorly tuned radio receiver. When the low frequencies are filtered off this turns into a high-pitched hiss and when it is low-pass filtered it resembles the distant rumbling of a jet aircraft.

White noise can be generated very simply, since the steady current passing through any electrical component contains a noise element, referred to as 'shot noise'. In essence, this simply needs to be amplified up to the required power level. Some synthesizers make use of 'coloured noise', in which the spectrum is not flat. By far the most common is 'pink noise' in which the power within each octave band is equal. With pink noise the height of the spectrum falls off towards the higher frequencies giving a much less harsh sound reminiscent of falling rain.

Sampling

The basic idea of sampling is that short fragments of sound from acoustic instruments or other sources are digitally recorded, to be replayed later by the synthesizer when notes on the keyboard are depressed or some other form of triggering device is brought into play. It is sometimes argued that sound-sampling instruments are not real synthesizers in that they simply replay recorded sounds, rather than construct them electronically. In reality though, a good deal of processing goes on between the recording and replaying processes and it is difficult to separate the sampling and synthesis approaches. Indeed, many modern synthesizers use techniques which combine the two concepts in a fairly complex manner.

Sampling takes on its simplest form in the 'drum synthesizer', since the sounds are of essentially fixed duration and short enough that they can easily be stored digitally in the sampling machine's memory. The other simplifying factor is that only a rather small number of different sounds are required, since drums are not capable of producing a whole range of different pitched notes, like say a flute or a piano. Each drum sound that is required is recorded digitally and is then replayed in its entirety when a trigger signal is generated by the percussionist striking the appropriate touch-sensitive pad. It is fairly easy to arrange that the volume of replay is increased when the pad is struck more vigorously or to make adjustments to the rate of decay of the sound.

Sampled sounds are generally stored in 'random access memory' or RAM. This is a form of electronic storage which allows digital records to be either written into it or read from it, as the occasion demands. This contrasts with another form of memory known as 'read only memory', or ROM, in which the digital records can only be stored at the manufacturing stage. A ROM retains its information indefinitely, but a RAM will normally lose it once the electrical power supply is switched off, unless of course there is a back-up battery; most sampling synthesizers in fact have battery back-up. If the synthesizer user wants to save large numbers of samples, these can be stored indefinitely by reading them out onto a computer disc.

In Section 2.6 we saw that an essential parameter which affected the quality of a sampled record was the sampling frequency. Let us examine this in a little more depth. A moment's thought will show that to resolve a signal of frequency f by a sequence of numbers the sample frequency needs to be at least $2f$; the highest frequency which can be sampled (known as the 'Nyquist frequency') is therefore half the sampling frequency. This means that the sample frequency should be at least twice the frequency of the highest component in the sound spectrum which is of musical significance. If it is less than this then the uppermost frequencies will not be handled adequately. Since the ear cannot resolve frequencies greater than about 20 kHz, it is common practice to set the sample frequency just above 40 kHz. The most commonly used sampling rate, which is standard for compact disc players, is 44.1 kHz. A sample rate of 48 kHz is sometimes used in high-quality recording work. Problems can be encountered if the sample frequency is set unnecessarily high since the storage available in the RAM will then be swallowed up too rapidly. In the case of a sampled drum sound the total length of the sample must be as least as long as it takes for the sound to die away completely, or else the tail will be clipped off when it is replayed.

If the sound contains significant components above half the sampling frequency then these are not simply lost: they are misrepresented as lower frequencies, and the sample is contaminated in a manner which cannot subsequently be remedied. This rather subtle effect is known as 'aliasing'. To avoid aliasing problems the analogue signal should be low-pass filtered to remove the frequencies above the Nyquist frequency before the digitizing process take place.

We saw in Section 2.6 that another parameter of importance was the resolution of the ADC. Whereas the sampling frequency determines the frequency response of the sampler, the resolution affects the levels of distortion and background noise. Most commercial digital audio systems, including those in compact disc players, operate with 16-bit resolution, but for high-quality recording 20-bit sampling is frequently used. The noise and distortion levels associated with even 16-bit resolution are extremely low, and far less than than those which will subsequently be introduced by the amplifier and loudspeaker system.

The full resolution capability of a digitizing unit can only be achieved when the input signal level has been correctly set. If the signal level is set too low then the range of voltage values spanned will be much less than those covered by the sampler; only a proportion of the available sampling levels (65,536 on a 16-bit sampler) will be utilized, thus effectively reducing the resolution. An even worse scenario is when the signal gain is set too high, such that the highest sampling voltage level is exceeded. In this case the tops of the signal peaks are clipped off, resulting in a gross distortion. Ideally when samples are being recorded the waveforms should be displayed visually; in this way clipping or too low input levels can be detected immediately. Many sampling synthesizers have a liquid crystal display (LCD) similar to the ones commonly used on electronic calculators and some have an output which can be plugged into a computer monitor. Some samplers incorporate a unit known as a 'compander' which automatically amplifies the signal level as its level drops, thus ensuring that the full resolution capability of the digitizer is utilized. On playback the original signal levels are restored by using an 'expander' unit. Companders and expanders can themselves introduce distortions and consequently are not in widespread use.

In the case of non-percussive sounds the role of the sampling synthesizer is somewhat more complex. Take, for example, the problem of sampling a trumpet sound and then using this to generate trumpet melodies from a keyboard synthesizer. The first difficulty encountered is that the duration of the notes in the melody need to be variable: when the key is depressed the sound should start and when it is raised the sound should stop, although not necessarily instantaneously. The second difficulty is that the melody could cover a wide range of pitches even though only one or two notes may have been sampled.

One way of dealing with the problem of variable length notes is to record a sound of very long duration in the first instance and then to cut this off on replay when the key is released. This is not a very practical proposition, however, first because it is difficult to obtain consistent sound quality over the full duration of a long sustained note, and secondly because very long samples take up a great deal of computer memory. The approach generally used to overcome this problem is to start with short sample sounds and create notes of arbitrary length using a 'looping' technique. The stored sample is replayed from the beginning when a note is depressed, in order to reproduce the starting transient, but the machine is programmed in such a manner that after a short fragment of the steady waveform has been replayed a jump is made back to an earlier part as shown in Figure 13.5. In this way a continuous loop is set up which sustains the sound for as long as the key remains depressed. When the key is released the signal is made to drop gradually to zero.

Producing a satisfactory loop is no simple matter and is a fundamental problem for sampling synthesizers. Loops may be set up manually with the aid of a graph-

13.5 Formation of a loop in a sampled signal

+ loop matching points

ic display of the sample. The procedure is to look for matching points on two different cycles of the waveform which the machine then links up, as indicated in Figure 13.5. The two points must be chosen so that the join between the beginning and end of the loop is absolutely smooth, otherwise clicks will be noticeable in the sound.

It must be remembered that we are dealing with a digitally sampled signal, and the period of the wave (the time for one complete cycle) will not generally be an exact multiple of the time between samples. For this reason it is not normally possible to loop a single cycle, for this will result in a change in pitch. Normally several hundred cycles are used. On the other hand, the number of cycles within the loop should not be too great, otherwise unwanted fluctuations in signal amplitude can result. Some machines have automatic looping systems whereby this procedure is carried out automatically using a microprocessor, but the resulting loops are often not as satisfactory as those set up by hand.

It is not necessary to record and loop samples for every note over the range of an instrument; this would be a very tedious task. Sampling synthesizers have the facility for replaying the digital record at different speeds, depending on which note is played. The principle here is the same as replaying a gramophone record at a different speed. Increasing the replay speed raises the pitch (by an octave for a doubling of the speed). Thus a single sample can provide a range of different pitches.

It may appear at first sight that a single sample would be enough for any particular instrument, but unfortunately this is not the case. The sound spectra for a particular instrument will vary quite significantly, depending on the pitch of the note played. For example a clarinet spectrum exhibits predominantly odd-numbered harmonics in the low register but the even harmonics become significant as the pitch ascends (see Section 3.3). Other instruments, such as the bassoon, have very strong formants which emphasize particular frequency components, independent of pitch; in these cases changing the replay speed will shift the position of the formants and completely alter the sound characteristics. This formant effect can easily be heard by replaying a recording of the voice at different speeds. The result of all this is that a single sample should not be replayed over a range of more than about an octave. For realistic synthesis half a dozen or so samples should be taken, covering the playing range of the instrument. In practice only one or two samples are sometimes used, in which case the player must be content with the sound being realistic only over a small range of the keyboard.

Wave tables

Many modern synthesizers manipulate and combine stored waveforms in complex ways in order to expand the range of sounds available. Such instruments usually rely heavily on preset waveforms stored in ROM at the manufacture stage. In storing large numbers of waveforms, use is sometimes made of a 'wave table', a term that is used in describing synthesizers using sets of stored samples. The waveforms are arranged in the form of a table, each one with its own address, which is used by the microprocessor when calling it up. The waveforms can then be manipulated using any of the techniques already described.

13.4 CONTROL TECHNIQUES

In Section 13.3 we have discussed the various techniques by which electronic sounds are generated. A complete instrument, however, requires some means of controlling the pitch, volume, and tone quality of the notes. These control techniques will be discussed in this section.

Keyboard control

The keyboard is far and away the most popular control device, since it is simple and positive in its action and also offers the possibility of allowing polyphonic music to be played. Synthesizer keyboards are typically five octaves in length and low-priced models designed for use in the home may be as short as four octaves. The shortness of length, compared to the piano, is partly overcome by the fact that selected sounds can be reproduced in different octaves.

Most modern electronic keyboards are 'touch-sensitive', although this is not the case with earlier electric organs, or indeed many of the low-cost home synthesizers today. A touch-sensitive key produces a control signal which depends on the velocity at which it is depressed. Usually there are only a finite number of volume levels that can be achieved, ranging from dozens of levels down to ten or fewer. The key velocity determines the overall level of the signal throughout its duration, the loudest available sound only being achieved when the key is struck very hard. Sometimes the degree of sensitivity can be altered to suit the player's particular liking. It is particularly important to have touch-sensitivity on a single-manual organ, since otherwise it is extremely difficult to achieve a satisfactory balance between notes in different registers. Most earlier electronic organs which did not have this feature achieved the balance by having two manuals.

Some instruments also provide an 'after-touch' facility whereby the volume can be altered once a key has been depressed, while it is being held down. Pressing harder on the key increases the volume, whilst releasing the pressure reduces it. After-touch is useful in the simulation of acoustic instruments which can sustain their notes, such as flutes, trumpets, etc. It allows crescendo or diminuendo effects to be introduced on long notes. Another useful facility is 'portamento' (sometimes termed 'glide') which allows the pitch to change gradually from one note to the next instead of in an abrupt step.

On an analogue synthesizer, depression of a note produces a control voltage which is standardized as being 1 volt per octave. Divided into twelve equal parts this gives 0.083 volts per semitone: the control voltage of any note is 0.083 volts greater than the note just below it. This is a linear voltage-to-pitch relationship. However, since pitch and frequency are logarithmically related, the relationship between keyboard control voltage and frequency is also logarithmic. The use of this logarithmic scale means that in most cases a non-linear amplifier has to be placed in front of any voltage-controlled units operated by the keyboard, since the unit will normally have a linear voltage-to-frequency characteristic; for example, equal increments in the control voltage to a VCO produce equal increments in output frequency. Early synthesizers used a linear scale for their keyboard control voltages, so that equal increments in control voltage gave equal increments in output frequency. The problem here was that the change in control voltage corresponding to a given pitch interval was dependent on the position on the keyboard.

It is sometimes possible to introduce a prescribed 'delay' between the striking of the note and the start of the control signal it generates. A short time interval then elapses before the sound is heard, characteristic of the pipe organ. A related facility sometimes available is known as 'hold'. When this is activated the control voltage which keeps that note sounding is maintained for a prescribed time after the key is released. The time for which the sustain level is maintained is therefore increased.

Early synthesizers were generally 'monophonic': they could only play one note at a time. Despite their limitations, monophonic synthesizers may still be used to good effect where only a solo voice is required. Normally they are played on stage with a second keyboard providing the accompaniment, or used for adding solo tracks in recording work.

Most modern instruments, on the other hand, are 'polyphonic': a number of separate notes can be sounded at the same time. Typically the number of notes that can be sounded simultaneously is sixteen; one then speaks of a 'sixteen voice' instrument. This is more than adequate for most purposes, since one rarely wants to play more than about eight notes at a time; nevertheless some instruments can play as many as thirty-two. The number of notes available at any one time is reduced when complex timbres are called up, or when the sounds are layered, with more than one sound at a time played from each note. Since the number of notes that can be played simultaneously is less than the total number of available notes, it is necessary to have some system of note priority. Usually the note that is played last has priority and robs a previous note of its sound.

A synthesizer may have 'multi-timbral' capability, in which case two or more different timbres can be played simultaneously, or it may be solely a 'homogeneous' system in which all the notes played at any instant sound the same timbre. The most common arrangement is to have a 'split keyboard' whereby one sound can be set for the bass and another entirely independent one set for the treble. This facility partially overcomes the problem of having only one manual, although the pitch range of each section is likely to become rather restrictive. On sophisticated instruments the split point can be chosen by the player, and it may be possible to split the keyboard up into as many as eight different units. Each different sound is referred to as a 'voice', and the electronics associated with producing a given timbre is sometimes called a 'voice module'. If, for example, a multi-timbral synthesizer has eight voices then this means that it can sound eight different timbres simultaneously. A word of warning here: in early literature the number of voices sometimes refers to the number of notes that can be played simultaneously.

Although keyboard synthesizers are usually mounted on legs in a fixed position and played in a manner similar to the more traditional organ, strap-on keyboards controllers are also available. These are lightweight instruments which are strapped across the player's neck like an electric guitar. The advantage of these is that the player is free to move about the stage, which has made them quite popular with pop bands.

Control without keys

In order to control a synthesizer all one needs in principle is some means of generating an electronic signal which the player can alter at will. Although the keyboard is by far the most commonly used way of achieving this, it does not by any means have a complete monopoly. In fact keyboard units themselves often incorporate some other control device, the most common being the 'pitch bend'. The hardware for a pitch-bend control is usually in the form of a wheel placed at the left-hand end of the keyboard, but various types of lever are also quite common. The device can be moved in either of two directions and is sprung in such a way that it returns to its central equilibrium position when released. As its name implies, the pitch bend simply alters the overall pitch up or down without otherwise varying the timbre. This allows the player to introduce slow vibrato effects, similar to those which can be produced by the tremolo arm on an electric guitar. It is frequently used quite liberally by pop artists using strap-on keyboard synthesizers when they want to imitate the effect of the electric guitar. A few instruments incorporate a 'ribbon controller' in the form of a slender metallic strip over which the player slides a finger. This allows continuous pitch variations to be made over a wide range for glissando effects.

Pedal controllers are also quite common. One of the simplest is the swell pedal, used for regulating the overall volume. This may take the form of a foot-operated variable potentiometer, similar to the ones commonly used on radio or television sets. A problem with this design is that with constant use the contacts tend to wear and crackly noises then come through when it is operated. Some swell pedals make use of a light-sensitive cell which has the property that it changes resistance when the amount of light falling on it is varied. Inside the pedal unit is a small bulb placed close to the cell; when the pedal is operated a mask moves into position between the bulb and the cell, so cutting off the light. The mask is designed so that the resistance variation changes gradually with the pedal movement. The photo-cell is included as one unit of an amplifier circuit such that the gain varies as the pedal moves. This produces a simple and almost noise-free swell.

It is also possible to control a synthesizer from the output of an electric guitar or indeed the signal from a microphone responding to the sound from an acoustic instrument such as a violin or even a vocalist. In this case processing electronics needs to be incorporated in order to convert the analogue audio signal into the appropriate control voltage levels required for an analogue synthesizer, or the voltage pulses required by a fully digital system.

In the case of drum synthesizers the control is relatively straightforward, at least in principle. Each particular drum sound is triggered by its own touch-sensitive pad which produces a voltage pulse when struck by a drum stick. The initiation of the pulse then triggers the drum sound and the pulse height determines its amplitude.

13.5 PERFORMANCE PRACTICE

MIDI systems

The term MIDI stands for 'musical instrument digital interface'. It is a standard specification for digital interfaces, or connections, which allows electronic instruments and related devices from different manufacturers to speak to each other. The original MIDI specification, known as MIDI 1.0, was introduced in 1983 and since then has become universally accepted. It gives standards for the digital language to be used by the microprocessors used in electronic instruments and also for hardware such as connecting plugs. Virtually all modern synthesizers and related processing units, except the very cheapest ones, are MIDI-compatible and can therefore be connected into a multi-instrument system.

It is normal for MIDI-compatible instruments to have three MIDI sockets, known as 'ports', which accept standard five-pin DIN plugs. The three ports are designated 'MIDI IN', 'MIDI OUT', and 'MIDI THRU'. In the simplest mode of operation the OUT from one synthesizer, known as the 'master', is connected to the IN of another, termed the 'slave'. When the master keyboard is played the slave also sounds, thus allowing timbres available on the two keyboards to be combined. Note that the MIDI connection only acts as a control, and does not alter the actual sounds available on either the master or slave.

MIDI ports can also be used to connect a 'sequencer'. This is a device used for controlling the synthesizer automatically; a sequencer will produce control signals for playing sequences of notes, either pre-recorded or programmed into the machine. It incorporates a clock which allows the notes to be played in rhythmic patterns. A drum machine is in essence a sequencer which also holds a number of its own percussive tones.

Often a sequencer will be used with a number of synthesizers in an arrangement known as a 'daisy chain', making use of the THRU ports. A problem with this type of series connection is that any fault or noise introduced by one sequencer will propagate through the system, so inaccuracies are likely to occur if too many units are daisy-chained. This problem can be overcome by connecting in parallel using a MIDI THRU unit. MIDI signals comprise sixteen channels, and individual instruments may be set up to respond to prescribed channels. In this way the separate instruments can be made to play different parts within a given sequence, hence sounds of orchestral dimensions can be produced.

MIDI signals contain more information than is simply required for switching notes on and off: for example, key velocity for the control of touch-sensitive keyboards, sustain, pitch bend, and control instructions for changing patches may all be accommodated. However, connecting through MIDI cannot produce effects which are not otherwise available on a particular instrument. If a synthesizer which is not touch-sensitive is slaved to one which is, for example, the slave will not respond to touch changes on the master.

With universal acceptance of MIDI, the 'remote keyboard controller' and the 'expander unit' have become popular. The remote keyboard controller is a keyboard which produces a MIDI control output but no sound of its own. The expander unit, on the other hand, produces a range of sounds but has no keyboard of its own. A remote keyboard controller together with an expander unit thus form a complete synthesizer package. The main advantage of having separate units is that it offers the player a greater degree of flexibility. Remote keyboard controllers can also be made very compact in size, which may be an advantage for stage use; strap-on keyboards are sometimes of this type.

Guitar and wind instrument controllers may also have MIDI outputs which can be connected directly to an expander unit or into a conventional keyboard synthesizer. The main problem with these is that they are not as positive in response as a keyboard, hence the inherent precision in the digital system is lost. In the case of the MIDI guitar, for example, there tends to be a delay between the time the string is plucked and the generation of the appropriate MIDI control signal. This delay, referred to as 'tracking', is normally rather short but nevertheless long enough to adversely affect the overall playing characteristics, particularly in fast passages.

Although the same MIDI code is universally accepted by instruments from different manufacturers, it is also possible to transmit commands known as 'system exclusive'. These are only recognized by instruments from a specific manufacturer. System-exclusive commands are particularly useful for sending instructions on patching between synthesizers and expander units of the same manufacturer. A patch determines the control settings within the instrument for the creation of a particular sound, for example the ADSR and filter settings.

MIDI is seen in its most sophisticated form when a computer is incorporated into the system. The output from a microcomputer can be made MIDI-compatible by using a suitable interface; indeed many computers have a MIDI interface as standard. The computer also needs to be supplied with a suitable program, and a range of software packages are available. With suitable software it is possible to build up a library of patches and to edit these as required. It is also possible to store and edit sampled waveforms on the computer and to generate rhythmic sequences using the computer clock. A great advantage of the computer is its enormous storage capacity. Even with a fairly modest personal computer it is now possible to store complete compositions, and the composer can have essentially a full orchestra at his or her fingertips. In order to simplify the writing of a musical computer program for the control of synthesizers and related devices, it is usually possible to specify the notes by playing them on one of the keyboards that is MIDI-connected to the computer. The sequence of notes played may then be recorded in real time by the computer or it may be 'auto-corrected'. In the latter case the time sequence is subjected to 'quantization': notes which are played slightly off the beat automatically have their timing reset. Once the sequence of notes has been recorded it may then be edited and replayed at any required speed.

With the aid of the computer and MIDI interfacing it is possible for a single performer to have complete control over a vast range of instruments in live performance on stage. For example the player of a keyboard instrument might arrange for different regions of the keyboard to sound different voices, let us say cello for the lower region and flute for the upper region, coupled with double bass on a pedal board. Certain bass notes might also be used to trigger into action specified percussion sequences and so on. On top of this the player can use prerecorded sequences and also sing parts which activate additional voices. A similar arrangement can be made with the guitar, using different strings to sound specific instruments or combinations of instruments.

There is an increasing tendency to combine electronic music reproduction with visual effects. This is seen in the current vogue of pop groups producing videos to accompany their chart recordings and in the use of lighting triggered by specific musical sounds. The crucial thing here is timing; it is important for example that climactic effects in the music coincide exactly with similarly dramatic visual effects. This is normally done by making use of the SMPTE (short for Society of Motion Picture and Television Engineers) code, which is the movie and video equivalent of the MIDI standard. Through the computer system MIDI and SMPTE can be synchronized together so that visual and musical events occur in their correct relative position throughout a complete performance. These devices are used in the production of film music or video recordings but can also be used live.

It is quite common to activate lighting systems from MIDI signals on stage; lights of different colour and intensity are often switched on when certain notes are played or when particular drums are struck. This is very effective in pop music; in this case the different coloured lights are usually made to flash in sync with the beat. An alternative approach is to trigger electronic sounds from movements on stage, usually those of dancers. This idea was pioneered by John Cage, for example in his composition *Variations V* (1965). Here he detected the movements of dancers using light beams and various electronic devices; the resulting signals were then used to trigger sounds from tape recorders, oscillators, and the like.

Computer music languages

Taking advantage of the explosive increase in speed and storage capability of computers, it is now possible to generate sophisticated electronic music compositions on a modestly priced home machine. There are numerous software packages that can be used to do this.

Some software packages generate MIDI signals as their output. These can be used as input to a synthesizer to realize the complete piece of music. An example of such a program is 'Max', written at IRCAM and named after one of the pioneers of digital synthesis, Max V. Mathews. Max is a graphic programming environment for developing real-time music software applications. Most modern computers have input and output ports for MIDI signals and also sound cards for recording and transmitting acoustic signals. In the Max language the user builds up patches from a bank of objects which can individually be pulled down using the computer mouse. The patches are elements of a flow chart which prescribes the way in which the computations proceed. The different objects within the patch define computational elements such as arithmetic operations, logical operators, random number generators, delay lines, input and output, etc. The programs are normally designed to run in real time. For example, MIDI signals can be put into the program from a keyboard or other control device and the output of the program can be used to play sounds from a sound generator unit. The program offers a very powerful tool for controlling music generation in real time.

A major limitation in Max is that the sounds cannot themselves be generated within the program. This is overcome in the Max MSP program which allows for the real-time generation of audio-rate signals. With Max MSP patches can be included for any of the standard synthesis techniques such as additive, subtractive, or FM synthesis. Thus the program is completely self-contained and will output musical tones directly to the sound card of the computer.

There are other programs which use a Graphical User Interface (GUI), notably 'Cubase'. This is in essence a software-based synthesizer offering audio and MIDI recording facilities, together with mixing and audio effects. It is possible to incorporate virtual instruments (referred to as 'plugins') within Cubase.

One of the most comprehensive and versatile software packages for electronic music is CSOUND. The programs for this are constructed by typing in instructions from the keyboard, rather than using a Graphical User Interface as in Max and Cubase. This makes CSOUND rather less user-friendly, but this disadvantage is offset by the enormous power of the program. A CSOUND program consists of two parts, an 'orchestra file' and a 'score file'. The orchestra file contains the individual instruments which generate the different sounds. Typically an instrument might be written for FM synthesis. The score file specifies the instants of time at which all the different notes are played, together with all the parameters that define how the notes should sound—the pitch, duration, and volume of the sound and the modulation parameters. Once the program has been 'rendered', the resulting sound file is opened with a sound editor and then played through the sound card of the computer. For some applications the score file is replaced by a sequencer-generated MIDI file or a MIDI controller.

The programs making up the CSOUND package have a long history of development, starting with the program 'Music4' written at Bell Telephone Laboratories by Max Mathews in the early 1960s.

Avant-garde techniques

The earliest avant-garde technique of significance in electronic music was *musique concrète*; this term signifies that sounds not normally associated with music—for example running water, wind, the sea, or machinery—are used as an integral part of a composition. This idea was first exploited by Pierre Schaeffer in 1948. For his earliest composition, *Etude aux chemins de fer*, he used multiple turntables to combine the sounds from steam railway locomotives in various ways. He could change the speeds, play the sounds backwards, and create loops, but by present-day standards the means he had at his disposal for manipulating the sounds were extremely limited. The advent of the tape recorder made the mechanics of this type of composition much simpler, since lengths of tape from different sound sources could easily be spliced together and multiple recording and replay heads could be used to produce echo and other similar effects.

With sampling synthesizers the scope for introducing *musique concrète* effects is even greater. Everyday sounds can be recorded digitally and then replayed using a keyboard. Certain transient sounds with no definite pitch, such as the sound of breaking glass, may be assigned to specific notes on the keyboard. Other sounds with recognizable pitch, perhaps a bird call or a mechanical band saw, may be replayed at different pitches depending on which key is pressed; in this way tunes can be played with the sounds. Modern synthesizers frequently have a range of preset sounds of this type.

For the purpose of live performance, it is generally desirable that the performer can interact with the electronic system generating the sound. As we saw in Section 13.1, acoustic feedback is normally an unwanted effect arising when an amplification system is incorrectly set up. However, many composers and performers of avant-garde music have used feedback as a means of extending the spectrum of sounds available to them and at the same time providing an interactive element. The pitch of the sound generated in this way can be altered either by electronic filtering or by introducing acoustic resonators in the vicinity of the microphone, thus effectively altering the resonance frequency of the feedback loop. The volume can also be controlled by moving the microphone position relative to the loudspeakers. An example of the use of feedback is the composition *A Mouth-Piece* by Mesías Maiguashca (1970); this makes use of the resonance of the performer's mouth cavity.

'Proximity detectors' of various type have been used to good effect to give interactive control in avant-garde performance. The idea of using detectors which respond to the proximity of a part of the body dates back to the theremin, which was discussed in Section 13.2. This used the capacitance in the hands to activate an electronic circuit. A more common approach nowadays is to use light beams focused onto photoelectric cells which produce voltages when interrupted. Often light paths are cut by dancers on stage as in Cage's *Variations V* (1965).

One of the interesting advances in modern computer technology is that, by using sophisticated programs, it is possible to make the systems interactive, i.e. responsive to external signals. For example programs have been devised which will create rhythmic patterns in sympathy with hand claps or percussive sounds from the performer. It is also possible for the computer to sense the different pitches of a melodic line and produce its own harmonically related accompaniment. Interactive systems of this type allow the full spectrum of electronic composition technique to be employed whilst still maintaining the human input. Interactive systems are rapidly becoming more sophisticated, incorporating techniques of artificial intelligence; this seeks to emulate the working of the human brain. Through artificial intelligence it is possible to introduce different stylistic elements and even improvisations.

The chance element is also one which is often used in electronic music. This concept is not new; it has been frequently employed by composers such as John Cage, for example in his compositions *Imaginary Landscape No 5* and *Williams Mix* (both completed in 1952), in which he combined the sounds from a large number of recordings onto a single tape using selection procedures derived from chance operations. The techniques used by some composers have been so bizarre that it is debatable whether the compositions can be classified as music at all. For example in *Pendulum Music* by Steve Reich (1968) microphones are suspended from the ceiling by their cables so that they can swing in a pendulum motion. The signals from the microphones are amplified and sounded through loudspeakers placed on the floor below, giving rise to a feedback squeal which is loudest when the microphone is in its stationary position above the speaker. The score then consists of a set of instructions for setting the pendulums in motion and finally for turning off the power at the end.

With computer technology, chance elements (or 'stochastic processes') can be incorporated into the programs using random number generators. A computer can be programmed to generate its own melodies and indeed complete compositions using stochastic processes incorporating certain restrictions, particularly on the range and on the number and size of intervals. The Serialist technique, for example, has a clearly defined structure which can be programmed into a machine. However, this application has not proved highly successful. The more fruitful approach seems to lie in the generation of certain sounds and musical fragments, for example chimings of bells, which are initiated by commands from the player. In this way the electronics operates as an aid to the performer, rather than usurping that role, so the human element is not lost.

A recent idea which is in its early stages of development but seems to offer promising possibilities is to make use of a computational procedure referred to as the 'cellular automata' (CA) technique. Computer programs based on the CA concept have been used in scientific research to study problems as diverse as crystal growth and fluid flows. The concept is that a computer model is constructed in the form of a lattice of cells, which can take on a finite number of possible values or states. Values of the cells evolve synchronously in discrete time steps according to identical rules called 'transition rules'. Any particular cell has its value determined by the previous values of a neighbourhood of cells around it. The operator specifies a set of starting numbers for the cells and then waits for patterns to develop; these are dependent on both the starting numbers and the transition rules. Many different CA models have been devised, for example the 'Game of Life', invented by Cambridge mathematician John Horton Conway and the 'Demon Cyclic Space', invented by David Griffeath of the University of Wisconsin at Madison, to name but two.

The idea that CA can be used in the present context stems from the observation that music may be thought of as a series of sounds related to each other in definable ways. It thus exhibits structural coherence akin to many physical problems in nature. In order to implement CA in a practical situation the computer is generally used to generate a series of control signals for pitch, volume, articulation, and timbre which are ultimately realized through a conventional synthesizer using the MIDI system. Various means have been devised by which the composer can set up a musical palette on the computer in advance of a performance and also interact with the program as it proceeds in order to influence the outcome. Possibilities also exist, however, for self-contained CA systems which do not require an external synthesizer.

The impact of electronics and computers in music has been as great as in any other field; clearly there are many more innovations to come in the future, although it is not easy to predict the directions which these will follow. Electronics has helped to make music accessible to a very wide audience in the twentieth century, and many people now come to musical instrument performance first through electronic instruments. It is worth recalling, however, that enthusiasm for acoustic musical instruments is probably also at a higher level at the start of the twenty-first century than at any time in the past. Some of the most interesting prospects for new musical paths in the new century involve fresh ways of combining acoustic and electronic musical instruments and techniques.

APPENDIX 1

TABLE OF PITCHES AND FREQUENCIES

In the table below we give, for each note of the chromatic scale in the frequency range between 16 Hz and 8000 Hz, the USA standard pitch notation (Roman font), the modified Helmholtz pitch notation (italic font), and the frequency in hertz of the note in equal temperament at $A_4 = 440$ Hz. The pitch notation systems are described in Section 1.3.

C_8	$D_8^\flat$	D_8	$E_8^\flat$	E_8	F_8	$G_8^\flat$	G_8	$A_8^\flat$	A_8	$B_8^\flat$	B_8
c'''''	$d_\flat'''''$	d'''''	$e_\flat'''''$	e'''''	f'''''	$g_\flat'''''$	g'''''	$a_\flat'''''$	a'''''	$b_\flat'''''$	b'''''
4186	4435	4699	4978	5274	5588	5920	6272	6645	7040	7459	7902
C_7	$D_7^\flat$	D_7	$E_7^\flat$	E_7	F_7	$G_7^\flat$	G_7	$A_7^\flat$	A_7	$B_7^\flat$	B_7
c''''	$d_\flat''''$	d''''	$e_\flat''''$	e''''	f''''	$g_\flat''''$	g''''	$a_\flat''''$	a''''	$b_\flat''''$	b''''
2093	2217	2349	2489	2637	2794	2960	3136	3322	3520	3729	3951
C_6	$D_6^\flat$	D_6	$E_6^\flat$	E_6	F_6	$G_6^\flat$	G_6	$A_6^\flat$	A_6	$B_6^\flat$	B_6
c'''	$d_\flat'''$	d'''	$e_\flat'''$	e'''	f'''	$g_\flat'''$	g'''	$a_\flat'''$	a'''	$b_\flat'''$	b'''
1047	1109	1175	1245	1319	1397	1480	1568	1661	1760	1865	1976
C_5	$D_5^\flat$	D_5	$E_5^\flat$	E_5	F_5	$G_5^\flat$	G_5	$A_5^\flat$	A_5	$B_5^\flat$	B_5
c''	$d_\flat''$	d''	$e_\flat''$	e''	f''	$g_\flat''$	g''	$a_\flat''$	a''	$b_\flat''$	b''
523.3	555.4	587.3	622.3	659.3	698.5	740.0	784.0	830.6	880.0	932.3	987.8
C_4	$D_4^\flat$	D_4	$E_4^\flat$	E_4	F_4	$G_4^\flat$	G_4	$A_4^\flat$	A_4	$B_4^\flat$	B_4
c'	$d_\flat'$	d'	$e_\flat'$	e'	f'	$g_\flat'$	g'	$a_\flat'$	a'	$b_\flat'$	b'
261.6	277.2	293.7	311.3	329.6	349.2	370.0	392.0	415.3	440.0	466.2	493.9
C_3	$D_3^\flat$	D_3	$E_3^\flat$	E_3	F_3	$G_3^\flat$	G_3	$A_3^\flat$	A_3	$B_3^\flat$	B_3
c	$d_\flat$	d	$e_\flat$	e	f	$g_\flat$	g	$a_\flat$	a	$b_\flat$	b
130.8	138.6	146.8	155.6	164.8	174.6	185.0	196.0	207.7	220.0	233.1	246.9
C_2	$D_2^\flat$	D_2	$E_2^\flat$	E_2	F_2	$G_2^\flat$	G_2	$A_2^\flat$	A_2	$B_2^\flat$	B_2
C	$D_\flat$	D	$E_\flat$	E	F	$G_\flat$	G	$A_\flat$	A	$B_\flat$	B
65.41	69.30	73.42	77.78	82.41	87.31	92.50	98.00	103.8	111.0	116.5	123.5
C_1	$D_1^\flat$	D_1	$E_1^\flat$	E_1	F_1	$G_1^\flat$	G_1	$A_1^\flat$	A_1	$B_1^\flat$	B_1
C'	$D_\flat'$	D'	$E_\flat'$	E'	F'	$G_\flat'$	G'	$A_\flat'$	A'	$B_\flat'$	B'
32.70	34.65	36.71	38.89	41.20	43.65	46.25	49.00	51.91	55.00	58.27	61.74
C_0	$D_0^\flat$	D_0	$E_0^\flat$	E_0	F_0	$G_0^\flat$	G_0	$A_0^\flat$	A_0	$B_0^\flat$	B_0
C''	$D_\flat''$	D''	$E_\flat''$	E''	F''	$G_\flat''$	G''	$A_\flat''$	A''	$B_\flat''$	B''
16.35	17.32	18.35	19.45	20.60	21.83	23.12	24.50	25.96	27.50	29.14	30.87

APPENDIX 2

KEYWORK TABLES FOR TYPICAL WOODWINDS

These tables do not attempt to provide fingering for instruments; this information is easily found in fingering charts and instruction books for each instrument. The information provided here is an indication of the keywork resources provided for the player in the common systems. Each key is named here after its principal function; in general any one key can be used in fingering for many notes.

'Tone-hole' here indicates a hole covered directly by the finger. An 'alternative key' is an alternative touchpiece acting on another keyhead. A 'duplicate key' is a duplicated touchpiece, keyhead, and key-hole. 'Ring-F' means a tone hole with a ring connected to the F key. The 'first octave key' is the first used in the ascending scale.

Key

L0	left-hand thumb	R0	right-hand thumb
L1	left-hand index finger	R1	right-hand index finger
L2	left-hand middle finger	R2	right-hand middle finger
L3	left-hand annular finger	R3	right-hand annular finger
L4	left-hand little finger	R4	right-hand little finger

8-key Transverse Flute

L0:	B♭ key	R1:	Tone-hole; C key
L1:	Tone-hole	R2:	Tone-hole
L2:	Tone-hole	R3:	Tone-hole; cross F key
L3:	Tone-hole	R4:	E♭ key; low C♮ key; low C key
L4:	G♮ key; long F key		

Boehm 1847 system Flute

L0:	B key	R1:	F key
L1:	Plate-C	R2:	E key; D trill key
L2:	A key	R3:	D key; D♮ trill key
L3:	G♮ key	R4:	E♭ key; low C♮ key; low C key
L4:	G key		

Modern Flute

L0:	B key; B♭ key	R1:	F key
L1:	Plate-C	R2:	E key; D trill key
L2:	A key	R3:	D key; D♮ trill key
L3:	G key	R4:	E♭ key; low C♮ key; low C key
L4:	G♮ key		

Müller's Clarinet

L0: Tone-hole; speaker key
L1: Tone-hole; A♮ key; A♭ key
L2: Tone-hole
L3: Tone-hole; B♭ key
L4: G♯ key; B♮ key; C♯ key

R1: Tone-hole; throat B♮ key; C♮ key
R2: Tone-hole
R3: Tone-hole; F♮ key
R4: Tone-hole; F♯ key; E♭ key; C♮ key

Klose-Buffet Boehm System Clarinet

L0: Tone-hole; speaker key
L1: Tone-hole; A♮ key; A♭ key
L2: Tone-hole
L3: Tone-hole; alternative B♭ key
L4: G♯ key; duplicate C♮ key; B♮ key; C♯ key

R1: Ring-B♭ (via correspondence); B♮ trill key; alternative A♮ key; alternative A♭ key; alternative B♭ key
R2: Ring-F♯ (and B♭ via correspondence)
R3: Ring-B♭ (via correspondence); alternative F♯ key
R4: duplicate C♮ key; E♭ key; duplicate B♮ key; C♮ key

Modern Clarinet

L0: Tone-hole; speaker key
L1: Ring-B; A♮ key; A♭ key
L2: Ring-A
L3: Tone-hole; B♭ trill key
L4: G♯ key; C♮ key; C♯ key; B♮ key

R1: Ring-F; B♭ trill key; C♯ trill key; F trill key; F♯ trill key
R2: Ring-E
R3: Ring-D; F♯ trill key
R4: C♮ key; C♯ key; B♮ key; D♯ key

(The note pitches are for the clarinet (second) register, corresponding chalumeau (first) register notes being a 12th lower.)

Saxophone

L0: Speaker key
L1: B♮ key; B♭ key; D$_6$ key; E$^♭_6$ key; alternative F$_6$ key
L2: C and A key; F$_6$ key
L3: G key
L4: G♯ key; C♯ key; B♮ key; B♭ key

R1: F key; alternative C♮ and B♭ keys and E$_6$ key
R2: E key
R3: D key; F♯ trill key
R4: C♮ key; C♯ key

Thumb-plate system oboe

L0: Thumb-plate; first octave key
L1: Perforated plate; second octave key; spat key
L2: Ring
L3: Tone-hole; D trill key
L4: G♯ key; low B key; low B♭ key; alternative E♭ key

R0: support
R1: Tone-hole; alternative key to thumb-plate
R2: Perforated plate
R3: Ring; F key
R4: low C key; C♯ key; E♭ key

Conservatoire system oboe

L0: first octave key; third octave key

L1: Perforated plate; second octave key; spat key

L2: Ring; alternative D trill key; spat key

L3: Ring; D♭ trill key

L4: G♯ key; low B key; low B♭ key; alternative E♭ key

R0: support

R1: Ring; G♯ trill key; B♭ trill key

R2: Perforated plate; D trill key

R3: Ring; F key; alternative low C key

R4: low C key; C♯ key; E♭ key closed standing forked F vent

French system Bassoon

L0: C key; B♭ key; first harmonic key; second harmonic key; alternative crook key; E♭ key; D key; C♯ key

L1: Tone-hole; G trill key; A♭₃ key

L2: Tone-hole; F♯ trill key

L3: Tone-hole; E♭ key

L4: C♯ key; crook key

R0: Tone-hole; alternative F♮ (enabling F♯ to G♯ trill) key; F♯ key

R1: Tone-hole

R2: Tone-hole; C♯ key

R3: G key; B♭ key; both with rollers

R4: F key; A♭ key; both with rollers

German system Bassoon

L0: C key; B♮ key; B♭ key; first harmonic key; second harmonic key; C♯ key; crook key; crook key lock; D key

L1: Tone-hole

L2: Tone-hole; F♯ trill key

L3: Ring giving C♯ to D♯ trill key

L4: E♭₂ key; C♯₂ key

R0: Plate; B♭ key; rest; F♯ key; A♭ key

R1: Tone-hole; C♯ trill key

R2: Ring-G₄ key

R3: G key; alternative B♭ with roller

R4: F key; duplicate F♯ key; A♭ key; rollers on F to A♭ key

APPENDIX 3

We use the traditional convention to denote the nominal sizes of brass instruments. This serves to distinguish between one instrument and another of the same nominal pitch but of double or half the tube length. The actual compass of notes will depend on the particular instrument and the repertoire. For instance, a french horn in 12-foot F will often play a higher lying part than an ophicleide in 8-foot C.

Note that this is a different conventional use of the word 'foot' from that used in specifying organ and harpsichord stops (see Sections 10.2 and 12.1), though both conventions stem from the useful coincidence that a conical or open-ended cylindrical pipe sounding a series of resonance mode frequencies approximating to a harmonic series based on the fundamental C_2 has a length of just about eight feet.

In the table below we show, for the more common conventional sizes, the actual length of a perfect cone sounding the corresponding series at $A_4 = 440$ Hz and some examples of instruments commonly built at that pitch.

The actual tube length of an instrument (ignoring valve loops etc) is, in fact, some 5–15 per cent shorter than the equivalent cone length, depending on the exact bore profile. The actual length will also depend on the pitch standard at which the instrument is designed to be played.

Nominal size	Equivalent cone length	Common examples
2¼-foot B♭	0.74m	piccolo trumpet
2½-foot A♭	0.83m	post horn
3-foot F	0.99m	high F trumpet
3¼-foot E♭	1.11m	soprano cornet
3½-foot D	1.18m	bugle horn, orchestral trumpet
4-foot C	1.32m	orchestral trumpet
4½-foot B♭	1.48m	bugle, cornet, flugel horn, B♭ valve trumpet
5-foot A	1.56m	post horn
5-foot A♭	1.67m	cornet crooked in A♭
6-foot F	1.98m	slide trumpet, low F trumpet, coiled posthorn
6½-foot E♭	2.22m	alto trombone, tenor horn
7-foot D	2.36m	natural trumpet

8-foot C	2.65m	natural trumpet, serpent, ophicleide, high C tuba
9-foot B♭	2.97m	tenor trombone, B♭ french horn, baritone, euphonium
10-foot A♭	3.33m	A♭ alphorn
11-foot G	3.53m	G bass trombone
11-foot G♭	3.74m	G♭ alphorn
12-foot F	3.96m	F french horn, F bass tuba
13-foot E♭	4.45m	french horn crooked in E♭, E♭ bass tuba
14-foot D	4.71m	trompe de chasse, natural horn
16-foot C	5.29m	natural horn, low C bass tuba
18-foot B♭	5.94m	french horn crooked in B♭ basso, low B♭ bass tuba

Lengths calculated for equal temperament at $A_4 = 440$ Hz,
c (speed of sound) $= 346$ m / s.

FURTHER READING

General

MARTIN AGRICOLA, *Musica instrumentalis deudsch*. A treatise on musical instruments (1529 and 1545) trans. and ed. William E. Hettrick. Cambridge: Cambridge University Press, 1994.

ANTHONY BAINES, *European and American Musical Instruments*. London: Batsford, 1966.

—— *The Oxford Companion to Musical Instruments*. Oxford: Oxford University Press, 1992.

—— (ed.), *Musical Instruments through the Ages*. Harmondsworth: Penguin, 1961.

ROBERT BARCLAY (ed.), *The Care of Historic Musical Instruments*. Edinburgh: CCI, MGC and CIMCIM, 1997.

ALEXANDER BUCHNER, *Colour Encyclopedia of Musical Instruments*. London: Hamlyn, 1980.

NORMAN DEL MAR, *A Companion to the Orchestra*. London: Faber, 1987.

ROBERT DONINGTON, *Music and its Instruments*. London: Methuen, 1982.

SIBYL MARCUSE, *Survey of Musical Instruments*. Newton Abbot: David & Charles, 1975.

JEREMY MONTAGU, *The World of Medieval and Renaissance Musical Instruments*. Newton Abbot: David & Charles, 1976.

—— *The World of Baroque and Classical Musical Instruments*. Newton Abbot: David & Charles, 1979.

—— *The World of Romantic and Modern Musical Instruments*. Newton Abbot: David & Charles, 1981.

MICHAEL PRAETORIUS, *Syntagma Musicum II, De organographia parts I and II*. Trans. and ed. D. Z. Crookes. Oxford: Clarendon Press, 1986.

MARY REMNANT, *Musical Instruments: An Illustrated History from Antiquity to the Present*. London: Batsford, 1990.

STANLEY SADIE (ed.), *The New Grove Dictionary of Musical Instruments*. London: Macmillan, 1984.

—— and J. TYRRELL (eds.), *The New Grove Dictionary of Music and Musicians*, 2nd edn. London: Macmillan, 2001.

ANDREW STILLER, *Handbook of Instrumentation*. Berkeley: University of California Press, 1985.

SEBASTIAN VIRDUNG, *Musica getutscht*. A Treatise on Musical Instruments (1511) ed. and trans. Beth Bullard. Cambridge: Cambridge University Press, 1993.

Journals

The Galpin Society Journal. 1948– .

Journal of the American Musical Instrument Society. 1975– .

Chapters 1 and 2

Murray Campbell and Clive Greated, *The Musician's Guide to Acoustics*. London: Dent, 1987; repr. London: Oxford University Press, 1998.

Diana Deutsch (ed.), *The Psychology of Music*, 2nd edn. San Diego, London: Academic Press, 1997.

Neville H. Fletcher and Thomas D. Rossing, *The Physics of Musical Instruments*, 2nd edn. New York and London: Springer, 1998.

Brian C. J. Moore, *An Introduction to the Psychology of Hearing*, 4th edn. San Diego and London: Academic Press, 1997.

Juan G. Roederer, *The Physics and Psychophysics of Music*, 3rd edn. New York and London: Springer, 1995.

Chapters 3 and 4

Anthony Baines, *Woodwind Instruments and their History*. London: Faber, 1977.

Bruno Bartolozzi, *New Sounds for Woodwind*, trans. and ed. Reginald Smith Brindle. London: Oxford University Press, 1982.

Philip Bate, *The Flute*, 2nd edn. London: Benn, 1979.

—— *The Oboe*. London: Benn, 1975.

Barra Boydell, *The Crumhorn and Other Renaissance Windcap Instruments*. Buren: Knuf, 1982.

Jack Brymer, *Clarinet*. Yehudi Menuhin Music Guides. London: Macdonald & Jane, 1976.

Paul Carroll, *Baroque Woodwind Instruments: A Guide to their History, Repertoire and Basic Technique*. Aldershot: Ashgate, 1999.

Adam Carse, *Musical Wind Instruments*. New York: Da Capo, 1965.

Stewart Carter, 'The String Tremolo in the 17th Century', *Early Music*, 19/1 (1991), 42–59.

Robert Dick, *The Other Flute: A Performance Manual of Contemporary Techniques*. Oxford: Oxford University Press, 1975.

James Galway, *Flute*. Yehudi Menuhin Music Guides. London: Macdonald, 1982.

Leon Goossens and Edwin Roxburgh, *Oboe*. Yehudi Menuhin Music Guides: London: Macdonald & Jane, 1977.

Bruce Haynes, *The Eloquent Oboe: A History of the Hautboy from 1640 to 1760*. Oxford: Oxford University Press, 2001.

Jacques Hotteterre le Romain, *Principles of the Flute, Recorder and Oboe*, ed. and trans. D. Lasocki. New York: Praeger, 1968.

Edgar Hunt, *The Recorder and its Music*. London: Eulenberg, 1977.

Günter Joppig, *The Oboe and the Bassoon*, trans. from the German. London: Batsford, 1988.

Jaap Kool, *The Saxophone*, trans. Lawrence Gwozdz. Baldock: Egon Publishers, 1987.

John Krell, *Kincaidiana: A Flute Players Notebook*. Culver City, Calif.: Trio Associates, 1973.

Oscar Kroll, *The Clarinet*, trans. from the German. London: Batsford, 1968.

Lyndesay G. Langwill, *The Bassoon and Contrabassoon*. London: Benn, 1965.

Colin Lawson, *The Early Clarinet: A Practical Guide*. Cambridge: Cambridge University Press, 2000.

—— *The Cambridge Companion to the Clarinet*. Cambridge: Cambridge University Press, 1995.

John Martin, *The Acoustics of the Recorder*. Celle: Moeck, 1994.

Raymond Meylan, *The Flute*. London: Batsford, 1988.

C. J. Nederveen, *Acoustical Aspects of Woodwind Instruments*, 2nd edn. DeKalb: Northern Illinois University Press, 1998.

J. PHELAN and M. D. BRODY, *The Complete Guide to the Flute*. Boston: Conservatory Publications, 1973.

J. J. QUANTZ, *On Playing the Flute* (1752), ed. and trans. by E. R. Reilly. London: Faber, 1966.

F. GEOFFREY RENDALL, *The Clarinet*, rev. edn. London: Benn, 1971.

ALBERT RICE, *The Baroque Clarinet*. Oxford: Oxford University Press, 1992.

EVELYN ROTHWELL, *The Oboist's Companion*, vols. i–iii. Oxford: Oxford University Press, 1974.

JOHN SOLUM, *The Early Flute*. Oxford: Clarendon Press, 1992.

S. W. STOKES and R. A. CONDON, *Special Effects for the Flute*. Culver City, Calif.: Trio Associates, 1976.

JOHN M. THOMSON with ANTHONY ROWLAND-JONES (eds.), *The Cambridge Companion to the Recorder*. Cambridge: Cambridge University Press, 1996.

NANCY TOFF, *The Development of the Modern Flute*, repr. of 1st edn. Urbana: University of Illinois Press, 1986.

—— *The Flute Book: A Complete Guide for Students and Performers*, 2nd edn. Oxford: Oxford University Press, 1996.

JOHANN GEORGE TROMLITZ, *The Keyed Flute*, trans. and ed. Ardal Powell. Oxford: Oxford University Press, 1996.

—— *The Virtuoso Flute-Player*, trans. and ed. Ardal Powell. Cambridge: Cambridge University Press, 1991.

MARION WHITTOW, *The Oboe: A Reed Blown in the Wind*. London: Puffit Publications, 1991.

Chapters 5 and 6

ANTHONY BAINES, *Brass Instruments: Their History and Development*. London: Faber, 1976.

ROBERT BARCLAY, *The Art of The Trumpet Maker*. Oxford: Oxford University Press, 1992.

PHILIP BATE, *The Trumpet and the Trombone: An Outline of their History*. 2nd edn. London: Benn, 1978.

CLIFFORD BEVAN, *The Tuba Family*, 2nd edn. Winchester: Piccolo Press, 2000.

ADAM CARSE, *Musical Wind Instruments*. London: Macmillan, 1939; New York: Da Capo, 1965.

RALPH DUDGEON, *The Keyed Bugle*. Metuchen, NJ: Scarecrow Press, 1993.

TREVOR HERBERT and JOHN WALLACE (eds.), *The Cambridge Companion to Brass Instruments*. Cambridge: Cambridge University Press, 1997.

KURT JANETZKY and BERNHARD BRUCHLE, *The Horn*, trans. from the German. London: Batsford, 1988.

REGINALD MORLEY-PEGGE, *The French Horn*, 2nd edn. London: Benn, 1973.

EDWARD TARR, *The Trumpet*, trans. from the German. London: Batsford, 1988.

SCOTT WHITENER, *A Complete Guide to Brass: Instruments and Pedagogy*. New York: Schirmer, 1990.

Journals

Brass Bulletin. 1972– .

The Historic Brass Society Journal. 1989– .

Chapter 7

JAMES BLADES, *Percussion Instruments and their History*, 3rd edn. London: Faber, 1980.

REGINALD BRINDLE SMITH, *Contemporary Percussion*, new edn. London: Oxford University Press, 1991.

THOMAS D. ROSSING, *Science of Percussion Instruments*. Singapore: World Scientific, 2000.

Chapters 8 and 9

TONY BACON (ed.), *Electric Guitars—The Illustrated Encyclopedia*. Thunder Bay, Calif.: Thunder Bay Press, 2000.

—— *The Ultimate Guitar Book*. London: Dorling Kindersley, 1991.

JAMES BEAMENT, The Violin Explained: Components, Mechanism, and Sound. Oxford: Clarendon Press, 1997.

DAVID D. BOYDEN, *The History of Violin Playing from its Origins to 1761, and its Relationship to the Violin and Violin Music*. London: Oxford University Press 1965; repr. Oxford: Clarendon Press, 1990.

—— et al., *Strings*. New Grove Musical Instrument Series. London: Macmillan, 1987.

PAUL BRUN, *A History of the Double Bass*, trans. from the French. Chemin de la Flanerie: the author, 1989.

ALISON CRUM with SONIA JACKSON, *Play the Viol*. Oxford: Oxford University Press, 1989.

CARLEEN M. HUTCHINS and VIRGINIA BENADE (eds.), *Research Papers in Violin Acoustics 1975–1893*. Woodbury, NY: Acoustical Society of America, 1997.

MARK LINDLEY, *Lutes, Viols and Temperaments*. Cambridge: Cambridge University Press, 1984.

MAURICE W. RILEY, *The History of The Viola*. Ann Arbor: Braun-Brumfield, 1991.

CHRISTOPHER SIMPSON, *The Division-Viol, or The Art of Playing ex tempore upon a Ground*, a lithographic facsimile of the 2nd edn. London: J. Curwen & Sons and New York: G. Schirmer, 1955.

PAUL SPARKS, *The Classical Mandolin*. Oxford: Clarendon Press, 1995.

ROBIN STOWELL (ed.), *The Cambridge Guide to the Violin*. Cambridge: Cambridge University Press, 1992.

JAMES TYLER and PAUL SPARKS, *The Early Mandolin*. Oxford: Clarendon Press, 1989.

IAN WOODFIELD, *Early History of the Viol*. Cambridge: Cambridge University Press, 1984.

Chapters 10 and 11

ANDERS ASKENFELT (ed.), *Five Lectures on the Acoustics of the Piano*. Stockholm: Royal Swedish Academy of Music, 1990.

ANNE BOND, *A Guide to the Harpsichord*. Portland, Ore.: Amadeus Press, 1997.

BERNARD BRAUCHLI, *The Clavichord*. Cambridge: Cambridge University Press, 1998.

MICHAEL COLE, *The Pianoforte in the Classical Era*. Oxford: Clarendon Press, 1998.

DAVID CROMBIE, *Piano*. San Francisco, London: Balafon, 1995.

CYRIL EHRLICH, *The Piano: A History*, rev. edn. Oxford: Oxford University Press, 1990.

LOUIS KENTNER, *Piano: Yehudi Menuhin Music Guides*. London: Macdonald & Jane, 1976.

EDWARD L KOTTICK, *The Harpsichord Owner's Guide*. Chapel Hill: University of North Carolina Press, 1987.

TOBIAS MATTHAY, *Muscular Relaxation Studies*. London: Bosworth & Co., n.d.

RICHARD MAUNDER, *Keyboard Instruments in Eighteenth-Century Vienna*. Oxford: Clarendon Press, 1998.

RUTH NURMI, *A Plane and Easy Introduction to the Harpsichord*. Albuquerque: University of North Mexico Press, 1974.

STEWART POLLENS, *The Early Piano*. Cambridge: Cambridge University Press, 1994.

EDWIN M. RIPIN et al., *Early Keyboard Instruments*. New Grove Musical Instrument Series. London: Macmillan, 1989.

RICHARD TROEGER, *Technique and Interpretation on the Harpsichord and Clavichord*. Bloomington: Indiana University Press, 1987.

SAMUEL WOLFENDEN, *A Treatise on the Art of Pianoforte Construction*. Henley-on-Thames: Gresham Books, 1916.

Chapter 12

POUL-GERHARD ANDERSEN, *Organ Building and Design*. London: George Allen & Unwin, 1969.

GEORGE ASHDOWN AUDSLEY, *The Art of Organ Building*, vol. i. New York: Dover, 1965.

DAVID BAKER, *The Organ*. Princes Risborough: Shire, 1991.

STEPHEN BICKNELL, *The History of the English Organ*. Cambridge: Cambridge University Press, 1996.

THOMAS DONAHUE, *The Modern Classical Organ: A Guide to its Physical and Musical Structure and Performance Implications*. Jefferson, NC: McFarland, 1991.

REGINALD FOORT, *The Cinema Organ*, 2nd edn. New York: Vestal Press, 1970.

EDWARD J. HOPKINS and EDWARD F RIMBAULT, *The Organ, its History and Construction*. London: Robert Cocks & Co., 1877.

OSWALD G. RAGATZ, *Organ Technique*. Bloomington and London: Indiana University Press, 1979.

PETER WILLIAMS and BARBARA OWEN, *The Organ*. New Grove Musical Instrument Series. London: Macmillan, 1988.

ARTHUR WILLS, *Organ*. Yehudi Menuhin Music Guides. London: Macdonald, 1984.

Chapter 13

TONY BACON, *The Ultimate Guitar Book*. London: Dorling Kindersley, 1991.

MICHAEL BOOM, *Music through MIDI*. Washington: Microsoft Press, 1987.

JOHN BORWICK, *Microphones, Technology and Technique*. London: Focal Press, 1990.

RICHARD BOULANGER (ed.), *The CSOUND Book*, Cambridge, Mass.: MIT Press, 2000.

J. CHOWNING and D. BRISTOW, *FM Theory and Applications*. Tokyo: Yamaha Music Foundation, 1986.

DAVID CROMBIE, *The Complete Synthesizer*. London: Omnibus Press, 1982.

—— *The Synthesizer and Electronic Keyboard Handbook*. London: Dorling Kindersley, 1984.

RICHARD DOBSON, *A Dictionary of Electronic and Computer Music Technology: Instruments, Terms, Techniques*. Oxford: Oxford University Press, 1992.

CHARLES DODGE and THOMAS A. JERSE, *Computer Music*, 2nd edn. New York: Schirmer Books, 1997.

JON F. EICHE, *What's a Synthesizer?* Milwaukee: Hal Leonard Books, 1987.

THOMAS B. HOLMES, *Electronic and Experimental Music*. New York: Charles Scribner's Sons, 1985.

HOWARD MASSEY, *The Complete DX7*. New York: Amsco Publications, 1986.

ALEC NISBETT, *The Sound Studio*. Oxford: Butterworth-Heinemann, 1962.

R. A. PENFOLD, *Computers and Music*. Tonbridge, Kent: PC Publishing, 1989.

—— *Synthesizers for Musicians*. Tonbridge, Kent: PC Publishing, 1989.

IAN R. SINCLAIR, *Introducing Digital Audio*. Tonbridge, Kent: PC Publishing, 1992.

GLOSSARY AND INDEX

For readers' convenience, the index to this book and a glossary of terms are combined into one alphabetical sequence. We give a brief account of the more important instruments which are nowhere described in the main body of the text; for those instruments and concepts which are treated briefly in the main text we give the page reference; and for those instruments and concepts discussed at length in the book we give a short definition together with references to the text.

Words in **bold** have their own entries in the index/glossary.

but with four **sympathetic strings** running between the **fingerboard** and the **neck**

Harmon, T., inventor, 205

harmonic, 15, 50, 52–3

harmonic series, a series of numbers which are exact integer multiples of the lowest (fundamental) member of the series. The frequencies of the **spectral components** of an sustained note on a wind or bowed string instrument form a harmonic series: the note has a **harmonic spectrum**

harmonic spectrum, 15, 18, 20–2, 23, 34–5, 52, 65

harmonica, name which has been used for various instruments, including the **mouth organ**

harmonicity ratio, in frequency modulation, 451

harmonics, bowed string instrument technique, 276–7

harmonics, brasswind, a term sometimes loosely used for the **natural notes**

harmonics, guitar technique, 304–5

harmonics, harp technique, 302

harmonium, free-reed keyboard instrument, activated by air compressed by pedalled bellows. There may be more than one **manual**. There are usually a number of **stops** and **couplers**

harp, plucked string instrument in which the strings are in a plane at right angles to the table or **soundboard**
   acoustics, 278–83
   ancient, 284
   medieval, 286
   modern, 297–8
   pedal, 288–9
   performance practice, 301–3
   Renaissance and Baroque, 287

harpsichord, keyboard plucked string instrument, with the strings mounted horizontally and more or less at right angles to the keyboard
   acoustics, 306–13
   construction, 332–9
   history, 313–14, 315–23
   modern, 323, 327–32
   performance practice, 342–5, 347–8
   tuning, 339–42

harp stop, harpsichord, 332

Hass family, clavichord and harpsichord builders, 319, 320

hautbois, Fr.: **shawm**, **oboe**

hautbois, early oboe, 87

haut-contre de hautbois, 87

hautecontre-taille violin, 244

Hawaiian guitar, a form of guitar held horizontally on the lap or on a stand, characterized by high **action** to facilitate glissando playing using a bar to stop the strings rather than the fingers, 442
   electric, 13.2.3

Haward family, harpsichord builders, 319

Hawkins, Coleman (1904–69), saxophonist, 115

Hawkins, John Isaac (fl. 1799–1845), pianoforte builder, 362

Haydn, Joseph (1732–1809), composer, 197, 397

Haydn, Michael (1737–1806), composer, 203

Haynes, flute makers, 128

head, drum, preparation, 226

head joint, flute, 131, 136–8

Heale, Michael (d. 2002), viol maker, 252

hearing, see **ear, human**

hearpe, medieval, 285

Hebenstreit, Pantaleon (1667–1750), dulcimer player, 296

Heckel family, woodwind instrument makers, 90–1

Heckelphone, double-reed conical-bore **woodwind** instrument, invented by the firm of W. Heckel in 1904; of wider bore than the **oboe** family, 98

heel, bow, 267

helicon, form of **tuba** with the tubing made in a wide coil to go round the player's body and rest on one shoulder

Helmholtz pitch notation, 16, 473

Helmholtz resonance, in wind instruments, 124, 152–3

Henry VIII (1491–1547), King of England, 125

Hertz, Henri (1803–1888), pianist, 380

hertz (Hz), unit of frequency, 4, 473

high C facilitator, flute, 131

high pass filter, 449, 450

highland pipes, mouth-blown Scottish military, pipe band and solo **bagpipe**; having conical bore chanter and cylindrical bore drones; **compass** G_4 to A_5

hi-hat cymbals, 216, 217, 220

historic instruments, surviving specimens of older forms of instrument contributing to knowledge of instrument history, 333

historical brasswind instrument-making, 201–2

historical instruments, modern instruments copied from or inspired by old models, drawing on knowledge of instrument history 252, 254

hitch pins, 324

Hitchcock, family, harpsichord builders, 319

Hofmann, Josef (1876–1957), pianist, 380

Hohlfeld, inventor, 356

Holborne, Anthony (d. 1602), composer, 245

hold, in sound synthesis, 463

Holliger, Heinz (b. 1939), oboist, 112

homogeneous system, in sound synthesis, 464

Honegger, Arthur (1892–1955), composer, 444

hook, harp, 288

hoop crack (drum technique), 229

Hope Jones, Robert (1859–1914), organ builder, 398, 399, 400, 407, 420

horn, in broad classification of lip-vibrated **aerophones** into **horns** and **trumpets**, the term 'horn' is preferred for instruments made from animal horn or tusk, or with a shape derived from these but in other materials, and thus of predominantly conical-bore profile such as the **bugle**. The term is often used without qualification for the **french horn** in the orchestra, the **tenor horn** in the brass band, and loosely for any wind instrument.

horn, English, see **cor anglais**

horn, french, see **french horn**

Hornbostel-Sachs classification, 40

hornpipe, a reed pipe terminating in an animal horn, usually with a single reed; many have two parallel pipes

horsehair, for bows, 265

hot potato, 124

Hotteterre family, wind instrument makers, 87, 121, 125, 143